Yearbook of Special Education

1980-81
Sixth edition

Contributing Editor

Glen R. Thompson, Ph. D.

with the assistance of
Rita Tatum

Marquis Academic Media
Marquis Who's Who, Inc.
200 East Ohio Street
Chicago, Illinois 60611

371.9
Y32
1980/81

Library of Congress Card Number: 75-13803
International Standard Book Number: 0-8379-3006-5
Product Code Number: 031100

Manufactured in the United States of America
1 2 3 4 5 6 7 8 9 10

Yearbook of Special Education

Reference books published by
Marquis Academic Media

Annual Register of Grant Support
Consumer Protection Directory
Current Audiovisuals for Mental Health Education
Directory of Certified Psychiatrists and Neurologists
Directory of Publishing Opportunities
Directory of Registered Lobbyists and Lobbyist Legislation
Environmental Protection Directory
Family Factbook
Grantsmanship: Money and How To Get It
Mental Health in America: The Years of Crisis
The Musician's Guide
NASA Factbook
NIH Factbook
NSF Factbook
The Selective Guide to Audiovisuals for Mental Health and Family Life Education
The Selective Guide to Publications for Mental Health and Family Life Education
Sourcebook of Equal Educational Opportunity
Sourcebook on Aging
Sourcebook on Food and Nutrition
Sourcebook on Mental Health
Standard Education Almanac
Standard Medical Almanac
Yearbook of Adult and Continuing Education
Yearbook of Higher Education
Yearbook of Special Education
Worldwide Directory of Computer Companies
Worldwide Directory of Federal Libraries

Contents

About the editor

Glen R. Thompson, Ph.D., is chairman of the Department of Special Education at Northeastern Illinois University in Chicago. Specializing in Behavior Disorders, Thompson has written a number of articles on various special education topics, including "Academic Achievement Patterns of 'Misgrouped' First Graders," "Creative Growth in the Fourth Grade as Related to Intelligence and Teaching Style," and "Language Evaluation Tests and Adult Retardates." His professional affiliations encompass a broad special education spectrum from the Council for Exceptional Children and the National Education Association to Phi Delta Kappa and the American Psychological Association.

Preface

The *1980-1981 Yearbook of Special Education* has revised its format as compared to previous editions. Certainly, the reader will promptly notice that this edition does not contain a solo chapter devoted to learning disabilities, for example. The editors deleted an isolated LD chapter in favor of addressing learning disabilities throughout the book. A LD approach is probably relevant with large numbers of exceptional children, regardless of the manner in which they've been labeled.

So every chapter contains at least one article that directly addresses learning disabilities. This approach was dictated by the recognition that learning disabilities have great impact in the field of special education generally. Indeed, this perspective also is reflected in the curricula of Northeastern Illinois University's special education department, chaired by Glen Thompson, Ph. D., contributing editor of the *Sixth Edition*. With the exception of the master's degree in Gifted, all the special education sequences at Northeastern contain learning disabilities courses as a part of a common curricular core.

The *Sixth Edition*'s chapters represent an attempt to be cognizant of current issues, trends and concerns, many of which relate to and emanate from attempts to implement Public Law 94-142. The law makes provisions for parent/family involvement mandatory in all aspects of identifying, diagnosing and planning for exceptional children, as well as requiring educational placement in an environment that is "least restrictive."

Thus, articles addressing parental involvement and mainstreaming comprise a significant portion of the "Introduction." The second section, "Minimum Competency Testing," contains articles of general interest. But the burning issue relates to MCT for handicapped students. (The Civil Rights Board ruling is covered in the *Fifth Edition*.) The debate simplifies to whether or not certain handicapped students would be permitted to graduate normally in districts and/or states that require passage of such a test as a prerequisite to graduation. In today's education, this problem must be promptly solved, hopefully in a manner that is equitable for all students. The editors opine the most equitable procedure currently available is to employ Individualized Educational Program goals as criteria of competence for handicapped students. However, a careful perusal of this section reveals there are many problems associated with even this seemingly simple approach.

"PL 94-142 and Uncle Sam" addresses the law and its implementation. Certainly, cultural diversity, as it relates to all aspects of special education and implementation of PL 94-142 is timely. In recognition of its importance, a separate chapter is devoted to "Cultural Diversity."

"Sensory Handicaps" and "Learning/Behavioral Handicaps" are less well-recognized as buzzwords in special education, but the editors have used them because we wished to de-emphasize the use of traditional categories. The primary objective in special education is providing exceptional children with appropriate educational programs. The provision of such programs must be based on an objective consideration of student strengths, weaknesses and needs. Unfortunately, traditional labels often fail to provide this kind of information. The editors sincerely hope the reader will find this approach meaningful. For more conventional terminology, please consult the index.

"Gifted/Talented" represents an extremely important section of this edition. PL 94-142 does not refer to gifted and/or talented children specifically. However, if a child is gifted and/or talented as well as handicapped, the concept of an appropriate education would imply that it must relate very directly. In the editors' opinion, such children are covered under PL 94-142. And the educational programs designed for them must recognize and respond to the special abilities they possess. However, specially trained personnel are required to identify these abilities in many handicapped children.

It is interesting to note the changes that have occurred in teacher preparation and teacher certification, partly as a result of PL 94-142's impact, but also because of advances in the profession itself. "The Professionals" covers these changes.

One special problem that deserves mentioning deals with the preparation and in-servicing of regular teachers. What courses and experiences should they have to make them even more effective in teaching exceptional children who will be mainstreamed into their classrooms?

This nation's future is its children. Currently, we possess the professional expertise to provide all children with an education that would best recognize and develop their talents. But, unfortunately, the priority given this task has been relatively low.

Special education and PL 94-142 enable the nation to take one big stride ahead by giving priority to financing and implementing the free and appropriate education to a certain segment of its school population—the handicapped. Perhaps the philosophical underpinnings of this great advance will give impetus to a similar commitment to the education of all children. Hopefully, the knowledge and experience gained in attempting to implement PL 94-142 will help make this goal more accessible.

—Thompson, Tatum

INTRODUCTION

by Glen Thompson, Ph.D. and Rita Tatum

There are a number of issues and trends in the field of special education today. One high priority is secondary special education and vocational preparation.

In the past, many special teacher preparation programs across the nation focused on educating young children. In fact, most special education programs commenced in elementary and junior high schools. When high schools initiated special education programs, they frequently hired elementary teachers with special education training, because secondary special education teachers were hard to find. Now, however, a concerted effort is being made to prepare secondary special education teachers. And there is a growing emphasis on vocational preparation as well.

After all, preparing a special education student so that he or she is capable of adjusting to the workaday world is an educational objective of overriding importance. In addition, there is a concomitant effort to provide teachers of special subjects with special education training.

Special education students should receive the same educational opportunities as their so-called normal counterparts. For example, they should receive courses in art, music, physical education and industrial arts from teachers who are aware of their special needs. And these teachers should be prepared to design appropriate educational programs. In fact, specialized teachers are embarking on graduate work in special education in ever-increasing numbers. Their motivation is a desire to work more effectively with special students who are programmed into their classes.

Mainstreaming

Though many states have been mainstreaming for years, a number of others have not. Under present statutes, a child's educational placement is to be in the "least restrictive alternative" setting. That includes, as frequently as possible, keeping the child within his or her own peer group.

Along with mainstreaming, educators must frequently provide Individualized Educational Programs (IEPs) that respond to each child's specialized needs. Some educators have hailed the shift from self-contained classrooms to mainstreaming as comparable to the recognition of civil rights.

But with the newly-recognized rights of the special education student also come some potential pitfalls. How is a teacher supposed to respond to the natural curiosity of the "other" children? What is an appropriate response to the second grader's question of an exceptional peer, "What do you see when you are blind?"

Handled correctly, mainstreaming can allow exceptional children to relate equally with other children. As one so-called normal child explained,"I think that just because they aren't the same they can sometimes do better things. Maybe because they can't jump, they can draw better or explain better than other people."

Ironically, a child suffering from one type of handicap will often be as ignorant of another child's limitations as are other children. The little boy in the wheelchair is as naive about being blind as the young blind girl is of being unable to run.

Parents

While children are learning how to relate to each other, another important segment in special education also is beginning to garner much-needed attention. When special education teachers prepared for parent conferences in the past, a script was often worked out among the professionals to insure the parent(s) would be sold on what the school wanted to do for their children.

Within education circles, those parents who were agreeable and who didn't question the school's opinions and recommendations were dubbed "cooperative." But those parents who questioned, objected or otherwise made waves were labeled "difficult to work with." During that time frame, school records were secret. Only those with professional training were permitted to examine the records of exceptional children. Or, indeed, any child's. After all, the rationale went, "We are the professionals. We know best."

Fortunately for both the children and their parents, as well as dedicated professionals willing to open their minds, school records are more available today. Many special educators now realize that paired with the parents they can often significantly improve the opportunities of their children.

1

Learning Disabilities: Lagging Field in Medicine

by Elizabeth Rasche Gonzalez

Up to 16% of American children have diverse difficulties that seriously interfere with their school performance. Primary care physicians can be helpful to these children but need considerably more information and training in such problems. Semantics also presents difficulties.

This was the consensus at a medical symposium on the need for interdisciplinary treatment of learning disabilities held as part of the recent Milwaukee International Conference of the Association for Children with Learning Disabilities (ACLD).

At the symposium, a report was given on an unpublished survey conducted by the American Academy of Pediatrics. All of 60 randomly selected pediatricians stated that they see patients with learning disabilities in their practices, according to Janet O. Lerner, PhD, professor of special education at Chicago's Northeastern Illinois University, and Susan L. Cohn, a senior at the University of Illinois College of Medicine. But 73% did not think that they had received adequate preparation for diagnosing and treating these children either in medical school or during their residencies; the same proportion reported a need for more training in the field.

The feeling that learning-disabled children often do not receive accurate diagnoses or appropriate treatment from physicians was expressed at the symposium. A typical physician attitude, some charged, was "Don't worry, he'll grow out of it." (Meaning: Now get this kid out of my office before he tears off the wallpaper.) The urgent need for preservice and continuing education courses in learning disabilities was stressed repeatedly.

Lerner and Cohn pointed out that under Public Law 94-142, the controversial Education for All Handicapped Children's Act that has led to widespread "mainstreaming" of handicapped children into regular schools and classes, medical diagnostic services are, implicitly, part of the yearly evaluations mandated for disabled youngsters. The law also prescribes "innovative and experimental inservice programs" for physicians and other professionals. The American Academy of Pediatrics is presently evolving inservice models for this purpose under a grant from the US Office of Education. As educational programs proliferate, pediatricians may have the option of subspecializing in child development.

In the meantime, how can primary care physicians who do not have much training in learning disabilities help these children?

First, the primary care physician often can pinpoint specific problems through a thorough history and physical examination. Charles D. Schoenwetter, MD, director of the University of Wisconsin's Learning and Behavior Clinic and associate professor of pediatrics, stresses that these should be conducted as early as possible—preferably by 1 year of age. At this time visual defects, hearing loss, interpersonal problems in the family, and other difficulties may be discernible.

Physicians who have not heretofore detected such problems, however, frequently are consulted when a child fails his preschool screening examination. At that time, "having been embarrassed by the deficiencies of the office screening," Schoenwetter comments, "it is best not to insist that Albert Einstein would have failed his preschool screening also [a reasonable assumption], but rather to ask how one can collaborate with the school to meet the situation."

Schoenwetter favors close physician-school liaison, admitting that this can sometimes cause tension and difficulty, at least at the outset. He himself spends much time with children and teachers in their classrooms but admits that this is not a practical option for many physicians.

Still, he and his associates believe that at least an occasional telephone call to the school about a disabled child can be helpful in mobilizing the school to meet the child's needs. In addition, Schoenwetter suggests that physicians, who generally are respected members of their communities and often serve on school boards, can help to build social awareness of the problems of learning disabled children.

Of course, not all learning problems can be handled at the primary care level. "If there is any uncertainty at all, the physician should refer," Schoenwetter told *JAMA* MEDICAL NEWS. He is part of an interdisciplinary team that also includes Raymond W. M. Chun, MD, professor of neurology and pediatrics; Charles G. Matthews, PhD, professor of neurology; and Jack C. Westman, MD, professor of psychiatry.

The Wisconsin team is currently studying a group of children whose problems stumped everyone. The 72 children, followed up for 20 months, received preliminary diagnoses of personality disorders (41%), "attention deficit disorders" (16%), or developmental disorders (14%). The children were referred for treatment with psychotherapy (46 children), special education (29 children), drug therapy (15 children), social services (5 children), speech therapy (5 children), or residential placement (5 children). Seventy-two percent of all children were considered improved on follow-up.

Nor is prevention of learning difficulties being neglected. Schoenwetter emphasizes the importance of parenting education, asserting that this should begin when future parents are adolescents. "We need to teach parenting in a primary care setting," he elaborates, "including such things as parental support, verbal interaction with the child, development of peer interactions, and exposing kids to content in the environment. These things are not even being taught in medical schools! Even if a learning disorder proves to be 'organic,' it will appear less to the degree that the child has a 'set of wellness' before it is biologically expressed."

(The idea of teaching parenting in a primary care setting is not as visionary as it sometimes seems but at present is largely limited to specialists like Schoenwetter and to younger physicians. In the tiny town of Española, NM, for instance, pediatrician Jim Waltner, MD, spends much of his professional life teaching parenting, both in courses he conducts for local residents and in one-to-one encounters with parents during office hours. While he focuses heavily on teaching basic home health care, Waltner is also committed to ensuring that parents know about the importance of early infant stimulation, verbal interaction with their children, and other "musts" for the prevention of intellectual and psychosocial impairment.)

'Refining' the Diagnosis

When preventive parenting has failed, optimal treatment of a learning disability begins with proper diagnosis—and not with the catch-all term "learning disability," according to the Wisconsin team.

"The learning-disability concept is simplistic and is not useful," Westman explains, adding that medical diagnosticians do not generally employ it. He told the symposium, "It is likely that the perpetuation of the concept of simple, specific learning disabilities is a result of the incomplete diagnostic study of these children." It is no longer appropriate, he stressed, to distinguish "organic" and "functional" disorders on the basis of the presence or absence of "cerebral dysfunction." Life experience modifies brain anatomy and physiology, he explained, and a multiplicity of genetic and environmental factors determines individual differences in cerebral structure and function. Hence, each child must be viewed as unique and his problem(s) evaluated holistically.

The Council for Exceptional Children defines a child with learning disabilities as "one with adequate mental ability, sensory processes and emotional stability who has specific deficits in perceptual, integrative, or expressive processes that severely impair learning efficiency," noted Westman. This and similar definitions suggest the presence of CNS dysfunction; such dysfunction often cannot be demonstrated, however, and in practice, the diagnosis "learning disability" is often predicated on the *absence* of any demonstrable dysfunction.

"The dilemma of inclusion and exclusion criteria is a semantic and conceptual nightmare," Westman told *JAMA* MEDICAL NEWS, "because you can go any way your biases lead you to, depending on your ax to grind. There's a whole controversy in the field: Are we talking about lesion, dysfunction, deficit, or developmental lag?"

The "nightmare" has been particularly evident in the area of what the American Psychiatric Association's third *Diagnostic and Statistical Manual* calls an "attentional deficit disorder" (formerly referred to by a variety of appellations, including minimal brain dysfunction, hyperkinesis, hyperkinetic impulse control disorder, learning disability, and cerebral dysfunction, and still commonly called hyperactivity). Explains Schoenwetter, "It's not a disease. There is no test to diagnose it. It's in the eye of the beholder." At one time, in the Denver school system, "they were describing upwards of 30% of the class as hyperactive," Schoenwetter says. "Their group included kids who were scratching their noses."

1

Schoenwetter, who uses a behavioral approach to helping very active children with short attention spans, believes that drugs are too often used diagnostically: "Give 'em a shot of Ritalin, and if it works, they're hyperactive."

Adds Westman, "I think that too many doctors see their role as that of saying a kid has minimal brain dysfunction and putting him on stimulants. If the child is restless and fidgety, you can reduce stimulation in the classroom. You can make the child understand what's expected of him and break down a task that's too large for him into small units."

Widespread diagnosis and pharmacologic treatment of "hyperactivity" is a peculiarly American phenomenon. Researchers have consistently found a much lower incidence of the disorder in the British Isles than in the United States and have rejected the broad diagnostic criteria used here (*Dev Med Child Neurol* 20:279-299, 1978). In the United Kingdom, most children who would be regarded as hyperactive by American diagnosticians are viewed-as having a "conduct disorder" and are rarely treated with drugs. Commenting on this phenomenon, Martin C. O. Bax, senior editor of *Developmental Medicine and Child Neurology*, wrote, "For children, movement seems to be as natural a way of coping with stress as does the proverbial cup of coffee—or something stronger—to the overstressed executive. There are many reasons why a child may display high activity. I listed seven some years ago, but I have thought of one or two more since then, of which 'iatrogenic' was the most obvious omission."

Another area rife with semantic and conceptual confusion is that of dyslexia. Practically, the term refers to any kind of difficulty in learning to read; it is commonly thought, incorrectly, to result from visual defects. Its multiple possible causes, Schoenwetter points out, include chronic absenteeism (for other reasons) from school; genetic factors; auditory problems; subnormal intelligence; CNS dysfunction; incomplete, crossed, or mixed cerebral dominance; difficulties with directional or spatial perception; and emotional or interpersonal problems. Most dyslexic children can be taught to read adequately, but they need to be identified and given remedial instruction as early as possible.

Children with particularly serious or elusive learning problems are best treated by interdisciplinary teams, a more common phenomenon these days than in the past. (The team at Ochsner Clinic's Child Development Center in New Orleans, for example, includes a pediatric neurologist, a child psychiatrist, a social worker, a special educator, an audiologist, and a hearing, speech, and language pathologist.) But perhaps even more important is closer cooperation between such teams (or individual practitioners) and the school systems in which impaired children spend so much of their time and have their most evident difficulties.

Says Schoenwetter, "This is one of the few areas in which medicine is asked to diagnose and education is asked to treat." But there are problems. "Economic pressures confronting local schools and the generalized training of educators have limited the focus of education to those students who can thrive in competitive, group-oriented schools," Westman told the symposium. "As a result most children with academic learning problems are the products of less than adequate schooling."

But at present, the idea of mobilizing already overscheduled physicians to work toward better educational help for their learning-disabled patients seems little more than a gleam in an interdisciplinarian's eye. Concedes Schoenwetter, "I don't think our society is set up that way."

At the ACLD meeting, as at many such meetings, various new "causes" of learning disabilities were announced. Through the years, investigators in the field have indicted fluorescent light in classrooms, allergies, vitamin deficiencies, otitis media, and numerous other factors. The Wisconsin team has recently evaluated one of the most famous of these factors, food additives, in a double-blind controlled study. Their conclusions are that a small group of children show an adverse behavioral response to additives and that preschoolers tend to be most responsive to the Feingold elimination diet but that the widespread favorable response to the diet that is sometimes claimed does not appear to exist.

JAMA MEDICAL NEWS asked the Wisconsin group for an opinion on a number of the aforementioned factors as possible causes of learning problems. Volunteered Westman, "Let me comment, because I'm predictably the one to be the most negative. I'm open to anything! For me everything is electrical and chemical and relates to metabolites. But so what? If changing dietary factors or lights in the school makes a difference, then do it."

Report Says Medical Model Hurts Handicapped Children

by *Psychiatric News*

CONTRARY TO traditional thinking and research on the subject, it is the social, not the biological, aspects of handicap that condemn a vast number of disabled children and adults to unrewarding and useless lives. This is one of the principal conclusions of the fifth report of the Carnegie Council on Children, entitled *The Unexpected Minority: Handicapped Children in America*, prepared by John Gliedman (associate professor of psychology, Empire State College of SUNY) and William Roth (associate professor of political science, SUNY at Albany).

Much of the blame for the discrimination against the handicapped must be laid to well-meaning professionals, particularly those in the medical profession, who, according to the report, view the handicapped only in the traditional medical model. This leaves the disabled individual to be perpetually viewed as a "patient," according to the authors, with the handicap being treated as if it were akin to an infection or a malignant tumor. "From this definition a host of consequences follows. Medically certified as 'ill,' the child becomes a full-time (and often lifelong) patient. Both the child and the parents are expected to accept passively the medical establishment's superior knowledge and therapeutic instructions." When defined this way, the authors state, success can only be perceived as the child's getting well, which is usually an impossible goal in the case of most physical handicaps. The report sees as one of the most destructive results of this attitude the fact that decisions about the future are frequently deferred indefinitely, i.e., until the child is "cured."

More often than not, Gliedman and Roth maintain, individual handicaps are not as restricting and confining as are the attitudes of a society that insists on labeling the handicapped as different or inferior. Society has, over the years, evolved lower expectations for the handicapped and discourages the same levels and types of achievements it encourages in "normal" individuals.

When handicapped individuals reach the levels society has set for them, society congratulates both them and itself, thus reinforcing this cycle of lowered expectations, according to the report.

To correct the long-standing problems of the handicapped, the authors of the report urge a "two-pronged strategy" consisting of both research and action. Research is most needed in the area of developmental stages of the handicapped. The report states that too often there is an attempt to force them to fit into developmental theories designed for the physically unimpaired, despite a growing body of evidence that their stages of development are unique, often in direct contradiction to traditional theories such as those of Piaget, Erikson, or Kohlberg.

The report stresses that action is needed to facilitate both social and political reform to benefit the handicapped. "Disability superstars" are needed to dramatize the seriousness of the situations in which handicapped people, particularly children, find themselves, according to the authors. "The Paul Robesons, Jackie Robinsons, and Ralph Bunches of disability" need to be mobilized to spearhead a civil rights movement for the handicapped.

Gliedman and Roth state that reforms could include giving disabled workers preference in hiring, or even taking away jobs from able-bodied, but less qualified, workers. Encouraged were tactics used by other civil rights movements such as fighting for quota systems and filing class action suits to enforce anti-discrimination laws.

An Observational Analysis Of the IEP Conference

by Sue Goldstein, Bonnie Strickland, Ann P. Turnbull and Lynn Curry

Abstract: Through naturalistic observational procedures, this study examined the dynamics of individualized education program (IEP) conferences. Participants present, the nature and frequency of topics discussed, and the length of conferences were considered. A followup questionnaire was administered to all conference participants to measure satisfaction. Results indicated that the IEP conferences studied generally involved the resource teacher, who was found to be the most dominant speaker, reviewing an already developed IEP with the parents, who were the primary recipients of the comments made at the conference. Implications point to the need to train parents in procedures and responsibilities associated with the IEP process and to train professionals to involve parents as active decision makers in defining an appropriate education for their child.

■ In the last decade professionals in special education have noted the need to involve parents in educational planning for their children as teachers, advisors, and advocates (Simches, 1975). Studies have indicated that parents' participation in education has a positive effect on their child's achievement (Bigler, 1975; Bittle, 1975; Edgerly, 1975; Locke, 1976; McKinney, 1975). Parent involvement has also brought about positive change in parental attitudes (Corrado, 1975; Lynch, 1976).

With the passage of Public Law 94-142, the Education for All Handicapped Children Act of 1975, a parent participation component of special education has been mandated for the public schools. Parents are now to be involved in all aspects of their child's placement process. This includes the presence of the parent at the individualized education program (IEP) conference. Communication has been emphasized as a major need by both parents and professionals in forming an effective alliance. The IEP conference can be viewed as an excellent means of exchanging information and as a mutual planning session between school and home. In this conference the professional can define his or her role as one of consultant to the parent, helping to set realistic goals for the child.

The role of parents in IEP development and on school planning teams has just begun to evolve. In a survey of professional members of school planning teams, a majority felt that parent participation in IEP development should consist mainly of presenting and gathering information relevant to the case, rather than contributing to the educational planning (Yoshida, Fenton, Kaufman, & Maxwell, 1978). Although many parents and professionals have advocated the role of parents of exceptional children as working partners in special education, the parent-professional alliance is still in an early stage of development.

The purpose of this study was to observe IEP conferences involving parents of mainstreamed children with mild learning problems. The observations were to delineate the frequency of parental involvement in the conference and the nature of topics discussed by

1

parents and educators. A questionnaire was also developed to ascertain each participant's satisfaction with the conference. The study provides a descriptive analysis of parent-professional interaction that is actually occurring in the development of the IEP.

METHOD

Sample

This study focused on the IEP conference process in three school districts in North Carolina: one rural, one suburban, and one in a university setting. Two schools within each district were chosen by the authors and local education agency directors of special education as being representative of that district. Conferences to be observed were selected by the special education teachers in the designated schools.

Two factors contributed to limiting the sample size of the study to 14 conferences. First, due to the exigencies of securing prior clearances, the study could not be implemented until early October of the school year. By that time the legislative deadline (*Federal Register,* August 23, 1977, Sec. 121a.342) had passed for developing IEP's for children previously classified as handicapped. Thus, the potential pool of handicapped children still in need of an IEP was limited. Secondly, although 21 conferences were scheduled to be observed, 7 of them were canceled because the parents failed to attend. These conferences were either re-scheduled or a copy of the IEP was sent to the parents' home for approval. Of the 14 remaining conferences, 11 involved children who were being considered for special education placement for the first time. The children whose conferences were observed were in grades two through six, and were classified as either mildly mentally retarded or learning disabled. These categorical areas represented the majority of handicapped children mainstreamed in the schools involved.

Procedures

As each IEP conference was scheduled, the special services teacher in the school contacted the observers. A coder-observer was in attendance at each conference reported in this study. An intercoder reliability of .87 was established by using videotaped conference segments for training and testing prior to initiating the observations. Written permission to code the verbal interaction in the conference was obtained from each parent before the session began.

A coding instrument was developed which enabled the observers to specify at 2 minute intervals the topic being discussed, the speaker, and the recipient. For example, through the use of numerical identifiers, it might be coded that the resource teacher was talking to the parent about a behavioral concern. Topics coded were selected through an analysis of the requirements of Public Law 94-142, as well as in consideration of the educational procedures that would produce these desired ends. The 2 minute time interval allowed the documentation of anecdotal information while still enabling accurate identification of major conference topics. Additional information coded included all participants by role at the conference and the starting and ending times of the conference.

A followup questionnaire to measure conference satisfaction was completed by all participants immediately after each conference. The questionnaire was comprised of eight questions rated on a five point scale with terminal points identified as *strongly disagree* and *strongly agree*.

RESULTS

Participants

In the 14 conferences observed, the mean number of participants was 3.7 (range 2-6). Table 1 indicates the percentage of observed conferences attended by the role of the participants.

When examining the IEP conference participants in light of the specifications for com-

TABLE 1

Percentage of Observed Conferences Attended by Role of the Participant

Role	Percent of conferences attended
Resource teacher	100
Parent	100
Classroom teacher	43
Student interns (student teacher or psychology intern)	36
Evaluator (other than resource teacher)	29
Principal	21
Counselor	14
Speech therapist	14
Reading teacher	7
Handicapped student	0

TABLE 2

Topics Ranked by Percentage of Total Citations

Topics	Percent of total citations	Mean citations per conference
Curriculum (goals and objectives)	20	3.6
Behavior	14	2.5
Performance	13	2.4
Miscellaneous conference procedures (signing papers, explaining forms)	12	2.2
Evaluation	11	2.0
Personal/family	7	1.3
Instructional materials	5	.9
Placement	4	.7
Special services	4	.7
Rights and responsibilities	3	.6
Individual responsible	2	.4
Health	1	.2
Future contacts	1	.1
Future plans	—	—

mittee membership set forth in the Rules and Regulations (*Federal Register*, August 23, 1977, Sec. 121a.344) for implementing Public Law 94-142, only 5 of the 14 conferences were found to be legally constituted. In the 9 conferences that did not have full representation, the missing participant was the representative of the public agency, other than the child's teacher, who was responsible for providing or supervising special education.

None of the observed conferences were attended by both of the child's parents. Of the 14 conferences, the child's mother was in attendance at 11 and the father at 3. The child was not included in any of the conferences observed.

Length of Conferences

The mean length of the 14 conferences was 36 minutes, the range being 6 to 72 minutes. No correlation was found to exist between conference length and the number of people present or the grade level of the child.

Topics

Table 2 provides a ranking of the topics discussed at the conferences according to the percentage of the total number of citations coded and the mean number of coded citations per conference. Although curriculum was the most frequently discussed topic, more than half of the coded curriculum statements were made in two conferences. Excluding these two conferences, the mean curriculum citations for the remaining 12 conferences was 1.9.

No one topic was recorded as being discussed at every conference. Curriculum, however, was cited in 13, and evaluation in 12 of the 14 conferences.

Conference Communication

The communication in the conference was coded according to which participant was speaking and which was the recipient of the information. Table 3 provides a breakdown of the participants ranked by the mean coded speaking citations per conference attended. The resource teacher was observed talking more than twice as much as the parent. Three of the 14 parents accounted for 63% of the parental speaking citations, all of which occurred in the three longest conferences. In examining the data from the four shortest conferences (6-20 minutes), the parents were recorded as talking 0 to 2 times. The resource teacher talked most at 11 of the conferences, while parents (both fathers) were cited as speaking the most at two conferences. At one conference the parent and classroom teacher were cited as speaking an equal amount, both more than the resource teacher.

The primary recipients of statements made during the conference were parents (63% of statements), resource teachers (17% of statements), and classroom teachers (10% of statements). Discussion at the IEP conference was directed toward the parent. The resource teachers were cited as directing 81% of their statements to parents, while the classroom teachers were talking to the parents during 76% of their cited statements. Typically, the professional who was speaking in the meeting directed comments to the parent, to the exclusion of other professionals who were present.

The topics most frequently discussed by the three major participant groups and the percentage of each group's total speaking citations devoted to that topic are outlined in Table 4.

Conference Satisfaction

Table 5 includes the mean responses for each participant group for the eight items on the questionnaire completed at the conclusion of the conference. No significant differences among groups were found in their report of satisfaction with the IEP conference proceedings.

DISCUSSION

Parent Participation

The two consistent participants at all observed IEP conferences were the resource teacher and the parent. In seven instances of previously scheduled conferences, the parents failed to attend. The conference was rescheduled in these instances, or the IEP was sent home for the parent to sign. (It should be pointed out that merely sending the IEP home for the parental signature does not meet the legal requirements for implementing Public Law 94-142.) The major reason that the educational personnel chose not to proceed with the conference was that in all seven instances of canceled conferences, the IEP had been written primarily by the resource teacher prior to the conference. Thus, the purpose of the conference could be viewed as informing parents of the nature of the already developed IEP, obtaining any suggestions from them for modification, and receiving their approval. If the parent was not in attendance, the purpose of the conference from the viewpoint of the educators could not be fulfilled.

The National Education Association's (NEA) *Study of Education of the Handicapped* (1978) reported that a common procedure for making placement decisions is for the resource teacher to confer informally with a classroom teacher concerning a child's placement. The IEP meeting then becomes little more than a "performance procedure" (p. 36). Of the 14 conferences observed, in only one instance was the meeting actually devoted to specifying goals

TABLE 3

Mean Coded Speaking Citations of Participants

Participants	Mean speaking citations per conference attended
Resource teacher	9.6
Parent	4.6
Classroom teacher	3.5
Counselor	3.0
Principal	2.6
Evaluator	2.0
Speech therapist	1.0
Reading teacher	1.0

TABLE 4

Topics Most Frequently Discussed by Three Major Participant Groups

Participant groups	Percent of group's total speaking citations devoted to topic
Resource teachers	
Curriculum	22
Evaluation	19
Performance	13
Parents	
Behavior	18
Curriculum	18
Personal/family	15
Classroom teachers	
Behavior	47
Curriculum	24
Performance	14

and objectives jointly between the parent and educators. It is noteworthy that in this instance the father was a psychologist who was familiar with the purpose and nature of the IEP, and had previously indicated to the resource teacher that his wife would attend the meeting and participate in writing the goals and objectives.

Scheduling

As reported in the previous section, none of the conferences were attended by both parents. Scheduling might have been an obstacle for some parents. Two of the conferences were held at 7:30 a.m. and the remaining 12 were conducted from 2:00 to 4:30 p.m. Evening meetings might have enabled more fathers to attend. The parents of learning disabled chil-

TABLE 5

Mean Responses for Each Participant Group on Followup Questionnaire (Scaled from 1 to 5)

	Resource teachers	Parents	Classroom teachers	Principals	Others (counselors, evaluators, student interns)
1. Has the IEP committee meeting been helpful in planning the child's educational program?	4.5	4.9	4.0	5.0	4.1
2. Can the goals set for the child be accomplished during the current school year?	4.1	4.4	3.5	4.5	3.9
3. Did you have all your questions concerning the child answered at the committee meeting?	4.1	4.8	4.7	4.5	4.0
4. Are you satisfied with the placement decision?	4.8	5.0	4.5	4.5	4.7
5. Can the school system offer the resources to effectively implement the IEP?	4.6	4.7	4.5	5.0	4.6
6. As a result of the IEP meeting, do you have a better understanding of the child?	4.4	4.3	4.0	4.5	4.2
7. Do you have a definite responsibility in achieving the goals of the IEP?	4.6	4.1	5.0	4.0	2.9
8. Do you feel that your time at the meeting was well spent?	4.9	4.7	4.7	4.0	4.6
Mean	4.5	4.6	4.3	4.5	4.2

dren in a survey conducted by Dembinski and Mauser (1977) stated a strong preference for the inclusion of both parents at conferences in which the concerns about the child are discussed. Local education agencies might provide encouragement for both parents to attend and explore alternative scheduling to increase the possibility of arranging a convenient time for parents.

Other Participants

The finding that the classroom teacher was present at fewer than half of the conferences is disturbing. It indicates that the person most responsible for implementing educational strategies to reach the objectives set for a mainstreamed child is not routinely involved in the development of these objectives.

The lack of correlation between the length of the IEP conference and the number of conference participants might be reflective of the findings related to major participant groups. It appears from these findings that the majority of the conferences consisted of the resource teacher reviewing the developed IEP with the parent, regardless of the number of other participants at the meeting. Other participants in the meeting might have participated only incidentally, and thus they would not have affected the length of the conference.

Topics Discussed

In analyzing the topics most discussed at the conferences, it was not surprising to find that curriculum, behavior, and performance ranked as the three most frequently discussed areas. It was surprising, however, that topics such as evaluation, placement, special services, rights and responsibilities, future contacts, and future plans received so little attention. An analysis of the anecdotal information related to evaluation revealed that standardized achievement test scores were typically reported to parents in terms of grade equivalencies. The explanations pertaining to evaluation could generally be characterized as confusing, and yet parents were not cited as asking questions for clarification. One contributing factor to this lack of questions could be the fact that evalu-

1

ation was discussed at the beginning of the conference, whereas parents were coded as participating more actively in discussions during the later portion of the conference when they apparently felt more relaxed.

Placement and special services each received an average of .7 citations per conference. Since this represents a major decision in the provision of an appropriate education to handicapped students, it is puzzling that such minimal attention was directed to it. Typically, parents were told that the child would be receiving resource help. This is consistent with the NEA findings previously reported. Parents generally seemed pleased that the child would be receiving extra help, but in one instance the parent questioned exactly how the resource program would be structured. On the followup questionnaire, parents reported total satisfaction (mean score of 5.0 on a 5 point scale) with the placement decision.

It is doubtful that the parents were aware of the day to day functioning of resource rooms or of issues such as the nature of coordination between resource and classroom teachers. The reason that parents did not ask placement questions could be that they did not realize the complexity of all of the issues involved in insuring that the child is, indeed, appropriately served. Further, parents made no requests for related services such as speech therapy or counseling even though these services would have been highly appropriate in several cases.

The legal rights and responsibilities of parents were glossed over in the majority of conferences. One observer noted that the resource teachers sometimes mentioned to the parent that they had discussed the parent's rights previously, and asked the parent whether he or she had any questions. This mention of rights was not always cited in the 2 minute observations. Two of the school systems gave parents a printed copy of their rights for future reference. Only one parent was noted as asking a question pertaining to rights, which was on the subject of confidentiality of records. Considering these observations, it could be inferred that either parents were already well aware of their rights or, more probably, that they remained relatively uninformed on this subject.

The lack of discussion of future contacts is troublesome. No comments were made regarding the legal requirement to review the IEP on an annual basis or to plan strategies for keeping lines of communication open between school and home.

The proceedings of the IEP conferences observed in this study can generally be characterized as the resource teacher taking the initiative to review the already developed IEP with the parent, who was the primary recipient of the comments made at the conference. Parents were given the opportunity to contribute additional information on the child that might result in modifying the IEP. This role is consistent with the findings of Yoshida and his colleagues (1978) regarding the responses of planning team members, who viewed the appropriate parental involvement activities as giving and receiving information. Further, the role was characterized in the Yoshida and Gottlieb (1977) model of parental participation as "passive participant" (p. 19). The majority of parental statements focused on the behavior of the child at home and at school. The anecdotal notes of observers indicated that the majority of the parents expressed the desire to work with their children at home; however, on the whole they received few suggestions from teachers on exactly what they should be working on.

The high frequency of classroom teachers' statements pertaining to behavior is an important indicator of their concerns regarding mainstreaming. Classroom teachers were cited as making statements concerning behavior almost twice as frequently as statements concerning curriculum. The IEP conference should be viewed as an opportunity to insure that the classroom teacher has sufficient information and backup support to manage the behavior of the child in the classroom.

Considering that the average length of the conferences was 36 minutes, it is not surprising that many important topics were not fully discussed. Additionally, several of the conferences were scheduled back-to-back; therefore, a time limit was imposed from the outset. Certainly, the time available for IEP meetings is at a premium. However, it is clear that an IEP meeting that covers all necessary topics related to providing an appropriate education to a handicapped child and creates opportunities for two-way communication between parents and educators cannot be limited to a half hour.

Satisfaction with Conference

The overwhelmingly positive reaction to the conferences on the part of all participants was an unanticipated finding. In one instance, for example, a mother walked 1½ miles to school in below freezing weather to attend her child's conference, which lasted only 6 minutes. On the followup questionnaire the mother circled "5's" on all 8 items, indicating a highly favorable reaction to the conference.

The response of parents to the item on the questionnaire asking whether they had all their questions answered was extremely positive (4.8). Considering how many topics received minimal attention and how short in duration the conferences were, this seems to be an inflated score. It is difficult to explain this reaction. It could be due to the parents' lack of knowledge of the purpose of the IEP meeting. They might have viewed the conference as an increase in communication over what had been experienced with teachers in the past, and felt a sense of relief that the purpose of the conference had not been to report that the child was "in trouble." They might also have anticipated positively the extra help the child would be receiving.

IMPLICATIONS

Due to the limited size, nature, and demographic restrictions of the sample, caution must be exercised in generalizing the conclusions and implications of this study. Further research and replication would more clearly delineate the extent and nature of parental involvement in the IEP conference. With these precautions in mind, several implications of this study will be considered here.

Availability of IEP to the Classroom Teacher

The limited involvement of classroom teachers in the IEP conference, the presence of the resource teacher at all conferences, and the frequency of speaking citations attributed to this representative, imply that the resource teacher assumes primary responsibility not only for the IEP conference, but also for the development and implementation of the IEP. For example, classroom teachers attended only 43% of the conferences. This raises a question as to whether or not the IEP is available to and being used by the classroom teacher. One resource teacher commented to an observer that not one of eight teachers whom she asked about an IEP knew what an IEP was, although they had children with IEP's in their classrooms for the entire year.

Further research is needed to determine whether this observation is a trend in all school districts and whether responsibility delegated in this way results in the IEP being simply a function of special education—developed by special educators and reflecting curriculum objectives of special education programs—rather than of the child's total curriculum. Further research might also determine the extent to which regular classroom teachers with mainstreamed handicapped students have access to and make use of the IEP in the regular instructional setting.

Definition of Roles and Responsibilities

The limited attendance and passive participation of other members of the IEP committee suggest that roles and responsibilities of these members are not clearly defined. A local education agency (LEA) representative, other than the child's teacher, was present at only 36% of the conferences, and each held a passive role in the conference attended. The role of this participant needs to be specified and, perhaps, training provided to help the LEA representative act as a parent advocate at the conference. Evaluation of a parent advocate role is needed to measure its effect on increasing parent participation in a conference. Unless each participant understands what his or her contribution is to be and actively assumes that role, the multidimensional purpose of the IEP conference will be defeated.

Parental Involvement in IEP

While parental participation and opportunity for such participation was quite limited in this study, further research is needed to explore the question of what constitutes effective parental involvement in IEP development and implementation. It should be pointed out that many parents may prefer not to be involved actively in writing goals and objectives. They may prefer the role of reviewing a previously developed IEP with the opportunity to make additions or deletions. The individual preferences of parents should be recognized. It should not be assumed that the most active involvement of parents in IEP development is always the goal for which to strive; or, on the other hand, that the mere presence of the parent at the IEP conference constitutes involvement. A caution in this regard is that some parents might wish to participate in the writing of goals and objectives but might lack the prerequisite skills for such involvement.

Replication of surveys to obtain data on parental satisfaction is needed prior to drawing definite conclusions in this area. The reaction of educators to the conference proceedings also requires further investigation. In a followup study currently under way, resource teachers have indicated that the major positive outcomes of IEP development are ease in planning for the handicapped child on a daily and weekly basis after the IEP is completed, and increased collaboration between special and regular educators. Increased collaboration between parents and educators was not identified by resource teachers in the study in process as a major positive outcome. It will be important in the continued development of the IEP process to build on the positive reactions of the initial implementation and refine it according to increased knowledge of this planning process.

CONCLUSION

The implications of this study point to the need for systematically training parents to fulfill their roles and responsibilities associated with IEP involvement and for training professionals to involve parents as *full* partners in this significant educational task. The competencies associated with successful shared decision making on the part of parents and professionals need to be specified and training models generated. This need was underscored by the NEA study (1978). It was pointed out in this study that, although the parent's involvement in the IEP is crucial and the need for systematic and humane parent education programs has been demonstrated, no evidence was found that such programs existed at the time of the study. Based on the results of this investigation, we have proposed training alternatives aimed at preparing both professionals and parents to share in educational decision making at the IEP conference (Turnbull, Strickland, & Goldstein, 1978). Evaluation of training programs should also be initiated. The ultimate outcome of the training for both parents and professionals should be a cooperative effort in developing the most appropriate educational program for the child.

REFERENCES

Bigler, M. A. G. Parental use of household literature to reinforce secondary school reading instruction. *Dissertation Abstracts*, 1975, *35*, 7146.

Bittle, R. G. Improving parent-teacher communication through a daily recorded telephone message: Evaluation of effects on academic and non-academic performance. *Dissertation Abstracts*, 1975, *35*, 7522.

Corrado, J. *The family hour: An experiment in parent involvement.* New York: Play School Association, 1975.

Dembinski, R. J., & Mauser, A. J. Considering the parents of LD children: What they want from professionals. *Journal of Learning Disabilities*, 1977, *10*, 49-55.

Edgerly, R. F. Effectiveness of parent counseling in treatment of children with learning disabilities. *Dissertation Abstracts*, 1975, *36*, 1301.

Locke, W. W. The effect of frequency of home visits on parent behavior and child achievement. *Dissertation Abstracts*, 1976, *37*, 4217.

Lynch, E. *Measuring involvement in an early intervention project.* Paper presented at the Annual International Convention of The Council for Exceptional Children, Chicago, Illinois, 1976.

McKinney, J. A. *The development and implementation of a tutorial program for parents to improve the reading and mathematics achievement of their children.* Maxi II Practicum, submitted in partial fulfillment of requirements for D.Ed, Nova University. Arlington VA: ERIC Document Reproduction Service, 1975. (ED113703)

National Education Association. *Education for all handicapped children: Consensus, conflict, and challenge.* Washington DC: National Education Association, 1978.

Rules and regulations for implementing Public Law 94-142. *Federal Register.* Washington DC: US Government Printing Office, August 23, 1977.

Simches, R. F. The parent-professional partnership. *Exceptional Children*, 1975, *41*, 565-566.

Turnbull, A. P., Strickland, B., & Goldstein, S. Parental involvement in developing and implementing the IEP: Training professionals and parents. *Education and Training of the Mentally Retarded*, 1978, *13*, 414-423.

Yoshida, R., Fenton, K., Kaufman, M. J., & Maxwell, J. P. Parental involvement in the special education pupil planning process: The school's perspective. *Exceptional Children*, 1978, *44*, 531-533.

Yoshida, R. K., & Gottlieb, J. A model of parental participation. *Mental Retardation*, 1977, *15*, 17-20.

Vocational Education And the Handicapped

by Terry Moynahan

"If I weren't getting training in school," said 17-year-old Gena, "I'd probably be going to work at a day-care center when I finish. I like kids, but I don't think I could take being with them all the time. I prefer what I'm learning now—typing, filing, and talking on the phone.

"I've had to work hard in the vocational classes, but if it weren't for them, I'd be skipping school, failing, and not getting anywhere in life."

This was Gena's reply when I asked her about the value of vocational training. She had found her niche in a clerical practices course.

In her first years in school, Gena's progress was slower than that of most of her classmates. In the sixth grade, she was diagnosed as having minimal brain injury and began receiving special education services.

She had problems until she entered vocational training. Now, her attitude and outlook are as beautiful as the glowing smile that lights her face when she describes her career plans—plans that had not even begun to develop until she entered her first vocational class.

As an instructor of a vocational education for the handicapped (VEH) class, I am interested in the impressions of students who are participating in vocational programs. I have spoken with many such students—both those presently enrolled in classes and those who were formerly enrolled—and know their opinions to be of great value in determining strengths and weaknesses of the programs.

When students discuss these programs, their comments usually center on several topics: the motivation and direction the programs give them, the self-confidence they develop as a result of developing skills, the pace of the classes and the number of students in them, the characteristics of their teachers, and the accessibility of various courses.

• Some students say vocational education motivates them to go to school and gives them direction. For example, Gena had had problems with attendance and lack of direction. She said, "I used to skip school a lot before I got into the clerical practices class. I really felt left out. I guess people thought because I was in a special ed class that I was stupid, that I didn't know anything. I think that once I began getting training and knew where I was going I didn't let them put me down anymore. I told them I could do just as good as they could, and I proved it, too."

In Gena's case, vocational education helped motivate her to a more serious approach to education and put an end to her attendance problems, also "Once I was in the clerical course I looked forward to it, so I was in school all the time. When you get into activities you really like, you don't skip."

• Students also repeatedly mention that vocational education builds self-confidence. Tracey, a student in a clerical course, discussed this subject. "I'm much better at typing now than I ever thought I could be, although I had taken a typing class before. The difference between the two is the confidence I have now because the teacher I have now understands that I learn slow and goof up. If the teacher gives you a hard time, you lose confidence. But you can regain it if the teacher takes time with you."

Gena agreed. "As I developed skills, I developed confidence. My vocational teacher told me I could handle anything if I put my mind to it. I didn't believe it at first, but once I really got into it, I learned things."

At the end of the year in the VEH class, Gena had progressed enough to be placed in a vocational office education (VOE) course and in an on-the-job training program. Confident of herself and her VOE teacher, Gena recognized that the new class was dif-

1

ferent from the VEH class. "In the VOE class, the work's a little harder, and they don't go as slow as I'm used to, but I'm catching on. If it weren't for the VEH class, I might be failing the VOE class."

A former student, Carlos, who was classified as language/learning disabled, agreed with Gena. "I got to the point [in the VEH class] where I was going just a little faster than before and got promoted to a more advanced program."

Both students had acquired enough skills, knowledge, and confidence in the VEH class to move into mainstream education.

Although many educators have expressed concern about integrating special-needs students into regular classes, the progress Carlos and Gena have made supports the contention that other special students who are placed in an appropriate environment can succeed also.

• Pace refers to the rate at which learning takes place. Class size determines the student-teacher ratio and therefore reflects the amount of help individual learners can get from the teacher. Because the pace and class size are right in VEH classes, students notice the lack of pressure associated with completing tasks within designated time intervals.

Gena: "The best thing about my vocational training is that the work is not so hard at first. It's at a pace that is comfortable. The work increases gradually as you go along with your lessons, but the deadlines are reasonable. No unnecessary rush, and you get your work done."

Richard, a former student who is now doing prefab residential framing, added, "If there were more students,

there wouldn't be enough time for everyone to get enough help." He said he had felt comfortable with a student-teacher ratio of about 10 to 1.

• In commenting on the characteristics of teachers, students expressed a strong preference for teachers who are sensitive and humane.

Tracey: "I had a lot of problems with attendance before I started Mrs. S's class. I wanted to quit school. But Mrs. S. understands me, and I'm bringing up my grades."

"We get more help and patience from our VEH teacher, and the students have more patience, too," Claire, another student in a vocational class, added.

These comments point out some distinct advantages that VEH teachers have over regular vocational teachers. The most important is their experience and training in dealing with handicapped students.

• In discussing accessibility of courses, special-needs students often feel that they get the "short end of the stick." It's difficult not to agree with them to some extent.

Handicapped students often find themselves training in fields for which they have little interest, simply because VEH course offerings do not include training in the area of their primary vocational interest.

Commenting on accessibility, Carlos, who is out of school and working successfully as a carpenter, ventured, "I don't think there are enough classes for special students. They can't get training for many careers. If a guy wants to take a regular vocational class and they know he's special ed, he may not be able to take it. And where's he going to be standing? Outside. He might have to settle for second or third choice."

Seven years after the passage of the Rehabilitation Act (PL 93-112) and five years after the passage of the Education for All Handicapped Children Act (PL 94-142), special-needs students are participating in a wide range of vocational programs. Some special students are progressing satisfactorily in regular classes, and many are setting their own pace in recently developed special-needs programs.

Yet a surprising number of students finish their education with embarrassingly limited vocational training. One reason is the limited funding available for expanding vocational programs for the handicapped.

Another problem is the difficulty of placing students in an appropriate program. Probably because of the limited number of programs, some students are placed inappropriately, and these students do not experience the success that others do.

Two important characteristics of students who are successful in these programs are a specific career interest in the particular training program and a general readiness for vocational training. Lacking these qualities, students seldom succeed in the class. More prevocational programs are needed to help students develop an interest in a particular career while acquiring readiness skills such as the ability to follow instructions, stay on task, and control behavior.

Special-needs vocational students do not doubt the value of vocational education. Rather, they take advantage of available opportunities to develop skills, knowledge, and attitudes that will prepare them for mainstream education and permanent employment. For the most part, they are overwhelmingly positive about their experiences. They speak proudly of the confidence gained from jobs well done and of their dreams for the future. □

Community College: New Opportunities For the LD Student

by Jeffrey Barsch

When the California State legislature passed Assembly Bill 77, providing for the educational rights and privileges of adult learning-disabled students, it created a brand new challenge for the State's community colleges. These schools were suddenly given responsibility for meeting the educational needs of the vast number of adults in California who are learning disabled but who, nevertheless, wish to continue their education beyond high school. At Ventura College, where I teach, we took this challenge seriously, and began planning a program for learning-disabled adults. I am recounting the major components of the program we developed at the college in the hope that our experience will aid other schools who are turning their attention toward similar comprehensive programs.

In September, 1977, when our program began, we had not yet formally assessed or diagnosed any students who might have learning disabilities; yet, a survey conducted earlier by several faculty members indicated that a substantial number of students had previously withdrawn from the college as a result of academic failure. As our first step in finding learning-disabled adults, we contacted the local Department of Vocational Rehabilitation and outlined our possible service to their clients. Members of our staff spoke to "core curriculum" college classes, suggesting to the students that, if they were experiencing failure, our learning disabilities center might be of value to them. We also displayed posters around the campus to publicize the presence and services of our center.

Students who had previously dropped out of college for academic reasons were invited to return to campus to make use of our services.

Within four months 24 students had been diagnosed as learning disabled (using results from the *Peabody Individual Achievement Test* [PIAT], the *Wechsler Adult Intelligence Scale* [WAIS], and the *Valett Perceptual Motor Inventory*).

Courses Developed

To meet the needs of these students, we developed the following courses:

Improving Your Learning Potential. The purpose of this course is to improve learning efficiency through perceptual-motor training. Designed as a laboratory experience, in this course each student receives individual instruction. Focus is on the pre-steps which we feel are necessary for proper memory retention and academic concentration. Activities to improve posture, bilaterality, rhythm, and muscular strength are provided. I cannot overemphasize the relationship which I have seen in the college student between physical clumsiness and inadequate academic skills.

Advances in Perception. This course is designed to help the student explore his or her learning style. The student needs to understand which sense is his best ally in the learning process. We emphasize to the student that some people learn best visually, while others learn best using the auditory sense, or perhaps through the tactual mode. Students who have taken this class have developed a learning style inventory which can be used to determine learning style preference.

Self-Adjustment to College. We have found that most of our students have experienced years of academic failure and generally have a very poor self-image. It is necessary to provide counseling experiences dealing with the self-fulfilling prophecy of academic failure, human sexuality, tension-release exercises, and assertiveness training. It has been very helpful in this type of class to have each student keep a daily diary on audio tape of his feelings and experiences. The idea of speaking thoughts out loud and listening to one's own voice is a meaningful educational experience.

Maximizing Occupational Potential. This class allows the student an opportunity to experience work tasks and the world of work. Students are required to maintain physical dress and appearance which is necessary to get a job. A time clock is used to record attendance hours. This punching in and out gives the student a feeling of working under the pressure of time. A variety of tasks to evaluate student efficiency is provided. A typical session provides a series of plumbing and woodworking tasks which each student performs. The next class session introduces typing and business-office practices. An evaluation of student potential in each job area is provided to the student.

Advanced Perceptual-Motor Training. This is a special program for those learning-disabled students who have completed the courses just described. Special emphasis is placed on the use of the metronome as an aid in studying. Generally, the metronome is associated with music. However, this is not always the case. Research indicates that the metronome has been used to aid reading rate, typing, relaxation training, and study skills. Several metronome ideas have been developed in this class:

1. Oral recitation of the times tables to the beat.
2. Increasing reading rate by finding a metronome beat with which the student is comfortable. After a comfortable speed is established, increase that speed by 20 beats per minute. When the student begins the reading assignment, the metronome beat should be ignored. This process will increase reading speed without a loss of comprehension.
3. Metronome spelling: Students make a list of words which they cannot spell. These words are written one letter at a time. The metronome rate is set at 40 beats per minute. Each letter should be touched, and said aloud, on the beat.

Continuous Assessment Model

Faculty in the program feel that standardized tests are of limited value to our learning-disabled students. As an alternative, we have developed a continuous assessment model which provides direct daily measurement of academic behaviors. This direct measurement of progress toward specific academic goals is usually displayed in the form of a histogram or polygon. We are presently attempting a statistical inference study to measure motivational levels toward academic tasks of students who use continuous assessment, as opposed to students evaluated by standardized assessment methods such as those mentioned earlier in this article.

Biofeedback and Other Methods

Biofeedback is also proving to be a surprisingly valuable tool in developing learning efficiency. A new technique for psychosomatic self-regulation, called autogenic feedback training, was developed by combining biofeedback techniques with autogenic training, which is a therapeutic method involving simultaneous management of mental and somatic functions. For example, one approach we have used to decrease test anxiety is to teach the student to control his autonomic nervous system functions by increasing blood flow to his hands, voluntarily. The student places his hands in hot water (or uses a heating pad), makes his hands into fists, and thinks about making his hands warm. Increased blood flow is associated with an increase in temperature of the hands. Researchers at the Menninger Clinic found, by chance, that recovery from anxiety, migraine headaches, tension, etc., coincided with a notable increase in hand temperature within a two-minute period, since temperature increases as blood flow increases. Our results so far, informal as they are, have been most gratifying.

Conclusion

It is my belief that the California community college system has been developed as a service-oriented institution to meet the needs of a local community area. Part of my feeling is that every student of community college age is entitled to a further educational experience. As a society we cannot afford to give up on students who have academic potential. The development of the program at Ventura College can be considered only a small step in the challenge which faces our society. As a former learning-disabled student myself, I must firmly urge other colleges to "get their feet wet" and provide services for the learning-disabled adult. If qualified professionals and my parents had decided that at age 18 there was no further help for me, I would not be the person I am today. Others should be given the same chance.

What's Happening In New Jersey?

by Charles W. Walker, Jr.

At the New Jersey Education Association (NJEA), an important part of our job is to provide organizational assistance to local associations on instructional issues. Recently, our phones have been ringing continually with calls from anxious vocational educators. They are seeking help with questions about the placement of handicapped students in their classes. Some of these questions and their answers follow:

What does the Education for All Handicapped Children Act (PL 94-142) say about mainstreaming handicapped children into regular school classes?

The word *mainstreaming* does not appear in the new federal regulations on PL 94-142. The federal regulations mandate that to the maximum extent possible, and where appropriate, handicapped students should be provided education in the "least restrictive environment." For some students this "least restrictive environment" is not a regular classroom.

The federal regulations mandate that decisions on the placement of handicapped students be made only after formal evaluation and classification of the student and development of an individualized education program (IEP) for the student. The student's teachers, the parents, and the student, where appropriate, are all supposed to take part in this process.

Some districts, without proper planning and consideration, have mistakenly scheduled all handicapped students into regular classrooms, thinking that by doing this, they are complying with federal law.

When this has happened—and it shouldn't—the phones at NJEA start to ring.

Recently, for example, a vocational education teacher called and said excitedly—

Yesterday, four handicapped students classified as emotionally disturbed were put into my metal shop class, which already had 22 students in it.

There are only 20 work stations in the shop. Now I have 26 students!

I received no instructions from my supervisors on how to work with these new students. I have no certification or course work whatsoever in education of the handicapped.

What's going to happen when we start to use machinery and tools that can be dangerous? I fear for the safety of the four new students and the other 22 as well.

The administration tells me that, in a month or two, they will provide an instructional guide to help me. Meanwhile, they say, "Stay cool. Mainstreaming is mandated by the government, and these students must stay in your class."

Is this true? Help!

What provisions have been made to ensure appropriate class size in classes that have handicapped students?

The class size issue is not adequately addressed in federal regulations. Moreover, most states and local districts have no requirements about maximum class sizes for regular classrooms.

Several states, however, have regulations on the maximum class sizes and/or pupil-teacher ratios for various kinds of self-contained special education classes that a certified teacher of the handicapped teaches. New Jersey is one. Chapter 28 of the New Jersey Administrative Code sets the following maximum number of pupils for self-contained classes for special students:

Auditorily handicapped—eight pupils
Chronically ill—15 pupils
Communication handicapped—eight pupils
Emotionally disturbed—eight pupils
Mentally retarded—educable—15 pupils
Mentally retarded—eligible for day training—nine pupils per classroom with a pupil-staff ratio of 3 to 1
Mentally retarded—trainable—10 pupils
Multiple handicapped—eight pupils
Neurologically impaired—eight pupils

1

Orthopedically handicapped—10 pupils
Perceptually impaired—12 pupils
Socially maladjusted—12 pupils
Visually handicapped—eight pupils.

These requirements recognize that handicapped students deserve special attention on an individualized basis when in the hands of a specially certified teacher. Unfortunately, the regulations for PL 94-142 set no requirements for maximum class size or pupil-to-teacher ratio for the regular classroom into which handicapped students are placed and where there is no specially certified teacher of the handicapped. Moreover, New Jersey and most other states have set no such requirements.

It is perfectly legal in most schools to integrate 20 or more handicapped students at one time into a vocational education classroom or any other regular classroom. The implications of this are perhaps most critical in the vocational ed class because of the possible danger to students from equipment. The job of the vocational education teacher becomes almost an impossibility.

Vocational education teachers are very aware of the responsibility they have to ensure that students are trained to use equipment properly. If students are injured in their classes, these teachers face the possibility of being sued or being held liable.

Therefore, they should be aware of what kind of liability provisions their state law contains. If it has no save- or hold-harmless provision to protect teachers against financial loss for acts of negligence committed in the line of duty, the teachers association, where state law permits, should bargain an indemnification and hold-harmless clause as part of its collective bargaining agreement.

Even if the state law does have a hold-harmless provision, it is advisable for teachers to incorporate it as a part of their contract. This would allow them to bring cases involving questions of teacher liability under the purview of an arbitrator.

Will prospective vocational teachers and those already in the classroom receive proper training on teaching the handicapped?

The key to making vocational education work and work well for handicapped students is proper preservice and in-service training for vocational teachers.

College students preparing for careers in vocational education need adequate courses at the undergraduate and graduate levels on educating the handicapped. These courses should provide specific experiences in the classroom and include methods of educating the handicapped.

Providing suitable preservice training for vocational ed teachers may sound like an easy task to accomplish, but few college courses on teaching vocational subjects to the handicapped exist—even though it has been more than two years since PL 94-142 went into effect. New teachers continue to be employed in new vocational ed positions with no preservice training on educating the handicapped.

In-service training programs for vocational ed teachers present special considerations. In 31 states where bargaining laws exist, the terms and conditions of a contract may dictate requirements for such programs. Negotiating provisions for these programs, such as costs, time schedules, and released time for teachers, can become complicated. Even in states where bargaining laws do not exist, boards of education must consider these aspects of in-service programs.

PL 94-142 provides money to states for in-service training through "comprehensive personnel development funds." These funds have not yet created many meaningful in-service training programs for vocational ed teachers, because of the time that elapses between the appropriation of funds and their use at the local level. The money filters from the federal government to the state and then the local district. The local district has ultimate responsibility for making in-service work, regardless of what seed money filters down from above.

Vocational ed teachers should be directly involved in determining what kinds of in-service programs will best help them meet the unique needs of their students. All too often, in-service programs are geared for the regular classroom teachers of academic subjects. At best, these programs give teachers general information about handicapped students.

Vocational ed teachers need this information, of course, but they also need to know how to ensure the safety of handicapped students around machinery, behavior characteristics of the different types of handicapped individuals, vocational teaching methods for the handicapped, and a long list of other subjects.

It takes four to five years of full-time college course work to become a certified teacher of the handicapped. The vocational ed teacher cannot be expected to gain similar—and necessary—knowledge for teaching the handicapped at one in-service session.

In some districts, some of the time, handicapped students are working well in vocational ed programs. Turning these superb exceptions into the rule will take time, money, consideration, and commitment. Federal and state regulations may have to be revised and enforced if vocational educators are to be equipped with the resources and support they need in order to meet the needs of all of their students. □

MAINSTREAMING

A Misinterpretation Hinders Mainstreaming

by Linda H. Parrish and Marilyn R. Kok

The person most responsible for successful mainstreaming — the receiving teacher — is often ignored in drafting IEPs.

When the individualized educational plan (IEP) is developed for a handicapped child, the person most responsible for successful mainstreaming — the receiving teacher — is often left out. This was not the intent of Congress when it passed Public Law 94-142 (the Education for All Handicapped Children Act) in 1975. It stems instead from misinterpretation of the regulations developed by the Department of Health, Education, and Welfare for implementing the law.

These regulations specify that three parties must be present at the IEP conference: 1) a representative of the public agency, other than the child's teacher, who is qualified to provide or supervise the provisions of special education; 2) the child's teacher; and 3) one or both of the child's parents. Ambiguity arises because the regulations fail to identify specifically which teacher (or teachers) should be present.

Too often the child's teacher is interpreted to mean the special education teacher. When 38 vocational teachers from 20 geographical areas in Texas were asked whether they had helped to prepare IEPs for their handicapped students, for example, 33 said that they had not.[1]

During the original discussion of P.L. 94-142 in Congress, Sen. Robert J. Stafford of Vermont, a member of the Senate Subcommittee on the Handicapped, made it clear that the receiving teacher should be included in the preparation of a child's IEP.[2] He saw the IEP conference as an opportunity for the receiving teacher to learn about the child's strengths, weaknesses, and preferred learning styles; to meet parents and support personnel; to understand why a specific program was chosen; and to help in identifying short- and long-term goals and necessary equipment and teaching aids.

The representative of the public agency is the person who is supposed to provide the essential input from special education, according to the regulations. In actual practice, however, this representative has often been the building principal or the district superintendent. Consequently, special education has taken over the role of the child's teacher. This, in turn, makes the receiving teacher's involvement optional.

We believe that, if states were to limit representation at the IEP conference to those individuals *intended* by P.L. 94-142, the committee would actually include: 1) a

representative from special education; 2) the receiving teacher(s), whether from special education, the regular classroom, or vocational education; 3) the parent(s); and 4) the student (when appropriate).

Many states have added considerably to this list, requiring the presence of administrative personnel, the diagnostician, the special education teacher who has been working with the student, the special education counselor, and — when a vocational placement is being considered — the vocational director and the vocational counselor. There is obvious wisdom to garnering this broader, more comprehensive input.

But regardless of who else is present, the receiving teacher must be included in the IEP conference if handicapped students are to reap the full benefits of P.L. 94-142.

---

1. Linda H. Parrish, *Final Report Including the Handicapped* (College Station, Tex.: Texas A & M University, College of Education, 1979).

2. *The Individualized Education Program: Key to an Appropriate Education for the Handicapped Child* (Washington, D.C.: U.S. Department of Health, Education, and Welfare, National Advisory Committee on the Handicapped, 1977). ☐

MAINSTREAMING

Mainstreaming: Getting Out the Word

by Thomas W. Todd, Ed. D., and Joseph B. Lazear, M.S.

Special education has always been flexible in its attempt to meet the needs of handicapped children. For the most part, the impact of special education has been internal and often isolated from regular classes. Since the passage of P.L. 94-142, regular education has been openly challenged to meet the needs of all children capable of being served in such a setting. Often this service falls under the rubric known as "mainstreaming."

Mainstreaming has caused professional personnel to alter their role and attitudinal approach. Central office administrators have had to find ways to smooth the flow of educational services. Principals have had to bridge programs within their buildings. Regular and special teachers have had to communicate as they never have before.

Expenditures of time, money, and staff inservice have been necessary to allay fears and misconceptions. New attitudes, knowledge, and techniques were needed by all those involved in a relatively short period of time.

Therefore, the teachers and administrators of the Princeton City School District requested that inservice training on mainstreaming of exceptional students be presented during the 1978-1979 school year. A group of interested regular and special education teachers from within the district volunteered to prepare and present the training. In researching the topic, it was found that few workshops had been developed specifically for regular teachers. The purpose of this article is to share the outline and information on how mainstreaming of exceptional children was introduced to the teachers of the Princeton City School District.

Fifteen teachers were involved in the training component. Three teams of five teachers evolved. Three of the teachers on each team were special educators, and the remaining two were regular educators. Wherever possible, the team was composed of teachers from the same building. This was done for several reasons:

1. they could meet easily with each other;
2. they could and were in fact working in a reciprocal relationship within their buildings; and
3. they believed in what they were doing, as did their principals and other teachers in their buildings.

The resource teams felt that regular classroom teachers would want answers to the following questions:

Why mainstream?

How do exceptional students differ from normal students?

How might exceptional students' behavior differ from normal students?

What instructional materials and techniques should be used?

In order to answer these questions, four general topics were developed: Due Process Procedures, Sensitivity Training, Behavior, and Instructional Techniques.

As the four topics were studied a resource book was developed, which would not only add structure during the workshop, but also provide future information and activities that teachers could continually use in teaching mainstreamed, handicapped students.

And finally, a must on everyone's list, the teachers involved in the training session would have opportunities to be "active participants" rather than "passive receivers." It was felt active participation would increase the teachers' empathy and give them activities for their classrooms the next day.

Format

The teacher trainers decided that the topics of Due Process Procedures, Behavior, and Instructional Techniques should be done in small groups while Sensitivity Training could be done with a large group. As a result, one special education teacher would take one-third of the inservice group and cover Due Process Procedures while two teams of a regular and special teacher would divide the remaining inservice teachers to cover Behavior and Instructional Techniques.

Twenty minutes was allotted for each topic. The groups rotated until each had been exposed and involved in all three topics. Then the participants assembled into one large group where a regular and

From *The Directive Teacher*, Vol. 2, No. 2, Fall 1979, published by NCEMMH, The Ohio State University.

special teacher, with the assistance of the other three teachers, conducted a sensitivity session.

The general format for all of the topics was fast moving with heavy emphasis on audio-visuals, audience participation, and instructor direction. The presentation itself followed a flavor similar to what is used on the TV programs "Laugh-In" or "Hee-Haw" in that a large number of ideas were covered in small sections in quick sequence.

Due Process

A brief explanation and reasons underlying P.L. 94-142 and due process were discussed. Many of the teachers did not know of the past abuses and neglect of handicapped children by educators, parents and agencies, and therefore the need to protect the rights of the handicapped was stressed. Definitions of each area of exceptionality served by the district were provided. Many regular teachers did not understand the specific differences of each exceptionality, nor the use of abbreviations (LD, EMR and SBD).

This section also covered the district's placement procedures, the Individualized Educational Plan (IEP) and the mainstreaming policy. Emphasis was placed on the importance of the regular teachers in the referral of exceptional students and their participation in the development of the student's IEP. Since, within the district's mainstreaming policy, each area (LD, EMR, SBD) has a different area of emphasis, each area was discussed separately. Within the Princeton School District the emphasis of the LD program is for students to be mainstreamed when they can work on grade level in the regular classroom without supplemental support. In order for a student to be mainstreamed from a SBD unit into the regular classroom, the student will be able to function academically in at least the lowest group in the receiving class, and will maintain a measurable decrease in pre-selected target behaviors for at least one month. EMR students can be mainstreamed into the regular classroom if they can function academically in at least the lowest group in the receiving class with or without supplemental support.

Remaining time was given to the roles of regular and special educators. The success of mainstreaming handicapped students depends on these two professionals' communication. Communications about areas such as parental contact, grades, homework, scheduling, and instructional and behavioral programs should occur before and after placement. It was suggested that the two teachers meet bi-weekly to confer on these and other issues. Two points were stressed:

1. If you or the student need help, get it immediately. The longer one waits, the worse the problem may become.
2. Do not be afraid to bend or change for an exceptional student.

Sensitivity Training

Sensitivity was defined as the ability to understand the feelings and experiences of others. Since many of the teachers had not had the opportunity to experience or understand the learning problems of exceptional students, the participants went through a series of awareness activities. These activities provided the teachers, as adults who had no learning problems, with an awareness of the difficulty experienced by handicapped students.

The activities were subdivided into four areas (visual, auditory, tactile-kinesthetic, and ego-interpersonal). There were additional activities within the resource book so that teachers could continue to improve their and their non-handicapped students' understanding of the handicapped.

Instructional Techniques

The third section of the inservice was designed to help teachers instruct exceptional children who are not able to learn as normal students. The participants were shown ways to identify the modality (visual, auditory or tactile) a student prefers for learning. The teachers were then shown numerous resource book activities, including how a skill can be introduced, mastered, or reinforced. Emphasis was placed on reading, language, spelling, and mathematics.

Teachers were urged to use multimedia presentations, grouping special students with their normal peers, games, and other activities that would improve the chances for a successful mainstreaming experience for themselves, the special student, and the other students in the classroom.

Behavior

The behavior of mainstreamed special students in a regular education classroom can be more crucial to their school success than academic skills. How a student behaves affects the amount and type of interaction with the teacher. The teachers were given examples of how behavior could be modified by increasing positive behavior and decreasing negative behavior. Also discussed were three behaviors: organization (the ability to bring together objects and/or ideas into a logical combination), attention (the ability of the learner to focus his attention on a task), disinhibition (the ability to control ones' reaction to internal or external stimuli). These areas were selected because of their importance in the learning process. Characteristics of these behaviors and suggested teaching methods to remediate behavior deficits in these areas were listed.

From a total of 273 elementary teachers within the district, ninety-six teachers voluntarily attended one of the six sessions offered. In general, their responses were quite positive. Most of the participants (77%) felt that the information presented was useful and relevant to their areas of responsibility. Seventy-seven percent of the teachers stated that they received ideas and techniques which could be used in their classrooms. A majority of the teachers (87%) would recommend the inservice to a fellow staff member who had a need or interest in this topic.

Art, music, and physical education teachers were more critical in terms of the workshops' usefulness to them, relevancy to their teaching area, and use of ideas and techniques covered. However, they strongly stated that the presentation was interesting and would recommend it to follow staff members. In the future, some of the content could be focused toward that group or they could attend a separate inservice session.

An added benefit to the workshop throughout the remainder of the year was the frequent calls for advice and information by regular teachers to the resource teachers who had developed the presentations. The presenters had, in fact, established themselves as authorities in this area. From a cost/benefit point of view, it was a very economical way of meeting regular teachers' needs.

Ongoing inservice plans for the coming year include a newsletter for teachers interested in increasing their awareness of mainstreamed students. Also, a followup questionnaire will be used to further evaluate the effectiveness of both the inservice and resource book. For new teachers and those teachers who did not attend previous sessions, another series of presentations will be offered.

MAINSTREAMING

1

Helping Mainstreamed Students Stay in the Mainstream

by Byrne B. de Grandpre', Ph.D., and Jo M. Messler

In special education teachers frequently use mastery learning (Block, 1971) or objective-based instruction (Smith, 1974) to improve their classroom instruction and evaluate procedures. Instead of teaching large amounts of content and then testing to see who learned what, teachers are directed to establish a set of specific instructional objectives for each child and to provide instruction until each child has achieved some pre-established criterion level.

Mastery learning or objective-based instruction includes many advantages for children who find learning difficult. The mind-set that leads some content oriented teachers to believe that "because I've covered it (the course content), I've taught it" is sharply challenged. The teacher does not blame poor learner performance on the child's learning disability, emotional disturbance or retarded mental development. Whenever a child fails to reach mastery on specific objectives, the task of the teacher is to change the instructional tactic.

Mastery learning represents an important advancement in instructional programming for handicapped learners. At the present time, however, it is not widely practiced in regular education programs. Children in regular classrooms, particularly in content area courses, are typically evaluated not in relationship to their mastery of specific objectives, but rather in terms of their skills in recalling large amounts of information, often referred to as units of instruction. Furthermore, an arbitrary percentage figure, (e.g. 65%) is used to determine a minimum pass. Any learner who scores below the arbitrary percentage fails the exam. To stay in the mainstream, handicapped learners need not achieve mastery levels in any subject matter area. They must, however, pass exams in each subject area in which they are mainstreamed.

Many handicapped learners at the junior-high level are receiving special education services in basic skill areas while being mainstreamed for various content areas such as social studies, science, and health. In this paper, a technique is presented in which self-instruction programs are used immediately before a scheduled test to help mainstreamed students pass content area examinations. These programs are designed to review only the most critical concepts to be tested.

In a large number of mainstreamed junior-high classrooms, students use a commercial textbook as the content base for the course. Day to day activities include reading from the text, discussions, viewing filmstrips and writing answers to questions. The classroom teacher typically evaluates a student's written responses in terms of right or wrong, does not alter instruction if some students are not doing well, and, does not assess a student's mastery of the text's content on a concept by concept basis. Assessment of student progress is usually determined by the end of chapter examination.

In most typical instructional settings, many handicapped learners fail exams. The end products may include disappointed learners and eventually less mainstreaming. Following is an example of how a simple instructional procedure is implemented to try to reverse the trend of mainstreamed learners failing content course examinations. Rather than telling the regular classroom teacher to demonstrate more responsibility and accountability for the failure of mainstreamed students by employing, for example, a mastery learning approach or some alternative instructional intervention, the special education resource teacher can elect to help the mainstreamed children by preparing self-instruction review packages for each chapter of the content area text in use. Naturally, if possible it would be desirable for the regular class teacher to carry out this task.

Most mainstreamed children spend some time in a resource program. Many attend for one or more periods each day.

From *The Directive Teacher*, Vol. 2, No. 2, Fall 1979, published by NCEMMH, The Ohio State University.

Where possible, on the day that the exam is to be given, mainstreamed children should spend part of their resource room session preparing for the content area exam. Since the review materials are self-instructional, many other settings for self study are possible. When the students arrive in the resource room, they pick up the self-instructional package (SIP) for the chapter on which the exam is based.

In developing the self-instructional package, the special education teacher reads through each chapter and reviews the end of chapter exercises. In many texts, it soon becomes evident that a small number of the end of chapter exercises summarize a large percentage of the concepts presented in the chapter. It is also frequently possible to review previous exams to learn if the format used (fill in the blank, true-false, matching, short answer, etc.) is consistent from test to test. Armed with this knowledge, the teacher develops a self-instructional package for each chapter.

Package development includes the following steps:
1. Identify the end of chapter exercises which incorporate at least 75% of the concepts presented in the chapter.
2. Prepare a brief definition/description of each concept.
3. Prepare the student task sheet. The format should be as close as possible to that of the actual test — if you are able to obtain this information.
4. Prepare an introductory statement and read it onto a cassette tape.

   Example:
   "Hi again! Let's get ready for the exam on chapter _____. We're going to review the most important terms in the chapter-one by one." "Before I begin, get out your task sheets; they're in the brown envelope next to the tape recorder."
5. Read the first term and definition/description onto the tape. Then say, "Now turn me off and answer the first question on your task sheet. If you're not sure of the answer, take a guess. When you're done, turn me back on."
6. Provide immediate feedback during each response period.

   Example:
   "Welcome back; the correct answer to number 1 is *(correct response)*. If you got it, great! If you did not write *(correct response)* in the blank, draw a line through your word and write *(correct response)* above it. (Pause for 10 seconds.)
7. Continue with the second term, then the third etc. following the guidelines provided in steps 5 and 6 above.
8. Prepare a closing statement including a brief pep talk and last minute directions.

   Example:
   "I hope this review of chapter_____ helped. That's it for now. If you have more time before the test, read over your task sheet. Read each statement 3 times in a row and read it slowly. Good luck on the exam; I'll be thinking of you."

As students proceed through the quickie review, they complete the following steps:
1. Get the cassette tape for the appropriate chapter.
2. Take a task sheet from the envelope and write their names at the top.
3. Turn on the tape and listen to the directions.
4. Turn off the tape at appropriate points and complete the task sheet items.
5. Correct task sheet mistakes immediately.

The procedure presented in this paper for helping mainstreamed children remain in the mainstream is presently in the experimental stage. Related procedures in which the special education teacher works directly with mainstreamed children to help them to prepare for an upcoming exam have proved effective in our setting, but often time consuming. When the special education teacher has not been available, handicapped learners have sometimes blamed the special education teacher for failure on the exam. It is hoped that the procedure presented in this paper will foster more self-reliance on the part of participating handicapped learners. It is furthermore hoped that this procedure will prove to be as effective as direct review sessions with the special education teacher.

References

Block, James H. (Ed.), *Mastery Learning: Theory and Practice*. New York: Holt, Rinehart and Winston, Inc., 1971.

Smith, R. M. Clinical Teaching: *Methods of Instruction for the Retarded*. New York: McGraw-Hill Book Company, 1974, 78-84.

MAINSTREAMING

Mainstreaming Versus An Appropriate Education

by Charles G. Davis

We stand witness to a new era in the right of a handicapped child to an education. The Fducation For All Handicapped Children Act of 1975 (Public Law 94-142)[1] coupled with the Rehabilitation Act of 1973 (Public Law 93-112)[2] have jointly been referred to as The Civil Rights Acts for the Handicapped. These statutes and their implementing regulations have embodied the basic rulings of numerous state and federal court cases. They are comprehensive and provide a yardstick by which every school district in this country must measure its program of education for the handicapped.

The Conflict:

Of the new rights recently granted to handicapped children, the one which generates the most heated discussions is the right to be educated in the least restrictive alternative. This right is commonly referred to as mainstreaming. Opponents of the concept claim it will jeopardize a child's right to an appropriate education.[3]

Mainstreaming has evoked a vision of severely handicapped children being "dumped" into already crowded classrooms of regular schools. There, these children are seen as a disruptive influence preventing other children from receiving their education. It is claimed that the regular classroom teacher, never trained in special education, will be forced to spend an inordinate amounts of time with the special children while ignoring the needs of the class as a whole. Neither the regular children nor the special children will receive an appropriate education in the midst of this chaos. If this conflict is to be resolved, we must go back to the legislative mandate. Just what does the law really require? Has

From *The Generator*, Vol. 10, No. 2, Spring 1980. Copyright 1980, American Educational Research Association. Reprinted with permission.

Congress gone too far in interfering with the educational process?

The Mandate:

The Education For All Handicapped Children Act of 1975 commonly referred to as P.L. 94-142[4] does not specifically define an appropriate education. It merely provides an operational definition, one which describes the process of arriving at an appropriate education.

The aim of the process is to prevent the double wrongs of discrimination and exclusion. These children are being discriminated against by their removal and segregation from their peers. Further, handicapped children have been excluded from the public schools either by actual or functional exclusion. A child is functionally excluded if not given the special services needed to allow him to benefit from an education.

The process may be summed up as follows:

   a)   a nondiscriminatory evaluation of the child's handicapping condition as it relates to his educational needs (not merely a medical diagnosis);

   b)   the development of an Individual Educational Program (IEP) which will place the child in an educational program tailored to his unique needs;

   c)   placement of the child in the most normal environment, i.e. least restrictive alternative;

   d)   the ability of the child, the parent, and the school district to participate in the challenge of decisions throughout the process.

The result will be an appropriate educational program. However, too many times we have seen children go through the process only to end up in a placement designed to meet the needs of the school district, not the needs of the child. Claiming they are under a mandate to mainstream, the district "dumps" the special child into the regular classroom. How can teachers prevent this?

Mainstreaming must be viewed within the context of the court decisions dealing with functional exclusion. In Lau v. Nichols,[5] the court ruled that placement of children who only speak Chinese in the mainstream public school classroom, which was taught only in English, excluded these children from a meaningful equal educational opportunity. These children were provided a true mainstream education but their unique special needs functionally excluded them from an education while causing the classroom teacher many problems. We need only substitute a deaf child for a Chinese child to see the parallel.

1

The Federal legislation states that:

> ". . . to the maximum extent appropriate, handicapped
> children, including children in public or private
> institutions or other care facilities, are educated
> with children who are not handicapped, and that special
> classes, separate schooling, or other removal of
> handicapped children from the regular educational
> environment occurs only when the nature or severity of
> the handicap is such that education in regular cases
> with the use of supplementary aids and services cannot
> be achieved satisfactorily . . ."[6] (emphasis
> added)

The key word in this definition is "appropriate". The key element
in the process of arriving at an appropriate education is the
"individualized education program." If an IFP is developed which
provides for the unique needs of the child, the program will be
appropriate because the child will not be functionally excluded.

The mandate is clear. It is not to mainstream but to provide the
least restrictive appropriate education.

The Key:

An educational program must be "tailored to the individual
needs"[7] of the child. The IEP is the heart of the new law.
It is both a shield and a sword, not only for the needs of the
child, but by necessity the needs of the teacher.

The IEP is defined in P.L. 94-142 and its implementation is explained in the Rules and Regulations of the Office of Education,
HEW.

§ 121a.346 Content of individualized education program.

The individualized education program for each child
must include:

(a) A statement of the child's present levels
     of educational performance;

(b) A statement of annual goals, including
     short term instructional objectives;

(c) A statement of specific special education
     and related services to be provided to the
     child, and the extent to which the child
     will be able to participate in regular
     educational programs;

(d) The projected dates for initiation of
     services and the anticipated duration of
     the services; and

(e)   Appropriate objective criteria and evaluation procedures and schedules for determining, on at at least an annual basis,
whether the short term instructional
objectives are being achieved."[8]
(emphasis added)

This section provides for the incorporation of mainstreaming as
part of the IEP. The degree of mainstreaming is only one aspect
of the decision to be made. The IEP is designed to prevent the
functional exclusion of a child from the classroom by the failure
to provide the necessary support services. The school district
must provide any support service necessary to assure that the
child is not functionally excluded.

In The Matter of Patricia J., Gordon M. Ambach, the New York State
Commissioner of Education, defined the test for supportive
services.

"The requirement that a board of education must provide
suitable educational opportunities for each handicapped
pupil who resides in the school district is necessarily
limited to instruction and related services which will
enable the pupil to benefit from instruction. The medical
needs of a handicapped pupil may, of course, require that a
particular educational methodology or particular related
services be provided for such pupil, so that the pupil may
benefit from instruction."[9]

The school district must first develop an IEP for the child based
upon the nature of the handicapping condition and the child's
special educational needs. Then the district must provide or
locate a placement in which the IEP can be fulfilled.

The participants in the development of the IEP are set forth as
follows:

"(1)   A representative of the public agency,
other than the child's teacher, who is
qualified to provide, or supervise the
provision of, special education.

(2)   The child's teacher.

(3)   One or both of the child's parents, . . .

(4)   The child, where appropriate.

(5)   Other individuals at the discretion of the
parent or agency.

(b)   Evaluation personnel. For a handicapped child who has
been evaluated for the first time, the public agency
shall insure:

(1)   That a member of the evaluation team

1

participates in the meeting; or

(2)   That the representative of the public
       agency, the child's teacher, or some other
       person is present at the meeting, who is
       knowledgeable about the evaluation
       procedures used with the child and is
       familiar with the results of the
       evaluation."[10]

Each participant is there to speak to the needs of the child in
the development of the IEP. The participants are experts within
their own areas and must be allowed to contribute if the process
is to be effective.

The parental involvment is necessary because the child does not
function only within the school building. The parents should be
able to provide the information as to the child's reaction to
various programs and approaches, as well as the child's more
general needs. Further, if they understand the school's approach
and program, they should be better able to support the efforts of
the teacher.

The "child's teacher" is unfortunately an ambiguous phrase. The
intent, however, is to include any teacher who can speak to the
child's needs. Therefore, it should be all teachers who are
presently dealing with the child. Those individuals are best able
to reflect upon the child's needs as they are operational within
the class. Does the child need a smaller class size? Is an aide
needed? Which subjects are successfully taught in the mainstream?
Does the child's behavior disrupt the class? Does the child need
a more protective environment away from the taunts of his classmates? What special training should the new teacher have?

The teachers of the various "specials" cannot be excluded from the
IFP conference. A handicapped child must be given music, art,
industrial arts, consumer and homemaking education, and vocational
education, if they are offered to his non-handicapped peers.[11]
Physical education must be provided specifically in conformity
with an IEP.[12] These teachers must be involved or the child
may well end up functionally excluded while attending these
classes.

Non-academic and extracurricular activities and services are also
covered by the new law. These may include lunchroom, playground
counseling services, athletics, transportation, health services,
recreational activities, special interest groups or clubs sponsored by the school district.[13]

Although lacking traditional academic curricula, these areas are
important. They provide the basis for the development of interpersonal relationships. The IEP must contain the degree and
manner of the integration of the handicapped child in these

activities and define the necessary support services required to allow the child to function within these programs.

A properly created IEP will result in a clear articulation of the educational needs of the child and a plan of interaction between the various teachers and special service providers which will result in the child being able to function adequately in whatever situation the IEP specifies. Since the IEP will contain a description of the specific services needed, the mainstream teacher will have available all that is required to be an effective teacher.

The IEP is a safeguard against:

a) Inappropriate mainstreaming

b) The failure to provide the teacher with the skills, equipment and supportive personnel needed to do the job

c) Overcrowded classrooms

d) Inappropriate scheduling of a child's special and regular classes

e) The failure to provide teachers with the time needed to provide the education for the child

f) The failure to provide the time necessary to develop the IEP

The IEP is a tool in the hands of educators. It is not a sword at their throats. Through the development of an IEP, the teachers have a unique opportunity to gain control over the classroom and the conditions under which they must work. The teachers must take an active and aggressive role in the development of the IEP. If they fail to seize the opportunity, the resultant "dumping and chaos" in their classrooms cannot be blamed on the new law.

The mainstream teacher who has a handicapped child in class, inappropriately placed, should not stand mute. The parent, the district's Committee on the Handicapped, and the Board of Education should be immediately notified. The teacher may then speak on behalf of the child, as a true advocate, to secure an appropriate placement. Whether the change will be as drastic as removal of the child from class, or as natural as the assistance of a specialty teacher, the classroom teacher must have a chance to be heard when the problem arises. The mechanisms are there. All that is needed is for the teacher to utilize the new law as a further tool for the betterment of education.

Conclusion:

There is no conflict between the doctrines of the least restric-

1

tive alternative and an appropriate education. We must provide these children with the least restrictive appropriate education. This will result from a properly developed IEP. The IEP is a shield which will protect both child and teacher from the dangers of "dumping". It is also a sword to guarantee these children the least restrictive appropriate education.

Footnotes:

1. P.L. 14-142, The Education of All Handicapped Children Act of 1975, 20 U.S.C. Sec. 1401, 1402, and 1411 through 1420.

2. P.L. 93-112, Rehabilitation Act of 1973, Sec. 504.

3. Readings in Mainstreaming, Special Learning Corporation, Avilford, Conn. 1978.

4. Supra N. 1

5. 414 U.S. 563 (1974) Court of Appeals Ninth Circuit

6. Supra N. 1 Sec. 612 (5)

7. In the Matter of Darren J., Decision of the Commissioner of Education of the State of New York No. 9525, October 12, 1977.

8. Rules and Regulations of the Office of Education, Department of Health, Education and Welfare, Implementation of Part B of The Education of the Handicapped Act. 121a.346 Federal Register Park II, Tuesday, August 23, 1977.

9. In the Matter of Patricia J., Decision of the Commissioner of Education of the State of New York, No. 9727, July 17, 1978

10. Supra N. 8 § 121a.344

11. Supra M. 8 § 121a.305

12. Supra N. 8 § 121a.307

13. Supra N. 8 § 121a.306

References:

H. R. Turnbull and A. Turnbull, Free Appropriate Public Education, Law and Implementation, Love Publishing Company, Denver, Colorado, 1978.

M. Kindred, Fditor, The Mentally Retarded Citizen and the Law, sponsored by The President's Committee on Mental Retardation, The Free Press, New York, New York, 1976.

J. P. Quirk, Publisher, Readings in Mainstreaming, Special Learning Corporation, Guilford, Conn. 1978.

R. Piazza and I. Newman, Readings in Individualized Educational Programs, Special Learning Corporation, Guilford, Conn., 1978.

PARENTS

Parent Involvement and PL 94-142

by Alan Abeson

In large measure much of the discussion of P. L. 94-142, The Education for All Handicapped Children Act of 1975, that has occurred since its passage, has centered upon the various legal, administrative, and fiscal provisions that it contains. This focus is quite legitimate since adequate understanding of these matters is necessary for implementation of the law to occur. To fully appreciate this significant legislation, however, another view must be recognized. This is the view that permits consideration of the major educational principles embodied in the law. Presented below is a brief description of these major provisions and an essential discussion of that provision dealing with parent involvement.

Principles of Education

Without question, the basic provision of P. L. 94-142 that all handicapped children be provided with a public education is reinforcement of the universal goal of American education being provided for all children. Despite the rhetoric to the contrary, such a goal was not in the past achievable for handicapped children because of various legally sanctioned exclusion clauses in State law and extralegal arbitrary and capricious decision making activities that often occurred within State and local education agencies.

Past rhetoric with regard to handicapped and, in fact, all children, also spoke of meeting the individual educational needs of children. Such an emphasis was fitting since all those involved in the schooling of children recognized that each and every child possesses individual characteristics that in some ways are unlike those of any other child. Such a recognition was evident as various strategies came to be used in grouping children in schools in various ways to reduce the child variance and permit more effective instruction to be provided to more similar children. It is in part from this progression that special education as a field emerged with the mandate to serve those children who presented the greatest qualitative and quantitative variance.

Over time what became clear in terms of special education and in general education, as well, was that regardless of the instructional groupings that were created, there still remained great difficulty in meeting individual needs. This in turn led to the use of team teaching, open schools, differentiated staffing, computer aided instruction and other similarly intended practices. Although such innovations were rarely employed with handicapped children, the same need persisted.

It is for this reason that the Congress included in P. L. 94-142 the requirement that each eligible handicapped child must be provided with an individualized education program (IEP), as indicateJ, a key educational provision. The IEP is in fact a major element of the law with its contents precisely stated:

"...a written statement for each handicapped child developed in any meeting by a representative of the local educational agency or an intermediate educational unit who shall be qualified to provide, or supervise the provision of, specially designed instruction to meet the unique needs of handicapped children, the teacher, the parents. or guardians of such child, and, whenever appropriate, such child, which statement shall include (A) a statement of the present levels of educational performance of such child, (B) a statement of annual goals, including short-term instructional objectives, (C) a statement of the specific educational services to be provided to such child, and the extent to which such child will be able to participate in regular educational programs, (D) the projected date for initiation and anticipated duration of such services, and appropriate objective criteria and evaluation procedures and schedules for determining, on at least an annual basis, whether instructional objectives are being achieved"
(Sec. 4(a)(19)).

A third example of the sound educational principles upon which P. L. 94-142 is based is the requirement that handicapped children be educated with the non-handicapped, wherever possible. This provision recognizes the desirability of promoting meaningful interaction in positive educational settings of handicapped children and their nonhandicapped peers. Further, by overcoming needless past segregation, all these children will be better prepared for the presence of the handicapped and possibly others with differenc kinds of individual differences in the adult world. One note of clarification, however, is that, contrary to misinterpretation, not all handicapped children will be placed in regular programs. Rather, it will be those children who can be expected to succeed and profit from such settings.

A fourth educational principle embodied within the Act and the one which is the focus of this article concerns the mandated opportunity for the parents of handicapped children to be involved in decision making regarding all aspects of educating their child. Once again, the desirability of parent involvement in the education of their children is a long sought goal of American education. Such a goal is based upon the belief that parents and teachers can work together to produce better learning opportunities for their children. It further sets aside the concept of "in loco parentis" in which the parents give to the schools alone, the right to make educational decisions about their children.

Baumgartner (1960) in a book about educating trainable mentally retarded children wrote that, "The conventional concept of parent-teacher relationships, with the connotation simply of occasional meetings, becomes outmoded when parents and teachers join forces to help the mentally retarded child. . . . The child, his parents, and his teachers become closely and inseparably united. The relationship might be compared to a three-legged milking stool that will collapse without any one of its legs" (p. 15). The milking stool concept is clearly applicable to all handicapped children.

The parent knows the child and knows the child well. As is perhaps obvious, this can occur simply because the parents of that child share the same environment. For many parents of these children, however, there is often a history of repeated contacts with varied professionals to verify parental suspicions about their child's development, to produce better understanding of the nature of their child and/or to find "cures" or treatment programs. This process, which may continue for years, frequently produces confusing and sometimes conflicting information which forces parents even further into the role of evaluators of their children.

Thus, because of living with a handicapped child and/or collecting and evaluating information about their child, the parents often possess extensive developmental, diagnostic and other information about their child that must be considered by school people in designing and implementing educational programs. To fail to consider this information and the frequent parental "hunches" that accompany it, would be a serious omission by educators. Further and perhaps a more intimate consideration is that as Winslow (1977) suggests, parents " . . . act as a resource for a whole set of personal values that they want and hope their children will incorporate into their own life styles" (p. 44). Parents then possess factual, interpretative, and aspiration types of information about their children that can contribute to the provision of an appropriate education.

While the above emphasis suggests that the primary purpose of parental involvement is related to the passing of information from parent to school in the design of programs, what must also be recognized is that there is necessity for continuing communication. As will be described, the essence of the IEP is that there will be continuous evaluation to assure that the educational program provided is appropriate to the changing needs of the child. While the schools will be the major monitor of this progress, the parent will similarly serve and can once again contribute to both major and minor program changes. In addition to contributing information, parents can under selected circumstances reinforce at home and in other settings, the daily educational program.

The Legality of Parent Involvement

In the past, school decisions about handicapped children often failed to consider any parent involvement. This occurred with regard to identifying children as potentially handicapped, evaluating them to determine the presence of a handicapping condition along with an understanding of the child's strengths and weaknesses, and finally, the educational placement. Since Congress was aware of this omission, it included specific provisions in P. L. 94-142 to insure that parents were provided with meaningful opportunity to be involved.

First, when a child is being considered by the schools as a potentially handicapped child who may be in need of an evaluation and a special program, before any activities are undertaken, the parents must be notified and provided with detailed notice regarding the proposed action. The purpose of the notice is to inform the parents of what the schools want to do, why they want to do it, and that they are seeking parental permission to move ahead. Such notice is to be provided prior to identification, evaluation or placement decisions.

It is important to note that the obligation of the schools is to do that which is in the best interest of the child, presumably that which is requested in the notice. By sharing their perspective with the parent, both formally with the written notice and hopefully through accompanying informal communication, the parents are being provided with opportunity to reciprocate and contribute to the best possible decision making about their child. Upon occassion, however, parents will resist the school's initiative and deny permission for the requested activity. The school, again acting in the best interest of the child, should try through various means of communication to help the parent understand what is needed. If this fails, another phase of the P. L. 94-142 procedural safeguard system can come into play.

Failure to achieve agreement regarding the notice can be followed by the impartial due process hearings required by P. L. 94-142. The purpose of these hearings and any subsequent appeals is to obtain a decision from an impartial hearing officer (officers if a panel is used) on the steps required of the public school in order to provide the child with an appropriate education. Consequently, hearings may be convened regarding identification, evaluation and placement decisions. In addition, they can occur with regard ". . . to any matter relating to . . . the provision of a free appropriate public education" (Sec. 615(b) (l)(E)). Worthy of emphasis is the fact that hearings can be a legitimate outcome of reasonable disagreements and can be initiated by parents or school officials.

The purpose of the total procedural safeguard system of the Act is to insure that the required opportunities for communication between parents and schools occur and that, when needed, impartial redress of issues can be obtained. In order to insure that all children have the benefits of adults representing their interest, the Congress recognized that some children do not have natural parents. Consequently, provision was made for assigning a surrogate parent to children"... to protect the rights of the child whenever the parents or guardian of the child are not known, unavailable, or the child is a ward of the state..." (Sec. 615(b) (l)(B)).

Traditionally, where parents of handicapped children were advised by the schools about the special needs of their children, it was generally in the context of an evaluation to determine if a program should be provided in a special education classroom. Today, however, it is recognized that there are a variety of special education programs that can be used to meet the unique learning needs of handicapped children. These can include intensive special education settings as well as regular education programs with limited special assistance. In fact, P. L. 92-142 requires that placement decisions be considered only after determination of the program needed by the child. This leads again to parental involvement.

As cited earlier, the individualized education program (IEP) must be developed at a meeting with school personnel and the child's parents. The child may also attend whenever appropriate. It is at this meeting that the specific program to be provided to the child is designed. Without a doubt the extensive information parents possess about a child can contribute to evaluation, but it is with regard to program that the full breadth of parent knowledge and aspiration can come into play. The law encourages the active participation of the parents in designing the IEP. What must be emphasized, however, is that the schools are obligated to provide parents meaningful opportunity to participate, but when such participation does not occur they are obligated to act on behalf of the child in terms of providing an appropriate education. Finally, the production of the IEP is also subject to the procedural safeguards that accompany the entire Act.

The Reality of Parent Involvement

Much has been and will continue to be written about parents and

1

schools working together. This is especially true with regard to
the education of the handicapped. Parents of these children often
come together to share their "war stories," their tales of "working" with the schools. P. L. 94-142 promises to bring meaning and
order to these fragile relationships. The degree to which the
effects of the law are positive is perhaps conditioned at least in
part by the expectations and related behavior parents hold for
schools and vice versa.

Schools today must suffer for a time the omissions of the past
with regard to the parents of handicapped children. These parents
were often denied, delayed, uninformed, and browbeaten. They came
to mistrust the public schools and unfortunately to categorize all
special and general educators and particularly administrators as
the enemy. So too, the schools learned to be wary of these parents who at best complained but at worst sought the assistance of
the courts to obtain an appropriate education for their children.
The negative expectations built upon yesterday's experiences
continue to be present in this new era.

Too often the schools say they want to work with the parents, but
they do not follow through. The parents, on the other hand, say
the schools don't appreciate the magnitude of demands upon time,
energy and other resources in living with a handicapped child.

Teachers, psychologists, administrators and others employed by
public schools have the responsibility of educating children and
are expected to know how to do it. These educators are well
trained, competent and want to serve all children well. Yet, it
is likely that there are some children, particularly some who are
handicapped, whose present needs defy total understanding. Parents of handicapped children have said that when educators encounter such children, they should avoid pretending to know all
the answers.

Similarly, educators sometimes fail to convey to parents the
concern they feel about the children as individuals. Perhaps this
practice is defensive in view of the historically hostile parent
of handicapped children who has been a recent fixture in America's
schools. Parents, however, want to feel that their children's
teachers are in fact concerned for the children as individuals,
not only as part of a group. Dr. Donald Trites*, in expressing
this concern from the parent perspective, described what he called
an anxiety factor: school people, like parents should understand
and convey that they understand, the implications of failing to
educate that child. Undoubtedly, school people believe they do
understand and would like to share this anxiety with parents in a
positive manner.

As with all aspects of P. L. 94-142, time will be required to

_____

*Dr. Donald Trites' presentation in Summer Workshop for Parents of
Handicapped Children, St. Simons Island, Georgia, August 17, 1978.

implement more than the letter of the law. The law attempts to build in protective mechanisms to insure that the schools and a child's parents act in his best interest. Further, safeguards are also provided when disagreements occur. At the heart of reducing disagreements between parents and schools is communication, which must be built on shared and expressed concern about each child as an individual. It is when this occurs and these collective energies are devoted, not to resolving disagreements, but to the design and implementation of individualized education programs that the spirit of P. L. 94-142 will be achieved.

References

Baumgartner, B. B. Helping the Trainable Mentally Retarded Child, New York, N.Y.: Teachers College Press, 1960.

Winslow, L. "Parent Participation" A Primer on Individualized Education Programs for Handicapped Children, Reston, VA: The Foundation for Exceptional Children, 1977.

PARENTS

1

Working with Angry Parents

by Fred H. Wallbrown and Ferguson B. Meadows, Jr.

Being human, parents show a wide range of feelings when they are first made aware that one of their children is encountering difficulties with school. Some parents feel confused, overwhelmed, and helpless whereas others react by becoming upset and angry. In other cases, the parents take more of a factual approach and come to the school seeking information. Conferencing almost always involves some form of emotional communication between the teacher and parents as well as the exchange of information, ideas, and suggestions. In problem-oriented parent conferences, the emotional aspect of the interaction between the parents and teacher often takes precedence over the informational aspects of the interchange. This situation is true when we are dealing with parents who are feeling angry, upset, and frustrated about what the school has been able to accomplish for their child.

When working with angry parents, the immediate issue is not whether this anger is justified by the behavior of the teacher. This point is critical if we wish to restructure the conference so it is concerned with what can be done to help the child *NOW*. Unless gross misinformation is involved, there is very little, if anything, to be gained by disputing what the parents have to say or arguing with them. Instead of arguing, it makes a great deal more sense to accept the parents' right to be angry and use some helping skills to show them that we not only accept their anger, but are even willing to help them express how they feel about us. The rationale for this approach is quite simple and

straightforward. When we are angry and upset there is a real need for us to express our feelings and "talk out" what is bothering us before we can get around to dealing with information in a more rationale manner.

Several skills from the area of behavioral counseling are helpful for teachers who wish to improve their communication with angry parents. One such skill is *active listening* (Gordon, 1970) or *attending* (Carkhuff, 1977). By this we mean paying careful attention to what the parents are saying, how they are saying it, and the quality of their nonverbal behavior. Furthermore, we need to make sure that the parents are aware that we are listening to what they have to say. Some of the ways that we can do this is to sit facing them squarely without barriers between us, maintain eye contact, and lean forward slightly. These are the very same kinds of nonverbal behaviors that we use when we are involved in an interesting conversation, even though we may not be aware of them. These are the kinds of behaviors that show parents we are interested in what they are saying and encourage them to go on sharing with us. On the other hand, if we sit behind a desk, look down, gaze around the room, fumble with materials, slouch in our chair, sigh deeply, or squirm and wiggle around in our chair, then we give the parents the impression that we are impatient, disinterested, and not listening to what they have to say. Such behaviors tend to increase the parents' anger and cut off further conversation.

At least two precautions are neces-

sary if we are to be effective in using the attending skills mentioned above. These involve interruptions and pauses. Most of us have difficulty allowing pauses when dealing with angry parents since we tend to talk fast and interrupt others when we are aroused by intense emotions such as anger, fright, or surprise. Such behavior is not helpful in a problem-oriented conference. One of the most serious mistakes we make in dealing with angry parents is talking too much rather than listening. Interruptions are especially inappropriate since they are a clear indication that we wish to cut off what the parents are saying rather than listening to them. In contrast, pauses are usually helpful because they are an invitation for the parents to collect their thoughts and go on with the conversation.

Several other procedures are also helpful in this regard. For example, a simple nodding of the head or brief verbal statement like, "um-hum," "oh," or "I see" usually encourages the parents to continue sharing their concerns. Some counseling authorities call these skills *minimal encourage* since they are brief and designed to encourage further expression (Ivey & Authier, 1978).

Another useful technique is for the teacher to occasionally pick up some part of what the parents are saying and repeat it so it takes the form of a question. This is accomplished by raising our voice at the end of the part of the statement we are repeating. Let's take a parent statement and see how this can work:

"What kind of teacher are you anyway! Don't tell me it's Karen's fault!

From *The Directive Teacher*, Vol. 2, No. 2, Fall 1979, published by NCEMMH, The Ohio State University.

She never had any trouble before she came to your class! You're the problem! Let's get that straight!!''

An appropriate response from the teacher might be, "I'm the problem?" Using this type of response not only encourages the parents to continue sharing, but also cues them concerning what part of their statement the teacher would like to know more about.

On the other hand, if the teacher had said, "She never had any trouble before?" then the parents would have been encouraged to pick up on this part of their statement and explain more about Karen's experiences with other teachers. Either of these two responses would have been appropriate depending on what aspect of the statement the teacher wished to pursue.

However, it would have been inappropriate for the teacher to have responded by saying "um-hum" or nodding the head. Either of these responses would probably have been interpreted by the parents as evidence that the teacher was acquiescing and agreeing that s/he was the cause of the problem when, in fact, the intent was only to indicate acceptance of the parent's feelings.

Asking *open questions* is another skill that can be highly effective in working with angry parents. Open questions are the kind that cannot be answered conveniently with a "yes" or "no" response. Open questions encourage further communication whereas closed questions tend to stifle conversation. To show how open questions are helpful, consider the following statement by an angry parent:

"We don't want Bob in a special class or any kind of resource room that will get him labeled! There's not that much wrong with him! Our doctor said he could make it in a regular class if he had a good teacher!"

We could question the physician's competence to make such a statement or use some sort of persuasive technique to convince the parents that "the school knows best." However, an open question such as, "How did the doctor describe a good teacher?" is much more likely to be effective. The advantage of this question is that it not only encourages the parents to continue expressing their feelings, but also leads them to be more specific and think about what kind of instruction they (or their physician) expect for their child.

Let us take another example of an angry statement by a parent and see how an open question can be used:

"Unless things change, we're going to make sure that Richard comes out of your class and gets put back in a regular class! We've already gone to the principal about you and we'll go to the superintendent and the board of education if we have to! We're going to get this thing straightened out if we have to go to court about you!"

Here again, we could argue with the parents or try to persuade them that what is going on in the special class is really okay. In contrast, an open question such as, "What would you like to see me change?" has the advantage of keeping communication open and encouraging the parents to be more specific about what they would like for their child.

The kind of helping skills we have discussed thus far are designed to help parents express and work through their emotions. We are not suggesting that they be used to manipulate parents or to avoid dealing with difficult issues. Rather, these helping skills are offered as a means of establishing an atmosphere of trust and mutual respect between the teacher and parents. When these skills are used effectively, we are likely to find that the parents gradually become less upset and angry. At some point their anger is likely to decrease enough so that we can begin to refocus the conference and begin to interact with the parents at an informational rather than an emotional level.

Needless to say, we do not mean to suggest that these skills are a panacea that will always enable us to be successful in our work with angry parents. We do maintain, however, that they can be very helpful for those teachers who are willing to invest the time and effort necessary to become proficient in using them.

References

Carkhuff, R. *The art of helping III.* Amherst, MA: Human Resource Development Press, 1977.

Gordon, T. *Parent effectiveness training.* New York: Peter H. Wyden, 1970.

Ivey, A., & Authier, J. *Microcounseling* (2nd ed.). Springfield, IL: Charles C. Thomas, 1978.

PARENTS

Communicating with Parents of Culturally Diverse Exceptional Children

by Robert L. Marion

■ Working with parents of culturally diverse exceptional children should be considered an exacting challenge to teachers and educators in this decade. The adoption of such an attitude by professionals does not negate or overly subscribe to the problems that might arise between parents and educators with conflicting ideologies, values, and feelings. Rather, such a view recognizes that relationships between parents of culturally diverse handicapped and gifted children and professionals have been drastically altered by recent court decisions and legislative enactments. These pronouncements have produced significant attitudinal changes among the affected groups.

Most of the changes brought about through the courts or by legislation have been viewed as positive by parents who had previously been identified as disadvantaged, disenfranchised, or deprived. There have been several reasons for this response from culturally different parents. The *Mills* v. *the Board of Education* (1972) decision spoke to the issue of tracking. It forbade the District of Columbia schools to use a system of placement that resulted in the assignment of disproportionate numbers of minority students to the general or lowest curriculum track in the schools. The *Pennsylvania Association of Retarded Citizens (PARC)* v. *Pennsylvania* (1971) case was a significant victory for handicapped students and parents. It established the right of every

mentally retarded child to have an opportunity for a free and appropriate public school education. The Education for All Handicapped Children Act of 1975 (Public Law 94–142) provided several guarantees to parents and clarified their roles as co-equal partners in the educational process. Protections that were of particular importance to parents of culturally diverse children were rights relating to due process, nondiscriminatory testing, and least restrictive environments.

To understand the significance that such parents attached to these developments, the similarities and differences in the educational process for culturally diverse gifted and handicapped children in the schools must be reviewed. The similarities can be summarized from the following viewpoints. First, parents of handicapped and gifted children should be considered parents of exceptional children. This statement can be interpreted within the framework that both categories of children have special educational, social, and personal needs (Cruickshank, 1975; Hoyt, 1976; Marland, 1972; Sato, 1974). Second, formal assessment has played a role in the assignment of numerous children to these divergent categories of exceptional children. This has been equally true for minority children and for nonminority children in society. Third, teacher perceptions have been a vital part of the total process of identifying gifted and handicapped students. Prior to Public Law 94–142, teachers were frequently the primary and even sole identifiers of handicapped children (Dunn, 1968; Hurley, 1969).

Some differences between the two categories of gifted and handicapped should be underscored, however. First, although both subsets are considered exceptional, giftedness has the connotation of excellence, of wisdom, of power. Handicapping conditions have the connotation of weakness, subnormality, and ugliness (Griffin, 1979). Second, assessment as utilized by the schools has played a far greater role in assigning culturally diverse populations to classrooms for mentally retarded children than to classes for the gifted (Dunn, 1968; Jones, 1972; Marion, 1979). Third, teacher nomination as a selection tool in the identification process has not been very successful in recognizing giftedness among culturally diverse children (Pegnato & Birch, 1959). It has been used with more accuracy in diagnosing culturally different pupils who are handicapped (Dunn, 1968; Hobbs, 1975; Jones, 1972).

REACTIONS OF PARENTS

The reactions of parents to these similarities and differences in the schooling process have led to a markedly different relationship between professionals and parents of culturally diverse gifted and handicapped students in contrast to their nonminority counterparts. The reactions of parents of culturally different children in both categories can probably be described differently from the way in which most of the literature to date has depicted them. Descriptions of the reactions of parents to the birth of their handicapped child include these terms: shock, disbelief, grief, mourning. A frantic search for a cause and a cure often accompanies these defense mechanisms. Many parents have been helped by professionals and other parents to accept the handicap of their child.

These reactions can be traced directly to studies of Anglo American parents. Much of the data was obtained from observing, examining, and reporting on the activities of nonminority parents. Not as much evidence on the same subject has been accumulated and documented with culturally diverse parents. One 3 year study (Marion & McCaslin, 1979) has served to substantiate the fact that many parents of culturally diverse handicapped children are not consumed with the same strong feelings as those that overwhelm nonminority parents. Luderus (1977) also supported the position that culturally different parents do

not fit the stereotype generally ascribed to parents of handicapped children. Frequently, parents of culturally diverse handicapped children have not expressed shock, disbelief, sorrow, and some of the other associated feelings of guilt and depression. On the contrary, prior to Public Law 94–142, feelings of protection and acceptance of the handicapped child was the more typical emotion (Marion & McCaslin, 1979). This was especially true of Mexican-American and Black families, both of whom had extended family networks (Billingsley, 1968; Hill, 1972). Much of the research during this period did not stress the strengths of minority and culturally diverse families and tended to ascribe pathological conditions to atypical family structures (Minuchin, 1967; Myrdal, 1944). Many researchers also ignored the role of religion and the feelings of acceptance and security engendered by its place of prominence in culturally diverse families (Billingsley, 1968; Cole, 1967; Hill, 1972).

The burden of having a handicapped child in the family was probably most strongly fixed in the minds of culturally diverse parents when their child entered school (Barsch, 1969). Faced with large numbers of culturally different children in urban areas, regular school systems showed their inability to accommodate these children by assigning increasing numbers of them to special education classes (Dunn, 1968; Hobbs, 1975; Jones, 1972). Special education aided in this movement by the reciprocal acceptance of these children into classes for the mentally retarded (Hurley, 1969; Hurley, 1971). Therefore, in the 1970's great numbers of culturally diverse children grew up in the special education system and, as adolescents, have become products of a self fulfilling prophecy (Larsen, 1975).

The greatest reaction expressed by parents of culturally diverse handicapped children has been one of anger and dismay at the policy of overinclusion of their children in classes for the mentally retarded and emotionally disturbed. This policy, as practiced by the schools, has permeated the thinking of culturally diverse families to such an extent that they have become desperate and confused. The anger displayed by these parents has been a reaction against an educational system that they feel has promoted these two categories as the only appropriate depositories for their children (Hurley, 1971; Marion, 1979).

Parents of culturally diverse gifted students have not reacted to a policy of inclusion but rather to school practices of exclusion. Although gifted children are considered exceptional children, parents of culturally diverse

1

gifted students have been less than optimistic about the chances that their children will gain entry into programs for talented students (Marion, in press). Pessimistic reactions to the heavy reliance by schools upon IQ tests as the major discerner of giftedness in students is common. Only when a marriage between "nature" and "nurture" theories is effected are parents of culturally diverse gifted children given to hope that their children might be included in these programs.

Many of the frustrations of parents of culturally diverse gifted populations have also revolved around the condition of schooling for adolescents. Parents are concerned that many culturally diverse problem adolescents of today were yesterday's gifted and talented children (Shaw, 1978). As younger children they might have been described as:

1. Members of large, financially insecure, and *a priori* love families.
2. Exhibiting inappropriate social behavior.
3. Popular with their classmates and possessing more social insight than their peers.

Parents are fearful that a goodly number of adolescents who demonstrated these tendencies to teachers were mislabeled *emotionally distrubed, socially maladjusted,* or *mentally retarded* on the strength of atypical family characteristics or culturally different mannerisms.

CONCERNS OF PARENTS

Many of the concerns of parents of culturally diverse gifted and handicapped children are creations of the negative image that education has projected. Consequently, many of the difficulties in the communication process can be traced directly to this undesirable image. For instance, special education has clung tenaciously to the view that the perfect family corresponds to an average US Census family, comprised of two parents and two children. Most culturally diverse families, especially the poor, exceed this family size, which immediately implies that they are atypical. Such an image strains the traditional concept of giftedness, when its presence is acknowledged solely in an only child or in the eldest of two children (Barbe, 1965). Likewise, parents of culturally different handicapped children have been made to feel guilty about their large families.

Testing

Perhaps the concern that has caused most friction to occur between schools and culturally diverse populations with gifted and handicapped children has been the issue of testing.

This issue has occupied the thinking of culturally diverse groups for a long time (Gay & Abraham, 1974; Oakland, 1974). Reasons for this preoccupation with the testing issue have been well documented through the courts (*Diana* v. *State Board of Education*, 1973; *Larry P.* v. *Riles*, 1972). The concern of parents of handicapped children has centered upon the use of tests to disproportionately assign their children to classes for the mentally retarded or the emotionally disturbed (Children's Defense Fund, 1974; Hurley, 1971). Parents of culturally diverse handicapped children have complained that prior to Public Law 94–142 their opinions were not solicited and they did not have any input into the placement of their children (Children's Defense Fund, 1975; Hickerson, 1966; Southern Regional Council, 1974).

With regard to culturally diverse gifted children, the uneasy truce between "nature" and "nurture" opponents has failed to quiet the differences of opinion concerning the potential for giftedness among this group. Although the definition of giftedness has been broadened, schools continue to support the idea that intelligence is measured by an IQ obtained through testing (Mercer, 1973).

Identification

A final concern that has troubled parents of culturally diverse gifted and handicapped children has been the question of teacher identification. This issue has emerged because many studies report on the inability of teachers to recognize giftedness among culturally different children (Malone, 1975; Pegnato & Birch, 1959). Traditional indicators upon which observations are based are usually middle class values, family stereotypes, and teacher expectations about conformist pupil behavior (Larsen, 1975; McCandless, 1967). In the eyes of many teachers, culturally diverse gifted populations fail to measure up to these indicators (Marion, 1979). On the other hand, many culturally diverse handicapped children are in fact identified and placed into special education (Prillman, 1975).

COMMUNICATING WITH PARENTS

Parents of culturally diverse gifted and handicapped students have exhibited a number of common needs. When these needs have been met, the views of culturally diverse parents have generally been changed to a more positive outlook and communication has been facilitated. Professionals who are attempting to work with these parents should have an understanding of these needs to effectively expand their roles in the communication process.

Need for Information

The need for information constitutes one of the primary requests from parents of culturally diverse gifted and handicapped children. In communicating with parents of handicapped children, much of this need can be satisfied through regularly scheduled meetings and conferences and planning sessions for the individualized education program (IEP). Many educators assume that their own familiarity with Public Law 94–142 is automatically bestowed upon the parents. Nothing is further from the truth. Some parents of culturally diverse handicapped children need to further understand the basic tenets of Public Law 94–142, including their rights and responsibilities. Educators working with parents should be certain that they:

1. Have a knowledge of the law itself and of corresponding regulations.
2. Have a thorough knowledge of their clients.
3. Can effect communication among staff members, between parents and the agencies which are to serve their child, and, in some cases, between staff and the client they are assisting.
4. Utilize appropriate times and settings for parent-teacher conferences.

Only well informed parents can be intelligent consumers of information. There should be agreement that parents and educators have one common denominator, their concern for the education and welfare of children.

Parents of gifted culturally diverse children have experienced many problems similar to those of their counterparts with handicapped children. They, too, have an information gap when qualitative and quantitative differences of giftedness are being discussed. Many parents have not been made aware of the broadened definition of gifted children as those individuals who excel consistently or show the potential for excelling consistently in any human endeavor—academic, creative, kinesthetic (performance skills), or psychosocial (relational and leadership skills). Parents must exchange information to be assured that the broadened definition will not perpetuate segregation within gifted education, that is, nonminority children being placed in all academically gifted classes and culturally diverse pupils going into what would be considered "talented only" sections.

Educators who are attempting to exchange information with parents of culturally diverse students should be prepared to engage in time consuming tasks. Sometimes the parents' lack of knowledge can actually be caused by educators who tend to hold back information under the assumption that culturally different parents are not sophisticated enough to grasp the material. Rather than assume this stance, professionals should be putting into effect the following guidelines:

1. Send messages home in language parents understand.
2. Work with children to prevent previous negative experiences from having a lasting impression.
3. Respect the parents enough to listen for messages being returned.

Communicating in a clear, concise manner implies that professionals and parents exchange information in layman's terms. Educators should have a sensitivity to Ebonics (Black dialectical differences) and bilingualism and not be offended by different syntaxes or speech patterns used by some culturally diverse populations. On the receiving end, educators should be understanding of the fact that some parents of culturally different children have not profited from all the established communication vehicles used by nonminority parents. Many parents of culturally diverse children have not actively gathered information by affiliating with professional organizations (Marion, 1979: Roos, 1976). Those individuals lacking the ability to handle the sophisticated reading level of much of today's literature have not been able to familiarize themselves with written material. Many do not belong to social cliques that obtain and exchange information on an impromptu basis.

In facing these situations educators must have an accepting attitude. When parents and professionals continue to exchange information, the apathetic and confused parent can be replaced by the parent who wants to know:

1. Whether or not programs for all ages exist.
2. How the schools go about identifying exceptional children.
3. About procedures for evaluating children.
4. How children are placed in programs.
5. About due process.
6. Who their allies are. (U. S. Department of Health, Education, & Welfare, 1976a, p. 4)

Educators will have to listen empathetically and realize that feelings of parents can change from trust to skepticism and/or curiosity. They may be critical of school policies and procedures. Teachers should realize that this reaction is normal and that parents may be hostile and desperate as they attempt to sort out facts from their fundamental beliefs about education.

Professionals who are attempting to work and communicate with parents are facing an important task (Rogers, 1961). They should be prepared to listen and be ready to join forces with parents concerning their rights and responsibilities. In essence, professionals should adopt the role of advocate with parents of culturally diverse children. Educators must report factual information in an objective fashion. By responding in this manner they can establish mutual positions of trust and respect.

Need to Belong

Another basic need of parents of culturally diverse gifted and handicapped children has been the need to belong. The same need applies to both categories in spite of obvious differences in the students. Parents with culturally different gifted and handicapped children are not well represented in the membership of parent organizations of either category. Some parent groups are unwilling to recruit culturally diverse populations into their organizations. Often an unstable family financial condition has contributed to the situation. Families struggling to meet basic survival needs may be unwilling to join dues paying associations. Moreover, if they have been experiencing basic survival needs, parents of culturally different children can be expected to be reluctant to associate with a membership comprised of people who have different socioeconomic and cultural backgrounds and interests.

The outcome of this nonalliance has been a feeling of isolation on the part of parents with culturally different children. These parents have often felt as if they were either unwanted visitors or undesirables. All too often the feeling of isolation has been brought on by an unfair appraisal of the family structure. It has not been easy for these parents to sit in on meetings where discussions about family characteristics and relationships are emphasizing issues foreign to their interests. Those who remain are often seen but not heard (Marion, 1979).

Schools have not successfully met the challenge of helping parents overcome their feelings of isolation and loneliness, either. They have practiced a policy of exclusion against the culturally different (Cohen, 1970). Language, speech, and racial differences have stamped certain groups of children as outsiders. Student pushouts, dropouts, and suspensions have characterized the schools' reac-

tions to people who vary from the nonminority population (Southern Regional Council, 1974).

Nevertheless, the major responsibility for alleviating parental feelings of indifference and isolation remains with schools and teachers. They have been ranked second only to the family in importance in the lives of children (Hobbs, 1975). Parents can be helped to shed the feelings of loneliness if professionals will not label them with such stereotypes as "rejecting," "hostile," or "demanding." Educators and other professionals should:

1. Assure parents that they should not feel guilty about their child's exceptionality or problem.
2. Accept the parents' feelings without labeling them.
3. Accept parents as people—not a category.
4. Help parents to see the positives in the future.
5. Respect the need for parents . . . to value their lives highly.
6. Recognize . . . what a big job it is to raise an exceptional child and help parents to find . . . the range of programs, services, and financial resources needed to make it possible for parents to do the job with dignity (U. S. Department of Health, Education, & Welfare, 1976b, p. 2).

Teachers and other professionals will have to become advocates for the inclusion of parents of culturally different children into organizations mainly frequented by nonminority parents. Culturally different parents should be encouraged to join parent organizations and present minority points of view. Educators will have to collaborate with parents to give them coping skills for joining and maintaining membership in such groups. Recruitment efforts might be strengthened with the addition of dues waivers for parents experiencing financial difficulties. Social isolation of culturally diverse parents will be reduced when their group numbers increase to the point where the majority membership acknowledges their presence.

Using these guidelines, teachers and other professionals will be assisting parents of culturally diverse gifted and handicapped children not only to combat feelings of isolation but also to achieve a sense of belonging.

Need for Positive Self Esteem

Maslow (1962) established the need for high self esteem as a fundamental issue in the hierarchy of needs. Parents of culturally diverse handicapped children have not experienced much enhancement of their self esteem as the schools have steadily increased the numbers of their children in classes for the mentally retarded or the emotionally disturbed. Their counterparts with gifted children have also suffered from a lack of self esteem. It has been pointed out to them that their children have consistently fallen short of measures of giftedness as determined by IQ tests. For both groups of parents it has been implied that family structures, economic class, and heredity all work to their detriment when they are compared to their majority counterparts (Jensen, 1969; Minuchin, 1967).

Parents in culturally diverse populations have a need to be understood. They are asking that professionals recognize their feelings and be responsive to them. Parents who have raised children in a cooperative atmosphere cannot be blamed for their alarm when this quality is not valued as highly as initiative in the school environment (Billingsley, 1968; Hill, 1972). Furthermore, Americans tend to pride themselves on "fighting against the odds and not giving up." Those persons who have not continually subscribed to this notion have often been accused of "sluffing off." Stoutheartedness and perseverance are expected of parents no matter what type of stress they may be confronting (Hudson, 1976). Parental reactions to these expectations have sometimes resulted in anger and loss of self esteem.

Professionals working with minority parents should capitalize on emotion to rebuild the self esteem of parents. Anger can be used to mobilize the parents into action. Parents should be urged to:

a) know the law
b) work with other parents
c) work with professionals
d) use their right to speak
e) stop pleading, education is a right
f) learn how to take part in planning conferences
g) not compromise and insist on full evaluation and clear goals
h) be an active citizen (U. S. Department of Health, Education, & Welfare, 1976b, p. 2)

Without question, educators and other professionals will have to continue their advocacy roles to assist parents of culturally diverse gifted and handicapped children in pursuing the prescribed actions. Parents are typically unwilling to undertake these assignments without the help of a committed, responsible professional.

However, these actions cannot be accomplished solely through teacher advocacy. The advocacy role for teachers will best be combined with an ombudsman approach. Educators are in a position to mediate any intense feelings that parents may have as they experience the stresses of rearing and educating their culturally different gifted and handicapped children. In these difficult times in the lives of parents, many will be heard saying that they do not need trials to build character (Hudson, 1976). Teachers should be prepared deal with that attitude. They should seek to strengthen the self concept of parents by aligning themselves with the parents. Teachers place themselves in an understanding position by acknowledging frustrations and anger. Working from this stance, professionals can resolve some of the temporary affective blocks that hinder communication. They can diminish the chance that they will be perceived as experts or authority figures. If parents are led to feel that they lack the qualifications necessary to meet the needs of their child, it can only serve to imtimidate them. As a result, the parents' self concept is further diminished and any additional attempts at communication are thwarted. Educators who are seeking to work effectively with parents of culturally diverse gifted and handicapped children have recognized that this outcome is in direct opposition to the intended goal of facilitating communication.

Instead, teachers should continually seek to mobilize the energy of parents toward productive ends. Professionals should help parents find satisfaction in learning what can be done for their child and working actively for the child's maximum potential development. As a result, the gains that parents see in their children will become a source of continued motivation. Using this approach, educators can increase the confidence of parents. Convincing parents to work for better public understanding of their children, to improve facilities and increase funding, will result in their increased self esteem.

CONCLUSION

Communicating with parents of culturally diverse gifted and handicapped children is a time consuming task. For these parents the realization that their children will be thought of as "special" students can be expected to produce varied reactions. Professionals who work with parents of culturally different students should be prepared to meet their needs for belonging, self esteem, and information. Also, educators must be guided by an appreciation of dialectical deviations, a respect for cultural differences, and faith in the concept of individualized instruction. Professionals must be prepared to provide help at the cognitive and affective levels as they work with parents who are traditionally outside the mainstream of American education. Successfully meeting these needs and expectations will help educators move toward the goal of improving communication between professionals and parents of culturally diverse gifted and handicapped children.

REFERENCES

Barbe, W. B. A study of the family background of the gifted. In W. B. Barbe (Ed.), *Psychology and education of the gifted.* New York: Appleton-Century-Crofts, 1965.

Barsch, R. *The parent-teacher partnership.* Arlington VA: The Council for Exceptional Children, 1969.

Billingsley, A. *Black families in White America.* Englewood Cliffs NJ: Prentice-Hall, 1968.

Children's Defense Fund. *Children out of school in America.* Cambridge MA: Author, 1974.

Children's Defense Fund. *School suspensions: Are they helping children?* Cambridge MA: Author, 1975.

Cohen, D. Immigrants and the schools. *Review of Educational Research,* 1970, *40*(1), 13–15.

Cole, R. *Children of crisis.* Boston: Little, Brown, & Co., 1967.

Cruickshank, W. W. *Psychology of exceptional children and youth.* Englewood Cliffs NJ: Prentice-Hall, 1975.

Diana v. State Board of Education. Civil Action No. C-70, 37RFP (N.D. Cal. January 7, 1970 & June 18, 1973).

Dunn, L. M. Special education for the mildly retarded—Is much of it justifiable? *Exceptional Children,* 1968, *35,* 5–21.

Gay, G., & Abrahams, R. Does the pot melt, boil, or brew? Black children and assessment procedures. *Journal of School Psychology,* 1974, *11*(4), 330–340.

Griffin, H. *Attitudes, opinions and general information concerning cerebral palsy.* Unpublished doctoral dissertation, University of Texas, 1979.

Hickerson, N. *Education for alienation.* Englewood Cliffs NJ: Prentice-Hall, 1966.

Hill, R. *The strengths of Black families.* New York: Emerson Hall, 1972.

Hobbs, N. The *futures of children.* Nashville: Vanderbilt University Press, 1975.

Hoyt, K. *Career education for special populations.* Washington DC: U. S. Government Printing Office, 1976.

Hudson, K. Helping parents to help their handicapped child. In *Proceedings, the Institute for Deaf-Blind Studies,* Sacramento, 1976, 75–78.

Hurley, O. *Special education in the inner city: The social implications of placement.* Paper presented at the Conference on Placement of Children in Special Education Programs for the Mentally Retarded, President's Committee on Mental Retardation, Lake Arrowhead, March 7–10, 1971.

Hurley, R. *Poverty and mental retardation: A causal relationship.* New York: Vintage, 1969.

Jensen, A. How much can we boost I. Q. and scholastic achievement? *Harvard Educational Review,* 1969, *39,* 2.

Jones, R. *Black psychology.* New York: Harper & Row, 1972.

Larry P. v Riles. Civil Action No. C-71-2270 343F, Supp. 1306 (N.D. Cal., 1972).

Larsen, S. The influence of teacher expectations on the school performance of handicapped children. *Focus on Exceptional Children,* 1975, *6,* 6–7.

Luderus, E. *Family environment characteristics of Mexican-American families of handicapped and non-handicapped preschool children.* Unpublished doctoral dissertation, University of Texas, 1977.

Malone, C., & Moonan, W. Behaviorial identification of gifted children. *Gifted Child Quarterly,* 19, 301–306, 289.

Marion, R. L. Counseling parents of the disadvantaged or culturally different gifted. *The Roeper Review,* in press.

Marion, R. L. Minority parent involvement in the IEP process: A systematic model approach. *Focus on Exceptional Children,* 1979, *10,* 1–14.

Marion, R. L., & McCaslin, T. *Parent counseling of minority parents in a genetic setting.* Unpublished manuscript, University of Texas, 1979.

Marland, S. *Education of the gifted and talented: Report to the Congress of the United States by the U.S. Commissioner of Education.* Washington DC: U.S. Government Printing Office, 1972.

Maslow, A. *Toward a psychology of being.* Princeton: Van Nostrand, 1962.

McCandless, B. *Children behavior and development.* New York: Holt, Rinehart, & Winston, 1967.

Mercer, J. *Labeling the mentally retarded.* Berkeley: University of California Press, 1973.

Mills v. Board of Education of the District of Columbia. 348 F. Supp. 866 (D.D.C. 1972).

Minuchin, S., et al. *Families of the slums: An exploration of their structure and treatment.* New York: Basic Books, 1967.

Myrdal, G. *An American Dilemma.* New York: Harper, 1944.

Oakland, T. Assessing minority group children: Challenges for school psychologists. *Journal of School Psychology,* 1974, *4,* 294–303.

Pegnato, C. W., & Birch, J. W. Locating gifted children in junior high schools: A comparison of methods. *Exceptional Children,* 1959, *25,* 300–304.

Pennsylvania Association for Retarded Children (PARC) v Commonwealth of Pennsylvania, 343F Supp. 279 (E.D. pa., 1972), Consent Agreements.

Prillman, D. *Virginia EMR study.* Bloomington IN: Phi Delta Kappa, 1975.

Rogers, C. R. *On becoming a person.* Boston: Houghton Mifflin, 1961.

Roos, P. Panel discussion. American Association of

Mental Deficiency National Conference, Chicago IL, 1976.

Shaw, C. *Imaginative investigations: Development of a creative writing course for gifted Black adolescents.* Unpublished masters thesis, The University of Texas, 1978.

Southern Regional Council. *The pushout.* Atlanta GA: Author, 1974.

U. S. Department of Health, Education and Welfare, Office of Education, Bureau of Education for the Handicapped. Know your rights. *Closer Look,* Winter, 1976a, 3–5.

U. S. Department of Health, Education and Welfare, Office of Education, Bureau of Education for the Handicapped. Professionals: Are you listening. *Closer Look,* Winter 1976b, 2–4.

PARENTS

1

Clinician and Parent: Partners for Change

by Lillie Pope

A major problem presented by the learning-disabled child is the abrasive interaction between him and his environment. He provides a constant source of friction to those around him, who in turn often react in ways that create further friction. To help this child, it may be necessary to modify his environment, and at the same time minimize his handicapping and abrasive behaviors. Modification of the home environment can be achieved only by employing the cooperation of the child's parents. Only by involving parents as collaborators (rather than as objects, patients, cases, or guilt-bearing child-abusers) can the clinician maximize the possibility of providing relief and assistance for the child. All of this must be accompanied by a program that helps him acquire the preacademic and academic skills that he needs.

The Learning Disabilities Clinic at Coney Island Hospital, part of a mental health unit in a public hospital setting, has enlisted the cooperation and assistance of parents of the learning disabled as therapists for other learning-disabled children, and as cotherapists in dealing with their own children. This is accomplished by means of a program involving the sharing of skills via workshops and training programs, foregoing technical terminology, and stressing the development of trust through open and reciprocal communication. In this program, parents and the clinic become collaborators in a joint effort.

The Parents

Parents whose children attend this clinic are, in the main, members of the working class, and some of them are unemployed. They are under constant strain. In most cases, the families are multiply handicapped (suffering from economic stress and many medical problems) in addition to having one or more children who fail to learn properly, and about whom the schools complain

From *Academic Therapy*, March 1980, Vol. 15, No. 4. Copyright 1980, Academic Therapy Publications, Inc. Reprinted with permission.

constantly. Familial histories of learning difficulties are frequently encountered. Many of the children have only one parent. Few parents have attended college, some have completed high school, and many have never gone that far. They are often inarticulate and poorly equipped to deal with the schools. They are generally mistrustful of mental health services, but are willing to have their children attend a "learning" clinic in the hope that success in learning will provide social and economic mobility for the child. In some cases, however, they come to the clinic only because they are forced to do so by the schools.

When he first comes to the clinic, the parent may be shopping for services, moving from one agency or clinic to another in search of a solution to his problem. The home may be troubled, or even turbulent. It is further strained by the child's behavior and failure to learn. The parent is bewildered, confused, resentful, frustrated, and often punitive. A feeling of helplessness and of general ineffectiveness pervades.

What do these parents need? They need guidance, reassurance, and answers to a multitude of troubling questions. They want to know why there are so many problems surrounding *their* child. If a label or diagnosis has been attached to the child, what does it really mean? What may be expected in the future? If medication has been prescribed for the child (or even suggested), they want to know more about it. What are its potential side effects and its potential long-term effects? What alternatives are available?

The parents need guidance in managing the child at home and in educational planning. They need advice regarding educational expectations for this child and guidance in obtaining services, including optimal class placement. They want to know how to deal with daily crises and with that insidious daily nightmare, homework.

Parents need support and guidance in dealing with grandparents, neighbors, pediatricians, fathers, teachers. These people can be friends and allies. Sometimes, however, they usually do not understand the problem, sit in judgment, and have inappropriate expectations. They may call the child lazy, uncooperative, and uncaring; they may fail to recognize that the child is doing his best and has very real handicaps. The mother is usually blamed for not "bringing up" the child properly.

Parents need help in understanding the language of the professional. They need help in walking the thin line that leads to getting the most and best services for the child (of the few that are available) without offending the professionals and the establishment.

Parent seek relief from harrassment, distress, and guilt; they seek a reversal of the cycle of failure, disappointment, and misery with this child. And they seek acceptance, respect, support, confidence, encouragement, compassion, humor, kindness, courtesy, and lots more. As clinicians, we try to give them all of these.

The Clinicians
The Learning Disabilities Clinic is staffed by a small group of

1

special educators, too few to stem the flood of problems presented by children from the local public and parochial schools. In order to deal wtih these problems, clinic and clinicians seek the cooperation of others. A constant effort is made to enlist the cooperation of school personnel, of other agencies, of volunteers, and, most important, of the parents of the children.

What, then, is the role of the clinician in working with the parents? The clinician can interpret to the parents the label or diagnosis attributed to the child. He can discuss the uses and misuses of labels. He can relieve the parents of destructive guilt. He can help set realistic expectations. He can coordinate the development of a viable treatment plan, including medical, psychological, educational, and home management components. He can help locate appropriate services, and serve as advocate in securing those services. He can provide guidance in dealing with social pressures generated by teachers, neighbors, relatives. To be effective in this role, the clinician observes several simple rules.

Do's and Don'ts of a Collaborative Clinician-Parent Program

1. Use simple language in communicating with teachers and parents. Language problems prevail among children with learning problems, and similar problems of communication exist among professionals, between professional disciplines, and between professionals and parents. Jargon and technical language are used by many to cloak confusion and lack of clarity. Simple, clear language expedites communication and builds trust. Rather than say, "I find it difficult to verbalize in terms that you will find comprehensible," the clinician should say, "It's hard to explain."
2. The clinician and the parent must be clear about the goals for this child, and for children generally. They must be honest and explicit. Are clinician and parents concerned with the child's learning to read? Or to have good table manners? Or are they even now concerned about his being accepted into medical school? Each of these requires a different plan; and some of them may be unrealistic for this child, or inappropriate for the moment.
3. Teachers and clinicians are more helpful when they explain to parents clearly what they are doing, and why they are doing this. For example, parents may think the use of games or motor activity during a tutorial session is a waste of time for their children, unless they are told how the games help teach Jane to sound out her short vowels, that the ball game teaches Peter the concepts of left and right which are important for his academic learning. Similarly, the value of an activity group or a therapy group may not be appreciated unless clinicians explain that the art activity group helps Peter and Jane improve their relationships with children and

adults. In this group Peter learns to wait his turn, while Jane learns to participate in activities which she has in the past tended to avoid. As they understand the "why" for each activity, parents become more cooperative (rather than resistant).

4. There must be acceptance of and respect for individual limitations—in parents, in teachers, and in clinicians.

> John was reported to have been physically abused by his father. For several years, John's father had refused to show his face at the clinic. Several months ago he started to bring John in for his appointments, and to sit in the waiting room while John was tutored. Though he had been reported to be an ogre, staff chatted with him casually and pleasantly during his visits. Treated with respect and acceptance, he relaxed. When a fathers' group was formed, he attended. And he spoke up. When the question of corporal punishment was raised, he announced, "I learned it. It doesn't pay." Apparently he now felt comfortable and trusting enough to share his experience.

Clinicians are forgetful and ineffectual at times. Parents can learn to accept the human limitations of the clinic and clinician, as they themselves are accepted.

5. Beware of the "mother abuse" bandwagon; avoid heaping guilt on the parents.

Parents of children with problems are often victims of home situations in which they are frustrated and helpless; much of this has developed from circumstances that were well beyond their control. They seek counsel on how to help the child, and how to change the relationship between the child and the parents or the siblings or friends or neighbors. Instead, they are burdened with abuse, with blame, and with guilt for having done an awful job. The mother, in particular, is subjected to much abuse and to great feelings of guilt.

This approach is destructive. It interferes with wholesome family relationships and hampers planning for good home and school management.

For example, consider the following example of Amy.

> At the age of 4½, Amy's speech was limited to a few words that were difficult to understand. She was always on the go, constantly moving, climbing, running, never pausing to concentrate on anything—"wild" they called her; but she was not retarded. Her mother was thin, worn, and drained. Near exhaustion, she

1

pleaded for help.

Amy was accepted and would attend a special class that would provide hope and help for Amy and her mother. Mrs. Kaye had to bring Amy daily—traveling one hour each way in the trolley car. The trip was a small price to pay for the schooling.

Every day, on the trolley car, Amy was her usual self—climbing, running, screaming (unintelligibly), and Mrs. Kaye, as usual, restrained her as well as she could, grateful that the trolley car provided natural boundaries so that she did not have far to chase the child.

And every day, some passenger would scold Mrs. Kaye for her failure to bring up her child properly. Several times a week, some neighbor would lecture to Mrs. Kaye on how poorly she had raised her child. They never considered the possibility that Amy's behaviors were based on constitutional problems, diagnosed as "brain injured" by the clinical team at the treatment center.

They were collaborators in one of our most handy and destructive social weapons—used by the teacher, by clinicians, fathers, mothers-in-law, and adolescents—mother abuse.

6. Share with the parents simple principles of child development, and of good management and educational practice.

a. Accentuate the positive. Every child has positives, and these must be recognized and encouraged. At the same time, the negatives must also be acknowledged and attended to. George is a remarkable skater, while his penmanship is illegible. He teaches other children to skate; at the same time, he receives special assistance with penmanship instruction. In addition, he is encouraged to use the typewriter. His self-esteem is supported by the respect given to him as a fine skater.

b. Because patience and objectivity are prime requisites for effective tutoring, parents should be urged not to tutor their own children. They are assured that they will be far more patient with the child of another family, and are therefore encouraged to tutor someone else's child. They will achieve, in addition, greater appreciation of their own child, as they become familiar with the problems and foibles of another child who has learning problems. Parents are cautioned not to nag.

c. Rather, they are taught to tell the child what is required, and let him suffer the consequences if he fails to do it. Nagging breeds nagging. If the child knows you will remind him again and again, he will hold you responsible for not reminding him the thousand and first time.

d. Do not compare the child with his siblings. Compare the child with himself: today he has moved far ahead of where he was two months ago. Every child in the family is different; it is unfair to compare them to each other. The concept of individual differences must be kept in mind.

e. Set realistic goals with small steps, so that the child may be assured of success. Only if he is successful will he be motivated to continue to learn.

f. Keep in mind that many of these children have problems in language, memory, and sequencing, and also difficulties with abstraction. Give one instruction at a time; avoid or explain idioms; teach concepts.

g. Parents should know how the schools *should be* so that they may be effective in making change, particularly for their own child with learning problems. Parents should understand the importance of gearing individual tasks and materials to a child's functional level rather than to his age or grade level.

The Parent Program in Action at the Clinic

The waiting room, where parents wait while their children are tutored or evaluated, acts as a "relaxercizer." Here a cup of coffee is always available. Parents chat with each other, share problems, and offer each other support. Staff members are available for "button-hole" conferences. Younger siblings are observed informally, and on occasion it is noted that it might be appropriate to evaluate one of them as a candidate for clinic service. A recipe book is on the table; parents and staff exchange recipes. The recipe book serves as an opener for conversation, and as a common denominator by means of which parents can share expertise with each other—and parents and professionals can do the same—speaking with each other as equals in one aspect of daily living—food preparation.

Here is the marketplace for mutual support, therapy, education, case finding, and the building of trust.

Parent groups meet with a staff member weekly on mornings when many parents bring in their children. Mainly, the participants are mothers; occasionally a few fathers attend. These are seen by the parents as problem-solving groups, and the clinicians as facilitators, rather than as therapy groups. In one group were a psychiatrist and an illiterate mother, both parents of learning-disabled children. Also present was a mother of four learning-disabled boys. One very anxious mother in the group saw her boy as a failure and applied too much pressure to him. Responding to group discussion, she was able to relax; as she relaxed, her son

1

began to make progress; and he is now in a class for the gifted.

A *for men only* group for fathers, led by a male staff member, met one evening a week last year. The response was enormous, and the series of meetings proved to be invaluable. Fathers had many questions, resentments, and biases that could be discussed only in this kind of nonthreatening atmosphere. This proved to be our most effective technique for reaching the fathers, usually the most difficult to reach. Unfortunately, the series had to be discontinued because of the unavailability of a staff member to meet with the group.

When the clinic was threatened with destruction because of New York City's fiscal crises, parents formed an association to save the clinic. They maneuvered to elect one of their members to the Community Board of the Hospital. And they organized plant sales, toy sales, and raffles to raise money for a scholarship fund to pay the clinic fees of those under greatest financial stress.

This type of mobilization is impressive in a group of parents who are not accustomed to group action, and who generally see themselves as helpless and ineffectual, and therefore usually deport themselves in that way.

The clinic runs courses to train parents in the community to volunteer as tutors in the schools. Many of the clinic parents take these courses. As a result of their increased understanding of child development and of educational concepts and problems, they are able to deal with their own children in an accepting and realistic way.

In addition, some of the parents are then invited to tutor at the clinic while their own children are being tutored. They have proven to be fine tutors; one of them remained in that capacity even after her daughter had "graduated."

Whenever possible, we share with the parents our reports, our joys, our problems and our work. When they read the psycho-educational evaluation describing their children, we gain their confidence and trust. When they see the films we have produced (one depicting a tutorial session, and two explaining psycho-educational assessment) they are once more impressed with the commonality of the scenes they view and the problems that they experience.

Parent-School Relations

We give parents confidence in dealing with the school, and with such typical issues as holdover, promotion, and homework. Frequently something is wrong with the child's school management, but the parents feel ineffectual in dealing with these problems. If it is warranted, we confirm their intuitions, and support them. Sometimes we disagree with their hunches. For example, a parent may insist that promotion will be better for her child than holdover for another year in the same grade. If we feel that in this case a holdover will be more helpful, but we cannot convince her, we nevertheless continue to work with her and the child.

In short, we work with the parents at their level, without patronizing them. We try to help them accept and cope with the problems presented by a learning-disabled child. We support their search for the best services available, and work with them for the development of more and better services. If there is any secret to the success of our program, it is contained in our working philosophy, which is to maintain a nondogmatic, nonauthoritarian approach to parents. We do not sit in judgment.

PART 2

2

MINIMUM COMPETENCY TESTING

by Glen Thompson, Ph.D.

Testing handicapped students has serious implications in identifying, diagnosing and evaluating the proper program for them. When a teacher notices that a child is having trouble hearing and/or learning in the classroom, the child is referred for psychological examination. The school psychologist arrives on the scene with a Wechsler, an achievement test, and possibly the Bender. Based on the results obtained in one or two testing sessions, the child is labeled as TMH, EMH, LD, BD or whatever. Staffings are held to determine the child's placement and programming, with the parents' involvement.

When I first began in the field, test results were often regarded as coming from heaven. They were not to be lightly questioned. Fortunately, today's educators are much more skeptical about test scores. Now educators consider the scores as bits of evidence that can be used to support or contradict hypotheses regarding the characteristics of particular children.

PL 94-142 requires more than one test be used to establish the presence or absense of a particular characteristic. Also, the law requires that those procedures and tests used not be discriminatory.

To meet that criterion, many school districts have taken to employing Black psychologists to test Black students; Hispanic psychologists to test Hispanic children. However, this can pose a problem. Some critics argue that minority psychologists who have successfully completed professional programs are really not very different from the majority of psychologists, because if

they were, they would not have succeeded.

Then there are the questions about truly fair tests themselves. Are they really based upon familiarity with the dominant culture, thus providing students from that cultural background with an unfair advantage? What about the assumption of equal exposure in the case of test of intelligence?

In the past, educators assumed that all examinees had nearly an equal opportunity to develop the abilities being sampled in the test. Assuming the equality, it followed that differences in test scores were related to heredity rather than environmental factors. This premise wasn't challenged for years. Yet decisions made on the basis of the resulting test scores often affected profoundly the future of those examined.

Slowly, the types of tests used and the interpretation of score data are beginning to correlate with the information needed to plan effective instructional programs. Test scores are now considered as one source of data. Other sources include the regular teacher, the special education teacher, the parents and other professionals. So the interpretation of test scores is not made by the psychologist in isolation. Rather they are considered with other information and all the data are integrated to support a given set of hypotheses.

Criterion reference tests and classroom observation indicate where any given child is in a sequenced curriculum. Together they indicate if and when short-term and long-term educational goals are obtained. Data derived from global tests of intelligence might indicate just how rapidly a child might progress through a planned and sequenced curriculum (if this information is important and otherwise unavailable). However, generally, a global IQ score has almost no value. Or as some argue, a negative value.

Across the states, a movement is stirring to use specially designed tests of minimum competency as a criterion for graduating and receiving a diploma from high school. Supporters feel that graduation from high school should symbolize a mastery of a certain level of academic achieve-ment. However, if this premise is accepted, then what does the teacher do in the case of handi-capped students? Should students who are unable to take or pass such a test be denied graduation or a regular diploma, even though they have achieved all goals established in their In-dividualized Educational Programs?

The questions are not new. For years, districts have denied graduation and/or regular diplomas to EMH and TMH students who completed their own curriculum but failed to achieve the academic levels of typical students.

2

Hearing Deficit
Misinterpretation Possible

by Margaret Markham

ANY PSYCHIATRIST confronted with the emotional turmoil experienced by some children with learning problems might be wise in asking if the youngster has ever had a thorough hearing test. Such a simple expedient might help explain the problem, at least in part, and could help smooth the way for youngsters who are themselves unaware of their perceptual limitations. This applies especially to those with a history of chronic middle ear infections, according to a study reported at the recent San Francisco gathering of the American Academy of Pediatrics.

In search of a possible link between recurrent otitis media and learning disability, at least in some youngsters, Forrest C. Bennett, M.D., University of Washington School of Medicine, and associates Susan H. Ruska and Roberta Sherman, tested the auditory status of 53 learning disabled pupils and 56 of their schoolmates without learning problems who served as controls. Most striking of their findings was the discovery that those with learning disability (LD) had significantly more middle ear malfunction than the controls.

Plays Role

This observation suggests to the Se-

attle pediatrician that "chronic, undetected middle ear problems may play a role in the etiology of some school learning disabilities." He reminded his audience that the basis of LD is often multifactorial and difficult to identify precisely. Central nervous system processing dysfunction, frequently involving a variety of perceptual problems, is considered by many physicians and educators to be a major underlying determinant in LD. Recent evidence suggests that progressive hearing loss might be one such culpable factor.

To test this hypothesis, Bennett focused his attention on students aged seven–12 who were attending full-time language and learning disability classes. To gain admission to these special services, the youngsters had to have a history of early school learning problems but to have achieved normal scores on psychologic testing, at the same time falling below expectations on achievement, perceptual ability, and frequently on language competence. Any child with known sensorineural hearing loss was excluded from the study, as were those with cleft palate or other craniofacial malformations predisposing to middle ear disease.

After extensive examination of the

youngsters' ears to gauge the patency of their auditory canals, pure tone audiometric screening was carried out at various tone frequencies. Each child also underwent bilateral tympanometry in order to plot the full hearing range. A history of the exact number of acute ear infections was also obtained from the parents; children with six or more episodes of acute otitis media prior to age six were regarded as "otitis prone." From such data the investigators uncovered the fact that a history of recurrent otitis media during childhood was more common among those with LD (23 percent) compared to the control group (nine percent). Over 50 percent of the LD group manifested abnormal tympanometry, pure tone audiometry, or both (those with acute respiratory infection of any kind were not tested while ill).

Other key points underscored by Bennett were:

• A significantly increased incidence of recurrent otitis media was found among children with documented language and learning disability;

• Significantly more ongoing middle ear dysfunction among LD children as evidenced by mild hearing loss and abnormal tympanometry; and

• A disturbingly high proportion of young LD children with evidence of active, *unrecognized* middle ear problems.

"Does this common childhood malady of middle ear dysfunction, as manifested by chronic and recurrent otitis media with middle ear diffusion, predispose children to the later development of language and/or learning problems? This important question is not new in the pediatric or otologic literature but is currently receiving increased attention because of the marked prevalence and therapeutic controversy associated with both these conditions," Bennett remarked.

"With the provocative hypothesis that early, chronic otitis media with mild, fluctuating hearing loss can have deleterious, irreversible academic sequelae receiving widespread dissemination in the popular press, some otologists and audiologists presently advocate a very early, vigorous medical, surgical, and educational approach to this problem, including liberal hearing aid placement and home stimulation programs for young children with recurring middle ear disease."

The Washington University pediatrician noted that one investigator has already coined the term Irreversible Auditory Learning Disaster (IALD) to describe such perceptually impaired children. He pointed out that highly sophisticated modern technology offers the potential for identifying such hearing defects much earlier, thus raising the possibility of large-scale screening programs for young children. Presumably, this would lead to earlier intervention in the disease process, and at least theoretically, to the prevention of associated developmental and psychological as well as educational complications.

Justification for such an approach has come from a number of directions. More than 20 years ago the Scottish Council for Research in Education made an analysis of the results of school transfer examinations of 310 children between 11 and 12 years. All of them had a history of otitis media. Children in this group were educationally retarded to a significant degree in comparison to those with a history of normal hearing; and most important, their level of achievement declined in relation to the severity and duration of hearing loss. V. A. Holm and L. H. Kunze a decade ago similarly attempted to determine the link between LD and hearing problems and focused their attention on a rather small group of children with chronic otitis media and fluctuating hearing loss who had been cared for in an outpatient clinic for such problems. The two researchers then compared the retrospective records of these children with those of youngsters treated at other types of hospital clinics. They found that those who attended the ear clinic were significantly delayed in all language skills requiring the receiving or processing of auditory stimuli or the production of verbal responses.

"A search of the literature reveals no long-term, rigorously controlled (ideally with siblings) prospective study of a middle-class pediatric population in which emerging language and learning function of children with chronic and recurrent otitis media is compared to that of their non-otitis controls. J. L. Paradise has recently called for this type of investigation, and we are in the early phase of such an effort within a health maintenance organization," Bennett declared.

"What seems to be clear from our study and the combined work of others is that chronic middle ear dysfunction may be a significant additional factor in the etiology of language and learning disabilities, particularly in children already at constitutional and environmental risk for development of these multifactorial problems."

That otitis media and its sequelae constitute a problem of major proportions was underscored at the same meeting by Sylvan E. Stool, M.D., and associates at the Children's Hospital in Pittsburgh. They characterized the condition as the most prevelant disease now encountered in pediatric practice—with an estimated 20,000,000 visits annually made in connection with its diagnosis and treatment. Despite this high prevalence, they believe there may be many other children in whom the condition is missed, or at least not diagnosed for some time.

2

Learning Disorder Found To Be Preventable

by *Psychiatric News*

Can the learning disability syndrome be nipped in the bud before it achieves full expression? Researchers in Florida and New York think it can and believe they have found a way to early identification of children vulnerable to learning failure.

According to Archie A. Silver, M.D., professor of psychiatry and director of child and adolescent psychiatry at the University of Florida Medical School, the requisite approach consists of three elements: a scanning battery to identify those at risk while still in their kindergarten years, an educational intervention program at the first and second grade levels for those vulnerable to learning failure, plus an interdisciplinary facility for diagnosis and evaluation of youngsters. This specific program, Silver told the American Academy of Child Psychiatry meeting in Atlanta, was designated about three years ago as a Child Demonstration Center by the U.S. Office of Education, Bureau of Education for the Handicapped.

The battery test consists of ten subtests that measure specific aspects of spatial orientation and temporal organization in various perceptual areas. Used with youngsters from 60 to 80 months of age, it can identify those kindergarten children who will subsequently fail in reading and pinpoint those who need additional diagnostic workup, Silver said.

The intervention aspect of the project is based on principles of deficit perceptual areas in a "prescriptive approach designed to build those neuropsychological skills we believe necesssary for progress in reading, writing, and spelling," Silver added. This "Search and Teach" program has now been replicated in 85 schools and 13 school districts.

The data compiled since the inception of the project has led Silver and co-workers Rose A. Hagin and Ronnie Beecher, both NYU psychologists, to conclude that such efforts can achieve secondary prevention of reading disability and its emotional consequences.

"Early identification of children vulnerable to learning failure, diagnostic evaluation, and specific educational intervention have yielded significant improvement in oral reading and reading comprehension. By the end of the fifth grade, children originally considered neurologically and perceptually impaired are not behaviorally distinguishable from the 'normal' peers," Silver reported.

From *Psychiatric News,* December 21, 1979, Vol. XIV, No. 24. Copyright 1979, The American Psychiatric Association. Reprinted with permission.

2

Neurological and Environmental Variables in Learning Disabilities

by Ronald L. Taylor, Ed. D., and Francisco I. Perez, Ph. D.

Behavioral approaches for the treatment of learning disorders in children typically disregard the role of the central nervous system (CNS) and its correlates. Conceptually, these approaches have also omitted the role of the CNS in the temporal sequence of events resulting in behavior. Psychoneurological approaches, on the other hand, have often failed to consider the role of the environment in the diagnosis and treatment of various disorders. This dichotomy has resulted in a failure to integrate knowledge from both fields. The present article is a discussion of the separate behavioral and neurological theories and a proposed behavior sequence which integrates and describes the importance of neurological and environmental variables in learning disabilities.

Neurological Approach

Although there is disagreement as to a precise definition of learning disabilities, most researchers agree that a variety of CNS impairments appear to be associated with learning disabilities and have noted a correlation between learning disabilities and positive neurological signs (Clements 1966, Rourke 1975). For instance, P. I. Myers and D. D. Hammill (1969) view learning disabilities as symptoms of internal conditions that exist within the child, such as suboptimal neurologic functioning or inadequate programing of an essentially normal nervous system. More specifically, D. J. Johnson and H. R. Myklebust (1969) propose the following definition of learning disabilities:

> . . . We refer to children as having a psychoneurological learning disability, meaning that behavior has been disturbed as a result of a dysfunction of the brain and that the problem is one of altered processes, not of a

From *Conference Report: Minimum Competency Testing and Handicapped Students,* printed by the State of Illinois, April 1980. Donald F. Muirheid, chairman, Illinois State Board of Education and Joseph M. Cronin, State Superintendent of Education.

generalized incapacity to learn.

These viewpoints of learning disabilities imply that learning and, conversely, the inability to learn are both functions of the brain. The implications of these approaches are evident in the treatment of learning disabilities. A. J. Ayres (1972) proposed a somewhat radical approach to treatment of learning disorders within a sensory integration/neurological dysfunction framework:

> A sensory-integrative approach to treating learning disorders differs from many other procedures in that it does not teach specific skills such as matching visual stimuli, learning to remember a sequence of sounds, differentiating one sound from another, or even the basic academic material. Rather, the objective is to enhance the brain's ability to learn how to do these things.

Thus, the objective of therapy is modification of the neurological dysfunction interfering with learning rather than dealing with the behavior associated with the dysfunction.

Behavioral Approaches

Behaviorists have typically considered learning disorders as being inherent in the circumstances of the environment in which children function (Throne 1978, Bijou 1966, Pennypacker 1973). Proponents of such a viewpoint look less inside of the learning-disabled child and more to the environment and situations outside the individual. W. D. Wolking and V. A. Schwartz (1973) noted that even severely brain-injured children and adults are able to relearn old verbal skills or learn new ones under the right conditions. They suggested that it was more functional to conceptualize learning disorders as deficits in either the history or the present conditions of learning, or both, rather than deficits in the learner.

The behaviorist viewpoint of learning disabilities suggests that the child is not learning disabled, only his academic behavior in the normal learning situation is disabled. This implies that it is not the neurological state of the child, but rather the environment which gives him the status of learning disabled. The implications of behavioral therapy are contrasted with Ayres in that the main objective is improvement of behavior through systematic arrangements of environmental events.

The Behavior Sequence

Indeed there has been little attempt to integrate knowledge from both fields in developing a system of diagnosis and treatment for the benefit of the learning-disabled child. One area of common agreement, however, is that whether the difficulties in learning are neurological or environmental in nature, the deficits will be observed in the behavior of the child. Thus, any attempt at integration of knowledge should include a precise analysis of behavior.

2

The approach presently offered conceptualizes behavior as an ongoing process continuous through time, and following an input-process outcome sequence constantly interacting with the environment. For practical purposes, however, we will intervene in this ongoing process and look at a sample of a single behavioral act. The following proposed sequence considers perception, CNS functioning, and the external environment as determinants of behavior.

1. Antecedent environmental events (stimuli, cues, and environmental history)
2. Registration (sensation and perception)
3. Organization (higher brain functions)
4. Integration (higher brain functions)
5. Behavior
6. Subsequent environmental events (consequences)

The environmental antecedent event can be subdivided broadly into two classes. The first is commonly termed stimuli or cues and corresponds to the environmental conditions which are unique to, and operating only at, the time of the behavior in question. The second class is referred to as the environmental history and includes such variables as the individual's prior reinforcement and punishment history. The ordering of stages 2 through 4 corresponds to the temporal sequence of events in the nervous system, beginning with stimulation and ending with activation of a muscle or gland. These various processes intervene between the occurrence of an environmental event and the subsequent appearance of a behavioral act, and are correlated with events in the organism's nervous system. The subsequent environmental events correspond to the consequences of the behavior.

Conceptually, this behavior sequence allows us to integrate both the neurological and environmental variables. Thus, in this sequence, behavior becomes the dependent variable and the other elements of the sequence become the independent variables. The implications of this statement are twofold. First, any one or a combination of these independent variables could have an effect on the dependent variable (behavior), including neurological and/or environmental effects. Second, improvements in behavior can only be achieved through manipulation of the environmental variables (i.e., antecedent and subsequent events). Even though stages 2 through 4 of the behavior sequence are occurring within the organism, external environmental manipulations (e.g., medication, sensory-motor exercises) are necessary to affect these stages which subsequently affect behavior.

Practical Implications of the Behavior Sequence

Many learning-disabled children display positive signs of neurological impairments. Professionals often identify many children with learning disabilities who show evidence of neurological abnormality. But other children with severe neurological impairments demonstrate no apparent difficulty in learning (Black 1973, Shields 1973).

The behavior sequence we have just described enables us to explain the discrepancy among these three statements in terms of interaction between the biological organism and the environment. For present purposes, we will consider the foregoing statements as three distinct categories. An attempt will be made to explain these three categories in terms of the proposed behavior sequence.

Category 1: learning disability—no neurological dysfunction. R. P. Edwards, G. R. Alley, and W. Snider (1971) found no significant differences between normal and retarded readers on the basis of neurological evaluation. Likewise, Black found many children with learning disabilities who demonstrated no neurological dysfunction and suggested that positive neurological findings should not be a criterion for the placement of children in remedial programs.

These findings can be explained in terms of the environmental variables in the proposed behavior sequence. Since children in this category demonstrate no neurological abnormality or problems in registration, stages 2 through 4 of the behavior sequence can be eliminated as the possible cause. This suggests that one or more of the following situational conditions could play an important role in the etiology of learning disabilities.

Antecedent environmental events—Some of the conditions included within this variable could be the social and academic history of the child, inappropriate curriculum or teaching strategies, inadequate physical arrangement of the classroom, or poor peer relationships.

Subsequent environmental events—Included within this variable are the effects of reinforcement and punishment on the child's behavior. Some deficits in learning could result from inadequate reinforcement (the teacher's "reward" is not reinforcing the child), withdrawal of reinforcement (the teacher ignores child's appropriate behavior), infrequent reinforcement (the child does not receive sufficient reinforcement while learning new skills), or inappropriate reinforcement (the teacher is reinforcing inappropriate or noncontingent behavior). Others include the inappropriate use of punishment (the teacher is punishing appropriate behavior) and high frequency of punishment (the teacher is making the classroom environment aversive).

Category 2: no learning disability—neurological dysfunction. Shields has indicated that many educators have identified children with extensive brain injury who demonstrate no impairment of learning abilities. This statement suggests that neurological impairment does not always result in learning disorders. This again can be described within the context of the behavior sequence.

In this category it is assumed that there is a dysfunction in one or a combination of stages 2 through 4. There is, however, no behavioral dysfunction in learning. It is possible that the antecedent and/or subsequent events are arranged in such a manner that the child is capable of emitting appropriate learning responses. This implies that the child's social and academic histories and the appropriate contingencies of reinforcement have developed an environment in which the child can learn regardless of the neurological impairment.

Category 3: learning disability—neurological dysfunction. Most researchers agree that groups of learning-disabled children display an unusually high incidence of positive neurological signs. In contrast with the previous category, this group of children displays behavioral difficulties in learning. The behavior differences in these two neurologically impaired groups could be attributed to the function of the environmental variables. In the previous category, the environment has been rearranged (through appropriate curriculum, teaching strategies and reinforcers, etc.), to facilitate learning in the neurologically impaired child. In the present category, however, the environmental variables have not been arranged in such a manner.

Implications and Summary

This article has attempted to describe the possible functions of neurological and environmental variables in learning disabilities. Research indicates that both types of variables can play an important role in the etiology of learning disabilities. The behavior sequence provides a conceptual framework to describe the relevancy and possible interactions of neurological and environmental variables.

The importance of the behavior sequence, however, lies in its implications for treatment. It must first be noted that all treatment of learning-disabled children is environmental. This does not imply, however, that environmental variables are the only determinants of learning disabilities. The objectives of treatment for children demonstrating learning disabilities with no neurological dysfunction, Category 1, is to arrange the environmental contingencies so that learning can occur. The goals of intervention for children in Category 3 is to move them, also through arrangement of environmental contingencies, to Category 2. It is extremely important to look at the behavior of the child and to monitor the daily changes in behavior caused by these environmental interventions. By studying the effects of various environmental manipulations on behavior, the most effective individual educational program can be developed for the learning-disabled child.

References

Ayres, A. J. 1972. *Sensory integration and learning disorders.* Los Angeles: Western Psychological Services.

Bijou, S. W. 1966. A functional analysis of retarded development. In *International review of research in mental retardation,* vol. 1, ed. N. R. Ellis. New York: Academic Press.

Black, F. W. 1973. Neurological dysfunction and reading disorders. *Journal of Learning Disabilities* 6:5 pp. 313-316.

Clements, S. D. 1966. *Minimal brain dysfunction in children.* Washington, D. C.: Co-sponsored by the Easter Seal Research Foundation of the National Society for Crippled Children and Adults and the National Institute of Neurological Diseases and Blindness, Public Health Service.

Edwards, R. P.; Alley, G. D.; and Snider, W. 1971. Academic achievement and minimal brain dysfunction. *Journal of Learning Disabilities* 4:3 pp. 134-138.

Johnson, D. J., and Myklebust, H. R. 1969. *Learning disabilities—educational principles and practice.* New York: Grune and Stratton.

Myers, P. I., and Hammill, D. D. 1969. *Methods for learning disorders.* New York: Wiley and Sons.

Pennypacker, H. S. 1973. Precision teaching: effective strategies and tactics for intervention on behalf of the disabled learner. In *The disabled learner,* ed. P. Satz and J. J. Ross. Rotterdam: Rotterdam University Press.

Rourke, B. P. 1975. Brain-behavior relationships in children with learning disabilities: a research program. *American Psychologist* 30:9 pp. 911-921.

Shields, D. T. 1973. Brain responses to stimuli in disorders of information processing. *Journal of Learning Disabilities* 6:8 pp. 501-504.

Throne, J. M. 1973. Learning disabilities: a radical behaviorist point of view. *Journal of Learning Disabilities* 6:543-546.

Vaughn, R. W., and Hodges, L. 1973. A statistical survey into a definition of learning disabilities: a search for acceptance. *Journal of Learning Disabilities* 6:658-664.

Wolking, W. D., and Schwartz, V. A. 1973. Applied behavior analysis and learning disorders. In *The disabled learner,* ed. P. Satz and J. J. Ross. Rotterdam: Rotterdam University Press.

MCT DEBATE

2

Minimum Competency Testing And Handicapped Students

by Illinois State Board of Education

The analysis of the relationship of minimum competency testing (MCT) to handicapped students in Illinois and other states has raised a number of legal, programmatic, and technical issues. This paper presents an overview of these major issues with specific references to the report resulting from a recent State Board of Education Conference on MCT and the handicapped student.

Policies on the application of MCT to handicapped populations stem from different interpretations of two federal laws: Section 504 of the Rehabilitation Act of 1973 and Public Law 94-142, The Education of all Handicapped Children Act. The former is often called a civil rights act for the handicapped individual since it prohibits discrimination against individuals because of their handicapping condition (O'Donnell and McCarthy). Public Law 94-142 requires free appropriate public education for handicapped students, ages 3-21. Illinois laws and regulations parallel the Federal ones. (Illinois Revised Statutes, Chapter 14 Rules and Regulations to Govern the Administration and Operation of Special Education.)

There are four provisions of Public Law 94-142 which are directly relevant to the implementation of an MCT program.

    1.   <u>Non-discriminatory testing</u> which requires that the test:
        a)   be conducted in the primary language mode of the student,
        b)   be validated for its specific use,
        c)   be administered by trained personnel,
        d)   be interpreted for placement decisions by a team of persons knowledgeable about the child,
        e)   measure the achievement or aptitude level of the student and not merely reflect the child's handicap,
        f)   not be a sole criterion for placement.

From *Conference Report: Minimum Competency Testing and Handicapped Students,* printed by the State of Illinois, April 1980. Donald F. Muirheid, chairman, Illinois State Board of Education and Joseph M. Cronin, State Superintendent of Education.

2. The Individualized Education Program (IEP) which includes:
   a) a statement about the present level of performance,
   b) annual goals and short term objectives,
   c) a specification of needed educational services, the dates of their initiation, and the anticipated duration,
   d) a statement of the procedures for evaluation,
   e) a statement of the extent of participation in regular educational programs.

3. Procedural and placement safeguards which require:
   a) a structure for recourse concerning proposed placement and treatment,
   b) the opportunity for the parent to obtain an independent educational evaluation of a student,
   c) the opportunity to have access to impartial due process hearings.

4. Free appropriate public education until the age of 21. An MCT/graduation requirement could affect the length of time handicapped students are in school thus adding substantial costs.

The application of these federal and state laws has been reviewed by the legal department of the Illinois State Board of Education, and they have suggested that a state policy on testing handicapped students should reflect the following elements:

(1) Equal protection: a testing policy must be applied to all appropriate parties.

(2) Fundamental fairness: the policy must not discriminate against any identifiable groups. The test must take into account the nature of the child's handicapping condition(s).

(3) The test results in reasonable classifications.

(4) The policy must reflect a concern which demonstrates a legitimate state interest.

The application of federal and state laws to testing handicapped students per se does not appear to be an issue unless an MCT is implemented as a graduation or promotion requirement, and/or the school district is issuing different types of diplomas. Both of these issues relate to whether one interprets the meaning of the high school diploma to be a certification of a specified level of achievement or the completion of a program of study.

Participants in the MCT/Special Education conference had numerous points of view on the issues, but they agreed that these differences resulted from their answers to the basic question about the significance of the high school diploma. If the purpose of a diploma is to certify a specified level of achievement, a single standard is appropriate, assuming that technical questions of test construction and administration have been answered (Lapan and Fisher). On the other hand, if the diploma signifies the completion of a program, the application of a single standard (even a specified minimum) is inappropriate for all students (Lapan).

The issue of awarding multiple diplomas relates to the interpretation of a single standard requirement. Some local school districts and other states have developed policies which result in the classification of students (by the type of diploma) based on the student's fulfillment of certain program requirements. "Special Education" diplomas are awarded instead of "regular" ones because the student is unable to fulfill the "regular" requirements.

What are practices in other states as well as some Illinois school districts in regard to special education students and MCT? Programs are neither uniform in philosophy nor in implementation, but rather reflect beliefs about the end result of a high school education.

New York

All New York students, beginning with the class of 1979, are required to pass a state MCT in order to receive a regular diploma. One other diploma is awarded for passing the Regent Examination. The state education office is suing a local school district because they awarded regular diplomas to two special education students who had not passed the state MCT but had completed their Individualized Education Programs (IEPs) at the ages of 20 and 21.

New Jersey

Students in New Jersey will have to pass a state MCT beginning with the graduating class of 1985. Special education students may have the requirement waived (which will be noted on their transcript) as a part of their IEP. Legislation presently requires that only one diploma may be awarded by local boards of education.

Massachusetts

In Massachusetts, the state education office requires all districts to administer basic skills tests based on state standards in elementary, middle, and high school. The districts may use the state developed test, develop a local test, or use a commercial one. The local and commercial tests must be approved by the state office. By 1983 a decision will be made concerning the implications of testing and high school graduation. Currently special education students take the test only if it is indicated in their IEP. All students currently enrolled in transitional bilingual programs are exempt from the testing program.

Vermont

Vermont does not have a minimum competency testing program, although there is a state process for checking the attainment of specified competencies (currently 51) through individual programs. It was initiated in 1976 and will be implemented as a graduation requirement for the class of 1981.

Local districts are to assess the competencies in appropriate ways and keep records of student progress. Assessment may include traditional tests, actual performance observed by a teacher, or some other alternative appropriate to the specified task. Achievement is then recorded on a standard form, the "Pupil Progress Record."

Students with handicaps, which would preclude their demonstration of any of the specified competencies, receive special consideration. If a child cannot meet a specified competency, the first consideration is whether or not the student could meet the expectation if it were assessed in an alternate manner. If not, the IEP team is allowed to file for a waiver.

The waiver must be approved through the local school board and sent to the State Department of Education. If approved, the IEP team is directed to develop an alternate program to be specified as a Multi-Year Plan. The Multi-Year Plan may reduce the difficulty of the competency or specify a substitute. Currently only 186 waivers have been granted for the class of 1981. If the students then complete their special education programs, they will receive diplomas.

Maryland

Maryland has a competency program entitled "Project Basic" which was initiated approximately two and one-half years ago. In order to graduate in 1982, students will be required to meet standards in reading. Mathematics and writing will be added for the class of 1984 and life skills in 1985. These skills requirements will be added to the existing requirements of four years of education beyond 8th grade in order to receive a State Diploma. It is illegal to automatically exclude anyone from these requirements including handicapped students.

In Maryland there are six levels of service for handicapped students. Students in the first three levels are provided service in conjunction with standard educational settings, and these students are expected to take the competency tests. Students in the last three levels are provided service in alternative settings. It is expected that students in these latter categories will receive preparation to meet the skills requirements until the multi-disciplinary assessment team determines that even with modifications the student would not be able to achieve the competencies. At that point a recommendation would be provided to the parent in the annual IEP meeting to provide an alternate educational program leading to a certificate of completion. If the parent agrees, the IEP will document that decision. For students not capable of performing tasks on the test because of their handicapping condition, alternative assessment mechanisms are allowable and the state has begun to specify the nature of those alternatives.

Illinois

Practices within Illinois are as varied as among other states. Some districts which require an MCT for graduation have set up special committees which make the final graduation determination for all students who fail the MCT. If they feel that the student has put forth the best effort and been remediated but continues to fail, an exemption may be granted.

Other districts have policies which reflect the single standard certification requirement. All students must pass the MCT in order to receive the only diploma which is awarded. Those students who have fulfilled all of their other requirements for graduation, with the exception of the MCT, receive a "certificate of completion." Some Illinois districts are giving different classifications of diplomas (as previously mentioned) which are determined by the program which the student has completed.

The School Code of Illinois does not specifically prohibit local boards of education from issuing different types of diplomas. Because the subject is not addressed, some districts have adopted multiple diplomas reflecting different achievement levels (or classifications) while others issue certificates to those who do not pass the MCT.

One additional area of concern in either local or state policies regarding MCT has to do with the administration of special education programs. Services for handicapped students in Illinois are often provided through joint educational agreements which generally serve more than one school district. Handicapped students served by separate school districts may have elementary level services provided by one special education service delivery unit and high school level services provided by a different unit. In those cases, the special education providers are faced with the need to articulate their services so that the student will be adequately prepared for an MCT.

In summary, decision makers will have to take into account a number of technical and programmatic considerations in adopting testing policies for special education students. This requires recognition of the fact that it may be inappropriate to classify or categorize all special education students into one group. As Dr. Lapan notes, ". . . handicapped children have many more personal and learning characteristics that differ from one another even though they show the same label . . ." and ". . . are just as likely to share personal and learning characteristics with non-handicapped persons as they would with their handicapped peers . . ."

The questions remain: If an MCT is to be a graduation requirement, should all students have to be certified at a specified level? Is it sound educational policy to award multiple types of diplomas?

MCT DEBATE

Response to Stated Issues

by Thomas H. Fisher, Ed. D.

Issue #1

The basic notion behind MCT's is often (but not always) that students should be expected to master certain minimum expectations (i.e., objectives) before being awarded a diploma. If children attend school for the purpose of accomplishing certain objectives and if a diploma is a document signifying that accomplishment, it is appropriate to think of performance expectations for various groups of exceptional students, e.g., TMR and EMR students.

These differing expectations probably would be reflected in the child's IEP. Their accomplishment would be a reasonable goal of the school and the student. Within this context, it would not seem proper to exempt exceptional students from the minimum competency requirements. Because there is such a wide range of difference, for example, between gifted and TMR students, it is improbable that a single set of expectations or a single test would be workable even if differential passing scores were established. The test would have to differ to the degree that the group's objectives differ, and different levels of passing scores are not likely to compensate for these wide differences.

The evaluation of the minimum expectations should be adapted to the particular needs of the exceptional students as far as possible. Such adaptations as large print and braille versions of the tests would be expected. It is not entirely clear which adaptations are really necessary for which students, however, and research in this area is limited.

Issue #2

If a student meets all requirements outlined by statute or regulation, the appropriate diploma should be issued. Failure to meet all requirements may result in a lesser document of recognition or in no document at all. Students could be given a certificate of attendance, a certificate of completion, or nothing other than a transcript of work accomplished. Exceptional

From *Conference Report: Minimum Competency Testing and Handicapped Students,* printed by the State of Illinois, April 1980. Donald F. Muirheid, chairman, Illinois State Board of Education, and Joseph M. Cronin, State Superintendent of Education.

education students could be given a certificate reflecting accomplishment of their IEP; however, it is difficult to see how one could complete an appropriate IEP and not simultaneously complete the requirements for the appropriate certificate or diploma, assuming differentiated diplomas were permitted.

Graduation exercises should be open to any student who accomplishes a diploma, a certificate, or lesser document (except, perhaps, just a transcript). No differentiation should be made in the ceremonies or related activities.

State and local education agencies should make every effort to make opportunities available for students receiving a lesser graduation document to up-grade their status. Further school work leading to a regular school diploma should be permitted and encouraged.

Issue #3

It would not seem appropriate to structure an MCT system in such a way that any students are precluded from attempting to meet performance expectations for a regular diploma. Statutes and regulations may be structured such that a special form of diploma is designed for certain exceptionalities, but the option of earning a regular diploma still should be available.

As far as litigation is concerned, it is possible that it will result regardless of the system which is designed. There is little which can be done to prevent litigation, but much can be done to lessen the probability of losing such cases.

Issue #4

As with Issue #3, there is no guarantee that the state or local education agency will not be sued on this issue. However, if the minimum competency system is designed to permit the issuance of an appropriate document to signify accomplishment of reasonable minimum standards, the chances of winning such challenges are enhanced. In this case, it would not seem to be appropriate to issue a regular high school diploma to two groups of students, even though they met different performance standards.

Issue #5

Whether or not grade-to-grade promotion should be tied to a minimum competency test is controversial among educators, many of whom have tried for years to decrease emphasis on grade levels in favor of the concept of continuous progress. Citizens, on the other hand, cling to the concept of grade levels. They are not likely to object to having a child retained in a grade level under appropriate conditions.

A system of minimum competencies could be designed around individual teacher evaluations of student progress. This would lessen attention paid to any single competency test but would increase the teacher's responsibility in certifying specific competencies. Many teachers feel insecure in this role and may be fearful of litigation from parents. A system involving special competency tests and teacher evaluation of student competencies may be a workable compromise.

Regardless of the system for evaluation of the competencies, it seems important to have special competencies for certain groups such as EMR and TMR students. Others, such as homebound students, would not necessarily need a special set of standards.

Issue #6

Technical issues related to minimum competency tests are varied and depend upon the system being implemented. A norm-referenced approach would lead to different technical problems and solutions than would an objective-referenced testing approach. In the former, the psychometric techniques are well defined and accepted, but, in the latter, the theories are in a state of development which leads to diversity of opinions among psychometricians.

Regardless of the testing system being implemented, certain issues will be of interest. These are test validity, test reliability, test renewal, establishment of passing scores, test bias, test security, standardization of test administration, test reporting, and test analysis. These issues are complex, and technical assistance must be available to anyone who attempts to implement an MCT program. This is a very real concern to small school districts charged with the responsibility of developing a local approach to MCT.

Adaptations of the minimum competency tests for exceptional students are appropriate and may include such things as large print versions, flexible scheduling, and audio versions of the test. Costs become an issue if, for example, a very small population demands access to an expensive test adaptation. Also, it is not entirely clear that certain exceptionalities really need a particular test adaptation even though such an adaptation leads to better scores. That is, where does one differentiate between (1) adaptations which will remove factors which prevent an exceptional student's accurate assessment, and (2) adaptations which make the test easier for an exceptional student regardless of handicapping conditions?

Issue #7

An important element of any minimum competency test is the availability of extra resources for students not meeting the minimums. It must be clear that students not meeting the minimums are going to receive extra help; otherwise, the threat of litigation on behalf of such students is likely to become very real.

It must be recognized that implementation of minimum competency programs will lead to restructuring instructional programs for certain students. Students who are likely to fail or who have failed to meet minimum standards will have to receive extra help in those areas. This may mean less time spent in other areas.

It is not correct to assume that art, music, social studies, optional courses, work study programs, etc. will disappear from the curriculum because of an MCT program. Such courses will continue. However, the purpose of an MCT program is to reveal which students lack certain minimums and to provide extra help to them until such minimums are met. It makes little sense to enroll a student in American Literature if he/she only reads at the second grade level. Whether or not to continue a student in a work study program would depend upon the circumstances. It may very well be that it would be more in the student's interest to be in school all day working toward removal of identified academic weaknesses rather than continuing in a work study program. Or, it may be necessary to alter the student's length of time in high school just as would be done in college for any student who only enrolls for half the normal course load. Implementation of an MCT program necessarily implies that many currently accepted ways of educating children will have to be changed.

2

MCT DEBATE

Minimum Competency Testing For the Handicapped

by Leonard W. Hall

I wanted to figure out a way to plan a meeting and not have the last session. We'd have more successful meetings. I was telling some of my newly found friends this afternoon that I am from Rockford, Illinois which is an adjacent city, and I am pleased that this discussion didn't take place on competency testing about 15 years ago. I might not have the privilege of being here with you. I am going back to see if I can hide the transcripts in case you take a look at it.

I have a couple of points of view and a couple of problems I want to share with you. This is very difficult. Cindy said "You cannot be opinionated; you must be neutral. You are the synthesizer." Let me tell you there is no such thing as a neutral state director. And there is also no such thing as synthesis or consensus among state directors on anything, much less competency testing. But I do believe that I can offer a point of view of not only one state director but of state directors because we are a family, and if I am wrong you will tell Joe Fisher, and he'll call me, and you'll know you heard from a maverick and not the group.

Reference has been made several times to the survey that NASDSE, the National Association of State Directors of Special Education, conducted. Let me just quickly highlight what NASDSE discovered, and then let me get to some of the responses or the thought-provoking issues that have come out of the last several hours of discussion, and for some of us, the last two days. I offer them to you as points of view, and as some hypothetical challenges for you to consider and think about as you go home, and hopefully to write back and feed some input to this very fine State Board of Education staff.

The first question that NASDSE asked the states, 57 states and territories make up NASDSE, was "Do you mandate minimal competency testing?" Seventeen states do mandate it, and 36 have no requirement prior to graduation. One

From a speech delivered at the Chicago MCT Conference, January 4, 1980, as printed in
Conference Report: Minimum Competency Testing and Handicapped Students, published by the
State of Illinois, April 1980.

state said that they have left it at the L.E.A. decision. One question was which categories of handicapped children are required to take such tests? Six states require all handicapping condition categories, others by some categories such as speech and language, and others specify just "mentally capable." There is no consensus; there is no state of the art. Issuance of regular diplomas to handicapped children - that was an issue that has been discussed extensively today. One state does not issue regular diplomas to handicapped children; 31 reported that they do issue regular diplomas, and 17 leave it up to the L.E.A. Do you issue special diplomas to handicapped children? One state did, 12 didn't, and 15 left it up to the L.E.A.'s. Do you issue a special certificate of attendance for handicapped children who do not receive a diploma? Nine do, 18 don't, 17 leave it up to the L.E.A.'s. Those are really impressive statistics - that aren't worth a nickel to you. You are plowing new ground, and if you had to come to Chicago to find that out, it was worth the trip for you.

Putting that aside, let's talk about what you have been discussing. And again I am going to kind of rechallenge you with some of the things that you have been challenging each other with for the past several hours. Think about whether or not you put the concept of competency testing in perspective. Is it really necessary? The question was asked yesterday - is it necessary to have competency testing? Evidently it must be: your legislature says so; many of your parents say so; the people for whom you work think it is. So, at least for now, it must be necessary that there be some kind of minimal competency measuring activity, which at least for today, you are calling a test. What is it then? What is this competency testing? I don't think you know! I really don't think you have the faintest idea of what you are talking about.

Are you talking about a competency test that you give as either an award to those that pass or as punishment to those who fail before they leave school? Or are you talking about a basic skills measurement that will be an instructional tool for you as you continue to work with that youngster after he or she has taken the test? Are you talking about an accountability system which provides you an opportunity to once again and perhaps more formally appraise and assess where youngsters are in the delivery system you call school? Are you talking about an assessment system? Are you talking about a look at a youngster at critical milestones down the 12 or 13 years the youngster spends in school, and at one point in time hope that you can now declare that youngster has met some kind of statistically-acceptable and society-acceptable competencies that mean reasonable expectation of the productive members of society? I think that this is what is in the back of your mind, but I never really heard anyone express it today. If all you're talking about is competency tests for the sake of competency tests, I submit to you that you are wasting your time, you're wasting your people's money, and you're wasting the time of the State Board of Education, because a competency test on the surface is a waste of time - absolutely worthless.

But a test of basic skills, a test where a youngster is at a given point in time, relating that youngster against what reasonable people feel that he or she should be to function in society is a very sound educational practice. And one that needs to be pursued. Are you pursuing basic skills as a teaching tool? I think it's worth thinking about. Are you looking at it as part of the total assessment program? Are you comfortable with the motives that have brought you here? Are you here to improve the quality of life of Illinois' handicapped children and youth? Are you here as a school accountability defense mechanism? Are here to figure out some way to devise some kind of test or procedure that you can finally get some results on which you can shut up the critics back home? Are you here because you are involved in a turf reaction to possible political usurpation of your right to govern your school? Hopefully we are here because we are concerned about the improved quality of life of the kids in this state. Hopefully the whole doggoned competency movement from Florida - we have been through it in Missouri and other states is because somebody out there has his eye on a youngster and says we need to find a way to be certain that we know just what this youngster knows when he or she leaves us, and that the youngster has a reasonable expectation of knowing what he or she knows when they leave us. It's really a pretty simple formula. I think it something worth thinking about. It's hardly worth a nickel, but take it home with you because those are some issues - the question of motivations - in some of the issues that I think undergirds all the discussions that we have.

Another thing I think we have to think about is what are the influences in our school environment which can hide behind the competency movement. Now I am not saying, "how can you hide behind competency testing;" but let's talk about the influences with which you deal that can hide behind the movement. One would be that which was suggested yesterday: teachers who don't teach, teachers who don't teach can hide behind the competency movement because they can teach the test. I heard it 4 times-teach to the test. If you have sense at all, you'll never say that in public. What a horrible selfindictment - suggest our field would teach to the test! Goodness knows we wouldn't do that or we wouldn't be professional. And we claim we are, at least at salary time. So we won't teach to a test, and those that would perhaps could hide behind the movement, unless we force them out. The administrators that hide from reality - do we have any? - those are the ones that permit folks to teach to the test. A weak administrator can hide behind the competency movement and just raise "holy heck" with it. And that goes sometimes for the way we administer our programs.

How about higher education irresponsibility? I can't believe how we are having inservice on a law that's been on the books now for going on five years. Surely, our graduates that are in schools now for the first year need no inservice, because they have had four years to get it in college. But they can hide behind the whole competency movement. How about the families that have no love for the youngsters - are there any out there? How about the sociological issues that you are trying to take into your schools? Can they hide behind the competency movement? The fact that the youngster hasn't seen a book until second grade and has never known the love of his parents or the feeling of a secure life or home. Can they hide behind the fact that he is not learning by saying you don't teach, and there's no competency in education. Can they hide behind the movement? Or could we glean that out as part of what we are looking at how the test or tests or system could be developed? How about the communities that don't support schools? How about you who can't get your levy passed? You can't get bond issues passed so you can't build buildings to have least restrictive environments - can they hide behind the test and have the chicken and egg thing go with you. If you start teaching Johnny to read, I'll support the levy - "but lady I can't teach Johnny until you vote me in some chalk!" But can they hide behind the competency movement and actually hope, maybe subliminally hope, that the scores aren't too good so they can justify their failure to support the system? As you know, we work for them.

How about the press whose only motive is to have a good story? How about the reporter who hopes that he finds bad results because good results don't sell papers? Can they hide behind the movement? How about inflated curriculum and grades - can we just continue to reinforce that? Keep in mind when you talk about what you mean by competency testing. Because you are talking about improvement of the quality of life of your state's handicapped children and youth. Talk about all those internal accountability measures that you have to be willing to deal with first, to respond to this symptom of education that is identified now as No. 1: back to basics; No. 2: competency, by whatever definition. Some of the issues that were addressed, I think, can also couple with some thought-provoking and some less than acceptable thoughts right now. Is the test the only way to measure competencies? Is the test the only way to measure your basic skills? What about the observation of the less formal, the ongoing kinds of things that a good teacher can do with or without any kind of law or mandate. Let's not hang our hat perhaps on the test. It's worth thinking about. Competency from whose point of view? - who wants to tell me I am competent? Probably nobody. Who does? - who wants to say that anybody in this room is competent? On whose standard? And, it's on your standard that you have just thrown the IEP out the window - because the IEP says it's got to be on my kid's standards. He's going to tell us when he's competent, because hopefully, we have been able to outline some reasonable expectations for him to achieve.

Who is going to superimpose a level of competency, and how are you going to defend that? We discussed the possibility of a single cutoff score that can be discriminatory because the test may not have been germane. That comment should have just been so basic that it need not have been mentioned, but you that spend any time in the schools know that we are pitifully weak as educators in understanding the whole basis of measuring, of monitoring the youngsters who receive the curriculum that we provide. It's critical that we know what our tests are doing and that we not use scores to measure things that were not germane to the effort.

What is a prescribed program? Are we serious about the IEP? What is the diploma? We have talked about it. If a diploma truly says that youngster has completed a prescribed program of study, and if we were honest about the IEP, then the issue about who gets the diploma is moot, because I get mine when I complete my prescribed course of study, and you get yours. You might be going to college and I might be going to work in the fields, and he may be going somewhere else, but if we have each completed our prescribed course of study, we deserve a diploma. And you know what? The employer may hire the handicapped kid who worked harder to get his than the gifted youngster who floated through and got theirs by putting in time. Someone mentioned that in a group, and I was so pleased to hear it because I think that's the real world out there. Just as the astute employer may look at your MCT scores down the pipe, they also look at the person, their character, and motivation, and tenacity, and the IEP can spell it out. It is something to think about as you look at minimum competency testing. Let's not hide behind the diploma issue. To me, it's an irrelevant issue. I agree with those that say that it's a dastardly thing to give them out in colors. It is a dastardly thing to keep from giving them out. The diploma is only any good to the youngster walking across the stage, and those in the audience waiting to see him or her get it. After that, the diploma is meaningless, and you know it as an educator. You absolutely know it. The diploma means nothing. The school can tell you if the child graduated. The school can tell you what the kid's about. The school can tell you how he or she behaves. But don't deny that youngster, for whom you have claimed a commitment to give a life of dignity and worth, the first chance that this youngster has to experience dignity and worth by taking away the darn diploma! And what do you do about the people who have paid for your salary, assuming that their child is going to graduate - but you are going to let that youngster go, but by the way, he or she doesn't deserve it. I don't know-think about it-it might not be worth a nickel. Or are we hiding behind it?

We have talked about state or local test development. If you develop your competency test or program - I want to say program-locally, but is it going to be safe if I move from Decatur to Chicago that there will be a reasonable semblance of the quality of education expectations, i.e. competency measurement that will be applied to my youngsters? Is it safe, then, if I go from Rockford to Cairo, that the same kind of expectations are going to be in effect? Are we going to have 1,000 independent states in Illinois, each with its own level of expectations, i.e. competency, that they are applying to their youngsters? If education is a state right - perhaps it should be a state test, if there is any testing program at all. Maybe not - because maybe there is too much state intervention of the right of local boards to govern schools. And you know what - if the board doesn't want a good school, the laws only have to say they have one - they can just stay one step ahead of the state and federal government, and they can just about do what they want. How consistent do you want to have education? Because we are a mobile society, we don't have the autonomy that we used to. So I think the state versus local issue is one that's pertinent. Nowhere in 94-142, nor in Section 504, nor in Illinois State law or any law that I know of, does it say that youngsters do not have the right to fail. Youngsters still have the right to fail. Just as the consumer has the right not to support the school while increasing his demands upon it. It is our obligation to see to it that if a youngster fails, it is despite the best that we could do to apply the art and science of education inside that kid. If we can sleep at night knowing that we have done everything possible in the classroom, in the teacher's lounge, and in the administrative offices - to climb inside and turn around that youngster, then the youngster can fail, and we can sleep. I suspect that if we are sleeping, the whole issue of competency testing is a moot issue. See if we can't go back home and think about that a little bit. Are we really applying the state of the art and science of education to the kids who can only look to us for a chance to advance to lead a life of dignity and worth? I think it is important.

We talk about remediation. We talked about whether or not the curriculum is

2

going to suffer. We talked about whether we narrow the curriculum. I don't think those are issues. I don't think that remediation is the only way to resolve the problem if the youngster fails to be moving forward on an assessment program as he or she should. Maybe acceleration is what it takes - maybe we have had the programs misprioritized, and we recognize by monitoring this kid's development, that we have to restructure priorities and then accelerate with the new priorities. Maybe the greatest remediation is acceleration. If we have had our perception of who that kid is, and how that youngster can learn as out of sync with what that youngster could have told us if we had asked him and looked at his properly administered test scores over a period of time and asked Mom how he behaves at home or she behaves at home. Maybe its something worth thinking about - maybe its something to think about compensation and acceleration, as well as remediation. And not about tunneling curriculum or about depressing curriculum, but about prioritizing curriculum based upon the information that youngsters are willing to tell us if we'll ask him or her.

Talk about separate standards for different handicaps - there's nothing wrong with that. Do you realize that I am convinced that Illinois has something it its water that causes genetic mutation, because in Missouri we don't have one homogeneous handicapped population. But evidently you do, because all I have heard all day long was the handicapped - the handicapped - I don't know who the devil they are! There are 2.8 million children in the nation going to school, according to 94-142 statistics, and that would be a heck of an "n" for some statistical study, because they must all be a control group. But you know, they are not. The deaf kid is not even close to that blind kid, nor that mildly retarded kid to that trainable kid nor that speech impaired kid that is smart as a whip. You can't talk about handicapped kids as a population. What you have to talk about is whether or not you are going to apply different standards of basic skills expectations at different levels of development for different youngsters exhibiting significantly different developmental characteristics to their peers. That's all you gotta do. It's really pretty simple. You do it in the classroom now - don't you? I think sometimes they call it a tracking system - other times they call special education. If we can deal with the handicapped as a population, we didn't need 94-142. In fact, we only had two groups: the normal and the handicapped - we didn't need all this other stuff. Get back into perspective, all of us - I think it is something we have to think about. The standard graduation level for a deaf student is rated in schools for the deaf at about 9 or 9 1/2 - 9th grade/4th month, roughly. But if that's the standard graduation academic equivalent for the nation's schools for the deaf, then I expect that's a competency test right there. I expect that it is pretty much expected that when a deaf 18 year old graduates and has mastered that much academics that they are generally, on deaf standards, ready to move on. That's a standard, and that standard doesn't clear any other standards that are normed on the right population - a truly homogeneous population with all the variables taken into consideration. Let's not think about the handicapped as a population. There are populations of individual kids that learn at different rates and different styles.

Let's not worry too much about litigation. Shoot - the lawyers don't know any more than we do, and sometimes they know less. Tom and I have a unique relationship - I have the highest respect for him - he is a tough attorney - he really is - he's tenacious, but I welcome him in my state because he's not frivolous and I need him - you need the attorney, because just as legislation shaped schools in the 70's, litigation is going to shape it in the 80's by answering the questions left unanswered. And government cannot lead - government must respond. You go out ahead of the group and you are going to get fired. You go out right with the group and let them lead, and you respond - you are going to be the leader. You sit back and gripe and react, and you are going to get fired. You pull back and be fearful of litigation, and the world's going to pass you by. Because the courts were here before we were. You go out and try to answer the questions too soon, and the auditors are going to get you. But you stay right in tune with litigation, and you monitor what the answers are, and you be there responding to that direction, and that's leadership. As long as you can deal with it to shape programs for kids and answer questions that won't go away. Don't become paranoid about litigation. It is costing too much money - that's not your problem - that's the public's problem that pays us to run the school. It's not your individual problem that you have 4-6-8 lawsuits against you, unless they are frivolous lawsuits. But the public has to wake up and realize that if litigation is answering the questions, then we must pay for litigation. So don't let that be an issue if you are willing to stand by the professional judgment, if you are willing to defend your position - there's no other answer until the courts tell you what it is. If there is an answer, then you have an obligation to answer it, and to go on with it.

The teachers' fear of the results of testing came up. That reminded me of the IEP anxiety of a few years ago that has nearly gone away. You know I have suggested to the people in Missouri that one of two things happened with the IEP - Number 1 - Congress had 6,000 parents of handicapped children parade before them saying - you and I didn't care about their youngsters - didn't know a thing about where the kids were or where the kids were going - and therefore they gave us the IEP, or Number 2 - Congress heard us say - I am really frustrated - I know I could do so much with this youngster if only the governing structure of my district would permit me to talk to other teachers and other administrators and to look jointly at the kid as they do in a medical staffing - I could be a better teacher. Now, one of those two things happened - I think it was the latter - the same thing is happening here - as teachers you should be grateful for competency measurement programs in your district; you should be grateful for a chance to find out who your kids are, where they are going, and how you can be with them. The least restrictive environment is not an issue as a result of MCT. It is an issue anyway - I don't think it is something you ought to worry about. It's something for you to think about.

Finally, don't handicap the disabled because of arbitrary governance with unclear purposes and even more unclear motives. Think about the kids in your school; think about how you want to assess them; think about how you want to determine their basic skills and how you want them to lead a life of dignity and worth. Convey that message to all, and you will have a competency testing program that may or may not include tests. But you will still be in charge of your schools, and you will still have the respect of the kids and parents whom you serve. Otherwise you are going to wonder where it went and wonder how you lost it. I think that is a point of view of a number of state directors. I thank you for this opportunity.

MCT DEBATE

2

Minimum Competency Testing For the Handicapped: A Report Prepared for Illinois State Board of Education

by Leonard W. Hall

On January 3-4, 1980, I served as a consultant to the staff of the Illinois State Board of Education to review the concept of minimum competency testing and its implications for handicapped children and youth. This report is presented as a summary of the issues which were brought forward during those two days of discussion and which appear to be the major areas of analysis to be pursued by the staff of the Illinois State Board of Education.

First, I think it is important for all to put into perspective the concept of minimum competency measurement. Is it necessary? Apparently it is wanted by the legislature and by the consumer, i.e., those to whom we are responsible and accountable. However, what is minimum competency measurement? Is it a test? Is it the "MCT" which has become an acronym in Illinois vernacular? Are those who are pursuing the "MCT" viewing it as a teaching tool? Are they putting the concern for the quality of life of the state's handicapped children and youth as a prerequisite to their attention, or are they responding to external pressures with motivations less than educational in nature? Are we looking at minimum competency measurement as part of a total assessment program? Have we analyzed the timelines of formal measurement, i.e., the test, and related it to the various strategic points in a child's formal learning experience when such measurement should be logically applied?

Are we comfortable with our motives? Are we concerned with improved quality of education? Are we responding to the minimum competency movement as a school accountability defense measure? Are we reacting to an attack upon our turf by politicians, and are we viewing their activity as an usurpation

From *Conference Report: Minimum Competency Testing and Handicapped Students,* printed by the State of Illinois, April 1980. Donald F. Muirheid, chairman, Illinois State Board of Education, and Joseph M. Cronin, State Superintendent of Education.

of our authority?

What other influences in school can hide behind the minimum competency movement? Will teachers who do not teach panic and claim irresponsibility on the part of administrators as a result of "MCT?" Will administrators who are hiding from the realities of the job dig more deeply into retreat as a result of the "MCT?" Will Higher Education irresponsibly use "MCT" as a way of passing the blame? Will families who have no love and who destroy children's spiritual and educational growth use the "MCT" as a means of projecting onto the establishment that which was generated at home? Will communities which fail to support public education use the "MCT" as a scapegoat? Will the press, which may have only a "story" as a motive, enjoy the "MCT" movement as a means of selling papers? Will we inflate curriculum and grades in order to keep the "MCT" from being a threat?

These are interesting challenges and may be self-indictments. However, they are issues with which we deal daily and which must be considered if the "MCT" movement is to be kept in perspective as a tool in the schools.

We can measure competencies in several ways; a test is one - it must not be disregarded out of hand.

Competency is a measurement based upon a point of view of someone. Who? If the child is to be kept in focus, we must not let one's self-perceived level of acceptable competency get in the way of the realistic implementation of the IEP.

A single cutoff score can be discriminatory if the test given is not germane to the issues measured.

What is a prescribed program? Are we serious about the IEP as being reflective of educational prescription? If so, we should pursue the goals, the objectives and the strategies of the IEP and not concern ourselves with the "MCT".

Are we hiding behind the issue of the diploma? Who gets it? How is it to be delivered? It is ironic that the diploma has become a major issue in the "MCT" efforts in Illinois. The diploma symbolizes for the graduate and his/her family an accomplishment which we have led them to believe is to be the result of efforts. It is not a license for a job. It is nothing more than a short-term symbol as part of a ceremony that has become a tradition in American education. For the handicapped learner who has been taught that quality of life, dignity and worth are experiences which he or she will enjoy at graduation, we are hypocritical in denying those experiences by cheapening the diploma through various kinds of alternative certificates, asterisks, et cetera, which make these people second class citizens. For one to be impeded by the diploma issue in discussing the "MCT" indicates that he/she is not ready to pursue the concept of competency as it relates to any dimension of education, either that of the competency of the school, the staff or, much less, the student.

The question of whether state or local tests should be administered as part of the "MCT" is an interesting issue. For such tests to be standardized and developed locally may permit the proliferation of individual fiefdoms in education which, when coupled with the reality of a mobile society, could make the "MCT" a meaningless measure.

The issue of teaching to the test is also a concern. For professional educators to even tolerate the accusation that we may teach to a test is an unnecessary self-indictment. Those who do so should be dismissed. Those who permit them to remain on faculty should be dismissed as well. Let us not cheapen a profession by indulging in proliferation of irresponsibility.

A student has a right to fail. However, it should only occur in spite of the best efforts of the art and science of education. The minimum competency testing program, when properly administered, helps not only the school know the extent to which a child has learned, but helps the child himself/herself know where he/she stands with his/her peers. We must not be afraid of the minimum competency movement.

The alternative educational strategies which may be considered as a result of a youngster failing an "MCT" are not necessarily remedial. Compensatory and accelerated instructions are also areas of intervention worthy of pursuit.

Qualified tests and instructional personnel are issues that must be considered. Separate standards for different kinds of handicapped children are an issue. Handicapped children are not homogeneous. They are as individual as the child himself/herself, and this must not be forgotten. There is concern about the threat of litigation as the result of an "MCT" movement. The threat of litigation is present as an entity of the eighties and should not be an issue in pursuing a responsible and professionally accountable "MCT" program.

It has been suggested that we should beware of haste, that we should not fall into the "new math" rut. This is correct and is advice to be considered.

In summary, let us not handicap the "disabled" because of arbitrary governance with unclear purposes and even more unclear motives. Let us look at the youngster as an individual learner. Let us worry about our obligation to be of service to that youngster and his or her family. Let us worry about the competency of the system and the child as part of the ongoing program and not permit ourselves to be railroaded into specific and arbitrary measures of competency for political purposes. Instead, let us provide a system of measurements throughout the experience of the youngster that will help us and the youngster himself/herself be comfortable at the point of graduation when the diploma is issued that the individually prescribed program for "the child" has been achieved, and it is with dignity, worth, self-accomplishment and a hope for a future that the graduate marches across the stage and out into society at ever different and individual levels of functioning. That is public education.

CLASSROOM APPLICATIONS

Communication Competence And Secondary Learning Disabled Students

by Gladys P. Knott

All secondary students are required to take high school English and some find literature, grammar, composition, and media rewarding. But others dislike high school English. Some who find English difficult among the latter group are learning disabled adolescents.

According to the U.S. Department of Education, learning disabled students have disorders in "basic psychological processes" (Federal Register, 1977) which result in difficulty in comprehending and expressing language in spoken or written form is the mainstay of the current definition of learning disabilities. The learning disabled student exhibits inherent problems in cognitive and linguistic behavior which decrease success in the English classroom as well as other areas.

Supporting data are sparse in defining cognitive and linguistic behaviors of learning disabled students. A major hypothesis of this article is that secondary learning disabled students manifest difficulties in communicative competence. The purpose is to suggest a framework for improving language and other communicative behaviors of secondary learning disabled students. Included are a definition of the term 'communicative competence," a review of research findings which assist in clarifying secondary learning disabled students' communicative problems, and suggestions for fostering improved communicative ability.

Communicative Competence Defined

The term 'communicative competence' has been defined as "competence in language use or as the language abilities of speaker and listener ("DeStefano. 1978, p. 2), and as secondary students' awareness of what linguistic behavior is and how it is used (Doughty, Pearce, & Thornton, 1971). Other researchers define the term more globally (Chafe, 1970; Moerk, 1977; Bates, 1976). Hymes (1974) defines communicative competence as:

. . . the child's acquisition of the ability to produce, understand, and discriminate . . . the grammatical sentences of a language. Within the social matrix in which it acquires a system of grammer, a child acquires also a system of its use, regarding persons, places, purposes, other modes of communication, etc., all the components of communicative events, together with attitudes and beliefs regarding them. There also develop patterns of the sequential use of language in conversation, standard routines, and the like (p. 75).

Linguistic behavior is only one aspect of the child's development of ability to communicate effectively. The child must also learn "how and when to use a language or languages or different varieties of a language, and with whom and, of course, when not to" (DeStefano, 1978, p.3).

Communicative Competence in Learning Disabled Students

Research evidence does not indicate learning disabled students demonstrate problems in acquiring and developing pragmatic aspects of linguistic behavior. Difficulties in receptive and expressive language (Johnson & Myklebust, 1967) or linguistic processing (Wiig & Semel, 1976) have not been shown to infringe on the concurrent development of pragmatic aspects of communicative behavior. The issue of 'use of linguistic behavior' as the precursor to dynamic symbolic representation has not been resolved with respect to normal language developing children or the learning disabled child.

The current state of knowledge is due partly to the youth of the field and partly from the focus, in past years, on construction of standardized language tests and development and remediation of syntactic abilities. In view of current psycholinguistic and sociolinguistic literature, however, the learning disabled students' communicative behavior warrants further and more intense investigation.

Support for the hypothesis that secondary learning disabled students manifest difficulties in various aspects of

From *The Directive Teacher*, Vol. 2, No. 3, Winter 1980, published by NCEMMH, The Ohio State University.

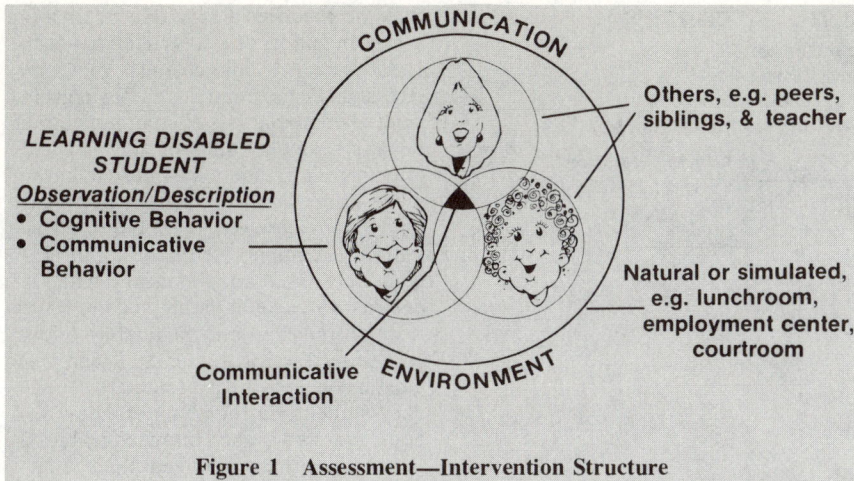

Figure 1   Assessment—Intervention Structure

communicative competence is reported in the literature. Descriptions of the course of development of communicative competence in normal children (Bates, 1976; Moerk, 1977; Halliday, 1975) suggest that young learning disabled children's problems in social perception (Johnson & Myklebust, 1967) may be the source of continuing problems in communicative behavior during adolescence. They describe learning disabled children's inability to perceive or attach meaning to nonverbal symbolic behavior of others (e.g., gestures, facial expressions and body movements) as well as other nonverbal symbolic behavior. Bates and Moerk assert that the child's understanding and use of nonverbal symbolic behavior constitutes the initial stage of the development of communicative competence. The young child's nonverbal communicative ability precedes verbal ability and is always a part of the child's and the adult's communicative repertoire. While this observation requires further exploration with learning disabled children, it does point to an aberration in development which may persist and affect communicative competence throughout adulthood.

Evidence suggests that young learning disabled children's problems in verbal and nonverbal communication may persist during adolescence. Bryan (1978) summarizes a series of studies on older learning disabled children's social status, relationships and interactions with peers in classroom and laboratory settings. Learning disabled boys were found to be ignored by peers and teachers twice as much as normal subjects, "white LD boys and girls are the least popular groups of children, followed by black LD boys and girls . . ."

(p. 109), and "LD children are less accurate in comprehending nonverbal communication than are peers" (p. 113).

Wiig and Semel (1976) define and summarize various aspects of nonverbal communication with specific references to learning disabled adolescents. The researchers assert that social perception, including nonverbal communication, is a component language and that academic performance and interpersonal relationships are affected by secondary learning disabled students' lack of competence.

Limited data suggest that young learning disabled children's communicative problems may persist through adolescence. This implies learning disabled students require continued intervention during their secondary education career. Their potential needs revolve around the improvement of communicative behaviors which affect academic success and interpersonal relationships.

Fostering Communicative Competence

There are unanswered questions related to process *versus* product intervention with secondary learning disabled students (Goodman & Mann, 1976) and to academic improvement *versus* vocational preparation. Research is needed regarding these questions before definitive statements can be made. The secondary learning disabled student's communicative competence is likely to be deficient and require intervention. In this regard, the following sections address characteristics of learning environments, materials, and methods for improving secondary students' communicative competence.

The Learning Environment

In most secondary schools, improvement of communicative behaviors is designated a responsibility of the teacher of English. The English teacher must have knowledge of the English curriculum and flexibility in accommodating student's needs, particularly the learning disabled students at the secondary level.

Arranging the learning environment to promote growth in academic and interpersonal communicative behavior is a primary concern of the teacher of English. Some students fail to recognize the relationships between themselves and the linguistic symbols of classroom material. To improve this condition and foster communicative competence, it is necessary "that the conditions for using language in the school be similar to those in the world outside . . ." (Doughty, Pearce & Thornton, 1971, p. 10). A major goal for students to perceive communicative competence is an essential part of their growth and development.

One implication of this construct is that the English classroom be arranged from the viewpoint of natural occurring or simulated social contexts. Conditions from the outside world are brought into the classroom to determine students' learning and communicative problems and to enable them to perceive their needs and improve their academic and communicative behaviors. For example, the classroom may be arranged as a special social gathering requiring introductions, announcements, etc., as a job placement center, as a vocational apprentice program which requires knowledge, understanding of the feelings of others and how they are communicated.

Determining Needs

What students need to learn is most often the language of content material. To determine student problems in oral and written form, their behaviors are examined in relation to specific channels, i.e., comprehension, expression and use of verbal-nonverbal communication in various social contexts, reading and written expression of information and ideas. Figure 1 illustrates major elements pertaining to observation-assessment-intervention strategies.

From a natural or simulated social context, students' communicative behaviors are systematically observed, recorded and described. The students' cognitive functioning, verbal behavior — phonology, semantic-syntactic relations and pragmatic aspects of linguistic

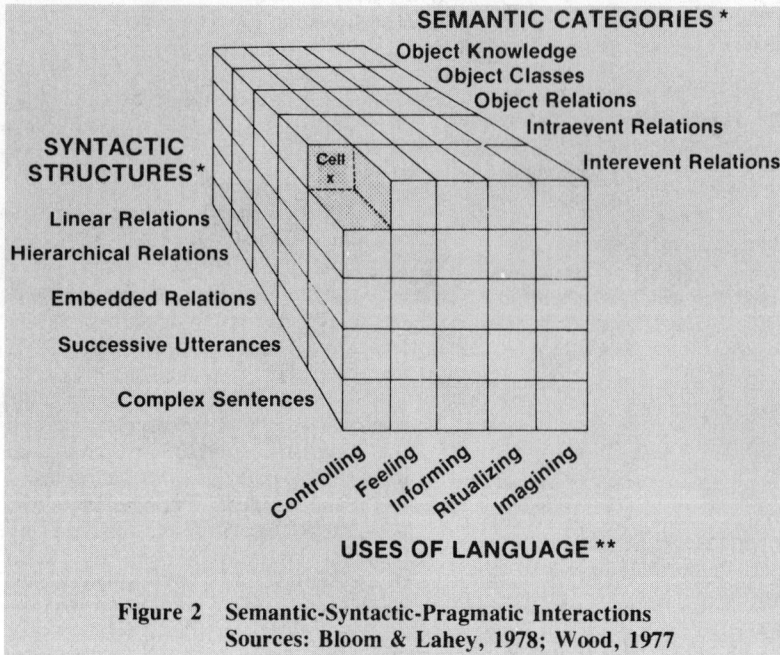

Figure 2 Semantic-Syntactic-Pragmatic Interactions
Sources: Bloom & Lahey, 1978; Wood, 1977

behavior and nonverbal communication (paralanguage, kinesics, and proxemics) (Knapp, 1978) are major concerns for determining interpersonal communicative needs. Academic areas include opportunities for students to read orally and silently and communicate information, and to engage in written expression of ideas based on the context of the situation. Based on the analysis and description of what students need to learn, materials and ongoing assessment-intervention strategies are selected.

Materials and Methods
Materials often require modification in order to accommodate secondary learning disabled students' needs. Some materials can be adapted to serve multiple purposes. For example, the textbook, *Lessons in Syntax* (McCarr, 1973) may be used in its published form to improve several aspects of verbal communication. The text may be adapted to reflect topics related to students' interest but still enable them to learn semantic-syntactic structures which are used in oral behavior, reading material and written language. In the latter use, topics are elicited from students anonymously. Then, the teacher develops units following the text or in relation to what students' needs dictate. Other suggestions for the use of this text have been reported elsewhere (Knott, 1979) which include practical ideas on improvement of reading and written language abilities.

A selection to foster competence in secondary students' use of linguistic behavior to achieve personal and social goals is *Development of Functional Communication Competencies: Grades 7-12* (Wood, 1977). The activities are selected and/or modified based on the needs of the learning disabled adolescent.

Finally, a selection pertaining to the dynamics of nonverbal communicative behavior is *A Handbook of Non-Verbal Group Exercises* (Morris & Cinnamon, 1975). The verbal and nonverbal channels of communication are used simultaneously in any communicative act but are separated in this discussion to give specific attention in helping students with details of communication.

As in the initial assessment of students' needs, on-going assessment-intervention strategies are implemented in simulated situations. Students may be selected to form small groups to provide learning models for one another. In situations where all students demonstrate the same need, the teacher assumes the responsibility for teaching specific communicative behavior. In any case, students are instructed as to the purpose and goals of the activity. One way of conceptualizing and planning activities representing the verbal channel is illustrated in Figure 2.

Figure 2 suggests that semantic-syntactic and pragmatic aspects of linguistic behavior are interrelated and interdependent. The content of the model

may be modified to include behaviors which members of a class need to learn.

A particular dimensions may be stressed. For example, Cell X suggests several combinations of communicative behavior which a student may need to improve. The student may need to know more information or content pertinent to relations between events in order to structure complex sentences; the student may have knowledge of what is desired to be communicated and for what purpose but may be unable to formulate syntactic structures. When linguistic concepts are presented to secondary students in this manner, they become more aware and knowledgeable of the relationships between their communicative abilities and what they need to learn to be more effective.

Role playing activities are amenable to improvement of students' verbal-nonverbal communication. Students can express ideas for group problem solving, to release frustration and emotional concerns and to assume roles they may actually desire to experience in real life. Guiding principles and suggestions for effective use of 'role playing' are reported by Thompson (1978).

Conclusion
Research data suggest that secondary learning disabled students manifest disorders in communicative competence. Such disorders infringe on the students social and academic success.

At the secondary level the English classroom can be arranged to provide an environment and instruction to improve communicative behaviors in learning disabled students. The suggestions presented here are not exhaustive, but they provide ideas for selecting alternatives to traditional materials and methods which often do not meet secondary learning disabled students' needs.

References
Bates, L. *Language and context: The acquisition of pragmatics.* New York: Academic Press, 1976.

Bryan, T. Social relationship and verbal interactions of learning disabled children. *Journal of Learning Disabilities,* 1978, 11(2), 107-15.

Chafe, W. *Meaning and the structure of language.* Chicago: University of Chicago Press, 1970.

DeStefano, J. *Language, the learner & the school.* New York: John Wiley, 1978

Doughty, P., Pearce J. & Thornton, G. *Language in use.* London: Edward Arnold, 1971.

Goodman, L. & Mann, L. *Learning disabilities in the secondary school*. New York: Grune and Stratton, 1976.

Halliday, M. Learning how to mean. In E. Lenneberg and E. Lenneberg (Eds.). *Foundations of language development*, Vol. 1. New York: Academic Press, 1975.

Hymes, D. *Foundations in sociolinguistics*. Philadelphia: University of Pennsylvania Press, 1974.

Johnson, D. & Myklebust, H.R. *Learning disabilities: Educational principles and practices*. New York: Grune and Stratton, 1967.

Knapp, M. *Nonverbal communication in human interaction*, 2nd. Ed., New York: Holt, Rinehart & Winston, 1978.

Knott, G. Developing reading potential in Black remedial high school freshman. *Reading Improvement*, Winter 1979, 262-269.

McCarr, J. *Lessons in syntax*. Beaverton, Oregon: Dormac, Inc., 1973

Moerk, E. *Pragmatic and semantic aspects of early language development*. Baltimore: University Park Press, 1977.

Morris, K. & Cinnamon, K. *A handbook of non-verbal group exercises*. St. Louis: CMA Publishing Co., 1975.

Thompson, J. *Using role playing in the classroom*. Bloomington, Indiana: Phi Delta Kappa Educational Foundation, 1978.

Wiig, E. & Semel, E. *Language disabilities in children and adolescents*. Columbus, Ohio: Charles E. Merrill, 1976.

Wood, B. (Ed.). *Development of functional communication competencies: Grades 7-12*. Urbana, Illinois: ERIC Clearinghouse on Reading and Communication Skills, 1977.

2

CLASSROOM APPLICATIONS

Modern Math
And the LD Child

by Mildred H. Wood, Ed. D.

Formerly, a learning-disabled child was frequently defined as one who was unable to read but who was good in math; today, because of changes in both reading and math instruction throughout the country, the learning-disabled child may be able to read with some degree of efficiency, but he may be totally unable to compute. It is my purpose in this article to point out the pitfalls of modern math for this select group of children.

What are the pitfalls? There may be others, but I have recognized at least five:

1. The language and vocabulary of modern math;
2. A lack of appropriate emphasis on mastery;
3. The use of set notation in the primary grades;
4. Inadequate teacher inservice education in modern math; and
5. The virtual elimination of a child's parents as partners in the mathematical teaching process.

The Language and Vocabulary of Modern Math

A film for teachers regarding the teaching of modern math clearly states: "Mathematics is a language. Once the language is mastered, math is mastered" (1972). By placing early and heavy emphasis on language, have we stacked the deck for the child who has a restricted language code? By deemphasizing computation and mastery, have we taken away the very aspects of math which some students could learn and in which they could develop some competency? Through the heavy emphasis on language, are we helping the child with limited language and vocabulary to achieve understanding and mastery, or are we introducing him to misunderstanding and mystery? The dilemma has been stated well by B. Carter and G. Dapper: "Mathematics is simple visually

From *Academic Therapy*, January 1980, Vol. 15, No. 3. Copyright 1980, Academic Therapy Publications, Inc. Reprinted with permission.

... but we get into trouble when we introduce language" (1972, p. 12).

The language of modern math is based upon the understanding and correct usage of an extensive vocabulary. For example, it is useful to consider some of the words commonly used in regard to sets: *set, subset, collection, elements, members, equal sets, cardinal number* of a set, *empty set, equivalent sets, finite set, infinite set, superset, universal set, intersection* of two sets, and the *union* of two sets. Consider the predicament of the child who does not even understand the words *set* and *subset* before being introduced to the other concepts regarding sets. I have observed the consequences in a classroom where the teacher said, "A subset of six may go to the fountain and get a drink." Joe sat at a table of six, but he remained seated when the other children left. Later, the teacher instructed her class: "A set of twenty-six may line up at the door for recess." Joe remained in his seat until he was told specifically that he could line up for recess.

Doris Johnson and Helmer Myklebust (1967) remind us that words, unlike numerical symbols, vary in meaning and are often confusing to a learning-disabled child. Even very ordinary words can create confusion for children. Consider the difficulty of a first-grade boy in following a teacher's instructions regarding the drawing of lines or the placing of numerals when he consistently uses the word *underalls* for *overalls, overwear* for *underwear,* and *undershoes* for *overshoes.*

Modern math requires not only an extensive vocabulary, but also the understanding and correct usage of many simple and complex language skills. An informal study by Angie Nall (1970, p. 44) revealed that 56 percent of the children in her sample had difficulty in visualization and auditory memory understanding. Nall cited an example of a thirteen-year-old boy who thought the difference between 28 and 38 was that one had a two in the number and the other had a three. He did not understand the phrase "difference between" to mean subtract. She also cited the case of a twelve-year-old boy who could not tell which was larger, 34 or 33. To him they were the same height (Nall 1970). Marianne Frostig and Phyllis Maslow (1973) suggest that a restricted language code is a characteristic of many children with learning difficulties. They further emphasize that limited language makes it difficult for a child to acquire basic language concepts such as the difference between *more* and *less, sooner* or *later, higher* and *lower.*

We might also consider the confusion of an elementary child who was referred to me for diagnosis. Ellen's personal language reflected, among other difficulties, a lack of understanding of the *if/then* construction—the ability to transform two sentences into one which denotes a causal relationship. However, her assignment in mathematics for the day consisted of answering questions such as the following: "If four jeeps equal 16 tires, then one jeep equals _____ tires." Questioning also revealed that she did not understand the meaning of the word *equals.*

One of the requirements of modern math is that the teacher, too, have the vocabulary, verbal facility, and language mastery to interpret and translate into the teaching process the mathematical terminology commonly found in the teachers' edition of any current modern math text. A simple analysis of the instructions to teachers regarding the teaching of various concepts reveals that, as stated, they may be very significant to mathematicians but less helpful and significant to the classroom teacher who must interpret the instructions and translate them for use with an entire class of children in which there is a wide range of ability and achievement levels.

By placing great emphasis upon language and vocabulary in modern math, we *are* stacking the deck against the child who has a restricted language code and a limited vocabulary.

The Lack of Mastery

In an otherwise unreported study, some years ago I interviewed 85 mathematics teachers in grades five through nine. Each was asked to respond to the question, "In what way would you like your students to be better prepared when they come to you?" The first answer given by 68 of the 85 teachers was, "I wish they had mastered their basic facts." The results of the informal study indicate the desirability of asking that same question of teachers in various school systems throughout the nation. An increasing number of newspaper editorials and magazine articles continue to point out that students and graduates lack competence in basic math skills.

If spending more time on teaching understanding was supposed to have resulted in skill acquisition, it simply has not happened. Children have not mastered the basic facts, and there has been a serious fall-off in students' ability to compute. The students whom I see are engaged in a lot of repetitious finger, toe, and tooth-counting. They are counting real number lines and imaginary ones. They are repetitiously counting the same number facts thousands of times with no sign of mastery forthcoming. We have a lot of powerless children, mathematically speaking. Surely, there has to be a more efficient way for a child to spend his time than to count out 8 + 7 every time he encounters it during his school career and, quite possibly, for the rest of his life.

Understandably, some children with learning disabilities are unable to tolerate drill or, for other reasons, are unable to master the facts. But, it has been my experience that the facts can be mastered and should be mastered by the majority of children with learning disabilities.

Mastery of the facts can provide or improve the structure of math for a child. It can improve his speed so that he can finish his assignments within a reasonable time. Mastery of the facts can make it possible for him to understand more fully and to have success in such processes as long multiplication, long division, fractions, and decimals. Mastery of the facts can give him power.

Ten years ago my diagnostic caseload consisted mainly of children who were referred because of their disability in reading. Diagnosis revealed, among other things, an absence of phonetic

2

skills. Remedial reading teachers found it necessary, in most instances, to teach phonics skills to third, fourth, fifth, and sixth graders. They found it a difficult task to do. The children wanted to continue guessing at words. Today, my diagnostic caseload has become increasingly weighted with children who were referred because of their disability in arithmetic. Diagnosis has revealed, in almost all of the cases, lack of mastery of the math facts or combinations. The remedial math teacher or the learning disabilities teacher endeavors to teach basic facts to third, fourth, fifth, and sixth graders; and she finds it a difficult task. The children want to continue to count on their fingers or to count on a number line.

It would appear that children are often mistakenly labeled "learning disabled" simply because they lack mastery; and the lack of mastery appears, all too often, to be related to the current method of teaching math. May I cite an example? Roger was a boy in second grade. His IQ as measured by the *Wechsler Intelligence Scale for Children* (WISC) was 149. He read with excellent comprehension at the eighth-grade level. He identified all of the words on the Reading subtest of the *Wide Range Achievement Test*. He was referred for diagnostic testing because he did not complete his math worksheets. During a classroom observation, he was noted to ignore the math sheet on his desk. But, with the greatest dexterity, he caught a fly mid-air, carefully dismembered it, arranged the pieces neatly in the pencil tray on his desk, then began to write around the edge of his math paper. A glance at his paper of the 100 unanswered addition facts revealed the word *supercalifragilisticexpialidocious* spelled backwards, a task he had designed for himself. Diagnosis revealed that he had never mastered any of the math facts. He felt counting to be too immature and the paper to be a waste of time since he had counted the same facts yesterday, the day before that, and the day before that. Learning disabled? Not at all. He simply had not mastered the addition combinations.

Let us now look at the cases of some children with learning disabilities. Jim was in the sixth grade two years ago. The following is an excerpt from the examiner's report:

> On a test of fundamental math processes, Jim became so confused that he stopped working. The numerals of the multiplication problems were too close together for him. His lack of hand coordination made it impossible for him to position his responses under the correct column or in the correct space. It was even difficult for him to add the numerals in one column when it was a two- or three-column problem. His eyes would focus on a numeral in the wrong column and he would include that numeral in his answer. On a survey of arithmetic facts, it was found that Jim, although accurate in counting, had not mastered the facts in addition, subtraction, multiplication, or division. He commonly referred to a related fact to arrive at an answer. In response to $9 + 6$, he said, "You take one off the 6 and put it on the 9." In response to $13 - 6$ he

said, "Six and six are 12; add 1 more." It should be noted that Jim twisted and finally pulled out a lock of his hair while responding to the math facts.

Rodney was repeating first grade when he was referred for diagnosis. He was obviously counting on his fingers to obtain answers to the facts. His answer to 8 − 2 was 5. When asked, "How did you get that answer?" he replied, "That was easy. I guessed that one."

Kevin, a fifth grader, was found to have a very poor auditory channel. When he was asked, "What are you studying in math now?" he said, "We are doing _____ now." (He used a word which only faintly resembled the word *geometry*.) When asked what geometry meant, he said, "A line going together." A survey of math facts disclosed that he knew only the zeros and the ones in addition and subtraction (Wood 1976). In response to 10 − 6, Kevin wrote 7. In explaining how he had arrived at the answer he said, "Well, I took 5 away. Then I had to take another one. It just turned out the right answer." When a few multiplication facts were shown to him he, too, began to pull his hair. His answer to 9 x 2 was 9. He explained how he arrived at the answer as follows: "I took 4 and another 4. Then I added 1 and another 1 and that gives me 9." He was asked to explain again what he had done. Very patiently he said, "I started with 9. I added 4, another 4, another 4, then 1, and 1, and I think 1 more. And then," he said with a sigh of relief, "I got 9."

It would appear that since modern math has been introduced into the primary grades, we have placed virtually all of the emphasis on understanding or getting meaning and we have placed very little emphasis on gaining mastery. Examples that are commonly found in the public schools have been cited. I can attest to the fact that, in some schools, it is very difficult to locate fact cards. But, every child can be seen taking timed tests over math facts on which he only learns to count in a more subtle, swifter fashion with each math test. And, a number line can be found in virtually every classroom. I sometimes think, a little irreverently I am afraid, and perhaps inappropriately, that if God had intended for children to use a number line forever, He would have placed one on the horizon.

It has been my experience that, because a child can use a number line or count his fingers, and thereby obtain a correct When asked how he used the number line to obtain answers to subtraction facts, a student told me last fall, "Well, I just look at the number line and turn my brain backwards a little bit." I asked, "How do you know how far to turn it back?" and he replied, "Well, I just guess."

Several years ago, L. J. Brueckner and G. L. Bond wrote:

When the learner has grasped underlying meanings of facts and operations and understands the processes involved, practice is necessary to assure retention . . . . Various forms of practice should be provided . . . including repetitive drill . . . . To assure retention, distributed "drills" systematically spread over a period of time should be arranged . . . accuracy on the facts is necessary to mastery of any of the processes . . . . The usual plan of having the pupils write the answers to a group of number facts given on a sheet of paper . . . is wholly inadequate (1955, pp. 271-272).

In describing the mathematics curriculum Frostig and Maslow state: "The child learns the number facts systematically, and practices them until they become automatic" (1973).

An interview with Dr. Robert Kane appeared in a recent edition of *Teacher* (1973, pp. 20-21). In describing modern math texts, he said, "One thing that teachers needed and that wasn't provided was a sort of road map to help them know when a lesson is introductory and at what point the child is expected to master a concept or skill."

While opposing rote memory which results in the mere storing of isolated pieces of information, Newell Kephart (1960, p. 67) said that there are basic pieces of information which must be committed to memory and that a rote memory process must be used. He described the basic addition and subtraction facts as isolated bits of information best learned through rote memory techniques. Brueckner and Bond (1955, p. 243) cautioned teachers that a math improvement program should be begun by remediating any lack of knowledge of the basic number facts. Carter and Dapper (1972, p. 13) gave this advice to volunteers in the schools today: "Don't worry about 'new math.' Work on basic facts."

It would appear that many of the problems of students being referred because of great difficulty in math have been created by a spiral math curriculum which has placed great emphasis on understanding and very little emphasis on mastery. I am convinced that we are not teaching for mastery when we give a child a page of 80 problems day after day on which he just learns to count faster and on which he also just learns to make counting a habit. By deemphasizing computation and mastery, we may have taken away the very aspects of math which some students could learn and in which they could develop some competency. A lack of mastery appears to be a real pitfall for learning-disabled children and quite possibly injures or cripples, in a computational sense, some of our future mathematicians.

The Use of Set Notation

A third pitfall of modern math for learning-disabled children appears to be the introduction to set notation in the early primary grades.

Symbol confusion is almost synonymous with learning disabilities. Surely, this was not taken into account when set notation was put into the math curriculum for young students. What elementary classroom teacher is not painfully aware of the *b* and *d* reversal, the *g* and *p* reversal, as well as the reversal of *on* for *no* and *was* for *saw*? What classroom teacher is not also aware that many of the same children who are reversing *b*'s, *d*'s, *p*'s, *g*'s, *on*, and *was* are also reversing brackets, braces, and parentheses?

Consider the child who has not yet internalized left and right, and who is making all of the reversals just mentioned, but who is expected to use correctly brackets, braces, and parentheses. And consider the child who does not yet comprehend the process of addition, and who has not mastered even the simplest addition facts, but who has been introduced to three, and possibly all four, of the following signs, plus the equal sign: $+, -, \times, \div$.

Further, consider the plight of the child who has mastered none of the facts, who is confused by symbols, signs, and braces, and who is expected to give an answer to the following problem: $\{$ 3, 6, +, 20, ___ $\}$. There is a need to measure empathically the depth and breadth of that child's failure when he is further unable to comprehend the nature of the task because he cannot read three of the words in the illustrative sentence at the top of his worksheet: $\{$ in, the, stars, heavens, are, the $\}$.

Frostig and Maslow (1973, p. 273) have cautioned that expanded notation should not be presented until a child understands place value and that the use of symbols of an empty set, as well as the use of symbols for more than and less than, should not be presented unless there is real understanding of the underlying concepts.

Concern for the children who were having great difficulty with set notation has led to the elimination of set notation in recent math texts and workbooks for use in the primary grades.

Inadequate Teacher Inservice Education

A fourth pitfall to understanding and mastery appears to be inadequate or inappropriate inservice education for the teaching of modern math.

When a fourth-grade teacher was told that only two children in her room had mastered all of the addition facts, that no one knew all of the subtraction facts, and that only one-half of the students could demonstrate any understanding of place value, she said, "Well, our text presents algebra now and I'm teaching that. I don't have time to go back and teach facts!" If inservice education had been provided in that school, it was either inappropriate or ineffective. Clearly, emphasis must not be solely on *what* to teach (which generally means what is in the book); rather, emphasis must also be placed upon *how* to teach a math concept or process and *when* to teach it.

Emphasis on sequential skill development is of paramount importance for learning-disabled children. Furthermore, inservice education which emphasizes how and when to teach facts to the level of mastery, how and when to teach place value, as well as how and when to teach algebra, would seem to be appropriate for teaching all children.

Classroom diagnosis of pupils' difficulties is another aspect of inservice education related to math which is too often neglected. Brueckner and Bond (1955, pp. 227-228) emphasized that a teacher needs to observe the methods used by each child and to determine the thought processes of those children who are having great difficulty in learning a new step or process.

Diagnosis can be very simple, and the classroom teacher can do it effectively by analyzing a student's work and listening to him as he explains what he is doing. Too frequently, a student is referred for diagnosis whose current problem can be diagnosed through a simple glance at his work. Diane responded to the facts on an informal fact survey as follows: $3 + 2 = 4$; $7 + 5 = 8$; and $2 + 6 = 3$. When asked to explain her answers she replied, "When you combine, you always get one more."

Todd was referred to me because, as the teacher said, "He does not even always know the zero facts." Diagnosis consisted of a simple question: "Todd, how do you figure out answers to the zero facts?" He said, "It's simple. When the zero is at the top, the answer is zero. When the numeral 6 is at the top, the answer is 6."

Some children's problems are more complex, but the diagnostic questions remain simple. Ron, a fifth-grade boy, missed most of the subtraction facts which had been put in front of him, but he had responded correctly to $8 - 6$. He was asked, "How did you know that the answer was 2?" He responded, "Well, first I added 8 and 16. That makes 14. Then, I subtracted 2. The rest I figured out in my head."

Inservice education for teaching math must stress how to teach math concepts and processes and when to teach them. It must also stress simple, ongoing, classroom diagnostic techniques. From my own viewpoint, the best single means of preventing math failure would be through the provision of appropriate, ongoing, inservice education.

The Elimination of Parents as Teaching Partners

The fifth pitfall of modern math is the virtual elimination of parents as partners in the mathematical teaching process. One editorial stated that one major problem with the new math all along has been that the parents could not do it (*Wall Street Journal* 1973). In another editorial, a parent was quoted as follows: "I tried to help my daughter with it and I just couldn't understand it. I was a math major . . . but it's got me. I'm suspicious of it" (*Sacramento Union* 1973).

Darryl was eleven years old and in the fifth grade when he was referred to me for diagnosis of his reading and math problems. He had repeated first grade and had then been pushed along from one grade to the next. He was found to have an extremely poor auditory channel, and I discovered that there had been a continual attempt, since kindergarten, to teach him math skills through the use of the texts and workbooks adopted by that school system. Those materials placed emphasis on understanding, which called for good auditory ability, and on the use of set notation. The teachers' manuals cautioned against the use of drill. Diagnosis revealed that although Darryl was eleven years old, he had acquired only the math skills of a beginning first-grade child. He was further handicapped by a deep sense of failure.

At the parent conference following the testing session, the

mother said apologetically, "I have never been able to help him with math because I don't understand new math, and he doesn't remember the instructions so that he can tell me what is to be done." She was told, "Your child has been instructed through the same methods for five and one half years to no avail. He does not learn well through his ears, he cannot remember the verbal instructions, and he is totally confused. It would appear that he can be taught traditional math and, with your approval, a traditional program will be set up for him."

The mother's response was unforgettable. Her face gleaming, she leaned forward, squeezed the examiner's hand and said excitedly, "Now, *I* can teach him!"

Math programs which have been used throughout the country for the past fifteen years or so have placed heavy emphasis upon language. This has made math very difficult for the child with a restricted language code. Math programs have given very little emphasis to mastery which has resulted in a lot of mathematically powerless students. The elimination of drill in some programs has prevented many students from developing at least the ability to compute. Use of set notation in the primary grades before there was an understanding of the necessary basic concepts has resulted in confusion for a large number of children with learning disabilities. It is heartening to note that an increasing number of schools are beginning to use a more traditional approach in the teaching of math in the primary grades.

References

Brueckner, L. J., and Bond, G. L. 1955. *The diagnosis and treatment of learning difficulties*. New York: Appleton-Century-Crofts, pp. 271-272.

Carter, B., and Dapper, G. 1972. *School volunteers: what they do and how they do it*. New York: Citation Press.

Frostig, M., and Maslow, P. 1973. *Learning problems in the classroom*. New York: Grune and Stratton.

Introducing sets. 1972. Film. Boston: Houghton Mifflin.

Johnson, D., and Myklebust, H. *Learning disabilities: educational principles and practices*. New York: Grune and Stratton, pp. 246-247.

Kane, R. 1973. The 'new' math as adolescent. *Teacher* 91:20-21.

Kephart, N. C. 1960. *The slow learner in the classroom*. Columbus, Ohio: Charles E. Merrill.

Nall, A. 1970. Teaching arithmetic by developing related areas. *Academic Therapy* 6:41-46.

Sacramento Union. 1973. Editorial, February 24.

Wall Street Journal. 1973. Editorial, May 31.

Wood, M. H. 1976. The dyslexic in the general classroom. *Bulletin of the Orton Society* 26:131-132.

CLASSROOM APPLICATIONS

2

Using Logic in Special Classrooms

by Miriam Cherkes, Ph. D., and Robert Pianta, M.A.

Historically, special curricula for the learning disabled have been based on the psychomotor needs of learning-disabled children. They have attended to modes of learning: input-output channels and perceptual processes. More recently, the curriculum emphasis in the field of special education in general, and in learning disabilities specifically, has shifted to content areas both in definition (*Federal Register,* November 1976) and in the nature of curriculum (Project Math, Mainstream, Me Now, and Me and My Environment). While the shift to subject area curriculum has been an important advancement, it provides only half of the needs of a learning-disabled child. The learning-disabled child is distinguished from other children who have not mastered content in that he or she has a specific problem in *learning* which disables him or her in the process of acquiring the content. There is, then, a great need for the inclusion of learning and reasoning considerations in the description and treatment of the learning disabled. The ultimate goal would be a developmental, empirically based diagnosis-curriculum system directed toward the information processing needs of the learning-disabled child which underlie learning in any of the content areas. Research has established that rules of logic are basic strategies for the processing and organizing of information (Flavell 1963, Furth 1970, Gagne 1965, Piaget and Inhelder 1969). Much work has been done, in special education and related fields, based on Piaget's conception of logic and logic development. Piaget's theory has been applied primarily to the definition and differentiation between sensory-motor, concrete, and abstract stages. Logic in this context is something different. It represents a shift to a more precise model of formal logic which emphasizes the specific aspects of information processing.

Since rules for logic are content free, are applicable in any

FIGURE 1
Curriculum and Entry System Model

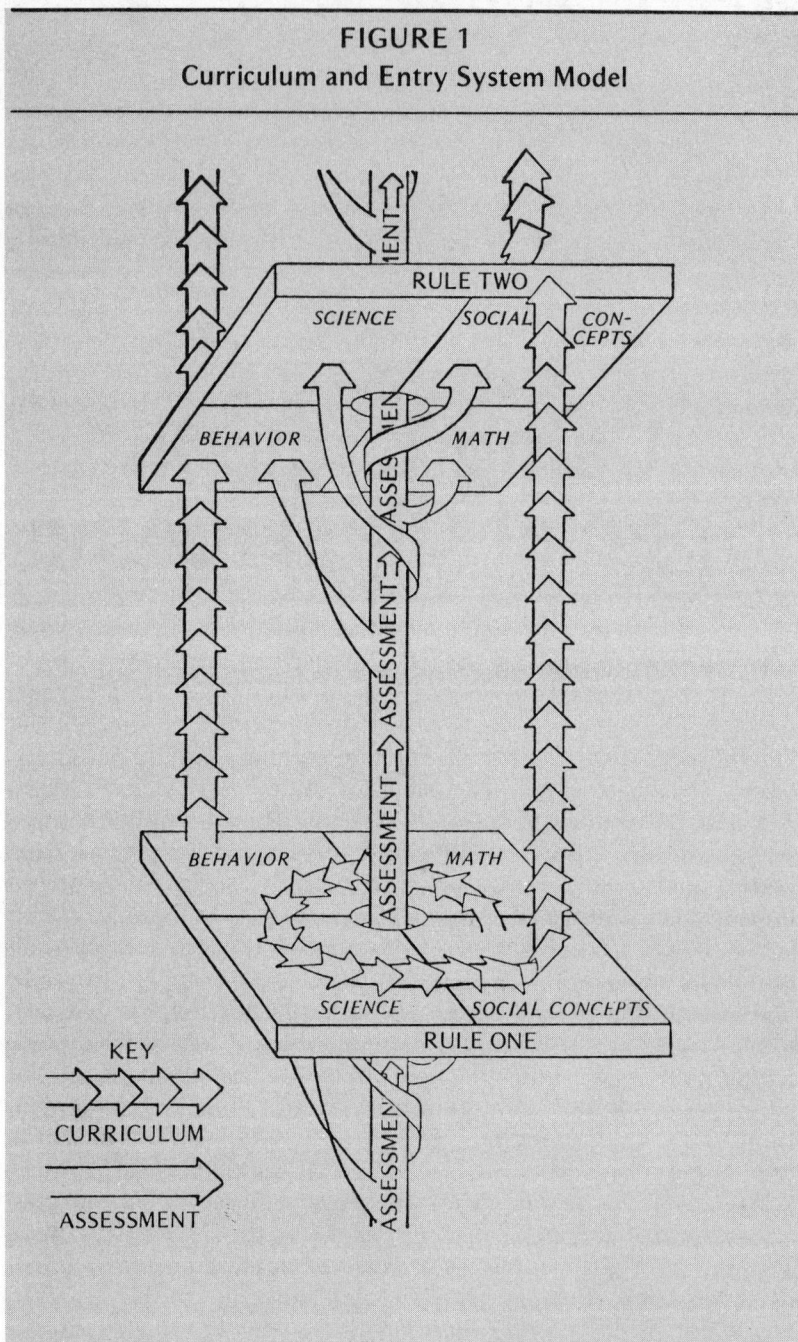

RULE TWO

SCIENCE SOCIAL CON-CEPTS

BEHAVIOR MATH

ASSESSMENT

BEHAVIOR MATH

SCIENCE SOCIAL CONCEPTS

RULE ONE

ASSESSMENT

KEY

CURRICULUM

ASSESSMENT

situation, and are limited in number, they provide a working foundation for the description and teaching of reasoning skills which can be transferred across content areas. This conception of rule and transfer is particularly appropriate for the typical profile of the learning-disabled child who demonstrates strengths in some subject areas, weaknesses in others. The implication is that poorly mastered rules can be taught in strong subject areas and poorly mastered subject areas can be taught through rule strengths. The aim of a concentration in logic is to design an individual education program for a child based on his *reasoning* and his *content* needs.

A Logic Curriculum

A curriculum in logic would include the essentials of sound curriculum characteristic of any instructional area:

1. An order of progression of rule difficulty;
2. Small transitional steps from one level to the next;
3. The use of strengths in learning which are most facilitative to the individual;
4. A system for maximum horizontal transfer (generalization) to the major subject areas;
5. A system for diagnosis of strengths and weaknesses as well as assessment of functioning level;
6. A system for evaluating mastery of lessons taught; and
7. A provision for additional opportunity to learn concepts and for overlearning.

Figure 1 describes the model according to which instruction can be developed. The model allows for rule instruction in various content areas. In the model presented here the areas of math, science, social concepts and behavior are included. Each rule for reasoning can be used in the context of each of these subject areas. The use of a given rule across content areas serves three functions. First, it gives the child an opportunity to learn the rule itself. Through repeated experiences both the identical rule applied to different attributes (math, science, etc.), the child can begin to identify the nature of the rule itself. Second, a given rule might be more easily learned within the context of a particular content area either because of a good rule-content match or because of a child's preference. Finally, repeated experience with a rule provides an opportunity for overlearning once mastery has been achieved.

The model is meant to provide a great deal of flexibility in the planning of individual programs. For example, if one child has a particular propensity for mathematics and has difficulties in behavior control, logic instruction could begin for him within the context of mathematics and be transferred eventually to behavior using the rule mastered in the context of mathematics as a foundation for instruction. Likewise, the child who demonstrates errors of overgeneralization in reading skills, language development, the application of mathematical algorithms and social judgments, might be served best by instruction in rules of logic which involve contradiction, exclusion, and fallacy. The intent of focusing upon rules themselves for a child like this is to give him a mechanism for structuring information which would be applicable and transferable in all relevant content areas. A third case would serve to illustrate another function of the model. Consider the child who is able to master what he is taught in separate content areas but seems not to "grow" and be able to transfer what is learned as a fundamental to a more complex situation. In this case the instructional sequence involves a vertical transfer of content and rules: perhaps instruction at level 1 in mathematics to level 2 in mathematics; level 1 in social concepts to level 2 in social concepts. The same procedure for

---

FIGURE 2
Sample Logical Rule in Four Content Areas

Rule: No S is P; All S is non-P.
Directions: Tell me if the picture fits the rule.

Content: Math. All squares are non-blue rectangles.

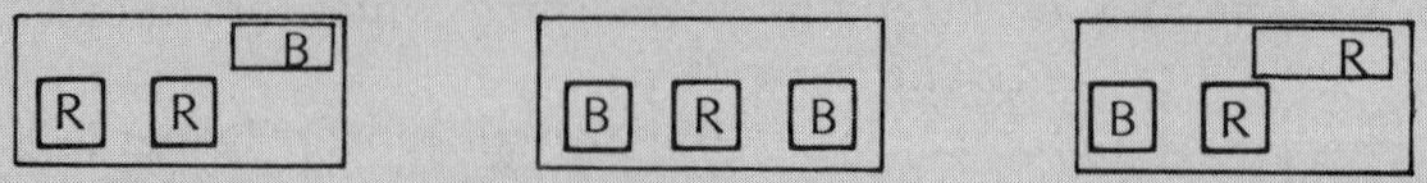

Content: Toys. All balls are non-red toys.

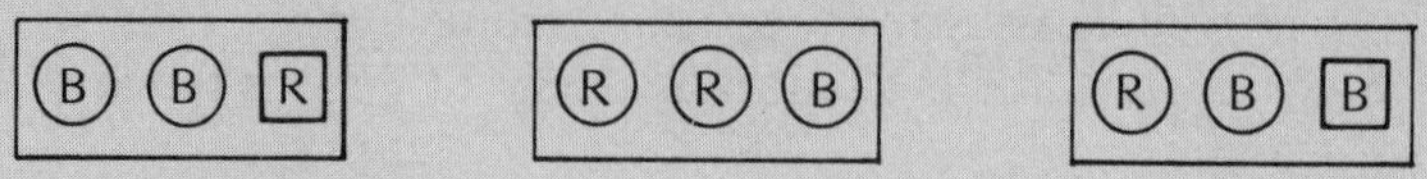

Content: Food. All lollipops are non-yellow food.

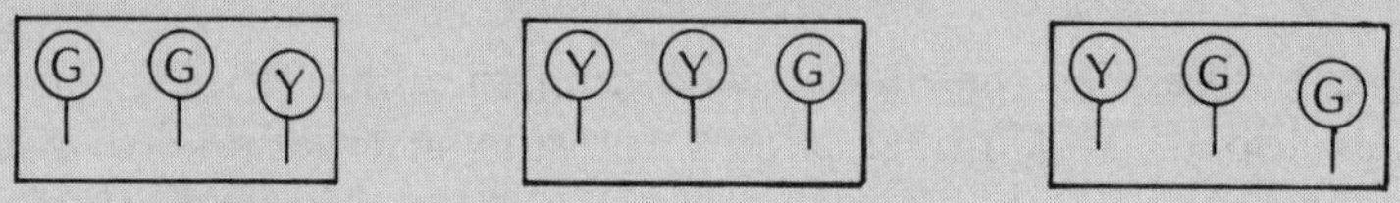

Content: Transportation. All cars are non-green things we ride in.

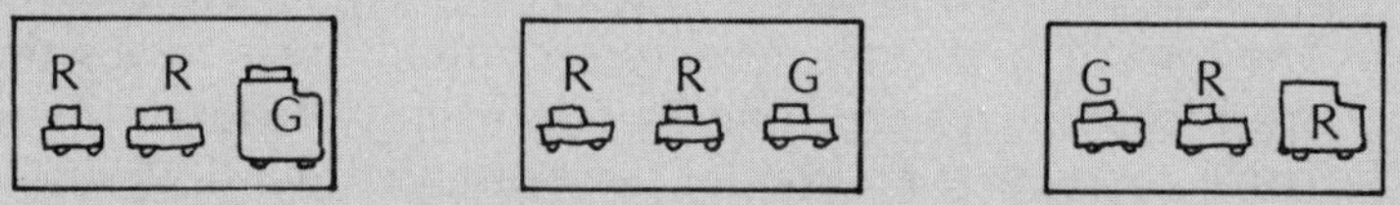

---

behavior and science would provide the opportunity for the child to experience the identical transition to a more complex level in several different situations. The intent is to allow the child to master the transition and finally to achieve a more complex processing of information.

Diagnostic Test

Clearly a crucial component to the entire approach to logic-content instruction is an adequate diagnostic test which controls for content while investigating rules for reasoning.* Such a diagnostic instrument (Cherkes and Pianta, in preparation) would form the foundation upon which curriculum could be developed as well as serve as a tool to assess reasoning-content strengths and weaknesses. The design of the diagnostic instrument includes the formulation of statements using each rule in different content areas, as well as the use of all rules in each content area. Test items take the form of sentences which state the rule. The child is instructed to select the picture which fits the rule. Alternate choices have been devised to reflect specific error patterns. Figure 2 provides an example of a rule applied across four content areas.

A single rule can be tested, then, in four different attributes or content situations. At the same time a single set of content can be tested in different rule circumstances. Figure 3 depicts

*I am indebted to John F. Cawley (1973) for the basis of this distinction between learning and content.

FIGURE 3
Sample Set of Logical Rules in a Single Content Area

Content: Math

Rule: If P, then Q; Q, therefore P.
Directions: If it is a square, it is a blue rectangle.
              It is a blue rectangle.
              Tell me if the picture fits the rule.

Rule: All S is P; No S is P (contrary)
Directions: All squares are blue rectangles.
              Tell me if the picture does *not* fit the rule.

Rule: Conjunction of Predicate.
Directions: A square is blue and white.
              Tell me if the picture fits the rule.

Rule: All A's are B's.
              X is an A.
Directions: All rectangles are blue.
              A square is a rectangle
              Tell me if the picture fits the rule.

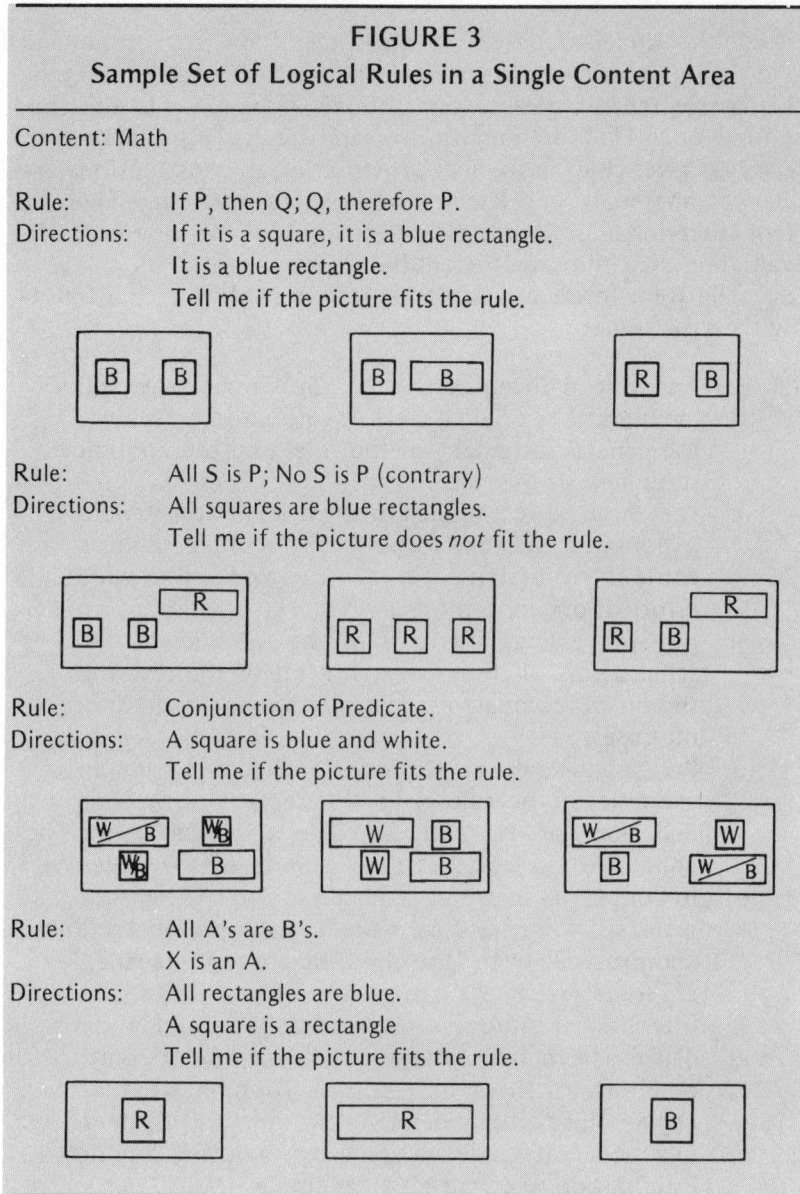

an example of math content as the context of a series of rules.

Item Interview

In addition, each item in the diagnostic instrument refers to a set of probes called the Item Interview Sequence. The Item Interview Sequence is constructed in order to probe the effects of input and output on forms of the understanding of the rule presented originally in the test. This Interview will give a more precise profile of the child's reasoning ability and pinpoint areas of strengths and weakness.

The Interviews are sequenced according to the order of the test items. Once a child has taken the original Logic Test and it has been scored, the tester may go back and administer the Interviews either on selected items or on all test items. We recommend, in order to get a more precise definition of the child's reasoning, that a selected set of the Item Interviews be given to the child at least once. The combination of the Logic Test and Item Interviews gives the basis for construction of instructional sequences, materials, and lessons for teaching reasoning. Then the Item Interviews come into play once again as the instrument for evaluating the child once lessons have been taught.

The Item Interviews are organized according to the following six-part format.

1. The title is listed across the top of the page and includes the original rule identification number, the general statement of the rule, and the content statement of the rule.

2. Part A is a direct replica of the original test item in a nonsense syllable form. It is intended to be a content-free statement of the rule and will provide information concerning the effects of content on rule processing. This part of the Interview is the same across all four content areas of the test and should be compared across content for evaluation purposes.

3. Part B allows the child the freedom to construct an example of the rule given a statement of the rule and appropriate materials. The tester gives the child two examples of each unit (e.g., two green lollipops, two yellow cupcakes, etc.). Then the tester asks the child to make an example of a rule and proceeds to tell the child the appropriate rule.

   In terms of evaluating reasoning abilities, this Interview technique requires that the child internalize a verbal formulation of a rule and translate that into a visual-motor output. It emphasizes the child's ability to understand the rule and to demonstrate that understanding by choosing among information to construct an example.

   The tester is to evaluate the child's performance on this section of the interview according to these three criteria:

   a. Number and correctness of each unit used.
   b. If the child used all possible correct units.
   c. If using all possible units can still be correct.

   In terms of administering the Interview, the tester should act as follows on each criterion:

   a. Simply observe the child's response (i.e., what units were used) and note their number and correctness. The reason for this is that the child could, in response to "All balls are red," place a red ball as the answer—which, while being perfectly correct, has not used the other red ball given and denotes some type of single-unit rigidity.
   b. For this criterion, the tester notes if the child

has used all possible correct units in the answer. For example, a correct answer to "All balls are red" could include anything given to the child except blue balls; thus red blocks, etc., all are correct examples of the rule. The processing of counter examples in deciding on rule truth has been found to be a critical skills in many areas of conditional reasoning (Wason and Johnson-Laird 1972) and is included here for the purpose of evaluating that ability.

c. In the third evaluative criterion, the tester asks the child directly if using all possible units in an example can still be correct. In this situation, this is a direct probe of the child's ability to evaluate counter-examples. If the child's answer were "two red balls" in response to "All balls are red," the tester would ask the child "Is it OK if I put a blue block (etc.) here?"—to which the child would answer "yes" or "no."

Part B thus allows a comprehensive evaluation of the child's ability to process the rule in terms of all possible examples of it, and in terms of the child's own output.

4. Part C is a technique that tests the child's ability to infer a rule, given examples of the rule and its intended subject. Thus, the child is presented with four examples of the rule, "All balls are red," including counter-examples, and is told that they formulate a rule about balls: "Can you tell me the rule for balls?" The evaluative criteria call for the tester to record the child's output in terms of correctness and type of rule statement. For exmaple, the child could respond, "All balls are red," which is correct. Or he could answer, "Some balls are red," which is not indicated, or "Balls are red and blocks are blue," which is also not indicated. Each error points to a specific processing breakdown. Part C, then, leaves the child free to respond in whatever manner he chooses. This gives the tester a precise statement of how the child will organize a given set of information and thus his preference for processing information.

5. Part D is intended to discriminate the child's responses and error patterns based on the linguistic information presented. Distinctions in the rule processing of such words as *all, some, none, or, and*, etc., are presented for the child in visual form and are once again evaluated on the basis of three questions, each of which gets progressively easier. A sample Interview in Part D would include:

a. The tester reminding the child that the rule is, "All balls are red."

b. Presenting the child with the distinction to be tested, in this case picture of an example of (1) "All balls are red," and (2) "Some balls are red."

c. Given the preceding information, the child is then asked how these two sets of pictures are different. His or her responses are recorded; and, if they include a statement that one picture has all red balls and the other has some, then the child is removed from the probe sequence, having demonstrated explicit knowledge of the distinction tested.

d. The next question is a further statement of the distinction and asks the child to point to the picture in which all the balls are red. Once again, if the child demonstrates knowledge of the distinction by pointing correctly, then he or she is removed from the sequence.

e. The final specification of the distinction is to state to the child that one picture represents "All balls are red," the other represents "Some balls are red"; and he or she is to point to "All balls are red." Here the child is actually told the distinction and asked to recognize it. A child who needs to come this far in the sequence in order for correct performance, or who does not get this one right, obviously needs much more work in the area of discrimination and rules involving *all* and *some*.

This section of the Interview (Part D) allows a progressively greater amount of information to be given to the child and allows for his or her reactions in terms of the processing of that information. In this manner, a systematic evaluation of the child's reasoning abilities in terms of differing amounts of information specificity is possible.

6. Part E of the Interview involves a different input-output combination and progression than has been tested to this point and it follows naturally from Part D. In this section the child is presented with a set of picture and a rule and told that the pictures fit the rule. The tester then adds one unit at a time. After each addition the tester asks the child if the pictures fit the rule now.

The presentation directs the child's attention to one unit at a time and the effect of one unit upon the whole rule. Thus, one unit can make the difference between *all, some,* and *none.* One unit can serve also as a specific example of the limits of a rule. For example, a contradiction arises when adding an item causes a rule to go from "All S is P" to "Some S is not P." In this case, a child who may have difficulty verbalizing that "Some S is not P" does "not fit" the original rule, should be able to see that the addition of an S that is non-P suddenly creates a set of pictures that does not fit "All S is P."

Once again the output is child-directed. While most responses are in a yes-no format, the tester should include all relevant statements the child may make.

At this point, the versatility of the Item Interviews should be apparent. Figure 4 clarifies the format. The Item Interviews can be used for (1) an overall evaluative instrument in conjunction with the Logic Test within one content area; (2) the basis of specific cross-content comparisons; (3) statements of reasoning style vis a vis different inputs and outputs; (4) pinpoints of specific breakdown areas in rule processing due to content, rule, or behavior; (5) direct placement at appropriate instructional level with specific materials and lessons; and (6) evaluation of those lessons and materials.

The flexibility of this system is left to be explored by the teacher. In order to maintain within-system integrity, however, certain procedures must be followed:

1. The child must be given the Logic Test in at least the content area of the intended Item Interview.
2. The Interview must be administered as directed; it is recommended that several sessions of 6-10 items be used instead of one long session.
3. The teacher should review the items before administering them to review her knowledge of rules for reasoning.

Within these broad guidelines the teacher is left to create as many learning experiences for children as desired.

Once appropriate diagnosis has been made and specific rules for reasoning and content areas have been selected, the challenge is to design instruction in rules of logic within the specified content. The goal for each lesson, as conceived in the framework of this model, is logical rule mastery. For a given subject area, the number of lessons to be developed depends upon the range of content relevant to that rule. For example, the rule of transitivity applied to the area of mathematics has several manifestations. Since the goal is rule mastery, the amount and specific nature of the content included is very much a concern of the individualized education program.

Three Levels of Instruction

Lessons to be developed from this model are identified by the rule and content area they cover. For each concept a lesson includes instruction at three different levels: thematic concrete, specific concrete, and abstract. The three levels reflect the theory of rule learning upon which this model of curriculum is built. At the first level, thematic concrete, concrete materials are selected because they are basic to the rule. To be basic, materials must conform to two criteria. First, they must have physical attributes which exemplify the rule. In the case of class reasoning

FIGURE 4
Sample Probe

Rule 8: No S is P; no P is S.
No lollipops are yellow.
No yellow things are lollipops.

A. *Nonsense Syllables*
This is a ming ✦   Point to "No mings are blue."

B. *Rule Instance (Child Demonstrates)*
1. Give the child the materials: two yellow lollipops, two green lollipops, two yellow cupcakes, two green cupcakes (two instances of each unit). Then ask the child to make an example of the following rule: "No lollipops are yellow."

   Check:
   a. Number and correctness of each unit used.
   b. If all possible units are used.
   c. If using all possible units can still be correct.

2. Then ask the child to make his set into an example of the rule, "No yellow things are lollipops."

   Check:
   a. If anything was changed.
   b. What was changed.

C. *Instance—Rule Inference*

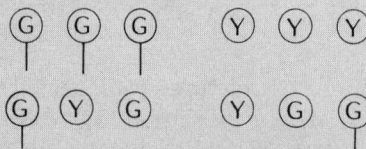

These are examples of a rule about yellow things. Can you tell me the rule about yellow things?
They are also examples of a rule about lollipops. Can you tell me the rule about lollipops?

D. *Linguistic Distinction*

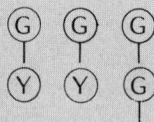

The rule is, "No yellow things are lollipops."
1. How are these different?
2. Point to "No yellow things are lollipops."
3. One of these is "No lollipops are yellow," the other is "No yellow things are lollipops." Point to "No yellow things are lollipops." and when they do not fit the rule. The rule is "No yellow things are lollipops."

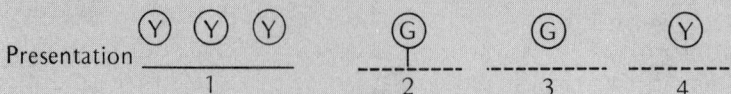

E. *Construction*
I am going to put some things in front of you. Then I will tell you a rule. I want you to tell me when the things in front of you fit the rule and when they do not fit the rule. The rule is "No yellow things are lollipops."

Presentation _____   _____ _____ _____
              1   2   3   4

they must have physical properties which form the criterion for inclusion in the class. Appropriate materials basic to class reasoning might include the objects belonging to the classes: *apples, chairs,* or *cars* (Rosch, Mervis, Gray, Johnson, and Boyes-Braem 1976). Second, materials and activities must illustrate the theme or basic relationship being taught. If the rule under consideration is, for example, transitivity, materials should be selected that elaborate the comparative relationship. Materials varying in size would provide thematic input for the child. On the other hand, concrete materials involving difficult or even deceptive physical attributes would confuse the transitivity process. Inappropriate materials would include those requiring conservation judgments.

At the second level, specific concrete, materials are selected to apply the rule rather than to focus attention on the understanding of the rule itself. Materials and activities at this level do not exemplify the theme of the rule. Nor do they have physical properties conducive to the form of reasoning being used. In this case the child is presented with objects whose attributes are easily perceived and manipulated but do not inherently specify the rule relationship. The abstract level discusses the rule and content verbally, in written language or written extra-linguistic symbols. This level requires that the child have some internal representation of the rule which would facilitate its application and transfer.

Reinforcement activities should be provided with each lesson to allow for additional trials to mastery and overlearning. Lessons should be designed to allow the teacher to use all, some, one, or more of the components, depending upon the needs of his or her students. A lesson is defined as instruction in a given concept, relating to a given content area, based on a given rule. All lessons should be designed to avoid the problems of reading which a learning-disabled child is likely to bring to the learning situation. Any lesson which employs written symbols (linguistic or logical) should provide for training on the recognition and understanding of those symbols.

Each lesson provides for assessment of the rule per se as well as the rule as it is used in that content and concept area. An assessment item using nonsense syllables can be used for rule understanding. In addition, mastery activities can be provided to test the understanding of the rule as it is used in each concept area. Figure 5 offers an example of the suggested lesson format including mastery and assessment items.

These illustrations have been offered as possible uses of a diagnosis-curriculum system which aims at instruction in rules for reasoning as well as the application of reasoning style in various content areas. The system is intended to have a maximum amount of flexibility and applicability so that it can be used appropriately for the wide range of learning disorders that exist. It is one attempt to uncover strengths and weaknesses in reasoning processes and to use them as bases for instruction in the content areas.

FIGURE 5
Sample Logic Lesson

Rule: Categorical Proposition
        Universal Positive   All S is P;
        Contradiction   some S is not p.

Assessment Item:

All caks have a nug.
These are caks [point to boxes], and these are their nugs [point to protrusions].

Point to the ones that are not caks.

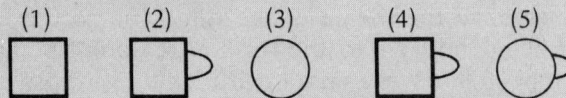

(1)   (2)   (3)   (4)   (5)

Note: Ideally, a student will express indecision about No. 5. Any other response indicates a failure to understand the full implications of the rule.

Content: Mathematics
Related Concepts: (1) cardinal property; (2) sets; (3) geometric shapes
Concept: (1) cardinal property

Thematic Concrete

The teacher tells the child or children that she is going to play a game with them. She will give them the rule for the game. The child is to look at a series of pictures and to select the ones that do not fit the rule. The rule is, "All dogs have four legs." First, the child is given a set of pictures of dogs, birds, and fish. The child is to select the pictures that do not belong. Next the child is given a set of pictures of dogs, birds, and cats. The child is asked to select the pictures that do not belong. The child should be asked to elaborate upon his decision concerning cats. Emphasis should be on the relationship of four legs to the original rule.

Mastery activity. The child is given the rule, "All people have two legs." The child is given a set of pictures of people, birds, and four-legged animals. He is asked to select the ones that do not fit the rule.

Specific Concrete

The teacher explains that she is going to give everyone in the class some balloons. All the boys will get exactly three balloons. The girls will have some balloons too. First she holds up three balloons for the class to see and gives them to one of the boys. She picks up two balloons and gives them to a girl. She then explains to the class that they are going to guess who gets the next bunch of balloons—a boy or a girl. She holds up four balloons. The students must answer that they will be given to a girl and explain why. This last procedure is repeated until the class responds four consecutive times correctly.

Now, the teacher tells the class she is going to try to trick them. She reminds them that the rule is the same: "All the boys will get exactly three balloons. The girls will have some balloons too." This time she will show them the balloons and give them to a child. The class has to decide whether she is following the rule or not. If the class guesses correctly, the child gets to keep the balloons, otherwise he must wait for another turn when the class does answer correctly. The following situations should be included to demonstrate the meaning of categorical proposition-contradiction:

—4 balloons given to a boy

—3 balloons given to a girl (the proper response here should reflect indecision but it is *not* incorrect to allow a girl to have 3 balloons)

—2 balloons to a boy

Materials needed: a large bag of balloons.

Mastery activity. Each student is given an opportunity to trick the class. Each must choose a number of balloons and give them to someone who, according to the rule, is not allowed to have them. The student must choose any number of balloons, except three, and give them to a boy to be considered correct. If a student gives three balloons to a girl and can defend his or her choice by the fact that the rule is unclear, this can be considered correct as well.

Abstract

The teacher tells the class (or small group, or individual) that she is going to tell them about a new kind of animal. The animal is called a zuk. All zuks have exactly five tups. The students are asked to repeat this several times until they have said the sentence three consecutive times without error. Each child is asked to draw a picture of what he or she thinks a zuk looks like. The children are asked to point to the tups.

The teacher continues to ask the students a series of questions about zuks:

1. What do you know about zuks?
2. Some animals have four tups. What do you know about them?
3. Some animals have six tups. What do you know about them?
4. Lots of animals have five tups. What do you know about them?

Note: The correct answer here is indecision and/or the conclusion that the animal is not necessarily a zuk.

Materials needed: paper and pencil and/or chalkboard

Mastery activity. Each student is asked to draw an animal that is *not* a zuk. The teacher has each child explain his drawing and why the animal is not a zuk.

References

Cawley, J. F., et al. 1976. *Project math.* Tulsa, Oklahoma: Educational Progress Corporation.

Cawley, J. F., et al. 1976. *Mainstream: an instruction program.* Tulsa, Oklahoma: Educational Progress Corporation.

Cherkes, M. G., and Pianta, R. *Logic test.* In preparation.

Mayer, W. V. 1975. *Planning and curriculum development.* Boulder, Colorado: Biological Sciences Curriculum Study.

Federal Register. November 19, 1976 (41 FR 52403).

Flavell, J. 1963. *The developmental psychology of Jean Piaget.* New York: Van Nostrand Reinhold.

Furth, H. G., et al. 1970. Children's utilization of logical symbols: an interpretation of conceptual behavior based on Piagetian theory. *Developmental Psychology* 3:1, pp. 36-57.

Gagne, R. M. 1965. *The conditions of learning.* New York: Holt, Rinehart and Winston.

Piaget, J., and Inhelder, B. 1969. *The psychology of the child.* New York: Basic Books.

Rosch, E., et al. 1976. Basic objects in natural categories. *Cognitive Psychology* 8:382-439.

Wason, P. C., and Johnson-Laird, P. N. 1972. *Psychology of reasoning.* Cambridge, Massachusetts: Harvard University Press.

CLASSROOM APPLICATIONS

Diagnostic Evaluation of Writing Skills

by Eva S. Weiner

The most accessible and useful material for diagnostic teaching is a student's own writing. The written production is especially valuable because in the process of transferring thoughts to words, the student learns everything necessary to become a proficient reader and a good writer. The student with deficiencies in both areas welcomes diagnostic teaching. It gives him concrete evidence that improvement is possible if his mistakes are analyzed one at a time, then corrected with the teacher's help until he is able to function independently in monitoring his own work.

The complexity of the writing task makes evaluation of the written product difficult unless the components are separated for diagnosis and remediation. An example of a simplified, individualized assessment instrument is presented in a form that facilitates the identification of specific writing problems.

The Diagnostic Evaluation of Writing Skills (DEWS) contains criteria of assessment divided into the following categories: graphic, orthographic, phonologic, syntactic, semantic, and self-monitoring (see Table 1). Each criterion serves as a guide to determine the individual student's need for direct teaching of a deficient skill. As the examples of errors are recorded in the appropriate column and space, the particular deficits become clearly defined. Targets for teaching emerge in concrete form; teacher and student can see at a glance what must be learned. Suggestions for implementing the plan of remediation are included in the explication of each category of the DEWS.

AUTOBIOGRAPHY

An autobiography is suggested as the initial writing assignment for diagnostic purposes because it reveals more about a student's problems and is less threatening than other writing assignments. Since the content involves only personal experiences, no student is overwhelmed by excessive demands on his knowledge. The writing can be done in groups or individually and completed in one class period with approximately 30 minutes for writing and 15 minutes for revision.

CRITERIA FOR ASSESSMENT

The criteria for assessment (Table 1) include most of the common types of errors encountered with learning disabled students. Elements may be added or deleted based on individual experience. The order of presentation is not suggestive of possible frequency or importance of the errors.

Graphic Category

This category of the DEWS contains criteria concerned with the visual aspects of writing. These visible features often represent the surface manifestations of more serious learning problems. Illegible handwriting and messy papers should be scrutinized for the particular difficulties they suggest. If the student uses excessive pencil pressure that creates grooves on the paper,

TABLE 1. Diagnostic Evaluation of Writing Skills (DEWS): Criteria for assessment.

Graphic (visual features)   Examples of errors
1. Excessive pencil pressure marks
2. Letter formation ambiguities; erasures
3. Capital and lowercase letter mixture
4. Size or spacing irregularities
5. Off-line writing
6. Margin slant or crowding

Orthographic (spelling)   Examples of errors
7. Sequencing of letters (reverse order)
   or three consonant clusters
8. Doubling final consonant
9. ed ending with sound of d or t
10. Prefix or suffix generalizations
11. ie becomes ei after c and with sound of a
12. y becomes i, except before ing
13. c or g, followed by e, i, or y
14. ch=k and sh; sh=si, ti, ci, ce, su
15. ph and gh = f
16. Silent letters in special spellings
17. Schwa sounds; related words
18. Word division by syllable

Phonologic (sound components)   Examples of errors
19. Nonphonetic spelling (bizarre)
20. Strictly phonetic spelling
21. Letter or syllable omissions
22. Words run together

Syntactic (grammatical)   Examples of errors
23. Subject and predicate agreement
24. Tense, plural, possessive endings
25. Word order; omissions
26. Incomplete sentences (fragments)
27. Run-on sentences
28. Punctuation; indentation of paragraphs
29. Variety in sentence structure
30. Coordination (and/but)
31. Complex sentences: subordination
32. Amount of information per sentence

Semantic (meaning)   Examples of errors
33. Flexible vocabulary, connotative-denotative
34. Coherence; focus and tense shifts
35. Logical sequencing
36. Transitions
37. Distinction between major and minor points
38. Inferential thinking; cause-effect
39. Idiomatic and figurative language

Self-Monitoring skills   Examples of errors
40. Self-correction: spelling and punctuation
41. Improvement through revision

2

tension might be the cause or if the student cannot write within the lines, the cause might be an inability to control the small muscles of the fingers. One solution is a thick pencil or a triangular slip-on plastic gripper for the pencil to help maintain a proper three-finger grasp with less pressure.

The left-handed, bent-wristed writer requires major positional changes to improve writing performance. This student needs to slant the paper in the opposite direction of that used by right-handed writers; otherwise the wrist must be bent and the pencil pointed downward toward the line to achieve the writing slant taught and demonstrated by most teachers. But with the paper slanted so that the side edges are parallel with the writing arm, the wrist can be straightened and the pencil can be pointed upward from the line, which produces the same writing slant as that of the right-handed writer.

The advantages of changing to a straight wrist are forcefully demonstrated when the hand is held in the bent-wristed position for a few seconds while noting muscle tension and fatigue. When the wrist is straightened the contrast in comfort convinces the student to change. With the straight wrist the student can write for a longer time without tiring and with less smudging of previously written lines. Neater and lengthier papers are the reward.

Cursive writing is neurologically easier than manuscript writing and is particularly advantageous for students who confuse reversible letters (b and d, p and q) or have spacing problems. Their spatial doubts are usually reflected in extreme crowding of letters or exaggerated spacing between words. In cursive writing, words are more easily recognized as entities because there are no spaces between letters, only between words.

In manuscript and cursive writing, repeated errors or ambiguities in letter formations and numerous erasures suggest a need for reteaching, with specific attention to directional aspects of letter formations and joining techniques for letters that have bridges to the next letter (b, o, v, w). If the student persists in mixing capitals and lowercase letters within a word, he probably does not remember the correct letter formation in the lower case; for example, he substitutes B for b because the lowercase b is confused with its mirror image d. He needs demontration and practice with each troublesome letter to discover the correct form, which eliminates the confusion of overlapping graphic features with similarities that cause doubts.

Differences usually have greater instructional value than similarities.

Orthographic Category

This category of the DEWS contains criteria relevant to spelling ability. Students with spelling errors that show sequencing problems need to pay greater attention to the internal structure of words than is possible for them during the reading process. They require practice in written spelling, which allows them to discover the form and internal structure of words in the kinesthetic act of writing and naming each letter in its proper spatial sequence. Those spelling mistakes that students make because they do not know the rules of orthography are most effectively remediated in the context of illustrative words applicable to a particular rule. Words suggested by students to augment the teacher's examples show evidence of whether or not the rule is comprehended. If necessary, further explication can help the student apply the rule.

Sometimes the wording of the rule compounds the difficulties, as in the case of the *ie* rule: *i* before *e* except after *c* and when the sound is *a* as in *neighbor* and *weigh*. Here the prepositions *before, except,* and *after* are particularly confusing for students with language disorders, and a change in wording is advisable. A simplified version of the rule using mnemonics makes it usable: *ie* in *piece of pie* and *friends to the end;* but *cei* in *receive* and *ei* when the sound is *a* as in *eight neighbors weighed the freight.* Students' suggestions, drawn from their own frame of reference, are especially effective in helping them remember unusual spellings.

The rule that governs doubling of a final consonant before adding an ending that begins with a vowel has two important parts. When a one-syllable word ends in a consonant with a vowel before it, the final consonant doubles (e.g., hopping). When a two-syllable word ends in a consonant with a vowel before it, the accent must fall on the second syllable for doubling to occur; the final consonant is not doubled if the accent falls on the first syllable. Thus in *occurring* the *r* is doubled, but in *offering* it is not doubled because the accent falls on the first syllable.

An *ed* ending must include *e* as well as *d,* though it sounds like *d* alone in *offered* or like *t* alone in *stopped.*

Prefixes and suffixes should be taught in the context of familiar vocabulary words: *pre* in *predict* and *preadolescent; est* in *latest* and *fastest.* Lists of unfamiliar Latinate forms and affixes are not easily learned by language deficient students.

Pretty to prettiest illustrates *y* changing to *i* before the addition of an ending that begins with a vowel. The *ing* ending is an exception to this rule, e.g., the *y* is retained in *trying, buying,* and *hurrying.*

C and *g* followed by *e, i,* or *y* have soft sounds: *s* sound for *c* in *cent, civil,* and *cycle;* and the *j* sound for *g* in *gem, giant,* and *gym.* Exceptions include *begin, girl,* and *get.*

Ch has three sounds: the *ch* sound in *chair* changes to the sound of *k* in *mechanic, school,* and *orchestra* or the *sh* sound in *chivalry, Chicago,* and *machine.*

The *sh* spelling for the *sh* sound usually occurs at the beginnings and ends of words (ship and dish), but for *si, ti, ci, ce* spellings, it occurs in the middle of words (mission, vacation, politician, ocean). Among the other uncommon spellings of the *sh* sound is *su* (sugar, sure, tissue).

Ph has the sound of *f* in *phone, alphabet,* and *trophy; gh* also has the sound of *f* in *cough* and *laugh,* but *gh* is silent in *fight* and *thought.*

Some silent letters create such a great spelling problem that students should be encouraged to sound the troublesome letters when spelling. These letters include the *b* in *lamb* and *doubt, c* in *scissors* and *science, d* in *Wednesday* and *handkerchief, g* in *gnaw* and *sign, h* in *ghost* and *honest, k* in *knowledge* and *knee, l* in *calf* and *folks, n* in *column* and *autumn, p* in *receipt* and *pneumonia, t* in *fasten* and *whistle,* and *w* in *answer* and *write.* When the silent consonant is pronounced in another form of the target word, the related word should be used to recover the silent letter as in *muscle* and *muscular, sign* and *signature,* and *bomb* and *bombard.*

Comparisons help students grasp the necessary generalizations for spelling proficiency. It is advisable therefore to work on similarities and differences appearing in the various categories of spellings. The *ch* in *march, lunch,* and *ranch* has a consonant before the *ch,* but the *ch* in *snatch, watch,* and *switch* has the consonant *t* before the *ch* (exceptions: rich, such, much). Multiple sounds for the same spelling include an *e* sound for *ea* in *steam* and an *a* sound for *ea* in *steak;* an *i* sound for *y* in *magnify* and the two other *y* sounds in *mystery;* a long *i* sound for *ive* in *survive* and a short *i* sound in *captive;* a long *a* sound for *ate* in *vacate* and a schwa sound in *private;* an *s* sound in noose but a *z* sound in nose. Multiple spellings for the same sound include an *e* sound for *ee* in *beet* and *ea* in *beat;* and *aw* sound with *aw* in *raw* and *au* in *fault;* a short *u* sound in *love* and *mother;* a long *i* in *fine* because of a final silent

e, and a long *i* in *find* and *kind* with no final *e* but two final consonants; and a short *i* in *will* with a doubled final consonant.

In ambiguous spellings in which either of two consonants could be used according to the pronunciation, a related word is helpful in the decision making. Critical determines the choice of *c,* not *s* in *criticize; medical* helps with *c* in *medicine.* A particular pattern of *t* and *c,* not *s,* alternations simplifies the spelling of certain pairs of words: *president* and *presidency; pirate* and *piracy; coincident* and *coincidence, present* and *presence.*

Reduced vowels, known as schwa sounds, might be spelled with a, e, i, o, or u. The correct spelling cannot be determined by any rule; but a related word, with stress on the syllable in question, provides the true vowel sound and spelling otherwise not ascertainable in an unstressed syllable. For example, in *democrat* the vowel *o* in the unstressed second syllable has a reduced sound that might be spelled with any other vowel. In the related word *democracy,* however, the *o* retains its sound in the stressed syllable *moc.* And the *o* of *democracy* is the same *o* of *democrat.* Other pairs of similarly related words (celebrate and celebrity, fantasy and fantastic, history and historical) provide clues for spelling schwa sounds and thus are important as self-help measures (Chomsky 1970). By compiling lists of related words, students become aware of the variant forms of words in different contexts and thereby learn to pay more attention to word endings than they ordinarily do. This technique is important in extending the student's skills in several categories in addition to the orthographic category.

Syllabication is a fundamental part of spelling and should receive the attention it warrants. The definition of a syllable, according to Webster, is a segment of speech typically produced with a single pulse of air pressure from the lungs. The requirement of at least one vowel in every syllable and the indivisibility of a written syllable therefore are logical expressions of the defined singleness of breath for a spoken syllable. Awareness of these essential characteristics of syllables prevents mistakes in word division when completion of a word is impossible in the remaining space on the line. Incomplete syllables are not permitted at the beginning or end of a line, and endings must never be divided (e.g., ous, ment, est, ble). If the student is required to spell in complete syllables orally and in writing, thinking of words as segments joined in a prescribed sequence is learned. This syllabic approach decreases errors of omission and increases general orthographic ability.

Phonologic Category

In this category of the DEWS the criteria focus on the oral and written sound components of language. Those students who are unaware of the phonetic structure of spoken words have difficulty in discriminating separate sounds in speech; they cannot segment an incoming stream of sounds into meaningful units (Mattingley 1972). Thus they act as though they have a hearing loss; they fail to respond to questions or they constantly ask "What?" Their real problem, however, is not hearing the message but decoding it. "What?" becomes a delaying tactic to gain time for processing speech sounds delivered too rapidly for them to understand.

The teacher can recognize this behavior as a coping strategy because the student belatedly begins to answer a question before his requested repetition is completed. Knowing that the student is not to blame for lack of attention, the teacher should try to speak more slowly and clearly, waiting without prodding for the student to decode the message and encode the response. If the student feels assured that he can have the extra time he needs, he discontinues his customary "what" response and concentrates on processing the message. Listening deficits signal speech and writing errors that accompany faulty reception. For example, a student might confuse the sounds of *th* and *f* unless he watches the lips of the speaker. The student who thinks the word *deaf* is pronounced *death* always pronounces and spells it incorrectly.

Despite years of listening, speaking, reading, and writing experience, the misperception persists unless someone discovers the mistake and corrects it directly. Language is not automatically absorbed in its proper form by mere looking or listening, or students would not be writing *would of* for *would have*, *alota* for *a lot of* and *are* for *our*. These visual representations of auditory misperceptions suggest the need for deliberate modeling of more precise speech and direct teaching to eliminate errors in listening, speaking, and writing.

Syntactic Category

The criteria in this category of the DEWS focus on specific grammatical problems identified in the context of student writing. Formal grammar lessons are less effective than the process of editing personal writing in making the abstractions of grammar rules meaningful. Even students who speak as ungrammatically as they

write eventually learn to detect their own errors after experience with this three-stage remedial procedure.

First, during a conference period the student reads his paper aloud to the teacher. Thus the visual stimulus is augmented by the oral reinforcement, which permits the student to recognize mistakes not discernable to him during silent reading. If he still cannot find his error, the second stage, the teacher's oral reading of the incorrect portion as it was written, provides additional auditory input. If the student still cannot identify the error, the teacher initiates the third stage of explaining the problem and the possibilities for revision. This approach enables the student to overcome the barriers of abstract grammatical concepts and to apply the rules of syntax in a concrete, meaningful way.

In the process of composing and correcting, the student discovers all the basic grammatical information needed. A sentence must contain a subject and predicate that agree in number, and capitalization is necessary for the first word in a sentence and for proper nouns. Sentences must be complete, unfragmented, and properly punctuated with a period, question mark, or exclamation point. A colon directs attention to what follows: a list, an explanation, a quotation. A semicolon signifies the equal importance of ideas on both sides of the semicolon, and a comma separates words in a series, in phrases, and in clauses but must not be used to splice two sentences into a single run-on sentence. An apostrophe resembles a comma in shape, but it is placed above letters or numbers to indicate possession, omission of letter, or plurals. Quotation marks indicate the beginnings and endings of the actual words of a quotation. Their shape, position, and number distinguish them from the comma and the apostrophe, but students who customarily see similarities and overlook differences might require explanation, demonstration, and practice to learn the correct forms.

Other syntactic errors revealed in student papers include word-order violations that result in awkwardness or faulty emphasis; omission of words and phrases or necessary word endings that signify tense, plurals, or possession; and subject focus or tense shifts that confuse the reader and interfere with comprehension. With supervised scrutiny of these deficiencies during oral proofreading, the student learns to pay attention to those details that determine the efficacy of his written communication.

Semantic Category

The criteria in this category of the DEWS are primarily

2

meaning oriented. Because the skills needed for conveying meaning in writing are inextricably bound to the skills necessary for extracting meaning from reading, the relationship of reading and writing assumes extraordinary significance. According to research data, it is through writing that a student acquires the differential sensitivity to structural characteristics and meanings that lead to efficiency in reading (Waller 1976). In fact, the syntactic level at which a student writes influences the level at which he reads (Smith 1971).

As the written language is practiced to express ideas in a variety of ways, the student learns to interpret the language of others and acquires facility in restating an author's ideas in his own words, which is the ultimate definition of reading comprehension (Adler & Van Doren 1972). The manipulation of complex language beyond the minimal level of ordinary concrete discourse helps students deal with abstractions in a way that actually transforms the nature of thought processes. These transformations result in general cognitive growth, with improvement not only in reading and writing but also in the capacity to learn. This ability is defined as analytical competence (Bruner 1975).

Self-Monitoring Category

This category of the DEWS encompasses all of the writing skills evaluated in the preceding categories. With the ultimate goal of self-monitoring being the independent functioning of the student, training in detection of errors is crucial. Diagnostic teaching develops self-monitoring skills through an uncomplicated direct modeling method; students learn by seeing concrete examples in their own writing of mistakes or weaknesses that require revision. As the teacher analyzes each error with the student and suggests possibilities for improvement, the student's uncertainty about the correctness of his writing is reduced, and he eventually is able to edit his own work.

The rewriting process embodies two elements that contribute to or possibly are prerequisites of improvement in reading: the ability to consider alternatives and to view writing from a new perspective (Gundlach & Moses 1976). As the student improves the handwriting, spelling, grammar, and ideation of his writing, he becomes increasingly competent in all areas of language, reception, and expression. Writing no longer frightens him, and he copes more effectively with educational demands.

REFERENCES

Adler, M., Van Doren, C., *How to Read a Book. New York: Simon & Schuster, 1972.*

Bruner, J., Language as an instrument of thought. In A. Davies (Ed.), *Problems of Language and Learning. London: Heinemann Educational Books, Ltd. (1976 rev.).*

Chomsky, C., Reading, writing, & phonology. *Harvard Educational Review,* 40, 2, May 1970.

Gundlach, R., Moses, R., Developmental issues in the study of children's language. *Paper presented at First Annual Boston University Conference on Language Development, Boston, 1976.*

Mattingley, I., Reading, the linguistic process, and linguistic awareness. In J. Kavanagh, I. Mattingley (Eds.), *Language by Ear and Eye — The Relationships Between Speech and Reading. Cambridge, Mass.: MIT Press.*

Smith, W., Reading and writing. *Paper presented at International Reading Association Conference, Atlantic City, N.J., 1971.*

Waller, T., Children's recognition memory. *Child Development,* 47, 1976.

Weiner, E.S., Improvement in reading through writing. *Academic Therapy,* 14, May 1979.

CLASSROOM APPLICATIONS

Resistive Activities Approach For the Learning Disabled

by Subhash Natwerlal Jani and Miriam L. Bender

Resistive activities are receiving increasing attention in education through the work of Miriam L. Bender, PhD, a physical therapist and a special educator. Bender (1971), completing her dissertation at Purdue University under the direction of Professor Earl J. Heath, noted that a high percentage of problem learners had some degree of residual symmetric tonic neck reflex (STNR). Basically, STNR involves involuntary changes in tonus of muscles with changes in head position. As the head is down, elbows tend to bend and hips and knees straighten. The converse is true with the head-up position. Heath and Bender explained how abnormal STNR adversely affected learning in a detailed article (1971). They cited several classroom situations where a learner's abnormal STNR resulted in limited abilities to explore his environment due to non-flexible movements and distorted feedback. Dr. Bender developed the *Bender-Purdue Reflex Test* (1976) to assess abnormal STNR.

At the Achievement Center, Purdue University, activities were successfully utilized by Dr. Bender in order to integrate STNR and facilitate learning. These were called "resistive activities." Resistive activities are so named because they involve resistance. In essence, the learner is offered "optimal resistance" as he is challenged to complete such developmental tasks as rocking on all fours, creeping, walking, etc. Optimal resistance increases and intensifies the feedback and improves feedback consistency (Heath and Bender 1971). Through improved consistency and feedback, the learner integrates the STNR and develops his own "unique" pattern of neuromuscular efficiency. The

From *Academic Therapy*, March 1980, Vol. 15, No. 4. Copyright 1980, Academic Therapy Publications, Inc. Reprinted with permission.

TABLE 1
Resistive Activities—A Summary of Rocking and Creeping Activities

	ROCKING (Push)	CREEPING FORWARD SHOULDERS (Push)	CREEPING FORWARD ANKLES (Pull)	CREEPING FORWARD HEELS (Push)	CREEPING BACKWARD BUTTOCKS (Push)
Space	Carpeted classroom	20 feet or so carpeted area			
Target	8 in. tin can above eye level	Nose	8 in. tin can or other paper targets of larger and smaller sizes, shapes, above eye level		
Generally Recommended Frequencies	10X	six days/week at a fixed predetermined time			
	10X with R & L Learner	2 round trips for 1st 6 wks., 2 round trips toward 2nd 6 weeks			
Learner (L)	Start with catsit	Hands and Knees Start with a box shape			
Educator (E) Position (General)	Close to and towards L's upper extremities	All Fours Facing Learner Parallel to the floor in the line with L			
(Specific)	a. Palm of hands on forehead clearing eyebrows b. Hands across buttocks	Palms on shoulder blades covering wide area. Avoid digging with fingers	Hold ankles such that thumb and forefinger meet on inside. Avoid fingers used like claws. Catsit positions.	Palm of hand in apposition to heels.	Palms on seat.
	Slide legs to get balanced graceful movement				
Commands (General)	a. Put your hands nice and flat, fingers pointing forward, toes pointing back, head up, watch the target. Simultaneously assist child towards this posture, while starting. b. Emphasize only Watch The Target during activities varying the command in rate and rhythm.				
Commands (Specific)	a. Now, I want you to push/pull (as appropriate) when I say push/pull. Ready? For optimal control, L must begin only when E says the command). Push/Pull. E concurrently gives tactual input through rebound to cue for movement initiation. CAUTION: Make sure to continue resistance till task completed. Beginning E's tend to let go resistance when verbal command is completed. b. Resistance is optimal when L is challenged enough to successfully complete specific tasks.				

learner now develops an improved overall sense of readiness to learn through tactual-kinesthetic, visual, and other sensory modalities. For example, Heath, Cook, and O'Dell (1976) did a controlled study comparing the effectiveness of the resistive, motor, and perceptual programs. They noted that the "Bender facilitating technique was significantly more effective in improving ocular-motor control than any other method used in the study" (p. 443). The improvement in the fixation ability of the eyes (and attention) were also reported by Bender and Jani (1975), at the annual meeting of the American Academy of Optometry.

Bonnie J. Swanson (1976) studied the relationship between resistive activities and memory. She noted that over a six-week period, her subjects receiving resistive activities showed greater gains on the visual and auditory memory subtests of the *Illinois Test of Psycholinguistic Abilities* (ITPA) compared with a control group.

Table 1 gives a brief description of these resistive activities and their application.

Full descriptions of the resistive activities are given in Dr. Bender's text (pp. 59-61). There are sections on general instructions and tips for trainers. In this section a brief description of the five exercises included in Table 1 will be given.

Rocking. The learner essentially rocks forward and backward, while fixating above eye level. The educator offers resistance to challenge learner's back and forth movements.

Shoulders—creeping forward push. The learner creeps forward, while fixating on educator's nose. The educator creeps backward, offering challenge level resistance at the learner's shoulders.

Ankles—creeping forward pull. The learner creeps forward while fixating a target above eye level at the finishing end of the room. The educator creeps forward, offering challenge level resistance at the learner's ankles. (Be careful to maintain resistance until the full forward movement of a given foot is complete.)

Heels—creeping backward push. The learner creeps backward while fixating a target above eye level at the starting end of the room. The educator creeps backward, offering challenge level resistance at the learner's heels.

Buttocks—creeping backward push. The learner creeps backward while fixating a target above eye level at the starting end of the room. The educator creeps backward, offering challenge level resistance at the learner's "sitting bones."

It should be noted that in all the preceding instances, the educator primarily offers challenge level resistance. The learner in turn, through his own experimentation, evolves an efficient pattern which is uniquely his own.

Generally, the program is conducted six days per week, for specified frequencies. For the interested educator or parent, appropriate work positions and some general and specific commands for each of the activities are presented.

It should also be noted that training, practice, and understanding are essential to proper implementation and successful results. However, with discretion, intelligent nonprofessionals could easily learn these and implement these with amazing degree of success (Heath, Cook, and O'Dell 1976; Bender and Heath 1971). Heath and Bender (1971) and I have noted successful application of these activities even with older school populations. Three representative reports are included in the following paragraphs indicating samples of responses from educators, administrators, and parents in Illinois.

Report 1: Ann

Ann is a child with learning disabilities. Two years ago she was very clumsy (always bumping into or spilling objects). She could not keep her eyes on a specific point on a page of print regardless of how large the print. Her eye-hand coordination was so poor that she could not follow a row of objects or line of print with her finger.

She began participating in a program of resistive activities at school. This participation coincided with a slight improvement in motor coordination. Ann's mother was asked to help with the resistive program at home and was shown how to do the resistive rocking and forward creeping activities. She was also shown several eye exercises to do with Ann. She did the exercises daily with Ann for about half an hour.

Within four months there was a noticeable improvement in Ann's abilities. She could keep her place on a printed page, and her eyes could follow a moving target such as her finger. Her clumsiness decreased, and she could perform many skills previously impossible for her, such as pouring milk or filling a salt shaker. There was a marked improvement in all academic areas—especially writing, math, and reading.

Reported by
Ms. Jan Dobbs, MS
Instructor
University School
Macomb, Illinois 61455

Report 2: Using the Resistive Activities

I have used resistive activities in various situations. Most recently, I worked with four learning disabilities teachers and in-serviced them to use the activities. Twelve children participated in the program on a daily basis for 15 minutes per day over a six-week period of time. The children who participated were learning-disabled students who were in first through fourth grade.

All children went through resistive rocking, resistive forward creeping, and resistive backward creeping. Other resistive activities were used at the teacher's option.

The activities are strenuous for both student and teacher and during the first week the 15 minutes had to be divided up in most cases.

The teachers noted that it was difficult to watch and make accurate observations on the basic *Bender-Purdue Reflex Test*. But after working with them on two or three occasions, teachers began to feel more at ease.

All teachers had positive feelings toward the activities and at the end of the six-week period said that they would continue with the activities. They noted improvement in all children they worked with. The improvement ranged from better performance with the activities themselves to two children having marked behavior changes in their respective classrooms.

One learning disabilities teacher told me that after three weeks, one classroom teacher commented, "What have you been doing with [name deleted]? It's as if the fog had lifted."

Another child with severe motor deficit made marked improvement in coordination within the six-week period.

The activities have great value because of the effectiveness of them over a short period of time. Also, these activities are easily adaptable to home use.

Reported by
Ms. Bonnie Swanson, MS
General Administrative Ass't
East Moline Public Schools
836 17th Avenue
East Moline, Illinois 61244

Report 3: Bill

Dear Dr. Jani:

First of all I want to thank you for the very thorough and complete summary of the testing done on Bill and the recommendations made in the report. His teachers and others involved were very impressed with the work you and your students did.

We have worked with Bill daily (with the exception of perhaps one day a week) on the resistive exercises, accommodation training, facilitated pursuits, "angels in the snow," and the gross-motor exercises. Following is a brief summary of my observations on each exercise:

1. *Resistive rocking.* The first few times we did this I had to resist uncontrolled rocking constantly, but now he only occasionally pushes back without a command. He will also move one of his hands sometimes. He does keep his eyes on the target almost constantly during this exercise, and the rocking is smooth.

2. *Resistive forward creeping.* Bill has gone from eye contact of about 25 percent to approximately 50 percent. We've been working on better hand control on this exercise, too; when he creeps his hands turn to the outside frequently. He no longer requires the constant commanding that he did at first.

3. *Resistive backward creeping.* We have moved from a very clumsy, wobbly backward creeping (his legs were going in and out) to a rather smooth one, with his feet now remaining on the floor for the most part. He keeps his eyes on the target almost constantly as he did pretty much from the start.

4. *Facilitated pursuits.* Bill started out squirming and moving his head quite a bit on this exercise. He now lies still and rarely moves his head. His eye contact with the target has gone from about 60 percent to 85 percent with both eyes. He has most difficulty when he covers one eye.

5. *Accommodation training.* This exercise was very difficult for Bill at first: He could not focus on the hand target at all. He would be looking at me when I would say "target" and claim he was looking at the target. I gave him a larger hand target (two-inch diameter); and he still had difficulty for a while. Now we are back to using the smaller target (one-inch diameter); and he is focusing on it. His eyes do wander quite a bit between commands and he looks at me often.

6. *Angels in the snow.* Of all the exercises I notice the most improvement on this one. Bill started with a great amount of hesitancy on each command and a lot of overflow. Lately he has good swift movements with hardly any hesitancy, but still some overflow. I do notice though that when I give a command to move two limbs, he will move one first, then the other.

7. *Gross-motor exercises.* Bill usually does these activities with his father. Mainly he does exercises that involve the leg muscles: bicycling, hopping,

knee-bends, "bunny hopping." They work on the balance beam often, sometimes catching and throwing a ball while Bill is on it. Also, because the weather is improving, they've been out pitching and batting balls often.

These exercises take a total of approximately 45 minutes a day. We seem to be having difficulty in finding the time to work on fine-motor activities. However, I feel from what I understand from our discussions, the preceding exercises we are doing have priority, and right now his school work seems to be directed almost entirely on fine-motor work. I will certainly try during the summer months to incorporate more fine-motor activities.

I have had a couple of conferences with Bill's teachers and the school principal. There is a general feeling that Bill has improved in the last few weeks. Most notably, he is now doing much more of his paperwork; and his printing and figures are better controlled. There also seems to be simply a more realistic and positive attitude on his part toward his schoolwork.

Again, the work and discussions with you and your students is proving increasingly valuable, and I will be waiting to hear from you regarding the exercise program and any other comments you might have.

Sincerely,
Bill's Mother

References

Bender, Miriam L. 1971. A study of the relationships between persistent immaturity of the symmetric tonic neck reflex and learning disabilities in children. Unpublished PhD dissertation, Purdue University.

Bender, Miriam L. 1976. *The Bender-Purdue reflex test and training manual.* Novato, California: Academic Therapy Publications.

Bender, Miriam L., and Jani, S. N. 1975. Symposium: resistive activities in the treatment of visual attention, fixations, and pursuits of the learning disabled child. Presented to the American Academy of Optometry.

Heath, Earl J.; Cook, P.; and O'Dell, N. 1976. Eye exercises and reading efficiency. *Academic Therapy* 11:4, pp. 435-444.

Heath, Earl J., and Bender, Miriam L. 1976. Motor and reflex evaluations: some new insights. *Academic Therapy* 11:4 pp. 413-415.

Swanson, B. H. 1976. The relationship of resistive activities on memory: a comparison study. Western Illinois University. Unpublished MS research paper.

PART 3

3

PL 94-142 AND UNCLE SAM

by Glen Thompson, Ph.D.

No other single thing has happened that has had as great an impact on education in general and special education in particular as has Public Law 94-142. As attempts are being made to implement it, the impact of the law is far reaching and seemingly ever increasing.

Most special educators are basically pleased with the law's intent. But not a few of them have voiced complaints relating to the time-consuming paperwork associated with PL 94-142. Composing Individualized Educational Programs (IEPs) can represent hours of additional work for already overtaxed teachers. However, experienced teachers use a systemized approach that reduces the time necessary for preparing IEPs.

For instance, computers equipped with set student characteristics can print out tentative IEPs, since common sets of student characteristics should suggest similar educational programs. Provided with the IEPs, most teachers are willing to implement them and to conduct assessments relating to long-term and short-term goals.

Most special educators are pleased that the rights of parents and students are guaranteed by law. But many are uneasy with extensive parental involvement. In addition, regular teachers may resent the additional responsibility required in mainstreaming, especially if they have not had any special education training.

Although local school districts must read parents their rights as it were, many parents are not familiar with the law, or with their own state's plans. Once aware of their rights, many parents

are relieved. In many cases, financial burdens are shifted because the public school assumes educational expenses for students they may formerly have refused because the children were, for one reason or another, uneducable.

Parents of more severely-disabled youngsters fear their children might be removed from a private school. Or that the child might be forced to move, unprotected into the mainstream of a regular classroom. However, parents have a strong voice in the educational placement and programming planned for their children.

Furthermore, PL 94-142 does not mention mainstreaming. In no way are mainstreaming and "least restrictive alternative" to be considered synonymous. In fact, mainstreaming a severely-retarded child, for example, into a regular classroom would possibly be more restrictive than placing the child in a self-contained room.

In the past, handicapped persons were isolated from the so-called normal mainstream. There were schools for the deaf and for the blind. And there were special schools for the physically handicapped. As a result, both the handicapped and the nonhandicapped suffered. Neither had any experience relating to the other. So they felt uncomfortable when they did come face to face.

In a sense, nonhandicapped persons benefit from the implementation of PL 94-142 almost as much as do handicapped people. In the end, regular education also benefits.

The law's philosophy is all children are to receive a free and appropriate education, which implies that all students' educational programs should be individually tailored for appropriateness. But applying such a philosophy to education suggests a high financial priority. Currently, PL 94-142 helps states establish educational programs for certain handicapped persons, while the education of regular children remains primarily the responsibility of state and local educational agencies. However, the trend has begun, and future generations of students may find the federal commitment to the appropriate education of all children more encompassing.

The Loophole in Public Law 94-142

3

by Lynne Raiser and Clint Van Nagel

Abstract: Public Law 94-142, the Education for All Handicapped Children Act of 1975, promises that no school aged pupil will be denied a free appropriate public education because of a handicapping condition. The authors propose that by regulatory exclusion, a great population of students with behavior disorders do not have this federally mandated guarantee and will continue to be at the mercy of local school districts, which may or may not choose to accept the responsibility for their education. Public Law 94-142 qualifies "emotionally disturbed" with the word "seriously," implying no responsibility for the moderately disturbed child. The law further specifically excludes "socially maladjusted" unless they are "seriously emotionally disturbed." The door is open for school districts to systematically exclude large numbers of behaviorally disordered students from special education classes and from school itself.

■ One of the common alternative ways to deal with disruptive children is to refer them to special education. In years past, a special education student was easily recognizable because of obvious blindness, deafness, physical impairment, or severe retardation. In recent years, more and more ordinary looking children with exotic labels such as "learning disability," "emotional disturbance," and "behavioral disorders" are being grouped in public school special classes. The distinction between the special and regular student has become blurred and the trend seems to be, when in doubt, refer to special education. As Dunn (1973) stated, "There has been a tendency to take pupils the regular teacher cannot handle and find something wrong with them so that they can be given a disability label" and thus be eligible for special class placement (p. 5).

In many cases, special education placement has become a panacea for regular education's inability or unwillingness to accommodate the mildly and moderately deviant child who seems unable to learn academics or appropriate behavior patterns in traditional school classrooms. Dunn (1973) suggested that before a child is placed in special education the total school setting should be carefully analyzed to determine if educators may be partially at fault by providing an inadequate or inappropriate education for the child in question. Why must teachers always assume the child is totally responsible for deciding when he or she cannot succeed in the mainstream of public education? Dunn (1973) further stated that placement in special education should be on a trial basis and only continue if proven to be a superior setting to what is available for the child in a regular class. Just because it is special does not mean it is better.

LEGAL REPERCUSSIONS OF EXCLUDING HANDICAPPED STUDENTS

Abeson and Zettel (1977) cited the two landmark court decisions that set the precedents for the enactment of Public Law 94-142, the Education for All Handicapped Children Act of 1975. The Pennsylvania Association for Retarded Children sued the Commonwealth of Pennsylvania in 1971 for its failure to provide all of its retarded school aged children with a free public education. *Mills* v. *Board of Education of the District of Columbia* in 1972 involved several exceptionalities, including the emotionally disturbed. Peter Mills and two of the other children in the class action suit had been excluded from school because of "behavior problems." The suit was filed on behalf of all District of Columbia school children who had been, or may have been, excluded from public education. The suit claimed that there had been no determination that these children would not benefit from specialized instruction adapted to their needs. The District of Columbia's compulsory school attendance law has an exclusion loophole which states that a child, upon examination by the school board, may be "excused" from school if found mentally or physically unable to profit from attendance at school or from specialized instruction adapted to his or her needs (Goldstein, 1974). The Court said "it need not belabor the fact that requiring parents to see that their children attend school under pain of criminal penalties presupposes that an educational opportunity will be made available to the children" (Goldstein, 1974). The Court found the District of Columbia in violation of its own statutes by not providing a publicly supported specialized education for these children.

THE RIGHT TO A FREE APPROPRIATE PUBLIC EDUCATION

What the District of Columbia had done to these children was not unusual. A school board may have extensive special education programs and find that a particular child does not fit into any one of them. Traditionally, programs are designed for a mythically homogeneous group of children such as the educable mentally retarded or emotionally disturbed. Specific criteria are developed for admission to each of the programs (District Procedures, Duval County, 1977-78). There may be no appropriate program for a child who fits the criteria for more than one disability, such as a severely emotionally disturbed mentally retarded child; or there may be no programing at all for a low incidence disability such as autism. Public Law 94-142 seeks to correct this by requiring an individualized education program (IEP) for each child enrolled in a special

education program. No longer will it be permissible for special educators to find ways to fit a child into a predetermined grouping system. The individual needs of students will determine the kind of programing they receive.

Except for previously excluding certain handicapped students who could not be expected to "profit" from an education, American school children have long been considered to have a legal right to a public education (Goldstein, 1974; Wilcox, 1880). Public Law 94-142 provides a dimension to educational opportunity previously undifferentiated: the legal rights of children to a free appropriate public education.

DISRUPTIVE STUDENTS DEFINED AS HANDICAPPED

The premise of the authors is that some, but not all, children with behavior disorders will be offered a free appropriate public education because of Public Law 94-142. Why not all? The problem lies in the very specific definition in the law:

"Seriously emotionally disturbed" is defined as follows: (i) The term means a condition exhibiting one or more of the following characteristics over a long period of time and to a marked degree, which adversely affects educational performance: (a) an inability to learn which cannot be explained by intellectual, sensory, or health factors; (b) an inability to build or maintain satisfactory interpersonal relationships with peers and teachers; (c) inappropriate types of behavior or feelings under normal circumstances; (d) a general pervasive mood of unhappiness or depression; or (e) a tendency to develop physical symptoms or fears associated with personal or school problems. (ii) The term includes children who are schizophrenic or autistic. The term does not include children who are socially maladjusted, unless it is determined that they are seriously emotionally disturbed (Education of Handicapped Children, *Federal Register*, Section 121a.5, 1977).

Yard (1977) took issue with the use of the term *seriously emotionally disturbed* as the label for the category "behavior disorders." The use of this term may eliminate a significant population of students with mild to moderate problems, some of whom are presently being served by state special education services. He further pointed out that none of the other definitions of handicapped conditions use the word "seriously." This implies that a student so labeled would primarily be considered for placement in greater restrictive services, rather than least restrictive services. Are we not inviting possible reverse discrimination suits from parents of normal children by leaving the mild and moderately disturbed in the mainstream with regular educators and no special services? What about the probable backlash from regular education teachers who are forced to serve these students in their classrooms (Yard, 1977):

Part of the issue here is the term *behavior disorders,* used by many professionals in the field, which includes both the emotionally disturbed and the socially maladjusted. It is difficult to differentiate between emotionally disturbed (ED) and socially maladjusted (SM) students because the overt behavior may seem the same although the causes are quite different. Socially maladjusted children may get along well within their peer groups which are often juvenile gangs, but this antisocial behavior is not culturally permissible at school, at home, or in the community. If adjudicated by the court system for behavior in conflict with the law, these socially maladjusted students are then labeled *juvenile delinquents* (Kirk, 1972).

Public Law 94-142 clearly excludes socially maladjusted students, except in cases where emotional disturbance can be proven. By excluding the socially maladjusted population, special education services for behaviorally disordered children must take on a new frame of reference, especially during the referral and placement process. Hewett (1977) pointed out that the first special class for children with behavioral disorders was established in New York in 1874 for boys who were "unruly and truant." This focus on disruptiveness and social nonconformity has continued to be a major criterion for placement in special education. It would seem to be a legitimate concern that regular educators will resist the responsibility for these students who have been taken off their hands by special education for the last hundred years.

It is a complicated matter to define, classify, and diagnose a behavior disorder. Whether or not the problem exists is not the issue. It is a matter of examining the context in which the behavior occurs and the expectations of all parties concerned (Hewett & Forness, 1977). Paul, Neufeld, and Pelosi (1977) described the problem as "the trouble or agitation which results from misfits between child and arrangements" (p. 12). He suggested treating the individual and the setting as a single complex system, but only after determining if the misfit is indeed a deviate by observing behavior in the "normal" environment to see if it is both unexpected and unacceptable. This ecological viewpoint, together with the influence of be-

haviorism with its concern with what a child does and not why he or she does it, further confuses the distinction between emotional disturbance and social maladjustment. As Hewett and Forness (1977) pointed out, "The definition of a behavior disorder is a statement of the actual behavior itself" (p. 92).

The task for the behavior modifier is to observe and systematically intervene through the rearrangement of environmental variables. Graubard postulated that "what is viewed as deviant behavior and how it is designated, interpreted, and treated are as much a function of the perceiver as they are of the behaver" (Dunn, 1973, p. 245). He further suggested that placement decisions should be based on the child's behavior, rather than interviews or tests administered outside the specific context of school where the problem has been identified, and the final diagnosis should be made on the basis of trial treatments.

If socially maladjusted students are excluded then who are the seriously emotionally disturbed children provided for in Public Law 94-142? Hewett and Forness (1977) defined this group as having childhood psychoses (childhood schizophrenia, infantile autism, and symbiotic psychosis), and/or severe psychosomatic disorders. Kirk (1972) described the emotionally disturbed child as one who exhibits inner tensions and anxiety and displays neurotic or psychotic behavior. Long, Morse, and Newman (1976) used the definition of the 1968 Joint Commission on the Mental Health of Children and Youth which states that an emotionally disturbed child is one "who has (a) impairment of age-relevant capacity to realistically perceive the external environment, (b) inadequate impulse control, (c) a lack of rewarding interpersonal relationships, and (d) failed to achieve appropriate learning levels" (p. 86).

The Joint Commission found that 0.2% of emotionally disturbed children were psychotic, 2 to 3% were severely disturbed, and 8 to 10% needed specialized services (Long et al., 1976). Bower, in 1960, found 0.5% of all school children were labeled overly aggressive, defiant, or overly withdrawn and timid (Kirk, 1972, p. 401). In 1968, the US Office of Education estimated that only 2% of the school population were emotionally disturbed (Kirk, 1972). With so many variations in definitions and points of view, it is not surprising that prevalence figures range from 0.02% to 15% throughout the United States (Dunn, 1973).

STUDENTS EXCLUDED FROM PUBLIC LAW 94-142's PROVISIONS

If we accept that possibly 2 to 3% of American school children are seriously emotionally disturbed, then regular educators may find that the remaining 8 to 15% of troublesome children may well stay in their classrooms. It is certain that socially maladjusted students will stay there, unless they get another placement through the juvenile court system. Socially maladjusted children between the ages of 10 and 17 are responsible for more than one-half of all serious crimes in the country. When they are caught by the police, most of them are quickly turned back out into society by the court system (*Time*, 1977).

The adjudicated and released delinquent and the socially maladjusted child who has not arrived in the court system will continue to disrupt schools. Public Law 94-142 does not guarantee these students a free appropriate public education. Mildly or moderately emotionally disturbed students will continue to demand too much of a teacher's time and attention because of their low tolerance for frustration, immaturity, inadequacy, and inefficient learning. Public Law 94-142 does not clearly guarantee these children a free appropriate public education.

The US District Court of South Carolina ordered a school district to evaluate Donnie, a 13 year old emotionally disturbed child who was expelled from school, and develop an individualized plan of special education services for him in the least restrictive environment. Without a clear cut definition of emotional disturbance, what if the South Carolina school district finds Donnie to be socially maladjusted instead of seriously emotionally disturbed? Will he again be excluded and end up in the court?

TOWARD A DEFINITION

To rectify the loophole in Public Law 94-142, the authors suggest that the definition be amended to read "behavioral disorders" with subgroups "emotionally disturbed" and "socially maladjusted" well defined. The qualifier "seriously" before "emotionally disturbed" should be eliminated because the required continuum of services from least to most restrictive assures appropriate education for all emotionally disturbed students, including the mildly and moderately disturbed not presently provided for in the law.

With the addition of the category "socially maladjusted" the following definition is proposed:

Socially maladjusted children are those children whose social, not emotional, behaviors inhibit meaningful, normative growth development. Specifically they:
consistently disregard or defy authority,
refuse to meet the minimum standards of conduct required in regular schools and classrooms,
have problems relating to society's normative expectations. Their problems are inter rather than intrapsychic in nature. They are chronic social offenders.

A TEMPORARY ALTERNATIVE

One stop gap alternative in the meantime is to place these children in a separate special education class under the label, *learning disability*. There is an abundance of information that suggests a majority of these students do indeed have learning disabilities (Hurwitz, Bibace, Wolff, & Rowbotham, 1972; Jacobson, 1974; Jordan, 1974; Mauser, 1974; Mulligan, 1969; Poremba, 1975; Stenger, 1975; Wacker, 1974).

While recognizing the need for special education programs for this distinct group, it should be kept in mind that although this group of children have many characteristics closely related to learning disabled children they should not be grouped with such children. It has been the authors' observation that children with social maladjustment problems tend to intimidate children who are learning disabled without social adjustment problems. What is recommended is that these socially maladjusted children be grouped and placed in special education learning disability classes as a separate group until Public Law 94-142 is amended.

CONCLUSION

As more and more socially maladjusted students are excluded from special education services, it is not unlikely that many more law suits will arise concerning the rights of these children to an appropriate educational placement, and the rights of teachers and other children not to have to cope with their disruptiveness. It is not inconceivable that parents will seek, through the court system, appropriate educational planning for their mildly or moderately disturbed children. It is not too unreasonable to view Public Law 94-142 as the precedent for requiring our public schools to give all American children a free appropriate public education based on individualized education programs. SAT scores are falling, children are not learning to read or do basic arithmetic effectively. Is it improbable to expect that the civil rights now granted to handicapped students may in the future be extended to all school children?

REFERENCES

Abeson, A., & Zettel, J. The end of the quiet revolution: The Education for All Handicapped Children Act 1975. *Exceptional Children*, 1977, 44(3), 114-128.

District Procedures, Exceptional Student Section. Duval County, Florida, 1977-1978.

Dunn, L. M. *Exceptional children in the schools.* New York: Holt, Rinehart & Winston, 1973.

Education of Handicapped Children: Implementation of Part B of the Education of the Handicapped Act, Rules and Regulations. *Federal Register*, 42(163), Tuesday, August 23, 1977.

Goldstein, S. R. *Law and public education.* Indianapolis: Bobbs-Merrill, 1974.

Hewett, F. M., & Forness, S. R. *Education of exceptional learners* (2nd ed.). Boston: Allyn & Bacon, 1977.

Hurwitz, I., Bibace, R. M., Wolff, P. H., & Rowbotham, B. M. Neuro-psychological function of normal boys, delinquent boys, and boys with learning problems. *Perceptual and Motor Skills*, 1972, 35(2), 387-394.

Jacobson, F. N. Learning disabilities and juvenile delinquency: A demonstrated relationship. In R. E. Weber (Ed.), *Handbook of learning disabilities: A prognosis for the child, the adolescent, the adult.* Englewood Cliffs NJ: Prentice-Hall, 1974.

Jordan, D. *Learning disabilities and predelinquent behavior of juveniles.* Report on a project sponsored by the Oklahoma Association for Children with Learning Disabilities, May 15, 1974.

Kirk, S. A. *Educating exceptional children.* Boston: Houghton-Mifflin, 1972.

Long, N. J., Morse, W. C., & Newman, R. G. *Conflict in the classroom* (3rd ed.). Belmont CA.: Wadsworth, 1976.

Mauser, A. Learning disabilities and delinquent youth. In B. Kratoville (Ed.), *Youth in trouble* (Proceedings of a symposium, Dallas-Fort Worth Regional Airport, May 1974). San Rafael CA.: Academic Therapy Publications, 1974.

Mulligan, W. A study of dyslexia and delinquency. *Academic Therapy Quarterly*, 1969, 4(3), 177-187.

Paul, J. L., Neufeld, G. R., & Pelosi, J. W. *Child advocacy within the system.* Syracuse NY: Syracuse University Press, 1977.

Poremba, C. D. Learning disabilities, youth and delinquency: Programs for intervention. In H. R. Myklebust (Ed.), *Progress in learning disabilities* (Vol. 3). New York: Grune & Stratton, 1975.

Stenger, M. *Frequency of learning disabilities in adjudicated delinquents.* Masters thesis at the University of Missouri-Kansas City, 1975.

The youth crime plague. *Time*, July 11, 1977, 18-28.

Wacker, J. A. *The reduction of crime through the prevention and treatment of learning disabilities.* Report to the National Institute of Law Enforcement and Criminal Justice, Law Enforcement Assistance Administration, September 1974.

Wilcox, S. M. Legal rights of children. U.S. Bureau of Education Circular, No. 3, 1880. Reprinted in *Legal rights of children.* New York: Arno, 1974.

Yard, G. J. Definition and interpretation of P. L. 94-142: Is behavior disorders a question of semantics? *Behavioral Disorders*, 1977, 24, 252-254.

3

FINANCING

Carter Delivers 1981 Budget

by Jeffrey J. Zettel

On January 28, 1980, President Carter delivered his fiscal year (FY) 1981 budget message to the Congress. The President's budget, on the one hand, represents a milestone to the Federal commitment to education. It contains, for the first time, a separate budget for the recently established Department of Education. Furthermore, the President has asked the Congress to budget $15.5 billion, representing an increase of over $1

PROGRAM	*Federal Financial Assistance for the Education of Exceptional Children (in millions of dollars)*		
	(FY) 1979	*1980*	*1981*
Education of the Handicapped Act (EHA)			
1. State Assistance:			
(a) State Grant Program (P.L. 94-142)	804,000	874,500	922,000
(b) Preschool Incentive Grants	17,500	25,000	25,000
(c) Deaf-Blind Centers	16,000	16,000	16,000
2. Special Population Programs:			
(a) Severely Handicapped Projects	5,000	5,000	5,000
(b) Early Childhood Education	22,000	20,000	20,000
3. Regional, Vocational, Adult and Postsecondary Programs	2,400	2,400	4,000
4. Innovation and Development	20,000	20,000	20,000
5. Media and Resource Services:			
(a) Media Services and Captioned Films	19,000	19,000	19,000
(b) Regional Resource Centers	9,750	9,750	9,750
(c) Recruitment and Information	1,000	1,000	1,000
6. Special Education Personnel Development	57,687	55,375	58,000
7. Special Studies	2,300	1,000	2,300
Gifted and Talented Education	3,780	6,280	6,280

From *Insight*, Vol. 11, No. 2, February 26, 1980. Copyright 1980, The Council for Exceptional Children. Reprinted with permission.

billion, or 7% higher than last year's 1980 appropriation level, for education programs. According to Secretary of Education, Shirley Hufstedler, this increase exemplifies the continuing "pattern which has seen funding for education increase by nearly 40% in the first 3 years of the Carter Administration." The Secretary added that the $15.5 billion budget request represents "the largest sum ever requested by any President in aid of education."

Proponents of exceptional education, on the other hand, need to take caution over such seemingly positive statements. A closer examination of the President's budget reveals that Federal monies for the education of exceptional children have not risen appreciatively. For the most part, as evidenced by the following chart, they have either remained the same, or in some instances, even declined.

It is very disheartening, therefore, that we feel compelled to bring your attention to at least the following five major budgetary categories related to the education of exceptional children:

1. *EHA-Part B, State Formula Grant Program (P.L. 94-142 Funds)*

As evidenced by the above chart, the FY 81 budget authorizes the expenditure of $922 million for school year 1981-82 of EHA-Part B funds. This represents an increase of $48 million over the $874 million appropriated in FY 80. According to justifications accompanying the budget, "the Federal Government will continue (its) 1980 policy of providing approximately 12% of the national per pupil expenditure." It should be recalled, however, that the original authorizing language of P.L. 94-142 projected that the Federal Government should be providing 40% of the national average per pupil expenditure at this time. The justification went on to further state that the $922 million will be used during the 1981-82 school year to serve approximately 3.85 million handicapped children. This amount will cause the per pupil reimbursement received by states under P.L. 94-142 to increase by $9 to $239 per student.

It should be pointed out that the rationale for the Administration's FY 81 authorization is based upon two very conservative and controversial estimates. First, there are many individuals who would argue that the figure of 3.8 million handicapped children to be served in FY 81 is rather low. Responsible authorities speculate that the number of handicapped children served at this point could be as high as 4 million. Second, there has been considerable debate with regard to the projected rate of future inflation as it affects the national average per pupil expenditure. The Administration used the figure of 7% to arrive at its FY 81 projection. Most experts, on the other hand, anticipate that the rate of inflation at this time will be between 10 and 13.5%.

In light of these discrepancies, if even moderate projection rates were used, one could very easily justify an FY 81 budget authority for state grant programs for the handicapped to exceed $1 billion even using the 12% rate. What becomes even more startling, is the fact that if one were to use the higher projection figures for child count and rate of inflation, the $48 million increase proposed by the Administration could, in actuality, be a decrease leading to a reduction in services to the handicapped. All of the foregoing, plus the fact that even a

AGES OF ELIGIBILITY FOR SPECIAL EDUCATION
DECEMBER 1979 *

The following survey of Ages of Eligibility for Special Education services for the 50 states and the District of Columbia has been prepared by the Policy Research Center of The Council for Exceptional Children. The survey includes figures for mandated and permissive ages obtained from 1979 state statutes. Mandated ages were obtained from states' special education laws. Thus, these are the ages for which school districts must provide special education; not the ages of compulsory attendance for the states. Permissive ages are the ages in which states allow districts discretionary authority to offer services, although education is not required at the permissive ages.—JPB, JM

State	Mandated Ages	Permissive Ages	0	1	2	3	4	5	6	7	8	9	10	11	12	13	14	15	16	17	18	19	20	21	22	23	24
Alabama	between 6 & 19								×	×	×	×	×	×	×	×	×	×	×	×	×	×					
Alaska	3 thru 19					×	×	×	×	×	×	×	×	×	×	×	×	×	×	×	×	×					
Arizona	between 6 & 21	5/K						•	×	×	×	×	×	×	×	×	×	×	×	×	×	×	×	×			
Arkansas	between 6 & 21	5/K						•	×	×	×	×	×	×	×	×	×	×	×	×	×	×	×	×			
California	4.9 - 18	3-4,9, 19-20				•	•	×	×	×	×	×	×	×	×	×	×	×	×	×	×	•	•				
Colorado	between 5 & 21							×	×	×	×	×	×	×	×	×	×	×	×	×	×	×	×	×			
Connecticut	5 - 21 C	*						×	×	×	×	×	×	×	×	×	×	×	×	×	×	×	×	×			
Delaware	4 thru 20						×	×	×	×	×	×	×	×	×	×	×	×	×	×	×	×	×				
Florida	6 & 18	3-6				•	•	•	×	×	×	×	×	×	×	×	×	×	×	×	×						
Georgia	6 thru C	0-5	•	•	•	•	•	•	×	×	×	×	×	×	×	×	×	×	×	×	×						
Hawaii	under 20		×	×	×	×	×	×	×	×	×	×	×	×	×	×	×	×	×	×	×	×	×				
Idaho	to 21		×	×	×	×	×	×	×	×	×	×	×	×	×	×	×	×	×	×	×	×	×	×			
Illinois	between 3 & 21	Deaf - 6 mo.				×	×	×	×	×	×	×	×	×	×	×	×	×	×	×	×	×	×	×			
Indiana	between 3 & 21					×	×	×	×	×	×	×	×	×	×	×	×	×	×	×	×	×	×	×			
Iowa	under 21		×	×	×	×	×	×	×	×	×	×	×	×	×	×	×	×	×	×	×	×	×				
Kansas	6 thru 21 C	5/K						•	×	×	×	×	×	×	×	×	×	×	×	×	×	×	×	×			
Kentucky	under 21			×	×	×	×	×	×	×	×	×	×	×	×	×	×	×	×	×	×	×	×				
Louisiana	3-21	*under 3	•	•	•	×	×	×	×	×	×	×	×	×	×	×	×	×	×	×	×	×	×	×			
Maine	between 5 & 20	4					•	×	×	×	×	×	×	×	×	×	×	×	×	×	×	×	×				
Maryland	under 21		×	×	×	×	×	×	×	×	×	×	×	×	×	×	×	×	×	×	×	×	×				
Massachusetts	3 thru 21					×	×	×	×	×	×	×	×	×	×	×	×	×	×	×	×	×	×	×			
Michigan	under 26	TMR-to 25	×	×	×	×	×	×	×	×	×	×	×	×	×	×	×	×	×	×	×	×	×	×	×	×	×
Minnesota	4-21						×	×	×	×	×	×	×	×	×	×	×	×	×	×	×	×	×	×			
Mississippi	under 21		×	×	×	×	×	×	×	×	×	×	×	×	×	×	×	×	×	×	×	×	×				
Missouri	5 & under 21							×	×	×	×	×	×	×	×	×	×	×	×	×	×	×	×	×			
Montana	between 6 & 18*	3-5, 18-21				•	•	•	×	×	×	×	×	×	×	×	×	×	×	×	×	•	•	•			
Nebraska	5-21	* under 5	•	•	•	•	•	×	×	×	×	×	×	×	×	×	×	×	×	×	×	×	×	×			
Nevada	5 & under 18	*						×	×	×	×	×	×	×	×	×	×	×	×	×	×						
New Hampshire	over 3 under 21						×	×	×	×	×	×	×	×	×	×	×	×	×	×	×	×	×	×			
New Jersey	between 5 & 20	under 5 & over 20	•	•	•	•	•	×	×	×	×	×	×	×	×	×	×	×	×	×	×	×	×				
New Mexico	school age	5/k						•	×	×	×	×	×	×	×	×	×	×	×	×	×	×					
New York	over 5 under 21							×	×	×	×	×	×	×	×	×	×	×	×	×	×	×	×	×			
North Carolina	between 5 & 18	0-5, 18-21	•	•	•	•	•	×	×	×	×	×	×	×	×	×	×	×	×	×	×	•	•	•			
North Dakota	6-21	3-6				•	•	•	×	×	×	×	×	×	×	×	×	×	×	×	×	×	×	×			
Ohio	between 6 & 18								×	×	×	×	×	×	×	×	×	×	×	×	×						
Oklahoma	4	*					×																				
Oregon	under 21		×	×	×	×	×	×	×	×	×	×	×	×	×	×	×	×	×	×	×	×	×				
Pennsylvania	between 6 & 21								×	×	×	×	×	×	×	×	×	×	×	×	×	×	×	×			
Rhode Island	between 3 & 21					×	×	×	×	×	×	×	×	×	×	×	×	×	×	×	×	×	×	×			
South Carolina	6-21	Hearing 4-21 5/K					•	•	×	×	×	×	×	×	×	×	×	×	×	×	×	×	×	×			

$1 billion appropriation represents only one third of the $3 billion-plus authorization ceiling for FY 82, suggests that advocates must push strongly for a higher figure than the $922 offered by the Administration.

2. Preschool Incentive Grants
The FY 81 budget calls for the authorization of $25 million to be provided for preschool incentive grants. This amount, however, represents a level funding of the program with no increase over the previous year's appropriation. Because the

*Ages of Eligibility for Special Education was prepared by Joanne P. Bunte and Jean H. Mack.

number of handicapped children who are identified and served at the preschool level will increase and in conjunction with the growing rate of inflation, the provision of $25 million for this program will in actuality cause the Federal Government's per-child allotment paid to local and state education agencies to decrease from $111 per child to $105. It should be remembered that the original authority for the Preschool Incentive Program called for a Federal reimbursement of $300 per handicapped preschooler. Instead of getting closer to this original authority, meaning an authorization level of at least $66 million, the FY 81 budget is actually taking us farther away.

3. *Personnel Development, Postsecondary, and Special Studies*
Slight increases in the authorization levels of the following three programs were approved in the Administration's FY 81 budget: Special Education Personnel Development (+2.6 million); Special Studies (+1.3 million); and Regional Vocational, Adult, and Postsecondary Programs (+1.6 million). It should be noted, however, that the increase in the authorization levels for the first two programs either brings them up to, or puts them slightly above their FY 79 appropriation levels. Both of these programs were reduced during the 1980 appropriation period. The $1.6 million increase in authorizations for Regional Vocational, Adult, and Postsecondary Programs will allow the number of projects funded by this program to be expanded from 8 to 23 in FY 81.

4. *Centers, Special Programs, and Services*
The Administration's FY 81 budget maintains the following programs at their FY 80 appropriations levels: Deaf-blind Centers—$16 million; Severely Handicapped Projects—$5 million; Early Childhood Education—$20 million; Innovation and Development—$20 million; Media Services and Captioned Films—$19 million; Regional Resource Centers—$9.75 million; and Recruitment and Information—$1 million. The problem with maintaining these programs at level funding, and as has been previously discussed, is the increased rate of inflation will lead to a reduction in the services offered to handicapped children by these programs.

5. *Gifted and Talented Education*
Even though Congress passed the Gifted and Talented Children's Education Act of 1978 during its last legislative session and called for a vastly expanded Federal role in the education of these youngsters, the FY 81 budget recommends the level funding of this program. Regardless of the fact that its authorization calls for $35 million in FY 81, the Administration, nevertheless, has requested the continuance of its $6.28 million appropriation figure of FY 80.

In summary, *Insight* readers should be aware that the submission of the Administration's budget is an important initial step in the eventual expenditure of limited Federal dollars. It should be regarded, however, as just that—an initial step. In the months to come, the Congressional budget and appropriations processes will have to be carefully monitored to ensure that all exceptional children will be provided with the necessary federal financial commitment to allow them to receive the free appropriate public education and related services they need.—*JZ*

State	Age range	
South Dakota	under 21	
Tennessee	between 4 & 21	
Texas	between 3 & 21	
Utah	5-21	
Vermont	under 21	
Virginia	2 & under 21	preschool
Washington	between 6 & 21	3-5
West Virginia	between 5 & 23	under 3
Wisconsin	3-21	5/k
Wyoming	over 6 & under 21	
D.C.	information not given	

*Connecticut — Permissive when necessary below age five
Louisiana — Children under three are permissive if they have a serious handicapping condition
Montana — After 9/1/80 ages will be between 3 and 21
Nebraska — For children under three parent training in the home is provided
Nevada — Gifted-4 MR-3
Oklahoma — No minimum for multihandicapped
X — Eligibility age
● — Permissive age
Key: C — Completion K — Kindergarten TMR — Trainable Mentally Retarded

FINANCING

State Financing of Special Education

by Jeffrey J. Zettel

An investigation of individual state funding patterns, state and federal financial assistance, and per pupil expenditures for special education has been recently completed by Margaret Hodge, a social science analyst for the U.S. Commission on Civil Rights.

The investigation, entitled "State Financing of Special Education," used the Bureau of Education for the Handicapped (BEH) child count and service rates in addition to adjusted service rates to identify changes in rates of services to handicapped children from 1975-1979. Data were also collected from State education agencies (SEA's) regarding FY 78 and FY 79 state aid for special education. With regard to the federal funds noted, only Part B (P.L 94-142) grants to states were analyzed. The total federal funds for special education are not indicated.

Although Hodge cautions that the FY 79 data reported by SEA's are estimates and not actual figures, she indicates that these could be useful in reporting trends in state aid for special education. Also, some of the factors that would make it appear as though state funds are low were discovered to be the accounting procedures used by certain states "which (in reality) 'hide' some of the support services provided for the handicapped."

The report found that nationally, state funds for special education increased at an annual rate of 13.3% during the initial years of P.L. 94-142. Since that time, the annual rate of increase has risen to 16.1% for FY 78 - FY 79. Furthermore, while it would appear that state funding for special education has increased generally, the percent of the total funds for elementary and secondary education used for special education has only dropped from 3.65% to 3.63%. This slight decrease, according to Hodge, indicates that the initial concern that state funds might be taken away from nonhandicapped children and used for handicapped children is largely

NUMBER OF HANDICAPPED CHILDREN SERVED AND FISCAL YEAR ALLOCATION UNDER P.L. 94-142, BY STATE PRESCHOOL INCENTIVE GRANTS

State	Children Served 1977-78 School Year (Ages 3-5)	Allocation for Fiscal 1979 (1978-79 School Year)	Children Served 1978-79 School Year (Ages 3-5)	Allocation for Fiscal 1980 (1979-80 School Year)
NATIONAL TOTAL	200,546	$15,000,000	215,637	$17,500,000
Alabama	1,092	81,677	1,643	133,338
Alaska	243	18,175	374	30,352
Arizona	0	0	0	0
Arkansas	1,348	100,825	1,802	146,241
California	22,412	1,676,323	22,560	1,830,855
Colorado	1,971	147,423	2,113	171,480
Connecticut	3,126	233,812	2,949	239,326
Delaware	510	38,146	465	37,737
District of Columbia	588	43,980	654	53,075
Florida	5,682	424,990	5,314	431,257
Georgia	3,916	292,900	5,062	410,806
Hawaii	336	25,131	195	15,825
Idaho	622	46,523	585	47,476
Illinois	18,489	1,382,899	17,900	1,452,673
Indiana	1,290	96,487	3,389	275,034
Iowa	4,010	299,931	5,046	409,508
Kansas	1,758	131,491	2,543	206,377
Kentucky	1,728	129,247	2,058	167,017
Louisiana	6,369	476,374	5,973	484,738
Maine	688	51,460	1,184	96,087
Maryland	904	67,615	4,879	395,955
Massachusetts	5,709	427,009	5,611	455,360
Michigan	13,116	981,021	12,844	1,042,354
Minnesota	5,786	432,769	6,767	549,175
Mississippi	1,062	79,433	1,130	91,705
Missouri	5,524	413,172	6,856	556,398
Montana	776	58,042	1,204	97,711
Nebraska	2,354	176,069	2,321	188,361
Nevada	724	54,152	402	32,624
New Hampshire	308	23,037	241	19,558
New Jersey	4,996	373,680	6,164	500,239
New Mexico	434	32,461	449	36,439
New York	5,127	383,478	5,057	410,400
North Carolina	4,695	351,166	5,651	458,606
North Dakota	578	43,232	603	48,936
Ohio	5,522	413,022	5,980	485,306
Oklahoma	3,236	242,039	4,225	342,879
Oregon	2,095	156,697	1,653	134,149
Pennsylvania	9,059	677,575	8,422	683,487
Rhode Island	922	68,962	854	69,306
South Carolina	4,885	365,378	4,028	326,892
South Dakota	883	66,045	986	80,019
Tennessee	6,648	497,243	7,464	605,740
Texas	20,960	1,567,720	19,694	1,598,265
Utah	1,376	102,919	1,750	142,021
Vermont	722	54,003	807	65,492
Virginia	5,352	400,307	6,714	644,874
Washington	2,279	170,460	1,965	159,469
West Virginia	896	67,017	1,293	104,933
Wisconsin	4,629	346,230	5,198	421,843
Wyoming	504	37,697	527	42,769
American Samoa	22	1,646	20	1,623
Bureau of Indian Affairs	182	13,613	116	9,414
Guam	22	1,646	85	6,898
Northern Marianas	1	75	11	893
Puerto Rico	1,877	140,392	1,754	142,346
Trust Territory	202	15,109	103	8,359
Virgin Islands	1	75	0	0

Figures from the U.S. Office of Education as reported in *Education Daily*, August 3, 1979.

unfounded.

To gain a better perspective as to the success of P.L. 94-142, the study also investigated state service rates. Figures indicated that from the fall of 1976 to the spring of 1979, 13 states reported a decline in numbers of children served. According to Hodge, however, "to get an accurate picture, these numbers need to be translated into an accurate service rate and demographic factors should be considered since the data in Table 5 do not tell anything about the decline in the population of school age children or migratory patterns across states."

Hodge's report further indicates that when one uses the service rates adjusted for ages of eligibility in addition to the factors mentioned above (which is BEH's method of computing service rates), the rates continue to drop in 10 states. On a national basis, the service rate of 7.9% falls to 6.5% when population and eligibility ages are considered.

Finally, FY 1978 and FY 1979 figures indicated that per pupil expenditures have dropped in 12 states while state funds per pupil increased in all states but two. The range of state per pupil expenditures was found to vary from $279 in Rhode Island to $2264 in Montana for FY 1979.

In summary, this particular investigation found the level of state special education funding, as well as most state per pupil expenditures for all but two states, has increased since 1975.

PL 94-142

Information sources PL 94-142: Education of All the Handicapped

3

by Barbara Clarke and David W. Parish

INTRODUCTION

Since the passage of P.L. 94--142, the Education for All Handicapped Children Act of 1975, on November 29, 1975, mandating that handicapped students be educated in the least restrictive environments possible, there has been an increasing demand for information related to the education of the handicapped. A common observation of teachers and administrators is that tedious hours of paperwork and conferences are required to plan individualized programs and meet governmental mandates.

Prior to 1975, as well as since that date, many individuals, institutions, state and federal government agencies have been involved in the identification and dissemination of special education information. As of 1979, sources on education of the handicapped include sophisticated data banks, detailed abstracts, and lesser--known government sources.

This two--part bibliographical essay is intended to suggest resources available to educators of exceptional children from a wide variety of sources. This overview is necessarily selective but it is hoped it will serve as a guide to some of the most important of the many special education resources currently available.

Part One of this essay introduces significant resources available for curriculum development and implementation in special education from mainly non--governmental sources.

Part Two focuses on information related to P.L. 94--142 available from federal and state government publications.

PART ONE
CURRICULUM RESOURCES

ABSTRACTS AND INDEXES

Although not exclusively concerned with special education, *Resources in Education*[1] (formerly *Research in Education*[2]), a monthly publication which abstracts and indexes non--journal literature dealing with all aspects of education, is an important source of special education information and may be the most widely available resource in this field at the present time.

Resources in Education indexes and abstracts materials originating mainly from non--commercial sources, such as state and locally developed curriculum guides, reports from institutions and committees, teacher developed handbooks and manuals, teacher/librarian developed bibliographies of professional materials and materials to be used by children and a wide range of other types of resources.

These materials are collected, indexed and abstracted by clearing houses established across the country for this purpose by the U.S. Office of Education. The various clearing houses together comprise the ERIC (Educational Resources Information Center) system, currently administered by the National Institute of Education. Most of the materials acquired by the clearing houses for indexing and abstracting are also filmed and reproduced in their entirety on microfiche. The microfiche and *Resources in Education* are available separately on a subscription basis. Many materials cited in RIE may also be ordered in hard copy from the ERIC Document Reproduction Service. *Resources in Education* is computer searchable through Bibliographic Retrieval Service, Lockheed Information Systems, System Development Corporation and many other data base search services.

Classroom teachers should contact their state department of education for information on computer searches of *Resources in Education* and copies of selected microfiche that may be available to them at no charge.

ERIC clearing houses are affiliated with educational institutions or nonprofit agencies, and each clearing house specializes in a certain subject area, e.g. teacher training, adult education. The clearing house concerned with the education of exceptional children is based in Reston, Virginia at the headquarters of the Council for Exceptional Children. In addition to serving as a clearing house for documents submitted to the ERIC system, the Council for Exceptional Children is also a major publisher and distributor of texts, monographs, journals and a wide variety of other resources in special education. *Exceptional Child Education Resources*[3] (formerly *Exceptional Child Education Abstracts*[4]) is a monthly publication of the Council for Exceptional Children that indexes and abstracts books, chapters in books, journal articles and ERIC documents concerned with the education of handicapped and gifted children. This publication is probably the single most comprehensive source of special education information currently available.

The indexing terms used in *Exceptional Child Education Resources* are the same as those used in *Resources in Education*. *Exceptional Child Education Resources* is searchable by computer through the same sources that provide computer searches for *Resources in Education*.

The recently discontinued *Developmental Disabilities Abstracts*[5] (formerly *Mental Retardation and Developmental Disabilities Abstracts*[6] and *Mental Retardation Abstracts*[7]), published by the Rehabilitation Services Administration of the United States Department of Health, Education and Welfare, provided indexing and abstracting coverage for books, chapters in books, journal articles and selected ERIC documents concerned

with theoretical and practical aspects of retardation from many professional perspectives including medicine, social work and education.

Indexing and abstracting coverage of the literature concerned exclusively with speech and hearingimpaired individuals is provided by the American Speech and Hearing Association's *DSH Abstracts.*[8] This quarterly publication covers books and journal articles, many of which are research oriented, although some resources of a more practical nature are also included.

The Chicorel Index to Reading Disabilities[9], published in 1974, provides indexing and abstracting information for more than 1400 books and journal articles concerned with various aspects of reading disabilities appropriate for teachers, librarians, psychologists and other professionals. Some parent resources and instructional materials for use by reading disabled students are also included. *The Chicorel Index to Learning Disorders: Books*[10], published in 1975, indexes and abstracts 2500 books for professionals, parents and learning disabled students.

These two works were merged to create the *Chicorel Abstracts to Reading and Learning Disabilities*[11], first published in 1975, and the *Chicorel Index to Reading and Learning Disabilities*[12], first published in 1976. Both these works are now published on an annual basis. The *Chicorel Abstracts to Reading and Learning Disabilities* indexes and abstracts the journal literature in these fields while the *Chicorel Index to Reading and Learning Disabilities* indexes and abstracts the book literature. (If this information on the Chicorel indexes sounds confusing, wait until you attempt to use the volumes.) The editor's intention in offering these volumes is to provide quick and easy access to the literature of these fields. Unfortunately, the confusing labeling and numbering of these volumes seriously hampers their use as ready reference aids.

Current Index to Journals in Education (CIJE)[13] indexes and annotates journal articles appearing in more than 700 education and educationrelated periodicals. Articles included in CIJE cover a broad spectrum of topics in education including much information of interest to educators of exceptional children. Indexing of articles in CIJE is done primarily by the network of ERIC Clearinghouses which also indexes documents for *Resources in Education*. The same indexing terms are used for both publications. CIJE is computer searchable through the same data base services as *Resources in Education*.

Education Index,[14] an H. W. Wilson publica

tion, provides subject indexing but not annotations for approximately 250 periodicals as well as year-- books and monographs concerned with education. Like CIJE, *Education Index* covers a wealth of material of interest to teachers and others concerned with the education of exceptional children. The subject headings used in *Education Index* are usually more specific than those used in CIJE. For this reason, searching in *Education Index* is often more rewarding than manual searching in CIJE. *Education Index* is not computer searchable.

ANNUALS AND LITERATURE REVIEWS

The Review of Special Education[15], now in its third installment, is a compendium of articles that provide reviews of the literature or state of the art surveys of selected topics in special educa-- tion. All articles include extensive references and a subject index is included for each edition. This publication is not intended to present a compre-- hensive review of developments in the field of special education. However, each volume of this publication treats a wide variety of timely topics covering both theoretical and practical aspects of this field. The latest edition of this work includes a review of mainstreaming issues.

While each article in the *Review of Special Education* is written especially for inclusion in that publication, much of the information in the *Year-- book of Special Education*[16] is excerpted from works originally published elsewhere. The *Year-- book of Special Education* is intended as a ready reference aid and addresses the informational needs of the handicapped, their families, professionals who work with the handicapped and others in-- terested in special education. The latest edition arranges information mainly under type of excep-- tional child with additional sections on "Special Education (General)," "Mainstreaming," "Rights and Litigation" and "Teacher Preparation." Among the information provided in this publication are a listing of agencies serving the handicapped and lists of reading materials about handicapping conditions appropriate for reading by parents and children.

Most of the articles included in *Exceptional Children: A Reference Book*[17] have also appeared previously in other publications. This work is mainly a collection of reprinted journal articles that provide basic introductory information on handicapping conditions and learning disorders. Several charts, glossaries of terms and various other miscellanea related to handicapping conditions and learning disorders are also provided.

Mainstream Currents: Reprints from Excep-- tional Children, 1968--1974[18] serves as a review of the literature on mainstreaming that appeared in this journal during the years cited. Articles are grouped into broad topical areas and reproduced in their entirety.

BIBLIOGRAPHIES

Mainstreaming Handicapped Children: Toward a Comprehensive Bibliography[19] is an unannotated listing of journal articles, books, reports and pre-- sented papers published from 1950--1977. This is an on--going bibliography and users are requested to submit additional references for inclusion in future editions. Citations are indexed by author and handicapping condition.

Blindness, Visual Impairment, Deaf--Blindness: Annotated Listing of the Literature, 1953--1975,[20] provides comprehensive coverage of the nonmedical literature related to blindness including books, reports and journal articles. Much information of practical use to educators can be found in this volume. This publication is updated semi--annually in the periodical *Blindness, Visual Impairment, Deaf--Blindness: Listing of Current Literature.*[21]

Bibliography on Deafness[22] is a classified listing of journal articles and reports concerned with deafness from a variety of professional per-- spectives including education.

The Bibliography of Deafness: The Volta Review, 1899--1976: American Annals of the Deaf, 1847--1976[23] is a comprehensive listing of articles that appeared in these journals from their inception until 1976. Citations are arranged chron-- ologically under various subject headings offering "a broad overview of the past and present history in the field of education of the deaf" (Foreword).

Those responsible for pre-- and in--service teacher training will find the *National Catalog of Films in Special Education*[24] a valuable resource. This publication indexes and annotates 900 films concerned with special education dating from the 1930's to 1975. More recent films will be included in the next edition of this catalog.

Materials for pre-- and in--service teacher edu-- cation can also be found in *Audio Visual Resources for Instructional Development*[25] which indexes approximately 1,000 resources that may be used as models for teaching, implementing and adminis-- tering programs for the handicapped. Pre-- and in-- service films and other audiovisual materials con-- cerned with physical education, recreation, sports, camping, outdoor education and perceptual motor activities for the handicapped can be found in *Annotated Listing of Films: Physical Education and Recreation for Impaired, Disabled, and Handi-capped Persons.*[26]

Both professional and child--use materials are listed in the *Exceptional Child Education Resources Topical Bibliography Series.*[27] These computer generated bibliographies contain abstracts of selected references from annual volumes of *Exceptional Child Education Resources*, cited earlier in this essay.

Up until very recently, the identification of child--use materials appropriate for special education was possible only by consulting numerous individual bibliographies. With the publication of the various National Information Center for Special Education Materials (NICSEM) indexes,[28,29,30,31,32] the bibliographical literature of special education instructional materials has finally come of age. These indexes truly represent a milestone in the bibliographic history of special education.

These indexes have been generated from the data base concerned exclusively with special education instructional materials developed by the National Center on Educational Media and Materials for the Handicapped (NCEMMH) at Ohio State University during the years 1974--1977. This data base, referred to as NIMIS I (National Instructional Materials Information System), was and is still used for generating lists of special education resources and for on--line searching. This data base was developed under a contract with the U.S. Office of Education which expired in August 1977. A new contract was awarded to the National Information Center for Education Media (NICEM) at the University of Southern California in October of 1977 to continue and expand upon the work begun at the Ohio State University. As a result of this new contract the National Information Center for Special Education Materials (NICSEM) was created. The NICSEM indexes are the first publications of this new National Center.

The *Master Catalog of NIMIS/NICSEM Special Education Information*[28] contains the entire NIMIS I data base in print form. The main section of this index is arranged alphabetically by title and contains abstracts for approximately 36,000 print and non--print instructional materials (films, textbooks, kits, games, etc.). Abstracts provide content and physical descriptions, grade level (K--Adult), author, publisher, date and series information. Although the NICSEM catalogs have been advertised as including prices for materials cited, prices are not included for most items listed in any of the NICSEM

catalogs. A subject index and a source directory listing publishers' names and addresses are provided. The *Index to Assessment Devices, Testing Instruments and Parent Materials,*[29] *Index to Media and Materials for the Deaf, Hard of Hearing, Speech Impaired,*[30] *Index to Media and Materials for the Mentally Retarded, Specific Learning Disabled, Emotionally Disturbed,*[31] and *Index to Media and Materials for the Visually Handicapped, Ortho-pedically Impaired, Other Health Impaired*[32] are all subsets of the *Master Catalog* from which information relevant only to particular audiences or handicapped populations has been extracted. These specialized indexes allow quicker access to appropriate materials than the more cumbersome *Master Catalog*. The format and abstract content is the same for these indexes as for the *Master Catalog*. All of the NICSEM catalogs are available in both print form and on microfiche. The NIMIS I data base is also computer searchable through Bibliographic Retrieval Service and Lockheed's DIALOG.

A related publication, the *NICEM Index to Special Education Non--print Materials,*[33] which has not yet been published, will index only non-print media. For further information on present and future products and services of the National Information Center for Special Education Materials (NICSEM) see issues of the Center's newsletter, *Frankly Speaking.*[34]

NIMIS Bibliographies[35] are yet further resources generated from the NIMIS I data base. These are very brief topical bibliographies containing anywhere from 20 to 100 abstracts of child--use materials. The content of the abstracts in these bibliographies is almost identical to the information provided in the NICSEM indexes for the same item since they are generated from the same data base. However, the NIMIS bibliographies provide price, ISBN and ISSN numbers (if available) for each item cited as well as audiovisual equipment required for use with the item (if any), information which the NICSEM indexes do not provide. All items cited in the NIMIS bibliographies are of course also included in the *Master Catalog of NIMIS/NICSEM Special Education* mentioned above. The purpose of the NIMIS bibliographies is to offer easy to use, inexpensive aids for the quick identification of resources targeted to meet very specific needs.

The NIMIS bibliographies are produced by the National Center on Educational Media and Materials for the Handicapped (NCEMMH) at the Ohio State University. With the termination of federal grant funds in August, 1977, NCEMMH became a project of the Faculty for Exceptional Children at the Ohio State University and still continues to disseminate information and publish products for special education. Further information about NIMIS bibliographies and other resources available from NCEMMH can be found in issues of the NCEMMH newsletter, *The Directive Teacher.* [36]

While the NICSEM and NIMIS publications cited above are much needed and very welcome additions to special education instructional materials resources, they certainly cannot answer every special education resource need. One of many other very useful bibliographies of learning resources available is *Films -- Too Good for Words* [36] which has become a "classic" in film bibliographies. This work presents brief annotations of non--narrated films that can be very useful for the entertainment and instruction of deaf and hearing--impaired persons of all ages. Three "classic" bibliographies of high interest/low vocabulary tradebooks and textbooks appropriate for the slow or reluctant reader are *Books for the Retarded Reader,* [38] now in its 6th edition; *Gateways to Readable Books,* [39] now in its 5th edition; and *Good Reading for Poor Readers,* [40] now in its 10th edition.

The latest (third) edition of *Large Type Books in Print* [41] lists 3300 titles of books for use by the blind and visually handicapped. Included is a "Children's Books" section which lists 300 titles (both fiction and non--fiction) as well as a "Text-book Section" which includes textbooks available in large print for both children and adults. Entries are arranged by subject, with author and title indexes.

An important concern of the mainstreaming movement is the development of understanding of the handicapped among the non--handicapped. *Notes from a Different Drummer: A Guide to Juvenile Fiction Portraying the Handicapped* [42] provides annotations and evaluative information for over 300 children's books useful for this pur--pose. This work also provides guidance for the use of these materials with children. *Special People behind the 8--Ball: An Annotated Bibliography of Literature Classified by Handicapping Conditions* [43] describes fiction and non--fiction books for children and adults that can be helpful for developing a sensitivity to and an understanding of the needs and concerns of handicapped persons.

I would like to close Part One of this essay by mentioning a very new publication that may be helpful to teachers, librarians and other persons concerned with locating resources appropriate for the mainstreaming of exceptional children. *Education Unlimited* [44] is a new journal scheduled for publication in April 1979 especially designed for "mainstream" educators. In addition to providing articles on topics of interest to teachers and administrators concerned with educating students in least restrictive environments, *Education Unlimited* will also provide reviews of new teaching resources.

Resources for curriculum development and implementation in special education are quickly multiplying. It is hoped that this overview has highlighted some of the most useful of the many resources presently available. Several additional curriculum resources produced by government agencies are cited in Part Two of this essay.

NOTES

1. *Resources in Education.* 1975– . M. $42.70. S.A. Cum. $18.00. ERIC–Educational Resources Information Center, Processing and Reference Facility, 4833 Rugby Ave., Suite 303, Bethesda, MD 20014. (Sub--scr. to Superintendent of Documents, U.S. Government Printing Office, Washington, DC 20402). Editor: Catherine Welsh. ISSN 0098–0897.

2. *Research in Education.* 1966–1974. M. ERIC–Educational Resources Information Center, Processing and Reference Facility, 4833 Rugby Ave., Suite 303, Bethesda, MD 20014. ISSN 0034--5229.

3. *Exceptional Child Education Resources.* 1977– . Q. $25.00 members; $50.00 institutions. Council for Exceptional Children, 1920 Association Drive, Reston, VA 22091. LC 78--640749. ISSN 0160–4309.

4. *Exceptional Child Education Abstracts.* 1969--1977. Q. Council for Exceptional Children, 1920 Association Drive, Reston, VA 22091. LC 76--6503. ISSN 0014–4010.

5. *Developmental Disabilities Abstracts.* 1977–1978. Q. Developmental Disabilities Office, U.S. Dept. of Health, Education and Welfare, 330 C St. S. W., Washington, DC 20201. LC 76–640457.

6. *Mental Retardation and Developmental Disabilities Abstracts.* 1975–1976. Q. Developmental Disabilities Office, U.S. Dept. of Health, Education and Welfare, 330 Independence Ave, S. W., Washington, DC 20201. LC 76–640457. ISSN 0361–3798.

7. *Mental Retardation Abstracts.* 1964–1973. Q. Division of Developmental Disabilities, U.S. Department

of Health, Education and Welfare, Washington, DC. Prepared by Herner Information Services, Inc., 2100 M St. N.W., Washington, DC 20037. LC 66--60248. ISSN 0025--9691.

8. *DSH Abstracts.* 1960-- . Q. $15.00. Co--sponsors: American Speech and Hearing Association and Gallaudet College. Available from: Deafness, Speech and Hearing Publications, Inc., Gallaudet College, Washington, DC 20002. Editor: Ernest J. Moncada. Also available in microfilm from University Microfilm International, 300 North Zeeb Road, Ann Arbor, MI 48106. ISSN 0011--5150.

9. Marietta Chicorel. *Chicorel Index to Reading Disabilities.* New York, Chicorel, 1974. $66.00. ISBN 0--87729--084--5.

10. Marietta Chicorel. *Chicorel Index to Learning Disorders: Books.* New York, Chicorel, 1975. $66.00. 2v. LC 75--9713. ISBN 0--87729--289--4; 0--87729--394--7.

11. *Chicorel Abstracts to Reading and Learning Disabilities.* 1975-- . A. Price varies. Chicorel Library Publishing Corp., 215 Central Park West, New York 10024. Editor: Marietta Chicorel. ISSN 0149--533.

12. *Chicorel Index to Reading and Learning Disabilities.* 1976-- . A. Price varies. Chicorel Library Publishing Corp., 215 Central Park West, New York 10024. Editor: Marietta Chicorel. ISSN 0149--5496.

13. *Current Index to Journals in Education.* 1969-- . M. $50.00. S--A cum. $90.00. Macmillan Information (Subsidiary of Macmillan Pub. Co., Inc.), 866 Third Ave., New York 10022. Editor: Thomas M. Wright. ISSN 0011--3565.

14. *Education Index: An Author--Subject Index to Educational Publications in the English Language.* 1929-- . M. (Sept.--June). Service basis. H.W. Wilson Co., 950 University Ave., Bronx, New York 10452. Editor: Marylouise Hewitt. ISSN 0013--1385.

15. *Review of Special Education.* 1973-- . Approx. A. Price varies. Grune & Stratton, Inc. (Subsidiary of Harcourt Brace Jovanovich, Inc.), 111 Fifth Ave., New York 10003. Editor: Lester Mann. ISSN 0091--5580.

16. *Yearbook of Special Education.* 1975/76-- . A. Price varies. Marquis Academic Media, 200 E. Ohio St., Chicago, IL 60611. LC 75--13803. ISSN 0146--2040.

17. *Exceptional Children: A Reference Book.* Guilford, CT, Special Learning Corporation, 1978. $64.00. 575p. ISBN 0--89568--077--7.

18. G. J. Warfield, ed. *Mainstream Currents: Reprints from Exceptional Children, 1968--1974.* Reston, VA, The Council for Exceptional Children, 1974. $5.50 pa. 250p. LC 74--29037.

19. *Mainstreaming Handicapped Children: Toward a Comprehensive Bibliography.* Completed primarily by JoAnn Van Schaik; foreword by Thomas M. Stephens. Columbus, National Center on Educational Media and Materials for the Handicapped, 1978. $8.75. (NCEMMH Publication no. NC--78:911)

20. Mary Kinsey Bauman, comp. *Blindness, Visual Impairment, Deaf--Blindness: Annotated Listing of the Literature, 1953--1975.* Philadelphia, Temple University Press, 1976. $25.00. 537p. LC 76--14724. ISBN 0--87722--067--0.

21. *Blindness, Visual Impairment, Deaf--Blindness: Listing of Current Literature.* 1976-- . S.A. $5.00. Nevil Interagency Referral Service, 919 Walnut St., Rm 400, Philadelphia, PA 19107. ISSN 0363--7689.

22. Gary Austin, comp. *Bibliography on Deafness.* Silver Spring, MD, National Association of the Deaf, 1975. $4.00 pa. 76p. LC 76--14529. ISBN 0--913072--20--6.

23. George W. Fellendorf, ed. *Bibliography on Deafness: The Volta Review, 1899--1976: American Annals of the Deaf, 1847--1976.* Rev. ed. Washington, DC, Alexander Graham Bell Association for the Deaf, c1977. $10.00. 272p. LC 77--86323. ISBN 0--88200--111--6.

24. *National Catalog of Films in Special Education: An Annotated List of Almost 900 Films for Teachers, Paraprofessionals and Parents on Various Aspects of Special Education.* Compiled by the staff of the National Center on Educational Media and Materials for the Handicapped and the New York State Education Department, Area Learning Resource Center, Albany, NY. 2d ed. Columbus, National Center on Educational Media and Materials for the Handicapped at the Ohio State University, 1978 (Distributed by Ohio State University Press, Publications Sales Division). (NCEMMH Publication No.: NC--78:201) $7.95.

25. Thomas Wilds, Barbara Lewis and Sharon Waldmon, comps. *Audiovisual Resources for Instructional Development.* Reston, VA, Council for Exceptional Children, 1975. 214p. LC 75--13595. Out of print.

26. Information and Research Utilization Center in Physical Education and Recreation for the Handicapped. *Annotated Listing of Films: Physical Education and Recreation for Impaired, Disabled and Handicapped Persons.* 2d ed. Washington, American Alliance for

Health, Physical Education and Recreation, 1976. $7.95. (ERIC Document ED 150 828) 128p.

27. *Exceptional Child Education Resources Topical Bib-- liography Series.* 19?-- . $4.00 per bibliography. Council for Exceptional Children, 1920 Association Drive, Reston, VA 22091. May also be available as ERIC Documents.

28. National Information Center for Special Education Materials. *Master Catalog of NIMIS/NICSEM Special Education Information: Contains the Total NIMIS I Data Base Developed at Ohio State University, Includes 36,000 Abstracts Describing in Detail Media and Materials Applicable to the Education of the Handicapped.* Los Angeles, National Information Center for Special Education Materials, University of Southern California, 1978. $121.00. 2v. LC 78--53042. ISBN 0--89320--014--X. Copies are available for reference at state and local Special Education Instructional Materials Centers.

29. _____ . *Index to Assessment Devices, Testing Instruments and Parent Materials.* Los Angeles, National Information Center for Special Education, University of Southern California, 1978. $33.00. 784p. LC 78--60575. ISBN 0--89320--020--4. Copies are available for reference at state and local Special Education Instructional Materials Centers.

30. _____ . *Index to Media and Materials for the Deaf, Hard of Hearing, Speech Impaired.* Los Angeles, National Information Center for Special Education Materials, University of Southern California, 1978. $60.00. 894p. LC 78--53036. ISBN 0--89320--015--8. Copies are available for reference at state and local Special Education Instructional Materials Centers.

31. _____ . *Index to Media and Materials for the Men-- tally Retarded, Specific Learning Disabled, Emotional-- ly Disturbed.* Los Angeles, National Information Center for Special Education Materials, University of Southern California, 1978. $55.00. 1090p. LC 78--53031. ISBN 0--89320--016--6. Copies are available for reference at state and local Special Education Instructional Materials Centers.

32. _____ . *Index to Media and Materials for the Visual-- ly Handicapped, Orthopedically Impaired, Other Health Impaired.* Los Angeles, National Informa-- tion Center for Special Education Materials, University of Southern California, 1978. $40.00. 1130p. LC 78--53103. ISBN 0--89320--017--4. Copies are avail-- able for reference at state and local Special Education Instructional Materials Centers.

33. _____ . *NICEM Catalog to Special Education Non-- print Materials.* Los Angeles, National Information Center for Special Education Materials, University of

Southern California, forthcoming. $47.00.

34. *Frankly Speaking.* 1978--. Q. Free. University of Southern California/National Information Center for Special Education, University Park (RAN) 2 fl., Los Angeles, CA 90007. Address subscriptions to: Harriet Cellini.

35. *NIMIS Bibliographies.* 1977-- . Approx. $4.00 per bibliography. National Center on Educational Media and Materials for the Handicapped at the Ohio State University, distributed by Ohio State University Press, Publications Sales Division, 2070 Neil Ave., Columbus, OH 43210. Copies of all NIMIS bib-- liographies have been distributed to all state and local Special Education Instructional Materials Centers. NIMIS bibliographies may soon be available as ERIC Documents.

36. *The Directive Teacher.* 1978-- . Q. Free. National Center on Educational Media and Materials for the Handicapped, Ohio State University, 365 Arps Hall, 1945 North St., Columbus, OH 43210. Editor: Thomas M. Stephens.

37. Salvatore J. Parlato. *Films -- Too Good for Words: A Directory of Non--Narrated 16mm Films.* New York, Bowker, 1972 (c1973). $13.95. 209p. LC 72--12831. ISBN 0--8352--0618--1.

38. J. A. Richardson, et al. *Books for the Retarded Reader.* 6th ed. Mystic, CT, Verry, Lawrence, Inc., 1977. $8.00 pa. 188p. ISBN 0--85563--152--X.

39. Dorothy Withrow, Helen B. Carey, and Bertha M. Hirzel. *Gateways to Readable Books: An Annotated Graded List of Books in Many Fields for Adolescents Who Are Reluctant to Read or Find Reading Dif-- ficult.* 5th ed. New York, H.W. Wilson, 1975. $12.00. 299p. LC 75--12933. ISBN 0--8242--0566--9.

40. George Daniel Spache. *Good Reading for Poor Read-- ers.* 10th rev. ed. Champaign, IL, Garrard Pub. Co., 1978. $5.95 pa. 284p. ISBN 0--8116--6013--3.

41. *Large Type Books in Print.* 1970-- . Irreg. Price varies. R.R. Bowker Co., 1180 Avenue of the Ameri-- cas, New York 10036. LC 78--647141. ISSN 0163--3198.

42. Barbara Baskin and Karen Harris, eds. *Notes from a Different Drummer: A Guide to Juvenile Fiction Portraying the Handicapped.* New York, Bowker, 1977. $15.95. 375p. LC 77--15067. ISBN 0--8352--0978--4.

43. June Mullins and Suzanne Wolfe. *Special Children behind the 8--Ball: An Annotated Bibliography of Literature Classified by Handicapping Conditions.*

Johnstown, PA, Mafex Associates, 1975. $9.95. 202p. LC 74–92371. ISBN 0--87804--255--5.

44. *Education Unlimited.* Scheduled to begin publication in April 1979. $12.00 individuals; $16.00 institutions. Educational Resources Center, 1834 Meetinghouse Rd., Boothwyn, PA 19061. Editor: Barbara Aiello. Coordinating Editor: Grace J. Warfield. Executive Editor: Floyd E. McDowell.

PART TWO
GOVERNMENT PUBLICATIONS

Federal and state publications concerning education of the handicapped are restricted according to the legal responsibilities of the particular issuing agencies. The subject index to the 1978 *United States Government Manual* lists eight federal agencies concerned with the handicapped population. The most important agency of these, the U.S. Office of Education, issues an extremely useful annual publication summarizing noteworthy provisions of Public Law 94--142. The 1977 annual report of the National Advisory Committee on the Handicapped, *Individualized Education Program; Key to an Appropriate Education for the Handicapped Child*[1], covered implementation, teacher preparation, and particular program categories such as physical education, recreation, and leisure activities. This latter title and the 1976 report, *The Unfinished Revolution, Education for the Handicapped*[2], both serve as starting points for administrators and teachers familiarizing themselves with program possibilities.

Although public--service librarians might consider the *Monthly Catalog of United States Government Publications*[3] a natural primary source for reports on the Education for All Handicapped Children Act of 1975, a search using the legal title as a subject proves futile. Instead, most entries are found under the category of "Handicapped Education." The *Monthly Catalog Semiannual Index* for 1978 produces a further bibliographic source, *The Handicapped, SB--037*[4], a member of the Special Bibliography series produced by the Superintendent of Documents. All 37 entries in SB--037 have at least a peripheral relationship with handicapped education ranging from *American Education* reprints to an actual copy of P. L. 94–142.

As with many other subject categories of federal publications, privately published bibliographic aids are very useful. Thus, the *CIS Index and Abstracts*[5] provide the earliest Congressional coverage of P.L. 94--142 directly under the official

title of the law. Those interested in legislative research may easily locate testimony by Terrell H. Bell, then Commissioner of Education, or the philosophic position of the Council for Exceptional Children, for instance. A second CIS Product, *American Statistics Index and Abstracts,*[6] proves useful in searching the categories of "Special Education" and "Handicapped Children." Data on federal funding of special education, children served by educational agencies, minority students placed in special classes for the mentally retarded, and those receiving individual instruction are examples of 1977 citations.

Government periodicals offer a meager source compared with the previously mentioned statistical and Congressional hearing sources. A search of the *Cumulative Index to U.S. Government Periodicals*[7] for 1975 finds slightly more than 20 articles on handicapped education with most pertaining to mainstreaming and individual education. Those from 1976 to the present offer little more. However, two government serials offer regular features of interest. *Programs for the Handicapped*[8], authored by the Office for Handicapped Individuals, contains a useful ongoing listing of new publications both government and non--governmental. *Mental Retardation and the Law, a Report on Status of Current Court Cases*[9] is invaluable for administrators needing to keep up--to--date on landmark opinions concerning classification, commitment, confidentiality, education, employment and even sterilization of mentally handicapped individuals.

Several lesser--known official sources are issued by the Department of Health, Education and Welfare. The *Publications Catalog of the U.S. Department of Health, Education and Welfare*[10], cumulative from July 1976 to December 1977, contains several fairly obscure titles such as "A Study: The Level of Awareness in a Low Income Community Regarding Handicapping Conditions in Children" as well as many other sources which can also be found in the *Monthly Catalog.* This catalog is the first by HEW since 1975 and is based on the GPO's automated information–gathering reviews system; it has received excellent commendation. A second valuable HEW product is *Research Related to Children*[11] which includes reports on research funded by the federal government, in progress or recently completed. The final products reported in this abstract sometimes are in the form of official publications, but more likely, are published as journal articles or books. Bulletin No. 40 (September 1977–February 1978) includes over 75 pertinent studies ranging from the "Special Education

Early Childhood Team Teaching Project" to "Methods for Language Development in Deaf Students." Much of this research is authored by professionals in the "field" and includes contact addresses. Usually a special bibliography is featured, such as "Cognitive Aspects of Reading and Mathematics Learning" (No. 39), "Child Abuse and Neglect" (No. 31) and "Perceptual Motor Abilities: A Bibliography" (No. 36).

In considering special curriculum materials for teachers of the handicapped, Uncle Sam does little more than distribute the funds as already noted. However, the *Catalog of NIE Education Products of 1975*[12] proved an outstanding venture in this area. It was the "first of its kind published by NIE and represented the accumulated knowledge of educational researchers in the form of products developed at a cost in excess of $100 million." Volume II is concerned solely with "Educational Equity," including over 100 texts, kits, multi-media and curriculum materials with abstracts, intended use and ordering information for the handicapped. A publication of value is the National Audiovisual Center's *Catalog of United States Government Produced Audiovisual Materials*[13] The 1978 edition, titled *A Reference List of Audio-visual Materials Produced by the United States Government*[14], includes over 125 sources listed under "Special Education." These are mainly of use for in-service education or teacher-training institutions. This basic catalog is presently updated with supplements. *Special Education*[15] includes over 300 additional sources and was issued in October 1977. The Bureau of Education for the Handicapped continues its popular *Catalog of Captioned Films for the Deaf*[16] supplemented by the *Catalog of Captioned Films for the Deaf, 1977-78, Theatrical Films and Educational Films for Adults*[17].

Publication lists can be a useful awareness source with several individual agencies issuing them irregularly. As examples, *Selected Publications Concerning the Handicapped*[18] from the U.S. Office for the Handicapped includes a section on education while many of the titles listed in the President's Committee on Mental Retardation *Publications List*[19] pertain to education of educable mentally retarded children.

Library of Congress Publications in Print, Spring 1978[20] is a comprehensive source for titles under its jurisdiction. Mainly concerned with the blind and physically handicapped, a mix of titles can be located ranging from *Update*, a newsletter reporting on current topics of interest to librarians

and volunteers to *Volunteers Who Produce Books: Braille, Braille Large Type, Tape.*

The scope of state publications covers a wide range of studies from broad developmental disability plans to practical curriculum guides. Fortunately, the ERIC information system includes many of these worthwhile titles. The *Monthly Checklist of State Publications*[21] issued by the Library of Congress lists 40 to 50 studies annually pertaining specifically to handicapped education, such as the Illinois Office of Education study on "Education for All Handicapped Children Act, P.L. '94-142' " found on page 125 of the February 1979 issue. However, perservering users must wait for the annual subject index or scan pertinent agencies involved in this field. A listing of state agencies concerned with the handicapped may be found in the *State Administrative Officials Classified by Function* under "Mental Retardation" and "Vocational Rehabilitation" categories[22].

Ingenuity becomes the "name-of-the-game" for lesser-known specialized bibliographies with *Child Abuse and Neglect Research, Projects and Publications*[23] as an example. Various studies on the problems of the mentally retarded at home are found in it as well as on brain injury caused by striking children. Issued by the National Center on Child Abuse and Neglect, this unique resource certainly would be useful for teachers and health specialists dealing with such professionally demanding situations. A *Resource Guide to Literature on Barrier Free Environments with Selected Annotations 1977*[24] by the Architectural and Transportation Barrier Compliance Board serves as another unique state-of-the-art with separate chapters on "Schools -- General" and "Schools -- Post-Secondary." The *Compliance Board Annual Report*[25], issued since 1974, proves an interesting resource for the latest goals and regulations. Another unlikely information source is the U.S. House Committee on Science and Technology which has a general commitment to improve the educational situation for the handicapped. *Research Programs to Aid the Handicapped Hearings*[26], issued in 1976, explained new products such as reading aids while it explored future government aid to the handicapped.

Several other representative bibliographies include the *Bibliography of Secondary Materials for Teaching Handicapped Studies* from the U.S. President's Committee on Employment of the Handicapped in 1977[27], and *Transportation for the Handicapped, Selected References* from the U.S. Transportation Department[28] Incidentally, the DOT is not assigned any responsibility for the handicapped in the *Government Manual.*

The gigantic three--volume U.S. National Institutes of Health *Indexes to the Epilepsy Access-- sions of the Epilepsy Information Systems*[29] of June 1978 is mentioned as another example of comprehensiveness thanks to the computer age. These indexes contain a collection of over 35,000 documents concerned with epilepsy and represent 90 percent of the worldwide literature on the sub-- ject since 1968. Although only a small percentage of the citations concern education, knowledge of this information system would be valuable to all educators working with the physically handicapped and learning disabled.

As previously noted, locating quality state government titles can be a time--consuming chore with the final result of questionable worth. A guide such as *Instructional Materials for Children with Learning Disabilities*[30], issued by the Illinois De-- partment of Public Instruction, is an unusual find. However, other excellent sources of quasi--state publications for the deaf--blind now are dissemi-- nated by the nine regional centers. In cooperation with the California State Department of Education, the Southwest Region Deaf--Blind Center issued a bibliography, *Proceedings and Publications of Regional Deaf--Blind Centers 1970--1077*[31] listing over 250 manuals, handbooks for parents, and curriculum guides covering subjects from sex educa-- tion to use of sign language. The same dual aus-- pices also produced *Literature on the Deaf Blind, an Annotated Bibliography*[32] in 1976.

A final burgeoning category of state publica-- tions related to Public Law 94--142 are the annual programs, amended plans, and special education handbooks issued by state departments of educa-- tion. These lengthy reports are fairly identical in their statement of goals, timetables, policy prior-- ities, child identification, individualized education programs (IEP), procedural safeguards, and explana-- tions of least--restrictive environments. Sometimes by--products of these plans include valuable book-- lets such as the Louisiana State Department of Education's public--relation pamphlets on "Child Search," the "Learning Resources System" and "Educational Services for the Homebound and Hospital." A second example is the Maryland State Department of Education Division of Special Education's "IED, Individualized Educational Plans." One example in the comprehensive program category is the *Georgia Special Education Annual Program Plan, Public Law 94--142*[33].

A further source provides a "reference guide to federal programs and private agencies that offer benefits, research materials and services for the disabled" (*Rehabilitation Literature*, January 1978, p. 29). This is the U.S. Rehabilitation Services Administration *Ready Reference Guide: Resources for Disabled People, a Handbook for Service Prac-- tioners and Disabled People*[34], including informa-- tion on the Education for All Handicapped Children Act of 1975. Finally, many educators are respon-- sible for guiding parents in establishing a positive home environment for a handicapped child. A *Reader's Guide for Parents of Children with Mental, Physical and Emotional Disabilities*[35] with over 600 annotated citations will aid in fulfilling this responsibility. It is divided into four sections: basic readings, books that train, those written by parents, and books dealing more intensively with particular issues in Part I. Part II includes books on particular disabilities divided by the four cate-- gories.

NOTES

1. U.S. National Advisory Committee on the Handi-- capped. *The Individualized Education Program: Key to an Appropriate Education for the Handicapped Child.* (3d Annual Report). Washington, U.S. Govt. Print. Off., 1977. $1.15. 37p.

2. _____ . *The Unfinished Revolution: Education for the Handicapped.* (2d Annual Report) Washing-- ton, U.S. Govt. Print. Off., 1976. $1.15. 48p.

3. U.S. Superintendent of Documents. *Monthly Catalog of United States Government Publications.* $45.00/ year. U.S. Govt. Print. Off., Washington, DC 20401. LC 4-18088. ISSN 0041-767X.

4. U.S. Government Printing Office. *The Handicapped, Special Bibliography No. 037.* Free. U.S. Govt. Print. Off., Washington, DC 20401.

5. Congressional Information Service. *CIS Index and Abstracts.* Congressional Information Service, 7101 Wisconsin Ave., Washington, DC 20014. ISSN 0007- 8530.

6. _____ . *American Statistics Index.* Congressional Information Service, 7101 Wisconsin Ave., Washing-- ton, DC 20014.

7. Infordata International Incorporated. *Index to U.S. Government Periodicals.* 1970– . $175/year. Infor-- data International, Inc., Suite 4602, 175 E. Delaware Place, Chicago, IL 60611. ISSN 0098-4606.

3

8. U.S. Department of Health, Education and Welfare. Office for Handicapped Individuals. *Programs for the Handicapped.* 1965– . Irreg. Free. U.S. Dept. of Health, Education and Welfare, Office for Handicapped Individuals, 200 Independence Ave., S.W., Washington, DC 20201.

9. U.S. Presidents' Committee on Mental Retardation. *Mental Retardation and the Law, a Report on Status of Current Court Cases.* 1974– . Irreg. Free. U.S. Govt. Print. Off., Washington, DC 20401. LC 75–64347.

10. U.S. Department of Health, Education and Welfare. Office of the Secretary. *Publications Catalog of the U.S. Department of Health, Education and Welfare.* Washington, U.S. Govt. Print. Off., 1978. Price on application to GPO. 675p.

11. _____ . Children's Bureau. *Research Related to Children, Bulletins.* 1950– . Irreg. U.S. Govt. Print. Off., Washington, DC 20401. S/N 1780–01373.

12. _____ . National Institute of Education. *Catalog of NIE Education Products.* Washington, U.S. Govt. Print. Off., 1975. $10.00 v.1; $12.00 v.2.

13. U.S. National Archives and Records Service. National Audiovisual Center. *A Catalog of United States Government Produced Audiovisual Materials.* Washington, U.S. Govt. Print. Off., 1974. Free. 356p. LC 75–314517.

14. _____ . *A Reference List of Audio-visual Materials Produced by the United States Government.* Washington, U.S. Govt. Print. Off., 1978. Free. 400p.

15. _____ . *Selected U.S. Government Audiovisuals, Oct. 1977, Special Education.* Washington, U.S. National Archives and Records Service, 1978. Free. 49p.

16. U.S. Department of Health, Education, and Welfare. Bureau of Education for the Handicapped. *Catalog of Educational Captioned Films for the Deaf.* Washington, U.S. Dept. of Health, Education and Welfare, Bureau of Education for the Handicapped, 1978. Free. 139p. LC HEW67–124.

17. _____ . *Catalog of Captioned Films for the Deaf, (1977–78), Theatrical Films and Educational Films for Adults.* Washington, U.S. Dept. of Health, Education and Welfare, Bureau of Education for the Handicapped, 1977. Free. 65p.

18. _____ . Office for the Handicapped. *Selected Publications Concerning the Handicapped.* 1974– Irreg. Free. U.S. Dept. of Health, Education and Welfare, Office for the Handicapped, 200 Independence Ave., S.W., Washington, DC 20201.

19. U.S. President's Committee on Mental Retardation. *Publications List.* 1966– . Irreg. Free. U.S. President's Committee on Mental Retardation, 1600 Pennsylvania Ave., N.W., Washington, DC 20500.

20. U.S. Library of Congress. *Library of Congress Publications in Print.* 1906–. Free. U.S. Govt. Print. Off., Washington, DC 20401. LC 6–35005. ISSN 0083–1603.

21. _____ . *Monthly Checklist of State Publications.* 1910– . M. $21.00/year. U.S. Govt. Print. Off., Washington, DC 20401. ISSN 0027–0288.

22. Paul Albright, ed., *State Administrative Officials Classified by Function.* 1935– . A. $10.00/year. Council of State Governments, P.O. Box 11910, Lexington, KY 40511. LC 35–11433.

23. U.S. Department of Health, Education and Welfare. National Center on Child Abuse and Neglect. *Child Abuse and Neglect Research, Projects, and Publications.* 1976– . Bi-A. $25.00/year. National Technical Information Service, 5285 Port Royal Rd., Springfield, VA 22161.

24. U.S. Architectural and Transportation Barrier Compliance Board. *Resource Guide to Literature on Barrier Free Environments with Selected Annotations, 1977.* Washington, U.S. Govt. Print. Off., 1977. Free. 223p.

25. _____ . *Report to the President and to the Congress of the United States.* 1973/74–. A. Free. U.S. Govt. Print. Off., Washington, DC 20401. LC 75–644292.

26. U.S. Congress. House. Committee on Science and Technology. *Research Programs to Aid the Handicapped, Hearings.* Washington, U.S. Govt. Print. Off., 1976. Free. 408p.

27. U.S. President's Committee on Employment of the Handicapped. *Bibliography of Secondary Materials for Teaching Handicapped Students.* Washington, U.S. Govt. Print. Off., 1977. Free. 27p.

28. U.S. Department of Transportation. Library Services Division. *Transportation for the Handicapped, Selected References.* Washington, U.S. Dept. of Transportation, Library Division, 1975. Free. (Bibliographic List – Dept. of Transportation, Library Services Div., No. 8) 39p. LC 75–602044.

29. J. Kiffin Penry, ed. *Indexes to the Epilepsy Accessions of the Epilepsy Information Systems.* Washing-

ton, U.S. National Institutes of Health, 1978. Price from NIH. 3v.

30. Jerry Baginski, comp. *Instructional Materials for Children with Learning Disabilities.* Springfield, Illinois Dept. of Public Instruction, 1976. Free.

31. California State Dept. of Education. *Bibliography: Proceedings and Publications of Regional Deaf--Blind Centers 1970--1977.* Sacramento, California State Dept. of Education, 1977. Free. 28p.

32. William A. Blea and Robert Hobron. *Literature on the Deaf Blind, an Annotated Bibliography.* Sacramento, California State Dept. of Education, 1976. Free. 45p. LC 77--620506.

33. Georgia. Dept. of Education. *Georgia Special Educa--tion, Annual Program Plan, Public Law 94--142 for 1979.* Atlanta, Georgia Dept. of Education, 1978. Free. 469p.

34. John D. Bailey. *Ready Reference Guide: Resources for Disabled People, a Handbook for Service Practioners and Disabled People.* Washington, U.S. Resources Rehabilitation Service Administration, 1978. Free. 115p.

35. Coralie B. Moore and Kathryn Gorham Morton. *A Readers Guide for Parents of Children with Mental, Physical and Emotional Disabilities.* Washington, U.S. Bureau of Community Health Services, 1979. (Dist. by U.S. Govt. Print. Off.) $3.00. (HSA 79--5290). 144p.

PL 94-142

PL 94-142 and the Changing Status of Teacher Certification/Recertification

by James M. Patton and Ronald L. Braithwaite

The Education for All Handicapped Children Act of 1975 (P.L. 94-142) provides federal legislative support to earlier philosophical and professional movements for "mainstreaming" and "normalization." A major intent of the law is that, to the maximum extent appropriate, handicapped individuals be educated in environments which progressively approximate those offered their peers. This mandate, together with the requirement that Individualized Educational Plans (IEP's) be developed for each handicapped child, seems to suggest changes in both teacher education and teacher certification and licensing of regular classroom teachers.

The mainstreaming of children with handicapping conditions into regular classroom environments requires that general educators develop competencies in providing differentiated, individualized instruction to all children, "normal" and otherwise. To meet this need, P.L. 94-142 mandates a Comprehensive System of Personnel Development to provide appropriate pre- and in-service education for regular classroom teachers. It logically follows that the education, certification, and licensing of these teachers will need to be changed to include special education courses and/or experiences which (a) provide some basic understanding of handicapped children, (b) develop skills in diagnostic and evaluative assessment, and (c) deal with appropriate curricular design, effective teaching strategies, and instructional media for those with handicapping conditions (Lynch, 1977). This study assesses the extent to which current special education requirements (courses and/or experiences) for the initial certification and recertification of regular classroom teachers throughout the country have been changed to meet the new requirements of P.L. 94-142.

METHODOLOGY

Sampling

State offices of teacher certification in the 50 states and the District of Columbia were contacted through use of a mail questionnaire during the month of April, 1978.

Of the 51 political units contacted, 48 useable questionnaires were returned, yielding a response rate of 94%. This relatively high response rate can be partially attributed to the rigorous follow-up procedures used, which involved follow-up letters and telephone calls to

TABLE 1
*Status of special education teachers
certification and recertification requirements for regular classroom teachers*

States	Requires courses or experiences	Does not require courses or experiences	Policy pending	States providing no information
Alabama		+		
Alaska		+		
Arizona		+		
Arkansas		+		
California		+		
Colorado	–			
Connecticut		+		
Delaware		+		
Florida		+		
Georgia	–			
Hawaii		+		
Idaho		+		
Illinois		+		
Indiana		+		
Iowa		+		
Kansas		+		
Kentucky	–			
Louisiana	–			
Maine		+		
Maryland		+		
Massachusetts			†	
Michigan		+		
Minnesota		+		
Mississippi		+		
Missouri	–			
Montana		+		
Nebraska	–			
Nevada		+		
New Hampshire		+		
New Jersey		+		
New Mexico		+		
New York				§
North Carolina				§
North Dakota		+		
Ohio		+		
Oklahoma	–			
Oregon		+		
Pennsylvania		+		
Rhode Island		+		
South Carolina		+		
South Dakota		+		
Tennessee			†	
Texas	–			
Utah		+		
Vermont		+		
Virginia	–			
Washington				§
West Virginia	–			
Wisconsin			†	
Wyoming			†	
District of Columbia		+		

state education agencies (SEA's) to clarify responses.

Instrumentation

A 10-item questionnaire was developed to determine the status of state-required special education coursework experiences for teacher certification and/or recertification. This instrument was designed to address the survey objective and to yield pilot data regarding the critical issue of special education requirements for the certification and recertification of regular classroom teachers. A mixed format including open- and closed-ended questions asked whether or not general classroom teachers were required to take special education courses and/or experiences to qualify for initial regular teacher certification and/or recertification, or whether such a policy was pending.

RESULTS

Certification Requirements

Special education courses for the initial certification of regular preservice teachers are currently required in 10 states, 21% of the political units sampled. Four states (9%) revealed that policies requiring special education courses for regular preservice teachers were pending. The remaining 33 states and the District of Columbia indicated that special education courses were neither presently required for teacher certification of regular preservice teachers nor pending. Identification of the status of the states regarding certification requirements is summarized in Table 1.

States which indicated that coursework in special education is required for prospective regular classroom teachers also described the nature and extent of the requirements. Two states, Georgia and Louisiana, indicated that "Introduction to Special Education" was required; Missouri and Nebraska require "Psychology of Exceptional Children"; Colorado requires a course entitled "Working with the Exceptional Child in the Regular Classroom"; and West Virginia, Kentucky, and Texas have specific special education program objectives which must be incorporated into all approved teacher education programs. A summary of program objectives required in the latter three states indicates that these objectives are related to (a) assessment/evaluation, (b) classroom management functions, (c) knowledge of characteristics and learning differences of handicapped pupils, (d) knowledge of the concept of least restrictive environments and its implications for the instructional process, and (e) knowledge of the admission, review, and dismissal processes and understanding the IEP for handicapped pupils.

Only one state, Virginia, requires prospective regular classroom teachers to obtain "experiences and/or coursework with exceptional children to qualify for initial teacher certification." Specifically, Virginia requires that prospective regular classroom teachers have only "experiences with exceptional children and knowledge in the detection of exceptional children." Virginia also requires information about referral procedures, including the role of the regular classroom teacher in the development, implementation, and evaluation of IEPs for exceptional children. Although the content of these experiences

is very specific, the mode and processes through which the content is presented are left to the training institution.

Recertification Requirements

Regular classroom teachers are required to take coursework in special education for recertification purposes in Georgia and Missouri; Kansas and Wyoming have policies pending. The majority of the states (44 states, or 92%) do not require special education coursework for the recertification of regular classroom teachers. None of the responding states require regular classroom teachers to have experiences with exceptional children to become recertified.

Factors Affecting Change

The 10 state departments requiring special education coursework for preservice or regular teachers were asked to rank order their reasons for requiring these changes. States were requested to rank the following reasons for changes in order of importance:

- P.L. 94-142 (Education for All Handicapped Children Act of 1975)
- Pressure or influence from professional organizations
- Pressure or influence from parent groups
- Pressure or influence from special education advocacy groups
- Genuinely felt need on part of state department
- Other _____

The category of "genuinely felt need on the part of the state department" was ranked as the most important change factor by 44% of the respondents. It is interesting to note that P.L. 94-142 and pressure or influence from parent groups were not ranked as strong reasons for requiring certification changes for regular classroom teachers. Apparently, P.L. 94-142 has not yet stimulated state Departments of Education to develop teacher certification policies which insure that practicing regular educators acquire competencies, skills, and/or experiences to deal with handicapped children.

DISCUSSION

To realize the promise embedded in the Education for All Handicapped Children Act of 1975, it is apparent that learners with handicapping conditions will increasingly be integrated into regular classroom programs, and that regular classroom teachers will need to be retrained for their work with these special populations. As mandated by P.L. 94-142, some local education agencies are providing special education in-service training for regular education personnel as part of their on-going Comprehensive System of Personnel Development. The question raised by this study, however, is whether state departments of education are requiring these changes as a part of their teacher certification requirements for prospective and practicing teachers. On the basis of the findings of this study, several conclusions may be drawn:

- A majority of the state departments of education (approximately 70%) do not presently require regular classroom teachers to complete courses in special education to qualify for initial certification.
- A large majority of states (approximately 92%) do not require special education coursework for the recertification of regular classroom teachers. In those states which do require coursework, general introduction to special education is the most commonly required course.
- Only the state of Virginia requires prospective teachers to obtain experience with exceptional children to qualify for initial teacher certification.
- Of those states which require coursework and/or experiences in special education for certification or recertification requirements, only two state departments of education indicated that these requirements resulted from P.L. 94-142 A majority indicated that changes resulted from a "genuinely felt need on the part of the state department."

There appear to be viable alternatives to the mere requirement of special education courses and/or experiences for regular education certification or recertification. West Virginia, Kentucky, and Texas' requirements of specific special education program objectives which must be incorporated into all approved teacher education programs warrant close attention. This requirement allows colleges and universities some flexibility, independence, and discretion as to how they will modify their curricula to provide training in special education for all teachers. In the implementation of such an approach, Turnbull and Turnbull (1978) suggest that all courses in the regular or general education curriculum that could have relevance to the education of the handicapped students be broadened to include the appropriate special education information. For example, modules on the historical and philosophical aspects of P.L. 94-142 would be integrated into the existing "History and Foundations of Education" course; a module on the use of specialized curricular materials for handicapped learners could be integrated into an existing "Materials of Instruction" course, and so forth. This integrated approach, notwithstanding unforeseen disadvantages, has merit and should be explored by state departments of education.

SUGGESTED FUTURE RESEARCH

This study focused on a very narrow range of questions on state certification and recertification requirements for regular classroom teachers, regarding their preparation in special education. The findings show that few states now have such requirements, but not why. Additional research is needed which (a) identifies reasons why a majority of states have not developed special education certification and recertification requirements for regular classroom teachers, (b) describes the nature and extent of modes of delivering special education courses and/or experiences developed by colleges and universities for regular classroom teachers, (c) describes the status of special education certification and recertification requirements for regular support personnel, such as guidance counselors, vocational counselors, principals, and so forth, (d) describes the legal implications and ramifications of compliance and the lack of compliance with both the letter and the spirit of the P.L. 94-142 mandate, and (e) describes innovative and creative ways of preparing regular educators to effectively work with handicapped learners.

REFERENCES

Lynch, W.W. Training educational personnel under the new law: Projects and prospects. In M.I. Semmel (Ed.), *The Education for All Handicapped Children Act (P.L. 94-142): Issues and Implications.* Bloomington: Indiana University, 1977.

Turnbull, H.R., & Turnbull, A. *Free appropriate public education: Law and implementation.* Denver: Love Publishing, 1978.

PL 94-142

Perspectives on PL 94-142

3

by Hana Simonson

One of the most significant educational developments since segregated schools were declared unconstitutional by the Supreme Court, was the passage in November 1975, of the Education of All Handicapped Children Act (PL 94-142).

Considered by many to be the Civil Rights Act for the Handicapped, this landmark legislation mandates that all physically, mentally, emotionally and sensorily handicapped children be provided with the opportunity to receive a free appropriate public education, no matter how severe the handicap.

Current estimates indicate that of the more than 8 million handicapped children in the United States, 4 million receive inappropriate educational services, while one million remain entirely excluded from publicly funded education. It is the aim of PL 94-142 to help each handicapped child become all he is capable of becoming, by developing educational programs designed to meet his individual needs.

In order to implement Congressional legislation to provide educational services for the handicapped (which would include children who were formerly in State institutions or at home) the Federal government has allocated more than 500 million dollars and will further assume increasing costs of 800 million by the fiscal year 1980. The Government's first priority is to reach the educationally unserved children and then, those who are inadequately served.

For a State to qualify for federal funds, each State Education Agency must submit its plan to the United States Office of Education detailing how such monies would be expended in accordance with the requirements of PL 94-142. Such plans are subject to annual review and revision by the Government.

From *The Generator*, Vol. 10, No. 2, Spring 1980. Copyright 1980, The American Educational Research Association. Reprinted with permission.

PL 94-142 has mandated specific goals which States must comply with in order to receive funds:

Least Restrictive Environment/Mainstreaming.

PL 94-142 requires that each handicapped child receive a free appropriate education in an environment which would be least restrictive for that child's normal development. Since "least restrictive" is interpreted as the "regular" classroom, handicapped children must be educated together with non-handicapped children, wherever possible.

Prior to the Act, handicapped children who had special needs were labeled, then separated from the other non-handicapped children in self-contained classrooms. They were kept away from the rest of the school population during academic work, recreation and lunch periods. Too often the special class became a dumping depot for the "incorrigibles" and a fertile medium for the segregation of ethnic or racial minority children.

It is the integration of handicapped children with their normal peers within the regular classroom that is currently referred to as "mainstreaming" although the word per se never appears in PL 94-142.

Individual Educational Program (IEP)

As part of the educational planning, each handicapped child must be provided with an IEP which is to be developed jointly by educators and parents. Each plan is to include a statement of the present educational level of the child as well as specific goals for short term and long term instructional objectives. Individual programs must be reassessed periodically to determine whether instructional objectives are being met, and reviewed frequently to keep pace with the child's progress.

Parental Involvement

The Education of All Handicapped Children Act has provided parents with unprecedented rights for direct participation in the education of their handicapped child. Parents have the right to question the procedures used to identify their child, to challenge the psychological and educational tests used to evaluate their child, and to disagree with and/or request change of a specific educational placement. If not satisfied with any educational aspect, parents have the right to an impartial due process hearing. PL 94-142 may be considered a virtual Educational Bill of Rights for Parents.

Personnel Development

In order to carry out the purpose of the Act, the Law requires each State to develop and implement a comprehensive system of personnel development, so that teachers are adequately prepared to educate the handicapped child. The great majority of regular classroom teachers have never had special education training, since colleges generally did not require special education courses for those who were preparing to teach in the elementary schools.

Special Education for All Teachers

Passage of a law is not enough to ensure compliance with that law. If the challenge of mainstreaming is to be realistically met, parallel changes must be made on State levels. The one indispensable factor for successful mainstreaming is a classroom teacher who will combine basic knowledge and skills in special education with those social attitudes which would readily respond to the needs of handicapped children.

The present special education elective course offerings by teacher training institutions for preservice teachers, and the variety of workshops, conferences, colloquia and seminars for in-service teachers are insufficient to keep pace with the demands of mainstreaming. Unless State Departments of Education amend their teacher certification requirements to include special education courses and field work as basic for all teachers, the great expectation of education for all handicapped children will remain the impossible dream.

Issues and Questions

The idea of the Education for All Handicapped Children Act is based on the principle of "zero reject"--every handicapped child has a right to an education qualitatively and quantitatively equal to the education of the non-handicapped child.

However well-intentioned, the Law's initial implementation is giving rise to some complex issues and questions:

> How can mainstreaming be realistically achieved when so many general teachers are neither adequately trained nor attitudinally prepared to accept the handicapped child?
> How can parents become involved in their child's education when so many lack knowledge of their newly-acquired rights while others lack the interest and/or the time for participation?
> Is it realistic to expect detailed IEP's with the frequently necessary revisions from busy overloaded teachers?
> Are we in danger of overflowing the banks of the mainstream by the disproportion of mainstreamed handicapped children to compete and qualified teachers?

PL 94-142

Problems and Prospects
Of PL 94-142

by Albert Shanker

For many years whether a handicapped child got an education was
a matter of geography, wealth or luck. Admission to special
education depended on programs and services available, and these
varied greatly from one community to another. Although good
special education was provided for many, schools traditionally
turned away significant numbers of handicapped children. Some of
the most severely handicapped were placed in public institutions
for what was largely custodial care. Those fortunate enough to
have wealthy parents or to be supported by charitable organizations were often placed in private schools. The rest were mostly
excluded from any educational system, public or private. Parents,
desperate to find help for their children, had nowhere to turn.

It was hardly surprising, then, that over the last decade a "quiet
revolution" occurred which culminated in passage of federal legislation guaranteeing the right of all handicapped children to a
free appropriate public education.

Following the lead of the States, particularly the State courts,
Congress enacted Section 504 of the Rehabilitation Act of 1973,
prohibiting discrimination on the basis of handicap in any program
or activity receiving federal funds. Finally, Congress overwhelmingly passed the Education for All Handicapped Children Act, P.L.
94-142, in November 1975.

P.L. 94-142 offers States basic grants and mandates procedures
for providing all handicapped children a free appropriate education in the least restrictive environment. Under this law, each
handicapped child must have an individualized education program
(IEP).

Almost all education organizations supported passage of P.L.

From *The Generator*, Vol. 10, No. 2, Spring 1980. Copyright 1980, The American Educational
Research Association. Reprinted with permission.

94-142 because they believed in handicapped children's right to a public education. The law was developed, however, with little input from educators. Since P.L. 94-142 took effect in October 1977, most educators have questioned its effectiveness. Prospects for the future of the law, as now written, are largely dependent on how seriously we deal with the problems which have emerged in its actual implementation.

IEPs Leave No Time to Teach

As school systems attempt to come into compliance with P.L. 94-142, the IFPs seem to generate the largest outcry. An IEP must be developed for each handicapped child which lists the child's present level of educational performance; annual goals and short-term instructional objectives; special education and related services to be provided; the extent of participation in regular educational programs; projected dates for initiation and expected duration of special services, and evaluation procedures to determine objectively whether instructional g"als are being met. In most cases, the additional duty of contacting parents to set up the IEP planning meetings has been assigned to teachers. If parents do not respond to the initial letter requesting their participation, documented efforts must be made to phone or visit them at their homes or worksites. Unfortunately, the latter is required with many parents. Additional time must be spent in the meetings themselves, sometimes held outside regular school hours, and with the extensive paperwork the IEPs require.

Teachers complain they have no time left to teach. A speech and hearing therapist, for example, working with 125 students, would be responsible for 125 contacts, 125 planning meetings, and preparation of 125 IEPs. consequently, throughout the country there were many such teachers who as late as February of the last school year had not begun to teach. Once the IEPs are finally completed, meetings must be set up again for their annual review and the whole process repeated. Immediate research is needed on whether IEPs, as defined under this law, actually enhance a child's education or work to prevent it. Too often, teachers have found the latter to be true.

The child's teacher is stipulated in the law as being one of the mandatory participants in the IEP planning meeting. More study is needed on how this is being interpreted from one school system to another. Is this teacher the special education teacher from the past school year or current school year, the regular teacher or a combination thereof? If it is the past year's special education teacher, does this create any problem for the current teacher in carrying out someone else's goals and objectives? If it is the special education teacher for the current school year, can the teacher develop reasonable goals without having worked with the child before? When are regular teachers involved in planning meetings? Many more questions regarding IEPs need to be investigated, including to what extent, if any, the IEP locks a child and teacher into a particular program and with what effect.

The majority of teachers feel that despite its intent, the IEP is diminishing the qulaity of education handicapped children receive They would like to see the IEP requirement revised or eliminated altogether. Unless teachers are freed from many of their present duties or have their workloads drastically reduced, the prospects of successful implementation of the present IEP concept are non-existent. Instead, the schools will be locked into a process which totally negates teaching and learning.

'Least Restrictive Environment' Required

Another requirement of P.L. 94-142, least restrictive environment placements, also needs further investigation. Although the Bureau of Education for the Handicapped (BEH) is now conducting a number of studies on various aspects of mainstreaming,* most of these will not be completed for at least another year. The last re-search review was done for BEH in 1975 by Wynne Associates on the effectiveness of mainstreaming children into the regular classroom in early childhood education. After reviewing all available research on mainstreaming, they found that it suffered from "methodological problems that render much of it virtually useless" and that "most of the views about mainstreaming held by its proponents are based on philosophical and political considerations rather than hard data." The report goes on to say:

> "At best, the research evidence suggests that a mainstream setting is at least as beneficial to mildly handicapped children (predominatly educable mentally retarded children) as a self-contained classroom.
>
> It is important to emphasize that research into these issues has not been able to substantiate conclusively that main-streaming is a 'good thing'."

Guidelines for Mainstreaming

The American Federation of Teachers supports mainstreaming on philosophical grounds. It makes sense that if a child is able to cope in a less restrictive environment, the child may be able to live a fuller, more normal life. Yet, such placements must be made with great caution and under the proper conditions.

We believe the following guidelines are essential to making less restrictive environment placements effective:

. Not all children benefit from a mainstream setting.

---

*As used here, mainstreaming refers to any placement in a less restrictive environment, rather than placement in a regular classroom only.

- Placement of exceptional children in regular classes and activities or other less restrictive environments should be decided on an individual basis, based on the readiness of the special student and the preparedness of the receiving classroom to meet individual children's special needs.

- Regular teachers should be informed in advance of all special placements in their classes.

- Staff-development programs to prepare teachers to work with students having various handicaps must be available prior to such placements, and continuous support and training are necessary to meet problems as they arise.

- Regular teachers should be involved in placement decisions, when appropriate, to assure acceptance of the exceptional child in the regular classroom and to evaluate the capability of the regular classroom to accommodate special needs.

- Transitional periods should be provided when necessary to prepare a child entering a less restrictive environment and other students in the class to adjust to new situations.

- Class sizes must be kept low in mainstreamed situations to assure the necessary individual instruction. (As the exceptional child is likely to require more of the teachers's time than other students, teacher-student ratios may be adjusted to weight the special student more Heavily, or they may conform to those classes from which the special student is transferred.)

- Certified special education teachers must be retained to continue to meet the needs of children in special classes and to work with regular teachers in developing appropriate instructional programs for mainstreamed children.

- Counselors, psychologists, psychiatrists and other auxiliary personnel must be readily available to special and regular teachers.

- Teachers should have regularly scheduled released time for consultations with support personnel.

- Instructional materials, equipment and facilities must be adapted to the needs of exceptional children in the regular classroom and throughout the school.

- Scheduling should conform to the needs of exceptional children rather than vice-versa.

3

.   Evaluations of student progress and placement should be
    carefully done on a continuous basis.

.   Safeguards should exist to see that funds designated for
    special education follow the child, even if in a main-
    streamed setting.

Supportive Services Are Mandated

These "common-sense" guidelines for mainstreaming are in fact
supported in the law. Under P.L. 94-142 each child receiving
special education is also to receive all necessary related services. These services are defined as "transportation and such
developmental, corrective and other supportive services as are
required to assist a handicapped child to benefit from special
education and include speech pathology and audiology, psychological services, physical and occupational therapy, recreation, early
identification and assessment of disabilities in children, counseling services, and medical services for diagnostic or evaluation
purposes. The term also includes school health services, social
work services in schools, and parent counseling and training." A
child is also to recieve all services needed, regardless of availability.

On paper these sound like nice quarantees, and no less so to the
teacher working with mainstreamed children. In reality, appropriate support services for each handicapped child are beyond the
current financial means of the public school system. The law
places on the schools the burden of proof that a handicapped child
cannot function in a less restrictive environment. Schools, short
on personnel and dollars and fearful of lawsuits or loss of federal funds, tend to "over-mainstream" in many cases. Severely and
profoundly impaired handicapped children are being places in
regular classrooms. Cases have been reported where this was done
on a weekend's notice. Mainstreaming saves money! If a child is
mainstreamed without adequate, mandated support services, even
more money is saved. No one has calculated the eventual costs -
to the the child, to his parents, to the society.

Less restrictive environment placements need more study and closer
monitoring to see whether placements are indeed based on individual needs and capabilities or on political or financial considerations. The law's intent should not be undermined. A continuum of
services must remain available, including residential institutions, hospitals, service centers, home-bound instruction,
self-contained special education classrooms, resource rooms and
regular classrooms. Services must follow the child. Otherwise,
the law will succeed only in dismantling an increasingly impressive special education program it took three quarters of a century
to build.

Lack of Training for Teachers

One of the most disastrous failings in the implementation of P.L.

94-142 is the real lack of the inservice training the law requires. To date, if teachers have received comprehensive workshops on the requirements of the law at all, it usually has been only through their union. The majority have received no inservice training for working with handicapped children already in their charge. Administrators are experiencing the same problem. Consequently, principals' directives for implementing the law vary enormously from one school to another within the same school system.

State education departments, responsible for seeing that inservice training is provided, are too busy carrying out the law's other mandates to address this issue seriously.

Some have given overview workshops to a relatively small number of teachers throughout the state, while others are only in the process of preparing such sessions.

Certainly, the lack of inservice training for teachers inexperienced in working with handicapped children is irresponsible. General workshops, sensitivity sessions and the like may be fine as far as they go. But good education can occur only if the handicapped child's teacher has an opportunity to work directly with someone knowledgeable about the particular handicapping condition prior to actual placement. Also essential is continuous access to such expertise as problems or questions arise. Several different specialists might be necessary to work with one teacher depending on the number of handicapped children placed in a class. If we are concerned with these children's fate, we must put the myth to rest that any teacher worth his or her salt should be able to teach any child. Many handicapped children have complex needs requiring specialized knowledge on the part of the teacher. Adding a few special education courses to the preservice curriculum of all teachers will still fall far short of creating a new teaching force immediately qualified to work with handicapped children.

Teachers finding themselves in new roles with handicapped children express great concern for the child's well-being when they find they are not qualified to teach the child, they lack the necessary resources or support services, or the child is obviously unable to cope with the classroom situation. It is important to note that placement or program decisions can be challenged only by the parent or the school system. P.L. 94-142 provides a due process procedure with local and state level hearings for such situations. But teachers have no access to this process. If a teacher for any reason finds that a child's education is inappropriate and the teacher is not supported by the parents or the school system, the teacher has no means of helping the child. We believe, therefore, that the law must be changed to allow teachers' use of the due process mechanism as child advocates. Appropriate placement of and the provision of needed services to all handicapped children would then be protected by three parties: the parent, the school system and the teacher.

It is profoundly naive to think all parents know or demand what is best for their children or that a school system always places a child's interest first. In one case, for example, the parents of a neurologically impaired child had their child moved from a school for the neurologically impaired to one for the orthopedic-ally impaired simply because it was closer to their home. The school system, which previously had challenged a number of par-ental placement requests, did not enter the due process mechanism on this one. Why? Because the effort was becoming burdensome, and it was easier to let the placement go unchallenged.

Teachers and other school employees also voice a second complaint about the law's due process procedure. At these hearings, only the parents and the school system are allowed legal counsel. The teacher who is often called in to testify is denied this right. Because teachers feel a concern about the accuracy and effective-ness of their testimony, and because such proceedings could con-ceivably affect their employment, teachers should have the same right to counsel.

Federal Funding Grossly Inadequate

The final and surest impediment to successful implementation of P.L. 94-142 is the lack of adequate federal funding. Congress authorized more money for P.L. 94-142 than for any single piece of education legislation since the Elementary and Secondary Education Act of 1965. Yet even if this law were fully funded and appro-priations matched authorization levels, federal funding would fall far short of what is actually required for implementation. At a time when schools are being closed for lack of funds or are threatened with this prospect through Proposition 13-type legis-lation, it is hard to see how schools can meet the mandates of P.L. 94-142.

The maximum allocation of federal funds a state may receive in any fiscal year is equal to the number of handicapped children aged 3 through 21 in the state who are receiving special education, mul-tiplied by the following applicable percentage of the average per pupil expenditure in U.S. public elementary and secondary schools: 5% in 1978, 10% in 1979, 20% in 1980, 30% in 1981 and 40% in 1982.

Several things are wrong with this funding formula. The per pupil expenditure in urban school systems is significantly above the $1,500 national average. States and school systems spending more than the average per pupil are discriminated against because they receive proportionately less than those which have not made educa-tion a priority.

Likewise, given the scarcity of resources in public education, the phase-in funding makes little sense when start-up costs are so

immense. BEH estimates that of 8 million handicapped children,
birth through 21, requiring special education, 2.5 million are
receiving an inappropriate education and another 1.75 million are
receiving no educational services at all. New or expanded programs, then, must be provided by the schools for several million
children. Federal funds, however, may be used only for the "excess costs" of special education. This is the amount the school
system must spend for special education over and above the cost of
educating a child in regular education. For each new handicapped
child served, schools first must search for money equal to that
spent on the education of children in the regular program.
One would think the federal government then would pay the true
excess costs. Not so. It contributes a fraction of the amount
needed for these costs. For the 1978-79 school year, federal
funding amounts to approximately $148 per handicapped child, of
which 25 percent goes to the States.
Take the problem of New York City. As of November 1978, the Board
of Education had 14,000 handicapped children on lists awaiting
placement. Of these, 5,000 had been evaluated but not placed.
New referrals were coming in at the rate of 1,500 per month. In
New York City, the cost of providing education to a handicapped
child can run anywhere from $4,000 to $7,000 per year - in extreme
cases, three or four times the higher figure - much more than the
$1,500 per year average expenditure throughout the country on
non-handicapped youngsters. The Board estimated that it would
take an additional $50 million this year to comply with the
mandates of P.L. 94-142, but, of course, it is getting nothing
like this from the federal government. To make matters worse,
additional money which was scheduled to come in from the state to
help with the excess costs (under a state law parallel to P.L.
94-142) had not come in by the fall 1978 term because the state
legislature could not agree on the proper funding formula.
Where is the money to come from - for New York, other cities and
other school districts? The likelihood of raising taxes is slim.
Is it any wonder schools find their only alternative is to remain
to some extent in violation of the law and hope no one notices?
Obviously, this choice is unacceptable. Violations will eventually be discovered, and court cases will result in the further
depletion of school resources. Headlines will again scapegoat the
public schools, and finally, fearful of losing federal funds
because of noncompliance, school districts will be forced to cut
regular education programs drastically to accommodate special
education requirements. Children deserve more, handicapped and
non-handicapped alike.
Only one viable course remains. School boards, administrators and
teachers cooperatively must document those things under the law
that they have been able to do using available resources and those
they have not been able to accomplish. This evidence must be
placed before Congress with the request that it either provide
sufficient funds to close the gap or change the law. Helping the
handicapped is a commendable goal. Promising help without providing the resources to make it possible is the cruelest kind of
hoax.

PART 4

4

CULTURAL DIVERSITY

by Rita Tatum

By definition, "minority" delineates the smaller segment of a given group. However, Americans frequently connect the term with nonEuropean cultural groups, thereby indicating that a culture with dominant European roots would be more easily assimilated in U.S. society. So the nation founded on Melting Pot principles emphasized English as the primary, if not exclusive, language of its educational system. And middle-class European aspirations guided the intellectual and academic bent of teaching the nation's young.

Because they didn't fit the mold shaped by a European heritage, other cultural and/or ethnic groups found the educational system malfunctioning for them. Often they found themselves in classes for "slow learners," where they were assumed to be less mentally capable of benefitting from the nation's educational system.

As recently as the 1960s, educators were privy to numerous studies that supposedly described the cultural characteristics of various ethnic groups. Rather than truly assist teachers, these studies fostered further stereotypes and more biases. For example, teachers were informed that they might expect motivational problems from Black children partially because Black children grew up in matriarchal familial settings.

Similarly, fatalism was suggested as a potential problem most frequently encountered with Hispanic American children. However, since that time, both generalizations have proven inaccurate. Once similar educational levels were compared, a Texas survey showed no statistically discernible difference in the occurrence of fatalistic attitude among Anglos and Mexicans.

And the motivational problems experienced by a number of the culturally diverse may relate to other elements. For the traditional Indian, reared to consider today over tomorrow, memorizing multiplication tables this year so division will be simpler next year seems remarkably inappropriate. But the Indian who grew up on Chicago's west side may suffer as much from being impoverished as from a contrasting cultural background.

Recent studies suggest that poverty can lead a child to perceive that he or she has less control over what happens than do children from more affluent upbringings. Some researchers are discovering that children from more affluent households often believe they are piloting their own destiny, while the impoverished often feel cast adrift.

Fortunately, at least one successful instructional program appears to amend a portion of the socio-economic difference. When children perceive they play a vital role in determining their activities, they seem more willing to assume personal responsibility for their success or failure. In classrooms employing a cooperative goal structure, failure is less likely to result in self deprecation than in those characterized by norm-referenced competition — the more traditional classroom structure even today.

Norm-referenced testing compares a child's performance with peers. Another method of testing being analyzed is criterion referenced. This test compares a child's performance with a certain standard of mastery. While criterion-referenced measures are certainly beneficial for the child (provided tests are not culturally biased), they could become so provincial as to restrict or retard a child's mobility. For instance, ghetto-ese still is not the prevalent boardroom tongue. Hence, provincial measurements could be even more confining than the present educational system for the culturally diverse.

Children from these background influences may be more accurately measured with modern intelligence tests, coupled with adaptive behavior scales. However, while a number of adaptive behavior models exist for determining mental retardation, no similar model for normal-to-intelligent is fine tuned.

In the past, the culturally diverse child ran the risk of being classified as Educably Mentally Retarded. That bias will not be completely eliminated solely with new testing procedures. Nor are current state and federal laws completely conducive to such a revision, since they require certain labels under their statutes.

In order to insure an accurate appraisal of the culturally diverse child, new testing systems would need to be evaluated by an unbiased inter-disciplinary team. That team would need to employ a measuring process that emphasized the specific skills required for survival in the academic setting. And the child's performance would need to be placed into the context of the total environment surrounding that student.

Accomplishing such a task may prove Herculean. But, at least one other interim direction emphasizes the use of multi-cultural programs that weave the experiences of the majority with the customs of the minority. Ideally, such programs will allow the adults of the future to incorporate the best of each culture into a truly American heritage.

Issues in the Education Of Culturally Diverse Exceptional Children

by Leonard Baca

Providing an appropriate and effective education for minority group students who are both exceptional and come from culturally and/or linguistically diverse backgrounds is without a doubt one of the greatest challenges facing special educators as we enter the 1980's. Five years have gone by since this journal first published a special issue devoted exclusively to the issues affecting culturally diverse exceptional children. During this time several important events have taken place that have served to promote the improvement of advocacy and services provided for these children.

Perhaps the most significant event that has taken place within The Council for Exceptional Children (CEC) is the establishment of an office of minority concerns at the national headquarters in Reston, Virginia. Within CEC, Black, Hispanic, and American Indian special educators have either further developed or recently established strong caucus organizations.

In the area of litigation we have witnessed the strong impact of the 1974 *Lau* v. *Nichols* Supreme Court decision on programs serving linguistically different children. This unanimous decision on behalf of 18 Chinese plaintiffs stated in effect that a monolingual curriculum denies equal educational opportunity and equal protection under the law. Schools must provide opportunities for learning in the students' native language. We are also now beginning to feel the impact of the 1979 Ann Arbor decision with respect to Black English. In this case, a Federal District Court held that since a child's behavior is influenced by an environment where Black English is spoken, it is mandatory that teachers become more familiar with the differences and characteristics of Black English. Legislatively, the most significant occurrence during the past 5 years has been the passage and implementation of Public Law 94–142, the Education for All Handicapped Children Act of 1975.

These three key events are among many others that have been instrumental in promoting stronger advocacy and improved services for culturally diverse exceptional children. Despite the modest progress that has been made thus far, much more remains to be done.

The difficulty in writing about this relatively new area of concern regarding culturally diverse exceptional children stems from the fact that there is a small amount of literature and research available. A second reason is that diversity exists both among the various minority groups and within each of the groups. The reader should be careful not to generalize from one diverse population to another. It is even difficult, if not impossible, to generalize within a single minority group because of the regional, cultural, linguistic, and other types of differences that prevail.

The major articles in this issue of *Exceptional Children* touch upon a broad range of topics and issues that have been identified as areas of pressing concern. It is hoped that the information presented in this special issue will call attention to the many critical and unique needs experienced by culturally diverse exceptional children. Having had their attention called to this tremendous and largely unmet need, it is anticipated that practitioners as well as scholars in the field will mount a renewed effort in response to this moral and professional challenge.

Cultural Diversity And Special Education

by Asa G. Hilliard, III

We must recognize at the outset that the history of the I.Q. test, and of special education classes built on I.Q. testing is not the history of neutral scientific discoveries translated into educational reform. It is, at least in the early years, a history of racial prejudice, of social Darwinism, and of the use of the scientific 'mystique' to legitimate such prejudices. (Peckham, 1979, p. 8)

■ In a landmark court decision, Judge Robert F. Peckham struck at the heart of poor educational practice in California. In California, as in most other states, the use of IQ tests has resulted in a disproportionate overrepresentation of African-American children in classes for the mentally retarded and in a disproportionate underrepresentation of African-American children in classes for the gifted. After reviewing nearly 10,000 pages of testimony, Judge Peckham found, among other things, the following situation:

These apparent over enrollments (of Blacks in EMR classes) could not be the result of chance. For example, there is less than a one in a million chance that the over enrollment of Black children and the under enrollment of non-Black children in the EMR classes in 1976-77 would have resulted under a colorblind system of placement. . . .
Even if it assumed that Black children have a 15 percent higher incidence of mild mental retardation than White children, there is still less than a one in a million chance that a colorblind system would have produced this disproportionate enrollment. (Peckham, 1979, p. 24)

Judge Peckham's ruling dealt only with a Black, non Black distinction. On further analysis, one finds that the classes for the educable mentally retarded are overwhelmingly male. There is little probability that a color and a sex blind system would find such a disproportion. Yet, the State Department of Education allowed surprising testimony in its defense.

Rather defendants' actions resulting in the adoption of the I.Q. requirement and the short list of accepted I.Q. tests can only be explained as the product of the impermissible and scientifically dubious assumption that Black children as a group are inherently less capable of academic achievement than White children.
Key officials of the State Department of Education, moreover, actually corroborated this explanation. They testified that they believed the over-enrollment of Black and Chicano children in the EMR classes actually reflected the incidence of mental retardation among those children. (Peckham, 1979, p. 88, italics added)

The testimony in this case documents racism in testing and education, the use of invalid tests by state mandate, and the revival or continuation of arguments which are the same as those of the eugenicists who were among the early designers and proponents of IQ tests (Kamin, 1974).

There are children who are handicapped in one way or another. Some, not all, of these disabled children require skilled special assistance in order to benefit most from education. The critical questions are these: Are we finding the right children? Are we providing valid services for those we do find?

HOW SPECIAL EDUCATION FAILS

Cultural diversity in education carries the suggestion that educational practice should be modified by cultural realities. *Compensatory education* suggests that something must be done for some children to make up for their lack of opportunity to obtain certain "normal" or required educational experiences. *Bilingual education* suggests that a child should not be penalized and prevented from obtaining an education simply by virtue of speaking a language other than English. Ordinarily, each of these terms is associated with "minority group" status in the minds of educators. All of the terms are ambiguous. They lack clarity. They are not precise professional terms. However, from them, certain issues, assumptions, or principles can be identified.

1. We must accept the reality of culture.
2. We must accept the reality of oppression.
3. We must accept the meaninglessness of *minority* as a term for group identification.

If educators are able to deal adequately with these three assumptions, the value of education in general, and special education in particular, will be greatly enhanced.

Special education fails when it ignores the obvious. With or without a systematic investigation, culture should be obvious to professional observers. *Culture* means the distinctive creativity of a particular group of people. *Creativity* includes world view, values, style, and above all language. No one culture is superior to another. Furthermore, mainstream American behavior is itself nothing more or less than a special case of culture. There are human universals at the deep structural level. However, those universals manifest themselves through learned cultural patterns, which show up as surface structures.

To recognize the existence of equivalent cultural forms among groups of people is to deal a fatal blow to standardization at the surface structural level. The mass production of tests and diagnostic devices can be achieved only when they tap deep structures. The confusion of these two levels of data is at the root of widespread confusion and error in education. For example, it comes as a shock to naive educators to learn that while language may reflect thinking patterns and structures, English will do so only for those who have had a chance to learn it. English is not language, but *a* language. Since educational assessment is primarily language dependent, no serious professional can afford to ignore the relevant scholarship on this subject. Yet, most special educators remain ignorant of such linguistic principles as variation and the surface deep structure distinction. The same may be said for relevant cultural anthropological principles. In general the principles of linguistics and cultural anthropology must be mastered more than the knowledge of particular languages and cultures. Diagnosis, interpretation, communication and rapport are all dependent upon a basic sophistication in these areas (Hilliard, 1976; 1979).

Special education fails when it cannot account for the presence and impact of oppression on professional practice and on the behavior of clients. The reality of oppression in America should require no documentation. Yet, the literature in special education tends to be devoid of both an historical and a contemporary political perspective. For example, few courses in tests and measurements in colleges and universities give attention to the history of IQ testing and the political activities and beliefs of the early advocates and developers. Yet, these matters are germane to the validity question (Brenner, 1973; Chase, 1977; Hilliard, 1978; Ryan, 1971; Thomas & Sillen, 1972).

Special education fails when it uses labels such as *minority*. Such a label may be consistent with the thinking of those who deny culture, or who ignore oppression, and who feel that a social class explanation can account for educational events. Yet, the term *minority group* refers only to the *number* of people in a group, not necessarily to culture or to class. The makeup of the minority group pool is fluid. It has neither character nor identity. No doubt that is because many educators seem to be so wed to an exclusive social class explanation for human behavior that they have been unable to experience or to perceive the realities of culture and oppression. Diagnoses, interpretations, communication, and rapport that are rooted in such theory will be seriously incomplete and misleading. Separate the rich from the poor and there still remain differences of culture and the experience of oppression within either group.

HOW SPECIAL EDUCATION SUCCEEDS

Special education will succeed with diverse cultural groups only when certain conditions prevail.

1. Culturally sensitive diagnostic validity must exist.
2. Professional practices must work significantly better than chance.

3. A valid link between special education assessment/diagnosis and teaching strategies must be present.

The situation is clear-cut when it comes to testing for eyesight and teaching braille, for example. Similarly, testing for hearing and the use of split-band amplification of sound to teach reading are validly linked. However, both the diagnoses and the teaching strategies become arbitrary, vague, and amorphous in such labels as "learning disabled" and "educable mentally retarded." Predictably then, the incidence of the disability skyrockets for these categories, especially for traditionally oppressed and excluded cultural groups, and more especially for males in those groups.

The professional definitions of *giftedness* or *retardation* must be rendered in something better than statistical rankings. What are the mental *functions* (not IQ test scores) that a gifted child can perform and a nongifted child cannot? What are the mental *functions* (not IQ test scores) that that educable mentally retarded child cannot perform and other children can? If the functions cannot be identified, how can the strategies be responsive? Further, the programs for the gifted and for the retarded must be described uniquely and the individual program validity must be established.

Above all, special education succeeds when it faces the major issue for disabled persons. Most of the normal fare in education can be mastered by a wide diversity of students. The disabled child can have more problems as a consequence of the attitudes of professionals and peers than as a result of his or her specific disability. In such cases the "therapy" must be directed toward the nondisabled population.

It is amazing that so little research on student learning controls for the quality of or equivalence of the school experience. Yet, the results are unmistakable. Good teaching works!

"IATROGENIC" TEACHING?

Illich (1976) has warned that physicians may be dangerous to your health—iatrogenic medicine. The same may be said for educators. The negative consequences of providing "treatment" for children who in no way need it, or of failing to provide good teaching for those who do need it are great indeed. The child can be made to respond to the stereotype. Does anyone today doubt the validity of the expectancy research? To offer "treatment" where none is needed is to signal misunderstanding and a low regard for the real person. The student usually has little power to make an impact on a negative assessment. As a result, many become depressed, fatalistic, intropunitive, or hostile. There is an ease with which some teachers are able to teach reading and other basic skills to traditionally oppressed and excluded groups (Hilliard, 1979). One can only regard the common failure to teach thousands of children who are much like these successful learners as irrefutable evidence of "iatrogenic teaching," "iatrogenic school leadership, " or "iatrogenic public policy."

THE PROMISE OF CULTURAL DIVERSITY

The lack of sensitivity to culture will produce professional error. The lack of comfort with another culture which one may recognize but at the same time dislike or fear, raises the question of the need for a professional to face, honestly, the ethical need for self disqualification. It also raises the ethical issue for supervisors who are in a position to observe.

On the other hand, to the special educator who is observant, sensitive, and sophisticated regarding the principles of culture, especially language, a whole world of possibilities open up at once. The fear of difference is reduced and the possibility for understanding is increased. The development of rapport is facilitated. The validity of professional practice is improved.

The knowledgeable educator is aware that culture per se presents no insurmountable pedagogical problems, indeed if it presents any problems at all. The thing that matters is how a child's culture is regarded by those who are charged with his or her care. A child's culture (i.e., world-view, values, style, language) is frequently used as a marker to target the child for a different treatment than the children of those who hold power in a society. It is the educator's professional responsibility to see that this does not happen.

A great deal is being written about "teacher burnout" and the burnout of educators at other levels as well. As more descriptions of what people mean by this term emerge, it is clear that at the root of the problem is often a tension that grows from teachers and students, or administrators and students and their communities who are alienated from each other. One hears most about burnout in the large cities where the heaviest representation of cultural economic diversity exists. Moreover, these cities have often had outmigrations of White children and a growth in the population of other children during the last two decades. In many of these same cities, there are declining enrollments and a resulting low staff turnover. There is the continuation of poor performance in affirmative action hiring. As a result there are frequent mismatches between the culture of educators and that of the children and their communities. The problems are minimized when cultural sensitivity and identification with children, families, communities, and their aspirations are high. Children and their families know the difference and feel it keenly. They respond to the differences as well.

At any point where a certain cultural group is overrepresented in a particular category of special education, the special educator should spare no effort to review the system of assessment for cultural bias. The burden of proof in establishing the validity of any assessment process which yields a gross disproportion in the distribution of groups to categories must rest with the educator. It is a shame and a disgrace that the courts and the legislatures are left to overrule the bad practices which are so widespread among us.

Neither teacher burnout nor child burnout is a normal condition. In any society that cares for its children, the truth must be told about the abilities of children regardless of their cultural background. The resources for teaching (i.e., class size, supplies and services, facilities, salaries) must be adequate. Institutional structures such as school size and governance must harmonize with the best in professional practice. At a policy level, education must be society's highest priority.

Special educators, teachers and researchers have contributed many new ideas and strategies to the teaching profession. Some say that the action is in innovation. Whatever good that has been done can be undone by allowing slipshod, arbitrary, culturally unsophisticated assessment to continue. The special educator, more than most others, has the chance to lead in the reform of education. The special educator has the skills to take the side of the children when that conflicts with the profiteers in standardized testing. The special educator can lead the way in showing how the culture of the child can be used as a building block for learning. This is the true meaning of teaching: going from the known to the unknown. The true educator can use culture as a building block for learning without the need to supplant or suppress children's native cultural forms. When this is done, special education will be seen as helping children reach for the possible rather than adjust to the expected.

CONCLUSION

It should be clear that cultural diversity requires no unusual special education. What is required is that normal valid professional practice be provided. That means that children from any cultural group have every right to expect that:

1. Communication with them be in a language that they understand and that communication be sensitive to cultural patterns which any particular person has given much energy to learn.
2. All diagnoses must use cultural information, therefore every diagnosis must reflect the culturally unique meaning of information which is collected.

Often pressures are placed upon professionals in education to do things that professional knowledge cannot support. Frequently these demands are made by people who do not understand the limitations of professional practice. To aquiesce in the face of these demands may bring temporary satisfaction and tension reduction. However, the long term consequences of such action are likely to be devastating. Special vigilance is required where traditionally oppressed and excluded groups are concerned.

The time is certainly ripe for assuring that children placed in special education programs for the mentally retarded have been properly identified and the merits of the individual cases carefully considered. . . . *The concerns expressed by John Chandler and John Plakos of the State Department of Education, and by Steve Moreno and his group within the Association of Mexican-American Educators [testify] that the labeling process at present is insufficient to accurately identify retardates among certain ethnic and racial minorities. The research of Dr. Jane Mercer of the University of California at Riverside has indicated that in the case of minority groups, individual I.Q.'s play a less significant role in determining of eligibility than do certain other indices. . . . some pressure has been exerted upon school districts to depart from traditional clinical practice in making the essential determination that a child is mentally retarded.*

. . . most psychologists . . . approve of the requirement that only individual intelligence tests of the stature of WISC, or recent revision of the Stanford Binet, be employed for the purpose of obtaining clinical data which will contribute to the labeling process. It is also obvious however, that many psychologists, special educators, and persons of varying levels of sophistication who have a particular interest in the education of the culturally disadvantaged child will disagree as to what kinds of alternative or additional psychometric information ought to be included. It is perhaps unfortunate that we find ourselves in the process of adding to the status of classical IQ instruments at a time when psychology is re-evaluating the appropriateness of IQ as a simple basis

for classification. (Peckham, 1979, pp. 117–118, italics added)

If the education profession is to serve all children well, it will take courage, integrity, and ethics to state clearly what we can and cannot do, what constitutes valid practice and what does not. Respecting cultural diversity is not a benevolent act but a prerequisite for science and valid professional practice.

BIBLIOGRAPHY

Brenner, M. *Mental illness and the economy.* Cambridge MA: Harvard University Press, 1973.

Chase, A. *The legacy of Malthus: The social costs of the new scientific racism.* New York: Knopf, 1977.

Fuller, R. *In search of the I.Q. correlation.* Stonybrook NY: Ball-Stick-Bird Publications, 1977

Hall, E. T. *Beyond culture.* New York: Anchor, 1977.

Hilliard, A. G., III. *Alternatives to IQ testing: An approach to the identification of gifted "minority" children.* ERIC Clearinghouse on Early Childhood Education, ED 145 957, 1976.

Hilliard, A. G., III. *Behavioral criteria in the study of racism: Performing the jackal function, part I.* Technical Report, Office of Naval Research. San Francisco: Urban Institute for Human Services, 1978.

Hilliard, A. G., III. The pedagogy of success. In Sunderlin, S. (Ed.), *The most enabling environment.* Washington DC: Association for Childhood Education International, 1979.

Hilliard, A. G., III. Standardization and cultural bias as impediments to the scientific study and validation of "intelligence." *Journal of Research and Development in Education,* December 1979, 47–58.

Illich, I. *Medical nemesis: The expropriation of health.* New York: Bantam, 1976.

Kamin, L. *The science and politics of I.Q.* New York: Wiley, 1974.

Peckham, R. F. (Opinion) *Larry P. v. Wilson Riles.* (US District Court F of the Northern District of California, No. C-71-2270 RFP).

Ryan, W. *Blaming the victim.* New York: Random House, 1971.

Thomas, A., & Sillen, S. *Racism and psychiatry.* New York: Brunner/Mazel, 1972.

Tyler, R., & White, S. (Eds.). *Testing, teaching, and learning: Report of a conference on research on testing.* Washington DC: National Institute of Education, DHEW, 1979.

4

Nondiscriminatory Evaluation

by Donald B. Bailey, Jr., and Gloria L. Harbin

■ Evidence of bias in our educational system has long been present. While the more visible instances of bias, such as separate schooling, are disappearing, questions of bias in assessment and placement of children with special needs are now rising to the forefront.

Bias in the schools occurs whenever educational decisions are inappropriately affected by a child's race, culture, economic background, or disability. Bias may enter into any facet of the educational program; however, the testing and placement of children in special education classes has become a major focus of concern by those interested in equality in the schools. Adding to the concern is the disproportionately high number of minority and low income children labeled as mentally retarded and the subsequent placement of these children in special education programs.

Much criticism has been aimed toward the use of standardized tests. It has been variously claimed that most standardized tests (a) are highly loaded with items based on White, middle class values and experiences (Williams, 1970); (b) penalize children with linguistic styles differing from that of the dominant culture; (c) sample cognitive styles directly opposed to those found in many children from low income families (Cohen, 1969) or culturally diverse groups (Kleinfeld, 1973); (d) are often administered in an atmosphere that may penalize culturally diverse children (e.g., White examiner, group administration); and (e) are scored based on norms derived from predominantly White, middle class standardization groups.

Current efforts to reduce these forms of bias include the development of new testing procedures, the use of adaptive behavior scales, the use of criterion referenced measures, and the interpretation of test results using local or special group norms. These alternatives are now in the developmental phase and have yet to be widely accepted as standard procedures.

This puts school systems in a difficult position. There is a clear mandate in Public Law 94–142 to insure that tests and other evaluative procedures are nondiscriminatory in nature. A firm theoretical and empirical basis for current evaluation options, however, has yet to be established. The purpose of this article is to delineate the current status of nondiscriminatory evaluation. The research on current attempts to reduce bias will be reviewed and some broad considerations will be discussed that have implications for school systems attempting to meet current legislative and societal mandates for nondiscriminatory evaluation.

THE SEARCH FOR A NONBIASED TEST

Historically speaking, the most common strategy employed by test developers to eliminate bias has been an attempt to minimize the cultural and verbal components of testing. Examples of such attempts include the Davis-Eells Games (Davis & Eells, 1953), the Culture Free Intelligence Test (Cattell, 1950), and Raven's Coloured Progressive Matrices (Raven, 1962).

Despite these attempts to desocialize evaluation instruments, research consistently indicates that children from low income or minority group backgrounds score lower than White, middle class children on these tests (Costello & Dickie, 1970; Drake, 1959: Higgins & Sivers,

From *Exceptional Children*, Vol. 46, No. 8, May 1980. Copyright 1980, The Council for Exceptional Children. Reprinted with permission.

1958; Kidd, 1962; Marquart & Bailey, 1955; Tate, 1952). This failure to equalize performance patterns has been attributed to differences in cognitive style (Cohen, 1969), bias in society at large (Ornstein, 1976), and unrealistic expectations for instruments that sample a limited range of school related skills (Ebel, 1972).

More recently, other strategies have been used to develop tests that, on the surface, should be free of bias. Williams (1972) developed the Black Intelligence Test of Cultural Homogeneity (BITCH), a 100 item test biased in favor of Blacks by selecting vocabulary items used in the Black culture but not in the White culture. De Avila and Havassy (1975) suggested that tests based on Piaget's stages of cognitive development are more likely to tap fairly the intellectual functioning of children from culturally diverse backgrounds. Budoff and Friedman (1969), Feuerstein (1979), and Kunzelmann and Koenig (1976) have all suggested procedures that measure the child's ability to improve test performance as a result of practice or training sessions. Each contends that postpractice or posttraining scores of low income or minority children are more accurate and less discriminatory than first day scores.

Unfortunately, none of these procedures has undergone the rigorous validation process necessary to determine whether, in fact, use of these instruments leads to reduced bias in labeling and placement. It may be that the search for one measure of general ability that is equally applicable to all cultural groups represents a simplistic approach to a complex problem. There are many reasons for school failure; there are also many reasons for low test performance. As these instruments are undergoing validation procedures, they should be viewed as experimental screening procedures that, as yet, tell us little about the nature of services needed to meet the needs of individual children.

ADAPTIVE BEHAVIOR SCALES

Adaptive behavior scales attempt to measure the ability of an individual to cope with the natural and social demands of the environment (Grossman, 1973), and thus should provide a more meaningful index of the individual's need for special services than does the use of intelligence tests alone. Many educators are now advocating the use of adaptive behavior scales in the placement process, since it appears that their use tends to reduce the placement of minority children in special classes. The use of dual criteria (intelligence tests and adaptive behavior scales) is assumed to result in a more valid diagnosis of mental retardation.

Brantley and Harbin (1978) divided adaptive behavior scales into three categories: developmental, psychosocial, and social systems.

Developmental Measures

Developmental measures are among the early adaptive behavior measures. The Vineland Social Maturity Scale (Doll, 1965) was designed to identify abnormal behavior and development as measured by sets of age related developmental milestones. Unfortunately, in the case of this and other developmental devices, the expectancies of the dominant culture were used in developing items. Most of these devices were normed on White, middle class populations, thereby ignoring the variations of a culturally diverse society. The norms have not been updated recently. For these reasons, developmental devices such as the Vineland Social Maturity Scale do not appear to meet the explicit and implicit mandates of nondiscriminatory testing (Harbin & Brantley, 1978).

Psychosocial Measures

Psychosocial measures, such as the AAMD Adaptive Behavior Scale (Nihira, Foster, Shellhaas, & Leland, 1974), were developed to provide a more comprehensive sampling of behavior than traditional norm referenced psychological or social devices. The devices in this category were originally developed as criterion referenced measures to aid in planning programs for institutionalized or low functioning mentally retarded persons. Other devices belonging in this category include the Devereux Child Behavior Rating Scale, Lakeland Adaptive Behavior Scale, Camelot, and Adaptive Behavior: Street Survival Skills Questionnaire. While these devices are useful for program planning, they have been criticized as not useful for identification of mentally retarded individuals because they are not norm referenced and because the content focuses on the low functioning child, and thus does not provide an accurate picture of normative functioning.

The AAMD Adaptive Behavior Scale: Public School Version (Nihira et al., 1974) is an attempt to transfer the measurement of adaptive behavior from an institutional setting to a public school setting and transform a criterion referenced device to a norm referenced device. A few items from the original Adaptive Behavior

Scale were eliminated and the remaining were standardized on a public school population, yielding separate norms for normal and handicapped children.

While some research has indicated that the Public School Version of the AAMD Scale may be useful in measuring the adaptive behavior of public school children (Lambert & Nicoll, 1976), there are two major concerns about the appropriateness of this instrument in the identification of mentally retarded children. First, the items in the scale were designed for a low functioning population, and thus do not sample a range of skills that is broad enough to encompass the functioning of mildly retarded and normal children. Second, it may be that the special group norms such as educable mentally retarded (EMR) and trainable mentally retarded (TMR) included children who were labeled erroneously because an adaptive behavior measure was not used when these children were labeled. For example, some minority children in California were labeled as mentally retarded but were later declassified and removed from special education when tested with both an intelligence test and an adaptive behavior scale. It is possible that some of these declassified children were included in the EMR norm group.

Social System Measures

The Adaptive Behavior Inventory for Children (ABIC) (Mercer & Lewis, 1978) is the only example of a social system measure available today. The ABIC assesses the child's ability to participate in social roles in the home and community. Mercer and others (Oakland, 1979) have demonstrated that the use of the ABIC eliminates the overrepresentation of minority children in some school systems, and have suggested that the ABIC is one answer to reducing bias in assessment. However, the ABIC has received some criticisms. The educational relevance of the instrument has been questioned (Goodman, 1977; Harbin & Brantley, 1978) because the arrangement of items into social roles makes it difficult for educators to translate the child's performance into an individualized education program (IEP). Gridley and Mastenbrook (1977) cited the need for local norms to accommodate the differences in experiences and societal demands from one locality to another.

Issues in Adaptive Behavior Assessment

At least three issues need to be resolved before the utility of adaptive behavior scales can be fully determined. First, there needs to be a consensus among professionals as to what comprises the adaptive behavior construct. Most people can agree on the AAMD definition (Grossman, 1973), but the operationalization of that definition into measurable behaviors has resulted in a wide range of items that vary greatly across adaptive behavior instruments. It must be asked whether these different instruments are, in fact, measuring the same thing. In an attempt to address that very issue, Goodman (1978) compared Mercer's early adaptive behavior scale and the Public School Version of the AAMD Scale and found no correlation between the two. If this finding is substantiated by subsequent research on current versions of these instruments, then adequate documentation of the content and construct validities of these instruments must be called for.

The second issue regards the instrumentation of adaptive behavior scales. Most of the scales depend on parent interviews or teacher reports for the collection of information. This approach may be logical and less time consuming than direct observation, but the reliability of the procedure is questionable. Millham, Chilcutt, and Atkinson (1978) compared a direct measure of adaptive behavior with the reports of floor counselors in a residential facility. Even after extensive training was given to the counselors, there was disagreement in 55.8% of the ratings. This is certainly an unacceptable level of agreement, indicating that much work remains to be done to insure the accuracy of the data collected.

The final issue regards problems in misclassification. Several studies have demonstrated that use of the ABIC has reduced the number of minority and low income children labeled as retarded to the proportion occurring in the general population (Mercer, 1973; Fisher, 1977; Reschly, 1978; Tebeleff & Oakland, 1977). In fact, Harbin (1980), in a study of rural Black children already classified as EMR, found that use of the ABIC resulted in the underrepresentation of that group in special classes. While it appears that bias has been reduced, there is no assurance that appropriate educational decisions are being made. Perhaps use of the ABIC means that some children who really do need support services to succeed in school will not be eligible for them. The impact of this procedure on the quality of education received by all children must be considered.

The impetus to use adaptive behavior measurement in the identification of mentally retarded individuals may be more political than evidentiary. Although the measurement of adaptive behavior makes theoretical sense because it provides a more complete picture of the child, there remains a need to adequately document the reliability and validity of these instruments.

CRITERION REFERENCED MEASURES

A number of professionals have argued that increased use of criterion referenced tests in the evaluation process would force decision makers to focus on the specific educational needs of children, as opposed to focusing on the labeling process. (A criterion referenced measure compares a child's performance with some standard of mastery, whereas a norm referenced measure compares a child's performance with that of other children.) This practice should facilitate nondiscriminatory decision making because the process then becomes one of (a) identifying basic skills that most children are expected to achieve, (b) assessing all children to determine which of these skills are present, and (c) designing appropriate instructional strategies to teach the remaining skills.

Bailey (1979) lent support to the contention that criterion referenced tests are an efficient and effective means of making some educational decisions. In a comparison of a number of screening procedures to identify high risk kindergartners, Bailey found a criterion referenced measure of kindergarten skills to be more accurate than the Stanford-Binet Intelligence Scale in predicting risk status. He concluded that educators should spend their time assessing specific school skills, rather than trying to sort children into various high risk groups.

This approach is appealing at first glance, but several problems present themselves. First, the current status of state and federal laws and funding systems necessitates a continuation of the labeling process. To suggest that school systems ignore mandatory guidelines for classification and placement of children would be unwise. Second, even if school systems *were* free to adopt a criterion referenced approach to evaluation, this would not necessarily insure nondiscriminatory decision making. Many of the discriminatory aspects of norm referenced measures, such as wording or content, can be found in criterion referenced measures as well.

Criterion referenced measures, however, can be extremely useful in making appropriate educational decisions. They can also fulfill the mandates for nondiscriminatory assessment when the following conditions are met:

1. The importance of the skills measured by the instrument and taught in the curriculum are agreed upon by culturally diverse groups within the school system.
2. Criterion referenced items are constructed so as not to measure the skills of children from a particular cultural group unfairly.
3. Alternative instructional strategies are incorporated to meet the learning needs of individual children.

For a long time information from criterion referenced devices was considered inadequate for making placement decisions. Actually, they provide information that is crucial in determining the program that best meets a child's educational needs. Both criterion referenced and norm referenced tests should be considered before making an educational decision, because each provides a perspective that the other does not. Decision makers should incorporate information from a wide range of sources before making significant placement decisions.

LOCAL OR SPECIAL GROUP NORMS

The purpose of norms is to provide a reference for interpreting a child's performance. Therefore, a set of norms must provide a meaningful and relevant standard for comparison. The current controversy over the use of local or special group norms concerns the conditions under which those norms are relevant (Oakland & Matuszek, 1977). Some professionals claim that many low income and minority children are constrained by a system that keeps judging their performance in light of norms of the dominant culture, and that the use of special group or regional norms allows comparison of the child to other children who have had similar opportunities and experiences. Professionals on the other side of the controversy claim that a useful standardization sample is drawn from different regions in the United States and is stratified by age, sex, socioeconomic status, and racial-ethnic groups in the same proportion as that in which these groups appear in society. These professionals feel that local and special group norms are, in the end, provincial. Although the practice of using local or special group norms sounds progressive and humanitarian, it actually works against the child's mobility. The end result of comparing a child to special and local norm groups is that of confining him to those groups.

The complexities of this issue do not lend themselves to easy resolution. At present the arguments for and against local or special group norms are philosophical in nature and are not empirically based. There is a clear need for systematic examination of the effects of local and special group norms, not only in relation to the question of bias, but also in the determination of whether all children are provided appropriate educational programs. A responsible decision concerning those instances where special norms are appropriate will be based upon sophisticated evaluation techniques reflecting the complexities of the issue.

CURRENT STATUS

While the legal status of nondiscriminatory evaluation is clear, the theoretical and technical status is uncertain at best. The movement toward bias free testing may be viewed alternately as a step backward that serves to emphasize and reinforce differences between cultural groups, a set of costly alternatives that have yet to be adequately validated, or a long overdue and appropriate response to a pressing human concern. Arguments in favor of one position or another range from the emotional to the empirical, and the final judgment of these procedures will probably be a long time in coming.

There are two major cautions which can and must be raised at this point, because the implications they bear will surely affect future research and development in this area. These cautions are concerned with the elimination of bias throughout the evaluation process and the selection of appropriate educational services for all children.

Elimination of Bias

Decision making is a step-by-step process. For example, the steps in the diagnostic and placement process typically include (a) referral, (b) testing, (c) interpretation of results, (d) determination of eligibility, (e) recommendation for placement, and (f) actual placement. While much criticism has been aimed at the testing component of this process, each step has the potential for bias against certain individuals or groups of children. The existence of this bias has been demonstrated by Mercer (1973). In a study of the labeling process in California, Mercer reported no socioeconomic bias and only slight ethnic bias in teacher referral of children for evaluation for special services. However, varying degrees of bias were found throughout the remainder of the evaluation process. A larger percentage of referred minority children were actually selected for formal testing. When those children were tested using a standard intelligence test, a greater percentage of minority children received IQ

scores below 80. Of the 134 children found eligible for special services, 47.4% were White, 32.7% were Mexican-American, and 19.8% were Black. However, of the 134 who were eligible, only 81 children were recommended for placement. Of these 81 children, 37.9% were White (a drop of 10%), 40.9% were Mexican-American (an increase of 8.2%) and 21.2% were Black (an increase of 1.4%). Finally, there were 71 children who were actually placed in special education classes. Of the 71 children, 31.1% were White (a drop of 15.3% compared to the percentage of Whites who were eligible), 45.3% were Mexican-American (an increase of 12.6% compared to the percentage who were eligible), and 22.6% were Black (an increase of 3.8% compared to the percentage of Blacks who were eligible). Each subsequent step resulted in greater bias against children from culturally diverse backgrounds.

Thus it appears that bias is not limited to the tests themselves, but is a problem permeating the entire decision-making process. The alternatives offered today have largely focused on the single evaluation step that is concrete and visible: the tests themselves. It is understandable that the focus is so directed, because the other steps in the evaluation process require human interpretation and decision making and the specific causes of bias are much more difficult to identify. There is a real need to continue to reexamine the tests, but bias does occur in human judgment and it would be a delusion to think that the elimination of test bias alone will result in nondiscriminatory decisions.

This is not to imply widespread intentional racial or economic prejudice in the education system. Prejudice may exist in some instances, but the problem in this case appears to be one of inadequate training in the decision-making process. Until teachers, administrators, school psychologists, parents, and others responsible for placement decisions gain skills in assessing and evaluating children from a pluralistic perspective within a team approach, school systems will continue to have difficulty in meeting legislative and social demands for nondiscriminatory evaluation.

Appropriate Educational Programs

The second caution regards the ultimate aim of educational decision making, which should be that of deciding the most appropriate program of services for each child. While this goal probably served as a major impetus for the movement toward nondiscriminatory evaluation, it has since taken a secondary role as professionals have focused on attempts to establish equality in testing. Little has been done to assess the impact of these procedures on the quality of the services children receive.

Children are not usually referred for evaluation on a teacher's whim. A referral indicates a significant educational problem that is unlikely to be remedied without some form of additional intervention with the teacher or child. It is the responsibility of the evaluation team to insure that the need for intervention is adequately documented and to determine the service approach that best meets the child's needs. Cultural background should play a major role in determining both of these decisions.

The elimination of bias and good decisionmaking are two separate goals. One is a social, legal, and ethical problem, the other is an educational programing problem. The achievement of one goal does not insure the achievement of the other. In the search for bias free assessments, evaluators must continue to examine educational programing options and make sure the assessment procedures used are directly related to these options.

CONCLUSION

The elimination of bias in decisionmaking will not be completely achieved through the development of new test instruments alone. At least three additional conditions must be met. First, the evaluation process must be conducted by an interdisciplinary team of professionals who (a) can select and use data gathering techniques in a nondiscriminatory fashion, (b) can truly work together as a team in making educational decisions, and (c) understand how bias can enter into the decisionmaking process and thus make systematic attempts to identify and control sources of bias.

Second, the evaluation process must focus on the specific skills necessary for survival in the academic setting. The major goal of the evaluation team should be that of identifying the discrepancies between skills the child possesses and those required in the classroom. Once this goal has been reached, the placement decision can be made on the basis of which service setting is most likely to meet an individual's needs.

Finally, the evaluation process must be conducted from an ecological perspective (Bronfenbrenner, 1976). This means that a child's performance must be evaluated within the total context of the settings in which he or she functions. These settings include the home, school, peer groups, and community, as well as the interrelationships existing between them.

It appears that education is currently making a concerted attempt to respond to legal and legislative mandates to reduce bias in testing by more carefully categorizing children. While this is an appropriate and necessary response, it will be a hollow victory unless the educational programs to which children are assigned actually meet the needs of those students.

REFERENCES

Bailey, D. B. *A comparison of non-biased screening procedures to identify high-risk kindergarten children*. Doctoral dissertation. University of Washington, 1979.

Brantley, J. C., & Harbin, G. L. *Adaptive behavior: Conceptual approaches and considerations in measurement*. Unpublished paper. Chapel Hill: University of North Carolina at Chapel Hill, 1978.

Bronfenbrenner, U. The experimental ecology of education. *Educational Researcher*, 1976, 5, 5–15.

Budoff, M., & Friedman, M. Learning potential as an assessment approach to the adolescent mentally retarded. *Journal of Consulting Psychology*, 1964, 28, 434–439.

Cattell, R. B. *Culture-free intelligence test.* Champaign IL: Institute for Pesonality and Ability Testing, 1950.

Cohen, R. A. Conceptual styles, culture conflict, and nonverbal tests of intelligence. *American Anthropologist*, 1969, 71, 828–856.

Costello, J., & Dickie, J. Leiter and Stanford-Binet IQs of preschool disadvantaged children. *Developmental Psychology*, 1970, 2, 314.

Davis, A., & Eells, K. *Davis-Eells Test of General Intelligence or Problem-Solving Ability*. Yonkers NY: World Book, 1953.

De Avila, E. A., & Havassy, B. E. Piagetian alternative to IQ: Mexican American study. In N. Hobbs (Ed.), *Issues in the classification of children*. San Francisco: Jossey-Bass, 1975.

Doll, E. A. *Vineland Social Maturity Scale.* Circle Pines MN: American Guidance Service, 1965.

Drake, R. M. Review of Davis-Eells games. In O. K. Buros (Ed.), *The fifth mental measurements yearbook*. Highland Park NJ: The Gryphon Press, 1959.

Ebel, R. L. *Essentials of educational measurement*. Englewood Cliffs, NJ: Prentice-Hall, 1972.

Feuerstein, P. *The dynamic assessment of retarded performers*. Baltimore: University Park Press, 1979.

Fisher, A. *Adaptive behavior in non-biased assessment: Effects on special education*. Paper presented at the Annual Meeting of the American Psychological Association, San Francisco, 1977.

Goodman, C. M. *Assessment and individual program planning uses of the AAMD Adaptive Behavior Scale with North Central Mississippi elementary students*. Unpublished doctoral dissertation. The University of Mississippi, 1978.

Goodman, J. F. The diagnostic fallacy: A critique of Jane Mercer's concept of mental retardation. *Journal of School Psychology*, 1977, 15 (3), 197–205.

Gridley, G. C., & Mastenbrook, J. *Research on the*

need for local norms for the Adaptive Behavior Inventory for Children. Paper presented at the Annual Meeting of the American Psychological Association, San Francisco, 1977.

Grossman, H. J. Manual on terminology and classification in mental retardation. Washington DC: American Association on Mental Deficiency, 1973.

Harbin, G. L. Comparison of the use of single versus dual criteria in the classification of the EMR black child. Unpublished paper. Chapel Hill: University of North Carolina at Chapel Hill, 1980.

Harbin, G. L., & Brantley, J. C. A comparison of measures of adaptive behavior. Unpublished paper. Chapel Hill: University of North Carolina at Chapel Hill, 1978.

Higgins, C., & Sivers, C. H. A comparison of Stanford-Binet and Raven Coloured Progressive Matrices IQs for children with low socioeconomic status. Journal of Consulting Psychology, 1958, 22, 465–468.

Kidd, A. H. The culture-fair aspects of Cattell's Test of g: Culture free. Journal of Genetic Psychology, 1962, 101, 343–362.

Kleinfeld, J. S. Intellectual strengths in culturally different groups: An Eskimo illustration. Review of Educational Research, 1973, 43, 341–359.

Kunzelmann, H., & Koenig, C. Nondiscriminatory assessment using learning screening. Kansas City MO: International Management Systems, 1976.

Lambert, N.M., & Nicoll, R. C. Dimensions of adaptive behavior of retarded and non-retarded public-school children. American Journal of Mental Deficiency, 1976, 81, 135–146.

Marquart, D. I., & Bailey, L. L. An evaluation of the Culture-Free Test of Intelligence. Journal of Genetic Psychology, 1955, 86, 353–358.

Mercer, J. R. Labeling the mentally retarded: Clinical and social system perspectives on mental retardation. Berkeley CA: University of California Press, 1973.

Mercer, J. R., & Lewis, J. F. System of Multi-cultural Pluralistic Assessment: Conceptual and technical manual. Riverside: Institute for Pluralistic Assessment Research and Training, 1978.

Millham, J., Chilcutt, J., & Atkinson, B. Comparability of naturalistic and controlled observation assessment of adaptive behavior. American Journal of Mental Deficiency, 1978, 83, 52–59.

Nihira, K., Foster, R., Shellhaas, M., & Leland, H. AAMD Adaptive Behavior Scale (1974 revision). Washington DC: American Association on Mental Deficiency, 1974.

Oakland, T. Research on the Adaptive Behavior Inventory for Children and the estimated learning potential. School Psychology Digest, 1979, 8 (1), 63–70.

Oakland, T., & Matuszek, P. Using tests in nondiscriminatory assessment. In T. Oakland (Ed.), Psychological and educational assessment of minority children. New York: Brunner/Mazel, 1977.

Ornstein, A. IQ tests and the culture issue. Phi Delta Kappan, 1976, 52, 403–404.

Raven, J. C. Coloured progressive matrices. New York: Psychological Corporation, 1962.

Reschly, D. Comparisons of bias in assessment with conventional and pluralistic measures. Paper presented at the Annual Convention of The Council for Exceptional Children, Kansas City MO, 1978.

Tate, M. E. The influence of cultural factors on the Leiter International Performance Scale. Journal of Abnormal and Social Psychology, 1952, 47, 497–501.

Tebeleff, M., & Oakland, T. Relationship between the ABIC, WISC-R, and achievement. Paper presented at the Annual Meeting of the American Psychological Association, San Francisco, 1977.

Williams, R. L. The BITCH Test (Black Intelligence Test of Cultural Homogeneity). St. Louis: Williams & Associates, 1972.

Williams, R. L. Black pride, academic relevance, and individual achievement. Counseling Psychologist, 1970, 2, 18–22.

Social and Emotional Needs Of Culturally Diverse Children

by Ronald W. Henderson

4

■ Teachers and administrators are now well accustomed to being admonished that schools must do a better job of meeting the special needs of children from socially and culturally diverse backgrounds. The prevailing assumption behind this advice seems to be that if children differ culturally from the White, middle class dominated traditions of the schools, their needs must also differ. Thus, for example, educators are advised to match instructional strategies to the cognitive styles that are assumed to differentiate culturally diverse children from their Euro-American peers.

The consequences of following this advice are not clear. While some attempts to match instruction to different cultural styles have been reported as successful, other attempts have produced effects opposite to the hypothesized benefits of instructional matching (Kagan & Buriel, 1977). Moreover, the research base upon which the notion that ethnic groups differ along such cognitive style dimensions as field dependence/independence does not provide entirely consistent results (Knight, Kagan, Nelson, & Gumbiner, 1978). Similarly, inconclusive findings have been reported for such developmental characteristics as self esteem (Gray-Little & Applebaum, 1979) and locus of control (Knight, et al., 1978). In brief, while there is wide agreement that instruction should take culturally determined characteristics into consideration in order to reduce the undesirable effects of discontinuities between home and school learning, there is disagree-

ment about the nature of the differences, their distribution within given groups, and how instruction should be adapted to take these factors into account.

If scientific information concerning the specific nature of cognitive needs among culturally diverse groups of children served by the schools is something less than definitive, knowledge of conditions required to promote their social and emotional well-being is even less clear. It seems unlikely that the basic needs of culturally diverse children vary on the basis of differences in their social and cultural characteristics. Rather it appears that a variety of social and cultural factors interact in ways that serve to curtail the probability that these needs will be met adequately within the context of schooling as presently constituted. While social scientists have shown a long standing interest in the ways in which sociocultural factors influence development, efforts to sort out the influences of complexly intertwined factors have been frustrated by both methodological and definitional problems.

Some of the problems that cloud the understanding of these interactions will be reviewed in this article, and a path model of reciprocal influences will be proposed with implications for the social and emotional well being of children whose cultural background deviates from the implicit expectations of the schools. Social and emotional well-being is too broad and ill defined a set of variables with which to explore the path model hypothesis. Therefore a more restricted aspect of social and emotional adjustment, functional adaptation, will serve to focus the premise explored in the latter portion of the article.

CULTURAL DIVERSITY AND STEREOTYPES

Basic Concepts

The terms *culture* and *society* are used in varied and often undefined ways by social scientists and educators. In their examination of uses of the concept of culture, Kroeber and Kluckholm (1952) found over 160 definitions of the term in the social science literature. What most of the definitions had in common was the idea that culture is composed of habitual patterns of behavior that are characteristic of a group of people. Those shared behavioral patterns are transmitted from one generation to the next through symbolic communication (Kroeber & Kluckholm, 1952) and through modeling and demonstration (Henderson & Bergan, 1976). Culture includes the goals and values that serve to instigate behavior and determine priorities within a social group.

While British anthropologists use the term society to designate the concept that most American social scientists call culture (Evans-Prichard, 1951; Radcliffe-Browne, 1957), Americans generally use the term society to designate an aggregation of individuals who live together in an organized population (Linton, 1936). Thus, *society* refers to a collective of people while *culture* focuses on the customary behaviors that are shared among people in the group. The terms are often used interchangeably when it is not considered important to distinguish between an aggregate of people and their customary patterns of behavior. The temptation to avoid making this conceptual distinction probably accounts for the popularity of the more general term, *sociocultural*.

People of differing statuses within a society play various roles, and the total set of roles make up the social structure of that group. These roles include those that define social stratification within a society.

The United States is a complex society in which a number of diverse groups may be identified. The members of any of these groups display a distinct way of life and social scientists often designate the group as a subculture. Valentine (1968, cited in Laosa, in press) has noted that the variety of units to which distinctive life ways have been attributed include such diverse groupings as ethnic collec-

tives, socioeconomic strata, age groups, and regional populations. From this perspective it is certainly possible to talk about the subculture of public education as well. But subcultures are distinct from the larger culture only in the limited sense that any part may be distinguished from the whole in which it is embedded (Laosa, in press), and it is in this limited sense that, for lack of a better designation, educators often refer to children who are members of identifiable groups—whose life ways deviate in certain ways from the dominant pattern—as *culturally diverse*, the term employed in this discussion.

Stereotypes

The pitfalls involved in distinguishing the influences of socialization experiences in a subculture are not easy to avoid, even by researchers who are aware of them. During the 1960's educators were introduced to studies that described the cultural characteristics of various ethnic groups. It was assumed that this information would help teachers to acquire a better understanding of the pupils in their charge. While every subcultural group is characterized by substantial heterogeneity (Laosa, in press), that diversity was largely ignored and stereotyped views were conveyed. For instance, motivational problems with Black children were attributed, in part, to a matriarchal family structure (Moynihan, 1967), a pattern that is less pervasive than the generalizations would suggest (English, 1974). Similarly, male dominance was seen as a hindrance to independence, mobility, and achievement among Mexican American youth (Heller, 1966); yet more recent work among migrant farm labor families found the most common mode of decision making to be egalitarian (Hawks & Taylor, 1975).

A number of studies have reported on the motivational characteristics of children from minority backgrounds. For example, the belief system of Hispanic Americans has been described as highly fatalistic (Heller, 1966; Madsen, 1964; Paz, 1961), a characteristic that has been blamed for hampering educational, social, and economic advancement. Yet when Farris and Glenn (1976) compared fatalism among Anglos and Mexican Americans in a Texas sample, they found no differences between the groups when they controlled for level of education.

Given findings that have helped to dispel cultural stereotypes, it should be remembered that in most ways members of subcultures within United States society are culturally more similar to each other than they are different, and in most cases within group variation exceeds between group variations. The world of subcultures is one of overlapping distributions.

Methodological Problems

In an ideal world it should be possible to distinguish between the influences of various intertwined cultural and social structural variables. Many studies that compare ethnic or racial minority and nonminority children fail to control for socioeconomic status (Laosa, in press). Thus the results are ambiguous at best and usually misleading. Chan and Rueda (1979) rightly argued that researchers should be careful to distinguish between the effects of poverty and culture in their analyses, but that is more easily said than done. There is little research available on the social or emotional development of ethnic minority children that has accomplished such separation with clarity. Chan and Rueda (1979) made the point that poverty mediates both biomedical health and the socialization environment. Their point is especially well taken with reference to health, but the distinction begins to get more vague when the socialization environment is discussed. For example, they attributed lack of socialization information among the poor to their reliance on the electronic media rather than books, which may be considered an expensive luxury. It is at least as reasonable to attribute this pattern to culturally patterned preferences and values as to poverty in itself.

The difficulty of making clear distinctions between cultural and social structural influences is important because a disproportionate number of children who are from minority group subcultures are also poor. Not all minority children are poor, and not all poor children are minorities. However, poor children, whether minority or not, may display culturally acquired behavior that deviates from the expectations implicit in the culture of the school. To the extent that this is true, they also may be considered "culturally diverse" for purposes of the present discussion.

Social and Emotional Well-Being

Problems of social and emotional well-being for culturally diverse children may be examined in a number of alternative ways. For example, as a result of discontinuities between home and school, many culturally diverse children encounter aversive experiences at school that could be explained by conditioning principles. The approach selected for present purposes is to focus on a specific aspect of social competence. The term *social competence* has an appealing ring to it, but as many observers have commented (Anderson & Messick, 1974; Zigler & Trickett, 1978), experts are far from agreement on the meaning of that construct. Recent work (Monson, Greenspan & Simeonsson, 1979) has conceptualized social competence with reference to interpersonal functioning in social settings such as classrooms. Dimensions of this conceptualization that have been examined include interest, curiosity, or assertiveness and conformity to rules and expectations (Kohn & Rosman, 1972; Monson, Greenspan & Simeonsson, 1979). These conceptions are compatible with Laosa's (1979) position that social competence involves functional adaptations to specific environments. Each environment may have its own specific demand characteristics for functional adaptation, and for a child success in two different environments may depend on the degree of overlap in the demand characteristics of the environments (Laosa, 1979).

Within the school environment, demand characteristics to which functional adaptations are required include such behaviors as appearing interested in school work, paying attention, and persisting at tasks. The present discussion focuses on the possible consequences for culturally diverse children who are unable to make a functional adaptation to the interpersonal setting of the school. But implicitly, the conceptualization presented here assumes that a condition required for primary prevention is for educators to know something about the child's environmental organization (Laosa, 1979), and to make adaptations in the interpersonal environment of the classroom that will enable the child to adapt to the requirements of school culture.

A PATH MODEL FOR CHILDREN AT RISK

A substantial body of research reviewed by Brophy and Good (1974) shows quite uniformly that teachers hold differential expectations regarding the academic performance of children who vary in personal characteristics such as sex, age, ethnicity, race, and even physical attractiveness (Brophy & Good, 1974; Henderson, in press). It could be argued that these expectancies are based on actual knowledge of children's motivation and achievement characteristics, but it is instructive to note that teachers may express stereotyped expectations based upon labels assigned to children even when the objective behavioral evidence runs contrary to those expectations.

This point is illustrated in a study (Foster &

Ysseldyke, 1976) in which teachers viewed a videotape of a normal fourth grade boy engaged in various test taking and free play activities. Different groups of teachers who viewed the tapes were told that the child whose behavior was depicted on the tape suffered from a different disorder: emotional disturbance, learning disability, or mental retardation. One group of viewers was informed that the child was normal. After viewing the tape, teachers expressed negative expectancies consistent with the deviance label they had been given. Differential expectations were expressed in spite of the fact that the behavior they witnessed was inconsistent with the label.

While the subjects in this study were not minority group children, the results seem particularly relevant to circumstances involving culturally diverse children, because these children have been so heavily overrepresented among those to whom deviance labels have been assigned (Richardson, 1979), and a number of studies have demonstrated that teacher expectations tend to be lower for minority than for majority children. The obvious question to ask, then, is whether or not variations in expectations are associated with differential behavior toward students. The answer seems to be yes.

Research reviewed by Good and Brophy (1974) revealed a fairly uniform pattern showing that whenever investigators have looked for differential treatment of students who vary in sex, achievement, or socioeconomic status, they have found it. An examination of the nature of these differences suggests that teacher communications toward children from lower socioeconomic status and/or racial and ethnic minority backgrounds is more likely to be aimed at controlling or managing behavior than is the case for their peers. Communications to majority, middle class children, in contrast, are more likely to be relevant to the content or skills of instruction than those teacher behaviors that are directed to children from culturally diverse backgrounds (Henderson, in press; Laosa, 1977).

While there is little direct information on the specific effects of differential teacher behaviors on the school achievement of culturally diverse children, an accumulation of research results does establish the general case that level of student involvement in academic tasks and the nature of teacher-student interactions are consistently related to achievement (Hoge & Luce, 1979). These findings are of particular interest when viewed in relationship to research on locus of control and learned helplessness, which provides a theoretical framework to explain how differences in teacher expectancies and interaction patterns may affect both the socioemotional development and achievement patterns of children with diverse socialization experiences outside the school.

PERCEPTIONS OF PERSONAL EFFICACY

Locus of Control

Locus of control is a personality construct that refers to the tendency of different individuals to perceive the events that influence their lives either as the consequence of their own actions (internal control), or as the result of external forces beyond their influence (external control). There is generally a positive relationship between internal perceptions of control and academic achievement (Henderson, in press; Lefcourt, 1976). Minority and poor children tend to score more toward the external end of the scale than their nonminority and more affluent peers (Henderson & Bergan, 1976).

Attribution Theory

Differences in locus of control have been explained on the basis of learned expectancies of reward as a consequence of behavior (Rotter, 1966), but more recently Heider's attribution theory (Weiner, 1979) has been used to amplify conceptions of locus of control and the closely related concept of learned helplessness. Individuals who find themselves unable to control aversive stimuli to which they are exposed often come to perceive themselves as helpless. Where the aversive experience is failure at a task that such individuals believe to be important, they may come to see themselves as incapable of overcoming failure. Failure leads to anxiety and deterioration of performance. Following failure experiences these individuals are likely to perform unsuccessfully even on tasks at which they were previously proficient. Children who experience repeated failure at the tasks assigned to them at school are likely to come to perceive themselves as incapable of accomplishing other tasks of the same kind. If the cognitive skills and behavioral norms a child has learned in the subculture of the home differ from those the school culture is prepared to build on, a disproportionate number of such children are likely to experience failure that is beyond their control and subsequently they will come to attribute failure to inability.

Causality may be attributed to a number of internal factors such as ability or effort, or to external factors such as luck or task difficulty (Heider, 1958). For example, an individual may perceive success or failure at a task as the result of ability (or inability), or level of effort. Within the norm referenced world of the classroom, children may be unable to discern their progress in relation to their own past performance, because implicit and explicit comparisons with peers are so salient (Henderson & Hennig 1979). The influence of failure experiences on the learning of helplessness has been documented in a large number of studies with animal (e.g., Abramson, Seligman, & Teasdale, 1978) and human (e.g., Wortman, Panciera, Shusterman, & Hibscher, 1976) subjects. In those studies that hold the clearest implications for children with exceptional needs, and more especially for those from culturally diverse backgrounds, the uncontrollable, aversive events that have led to perceptions of inability have involved the manipulation of feedback that lead subjects to believe they have failed problems that measure important human abilities (Roth & Kubal, 1975).

Effects of Learned Helplessness

In a series of studies, Dweck and her associates (Diner & Dweck, 1978; Dweck, 1975; Dweck & Busch, 1976; Dweck & Reppucci, 1973) found that children who have learned to feel helpless when confronted with difficult problems tend to attribute their failure to inability, while their nonhelpless peers often display improved performance following failure. Their improvement may be attributed to increased effort.

Helpless children are likely to see aversive situations as insurmountable and thus fail to display effort on subsequent tasks of the same sort. They are less likely to be willing to initiate a task or persist at it than are individuals who perceive their own effort as an important cause of success or failure outcomes. This is an important point, since there is evidence that differential instructional behaviors of teachers may be more associated with teacher judgments of pupil motivation to do school work than with achievement expectations (Luce & Hoge, 1978). This finding is particularly relevant in association with data showing that the behavior of teachers is markedly influenced by aspects of functional adaptation such as attending and nonattending behavior of students. Together these strands of evidence suggest that if helpless children respond to failure by declining to expend effort on subsequent tasks, teachers may react with negative expectations. Consequently, their interactions may be directed toward behavioral control rather than skill and content instruction.

Thomas (1979) has drawn attention to the striking parallels between the learned helplessness pattern and the characteristics of children classified as learning disabled. While the learning disabilities concept designates a diverse array of problems, Thomas noted that a common characteristic of children to whom this label is applied is that they are often convinced that they cannot learn. Consequently, a good deal of teaching is aimed at getting them to expend sufficient effort to achieve success (Thomas, 1979). The stronger a child's history of failure is, the more likelihood there is of self attributions of inability, and the likelihood of effortful, attentive behavior is concomitantly reduced. It seems that the nature of some schools in the United States almost predestines certain children to experience repeated failure, beginning with their earliest classroom experience. Since the socialization experience of culturally diverse children may not be highly congruent with the curricular and behavioral expectations of the middle class oriented school, a disproportionate number of them are at risk of falling into this group.

Failure, linked to perceptions of personal inability, may be coupled with negative affect (Ames, Ames & Felker, 1977). Failure may be experienced as a painful, punishing event, and the nature of responses to aversive stimuli are well documented. One response is escape or avoidance. Another is counter aggression (Henderson & Bergan, 1976). In the school context, either may be interpreted as alienation. Aversive failure experiences often produce anxiety, and a substantial body of research has documented the inverse relationship between anxiety and student ability to profit from instruction in school. Anxiety is linked to a range of academic indicators, including academic achievement and dropout rates (Tobias, 1979).

FACILITATING ENVIRONMENTS AND THERAPEUTIC APPROACHES

A number of instructional characteristics appear to facilitate perceptions of internal control and efficacy, while other procedures have been effective in increasing children's effort attributions. When children perceive a role in determining their own activities, they appear more likely to accept personal responsibility for success or failure than children in classrooms where no such opportunity to participate in the setting of objectives is provided (Arlin & Whitley, 1978; Wang & Stiles, 1976). It has also been demonstrated that the effects of success and failure are mediated by the kinds of social situations in which they occur. Classrooms constitute one of the few social settings in which children are routinely subjected to public comparisons of performance, and social comparisons are especially salient in those classrooms that employ competitive goal structures (Ames, Ames, & Felker, 1977; Henderson & Hennig, 1979). Failure is less likely to result in self deprecation in classrooms that employ a cooperative goal structure than in those characterized by norm referenced competition (Ames, Ames, & Felker, 1977).

A variety of therapeutic procedures have proved effective in changing dysfunctional attributions of cause (Henderson, in press). Since repeated failure experiences are implicated in the development of maladaptive attributions, it may seem logical that the way to change attributions from perceptions of inability to those of insufficient effort would be to provide generous portions of success. This appears not to be the case. Dweck (1975) found that a success-only intervention did not improve the ability of helpless children to sustain effort following a failure experience. In fact, after a success-only intervention, many children showed a subsequent increase in sensitivity to failure. Children who were given a program of cognitively oriented attribution retraining displayed subsequent increases in effort attributions and improved adaptation to failure.

Both environmental control programs and self regulation programs have been found effective in changing socially and academically maladaptive classroom behavior. However, the effectiveness of a given procedure seems to interact with children's perceptions of causation. Bugenthal, Whalen, and Henker (1978) have recommended beginning with therapy that is in line with the child's perceptions of causation, and moving toward procedures that provide greater self control through the application of self regulation strategies.

CONCLUSIONS AND IMPLICATIONS

Culturally diverse children are at risk of entering school with behaviors that differ from the cognitive and social norms governing the expectations of teachers who have been socialized into the school culture. These differences appear to play an important role in the reciprocal relationships among the child's capabilities, his or her actual behaviors, the teacher's expectancies, and the teacher's responses to the child. Differences in children's ability to adapt to school norms appear closely related to the level of formal education their own mothers have attained (Laosa, in press). Behaviors such as attentiveness and persistence at the kinds of tasks teachers consider important tend to influence the expectancies teachers hold, and these expectations, in turn, often influence the manner in which they interact with children.

Children whose behavior is discrepant from the norms of the school culture are likely to experience repeated failure. If, as a result, they develop feelings of helplessness in the school setting, they may well exert less and less effort, which in turn leads to more failure. An important social need of these children is to experience a feeling of personal efficacy. While it has been suggested that patterns of failure among culturally diverse children might be eliminated if the school would build systematically on abilities acquired by children in their home environments, it has proved more difficult than anticipated to put this suggestion into practice (Gallimore & Au, 1979).

One thing that can be done is to help teachers become aware of their own expectancies and variations in their instructional interactions with different children. Research on learned helplessness also suggests that it may help to structure classroom social environments in less competitive ways than has been traditional. In addition, children may be helped to gain a greater sense of efficacy if they are taught to set some of their own goals and to employ self regulation procedures. But therapeutic procedures based on experimental demonstrations are doomed to fall short if they are tagged on as remedial procedures in isolation from the on-going activities of a classroom. To do so would only provide an illusion of personal control, and set children up for additional failure.

Bilingual and multicultural programs that enable children to experience cultural and linguistic pride certainly have an important role to play in meeting the social and emotional needs of children from diverse backgrounds (Gibson, 1978; Goebes & Shore, 1978), but they cannot fully accomplish their purposes unless children are helped to experience genuine feelings of personal and social competence within the total school setting. Existing research provides only indirect evidence relative to how reciprocal influences in classrooms might be turned to a better advantage for culturally diverse children. More specific research addressed to these dynamics is urgently needed.

REFERENCES

Abramson, N. L., Seligman, M. E. P., & Teasdale, J.

D. Learned helplessness in humans: Critique and reformulation. *Journal of Abnormal Psychology*, 1978, *87*, 49–74.

Ames, C., Ames, R., & Felker, D. W. Effects of competitive reward structure and valence of outcome on children's achievement attributions. *Journal of Educational Psychology*, 1977, *69*, 1–8.

Anderson, S. B., & Messick, S. Social competence in young children. *Developmental Psychology*, 1974, *10*, 282–293.

Arlin, M., & Whitley, T. W. Perceptions of self-managed learning opportunities and academic locus of control: A causal interpretation. *Journal of Educational Psychology*, 1978, *70*, 988–992.

Brophy, J. E., & Good, T. *Teacher-student relationships: Causes and consequences.* New York: Holt, Rinehart & Winston, 1974.

Bugenthal, D., Whalen, C. K., & Henker. Causal attributions of hyperactive children and motivational assumptions of two behavior change approaches: Evidence for an interactionist position. *Child Development*, 1977, *48*, 874–884.

Chan, K. S., & Rueda, R. Poverty and culture in education: Separate but equal. *Exceptional Children*, 1979, *45*, 422–428.

Diner, C. I., & Dweck, C. S. An analysis of learned helplessness: Continuous changes in performance, strategy, and achievement conditions following failure. *Journal of Personality and Social Psychology*, 1978, *36*, 451–462.

Dweck, C. S. The role of expectations and attributions in the alleviation of learned helplessness. *Journal of Personality and Social Psychology*, 1975, *31*, 674–685.

Dweck, C. S., & Bush, E. S. Sex differences in learned helplessness: I. Differential debilitation with peer and adult evaluators. *Developmental Psychology*, 1976, *12*, 147–156.

Dweck, C. S., & Reppucci, N. D. Learned helplessness and reinforcement responsibility in children. *Journal of Personality and Social Psychology*, 1973, *25*, 109–116.

English, R. Beyond pathology: Research and theoretical perspectives on black families. In L. E. Gary (Ed.), *Social research and the black community: Selected issues and priorities.* Washington DC: Institute for Urban Affairs and Research, Howard University, 1974.

Evans-Pritchard, E. E. *Social Anthropology.* Glencoe IL: The Free Press, 1951.

Farris, B. E., & Glenn, N. D. Fatalism and familism among Anglos and Mexican Americans in San Antonio. *Sociology and Social Research*, 1976, *60*, 393–402.

Foster, G., & Ysseldyke, J. Expectancy and halo effects as a result of artificially induced teacher bias. *Contemporary Educational Psychology*, 1976, *1*, 37–45.

Gallimore, R., & Au, H. The competence/incompetence paradox in the education of minority culture children. *The Quarterly Newsletter of the Laboratory of Comparative Human Cognition*, 1979, *1*, 32–37.

Gibson, G. An approach to identification and prevention of developmental difficulties among Mexican-American children. *American Journal of Orthopsychiatry*, 1978, *48*, 96–113.

Goebes, D. D., & Shore, M. F. Some effects of bicultural and monocultural school environments on personality development. *American Journal of Orthopsychiatry*, 1978, *48*, 398–407.

Good, T. L., & Brophy, J. E. Changing teacher and student behavior: An empirical investigation. *Journal of Educational Psychology*, 1974, *66*, 390–405.

Gray-Little, B., & Applebaum, M. I. Instrumentality effects in the assessment of racial differences in self-esteem. *Journal of Personality and Social Psychology*, 1979, *37*, 1221–1229.

Hawkes, G. R., & Taylor, M. Power structure in Mexican and Mexican-American farm labor families. *Journal of Marriage and the Family*, *37*, 1975, 807–811.

Heider, F. *The psychology of interpersonal relations.* New York: Wiley, 1958.

Heller, C. S. *Mexican-American youth: Forgotten youth at the crossroads.* New York: Random House, 1966.

Henderson, R. W. Personal and social causation in the school context. In J. Worell (Ed.), *Developmental psychology for education.* New York: Academic Press, in press.

Henderson, R. W., & Bergan J. R. *The cultural context of childhood.* Columbus OH: Charles E. Merrill, 1976.

Henderson, R. W., & Hennig, H. Relationships among cooperation-competition and locus of control in academic situations among children in traditional and open classrooms. *Contemporary Educational Psychology*, 1979, *4*, 121–131.

Hoge, R. D., & Luce, S. Predicting academic achievement from classroom behavior. *Review of Educational Research*, 1979, *49*, 479–496.

Kagan, S. & Buriel, R. Field dependence-independence and Mexican-American culture and education. In J. L. Martinez (Ed.), *Chicano psychology.* New York: Academic Press, 1977.

Knight, G. P., Kagan, S., Nelson, W., & Gumbiner, J. Acculturation of second and third generation Mexican-American children. Field independence, locus of control, self-esteem, and school achievement. *Journal of Cross-Cultural Psychology*, 1978, *9*, 87–98.

Kohn, M., & Rosman, B. L. A social competence scale and symptom checklist for the preschool child. Factor dimensions, their cross-instrument generality, and longitudinal perspectives. *Developmental Psychology*, 1972, *6*, 430–444.

Kroeber, A. L., & Kluckhohn, C. *Culture: A critical review of concepts and definitions.* New York: Vintage Books, 1952.

Laosa, L. M. Inequality in the classroom: Observational research on teacher-student interactions. *Aztlan International Journal of Chicano Studies Research*, 1977, *8*, 51–67.

Laosa, L. M. Maternal behavior: Sociocultural diversity in modes of family interaction. In R. W. Henderson (Ed.), *Parent-child interaction: Theory, re-*

search and prospect. New York: Academic Press, in press.

Laosa, L. M. Social competence in childhood: Toward a developmental, socioculturally relativistic paradigm. In M. W. Kent & J. E. Rolf (Eds.), *Primary Prevention of Psychopathology* (Vol. III). Hanover NH: University Press of New England, 1979.

Lefcourt, H. M. *Locus of control: Current trends in theory and research.* Hillsdale NJ: Lawrence Erlbaum Associates, 1976.

Linton, R. *The study of man.* New York: Appleton-Century-Crofts, 1936.

Luce, S. R., & Hoge, R. D. Relations among teacher rankings, pupil-teacher interactions, and academic achievement: A test of the teacher expectancy hypothesis. *American Educational Research Journal,* 1978. *15,* 489–500.

Madsen, W. *The Mexican-American of South Texas.* New York: Holt, Rinehart & Winston, 1964.

Monson, L. B., Greenspan, S., & Simeonsson, R. J. Correlates of social competence in retarded children. *American Journal of Mental Deficiency,* 1979, *83,* 627–630.

Moynihan, D. P. *The Negro family: The case for national action.* Washington DC: US Department of Labor, March, 1967.

Paz, O. *The labyrinth of solitude: Life and thought in Mexico.* New York: Grove Press, 1961.

Radcliffe-Browne, A. R. *A natural science of society.* Glencoe IL: The Free Press, 1957.

Richardson, J. G. The case of special education and minority misclassification in California. *Educational Research Quarterly,* 1979, *4,* 25–40.

Roth, S., & Kubal, L. The effects of noncontingent reinforcement on tasks of differing importance: Facilitation and learned helplessness effects. *Journal of Personality and Social Psychology,* 1975, *32,* 680–691.

Rotter, J. B. Generalized expectancies for internal versus external control of reinforcement. *Psychological Monographs,* 1966, *80,* (1, whole No. 609).

Thomas, A. Learned helplessness and expectancy factors: Implications for research in learning disabilities. *Review of Educational Research,* 1979, *49,* 200–221.

Tobias, S. Anxiety research in educational psychology. *Journal of Educational Psychology,* 1979, *71,* 573–582.

Wang, M. C., & Stiles, B. An investigation of children's concept of self-responsibility for school learning. *American Educational Research Journal,* 1976, *13,* 159–179.

Weiner, B. A theory of motivation for some classroom experiences. *Journal of Educational Psychology,* 1979, *71,* 3–25.

Wortman, C. B., Panciera, L., Shusterman, L., & Hibscher, J. Attributions of causality and reactions to uncontrollable outcomes. *Journal of Experimental Social Psychology,* 1976, *12,* 327–345.

Zigler, E., & Trickett, P. K. IQ, social competence, and evaluation of early childhood intervention programs. *American Psychologist,* 1978, *33,* 789–798.

Teacher and Social Worker Agreement on Behavioral Expectations of Special Children

by Jon R. Conte and Linda McCoy

4

Special children in therapeutic educational programs receive intensive help for a period of time to enable them to develop the behaviors necessary to move to less restrictive environments. Concern has been expressed by some professionals working with these children that the behavioral expectations within these programs may not be consistent with those of postprogram placements. The isolation experienced by professionals working with special children may change their perceptions about typical behaviors and capabilities of children. As a result, their expectations of children within therapeutic educational settings may be at considerable variance from the expectations of professionals who will receive these children in their postprogram placements.

This issue was addressed as part of a larger evaluation of a day treatment program for severely behavior disordered children. Teachers and social workers who worked in this treatment program and teachers who worked in classrooms for behaviorally disturbed children in regular schools in the district were asked to participate in the study. The latter group was chosen because children were transferred to the classrooms for the behaviorally disturbed after termination from the day treatment program.

The study was designed to examine the within group and between group agreement on behavioral expectations of special children. Respondents were asked to rate each of 83 behaviors on a five point scale indicating the degree to which that behavior would impair a child's ability to function in a special education classroom within the district.

A 1 week test-retest reliability study of two ratings by the same day treatment staff member ($n=11$) indicates a moderately high level of agreement (Spearman's rho, $\overline{X}=73.7$). Three tests of within group agreement which describe the agreement among day treatment teachers ($n=5$), day treatment social workers ($n=6$), and district teachers ($n=7$) are all significant. In addition, the between group agreement for all three groups is also significant (Kendall's coefficient of concordance, $W=.8558$, $Chi^2=210.5$, $df=82$, $p=.00001$).

However, in spite of significant overall agreement on the rankings of items, an item by item comparison for each of the 83 behaviors found 22 significantly different ratings between day program social workers and district teachers; 14 significantly different ratings between day program teachers and district teachers; and only 1 significantly different rating between day program teachers and social workers. The number of significantly different effects exceeds the number which might be expected simply from chance in this large a number of analyses.

Visual inspection of the mean ratings for

each of the three professional groups shows that district teachers consistently rated items higher (i.e. rated the behavior as "extremely" or "very likely" to affect a child's ability to function in a district classroom) than did either day program teachers or social workers.

These data would seem to provide preliminary evidence to support the concerns of professionals working in therapy programs. These professionals may in fact have significantly different expectations, at least on some behaviors, than do professionals in postprogram placements. While additional research is needed to investigate the nature of these differences with other professional groupings in other programs, the differences among the professional groups in this study were in the direction of lower expectations on the part of program personnel. This is of concern in preparing special children for successful adjustments to less restrictive environments and is an area that personnel in intensive programs might wish to address in their intervention planning.

Curriculum Adaptations and Modifications for Culturally Diverse Handicapped Children

by Helen P. Almanza and William J. Mosley

4

■ Due to recent enactments of federal and state legislation, the country is now required by law to provide an appropriate education for all handicapped children. Part of meeting this mandate appears to be largely mechanical: a matter of bringing existing teaching skills and improved instructional techniques to bear on the varying educational needs of exceptional children. The problem of providing an appropriate education would seem to be within reach. Recent research (Semmel, Semmel, & Morrissey, 1976; Shores, Roberts, & Nelson, 1973) and an abundance of texts designed to show teachers how to meet a variety of instructional needs (Barnard & Erickson, 1976; Charles, 1976; Hawisher & Calhoun, 1978; Stephens, Hartman, & Lucas, 1978; Turnbull, Strickland, & Brantly, 1978; Wallace & Kauffman, 1978; Wiederholt, Hammill, & Brown, 1978) provide clear evidence of our ability to teach the exceptional child, given adequate personnel and sufficient funding.

THE PROBLEM

Problems emerge, however, when educators move from a consideration of providing an appropriate education for the exceptional child to that of providing an appropriate education for the exceptional minority child. Recent writings indicate that culture, as it relates to racial and ethnic differences in children, can strongly affect various aspects of learning (Bortner & Birch, 1974; Coop & Sigel, 1974; Deutsch, Katz, & Jensen, 1968; Hannerz, 1969; Lesser, Fifer, & Clark 1965; Mazur & Robertson, 1972).

However, until quite recently instructional planning and curriculum development activities for racially or ethnically different children receiving special education services have been implemented with little or no consideration given to the effects of race, ethnicity, or culture on learning. In special education the prime factor for determining the curriculum used with a child has been the category of handicap with which he or she is labeled. Curriculum developers in special education have regarded categories of handicap as the basic variable for appropriate curriculum differentiation (Gardner, 1978). Racial-ethnic and other cultural distinctions have been viewed as irrelevant to the task.

Curriculum practices in American schools have traditionally had a monolithic orientation relative to race, ethnicity, and culture. They have had a Euro-American orientation which, while reflecting the larger society (Guerra, 1973; Mosley & Spicker, 1975), ignores the pluralistic makeup of our schools. Hazard and Stent (1973) stated:

Some data on school populations may give needed perspective to the reality of cultural diversity. In

From *Exceptional Children*, Vol. 46, No. 8, May 1980. Copyright 1980, The Council for Exceptional Children. Reprinted with permission.

the fall of 1970, over 51 million children were enrolled in public and private elementary and secondary schools. The most recent (1968) data indicate that 14.5 percent (6,282,200) pupils were Black, 4.6 percent (2,003,000) were Spanish Americans, and 142,630 (less than .05 percent) were American Indians. Predictably, the twenty-one largest school systems reported substantially different racial-cultural "mixes" in their school districts for the same year (1968). Of the total pupil population of 4,728,886, Black pupils numbered 1,921,465 (40.6 percent); 502,528 (10.6 percent) were Spanish American; 7,912 (0.2 percent) were American Indians, and 68,680 (1.5 percent) were Oriental. . . . . . to postulate our education on bases other than cultural diversity and pluralistic notions seems to ignore the realities of our schools' population. (pp. 17–18).

The need for cultural pluralism to replace traditional monocultural approaches has been raised at various times in regular education (Castaneda, 1974; Epstein, 1978; Stent, Hazard, & Rivlin, 1973; Valverde, 1978) as well as in special education (Dunn, 1968; Hall, 1970). A great problem in special education relative to a monolithic approach to curriculum is evident when one considers the documentation of the disproportionate overrepresentation of racially and ethnically different children in special classes (Garrison & Hammill, 1971; Mercer, 1971).

If student learning is affected by the child's culture, specifically as this culture relates to racial or ethnic differences, then curriculum development activities must address this need. Curriculum should be designed in such a way that concern for racial and ethnic differences is translated into curriculum components.

MEETING CURRICULUM NEEDS

Materials

The issue becomes how to accomplish this translation. One response has been to introduce culturally relevant teaching materials and resources into the curriculum. Hence, there now exist reading lists for secondary schools that include such books as *Bury My Heart at Wounded Knee* (Brown, 1971) and *Great Negroes, Past and Present*, (Adams, 1969) preprimers that include pictures of culturally diverse children, and kits designed to teach about specific cultures, (Gay, 1979; Tiedt & Tiedt, 1979).

There can be little doubt that this approach can have an impact; however, culturally relevant materials in the curriculum, by themselves, will not address the instructional needs of racially and ethnically different children.

Values

A far more basic issue exists in which the culture, history, and values of the individual child must be taken into consideration. Both curriculum and instruction need to be based on the knowledge of the specific minority culture and student attitudes about school and themselves, as well as knowledge of the social goals and aspirations of the particular community involved (Short, 1975). This is fundamental to the development of any curriculum. If teachers want to impart information and skills to students and have them valued, then the content has to be more personally meaningful (Weinstein & Fantini, 1970).

Pepper (1976) presented a comparison of the values held by Indian people contrasted with those held by people in the dominant group. Examination of this comparison reveals the importance of considering the basic values of a group of people in order to develop and/or modify curriculum. For example, the values related to time were described as follows (p. 135):

Indian	Dominant Society
Time is present oriented— this year, this week— NOW—a resistance to planning for the future	Time is planning and saving for the future

It is evident that this difference in values creates problems in curriculum if the differences are not accounted for and some modifications made. There is little reason to learn multiplication tables just because they are needed next year to do long division. Pepper described the many conflicts in values between the two cultures as well as unique characteristics of the Indian child in the classroom. She quoted Sando (1974) on how the Indian's concept of time affects his school performance, citing problems with attendance, scores on timed tests or test-like assignments, attention, and the willingness to plan ahead and delay gratification.

The need for curriculum adaptation and modification is never clearer than when an attempt is made to teach about sex roles to Mexican American students. The values of the particular Mexican American community need to be examined. Sex roles are often clearly defined within Mexican American communities, and parents frequently place as much emphasis and value on social roles and behavior as they do on academic education (Castaneda, 1976). To attempt to teach about this subject only from the point of view of the dominant society without making any adaptation to account for the conflict in values may be a fruitless exercise.

Values must be considered in the development of any curriculum. Each respective culture has a basic set or common core of values that holds it together, although it would be a mistake to assume that all children within a designated culturally diverse group are alike.

Individual Traits/Learning Styles

There is a great diversity among children within any group. This is true not only in relationship to their values but also in terms of their individual traits and learning styles. If teachers are concerned about translating racial and ethnic differences into curriculum components, then they must attend to individual traits and learning styles.

Again, information about the specific culturally diverse group can be of value. This information can be taken into consideration when the learning style and traits of an individual child are matched to the teaching task.

Movement repertoire. Boykin (1978) discussed the work of Guttentag (1972) whose research related to active/passive behavior. Guttentag observed and recorded the movement activity of Black and White preschool children in a number of different free play situations. The most passive behaviors (lying, sitting or squatting) were engaged in by Euro-American children approximately 60% of the time. Black children engaged in this behavior only 25% of the time. The most active behaviors (running, kicking, jumping) were engaged in by Black children 46% of the time, while Euro-American children engaged in it 22% of the time. Additionally, certain movements such as intricate rhythmical tapping with the fingers were engaged in by over 25% of the Black children but by none of the Euro-American children. The study suggests that Black children possess a richer movement repertoire than Euro-American children.

In many American schools and especially in inner city schools, children are expected to talk or to move about only when directed to do so by the teacher. Those children whose style in the classroom is passive and who talk and move about according to teacher directions meet the normative standards and expectations common to elementary classrooms. Those children whose style is much more active and who talk and move about with or without teacher directions do not meet normative standards and expectations. They can conceivably become labeled as behavior problems because of their behavioral style.

Boykin (1978) concluded that Euro-American children possess the movement repertoire that will satisfy the normative standards and expectations governing child behavior in elementary classrooms while the richer movement repertoire of Black children does not satisfy those normative standards. This information suggests that curriculum development activities for the Black child should consider movement repertoire. If the learner has a movement repertoire that is active rather than passive, then the curriculum probably needs to be broken down into segments that would allow tasks to be of short duration. There should be a variety of activities, and task completion should not necesarily require the child to remain in a stationary position. This approach would use the movement repertoire as a means of facilitating academic performance.

A child's Blackness does not mean that he or she will be more active than others; however, this research suggests that the possibility does exist and should be taken into consideration as teaching tasks are matched with individual learning style and traits.

Perceptual and cognitive style. Other aspects of individual traits and learning style that have implications for curriculum adaptation or modification in relationship to culturally diverse children are the concepts of perceptual style (Witkin, 1950, 1962) and cognitive or conceptual tempo (Kagan, 1965). Research has revealed differences in the perceptual style and in the cognitive style between disadvantaged and nondisadvantaged children (Davey, 1976; Hallahan, 1970). This research is of interest because of the large numbers of disadvantaged children who may also be classified as minority or culturally diverse group members.

Perceptual style. In investigating perceptual style, Witkin (1950; 1962) developed the concept of field independence/dependence. *Field independence* indicates the ability to perceive specific objects within a perceptual pattern as discrete entities. This concept describes a perceptual style in which the stimulus effects of specific aspects of a perceptual pattern are not overwhelmed by the stimulus effects of the general or total perceptual pattern. *Field dependence* describes a perceptual style in which the stimulus effects of specific aspects of a perceptual pattern are overwhelmed by the stimulus effects of the general or total pattern. This concept indicates the inability to make critical discriminations among competing perceptual

4

stimuli. Within this context, objects that are parts of an overall pattern are not perceived independently of the total pattern. These two concepts are simply two different ways of looking at one's world.

Field independence has been found to be positively correlated with skill in such aspects of reading as word recognition, word meaning and comprehension (Gardner & Long, 1961; Gluck, 1972; Schwartz, 1972). Since field independent children are able to selectively identify discrete features within a perceptual frame, it follows that these children tend to possess appropriate analytic and attentional skills for the traditional learning environment. These children can also meet the attention requirements of such traditional instruction.

The field dependent learner tends not to be able to make selective discriminations within discrete units in perceptual patterns. These children seem unable to focus on specific sub-effects, but rather tend toward a more global approach. The field dependent learner does better with activites that require a shorter attention span. This type of learner also tends to use relational instead of analytical strategies in making discriminations among stimuli. The field dependent learner appears to require clear, concise directions (and redirecting as necessary) and specific instructions regarding task assignments.

Cognitive style. In order to characterize different problem solving approaches used by learners, the concepts of reflectivity and impulsivity have been used (Kagan, 1965). Reflective learners examine critically, show few signs of distractability or hyperactivity, and are persistent when responding to an academic task. Learners who appear impulsive seem to rely on guesses or "hunches" for problem solving, when actually they may be attending to different stimuli. They do not appear to examine critically, often show signs of distractibility or hyperactivity and may not persist at task completion. Children using reflective cognitive styles have been found to perform better than those using an impulsive cognitive style on a number of reading measures (Kagan, 1965; Hood, Kendall, & Roettger, 1973).

It is important to note that most academically proficient students in the traditional setting are much like what can be called *field independent* learners. Analysis and/or deduction is second nature to them; they seem to have thoroughly assimilated a reflective problem solving style (Mosley & Spicker, 1975).

The students who require the greatest amount of task structure and teacher attention and who also show signs of distractibility and hyperactivity often tend to be minority children of low income parents. These children tend to perform below grade level in the regular classroom, and are likely candidates to become exceptional culturally diverse children. Teaching such children according to their own cognitive style may be a preventive measure and may prevent labeling them falsely as being handicapped.

It is possible to hypothesize that children who vary on field dependence/independence measures probably vary similarly in terms of cognitive style. In many ways the characteristics of the field independent (analytical), reflective child represent a profile of the typical middle class Euro-American child who performs at or above grade level in school. The characteristics of the field dependent (relational) impulsive child seem to represent a profile of the exceptional culturally diverse child, but many individual gradations fall along the continuum.

CURRICULUM INTERVENTION

This type of description is used because it allows the operationalization of certain academic performance problems leading to needed curriculum intervention for culturally diverse exceptional children. For example, if these children have difficulty identifying independent units within a perceptual pattern, it follows that they will process information relying on relational instead of analytical cues.

The point of all this is simply that, relative to academic performance problems and curriculum needs of exceptional culturally diverse children, notions of cognitive and perceptual style allow the professional to focus on the process instead of the products of learning. Such an approach may provide needed information about how a student does something relative to task completion instead of information that merely tends to focus on the results of the completed task.

A major assumption is that curriculum design should relate more directly to the adaptive styles of exceptional culturally diverse learners. If these students are in fact relational/impulsive in learning situations, the curriculum should be developed with the aim of helping them develop more analytical and reflective skills. This approach, if successful, would show that the major problem of instruction has to do with cognitive style, that is, the inappropriate use of a relational/impulsive style when most learning tasks in school require an analytical/reflective style.

Developing Analytical/Reflective Skills

If this assumption is conceptually sound, then one of the objectives for curriculum development must be to provide instruction that will enable the exceptional culturally diverse child to employ analytical approaches in processing information and reflective approaches in solving problems.

Since a critical subject area for these children is reading, an example is presented showing how such an objective might be met through curriculum development in reading. One approach for meeting the objective might be to design a reading curriculum that is consistent with the basic style of the exceptional minority child but alters the approach in line with the developing skills of the student in reading. For example, the whole word approach has been advocated by some as being the best method to use when teaching reading to slow learners or other students with low performance.

The whole word approach has been shown to result in greater immediate gain on the part of these students (Chall, 1967). An important feature of this approach is that it relates directly to the information processing style used by many exceptional minority students; that is, it requires the student to process information relationally. With this approach, students learn words by using such relational cues as basic word shape and length, shape and size of initial letters, and shape and size of final letters. Because the whole word approach is consistent with the information processing style believed to be used by many exceptional culturally diverse children, it is logical to assume that they would initially experience greater success with this method.

Since the concern is to develop higher rates of performance in reading on the part of these students, the reading curriculum should provide initial reading instruction using the whole word approach. However, once these students begin to learn to read, the reading curriculum should gradually provide more reading instruction in phonics and less instruction based on the whole word approach. The phonics approach will provide the student with analysis training. Through the use of analytic skills the student should begin to use a reflective problem solving approach. It is important to note that phonics and/or the word analysis approach require a child to move from a relational to an analytic mode of information processing. Earlier in this article it was pointed out that the child who is relational in terms of information processing is likely to show impulsivity relative to problem solving strategies. If the goal is to move the child from the relational to the analytic dimension and from the impulsive to the reflective dimension, the task becomes one of moving the child through a self reflective problem solving mode.

Developing Reflectivity

Impulsivity in problem solving is evident when the child responds to problems posed or questions asked with immediacy and spontaneity. Often the child seems to simply blurt out an answer. Sometimes answers are correct; often they are not. Generally the child does not know whether the answer is right or wrong. Such a child tends to be field dependent and does not appear to focus on the appropriate aspects of the stimulus field when responding.

Two methods might be used to develop reflectivity in this case. The first method consists of providing reflective type directions. Before responding in class, the child should be instructed to pause, to think, and to make decisions. The pause is designed to eliminate spontaneous replies and to give the child the necessary time to examine the referent to the question. When the child is instructed to think, specificity is essential. He or she must be taught how to think in a reflective style. To accomplish this the child is instructed to think of the referent of the question. The information being requested in terms of the referent is reviewed and then the child is led into decision making. Essentially at this point the child is testing all the hypotheses relative to the question asked.

The second method proposed to increase reflectivity is modeling and imitation. Here the teacher literally dramatizes reflective behaviors by, for example, exaggerating an audible pause. The search for the relevant aspects of the stimulus field are verbalized by the teacher and possible alternative answers to the question are stated aloud as hypotheses relating to the question. The teacher then has the children imitate his or her reflective problem solving behaviors.

DISCUSSION

These approaches should be successful in stimulating the exceptional culturally diverse child to use those cognitive processes that are used by children who are regarded as successful students and that are required in traditional classrooms. While curriculum development in reading has been used here as an example, similar approaches could be built into curriculum units in mathematics and other subjects. Of key importance, however, is the need to focus on the processes of learning and the way in which these processes vary among different groups of students. Such an approach might enable teachers to be much more successful in helping different types of learners to learn successfully.

REFERENCES

Adams, R. L. Great Negroes past and present. Chicago IL: Afro-Am Publishing Co., 1969.

Barnard, K. E., & Erickson, M. L. Teaching children with developmental problems (2nd ed.). Saint Louis MO: C. V. Mosby, 1976.

Bortner, M., & Birch, H. G. Cognitive capacity and cognitive competence. In R. L. Jones & D. L. McMillan (Eds.) Special education in transition. Boston: Allyn & Bacon, 1974.

Boykin, W. A. Psychological/behavioral verve in academic/task performance: Pre-theoretical considerations. The Journal of Negro Education, 1978, 67(4), 343–354.

Brown, D. Bury my heart at Wounded Knee. New York: Holt, Rinehart & Winston, 1971.

Castaneda, A. Cultural democracy and the educational needs of Mexican American children. In R. L. Jones (Ed.), Mainstreaming and the minority child. Reston VA: The Council for Exceptional Children, 1976.

Casteneda, A. The educational needs of Mexican-Americans. In A. Castaneda, R. L. James, & W. Robbins (Eds.), The educational needs of minority groups. Lincoln NB: Professional Educators Publications, 1974.

Charles, C. M. Individualizing instruction. Saint Louis MO: C. V. Mosby, 1976.

Chall, J. Learning to read: The great debate. New York: McGraw-Hill, 1967.

Coop, R. H., & Sigel, I. E. Cognitive style: Implications for learning and instruction. In R. L. Jones & D. L. MacMillan (Eds.), Special education in transition. Boston: Allyn & Bacon, 1974.

Davey, B. Cognitive styles and reading achievement. Journal of Reading, November 1976, 113–120.

Deutsch, M., Katz, I., & Jensen, A. R. Social class, race and psychological development. New York: Holt, Rinehart & Winston, 1968.

Dunn, L. M. Special education for the mildly retarded—Is much of it justifiable? Exceptional Children, 1968, 34, 5–22.

Epstein, N. Language, ethnicity, and the schools. Washington DC: Institute for Educational Leadership, 1978.

Gardner, W. I. Children with learning and behavior problems. Boston: Allyn & Bacon, 1978.

Gardner, R., & Long, R. Field-articulation in recall. Psychological Record, 1961, 7.

Garrison, M., & Hammill, D. Who are the retarded? Exceptional Children, 1971, 38, 13–20.

Gay, G. On behalf of children: A curriculum design for multicultural education in the elementary school. The Journal of Negro Education, 1979, 68(3), 324–340.

Gluck, E. Psychological differentiation and reading achievement in first grade children. Unpublished doctoral dissertation, Boston University, 1972.

Guerra, M. H. Bilingual and bicultural education. In M. D. Stent, W. R. Hazard, & H. N. Rivlin (Eds.), Cultural pluralism in education. New York: Appleton-Century-Crofts, 1973.

Guttentag, M. Negro-White differences in children's movement. Perceptual and Motor Skills, 1972, 35, 435–436.

Hall, E. Special miseducation: The politics of special education. Inequality in Education, 1970, 4(3), 17–29.

Hallahan, D. P. Cognitive styles—Preschool implications for the disadvantaged. Journal of Learning Disabilities, 1970, 3(1).

Hannerz, U. Soulside: Inquiries into ghetto culture and community. New York: Columbia University Press, 1969.

Hawisher, M. F., & Calhoun, M. L. The resource room. Columbus OH: Charles E. Merrill, 1978.

Hazard, W. R., & Stent, M. D. Cultural pluralism and schooling: Some preliminary observations. In M. D. Stent, W. R. Hazard, & H. N. Rivlin (Eds.), Cultural pluralism in education. New York: Appleton-Century-Crofts, 1973.

Hood, J. E., Kendall, J. R., & Roettger, D. M. An analysis of oral reading behavior of reflective and impulsive beginning readers. Paper presented at the annual meeting of the American Educational Research Association, 1973.

Kagan, J. Reflection-impulsivity and reading ability in primary grade children. Child Development, 1965, 36.

Lesser, G. S., Fifer, G., & Clark, D. H. Mental abilities of children from different social-class and cultural groups. Monographs of the Society for Research in Child Development, 1965, 30(4).

Mazur, A., & Robertson, L. S. Biology and social behavior. New York: The Free Press, 1972.

Mercer, J. R. Sociocultural factors in labeling mental retardates. Peabody Journal of Education, 1971, 48, 188–203.

Mosley W. J., & Spicker, H. H. Mainstreaming for the educationally deprived. Theory into Practice, 1975, 14(2), 73–81.

Pepper, F. C. Teaching the American Indian child in mainstream settings., In R. L. Jones (Ed.), Mainstreaming and the minority child. Reston VA: The Council for Exceptional Children, 1976.

Sando, J. Educating the Native American: Conflict in values. In L. A. Bransford, L. Baca, & K. Lane (Eds.), Cultural diversity and the exceptional child. Reston VA: The Council for Exceptional Children, 1974.

Schwartz, F. The effects of field dependence-field independence upon word recognition ability of second grade subjects. Unpublished doctoral dissertation, University of Michigan, 1972.

Semmel, M. I., Semmel, D. S., & Morrissey, P. A. Competency-based teacher education in regular education: A review of research and training programs. Bloomington IN: Center for Innovation in Teaching the Handicapped, Indiana University, 1976.

Shores, R., Roberts, M., & Nelson, C. M. An empirical model for the development of competencies for teachers of children with behavior disorders. *Behavior Disorders*, 1976, *1*, 123–132.

Short, E. C. Keeping up with research: A method for curriculum planners. *Curriculum Trends*. Waterford CT: Croft NEI Publications, August, 1975.

Stent, M. D., Hazard, W. R., & Rivlin, H. N. (Eds.). *Cultural pluralism in education*. New York: Appleton-Century-Crofts, 1973.

Stephens, T. M., Hartman, C. A., & Lucas, V. H. *Teaching children basic skills: A curriculum handbook*. Columbus OH: Charles E. Merrill, 1978.

Tiedt, P. L., & Tiedt, I. M. *Multicultural teaching*. Boston: Allyn & Bacon, 1979.

Turnbull, A. P., Strickland, B. B., & Brantly, J. C. *Developing and implementing individualized education programs*. Columbus OH: Charles E. Merrill, 1978.

Valverde, L. S. (Ed.). *Bilingual education for Latinos*. Washington DC: Association for Supervision and Curriculum Development, 1978.

Wallace, G., & Kauffman, J. M. *Teaching children with learning problems*. Columbus OH: Charles E. Merrill, 1978.

Weinstein, G., & Fantini, M. D. *Toward humanistic education: A curriculum of affect*. New York: Praeger, 1970.

Wiederholt, J. L., Hammill, D. D., & Brown, V. *The resource teacher: A guide to effective practices*. Boston: Allyn & Bacon, 1978.

Witkin, H. A. Individual differences in ease of perception of embedded figures. *Journal of Personality*, 1950, *19*, 1–15.

Witkin, H. A. *Psychological differentiation*. New York: John Wiley, 1962.

4

Career Opportunities For Culturally Diverse Handicapped Youth

by George W. Fair and Allen R. Sullivan

■ Critical and somewhat contradictory concerns have been expressed relative to the provision of career and vocational educational opportunities for culturally diverse youth (Wells, 1978). There is little research specifically addressing issues related to the provision of educational opportunities for culturally diverse youth with handicaps. This article first provides an overview of the employment situation for minority individuals and its implications for career and vocational education of culturally diverse handicapped youth. Second, the article delineates the enigma presented by being a member of a doubly stigmatized population, that is, culturally diverse handicapped youth. Attention is given to the barriers to effective educational and employment opportunities for this population. Finally, the article forecasts the prospects of career and vocational education and makes recommendations for future programing and research.

RACE, CULTURE, HANDICAPS: EMPLOYMENT

"Changes in Society Holding Black Youth in a Jobless Web" (Herbers, 1979), along with a series of four other articles, described the plight of the Black youth in reference to employment opportunities. In this article, Labor Secretary Ray Marshall indicated that unemployment among Black youths between the ages of 16 and 19 was as high as 38.3%. This is considered a conservative estimate by many. The unemployment picture for minority youth, particularly Blacks, is now roughly what it was for the entire nation during the Great Depression. Although racial discrimination in employment was made illegal by the Civil Rights Act of 1964, and although successive court decisions have upheld the right of equal access to jobs, job discrimination, while more subtle than before, still remains (Herbers, 1979).

Stereotypes exist in society that make securing employment extremely difficult for culturally diverse handicapped youth. Little professional attention has been paid to the interaction among race, gender and handicapping conditions, which, when combined, may identify the most discriminated class of people within our society. Paradoxically, these persons, when employed, may well be the most stable working force. An illustration of this point can be found in a survey conducted by the US Office of Vocational Rehabilitation (Halloran, 1978) on the experiences with handicapped employees of more than 100 large corporations. Of the corporations reporting, 66% said there were no differences between handicapped individuals and able bodied individuals in productivity. Furthermore, 24% rated handicapped persons higher in productivity. Thus, 90% were perceived to be equal to or surpassing the productivity of nonhandicapped individuals. The study further indicated that 57% reported lower accident rates, 55% reported lower absenteeism rates, and 83% reported lower turnover rates for handicapped persons. Providing this information could go a long way in reducing the xenophobic response expressed or implied by potential employers, that is, the fear that employing handicapped individuals will present personnel problems for the company.

OVERVIEW OF VOCATIONAL TRAINING OPPORTUNITIES

For women and minorities, vocational education has been used to reinforce society's notion of their proper or realistic role in society. Halloran (1978) suggested that vocational institutions should focus their attention on the effects of handicapping conditions that can be remedied. He further pointed out that more than two-thirds of vocational education for the handicapped is not intended to prepare students to compete on the open labor market in a given skill, craft, or trade. Lee (1975) indicated that approximately 1.7% of students enrolled in vocational education programs are handicapped youth. Because of the criticism of traditional vocational education and because so few poor, minority, and handicapped youth were included, the Comprehensive Employment and Training Act (CETA) program was developed and included more than double the number of handicapped persons (4%) that were in traditional vocational education programs. Levitan and Taggart (1976) found that 40% of disabled adults are employed compared with 75% of the nondisabled population. Average weekly wages of employed disabled males are 22% lower than those of their nondisabled counterparts. In summary, these findings indicate that, to date, programs that have legislative, professional, and moral responsibility for providing meaningful training opportunities for handicapped individuals have been less than adequate. Thus, the very programs designed to address the needs of bypassed populations, victims of systematic discrimination and exclusion, perpetuate the identical practice and philosophy. One reason this practice continues may be fear or apprehension on the part of potential employers and trainers in terms of working with handicapped individuals. This concern was addressed by Wright (1960) in her classic book concerning physical disability. She indicated that "existing values, concepts, and factual information can go far in relieving suffering and aiding social and psychological rehabilitation, if only applied more genuinely and generally in the ordinary affairs of life as well as among the many special enterprises that society as a whole needs to undertake" (p. 380).

The Comptroller General's 1974 report to Congress indicated that the federal government's priority of providing vocational opportunities for disadvantaged and handicapped students had not cascaded to the state and local level. The report further expressed concern about the small number of students receiving these services compared with the large number needing them. One of the dangers currently confronting the provisions for handicapped and culturally diverse youth is the back to basics trend in education. The back to basics or back to the good old days phenomenon presents problems for populations who were denied equal opportunities in those "good old days." Those days were good for only some people. Valverde (1977) postulated that the back to basics trend is attempting to solve novel problems of education's advancement by simply reverting to former practices with their familiar frustrations.

BARRIERS TO ACHIEVEMENT

There are several specific barriers to the education and employment of handicapped individuals and their quest for educational equity and excellence:

1. *Architectural barriers* deprive mobility limited persons from access to the place of employment and instructional facilities.
2. *Ideological barriers* are imposed by limited vision or myopic response to the abilities of culturally diverse handicapped persons, therefore limiting the perception of what skills a student can master.
3. *Procedural barriers* are created by procedures that do not adequately search for, identify, counsel, and select culturally diverse handicapped students in the full continuum of vocational and career training opportunities.
4. *Substantive barriers* are imposed by limiting the scope and sequence of the curriculum. This occurs by focusing on a narrow band of vocational skills without taking into consideration an individual student's motivation, personal preference, and need to develop social competencies. These barriers are also reflected in the type of clusters offered in vocational programs that exclude areas such as retailing, technical, and scientific services and emphasize instead human service areas such as food preparation and delivery, housekeeping, and maintenance.

5. *Affective barriers* are personal in nature, and influence an individual's feelings about culturally diverse handicapped persons, engendering inappropriate sympathy or apathy, or fostering protective or rejecting behaviors, respectively.

THE CHALLENGE TO CHANGE

When specifically focusing on minority youth, the whole specter of racism enters the picture. The history of negative responses to minority and racial groups has been well documented. Any solutions to problems concerning this topic as it relates to handicapped youth would have to be blended into a systematic civil rights thrust. Many groups such as the Urban League, the Urban Coalition, and several Black fraternal and social groups have attempted to address the issues of motivation and effective educational programing for minority youth. These groups should be encouraged to add a component for handicapped youth.

As reported by Wells (1978), the US Office of Education conducted a study of the attitudes of more than 1,000 Black leaders, including vocational educators, and found a general lack of enthusiasm for vocational education programs as generally constituted. "The study concluded that Blacks believe formal vocational education programs 'limit the employment and leadership potential of the student more than some alternative types of job training programs'" (p. 46). The criticism could continue. For example, one major criterion for the selection of teachers in vocational programs is that they have had significant experience in the field. When this requirement is coupled with documented failures of the labor movement to affirmatively involve minority and racial groups into the mainstream of employment opportunities, there is a strong possibility that vocational teachers may lack experience and sensitivity in addressing issues that provide legitimate vocational opportunities for culturally diverse youth. The selection and hiring practices of schools reduces the possibility that culturally distinct students will have relevant vocational role models.

DIRECTIONS

Adelman and Phelps (1978) identified several program components that they believe are essential in developing a vocational program for handicapped youth. These same components are necessary for culturally diverse handicapped youth.

1. *Individualization* does not mean a student is taught in isolation, but it suggests that there may be special and unique needs for particular individuals.

2. *Student analysis* is an assessment of the strengths, interests, and skills that a student has including manual dexterity, work capacity, and motivation.

3. *Task analysis* is matching the student's skills to the specific occupational competencies he or she will be learning.

4. *Program analysis* is deciding whether general or specific training in an occupational cluster will be provided to the student.

In general, Adelman and Phelps indicated that the handicapped student should be given a good faith opportunity to learn through the presentation of clearly thought out experiences.

Strategies for Success

In a paper entitled "Retaining Blacks in Science: An Effective Model," Young and Young (1979) identified strategies for enabling unprepared or disadvantaged students to succeed in technical college level programs. Many of these strategies are applicable to enabling culturally diverse handicapped individuals to succeed in technical career development programs. The following is an expansion of the suggestions by Young and Young (1979) that can be used in career and vocational education programs in which culturally diverse handicapped students are enrolled.

1. *Begin Instruction at Students' Present Level.* The first suggestion deals with the process of beginning instruction. Many programs in secondary schools make assumptions about the prerequisite skills that a student possesses upon entering the program. The recommendation is that the instructor take enough time to adequately assess each student in reference to these prerequisite skills and begin instruction based on this data. Reading and math grade level scores obtained by standardized testing are often used to convey the degree of competence in these areas, and instruction often begins based on this data. Such a procedure is not satisfactory for culturally diverse handicapped students. These judgments should be based on valid assessment activities that are nondiscriminatory in nature and that are employment and job related.

2. *Utilize Mastery Learning Objectives.* The second suggestion is related to the mastery learning concept. Many persons with stereotyped ideas immediately think of lowering standards when culturally diverse or handi-

capped persons are concerned. If there is a clear articulation of what the standards and objectives are, a lowering of standards is not necessary. The objectives should be clearly defined and alternative modes of instruction should be made available in order to meet these objectives. If appropriate and adequate opportunities are made available to culturally diverse handicapped students the lowering of standards need never be considered.

3. Accommodate Differences in Learning Styles. Most professionals in special education understand that students with learning problems may have different learning styles. This is obviously true for culturally diverse handicapped students as well. The important point to remember is that this group does not, within itself, have any homogenous learning style. The statements that attempt to attribute particular learning characteristics to certain minority groups are simply not valid.

4. Provide a Positive Psychological Climate. A positive psychological climate is one where a good rapport exists between students and teachers, and an expectation of success prevails. It is developed from mutual respect on the part of both students and teachers. Teachers need to have a pluralistic frame of reference which acknowledges that all people have something of value to offer and that cultural and linguistic differences are societal assets. Success experiences are also a part of a positive psychological climate. Such experiences are fostered by the adoption of appropriate expectations and provision of sufficient opportunities to succeed.

5. Enable Students to Build an Internal Sense of Responsibility. Enabling students to build a sense of personal responsibility means that students should be encouraged to feel that they have a degree of involvement in determining their own fate. Culturally diverse handicapped students need to realize that there exists a relationship between their behavior and what happens to them. As a culturally diverse handicapped person it is understandable and somewhat realistic to think that people will make prejudgments about one's ability and that certain opportunities will not become available. This type of orientation may be counterproductive to developing the degree of competence that is needed to be the master of one's own fate.

6. Provide a Well Articulated, Comprehensive, Cohesive Program Structure. Successful programs for culturally diverse handicapped students should be comprehensive and cohesive. Special education and vocational education instructors, counselors, and other helping professionals need to work together for the benefit of these students. Such cooperation should take the form of planning and organization that will be proactive and participatory, therefore preventing problems from developing rather than being remedial and providing only temporary solutions to crises. Coordination has been lacking in many programs that require the contributions of a significant number of people, disciplines, and agencies. Without question, if culturally diverse handicapped children are to be meaningfully served in career and vocational education programs, cooperation and coordination must improve.

7. Provide Comprehensive Personnel Development. For success to occur a systematic and comprehensive staff development component should be added to career and vocational education programs. The majority of occupational education teachers state that they were not trained to work with special needs students. Their training should not be independent from the training of other staff members who are involved with handicapped youth. The special education staff should become more familiar with vocational assessment and programing. Sheppard (1966) and Schwartz (1967) stipulated that preservice and inservice training must provide teachers with many opportunities for solving problems related to adapting programs and practices for handicapped youth, clarifying their own values, and recognizing ambiguities and ambivalence in their own beliefs and in the beliefs of others.

8. Facilitate Career Planning. Career planning is an area where monumental efforts are needed for culturally diverse handicapped students. People think about potential occupations on the basis of perceptions that are often sketchy or inaccurate. This is particularly significant for culturally diverse handicapped students because of the lack of exposure they may have to occupations. The decisions that one makes based on incomplete information can affect an entire lifetime. It is difficult for most students and especially for culturally diverse handicapped students to obtain informal exposure to a variety of occupations because of the barriers and other conditions discussed earlier.

Appropriate career planning encompasses many activities. It should include early occupational experiences that permit individuals to expand their knowledge and increase their est force in providing for the needs of culturally diverse handicapped students.

The focus of school programs for these young people needs to center on long term employability and job related skills. Special education, with its work-study programs, has not always focused on long term employment needs. Programs must be expanded to provide vocational training and job related skills before job placement is considered. Such programs must have adequate resources and equipment, and provide for continuous job supervision and rewards for exemplary performance.

A coordinated governmental thrust is necessary to ensure that programs developed to focus on career and vocational needs have processes that include culturally diverse handicapped youth. Such programs should be strongly encouraged to incorporate successful graduates of these programs as resource persons and instructors in an attempt to provide appropriate role models for program constituents. A dissemination process providing information related to practices that have been effective in providing psychologically sound and well articulated vocational experiences for culturally diverse handicapped youth should also be provided. Inherent in this process is establishment of validation procedures through demonstration, research, and evaluation.

There is also a need to encourage and provide financial support (federal, local, and private foundations) for institutions that have had a significant track record in developing and implementing educational and vocational programs for bypassed and unserved populations. These institutions (namely, historically Black oriented colleges and selected junior college systems) should be encouraged to conceptualize, develop, and implement vocational efforts for culturally diverse handicapped youth.

Finally, school personnel must broaden their vision and think about the year 2000. Rather than predicting fewer opportunities for employment of handicapped persons, the provision of training opportunities and experiences should enable more and varied employment situations to become realistic options. Discrimination and a lack of attention to the problems of culturally diverse handicapped persons has existed too long. Suggestions and strategies are at hand that will enable more culturally diverse handicapped students to become productive members of society. The awareness of the range of occupational alternatives. Such planning should recognize the contributions that persons of specific cultural and ethnic backgrounds have made to society.

Students must also be made aware that racism does exist in society and that it places additional demands on certain students.

In light of the fiscal considerations, workload, and training of present counselors, the one to one counseling model will not meet the needs of the culturally diverse handicapped student who should participate in such a program. The new model should be community based and include contributions by parents and other nonschool personnel. Advantages of such a model enable culturally diverse handicapped students to identify their own abilities, interests, and values. Occupational information should be combined with a personal evaluation. The individuals can then be helped to identify job market trends and characteristics and relate the characteristics and requirements of various occupations to their individual abilities, interests, and values. Pertinent occupational information should also allow the student to identify the sequence of activities that are required to enter a given occupation. In this way, appropriate career planning becomes an effective vehicle in providing more opportunities for culturally diverse handicapped students.

FUTURE

Particular trends and issues will merit critical attention in the next 10 years. It is evident that the schools will have the major responsibility for preparing culturally diverse handicapped youth with basic skills and work skills. The schools, although criticized by many persons, are still best prepared to accomplish this task. Innovative and dynamic school leadership that interfaces with all aspects of the community will be demanded to a greater extent than ever before. Alternative institutions have developed for those students for whom the school has not been effective. Cooperation between these institutions and the schools should be encouraged. Such institutions provide a healthy diversification of approaches and vary in their vocational focus, methods of delivery, institutional structure and means of support. However, the schools will continue to be the greatknowledge is available. Now the commitment to implementation is needed.

REFERENCES

Adelman, F. W., & Phelps, L. A. Learning to teach handicapped learners. *American Vocational Journal*, 1978, *53*, 27–29.

Halloran, W. D. Handicapped persons: Who are they? *American Vocational Journal*, 1978, *53*, 30–31.

Herbers, J. Changes in society holding Black youth in jobless web. *New York Times*, March 11, 1979, pp. 1;44.

Lee, A. Learning a living across the nation, Volume IV. *Project Baseline*. Flagstaff: Northern Arizona University, October, 1975.

Levitan, S. A., & Taggart, R. *Jobs for the disabled*. Washington DC: George Washington University, Center for Manpower Policy Studies, 1976.

Schwartz, L. An integrated teacher education program for special education—A new approach. *Exceptional Children*, 1967, *33*, 411–416.

Sheppard, G. What research on the mentally retarded has to say. *Journal of Secondary Education*, 1966, *41*, 339–342.

Valverde, L. A. Multicultural education: Social and educational justice. *Educational Leadership*, 1977, *34*, 196–199.

Wells, J. Outside looking in. *Journal of the American Vocational Association*, 1978, *53*, 45–47.

Wright, B. A. *Physical disability—A psychological approach*. New York: Harper & Row, 1960.

Young, H. A., & Young, B. *Retaining Blacks in science: An effective model*. Unpublished paper, University of Louisville, May 1979.

4

PART 5

SENSORY HANDICAPS

by Glen Thompson, Ph.D.

PL 94-142 is having an impact on the education of children with physical and/or sensory handicaps. As with other handicapped children, nondiscriminatory assessment must be used, staffings must be held with both parent and student involvement and Individualized Educational Programs (IEPs) must be developed.

Of course, the problems associated with the educating of the blind or partially sighted, the deaf or those with partial hearing and the physically handicapped have been addressed quite effectively in the past. Those with vision and hearing problems require highly specialized approaches and materials in the classroom, while those with a physical handicap may require ramps for access to transportation and buildings, as well as other provisions that would enable them to compensate for the nature of their disabilities.

Physical therapy frequently is included in their school program. However, the law's greatest impact may not be in the design of educational programs. Rather it could be in increasing substantially the amount of contact occurring between these students and their so-called normal peers.

The contact is occurring. And it's occurring because for many sensorially-disabled students, the least restrictive alternative is at least part-time placement in the mainstream.

With the concurrent increase in the accessibility of public facilities to handicapped persons—and with a happy upsurge in the militancy of handicapped people who are aware of and fighting for their rights—the number of handicapped students going on to regular colleges and universities is increasing dramatically.

A few years ago, college represented the first on-going contact between handicapped and non-handicapped students. As a result, both often felt uncomfortable in their initial contacts. Today, many handicapped students attending regular colleges come from grade and high schools that mainstreamed them and the results overall have been very favorable.

During my undergraduate days, I was a reader for a blind veteran, who was an excellent student at a scholastically difficult liberal arts private college. After graduation, he applied for admission to several schools of social work. All but one turned him down because he was blind. Undaunted, the veteran completed his master's and became quite successful in the field. Today, I doubt he would be turned down by any school on the basis of his blindness.

Even relatively recently, some universities hindered or blocked the progress of handicapped students because the schools felt the handicaps might interfere negatively with teaching performance. (And I'm speaking about special education departments!) However, at least with the cases about which I am familiar, legal action, or the threat of legal action, remedied the situation for the handicapped student.

I don't maintain that handicapped people can be prepared to perform any task. Airline pilots probably shouldn't be blind. But it is the responsibility of the educator to find ways that people with given physical or sensory handicaps can adapt and compensate so that they might successfully perform certain societal positions. Interestingly, many creative adaptations have been conceived by the handicapped.

Fortunately, the incidence of physical and sensory handicaps are dramatically declining through advances in medical and technological developments. New procedures for improving vision and hearing in people with certain kinds of loss have been devised in the last two decades, as has acoustical and visual assisting equipment that helps correct or otherwise compensate for the loss.

Among the economically deprived, however, the incidence of handicapping conditions is significantly higher than among the more affluent. What's needed is a higher investment in health and education for the poor. The investment would more than likely decrease handicaps greatly and be humanitarian. Also, prevention is almost always a much less expensive alternative than the cure. Unfortunately, the latest and most advanced practices in medicine and education presently are more frequently applied in affluent areas. And we need to be attuned to those pockets of society in which people are victims of neglect.

Liberal Education
For the Handicapped

by Robert Russell

What I am going to say is quite intentionally general, because I want to set up a framework within which you can raise specific questions that I have not touched on or that relate somehow to general observations I am going to make. So keep that in mind.

First, let me define my topic. A lot of people are struggling long and hard trying to define education, but I am going to content myself with simplicity. It seems to me that education can be divided into two kinds. The two refuse to stay separate, but for the sake of clarity I am going to pretend that they do.

The two kinds of education are vocational and liberal. Vocational education is the kind we take so that we can do something that we could not do before because we did not know how. An example would be learning to saw a board at a 90-degree angle—90 degrees from the beginning to the end of the cut, and 90 degrees from the top to the bottom. Although I have sawed many a board in my day, I still cannot make that perfect cut. When I do, it is by accident; and as you probably know, good accidents do not happen very often. If I were a carpenter and not in literature, I would have learned the skill of making that kind of cut plus a whole lot of other cuts. That kind of knowledge is very practical, because with it a person can make a chair, patch a roof to keep the rain out, etc. If I were really good at that sort of thing, I could hire myself out to do those things for somebody else, thus translating my knowledge and skill into money, which I could retranslate into a variety of other things.

The education of lawyers or doctors is equally vocational. They translate their education into practical use for hire, and they hire themselves out to patch kidneys instead of roofs or to serve as guides through the jungles of the law, and they do very handsomely for themselves in the process. In the use of their knowledge, they are no different from the carpenter or the bricklayer. To my way of thinking, then vocational education is the kind of education that the possessor *uses*—most often for making money. This is certainly the most popular kind of education, and it is going to become increasingly so. You may be asking yourselves, "Is there actually any other kind of education?" If so, you may wonder of what value it is, if it is not practical and not

From Chapter IV of *Disability: Our Challenge,* published by the Project for Handicapped College Students, based at Teachers College, Columbia University. Reprinted with permission.

translatable into cash?

Well, I think there is another. I call it liberal. And I even think it is the primary, most important kind, for reasons I shall try to explain. First, I must go back to the term "education." It comes from the Latin *ducere*—that is a verb meaning "to lead." And when you have the prefix *e-*, it means "to lead forth." That is probably nothing new to you. So "education" means an activity or a set of activities that have the effect of leading something forth from the student. But—leading what? That is the question. Well, leading forth the intellect and the emotional capacities of the learner; in short, his or her entire personality, enticing it out of its most secret retreats and challenging that personality to a sort of wrestling match, a full-scale struggle to understand and cope with all the complexities of being human. That struggle is immensely exciting and immensely stimulating and pleasurable as well and not merely to the intellectual faculties or the muscular skills but to the whole person. In other words, a liberal education does not offer the development of a marketable skill; rather, it promises the excitement of a full engagement with one's whole self, the reward being the pleasure of being more fully alive. Now, I know these are very abstract terms, but I am going to try to clarify them.

Traditionally, liberal education is confined in its definition to the study of philosophy, history, literature, subjects like that. But I do not believe that the terms "liberal" and "vocational" actually have anything to do with the subject matter of study. What determines whether a study or an activity is liberal or vocational lies entirely in the way the student feels about the subject. For instance, I could study philosophy with the specific purpose of making myself a teacher of philosophy so that I could make a living at it. For me, that study would be just as vocational as carpentry. Or, I can (and have) study for instance, automobile mechanics. I am no better as a mechanic than I am as a carpenter, as a matter of fact, so I only tinker around with my own car. I have reduced my garage bill, so there is some economic benefit for what little knowledge I have; but that is not the main reason why I inquired into the subject. I inquired into it because I was interested. Why an engine does or does not run actually fascinates me. A badly running outboard or car is a challenge to me; diagnosis of the problems forces me into a rigourous logical exercise that leads all of me forth, not just my mental faculties—I become desperately excited. When I occasionally find the cause of a problem, fix it, put things back together, step on the starter or pull the cord, no words can possibly express my joy when the thing runs.

Now, I have saved some money, which is nice. I need money, I like money, just as much as anybody else I know. But the pleasure that has streaked through me whenever I have dealt with one of those casual problems is not measurable in dollars and cents. So, mechanics is for me a liberal pursuit, and what makes it liberal is the way I feel about it. It leads me forth, it invites me to grapple with complex reality, it taxes my faculties, my patience, and my intelligence, and it thrills me deeply. Do not try to hire me—I am not worth it. Besides I only work on engines for love, and love is just shorthand for those feelings I mentioned that consume me when my efforts prove to be successful.

But what does all this have to do with the subject I was asked to talk about? So far I have started by defining my key terms. Education is the main one, and I have said there are two kinds, the liberal and the vocational. And then I said the liberal is the more important, the more exciting kind. But my talk concerns education for the handicapped, so let us move on to the handicapped.

Now, to be handicapped simply means to be limited, not able to do everything. No human being is able to do everything, so to be human is to be limited. Most people, however, when they first meet me think that I am an oddity, because in addition to the usual set of human incapacities, I cannot see. I am stuck with that, or rather with both of those things. I am stuck both with my blindness and with other people's reaction to it. They are separate things, but combined they make a pretty marvelous mess to deal with. They constitute a rather special degree of limitation or handicap. Not too special, I know, when compared to others in this room. But special with regard to those so-called average or normal persons. I presume that in this audience, as in every audience, you can find the most wonderful collection of incapacities. I hope that perhaps you can see some relation between mine and yours.

I am not about to stand up here and ask you to believe the pious and heroic lie that my blindness has not been, is not now, and will not continue to be a most constant, profound, and infernal nuisance. To pretend that I have overcome it would be as foolish and dishonest as if I were to pretend to you that through great courage and moral virtue I have overcome the necessity to breathe. Just absurd. It was a fact, it is a fact, and it will continue to be a fact that because of my blindness I cannot, for instance, enjoy the beauty of the world at a distance. I do not know what my wife or my children look like. I cannot as my colleagues regularly do, which infuriates me, pick up a book and read it. I cannot gracefully pass the salt to a guest at my dinner table. I consider these serious and very terrible deprivations. What is worse is that they force me into a dependence on other people, and I resent those dependencies; but I have to learn to live with them as gracefully as I can, to accept them, as I must learn to live with the fact that I cannot watch the cardinal feeding its young in the nest just outside our bathroom window. So, my blindness causes me a lot of personal distress. Keep the word "personal" in mind.

As annoying as this distress is, it is not comparable to other people's conception of how blindness must limit me. I know through experience what some of these limitations are. They do not. But they think they do. And this is what gives rise to most of the trouble. Since I cannot see, they assume that I am either sub or superhuman. Whether sub or super, the result for me is exactly the same. I cannot be communicated with. I am outside the pale. I do not belong. People separate me from the warm brotherhood of mankind, either by excessive pity or excessive admiration, and by either emotion they show that I am closed out of any possibility of ordinary relationships with them. In Paris, in London, in Sarajevo, in Stockholm, and in Watertown, New York, the waitress says to my companion, "Does he take sugar in his coffee?" If she were to think about it, which she does not (nobody does), she would have to explain that I seem to her like some marvelously trained dog, who has learned how to sit up and eat at the table and drink almost like a person, and can only be communicated with through my trainer. Now, am I angry? Yes. Is my anger a solution or a small step toward solving the problem? No. A joke might be, something or other that would suggest that I actually share lots of feelings with her. Something like, "I like my coffee just exactly the way you like yours, Sweetie." Then maybe she might giggle and go on to say to my master, "Isn't he wonderful?" With the word "wonderful" she has flipped me over from the sub to the super. Which is no progress for me, but it is at least a change. She has flipped me into that same box, at the other end of the spectrum, into which I am tossed by prospective employers.

I have applied for teaching jobs in every respectable four-year institution in the United States—and some that are not even respectable. I have received all kinds of letters in reply. But when they start out with a compliment, I know what the end is going to be. I send off a description of my background, qualifications, publications, and all that, and the reply comes back with "Dear Mr. Russell, you're obviously just an amazing person. It's incredible what you've done. Yale, Oxford, those fellowships, won an international competition, all those books, those stories, those articles you've written, and all those years of chairmanship with that big English Department, why, you're just miraculous that's all. Just miraculous, that's all I can say. As to this job, we just don't see how you could possibly manage it, there are people to see, and well, we're just really sorry, we're sure you understand. With cordial admiration" and then the signature. Oh, I understand all right. Angry? Very. Solution? No more than with the waitress. Should I write back to this dean or president and point out the logical contradictions between his praise and his rejection? He is no dummy. He understands the contradictions as well as I do. He just does not want me around, that is all. And he does not because he thinks I am different. That would make him uneasy. Because it would make him and everybody else uneasy, it is more simple just to write me off. So, what might help? What might help is almost always impossible. What might help would be to get him out for a cup of coffee or a drink. Or lunch. To talk. In that talk we might get our ideas colliding, our values engaging each with the other's, and at the end of an hour, maybe two, he might feel, "Yes, while there are differences, they are superficial. But more important, there are basic similarities—concerns that we share, sensibilities and attitudes. Above all, the things that we share are far more important than the differences that appear to separate us."

Do you recognize any of these things? This situation? If you do, then we can proceed with the subject that I am supposed to be discussing here. And that is, education for the handicapped. Remember what I said about education, the vocational and the liberal and the first aims of each? The first aim of the vocational is producing a marketable skill. The first aim of the liberal is the leading forth—it is an invitation, a challenge, to a kind of wrestling match with reality, a full engagement of personality. I said this second kind was most important for everybody. Now that I have defined the handicapped, I want to say that this kind of education, the liberal, is more important for the handicapped than for the "ordinary" person. I use myself as an example, and I hope you can see what I think my major problems are and that they have nothing to do with whether I am skillful as a carpenter or as a mechanic or as a teacher. My problems have nothing to do with whether I am good at my job. My main problem, and I think it is a peculiarly central problem for every handicapped person, is to convince the waitress and the college principal that we are human, that we are neither below nor above that classification, neither sub nor super.

If, for example, I were to bet all my marbles on carpentry and make myself the best carpenter in the world, that would not be any good if I could not get someone to hire me. My central and continual job is to calm those fears in the other, whether an employer or a waitress, that spring from his or her sense that I am an oddity. I have got to show others that I understand and care very much about the same basic concerns that fascinate and perplex all sensitive human beings. A liberal education stimulates precisely the kind of understanding and the kind of caring that holds the possibility of uniting all human beings. This sense of the the world communicates itself to other people and puts them at ease in one's presence. They no longer think of one as sub or super but simply as a person.

Too often we are inclined to confine the notion of education to schools and books, and this is really a disastrous restriction. It is unfortunate that we do this; because not only do we separate school from life, but we assume there is going to be no carry-over from books to living. And because we do not expect any carry-over there is none, or very little—which is too bad, since potentially there is a great deal. Let me tell you about a friend of mine who was, I will say, trying to get an education. Fred and I met at school for the blind in New York City. Fred had previously attended a public high school; I do not know if they are still in existence, but in those days there were Regent's—exams that you had to pass in order to get your high school diploma. Fred came to the school, the New York Institute, for what they called a year of "postgraduate" work. When Fred came in he had passed all his Regent's, which most of us were in the process of trying to do. He was sporting a Regent's average of 94 or 95. So our impression was that Fred was pretty bright. One day I confessed, "Fred, I'm really impressed with your average in Regent's; mine isn't anything as good as that." And he said, "Don't be impressed, that doesn't mean a thing." I said, "Why doesn't it?" He said, "I took it at the public high school, and the teachers didn't know how to handle me. They couldn't give me the questions in braille, nor could they let me write out the answers in braille because if I had written them out they wouldn't have known how to read them. So they just read me the questions verbally, and when I couldn't tell them the answers, well, they told me; but it didn't mean that I learned anything. They were awfully nice to me, too nice to me, all the time. That's one thing I regret." The niceness of those teachers did not lead Fred forward. They did not invite him to engage with any subject matter. They, in fact, said with their actions—naturally they did not put it into words—something like this: "Fred, you're a poor blind boy and we know you've had a lot of suffering, so why don't you just stay there, secreted in your own person, and we'll deal with the problems of life for you. We'll give you the answers and you can just trot along. We'll take care of you. We'll shuffle you off to a sheltered workshop. You'll be all right, just don't worrry about it." That was not education although it happened in a school. They were actually holding Fred back, not inviting him forth. They were giving him neither a vocational nor a liberal education. They were asking him merely to serve time. That was a shame, because Fred had a lot to give, and he may in fact be giving it in ways that I do not know about. I have not been in touch with him in thirty-five years, but his story stands out because it spoke to me of the cruelty of kindness.

I desperately wanted to get out of that school. I wanted to go to college. I did not so much want to go to college as I wanted to enter a world where people could see, and I wanted to be accepted in that world. So I applied and was accepted at a college in upstate New York, a place called Hamilton College, a marvelous place, and I even got a scholarship. I did so abominably in my first semester that they took my scholarship away. I think I got four D's, as in "dog," and a D minus, as in "less-than-dog." I do not know what my average was, but it was appalling. No one had the guts to fail me. Yes they did, there was a marvelous chap in math, and he failed me. I respect him for it.

Academically, my freshman year was a bust. But my education did not suffer. At least in the sense of liberal education it did not suffer. I engaged in some very crucial activities that invited the wholeness of self out to an engagement with this new world in the middle of which I had landed. I learned how to drink beer. That mattered. That mattered desperately. I did not know it, I am not pretending that I was conscious of what I was doing, but the instinct of necessity drove me to learn these things. I played cards—poker, blackjack—long into the hours of the morning with other wastrels and academic no-goods. I went to the gym. I had wrestled in school, and I wrestled in freshmen class the first day and pinned a sophomore that they had sent up against me. That did

5

not hurt at all. It made me feel that I had to be dealt with, made them feel that I had to be dealt with.

The point is that while that first year was a great academic bust, educationally, liberal educationally, it was immensely important. I do not look upon it as a waste at all but as an exceedingly valuable time. Of course I made a fool of myself, with the excess of the young. That is the privilege of the young. But I needed to do that, and I had to do it there. I could not do it at the school for the blind; I did not need to do it there. It was not until my second year that I began to respond to academic subjects, to literature. I had to make my life in some way connected with books and reading. So that while I failed at Hamilton, academically, in my freshman year, educationally it was a great experience. It has continued to be that way throughout the years since that freshman year. I learned how to reach out to people. And all the important contacts of my life have been made not through the exchange of money but through the sharing of interests, liberal interests. That is, those interests that invite the coming forth of the whole person. Those interests that I pursue with others— sharing. This was and is and will be my liberal education. Sometimes these interests are and were academic, sometimes not. I have bent toward another and that other has bent toward me, over beer, over a dialogue of Plato's, over a cranky engine or a poem of Gerard Manley Hopkins, over a game of poker, a Beethoven quartet, the buzz of the reel when the fish strikes, the sound of waves, the feel of spray, a child crying in the night with no language but a cry—these interests and countless others have led me forth and challenged me to engage with another person, who, him- or herself, was tempted forth to engage with me at that point of our shared interest. And where we met, where we became friends, became lovers, was in the width of that foaming glass, at that word on the page, at that point in the cylinder where the spark did not flash to ignite the fuel, in that movement of the large, warm cello, that stepping down note by note from the cheerful major to the exquisite sadness of the minor.

Each of us nervous, uncertain what the other knew or felt, reluctant—each reluctant—to advance but still drawn forward by that thing between us, whatever that thing was. We came closer as if unable to help ourselves, the excitement about that thing growing all the time and our pleasure growing in the increasing closeness with the other; and then our meeting, always partial but always wonderful, and the parting, the withdrawal back to where each had been hiding, but never all the way back, not for each other any more, because each now felt relaxed with the other, comfortable in the closeness because each knew that the other was human too.

Since this is what I think happens, I suppose I ought to call this kind of comfortable sharing of thoughts and feelings the product of a liberal education. But I do not like that idea of product, because it sounds too confining. It sounds as if now that it has happened, the education is over; and it is not, it goes on and on and on. There will always be marvelous books that I have not read. There will always be peculiar spasms in the outboard engine that I cannot figure out, that somebody will love to work on with me. There is actually an inexhaustible supply of fascinating people to meet as you actively pursue your liberal interests, whatever they may be. Now, "actively pursue" is obviously a key expression because it means going forth, energetically exercising your interest—all of you, not just your mind but your heart as well. In that going forth we entice others to do the same. This means we will meet others there, at that point. After meeting, through the engagement of personalities, we learn to accept each other as human. That is why I think liberal education is the most important kind for everyone but especially for us, the handicapped; because others who do not know us are inclined to exclude us from the club without thinking.

Once we can meet them, once we can make of them friends, the handicap, while it will never disappear, will take on its genuine significance—which is, very minimal.

PANEL DISCUSSION

Panelists: John Kemp, Kemp and Young, Inc.
Lorna McIntyre, Teachers College
Jim Reitwiesner, New Jersey Commission for the Blind

Contributors: Armand Bakalian, In Touch Networks, Inc.
Susan Beidel, St. John's University
Elizabeth Scott, Teachers College

QUESTION: I am rather disappointed that there are not more blind people in the audience. Why is that? Was this lecture announced on the "In Touch" radio program?

MR. BAKALIAN: I was not in charge of publicity. Perhaps I should have taken a little more initiative and contacted more organizations.

MR. RUSSELL: I did not mean to address myself only to blind people. I hope everyone in the audience found it worthwhile.

MR. KEMP: I would like first to react to one part of the lecture, the part about liberal education in conjunction with a college education. I, as a handicapped person, relate very well to that. I too had a bust first year, and not only that I had a bust second year. I enjoyed getting the liberal education more than I enjoyed the academic parts, but I had a lot of trouble persuading my dad about the significance of the liberal education I was receiving, the social advances that I was making, the participation with other people, the socialization process. While my grades suffered, I relate very much to the feeling that there was an element of need and an element of success in spending my time doing that. I went to Georgetown University in Washington, D.C., where eighteen was the legal age for beer and white wine. I, too, had a great time learning how to drink, did a very good job of leaning how. It was very, very important for me to learn how to begin the process—of knowing women and men, of talking with women and men, of learning about areas of life beyond the mental ken of "I'm a handicapped person going to a big school for the first time." So I relate directly to what was said by Dr. Russell, and I feel that there is great value in urging that a liberal education be obtained by handicapped individuals.

QUESTION: During freshman year I went through a lot of the same experiences that you were talking about, and I did not go to class as much as I should have for that reason. I really relate to what you have said, because when I went off to college I was very short on socialization. Although my freshman year, and even my sophomore year, was as you might say an academic washout, I enjoyed it and I grew tremendously as a person. I learned to relate to people on an equal level, the way you were talking about, getting just as much from them as they were from me. I would not trade that for a few years of straight A's.

DR. RUSSELL: I am glad to hear that it was a valuable experience, although not necessarily academically. The academic rewards do not matter as much as the others.

QUESTION: There is one problem with your promotion of liberal education. Many disabled college students are supported by state vocational rehabilitation agencies, which are very clearly vocationally oriented. Students have to justify their education in those terms. Can we change those policies?

MR. REITWIESNER: I think too much emphasis is put on employability; we put a lot of funding into training students, with the ultimate goal of their getting jobs. But I think that, as Dr. Russell has said, there is a lot to be said for developing the whole person. You cannot expect a person to get a job if he is not developed physically, socially, emotionally—in `every way. I wanted to ask Dr. Russell something relating to social development. You mentioned, for example, that you wrestled. You mentioned some personal distress that you had encountered in various experiences. Among the students I work with I have found that such sports as wrestling and swimming are not as socially acceptable as tennis and golf, and I was wondering how you overcame the problem.

DR. RUSSELL: I did not. I did not. But you see, wrestling was a very valuable thing for me. Not that I was especially good at it, but it brought me into combat—the basic archetypal human conflict, man against man. The other chap says, "I can see. You can't. Boy, you're a poor chap." And I say, "Am I? Come on, let's find out." And we get right down to the absolute basics. I have gained the respect of quite a few people that way. I worked at that because I liked it and it brought me into real and continual contact with people whom I might otherwise never have met; and they had to deal with me, they were forced to deal with me, as a person. They could not just back off the mat and say, "Well, dear, goodbye, it was nice to meet you." They had to face up to the fact that I was there. It is not a carryover sport like tennis or golf, but I still roll around on the mats with the wrestling team at Franklin and Marshall. I cannot compete with them, but that does not matter, I get a workout. I mentioned wrestling. But there is no particular virtue in wrestling. If you are good at checkers, try that, work at that. Anything. Playing the piano. I did not play the piano; if I had, that probably would have been immensely useful. Or the guitar. But that was before the "discovery" of the guitar. Solitude is the real pit. It invites suicide for the handicapped. How does one get out of that solitude? Wrestling is just symbolic of a way to begin coming forth socially. Any kind of skill or interest brings forth, whether it be checkers or dirty jokes. The focus does not matter. What matters is that it provides the opportunity and even creates a necessity for human contact, and that is what counts. The things that have brought me together with some of my very best friends were, in themselves, trivial things, such as a broken spark plug wire. But out of dealing with that, I made friends. And this is what happens—it creates contact. I do not care what the interest is. So long as you pursue it, you are going to find somebody else who also cares about it. We are marvelously unpredictable human creatures, and you will find somebody to share your interest, whatever it may be.

But you are going to have to do something. You cannot just sit and hope that they will come to you. It is an active pursuit. So, anything that creates a joint pursuit is valuable. That is why cocktail parties are, for the most part, just a waste, they are not a pursuit of anything. I have met people at cocktail parties that I thought were absolute blobs. But when I get them out in the garage or in a boat fishing—doing something together because we are both interested—then they come alive as people. You begin to move toward each other. That is when you begin to make contact for the most part. It is the active pursuit of an interest—whether it be wrestling or checkers or whatever—that is going to count as the most important thing for anybody, but particularly for the handicapped.

QUESTION: I went to a school for the deaf and I was trained to be a commercial artist even though I had a high IQ, a high academic score, and so forth. I got married and had three children, but I was never happy being a commercial artist. So at a late stage in my life I had to change careers. Now I am an administrator at a school for the deaf and I am the happiest person in the world. I find that now I relate better to my family, too. And I am making three times the amount of money that I ever made as a commercial artist.

QUESTION: As someone who worked for a number of years with the Office of Vocational Rehabilitation (OVR) in New York State, I would like to say that the first year is generally regarded as an "experience year." Students do not necessarily have to be that successful academically to maintain their sponsorship. If they are not successful for two or three years, then there is a problem with the client's educational situation, anyway.

QUESTION: I wanted to major in philosophy, and OVR would not sponsor me. So for four years I borrowed money. The fifth year they agreed to sponsor me, but then they tried to place requirements on my program above and beyond what the college itself required.

MS. BEIDEL: Let me say a word on behalf of OVR. Had it not been for them, I would not have made it through college; I would not be here except for them. About the standards they have for grades: They forced me to study deep into the night. I had been educationally disadvantaged but I graduated with a grade point average of 3.85 because of the standards they set for me. Also, if they had not required me to pursue a vocational education, I would not have received the offer I did—as a recruiter/counselor for the handicapped at the New York City Board of Education. So it depends on how you deal with the setting of high standards. For me it has been a great source of enrichment in my life.

QUESTION: I have had some experiences with OVR too. I remember one time when I told a counselor everything about myself and he did not know what to say to me. At that moment, I saw that he was human like everyone else. Sometimes when you need something from somebody you have to work through with them the common factors you enjoy. Some counselors at OVR are more receptive than others.

QUESTION: Dr. Russell, would you say that the waitress you talked about was also likely to be racist?

DR. RUSSELL: There is a similarity, of course, between racial prejudice and prejudice against the handicapped; and I suspect that the laws have not wrought much change. The kind of thing that will bring change is the gradual making of friends. I have never believed in separatistic solutions. In the 1960s there were very strong separatist movements among black students that taught, and I argued vigorously with them trying to explain that from my experience, separatism was badism. Separatism is what I have been trying to fight all my life and will continue to fight. I will never be able to complete the fight. There is always going to be that other waitress in the next diner, and you are going to meet her. That meeting is an opportunity. It is an infuriating one, I know; but if enough people go around, she is going to get used to us. We are just using the waitress as a symbol, right? She is no different from the college president.

MS. SCOTT: One of the goals that the Distinguished Lecturer Series planners had for the panel discussions was that everybody should pool their ideas and direct them toward particular issues; we wanted people to talk about some of the ways we can organize and bring about changes, such as having buildings made more accessible and having admissions training programs set up so that admissions officers will not discriminate. I was wondering if anyone on the panel would like to address themselves to the issue of what we can do about some of these problems?

MS. BEIDEL: The New York City Board of Education at 65 Court Street in Brooklyn will be servicing the handicapped population as soon as I get on the payroll. We would like you to start writing or visiting us. Our office came about as a result of affirmative action. I want you to know that this is just a beginning. We do not yet have all our resources and I would appreciate your sending us any relevant material.

QUESTION: I would recommend that if this lecture series is published it be sent to vocational rehabilitation offices all over the country—especially this session stressing the importance of extracurricular activities and liberal education, because OVR does not consider that a part of the academic function. As for being "indebted" to OVR, I think that is not right. OVR receives funds to educate disabled people. They are not doing us a favor. I think it is critical that they see that higher education is more than mere academics.

DR. HOURIHAN: I want to mention that right now, in Washington, Congress is working on amendments to the Rehabilitation Act of 1973. Every five years particular pieces of legislation are worked on, and the rehabilitation legislation is now being worked on in the Senate. If you want to be an instrument of change, whatever your viewpoint, write to your senator. And do it this week, because next month it will be acted upon. Congress will enact new legislation incorporating all the amendments. If you want to have input into the process, now is the time to do it. Disabled people can, if interested, provide input at this time and be instrumental in bringing about changes.

QUESTION: I am thoroughly delighted that the legislation is being worked on and that it does initiate certain changes relating to mainstreaming. But I want to mention another dimension, in addition to architectural change, that has to be worked on—and that is resistance. There are teachers who are resistant to having students who are disabled because they find it too uncomfortable to deal with their presence. I think that interpersonal relationships, which Dr. Russell spoke about today, are important for all of us; they must be worked on. We also must work on the resistances that students have in dealing with others who might be different in some way. We are missing a whole dimension that is necessary, and we can never legislate that. That has to be part of the guidelines that are sent to the schools along with architectural guidelines. We need to set up sensitivity workshops for teachers and students.

QUESTION: One man I know is attempting to organize committees for the handicapped in every community in New Jersey. We should actively inquire of the mayor and the local government in our communities, "Do you have an active plan to organize an office for the handicapped?" An effort such as this would contribute greatly to the organization of the handicapped people, while also helping to achieve their goals.

MR. KEMP: I would like to mention briefly that awareness training is included in Section 503—in the affirmative action section of Title V of the Rehabilitation Act of 1973. It stipulates that supervisors should be taken through an awareness training that will make them more familiar with the problems that handicapped persons face and with the functional capabilities of many handicapped people in a variety of limiting conditions. This is something that our company does, and it can be done by many people as long as it is done properly. An attempt should be made to show in a very positive way the problems faced by handicapped individuals. Awareness training is also included in PL 94-142, the Education of Handicapped Children Act. Second, the Rehabilitation Act was addressed by Dr. Hourihan, and it is quite true that Congress is trying to amend it, to expand it beyond a vocational rehabilitation concept with just employment as the ultimate goal of rehabilitation. They are trying to include the concept of independent living—which hopefully expands the capabilities and objectives of handicapped people—by providing much broader social, cultural, legal and financial services. I think this is very good and very positive. The big concern in Congress right now is that it is going to be very expensive. I do not know how the rehabilitation departments are ever going to be able to handle it. Rehabilitation counselors still are job-oriented because the legislation has been pushing them in that direction. If the amendments are put through, I think we are going to see a broad change—a better deal for handicapped individuals in general. My third point is a commercial, because people from Mission, Kansas do not get to Cranford, New Jersey very often. I have about twenty-five copies of the *Section 504 Compliance Report*, which is a newsletter published by Kemp & Young, Inc., as well as other types of publications. You are welcome to look at them and see if there is anything of interest to you.

QUESTION: I personally believe that the way we disabled people will get our rights is not necessarily by asking the government for them but by organizing ourselves. I think we should take advantage of this meeting today to pursue that objective.

5

VISUALLY IMPAIRED

A Preliminary Assessment Of the Validity and Usefulness Of the WRAT with Visually Handicapped Residential School Students

by David W. Alford, Mary W. Moore and Janet L. Simon

Abstract: A pilot study was conducted to provide a preliminary assessment of the validity and usefulness of the Wide Range Achievement Test as a teacher aid for IEP development and educational programming for visually handicapped students. Twenty-one residential school students (12 large print readers; 9 braille readers) were administered the WRAT. Correlations were computed between test grade equivalents and teacher ratings and between WRAT SS's and Verbal IQ's. Significant results suggest the valid use of the WRAT with visually handicapped students. Test and pilot study weaknesses are noted along with recommendations for further study.

The requirements of PL 94-142 mandate that all exceptional persons, age 3 to 21 by 1980, be provided not only an appropriate educational program in the least restrictive environment, but also, a parent-approved individualized educational program (IEP) (Beekman, 1977). In the development of an IEP, the educational team is required to assess the student's current level of functioning as well as to plan programs with specific goals and objectives. Standardized achievement tests, in addition to teacher assessments, may be appropriately used to provide achievement grade levels in order to measure student progress (Duffey, 1978). A number of achievement tests are frequently used, including the Wide Range Achievement Test (WRAT), Peabody Individual Achievement Test (PIAT), Key Math Diagnostic Arithmetic Test, and Woodcock Reading Mastery Test (Wallace & Larsen, 1978).

For teachers of blind and partially sighted students, the problems of describing functioning levels for IEP development are compounded by the limited availability of appropriate achievement tests. Several group achievement tests are available on which some non-sighted norms have been established. However, deficiencies exist which make them inappropriate for IEP development. For example, the Iowa Test of Basic Skills (ITBS) is published in both braille and large print editions, but non-sighted norms are provided for only grades three through nine (Scholl & Schnur, 1976). Morris (1974) reported that a great deal of work was expended in adapting the Stanford Achievement Test (SAT) for blind and partially sighted students but administration of the test can require up to three days. Trisman (1976) related braille test scores to existing sighted norms on the Sequential Tests of Educational Progress (STEP), but a continuous standard score is provided for only grades four through fourteen. Braille and large print editions of the School and College Ability Tests (SCAT) are available, yet non-sighted norms were established for only grades four, five, and six (Pearson, 1963). While these group achievement tests can be used with blind and partially sighted students as a comprehensive measure, the length of time required for administration and the non-inclusion of lower grade level norms reduce the utility and practicality of the tests as a means of obtaining relatively quick achievement levels for IEP development and educational programming.

In addition to group tests, several different reading tests are reported to have been used with blind and partially sighted students. The Diagnostic Reading Tests, available in both braille and large print editions, yield reading scores involving word recognition, comprehension, vocabulary, and story reading for grades four through thirteen (Scholl & Schnur, 1976). Bauman (1974) reported that the Gray Oral Reading Test has been used with partially-sighted students since 1923 but currently is infrequently used. The Durrell Analysis of Reading Difficulty Test is also reported to have been used with partially sighted students (Nicholson, 1975). The use of these reading tests for IEP development is limited since the Gray and Durrell are available neither in braille nor large print and the Diagnostic Reading Tests provide no norms for grades one through three.

A number of other academically related tests have been used with blind and partially sighted students. Morse (1970) adapted the Academic Promise Test (APT) for blind students to provide percentile norms for each grade level in abstract reasoning, numerical, verbal, and language usage. The Blind Learning Aptitude Test (BLAT), measuring learning ability, was

developed for and standardized on a blind population (Newland, 1964). Nicholson (1975) indicated the following academically related tests to have been used with blind or partially sighted students: Detroit Tests of Learning Aptitude, Mecham Language Development Scale, Peabody Picture Vocabulary Test, Wepman Auditory Discrimination Test, Slingerland Screening Tests for Identifying Children with Specific Language Disability, and the Wide Range Achievement Test. Except for the WRAT, these tests measure specific areas of learning ability or disability which, while useful, do not provide the teacher a practical means of assessing current academic achievement levels necessary for the development of an IEP.

The brief review of academically related tests which are reported to have been used with blind and partially sighted students reveals that the availability of a quick achievement test for reading, spelling, and arithmetic, encompassing all grade levels, is limited. While not recommended as a diagnostic tool nor as a comprehensive measure of achievement, the WRAT meets the criteria of availability in both braille and large print editions, quick administration (mean = 30 minutes), measurement of basic skill areas (reading, spelling, and arithmetic) and normative data of grade levels, SS's and percentiles.

Warren (1977), however, has cautioned against the indiscriminate use of sighted-normed tests with blind and partially sighted students. The scores attained reflect the students' relative standing compared to sighted children so should not be used as a basis for prediction of future behavior. However, such scores can be useful as a measure of academic growth of an individual child.

Since the braille and large print editions of the WRAT provide no data as to the applicability of the test with visually handicapped students, a pilot study was conducted at Western Pennsylvania School for Blind Children to provide a preliminary assessment of the validity of the WRAT as a teacher aid for IEP development and educational programming.

Method

Subjects

The subjects were 21 blind and partially sighted non-graded intermediate school students at the Western Pennsylvania School for Blind Children, a residential school serving western Pennsylvania. The subjects ranged in age from 9 to 15 years at the time of testing. Nine were braille readers and 12 read large type print. The mean length of time that subjects had attended the residential school was four academic years. Subjects, enrolled in the school, had among them 14 different diagnosed visual disorders. The most frequently recurring diagnosis was congenital nystagmus (n = 5); retinitis pigmentosa and congenital glaucoma each appeared in two subjects.

Materials

The 1965 braille and large print editions of the Wide Range Achievement Test (WRAT) were provided by the American Printing House for the Blind, and used in the testing.

The WRAT was first standardized in 1936 as a tool for the study of the basic school subjects of reading, spelling, and arithmetic computation. The test is divided into two levels; level I is for students between the ages of 5 years 0 months and 11 years 11 months and level II is for students aged 12 years 0 months to adulthood. The manual provides explicit administration directions and scoring procedures.

Reliability coefficients, established on a sighted population, range from .92 to .98 for the reading and spelling tests, and .85 to .92 for arithmetic (Jastak & Jastak, 1976).

Procedures

The WRAT was administered individually by graduate students enrolled in the master's degree program for the professional preparation of teachers of visually handicapped children at the University of Pittsburgh. The graduate students were trained in the administration of the WRAT and supervised by two certified school psychologists.

All test directions as stated in the examiner's manual were followed except the adherence to time limits in reading and mathematics, since it has been shown that eliminating time limits for visually handicapped students does not positively skew scores (Birch, Tisdall, Peabody, & Sterrett, 1966). Braille readers were permitted the use of an abacus but no other aid. Spelling responses for braille readers were oral. Prior to the testing, teachers of each subject were requested to estimate each student's achievement level in grade equivalents for each subject area, based on their knowledge of student performance. A mean grade equivalent for each student was obtained by averaging the ratings of the reading/spelling, math/social studies and science/health teachers for each of the test areas of reading, spelling, and arithmetic.

Results

A summary of results is provided in Table 1 which includes the means and standard deviations of WRAT test scores, mean teacher ratings, and IQ's.

Table 1 Data Summary		
WRAT	**Mean Grade Levels**	**SD**
Reading	4.6	1.8
Spelling	4.3	1.7
Mathematics	3.6	.9
Mean Teacher Ratings		
Reading	3.9	1.1
Spelling	3.5	1.0
Mathematics	3.5	.9
IQ	90.43	13.8

Although most WRAT scores and teacher ratings were significantly correlated, a greater range of scores in reading and spelling was obtained on the WRAT than by teacher assessment which affected the means. For example, WRAT scores ranged from 2.0 to 7.2 in reading and 2.5 to 10.9 in spelling vs. teacher ratings of 2.2 to 5.8 in reading and 2.0 to 5.8 in spelling.

A computer analysis of the data was made. Table 2 presents correlations between WRAT test scores and mean teacher ratings using the Pearson Product Moment correlation formula. Separate correlations were made between braille and large print test scores. Highly significant ($p < .001$) correlations were obtained between teacher ratings and WRAT test scores in reading, spelling, and arithmetic for the large print readers. Significant correlations ($p < .01$) were obtained in reading and spelling but not in arithmetic for braille readers.

Table 2
Correlations Between Obtained WRAT Grade-Level Scores and Teacher Assessment of Grade Level Functioning

	Large Print	Braille	Total
Reading	.92**	.82*	.84**
Spelling	.85**	.85*	.82**
Arithmetic	.88**	.26	.62**

** .001
* .01

Since the WRAT manual provides correlations between WISC-R IQ's and WRAT SS's as a measure of criterion validity, Pearson Product Moment correlations were computed between the subjects' WISC-R Verbal IQ's and WRAT SS's. Verbal IQ scores ranged from 69 to 120 (mean = 90.4) and WRAT SS's ranged from 64 to 124 (mean = 84.5). As presented in Table 3, a significant correlation ($p < .01$) was obtained between Verbal IQ's and spelling SS's, but a correlation between reading SS's and Verbal IQ's failed to attain significance. A correlation between arithmetic SS's and Verbal IQ's was significant at the .05 level.

Table 3
Correlations Between WRAT SS's and WISC-R Verbal IQ's

	p
Reading	.40
Spelling	.57
Arithmetic	.55

Finally, Table 4 presents correlations of inter-test consistency among subtests. A highly significant correlation was obtained between reading and spelling subtests ($p < .001$) a significant ($p < .05$) correlation was obtained between reading and arithmetic and between spelling and arithmetic.

Table 4
Correlations Among WRAT Subtests

Subtests	Braille	Large Print	Total
Reading vs. Spelling	.77	.78	.75**
Reading vs. Arithmetic	.47	.44	.46*
Spelling vs. Arithmetic	.51	.49	.48*

** .001
* .01

Discussion

The purpose of the pilot study was to determine the validity and usefulness of the WRAT as a teacher aid for IEP development and educational programming with visually handicapped, residential school students. The results of the study suggest concurrent validity as indicated by significant correlations between WRAT scores and teacher ratings and between WRAT standard scores and WISC-R Verbal IQ scores.

IEP Development

From discussion with teachers, it was established that they accepted the results of the WRAT and were able to use the test information in developing the IEP. The description of a student's functioning level is a critical component of the IEP. Unless the functioning level accurately reflects the current performance of the student, there is a possibility that IEP goals and objectives could be unrealistically stated. Teachers often use their own observations as the foundation for describing student performance. This practice frequently proves to be satisfactory, especially for experienced teachers. However, utilization of WRAT

5

results can be an asset to the teacher. As this study suggests, teacher observations of student performance can be supported through scores obtained from the WRAT. Standardized test information coupled with anecdotal classroom information can provide the teachers with a comprehensive means for stating the students' present academic levels. Administration of the WRAT furnishes teachers with objective data so that they will not need to rely solely upon observation and results from teacher-made evaluations for determining functioning levels for students.

Inclusion of data from the WRAT is also proving to be useful in discussing student performance with others outside the school. Specifically, parents and school district representatives are better able to understand functioning levels when information obtained from the WRAT is included in the IEP. Being able to view student performance in terms of standard norms has been helpful in situations where the return of the student to the public sector is being considered. WRAT scores, in addition to other data and evidence, can be beneficial when such a return is being considered.

Diagnostic Usage

In addition to being a teacher resource for IEP development, the WRAT has been found useful in the identification of problem areas. While the WRAT was not selected because of its diagnostic properties, it was especially useful in several instances. The WRAT arithmetic subtest is brailled in Nemeth Code (1973). Not all of the students had mastered the code, so their lack of familiarization may account for test scores differing from teacher ratings of the student's actual arithmetical abilities and achievement levels. While the students functioned effectively when performing mental arithmetic, the results of this study suggested that better braille Nemeth Code skills were needed in order to achieve a score on the WRAT commensurate with their classroom performance.

In addition to suggesting the need for better braille Nemeth Code skills, the WRAT proved useful in yet another way.

Many students enrolled in the subject population were boys and girls who evidenced behavioral problems that limited their potential for successful enrollment in schools with non-handicapped children. The results of this study suggest that the pupils' interfering behavior in the classroom may have masked their true academic ability, causing the teacher to underestimate pupil performance. One such incident involved a student who was observed as having difficulty complying with classroom standards. WRAT grade level scores of 7.2 in reading and 10.9 in spelling were obtained, although the teachers had assessed the student as functioning at 5.8 and 5.2 grade levels in reading and spelling respectively.

Advantages and Weaknesses of the WRAT

While the WRAT appears to be a valid instrument for use with visually handicapped students and offers advantages in comparison with other academic tests, there are also several weaknesses of the test. The following list summarizes both the advantages and weaknesses.

Advantages:

It appears to be a valid test for use with visually handicapped students.

It can be administered in about 30 minutes.

Scores can be reported in grade equivalents, percentiles, or standard scores.

It measures a full range of grade levels from kindergarten through 18.

Both braille and large print editions are available from the American Printing House for the Blind.

Weaknesses:

The reading subtest is actually a measure of word recognition. No measure of reading rate or comprehension is provided.

The arithmetic subtest measures only computational skills, so concepts are not taken into account.

Reading of the Nemeth Code is difficult due to braille spacing.

An alternate test form is not available for test-retest purposes.

Recommendations

Prior to the comprehensive use of the WRAT with visually handicapped students, additional study is needed. Although the validity of the WRAT is suggested by this study, the sample population should be expanded to include all age groups as well as public school students. A longitudinal study is needed to determine the reliability of the test for use with visually handicapped students. Finally, an investigation of the face validity of the Nemeth Code translation for the arithmetic subtest is needed.

REFERENCES AND SELECTED RELATED READINGS

Bateman, B.D. Psychological evaluation of blind children. *New Outlook for the Blind,* 1965, 59, 193-196.

Bauman, M.K. Blind and partially sighted. In M.V. Wisland (Ed.), *Psychoeducational diagnosis of exceptional children.* Springfield, Ill: Charles C Thomas, 1974.

Beekman, L. The impact of implications of state and federal legislation affecting handicapped individuals. In G. Markel (Ed.), *Proceedings of the University of Michigan Institute.* Ann Arbor: University of Michigan School of Education, 1977.

Birch, J.W., Tisdall, W., Peabody, R.L., & Sterrett, R. *School achievement and effect of type size on reading in visually handicapped children.* (Cooperative Research Project No. 1766, Contract No. OEC-4-028) Pittsburgh: University of Pittsburgh, 1966.

Duffey, J. *An introduction to individualized education program plans in Pennsylvania.* Pennsylvania Department of Education, 1978.

Ferguson, G.A. *Statistical analysis in psychology and education* (2nd ed.). New York: McGraw-Hill, 1966.

Jastak, J.F., & Jastak, S.R. *Manual: The Wide Range Achievement Test.* Wilmington, Del.: Guidance Associates of Delaware, 1975.

Morris, J. The 1973 Stanford Achievement Test series as adapted for use by the visually handicapped. *Education of the Visually Handicapped,* 1974, 6, 33-40.

Morse, J.L. The adaptation of a non-verbal abstract reasoning test for use with the blind. *Education of the Visually Handicapped,* 1970, 2, 79-80.

Nemeth braille code for mathematics and science notation (1972 revision). Louisville, Ky: American Printing House for the Blind, 1973.

Newland, T.E. Prediction and evaluation of academic learning by blind children. Study II: Problems and procedures in evaluation. *International Journal for the Education of the Blind,* 1964, 14, 42-51.

Nicholson, G.P. Psychological evaluations of visually impaired children. *DVH Newsletter* (Division of Visually Handicapped, Council for Exceptional Children), 1975, 29, 6-12.

Pearson, M.A. The establishment of school and college ability test norms for blind children in grades 4, 5, and 6. *International Journal for the Education of the Blind,* 1963, 12, 110-112.

Scholl, G., & Schnur, R. *Measures of psychological, vocational, and educational functioning in the blind and visually handicapped.* New York: American Foundation for the Blind, 1976.

Trisman, D.A. Equating braille forms of the Sequential Tests of Educational Progress. *Exceptional Children,* 1967, 66, 419-424.

Wallace, G., & Larsen, S.C. *Educational assessment of learning problems: Testing for teachers.* Boston: Allyn & Bacon, 1978.

Warren, D.H. *Blindness and early childhood development.* New York: American Foundation for the Blind, 1977.

Wide Range Achievement Test (1965 edition, braille and large print). *Catalogue of Mental Tests and Measurement.* Louisville, Ky: American Printing House for the Blind, 1978.

5

VISUALLY IMPAIRED

The Usability of the Adopted Durrell Listening-Reading Series With Students In the Intermediate Grades

by Thomas A. Wood

Abstract: The use of the newly adapted Durrell Listening–Reading Series (DLRS) with visually handicapped students in the intermediate grades is discussed. A total of seventy-one students in four residential schools for the blind were tested according to their primary mode of learning: large print, or braille. Scores on both the listening section and reading section of the test were evaluated for reliability and validity. Pearson Product Moment correlations derived from the split-half technique showed a high degree of internal consistency. A comparison of the DLRS scores with scores of the Stanford Achievement Test demonstrated external validity. Based on this study, the DLRS seems well suited for use with this population; however, additional research efforts are recommended.

The adaptation of standardized ink-print tests for use with the visually impaired is a long-established practice (Ozias, 1975). Included among these adopted tests are numerous instruments designed to measure academic or scholastic achievement. Although a number of these achievement tests have proven to have great usefulness in the educational assessment and programming for the visually impaired, a standarized instrument to evaluate and compare listening and reading abilities has just recently been made available.

In 1973 a test-advisory group con-

vened at the American Printing House for the Blind (APH), Louisville, Kentucky, to recommend tests for adaptation. The Durrell Listening-Reading Series (DLRS), published by Harcourt, Brace Jovanovich, was one of the tests recommended by the group for adaptation (Morris, 1976) and was made available in both large print and braille editions by APH in the spring of 1977.

Description of the DLRS

The DLRS is an instrument which has been widely used to assess listening and reading skills of school-age children. The standardization program for the DLRS consisted of a norm sample of 35,408 students. The sample was drawn from eight regions in the United States and was checked against census figures with regard to two socioeconomic indexes, median family income and median number of years of schooling completed by persons 25 years of age or older (Durrell and Brassard, 1970).

According to Durrell and Brassard:

The Durrell Listening–Reading Series is designed to provide a comparison of children's reading and listening abilities. Its purposes are to identify children with reading disabilities and to measure the degree of retardation in reading as compared to listening. Knowledge of discrepancies between a child's understanding of spoken language and of printed words is basic to analysis of reading disabilities and diagnosis of remedial needs [p. 3].

The DLRS is available in two equivalent forms (DE and EF) and at three levels: Primary (for Grades 1 – 3.5); Intermediate (for Grades 3.5 – 6); and Advanced (for Grades 7 – 9). At each level the DLRS consists of both listening and reading subtests which are as follows:

Primary

    Test I   Vocabulary Listening
    Test II Sentence Listening
    Test III Vocabulary Reading
    Test IV Sentence Reading

Intermediate and Advanced

    Test I   Vocabulary Listening
    Test II   Paragraph Listening
    Test III Vocabulary Reading
    Test IV Paragraph Reading

Since a few differences exist between the Primary level and the Intermediate and Advanced levels, the description which follows will be limited to the Intermediate. A complete review of the Primary level of the DLRS has been provided by Morris (1976).

The listening section of the DLRS is administered orally. For the Vocabulary Listening Test (Test I), four key words are printed across the top of the page under pictures which graphically represents each key word. For example, the word "house" might be printed with a picture of a house just above it. The examiner reads the key words then a series of words which the student must match to one of the key words.

The Paragraph Listening Test (Test II) requires the student to listen to a short paragraph and then respond to statements presented orally by the examiner regarding the content of the para-

graph. For each statement the student must respond by selecting one of four phrases which most closely parallels the statement. The statements are: (a) True only of___; (b) True only of___; (c) True of both; and (d) Answer is not given.

The reading section (Tests III and IV) of the DLRS is almost identical to the listening section in format. The Vocabulary Reading Test provides the student with a column of words to read which must be matched to the key words and pictures presented across the top of the page. For the Paragraph Reading Test, the student reads a paragraph and then reads and responds to the four statements regarding the content just as was required for the Paragraph Listening Test.

The total test requires approximately 85 minutes' administration time; the manual recommends two separate testing sessions rather than giving the entire test at one administration. For both sections and all four subtests the student responds by darkening in a block with a pencil to indicate the answer. A machine-scorable answer sheet is also available.

The test manual provides tables which convert raw scores into age equivalents, grade equivalents, percentiles, and stanines for both listening and reading performance. Also provided in the manual is a section on the interpretation of test results and recommendations for using the test results in educational programming.

The content of the standard version of the DLRS and the APH-adapted version for large print and braille readers is identical. The format of the regular print and enlarged print version is also identical. Format differences between the standard versions of the DLRS and the braille edition are reflected primarily by the absence of pictures associated with key words. The test booklets also differ slightly in arrangement of key words and sentences. The user of the large print edition indicates his or her answer in the same fashion as the regular print user by darkening in the appropriate boxes with a pencil. The student using the braille edition must mark across a raised word or sentence with

5

a pencil or a crayon to indicate the answer.

Special Directions

The adapted DLRS is provided with specific directions developed by APH for both large print and braille editions. These directions also recommend that the examiner be thoroughly familiar with the DLRS as well as the general directions for its administration.

These directions recommend that braille readers who have not had previous experience with multiple-choice tests be given an opportunity to practice the answer-marking technique of drawing a line with a pencil or crayon through answers of their choice.

Some children to whom the large print version is administered may experience difficulty following the rows across the pages visually which may result in marking answer choices in the wrong rows. In incidences where difficulty of this nature is experienced, children may use a rule or strip of colored construction paper to keep their place. Of course, children who normally use magnification for academic work should be permitted to use it for the test.

Reliability and Validity

The reliability information presented in the DLRS test manual includes split-half odd-even reliability (corrected), Kuder-Richardson Formula 21 reliability coefficients, and reliability of the difference scores computed between listening and reading. The odd-even and Kuder-Richardson reliability coefficients approximate or exceed .80. The coefficients for the difference scores between listening and reading are .80, .74, .76, and .77 for grades 3, 4, 5, and 6 respectively.

Information regarding concurrent validity is presented in the form of correlations with other tests. The Metropolitan Achievement Tests and the Iowa Test of Basic Skills were utilized; correlation with the Durrell Tests ranged from .15 to .85. According to Spache (1972), the content validity of the DLRS is insured by using representative word lists and by varying the types of words used in the construc-

tion of the test.

Purpose

The purpose of the study was to gather reliability and validity data related to use of the DLRS with visually impaired children. Prior to the adaption of the DLRS for use with the visually impaired, only one attempt had been made to use the DLRS with this special population (Morris, 1976). Since no reliability or validity data were available on the DLRS for use with visually impaired subjects, acquiring such data seemed to be a prerequisite to the utilization of this instrument with the visually impaired.

Method

Subjects. Subjects were selected from residential schools for the blind which indicated willingness to participate, had a sufficient number of students enrolled who met the selection criteria, and were geographically accessible. Due to the widely scattered and low-incidence nature of the population of visually impaired children, it was not feasible to draw subjects for this study in a random fashion.

Seventy-one subjects were selected from four residential schools for the blind: Kentucky School for the Blind, Indiana School for the Blind, Missouri School for the Blind, and Illinois Braille and Sight Saving School. Since this study involved only the intermediate grades, all children in grades four, five, and six were included with the exception of children with a tested Verbal IQ below 60 and children possessing an additional handicap to their visual impairment, such as a hearing loss. Subjects were divided into 2 groups according to their primary mode of reading: print (39) and braille (32). The subjects in the braille group ranged in age from 9 years 9 months to 14 years 4 months with a mean age of 12 years 1 month. The age span of the large print group ranged from 9 years 1 month to 15 years 8 months with a mean of 11 years 9 months.

Procedure. Both the braille and print groups were administered the appropriate forms of the Intermediate Level Listening and Reading Sections of the DLRS. All of the testing with the DLRS was conducted during the month of May 1977. The investigator conducted all the Durrell testing at each participating test site. The subjects at each participating residential school were tested according to the following schedule:

Groups	First Day	Second Day	Time
Print	Listening Test	Reading Test	AM
Braille	Listening Test	Reading Test	AM

The tests were administered according to the special directions and time allowances provided for the APH-adapted version of the DLRS.

Since no data were available to determine the validity of the DLRS with visually handicapped children, scores from the reading comprehension subtest of the Stanford Achievement Test (SAT) were used as a measure of external validity. The SAT is a commonly used achievement test which was adapted for large print and braille students by APH; the modification also includes special directions and time allowances. The SAT had been administered by teachers under standardized conditions in all four residential schools as a part of the regular school testing program. All subjects selected for this study, with the exception of the fifth-grade print readers at one school, had SAT scores on file which were less than two months old. For this particular group of subjects the investigator administered the SAT reading comprehension subtest under standardized conditions following the DLRS testing sessions.

To determine reliability, the Listening Test and Reading Test raw scores were divided into two groups using the odd-even split-half reliability technique (Anastasi, 1968). The total score (Listening plus Reading) of the DLRS was also correlated using this technique.

Data Analysis. The data analysis involved computing Pearson Product-Moment correlations (r), means and standard deviations for each comparison (Hays, 1973). The coefficients derived from the split-half reliability technique

were corrected for full length by the Spearman-Brown formula (Guilford, 1954). Pearson Product-Moment correlations (r) were also obtained between the Reading Comprehension subtest of the Stanford Achievement Test (SAT) and the Listening-Reading sections of the DLRS.

Results

The reliability coefficients, means and standard deviations for the Listening and Reading sections of the DLRS are presented in Tables 1 and 2. Table 3 presents reliability coefficients, means and standard deviations for the total DLRS (Listening plus Reading) raw scores.

TABLE 1
Listening Test Reliability

Test	Mean	Mean Difference	sd	r
Odd Half	44.26		12.42	
		1.88		0.91*
Even Half	42.38		13.98	

*$p < .01$

TABLE 2
Reading Test Reliability

Test	Mean	Mean Difference	sd	r
Odd Half	37.91		13.42	
		2.07		0.93*
Even Half	35.84		13.98	

*$p < .01$

Mean differences were not significant for listening, reading or total test scores and reliability coefficients were significant at $p < .01$ for listening, reading and total test scores.

TABLE 3
Total DLRS (Listening and Reading) Reliability

Test	Mean	Mean Difference	sd	r
Odd Half	82.09		24.52	
		3.78		0.96*
Even Half	78.31		26.49	

*$p < .01$

Tables 1, 2, and 3 indicate that the halves of each comparison have unequal *sd*s and therefore unequal variances. Since the use of the Spearman-Brown formula assumes equal variance in each half of the test, an error is introduced when this condition is not met. According to Cronbach (1951), if the ratio of the *sd*s is not greater than 1.2, the error is not greater than 2 percent.

The ratio for the Listening Test is 1.13, for the Reading Test 1.04, and for the total DLRS 1.08. It can be assumed then that the coefficients reported in Tables 1, 2, and 3 do not exceed a 2 percent error due to the Spearman-Brown correction for test length.

Table 4 presents the correlation coefficients between the Reading Comprehension Subtest of the Stanford Achievement Test and the Listening and Reading Sections of the DLRS. Correlation coefficients were significant at $p < .01$.

TABLE 4

SAT and DLRS Grade Equivalent Comparison

DLRS	SAT
Listening Test	.69*
Reading Test	.89*

*$p < .01$

Discussion

The Listening Test, the Reading Test, and the total DLRS all appear to have a high degree of internal consistency. The highly significant correlations indicate that the DLRS seems to be a reliable instrument for use with visually handicapped children in the intermediate grades. The correlations between the DLRS and the SAT also were significant, indicating that the DLRS has sufficient criterion-related validity to warrant its use with this population of children.

The DLRS is a test which can provide valuable assessment information regarding a student's level of achievement in listening skills, reading skills and a comparison between these two skills areas. The conversion of raw scores to grade equivalent scores enables the comparison of a student's achievement in these basic skills with achievement in academic areas or with aptitude scores.

A word of caution should be mentioned regarding the use of the DLRS with visually handicapped students. Since this research was conducted with a relatively small sample, and this sample was somewhat homogenous in nature, generalization should not be applied too liberally. Additional experience is needed using the DLRS with all ages of visually handicapped students in both residential and public school settings.

REFERENCES

Anastasi, A *Psychological Testing* (3rd ed.). New York: Macmillan, 1968.

Cronbach, L.J. Coefficient alpha and internal structure of tests. *Psychometrika,* 1951, **16,** 297-334.

Durrell, D.D., & Brassard, M.B. *Durrell Listening-Reading Series Intermediate Level Manual: Form DE.* New York: Harcourt, Brace Jovanovich, 1970.

Guilford, J.P. *Psychometric Methods.* New York: McGraw-Hill, 1954.

Hays, W.L. *Statistics for the social sciences* (2nd ed.). New York: Holt, Rinehart and Winston, 1973.

Morris, J.E. Adaptation of the Durrell Listening-Reading Series for use with the visually handicapped. *Education of the Visually Handicapped,* 1976, 8, 21-24.

Ozias, D.K. Achievement assessment of the visually handicapped. *Education of the Visually Handicapped,* 1975, 7, 76-84.

Spache, G.D. Review of the Durrell Listening-Reading Series. In O.K. Buros (ed.), *The Seventh Mental Measurement Yearbook* (Vol. 2). Highland Park, N.J.: Gryphon Press, 1972.

VISUALLY IMPAIRED

Relevant or Obsolete Technique: Use of Programmed Instruction With Visually Handicapped And Hearing Impaired Subjects —A Review of the Research

by Frank P. Belcastro

5

Abstract: The research literature in the use of programmed instruction with visually handicapped and hearing impaired subjects was reviewed. The small number of experimental studies using programmed instruction with the visually handicapped was noted. The applications of behavior modification and programmed instruction were compared. Among the various recommendations and conclusions made were that brailled programmed materials and programmed lectures should be written specifically for the visually handicapped; that educators of the visually handicapped and hearing impaired should help in developing programmed materials; that programmed instruction be used more often, especially in the teaching of academic subjects; that the use of programmed instruction could alter the traditional roles of the teachers of the visually handicapped and hearing impaired, could help solve the teacher and classroom shortages, and could help solve the problem of individualizing instruction.

During the early and middle sixties, programmed instruction held high promise as a technique for teaching subject matter to students in a variety of situations and under a variety of conditions. Just at the time this promise was being fulfilled, programmed instruction was superseded by a technique of greater diversity, flexibility, and adaptability, namely, behavior modification.

Although both programmed instruction and behavior modification are based on the same psychological principles of operant conditioning, behavior modification has the added advantage of being flexible enough in format to focus upon an extensive variety of objectives, contingencies, and techniques. In addition, the crucial and exclusive superiority of behavior modification over programmed instruction is in its use of the experimenter (a) to identify the behavior to be modified, (b) to record this behavior in a natural setting, (c) to identify environmental variables, (d) to establish final goals, and (e) to consistently and systematically apply the variables which could change behavior, especially social behavior, and to modify these variables when necessary.

However, where behavior modification has been used almost exclusively in changing social behavior, programmed instruction has been used exclusively in modifying academic behavior. Because a subject's maladaptive social behavior often prevents his acquiring academic learning, the possibility exists that these two techniques both might be necessary and could be used in combination: behavior modification to modify social maladaptive behavior and then programmed instruction to modify academic maladaptive behavior.

This review will limit itself to the use of programmed instruction with visually handicapped and hearing impaired subjects and further limit itself to the research literature.

Additionally, this review will not consider computerized machines even though this instructional medium holds tremendous potential for the education of hearing impaired students. Some hearing impaired students have already learned through the use of computers at Columbia University, National Technical Institute for the Deaf, Gallaudet College, and Kendall School for the Deaf, and learned such subjects as speech (Boothroyd, Archambault, Adams, & Storm, 1975), language (Layzer, 1976), and elementary mathematics (Suppes, Fletcher, Zanotti, Lorton, & Searle, 1973).

The study by Mladejovsky, Eddington, Evan, and Dobelle (1976) reports on the great potential of computers for teaching the blind and the deaf. In this study, successful computer-controlled electrical stimulation of the visual and auditory cortexes of the brain through implantation of arrays of electrodes suggests that the theoretical concept of producing artificial vision for the blind and artificial hearing for the deaf may not be far from realization.

At present, the primary disadvantages of computerization are its inability to teach the severely visually handicapped, its high initial cost, its relatively expensive line costs, the lack of sufficient programs of instruction at various levels and in the different subject matter areas, and the lack of a large enough target population among the hearing impaired and visually handicapped to justify not only a wide scale development of software but also either the purchase of the needed computers or the leasing of computer terminals.

Although Ashcroft (1961) taught braille by programmed instruction to would-be transcribers and teachers, and Harley, Wood, and Merbler (1975) taught orientation and mobility procedures through programmed instruction to teachers of multiply impaired blind children rather than the blind students, in only three studies were the visually handicapped students taught academic subjects by programmed instruction: Coffey (1963) used grammar and algebra; Russell (1971) used braille; and Tobin, Clarke, Lane, and Pittam (1970) used braille, social studies, and science as academic subjects.

The vast majority of the research literature reviewed here focussed on teaching academic subjects through the technique of programmed instruction to the hearing impaired. Academic areas taught were written language (Birch & Stuckless, 1963; Rush, 1966), high school mathematics (Bornstein, 1964), vocabulary (Devine, 1970; Falconer, 1961), beginning reading (Karlsen, 1966), receptive visual language (Lennan, 1974), language of written directions (Rush, 1964), and arithmetic (Ogawa, 1965).

Conclusions and Discussion

The dearth of experimental studies on the use of programmed instruction with the visually handicapped must be noted. Because of the successful use of programmed instruction in teaching academic subjects to the visually handicapped in the three studies reviewed, it is recommended that programmed instruction be utilized with the visually handicapped with much greater frequency and that more studies be conducted to determine the variables necessary for optimum programming of materials for use in teaching the visually handicapped.

It seems obvious that programmed materials in their present format cannot be used with the blind and severely visually handicapped. Tactile and/or aural communication must be established through brailled programmed materials or programmed lectures.

Since translating programmed materials

written for the sighted into a form usable by the blind does not appear to result in optimum programmed materials for the blind (Coffey, 1963), then programmed materials for the visually handicapped should be written specifically for the visually handicapped and empirically tested with visually handicapped students in order to maximize performance on external criteria such as post-tests.

Because practical considerations such as cost, availability of space, and efficiency of labor are determining factors in the use of programmed instruction, the possibility of programmed lectures rather than brailled programmed materials should not be overlooked.

Volunteer transcribers, rehabilitation workers, school teachers, home-bound instructors, parents, and others who work with the visually handicapped and need quickly to acquire both braille skills and a positive attitude toward braille should make use of programmed materials that instruct in the skills of braille.

Programmed instruction should be used with hearing impaired students to remediate those errors that are consistently and markedly different from errors made by hearing children of the same chronological age, i.e., following directions, and written composition errors of omissions, additions, substitutions, and word order (Conrad & Rush, 1965).

For those learning English as a second language, the neurologically impaired, the mentally retarded, and other language-impaired students, programmed instruction should be useful in teaching them language.

Educators of the visually handicapped and hearing impaired should become involved with behavioral psychologists and commercial firms that write programmed materials in order to direct the development of these programmed materials and then should integrate them into the school curriculum.

Because the itinerant teacher of the visually handicapped or of the hearing impaired has a limited amount of time for each student, the use of programmed instruction could permit that teacher to assume the role of resource person; the role of the specialized teacher of the visually handicapped or of the hearing impaired could be changed into that of skilled tutor, facilitator, intellectual gadfly, and consultant to highly motivated students instead of being a teacher of basic skills that could easily be taught by programmed instruction.

The shortage of educators of the visually handicapped and of the hearing impaired represents a formidable barrier to progress in these areas of special education. Yet, programmed instruction could reduce the shortage in two ways: by covering areas of knowledge (e.g., Russian) whenever no teachers are available to the schools for such areas, and by teaching up-to-date subjects (e.g., metric system) in schools whose teachers are not abreast of the new approaches in these fields.

Any classroom shortages could be relieved by programmed instruction, for many visually handicapped and hearing impaired students could take their programmed materials to their rooms or a study hall or the school library thus reducing classroom attendance to those occasions when assistance would be needed or when group instruction would be necessary. Further, classroom attendance would be eliminated for those students using special programmed materials dealing with subject matter beyond the instructors' competencies.

With the visually handicapped and hearing impaired students there is the danger that entirely self-paced learning might isolate them still further; clearly, programmed instruction should be only one of many teaching methods used, some group work should be mandatory, and both teachers and counselors should be alert for adverse effects.

As noted earlier, behavior modification and programmed instruction could be used in tandem: behavior modification used initially to change socially maladaptive behavior so that a subject can be free to acquire academic learning, afterward programmed instruction used to free the experimenter by its teaching the academic subject matter to the student.

The problem of how to teach all the

students in a class equally well could be partially solved by programmed instruction: the brighter student could proceed through programmed materials rapidly while a slower classmate could proceed through the same subject area at his/her own pace without the pressure of maintaining the learning rate of the other students. Thus, instruction could be individualized.

Also, the number of programmed materials from which the visually handicapped or the hearing impaired student could select, including the number of programmed materials for each ability level and each grade level, could grow each year. Too, the variety of subject areas available in programmed materials will always exceed the educators available to an institution to teach in these same areas.

Unlike some of its human counterparts, programmed instruction does not discriminate as to race, color, creed, or educational or socio-economic levels. It is always patient, never loses its temper, never punishes and always rewards.

The possibilities of programmed instruction for the visually handicapped and the hearing impaired should be vigorously pursued. There is every reason to believe that the benefits of programmed instruction that have been demonstrated for the sighted and the hearing can be reaped for the visually handicapped and the hearing impaired.

REFERENCES

Ashcroft, S. Programmed instruction in braille. *International Journal for the Education of the Blind*, 1961, **2**, 46-50.

Birch, J.W., & Stuckless, E.R. Programmed instruction in written language for deaf children. *American Annals of the Deaf*, 1963, **108**, 317-336.

Boothroyd, A., Archambault, P., Adams, R.E., & Storm, R.D. Use of a computer based system of speech training for deaf persons. *Volta Review*, 1975, 77, 178-193.

Bornstein, H. *An evaluation of high school mathematics programmed texts when used with deaf children.* Washington, D.C.: Gallaudet College, 1964. (ERIC Document Reproduction Service No. ED 003 292)

Coffey, J.L. Programmed instruction for the blind. *International Journal for the Education of the Blind*, 1963, **2**, 38-44.

Conrad, R., & Rush, M.L. On the nature of short-term memory encoding in the deaf. *Journal of Speech and Hearing Disorders*, 1965, **30**, 336-343.

Devine, F.S. An attempt to increase specific reading vocabulary by means of programmed instruction among children with impairment of hearing. *Dissertation Abstracts International*, 1971, **31**, 3950A-3951A.

Falconer, G.A. A mechanical device for teaching sight vocabulary to young deaf children. *American Annals of the Deaf*, 1961, **106**, 251-257.

Harley, R.K., Wood, T.A., & Merbler, J.B., Jr. Programmed instruction in orientation and mobility for multiply impaired blind children. *New Outlook for the Blind*, 1975, **69**, 418-423.

Karlsen, B. *Teaching beginning reading to hearing impaired children, using a visual method and teaching machines.* Minneapolis: University of Minnesota, 1966. (ERIC Document Reproduction No. ED 015 603)

Layzer, A. Computer animated and textured presentation of language for the deaf. *American Annals of the Deaf*, 1976, **121**, 38-43.

Lennan, R.K. A comparison of four strategies to teach receptive visual language to young deaf learners. *Dissertation Abstracts International*, 1974, **35**, 2088A-2089A.

Mladejovsky, M.G., Eddington, D.K., Evan, J.R., & Dobelle, W.H. A computer-based brain stimulation system to investigate sensory prostheses for the blind and deaf. *IEEE Transactions on Bio-Medical Engineering*, 1976, **23**, 286-296.

Ogawa, S. The progammed arithmetic study applied to deaf children. *Japanese Journal of Educational Psychology*, 1965, **13**, 21-27.

Rush, M.L. Programmed instruction for "the language of directions." *American Annals of the Deaf*, 1964, **109**, 356-358.

Rush, M.L. Use of visual memory in teaching written language skills to deaf children. *Journal of Speech and Hearing Disorders*, 1966, **31**, 219-226.

Russell, H.K. The effect of order of presentation in the programmed learning of Braille. *Dissertation Abstracts International*, 1971, **31**, 5038B.

Suppes, P., Fletcher, J.D., Zanotti, M., Lorton, P.V., & Searle, B. *Evaluation of computer-assisted instruction in elementary mathematics for hearing impaired students.* (Tech. Rep. No. 200). Palo Alto: Stanford University, March 1973.

Tobin, M.J., Clarke, D., Lane, I., & Pittam, V.G. Programmed learning for the blind. *Education of the Visually Handicapped*, 1970, **2**, 11-23.

VISUALLY IMPAIRED

Optacon — A Tool For Independence

by Karl S. Gutnecht

Asking for help is sometimes the only way blind people can do some very ordinary things, like reading the label on a can of soup or counting money at the check-out counter. But asking can be tiresome, sometimes help isn't there, and some things a person wants to do alone.

The printed words and numbers which most of us rely on almost unconsciously are now being made accessible to people who are blind. Carefully and slowly, but for the first time unaided, a blind person using a machine called the Optacon can read typed or printed information.

The Optacon is the result of five years of intense collaboration between a California inventor and the Office of Education's Bureau of Education for the Handicapped. The device today is a tape recorder-sized unit consisting of a tiny TV camera and a screen of 144 vibrating points which can be covered with a fingertip. The user moves the camera across the printed page with one hand and feels the vibrating image with the other.

At the Wisconsin School for the Visually Handicapped in Janesville, students say the Optacon gives them a new way of getting information. They talk of gaining confidence in themselves as they learn a new way of looking at the world—the world through print in stories, verses, the phone book, and letters from home and friends. In short, anything that is printed in a reasonable size can now be read by the blind person. For the Wisconsin students, the Optacon is a way to be involved in today.

Preparation for real life world

Instructor-coordinator of the Optacon program at the Wisconsin school, Mrs. Anne Lyhus, works 30 or more Optacon classroom-instruction hours a week with 23 students. She states the Optacon means her students "are tactually learning today about a world they will be experiencing tomorrow." She emphasizes that the Optacon in no way replaces traditional braille instruction, which is received by all 158 visually handicapped students at the school.

The Janesville Optacon program is integrated into the traditional classroom instruction with Mrs. Lyhus having full responsibility for the entire. program.

"Direct access to print sources is the most efficient way to communicate. In the 'real life world' there aren't always readers and braille transcribers. Our Optacon program helps to awaken children to this reality. We try to give them an appreciation of real life needs

From *American Education,* January-February 1980, published by the U.S. Department of Health, Education and Welfare.

5

so the transition from the school world to the real world is not such a shock," Mrs. Lyhus explained.

Her introduction to the Optacon came in the summer of 1976 at a two-week Optacon workshop held on the campus of Northern Illinois University, Dekalb.

"I came away from that convinced it was virtually impossible for anyone to learn to read in this way. Experience and the students themselves have taught me otherwise."

Now the school has 31 Optacon machines. The 23 students receiving instruction are each issued an Optacon which they can use in dorm rooms on assignments, during study halls, or for use at home on weekends.

When should a person begin Optacon instruction?

"The sooner, the younger, the better," Mrs. Lyhus says emphatically.

Constant pupil-teacher exchange

Her Optacon classroom instruction technique might best be characterized as an "exchange" method. The students trade their confusion, indecision, and difficulties in working and in comprehending for the constant verbal diagnosis and guidance. She is able to watch each student's work (as many as five work with the Optacon during a single class period) from any place in the room with the aid of large visual arrays which project the exact image being felt by the student.

What is felt by the student and seen by the teacher, the electronic image, is not felt and seen as a whole unit simultaneously. The image slides across the index finger from right to left as the camera is slid across the letter from left to right. This sensation is described by students as "a series of pins pricking," caused by 144 electronic sensors which vibrate to form the raised image.

The verbal give-and-take between sighted teacher and blind student is continuous. The two Optacon control dials must be adjusted. One controls the delicate camera's magnification, the other, a "threshold" dial, controls the density of electronic impulse to be read by the student.

Discovery of images

For 10-year-old Anna Lisa Anderson of Grantsburg, Wisconsin, who is in her third year of Optacon instruction, "big blobs" caused confusion at a recent lesson's beginning.

"Nothing is making sense here, Mrs. Lyhus."

"Those are blobs of color, Anna Lisa," Mrs. Lyhus explained, as she firmly guided her right hand down the page to be beginning of the text.

"One of the first things children are shown after they learn the alphabet is what their name looks like," Mrs. Lyhus said.

"Three years ago Anna was slowly going through an A followed by two Ns and another A. Then stopped and said, 'Oh, that's what my name looks like!' It was as if she had gotten a new identity."

This day, after 30 minutes of Optacon instruction, Anna Lisa complained to Mrs. Lyhus of being tired.

"This points out a potential limitation of the Optacon's use," Mrs. Lyhus observed. "Each child has a different tolerance level for learning. Reading with the Optacon requires intense concentration. Students do get tired and must not be pushed beyond their tolerance."

Donna Natarelli is a demure, brunette, 13-year-old freshman from Milwaukee who has ambitions to become a psychoanalyst with additional aspirations for "a part-time career in country and western music."

"Why take someone else's time?"

She said the Optacon has given her "a new outlet, a new way of getting answers. I hope I'm headed for college and the Optacon will be important for me there. Sure, I could hire a reader for books that aren't in braille, but why take someone else's time when you can do it yourself."

Donna also has an Optacon unit at home which she uses on weekends and vacations.

"I'm not interested in having my brothers reading my mail, especially now," she said, smiling.

Mrs. Lyhus elaborated, "The ability of students to read their own mail independently and privately has meant very much to them." She added that Donna's Optacon work with telephone directories has given her an added flexibility of being able to look up her own telephone numbers.

"I don't believe many teenagers like to ask their family to look up the number of their boy or girl friend for them." Mrs. Lyhus said.

Learning the letters

Matthias "Matt" Norfleet, a 12-year-old sixth grader from Milwaukee, entered for his Optacon lesson with rambunctious enthusiasm. After only six weeks of work with the Optacon he knows the alphabet.

"By the way, Mrs. Lyhus, I heard this weekend there are two kinds of Ns—one has two humps, doesn't it?"

"I believe that's an M you are talking about, Matt," Mrs. Lyhus said.

"We'd better read a story to help you understand the difference," she continued.

Matt endured his way through an Optacon short story, "The Man and the Girl. This is a Man. This is a Leg. This is a Neck. This is a Pan."

" See what you mean, Mrs. Lyhus," he admitted.

Peter Atkinson, a 13-year-old eighth grader from Delavan, Wisconsin, began with the Optacon only two years ago when print characters became impossible for him to read.

"Since I already knew print letters, it was really difficult at first learning how they felt, what they looked like on my hand. All I could feel were the 144 pins vibrating up and down."

Now Peter receives Optacon instruction two days a week. He said the capital letters A, E, and S, because of their similarities, had given him the most difficulty. Similar problems were encountered with the lower case a, e, s, and c. He is now reading at a pace of about 25 words a minute.

Peter has career plans to be a radio announcer.

Students are first taught to distinguish between a vertical and a horizontal line, according to Mrs. Lyhus.

"Then we move to the circle and attempt to distinguish the circle from the letter C.

"Then we move to the more vertical letters such as I—IC and the word ICE is formed."

She said it is very common for students to get stalled after learning letters and that for many, the comprehension jump to words is difficult.

"Then they have to be taught to put chunks of words together to make meanings. Obviously someone who is a good braille reader will tend to be a better Optacon reader. It becomes a question of comprehension."

School Superintendent William English echoes the enthusiasm of Mrs. Lyhus and the students about the Optacon.

Feeling a new sense of freedom

"I said, not very long after I had observed our first instruction here with the Optacon, 'Hey we've got something here that's going to work.' The Optacon is a valuable addition to our program. There is additional feeling of freedom with it that the totally blind person has not had," English said.

Mrs. Lyhus has introduced several innovations with the Optacon which she uses interspersed with lesson materials.

"We attempt to teach our older students to type their own checks, and with the Optacon they can proofread their checks and even balance their checkbook."

She also teaches a method to distinguish between various currency bills. "The $5 bill has 11 columns on the Lincoln Memorial, which gives a much different sensation on the Optacon from the four-floored U.S. Treasury on the $10 bill and the five columns of the White House on the $20 bill.

"This too, does not come easy, and takes a lot of practice."

Mrs. Lyhus also encourages her students to write their own stories and verses which they can then proofread with the Optacon.

"The Optacon is a confidence booster, an ego booster, especially when students are able to read back what they have written," she said.

The fundamental Optacon skills

Speed and reading with the Optacon are dependent on particular skills which Mrs. Lyhus is constantly stressing:

Finger Position: A slight error in finger placement can make a big difference in tactual sensitivity. The student

5

needs to keep finger position in mind at all times.

Tracking: Tracking, according to Mrs. Lyhus, is the most difficult skill for the Optacon user to master. If the camera is not held perpendicular to the line of print, the letters become skewed. A specially designed tracking tray is used during the initial training period.

Controls Adjustment: If controls for a type style are set incorrectly, oversized or undersized letters may be the result. Practice with the magnification controls on the hand-guided camera and the threshold control, which determines the size of the letter impulse transmitted, is essential.

Language Skill: When readers begin to perceive words instead of simply letters, speed of recognition can be increased. Word comprehension or "word chunking" is crucial to increasing reading speed.

Nearly 50 students have been trained on the Optacon by Mrs. Lyhus since 1976.

"My greatest satisfaction in Optacon instruction is watching the student grow in confidence. It is a real confidence builder.

"I believe it gives our students a more realistic grasp of what they will face when they leave the protection of routine, braille transcribers, and the attention of faculty and staff in a school setting. The Optacon cannot answer or take over all real life reading needs for the blind, but it is an important additional tool," Mrs. Lyhus said.

In 1971, the Bureau of Education for the Handicapped (BEH) began funding the Optacon after experiments at Stanford University and Stanford Research Institute had shown the feasibility of such a device.

During the ensuing five years, BEH invested approximately $2.5 million in such phases of the project as research, development of prototypes, field tests of the machine in actual teaching situations, and evaluations of the Optacon's effectiveness. During the latter part of the five-year period, an additional

$300,000 was used to train teachers so they could train others to work directly with blind students in the use of the Optacon.

In June 1976, the Bureau began a related new venture—the Optacon dissemination project. This three-year project helped make Optacons available both to teachers trained to instruct the blind and to blind students on a demonstration basis.

The project's purpose is three-fold: to make some of the estimated 6,000 school-aged blind students aware of the uses of the Optacon; to stabilize the price of the device; and to stimulate public schools, colleges, and other agencies to help purchase Optacons and make them available as learning aids.

BEH has invested about $1 million per year over four years in the dissemination project.

To date, BEH has purchased 1,246 Optacons. Of that total, 628 have been distributed to teachers, 105 to universities which offer teacher training programs involving the Optacon, and 483 to students. The 628 teachers have trained 1,600 students in the use of the Optacon, and there are Optacons in virtually every state. Optacons also have been purchased privately by colleges, service clubs, school districts, and individuals.

In 1971, the cost of an Optacon was $5,000. Today it is $2,995—a decreased price which has remained constant throughout the three years of the project.

Approximately 400 student teachers have received training in the use of the Optacon. These sessions were conducted by universities which were already running inservice sessions for active teachers and wanted their beginning teachers to be trained.

With these purposes accomplished, BEH is phasing out its dissemination activities. BEH will continue to train teachers in the use of the Optacon and has just completed a series of summer seminars.

The Optacon was developed, and is manufactured, by Telesensory Systems, Inc., Palo Alto, California.

VISUALLY IMPAIRED

The Kurzweil Reading Machine

by Ruth-Carol Cushman

"It's the most wonderful thing in the world —I can't describe the joy of putting a piece of paper on the machine and hearing what is there!" The speaker is Linda Skroski, a music graduate from the University of Colorado who has been blind since birth. Linda can do almost anything: She skis, she sings, she can play a tune on a cash register or on a piano. And now for the first time, she can read a book without using Braille, without asking someone else to read it to her, and without waiting for a pre-recorded tape.

Homer Page, head of the program for disabled students at the University of Colorado, is also blind. He ran for the State legislature in 1978 in spite of what some people might consider a handicap, and during the campaign he read "hundreds of things from letters to summaries of legislative documents." Although he narrowly lost the election, he did prove that blindness need not be an obstacle to holding a government office.

Mike Smith is a blind taxpayer service representative for the Internal Revenue Service in Des Moines, Iowa. "In the four years since I have been on this job, tax rules and regulations have changed substantially, and they continue to change. I am required to do a tremendous amount of reading just to keep current." He does that reading on his own.

The Kurzweil Reading Machine makes all this possible. Physicist Mike Hingson, also blind, travels around the country for the National Federation of the Blind demonstrating the machine and teaching people how to use it. "It's the greatest thing since Braille," he said on a visit to Norlin Library at the University of Colorado, where the first machine to be installed in a university library has been in heavy use since the beginning of 1978.

A new era of independence

Designed by Ray Kurzweil, an engineering graduate from M.I.T. who started programming computers when he was twelve, the machine uses an electronic scanner with a speech synthesizer to read printed material aloud. It is programmed for one thousand linguistic rules plus two thousand exceptions, and it can read 200 different type faces at up to 225 words-per-minute. A new era of independence has opened for the blind who can now—on their own—read a wide variety of materials: books, magazines, newspapers, business memos, job training manuals, or typed correspondence.

No longer must a blind person wait for a reader in order to dive into the latest bestseller or today's newspaper. As one user pointed out, "It's sort of embarrassing to have to ask someone you don't know to read a risqué novel out loud!" A blind University of Colorado journalism student was thrilled to discover that she could use the machine to read her own articles back to her, and other students have used it to read back their term papers and creative writing assignments.

Out of about 40,000 books published each year, only about 350 are available in braille. "The Kurzweil machine means blind persons can select from the whole range of written materials," says Julia Brody, chief of a Manhattan branch of New York Public Library

5

where several machines are in heavy use.

At the Library for the Blind and Physically Handicapped in Virginia Beach, Linda Midgett and Barbara Style (two blind staff members) can now work directly with print for the first time. Linda has the Kurzweil machine read a text aloud, while she proofreads the braille transcription. The machine can also be used to help people suffering from dyslexia, a reading disability, by allowing them to hear the words at the same time they see them on a page. Marilyn Mortensen, special services coordinator at the Virginia Beach Library, says the machine is used by a wide variety of people, including lawyers, authors, physicians, opthalmologists, psychiatrists, an architect, an electrical engineer, a navigation specialist, blind teachers, and teachers of blind students.

The voice inside a box

Even children as young as first-graders learn to use the machine quickly and love it. At the Beethoven School for the Blind in Boston, the children have nicknamed the machine "Kurzie" and regard it as almost human. One happy child summed it up: "What it does, it takes a picture and comes out in a voice. It's like a radio: You're like the radio announcer —you decide what you want to hear."

Originally this voice had a "heavy foreign accent," but a newly developed synthesizer has a deep, resonant "baritone" voice that produces a more natural sound. Like most standard synthesizers, the Kurzweil reproduces the sixty or so phonemes (basic units of sound) that make up English speech. But in addition, the machine has a system that analyzes the syntax of each sentence. It duplicates nuances in pronunciation by differentiating sounds according to their relationship to other elements in the sentence.

"Sometimes you feel as though there's really a tiny, little person sitting inside the box, and maybe you should invite him out for coffee," says Nancy Cateora, a volunteer who works with the machine at the University of Colorado Libraries.

Nancy sees the Kurzweil as one way of helping end prejudice against the blind. Although few people would admit to such prejudice, there is no doubt that it is harder for a blind person to get a job than it is for the sighted. "This machine should bring about a lessening of preconceived notions of what the blind are capable of doing," says Nancy. "In the four years I have worked with the blind, I have found their limitations are ones *I* set for them. It's *my* hangup, not theirs. . . .

These minds shouldn't be wasted by being shunted into niches *we* think are appropriate." Nancy is especially enthusiastic because of the independence the Kurzweil machine gives to the blind. Within eight to ten hours of training most people can operate the machine without assistance.

It took only one hour for Linda Skroski to become adept at the keyboard, and now she trains all users as part of her job as coordinator in the Office for Disabled Students at Colorado University. "In an average week the machine is in use about forty hours, but sometimes I can't get everybody in, it's so busy," she says. Approximately 45 people have been trained to use the machine, which is usually available from seven in the morning till eleven at night at the library.

Financing the machine

By the beginning of 1980 more than a hundred reading machines have been placed in schools, libraries, rehabilitation centers, and work settings around the country. During 1979 approximately 250 orders were filled, 64 of them through the Bureau of Education for the Handicapped, a division of the Department of Health, Education, and Welfare. (See the list of libraries that own the Kurzweil machine on page 314.)

Because of the cost of the machine, many libraries have obtained financial aid for their purchase. Two private foundations, for example—The Swan Foundation and the Hill Foundation—purchased the reading machines for the University of Colorado.

In Massachusetts, $110,000 was funded as part of the Blind and Physically Handicapped area of the Library Services and Construction Act (Title 1) that enabled five public libraries (Lawrence, Newton, Peabody, Weymouth and Worcester) to purchase machines and train staff in their use. Thomas A. Ploeg, consultant for the physically handicapped at the Massachusetts Board of Library Commissioners, listed the project objectives:

- "To provide blind and physically handicapped persons with access to their community's information resources;

- to provide a reading machine which will provide one method of access to information resources;

- to provide trained staff that can effectively deal with client group and reading machine;

- to provide 'model situations' that can be

observed by other libraries; and

- to provide information on the feasibility of using a reading machine in a variety of public library settings."

In New York the machines were considered so vital that Assemblyman Edward Sullivan and Senator Hugh Farley introduced a bill to the state legislature that would put a reading machine in each of the twenty-two public library systems. The bill was passed in July.

Improvements and operation

One reason the Kurzweil Reading Machine suits blind people so well is that it was field-tested by blind users through the National Federation of the Blind. This testing resulted in many improvements in early models: For example, the machine was modified to read photocopies, to handle italics and columns, and to respond to additional user commands. A new compressed speech feature enabled the blind to read print at a rate fifty percent faster than normal human speech. As improvements continue to be made, older models are quickly updated by insertion of a reprogrammed cassette; it is not necessary to purchase a new machine to benefit from new developments.

To operate the machine a user places readable material on the glass surface, and then commands the machine by striking control keys on a small computer terminal. Under the glass a camera moves back and forth across the page; it can be stopped at any time by the user and commanded to spell a word, to give punctuation, or to back up and repeat. The user can also speed up or slow down the voice and adjust its tone.

The original 1974 prototype, which could read only print typed on Ray Kurzweil's personal typewriter, occupied half a room and cost a fortune to build. The machine at the University of Colorado, manufactured about two years ago, is about the size of a photocopier and was originally priced at $50,000. Although this model seems a miracle to those who use it, current models have superseded it.

New models have been reduced to less than one-third the size of the University of Colorado model. They weigh only 90 pounds (light enough for one person to lift), and the cost has been reduced to $23,800. This new desktop machine has a hand-scanning option that enables users to "browse" a page, explore its format, and then read material selectively. It also has a compressed speech device. At the

U.S. libraries owning the Kurzweil Reading Machine:

California
California State Library, Sacramento
San Diego State University Library
San Francisco Public Library
Colorado
University of Colorado Libraries, Boulder
Georgia
South West Georgia Regional Library, Bainbridge
Kansas
Topeka Public Library
Massachusetts
Cambridge Public Library
Haverhill Public Library
Lawrence Public Library
Newton Free Library
Peabody Library
Tufts Library, Weymouth
Worcester Public Library
Maryland
Enoch Pratt Free Library, Baltimore
Minnesota
Mankato State University
Missouri
University of Missouri, Columbia
Montana
Montana State Library, Helena
Nebraska
University of Nebraska, Lincoln
New Hampshire
Manchester Public Library
New Hampshire State Library, Concord
New Jersey
Ocean County Library, Toms River
Ramapo College, Mahwah
New York
Mid-Manhattan Library, New York City
New York State Library, Albany
North Carolina
East Carolina University, Greenville
University of North Carolina, Chapel Hill
Western Carolina University, Cullowhee
Ohio
Ohio State School for the Blind Library, Columbus
Pennsylvania
Free Library of Philadelphia
Virginia
Department of Public Libraries, Special Services Division, Virginia Beach
Washington, D.C.
Library of Congress

5

beginning of the fall semester, the University of Colorado Libraries added a desk top model. "Since this model is portable," says Linda Skroski, "a student can check it out the night before a final exam or for a special project."

The corporation is still working on improvements. Eventually the machine will be the size of a briefcase at a cost of about $5,000. Kurzweil has also developed new products: the Kurzweil Talking Terminal, that will enable voice-impaired people to communicate orally when it is attached to any computer terminal, and a print-to-braille machine, developed for the Library of Congress.

Blind user Gayle Dougherty, who formerly directed the Kurzweil project at the University of Colorado Libraries, looks forward to the day when blind people can buy their own Kurzweil: "When we can read our own office memos, instructional materials, and letters," she says, "we can become truly independent and can end job discrimination against the blind."

VISUALLY IMPAIRED

Learning Enhancement Through Visual Training

by Donald J. Getz

Problem: Programs to improve the reading ability of pupils diagnosed as learning disabled due to visual perception deficiencies have met with varying degrees of success. Alternate strategies that have been used include language experience and phonics programs to teach the child through the auditory channel. High-interest material, individual tutoring in basic texts, rote memorization of word lists, and programs to train the child in the necessary prerequisite visual skills for reading, have also been used.

Current research concerning the success of vision training for students is contradictory in its findings. Both significant positive results, and no correlation between reading and visual perception, have been reported by researchers! The most positive results appeared to occur when an optometrist was utilized as a consultant to help design the program (Breslauer et al. 1978, Ryan 1973).

In the Sulphur Springs Union School District, programs for learning-disabled students, it had been observed, on an informal basis, that students receiving some form of vision training (Frostig materials, *Michigan Tracking Program*) showed improved performance. It was the feeling of the special education staff that, for students with visual perception deficiencies, vision training was a more effective method of improving reading performance than alternate methods that had been utilized.

Most researchers agree that certain visual skills are necessary for a pupil to read fluently and with comprehension. These skills are both hierarchical and concurrent in terms of developmental stages. These skills involve the ability of a student to identify his body parts, learn to team the two halves of his body together, learn control of his gross musculature system, and to learn to move in space.

Laterality must then be developed. Laterality is the ability to distinguish and differentiate right sidedness and left sidedness. A sense of left-to-right directionality, which is the conventional direction of the English language, might be developed. The student must now develop the ability to differentiate the correct orientation of objects he has seen. This skill is necessary, for example, to correctly identify a *b* from a *d*. The ability to remember a series of symbols (such as letters that make up a word), and visualize the correct ordinal position of these symbols, constitute one of the primary visual skills needed for successful reading and spelling performance.

Eyes are equipment for gathering information, as are all the other senses. They should be able to maintain an awareness of a wide field of view while centering on a specific task. If the skill has not been developed, the child is too aware of every possible visual (and auditory) distraction, and has not developed the ability to center visual attention and maintain that self-directed attention.

Quick Eyes

Eyes should be able to change focus quickly and easily from far to near and near to far—chalkboard to desk, desk to teacher, chart to books, etc. The child whose eyes perform this change of focus at half the normal speed is the child who is only half finished copying an assignment from the chalkboard when most of the others are finished. He is not necessarily dawdling—he lacks the visual flexibility to keep up.

Another major area of visual-perceptual readiness involves the student's ability to team his eyes correctly. He must be able to coordinate the muscles of both eyes and make smooth and accurate movements from word to word for rapid and accurate reading. If he overshoots (moves his eyes past a word), then the context of the reading material will be altered and comprehension will decrease. An excessive amount of energy and concentration is required if ocular tracking is not an efficient process. This tires the student, makes reading an unenjoyable task, and reduces comprehension. An avoidance reaction to near-point work generally ensues, and the child is often observed daydreaming and displaying a short attention span.

The child who cannot move his eyes smoothly and easily to follow a moving target will lack the visual skill to follow a line of print smoothly, and will need his finger or a marker to help his eyes keep their place.

A youngster who cannot make quick, accurate fixations will be in trouble with both math and reading. He will pick up the wrong digit in math, or skip words, reread the same word, or miss an entire line when he is reading.

The amount of information gathered during each fixation is also of great importance. An individual who can grasp only two symbols with each fixation has to move his eyes twice to read the words *look* or *come*; and, if the fixation is inaccurate, his eyes may not even land on the same word at the second fixation.

Visual form perception is another skill which needs to be developed. Letters, words, and numbers are all forms; and the pupil who has difficulties discriminating and reproducing simple geometric forms is likely to have even more difficulty with the more complicated shape of symbols.

Rhythm, stressed in a great many of the activities in the Sulphur Springs Visual Training Program, is at the root of mathematical concepts and is important for reading fluency, as well as an integral part of normal body functioning.

Visualization, the ability of the pupil to "look at" something within his mind and see it clearly enough to be able to use it to assist in activities during which his eyes are otherwise involved, is directly related to the ability to utilize intelligence, and is trainable in almost all individuals. Increasing a child's ability to visualize has, in many cases, improved achievement test scores. It also benefits spelling, reading comprehension, and all scholastic activities involving logical reasoning.

Inservice Training

It was decided by the district to employ an optometrist who specializes in vision therapy to provide a thirty-hour inservice training program in the theoretical aspects and in the methodology of training for the special education staff. I was selected to perform in this capacity. It was reasoned that it is difficult, or impossible, for anyone who has not had some special highly specific training in the area of visual performance to identify what he is seeing in the pupil's visual behavior, or evaluate that behavior in terms of its adequacy for classroom learning.

Upon completion of the above program, it was decided that a pilot study in the effectiveness of vision training in improving reading and spelling ability should be implemented before introducing a district-wide program in this area.

It was further decided that the optometrist would be commissioned to prepare a teacher's manual of classroom visual training activities to be employed in the pilot study.

Is there a relationship between vision training, reading, and spelling achievement in second-grade pupils identified as being poor readers with visual-perceptual deficits?

Null Hypotheses

First, there will be no significant difference on a standardized reading test between students receiving vision training and students receiving no training.

Second, there will be no significant difference on the spelling section of the *Wide Range Achievement Test* between students receiving vision training and students receiving no training.

Third, there will be no significant difference in word recognition skills on the reading section of the *Wide Range Achievement Test*.

Definition of Terms

Small-group training. Small-group training performed by special education teachers to improve body image, coordinated body integration, laterality, directionality, span of perception, focus flexibility, eye teaming, eye movements, form perception, and visualization.

Students with visual-perceptual deficits. These pupils will have failed an initial screening by obtaining a score on the *Bender Gestalt Test* of one year or more below chronological age. Each child was then screened by a team of optometrists. The tests performed by the optometrists included:

1. Visual acuity—right eye and left eye at far point
2. Visual acuity—right eye and left eye at near point (reading distance)
3. Cover test at far point and near point
4. Near point of convergence—break and recovery
5. Retinoscopy
6. Versions
7. Accommodative rock
8. Stereo fly
9. Keystone visual skills
    a. lateral posture
    b. fusion
10. Brock string
11. Balance board
12. Knowledge of right and left
13. *Leavell Language Development Directionality Test*
14. *Children's Perceptual Achievement Copy Forms*

In addition, it was felt that one of the best screening methods to detect a visual problem would be the classroom teacher who is trained in what symptoms to look for that could possibly indicate the existence of a visual problem. Consequently, a teacher observation checklist was prepared which included the following signs:

1. Confuses letters or words
2. Reverses letters of words
3. Skips or rereads
4. Vocalizes when reading silently
5. Reads slowly
6. Uses finger as a marker
7. Poor reading comprehension
8. Covers or closes one eye
9. Moves head excessively
10. Tilts head to one side
11. Holds reading close
12. Head close to desk when writing
13. Frowns or squints
14. Rubs or blinks eyes excessively
15. Writes or prints poorly
16. Tires easily
17. Inattentive
18. Daydreams
19. Poor general body coordination
20. Short attention span
21. Learns more effectively auditorily than visually
22. Performance below potential

Students who failed the *Bender Gestalt Test* or the optometric screening were eligible for inclusion in the program.

Poor readers: Second-grade students who scored in the bottom 25 percent on the first-grade *Cooperative Primary Test.*

Design and Methodology

Second-grade students at four elementary schools were identified as poor readers and were screened first by the school psychologist and then screened by the team of optometrists to determine if they were deficient in visual-perceptual skills. One hundred twenty students were randomly selected from this group. Half of these students were randomly assigned to the control group. Students in the treatment group were seen for one-half hour a day, five days a week for a four-month period of time. These students received the vision training program in groups of six to eight pupils. A total of 40 hours of training was available for each student. Pupils who were not present for at least 80 percent (32 hours) of the sessions were excluded from the experimental analysis of the data.

The learning disabilities teacher at each of the four schools instructed the students in the visual training program. These persons received a thirty-hour inservice program in the theory and methodology of vision training and an additional twelve hours of inservice training in the correct application of each of the procedures in the vision training manual.

The specific procedures included in the manual are:

1. Homolateral creeping
2. Herman
3. Marsden ball
4. Simon Says
5. Penlight Versions
6. Cross-pattern creeping
7. Pre-writing designs
8. Fixations
9. Chalkboard templates
10. Balance board or block
11. Chalkboard circles
12. Geoboard
13. Balance board on a two-by-four
14. Chalkboard bimanual lines
15. Parquetry blocks
16. Chalkboard left-to-right patterns
17. Jigsaw puzzles
18. Walking rail
19. Box of cube blocks
20. Perceptual development motor activity cards
21. Tracking work book
22. Slant desk
23. Jump board
24. Perceptual-developmental skill builder (light and buzzer)
25. Toss back with tooties

5

26. Angels-in-the-Snow
27. Visual-fields card
28. Tachistoscope with circles
29. Tachistoscope with forms
30. Chalkboard animal fixations
31. Road map
32. Beads and patterns
33. Kirshner arrows
34. Tumbling *E* and number charts
35. Flannel boards with fish
36. Templates on paper
37. Brock string
38. Perceptual developmental drawing cards
39. Wide View
40. Small geoboards
41. Designs for large parquetry blocks
42. Flannel boards with geometric forms
43. Accommodative rock
44. Alphabet pencils
45. Tachistoscope with tic-tac-toe grid
46. Tachistoscope with arrows
47. Parquetry chips
48. Flipped forms
49. Tachistoscope with digits
50. Motor control stick with Marsden ball
51. Rotated forms
52. Outline patterns for parquetry blocks

At the end of the four-month period, all pupils who completed 80 percent of the program and all control pupils were assessed on the three posttest measures selected:

1. A standardized reading test (*California Cooperative Primary*, second grade).
2. The Spelling section of the *Wide Range Achievement Test*.
3. The Reading section of the *Wide Range Achievement Test*.

It was decided that analysis of the data would involve a posttest-only control group design, with random assignment of subjects using a two-tailed t test with a level of significance set at a 0.05 level.

Results

Of the original 120 children in the study, a total of 70 students completed 80 percent (32 hours) of vision training and all pre- and posttesting. An additional 17 children completed 80 percent of the vision training program and sections of the pre- and posttesting. Students were included in the statistical analysis of the data only if they completed 80 percent of the vision training and the pre- and post- data of a given measure.

In addition to the three tests just indicated, the *Slosson Intelligence Test* and the Math portion of the *Wide Range Achievement Test* were also given to some of the children. Results of the measures were not included due to the fact that not enough of the children completed these sections of the testing.

A pre- and post- optometric screening of the children was performed. The individual tests were enumerated earlier. This testing, however, was not part of the experimental design. For this reason, it is not being presented in this report.

Of the three measures administered, significant results at a .05 level were found for two measures. A t of 2.34 was obtained for the group reading measure. This was significant at the .05 level. The experimental group obtained a mean growth of ten months and eight days in reading scores. The control group obtained a mean growth of eight months and nine days. A t of 2.71 was obtained for the Reading section of the *Wide Range Achievement Test.* The significance level of this measure was .01. An average growth of eight months was obtained for the experimental group and an average growth of five months and three days was obtained for the control group. A t of .51 was obtained for the Spelling section of the *Wide Range Achievement Test.* These results did not prove to be significant at a .05 level. The mean gain for the experimental group was five months. The mean gain for the control group was four months and five days.

Summary

Students receiving vision training did significantly better in tests measuring reading comprehension and word recognition skills than students who did not receive this training. The spelling scores of children in the experimental program showed approximately one month of additional growth over students not receiving visual training. This level of growth on the spelling measure was not significant, however, at the level (.05) selected in the experimental design.

The results obtained on the test measures were consistent with the improvement expected from the vision training design and theory. It was expected that the visual skills taught in the vision training program would most directly benefit word recognition skills. The higher gain of experimental students on the test measuring this skill confirmed this expectation.

The measure involved with reading comprehension showed significant results, but to a lesser degree than the measure involving decoding. This is consistent with a view of reading as a hierarchal skill. The vision training then made the most impact at the basic level of reading skills upon which higher-level reading skills (i.e., comprehension, fluency) are necessarily based. A child must first recognize the individual symbols upon which reading is based before he can progress to a higher level of abstraction in the interpretation of these symbols.

The lack of significant gain in the spelling measure can be analyzed in a variety of ways. It was felt that the visualization skills taught at the end of the training would directly improve performance in this area. Many children, for a variety of reasons, did not receive the visualization training before the allotted time ran out. It is hypothesized that the relatively short time of the study (four months) did not allow for enough practice in the final skills taught to effectively teach the children to use these skills in a practical way so as to be able to apply them in the classroom.

Recommendations

Based on the higher level of significance obtained at the decoding level, this program would be seen as most benefitting kindergarten and first-grade students in the regular school program. Inclusion of this program for all students who fall in the lowest 25 percent on district reading measures should also be considered. It is also believed that this training would benefit those students who have been placed in special education programs.

The time period of the experimental program did not allow for effective learning of the final skills. The program should be restructured to allow for more complete learning of the visualization tasks. Increasing the program to cover 32 weeks with tasks introduced at a slower rate has been recommended and the manual has been revised accordingly.

Conclusions

The results of this study showed a positive relationship between classroom vision training and academic performance. It is felt that the results will be even more significant as the teachers involved in the administration of the program become more experienced as observers and trainers of visual skills. It is also felt that the program could be even more successful if an optometrist specializing in vision therapy was employed by the district to help in the administration of the program as well as in the service training of the teachers involved.

References

Breslauer, A.; Mack, J.; and Wilson, W. K. 1978. *Vision, its impact on learning,* ed. R. M. Wold. Coronado Unified School District Perceptual Project. Seattle: Special Child Publications, pp. 349-362.

Ryan, P. J. 1973. *The Cambrian project.* San Jose, California: The Cambria School District.

VISUALLY IMPAIRED

An Orientation and Mobility Program for Multiply Impaired Blind Children

by Randall K. Harley, Thomas A. Wood and Jon B. Merbler

Abstract: The purpose of this study was to develop programed instruction in orientation and mobility for multiply impaired blind children. Scales were developed for each of four major areas: motor development, sensory training, concept development, and mobility skills. Programed instruction was written for each of these scales. The programed instruction was validated with 40 multiply impaired blind children in nine facilities in a 16 week field test. The experimental group using the programed instructional materials demonstrated significant overall performance gains over a control group.

■ In recent years, a demand has grown for extending basic orientation and mobility instruction to include multiply impaired blind children. Some teachers have felt that the basic skills necessary for sighted-guide and independent travel can be learned by low functioning multiply impaired children who have a variety of handicapping conditions. This article presents a detailed description of the events and activities of a project funded by the Bureau of Education for the Handicapped over a 1 year period to develop programed instruction in orientation and mobility for use by teachers of multiply impaired blind children. The project included the development of measurement scales and programed instruction in four basic areas of precane instruction, the results of field testing, and the dissemination activities.

BACKGROUND

Related Studies

The identification of the orientation and mobility skills needed by multiply impaired children and the construction of an instrument to measure these skills were the first steps in designing appropriate instruction for these children. A review of the literature was undertaken to determine the basis for developing a measurement scale and programed instruction appropriate for multiply impaired blind children.

The literature indicated that some effort has been made to define the areas in mobility instruction needed by low functioning blind children and youth. Scales have been developed to measure orientation and mobility competency in young blind children. Lord (1966, 1967, 1969) used a developmental task approach to develop a scale for appraisal of orientation and mobility skills in young blind children. Significant and appropriate developmental tasks were taken from child development data and lists of skills were compiled from experienced teachers. The scales included self help skills; precane orientation and mobility skills, such as movement in space; use of sensory cues in travel; and use of direc-

5

tions and turns in travel.

A pilot study by Harley, Wood, and Merbler (1975) was completed prior to the beginning of the project. The objectives of the pilot project were to determine the feasibility of programed instruction in orientation and mobility for use by teachers of multiply impaired blind children, to develop a scale, and to prepare a program of instruction. The most important conclusion from the pilot study indicated that programed instruction in orientation and mobility was feasible for use by teachers of multiply impaired blind children.

Overview of Project

The objectives of this project were to develop and to validate a programed course of instruction in orientation and mobility for multiply impaired blind children. The manual was to consist of an assessment instrument and programed instruction for use by classroom teachers and parents. The assessment instrument was to be designed to evaluate children's developmental levels in the areas of concept development and motor, sensory, and mobility skills. The programed instruction was to be designed so that the purpose, task objectives, a pretest, materials, educational program, and enrichment activities were provided for each subscale. Each lesson was to be programed in small, sequential steps with directions to the teacher or parent showing when to give commands, provide reinforcement, repeat cycles, or proceed to the next step.

Development of the Scale

The first step in developing the Peabody Mobility Scale (PMS) was to define the scale's item content. Content definition occurred in two phases. The first phase dealt exclusively with the mobility section of the scale. Information for defining the content of the mobility section of the PMS came from three sources: the research literature on orientation and mobility; direct, informal observation of low functioning children who were proficient travelers to determine what mobility skills they demonstrated; and the joint experience of the investigators in providing mobility instruction to low functioning children. Through these sources of information, six basic orientation and mobility skills were identified, including (a) using sighted guide; (b) seating, (c) trailing; (d) turning and maintaining orientation; (e) using discriminable landmarks; and (f) mastering environmental travel.

The second step of the definition of the item content of the PMS pertained to the prerequisite skill domains, specifically, the motor, sensory, and concept sections of the original scale. These revisions were based on the research literature and task analysis of the criterion behaviors essential for independent travel. The final form of the Peabody Mobility Scale included four basic areas: motor development, sensory skills, concept development, and mobility skills. Each of these scale areas were divided into subscales, which can be seen in Figure 1. A total of 25 subscales comprised the total scale.

The next step in developing the revised edition of the PMS was to translate the identified content of the scale into an assessment format. The format for the revised PMS was designed to adhere to four guidelines. The first guideline was that the scale would follow a criterion referenced format with scores based on direct observation of the behaviors of interest. The second guideline was that the scale could be administered with minimal verbal interaction between the examiner and the child. The third guideline was that the items would be arranged in developmental order with each item partitioned into five developmentally sequenced subitems. The fourth guideline was that the instrument could be administered easily by teachers or parents. The administration procedures were carefully described for each item and subitem, including position of the examiner and the child, context, materials, and presentation procedures. In the scoring section, the criterion behavior was precisely defined and a scoring grid was provided for recording the examiner's evaluations.

The general assessment procedure was that the examiner presented the tasks to the child, observed the child's response, rated this response, and recorded the rating on the test protocol. The administration time for the PMS varied between approximately ½ hour and 2 hours.

Several statistics have been computed on various parameters of the revised PMS. Interrater reliability, which provides a measure of how well the criterion behaviors are defined in observable terms, was computed using a percentage of agreement method. An examiner and a second observer simultaneously and independently rated a group of 10 multiply impaired blind children as the children were administered the revised PMS. The obtained agreement was 92%, which indicates that the revised PMS had high interrater reliability.

I. *Motor Development*	III. *Concept Development*
1.1 Basic movement	3.1 Body image
1.2 Creeping	3.2 Spatial relations (front/back; up/down; on/under)
1.3 Standing	3.3 Left-right discrimination
1.4 Walking	3.4 Shape discrimination
1.5 Ascending stairs	3.5 Size discrimination
1.6 Descending stairs	3.6 Organization
1.7 Running	
1.8 Jumping	IV. *Mobility Skills*
1.9 Climbing	4.1 Sighted guide
	4.2 Seating
II. *Sensory Skills*	4.3 Turning and maintaining orientation
2.1 Sound localization	4.4 Trailing
2.2 Tactual discrimination (hands)	4.5 Utilization of discriminable landmarks
2.3 Tactual discrimination (feet)	4.6 Environmental travel
2.4 Olfactory discrimination	

Figure 1. Peabody Mobility Scale category and items.

A multiple linear regression analysis was computed on the PMS to determine the validity of the assumption that the motor, sensory, and concept sections of the scale measure behaviors that are, in fact, prerequisites for mobility. The mobility section of the scale was the criterion measure, and the motor, sensory, and concept sections were used as predictor variables. The PMS scores of 40 multiply impaired blind children were used as data for the regression analysis. The significant results of the analysis of variance performed on the regression data indicated that a child's performance on the motor, sensory, and concept portions of the PMS was a good predictor of performance on the mobility section of the scale.

Development of the Programed Instruction

The programed instructional packets were organized into the same four separate components as the PMS: motor development, sensory skills, concept development, and orientation and mobility skills. All of the items within each area of the program were divided into 5 subitems that also corresponded to the scale. The tasks in the program were sequenced developmentally to facilitate the child's progress from the entry point to the terminal objective through successive approximations. The entire program was based on behavior modification procedures, using positive reinforcement exclusively. Each lesson was divided according to purpose, task objective, materials needed, pretest, and suggested educational program. The tasks included in the instruction were designed to be developmentally sequenced. This developmental sequencing was maintained both within lessons (e.g., progressive stages of learning to walk) and between lessons (e.g., crawling lesson before walking lesson).

METHOD

Following the development of the programed instructional system, the next phase of the Peabody Mobility Project consisted of field testing to determine the system's effectiveness as a teacher implemented orientation and mobility program for severely handicapped blind children.

Subjects

A total of 42 children enrolled in nine selected facilities met the selection criteria. These criteria included:

1. Range in chronological age from 4 years to 13 years, 11 months.
2. Possess a visual handicap of light perception or less.
3. Possess one additional handicapping condition.
4. Function on the preschool level between the ages of 1.5 and 6 years as measured on the Maxfield-Buchholz Social Maturity Scale (1957).
5. Respond to verbal or manual communication.

The mean chronological age (CA) of the children was 10 years, 8 months, with a range from 5 years, 2 months, to 13 years, 9 months. The social ages of the children ranged from 1.92 to 5.79 with a mean of 4.00. All were low functioning children.

Nine classroom teachers located at the sites from which the children were selected provided instruction in basic mobility skills to the experimental group children using the programed instructional materials. The Peabody Mobility Scale was used for the assessment of each child's level of skill development in motor, sensory, concept, and basic mobility domains. The Peabody programmed instructional system in orientation and mobility was used as the basis of the training program to determine its instructional effectiveness.

Experimental Design

The study employed one experimental group and two control groups within pretest-posttest design. The subjects in the experimental group received daily intervention using the programed orientation and mobility instruction materials. In contrast, children in the control groups continued their daily educational routines without special intervention programing.

Two types of control groups were employed in the study. The first control group consisted of children located within the same classroom as the experimental group children. The presence of control group children within the same classrooms as experimental group children insured that both experimental and control group children within sites had essentially identical educational opportunities with the exception of the experimental instructional materials. To reduce the likelihood of experimental-control condition contamination, a second, distal control group was employed in the study. Distal control group subjects were located at three sites where no experimental intervention was planned.

The experimental and control groups were established through two levels of randomization. The distal control sites were chosen at random from among the nine facilities participating in the study. Within each of the remaining six facilities, children were randomly assigned to either the experimental or on-site control conditions. Eighteen children were assigned to the experimental group, and nine children were included in each of the two control conditions.

The primary data analyzed in the field test study were the scores the children attained on the PMS. Each behavioral description was point weighted as follows:

Independent (I) = 2 points
With assistance (WA) = 1 point
Not performed (NP) = 0 points
Not applicable (NA) = —

Assessment Procedures

The PMS assessments were conducted in accordance with the general guidelines for its administration (Harley, Wood, & Merbler, 1975). Each child was assessed in all PMS content areas that were applicable, given his or her particular handicapping conditions. The results of the pretesting were graphed on special score profiles that provided a convenient visual summary of the child's strengths and weaknesses across the various PMS content areas. The postintervention assessments were concluded following the same procedures as those used during pretesting.

Intervention Procedures

The field testing of the programed instructional materials was conducted during a 16 week period. The 16 week field testing period was divided into two 8 week phases. The first 8 week period focused on sensory and motor components of the instructional materials. During this phase, the teachers worked on an individual basis with the experimental group children in their classroom on the motor and sensory skill deficiencies indicated in the children's instructional prescriptions. The teachers worked on two programed lessons a day—one motor and one sensory. The teacher spent a mean time of 20 minutes per lesson per day.

The second 8 week period was devoted to the concept and mobility portions of the instructional materials and followed the same procedures as those used during the first phase of the field testing. The children were posttested on motor and sensory skills at the completion of the first 8 week period. Posttesting on concept and mobility skills occurred at the completion of the second 8 week period.

RESULTS

Although the groups were constituted at random, the mean pretest scores of the groups were markedly different (see Table 2). Consequently, an analysis of covariance (Winer, 1971) was conducted on the PMS scores to statistically equate the experimental and control groups. The social ages of the children were used as the covariate to adjust both the pretest and posttest means. Social age was selected as the covariate because of the high positive correlation between the children's total PMS scores and their assessed social age ($r = .87$).

The results of the 2×2 analysis of covariance are summarized in Table 1. The significant main effect for the groups factor ($F = 7.33$,

TABLE 1

Summary of Covariance Analysis

Source	Adjusted sums of squares	Degrees of freedom	Mean square	F
A	10774.298	1	10774.298	7.33**
Subj. W.A.	48488.37	33	1469.34	
B	6825.01	1	6825.01	87.83*
AB	5356.125	1	77.70	68.93*
Residual	2564.361	33		

*p <.01
**p= .05

TABLE 2

t Test Results for Pretest-Posttest Differences in the Four Skill Areas for the Experimental Group

Instructional areas	Pre-post mean PMS score difference	t* observed
Motor	6.05	5.34
Sensory	7.29	6.46
Concept	9.83	5.31
Mobility	14.11	6.72

*p <.01

1/33 $d.f.$, p = .05) indicates that the PMS scores of the experimental group children were higher than those of the control group. A significant F ratio was also obtained for the test condition factor (F = 87.83, 1/33 $d.f.$, p = .01). This significant finding indicates that the postintervention scores of the subjects were significantly higher than their preintervention PMS scores.

Table 2 presents the results of t tests performed on the preintervention and postintervention scores of the experimental group children for motor, sensory, concept, and mobility components of the programed instructional materials. Significant t statistics were found for motor (t = 5.34, 18 $d.f.$, p = .01), sensory (t = 6.46, 18 $d.f.$, p = .01), concept (t = 5.31, 18 $d.f.$, p = .01), and mobility (t = 6.72, 18 $d.f.$, p = .01) instructional components. These findings indicated that substantial postintervention performance improvements were demonstrated by the children across all intervention system content areas.

DISCUSSION

The purpose of this study was to develop an effective programed intervention system in orientation and mobility for multiply impaired blind children. The positive results of the field test study indicated that this objective was fulfilled. The children who received instruction based on the programed intervention system demonstrated significant overall performance gains as indicated by the results of the analysis of covariance. The significant F ratio obtained for the interaction of the groups factor and test conditions factor indicated that the difference in performance between the preintervention and postintervention period measures was higher for the experimental group than for the control group. Since extraneous factors such as teacher or site effects were controlled (i.e., through the site control group), the most plausible explanation of this differential performance between the groups was the intervention the experimental group children received. The results of the individual t tests indicated that the four instructional areas of the intervention system (i.e., motor, sensory, concept, and mobility) were all effective as a basis for a training program.

In addition to validating the intervention system, the results of the field test study also provided information on several relevant educational issues concerning multiply impaired blind children. First, the significant performance gain demonstrated by the experimental group children indicates that severely multiply impaired blind children can learn basic motor, sensory, concept, and mobility skills. The results of the field test study also indicate that classroom teachers can effectively train multiply impaired blind children in basic orientation and mobility skills if they are provided with programed instruction.

REFERENCES

Harley, R. K., Wood, T. A., & Merbler, J. B. Programmed instruction in orientation and mobility for multiply impaired blind children. *New Outlook for the Blind*, 1975, 69, 418-423.

Lord, F. E., Manshardt, C. E., Adams, G. S., & Bailey, M. J. *Identification of orientation and mobility skills relating to developmental tasks for young blind children.* Project No. 5-0980-4-11-3. Washington DC: US Department of Health, Education and Welfare, Office of Education, Division of Handicapped Children and Youth, 1966.

Lord, F. E. *Preliminary standardization of a scale of orientation and mobility skills of young blind children.* Project No. 6-2464. Washington DC: US Department of Health, Education, and Welfare, Office of Education, Bureau of Research, 1967.

Lord, F. E. Development of scales for the measurement of orientation and mobility of young blind children. *Exceptional Children*, 1969, 36, 77-81.

Maxfield, K. E., & Buchholz, S. *A social maturity scale for blind preschool children.* New York: American Foundation for the Blind, 1957.

Winer, B. J. *Statistical principles in experimental design* (2nd ed.). New York: McGraw Hill, 1971.

Note: The Stoelting Company (1350 S. Kostner Avenue, Chicago, Illinois 60623) has accepted the Peabody Mobility Kit for publication.

VISUALLY IMPAIRED

Science Activities for The Visually Impaired: Developing a Model

by Linda DeLucchi, Larry Malone and Herbert D. Thier

Science Activities for the Visually Impaired (SAVI) introduces blind and visually impaired children between 9 and 12 years of age to physical and life sciences in a multisensory way. In the process of using SAVI activities, students can strengthen logical thinking skills, improve their manipulative skills, and discover ways to apply these skills to everyday life situations. Students learn by doing and observing; the organisms are live and the activities strictly hands-on.

CONSIDERING SPECIAL STUDENTS AND TEACHERS

Students who have reduced sensory input in the area of vision are of great concern to special educators. Many students are educationally handicapped because of lack of appropriate educational materials and techniques. Others are socially isolated and lack experience in the real world as a result of over protective environments.

SAVI activities are developed to remediate and stimulate learning. Materials are designed to be both appropriate for learners with limited experience and ability and challenging for the most capable students.

It is often difficult to integrate science into a curriculum for visually impaired students. These activities are interdisciplinary, drawing in opportunities for experiences in the aca-

demic fundamentals and living skills. The distinction between science and other learning areas is softened.

Activity write-ups appear in folio format—one activity per folio. Individual experiences can be selected from the broad range of offerings. The activities, designed for both inside and out of doors, are as adaptable for a teacher with one student as they are for small groups in a learning center or an entire self contained classroom.

EVOLUTION OF SAVI ACTIVITIES

This rationale influences each SAVI activity as it evolves from an idea to a printed interdisciplinary, science based learning experience. The stages of development are as follows:

1. *Exploration.* An idea presents itself and the originator gathers some materials and works out preliminary procedures before meeting with students. The idea is taken to the classroom, and the developer teaches the concept to visually impaired children. The developer turns author and prepares the first draft of the activity.
2. *Local trials.* The lesson plan is reproduced and the materials manufactured in a limited production. Local teachers of the visually impaired are trained and sent back to the field to test the activities. Staff members observe and the teachers provide feedback.

5

3. *National trials.* Activities are revised, organized into modules, and printed. Materials are prepared in an inhouse production run and shipped to six national trial testing centers. Extensive feedback is collected, after which the final revision for general distribution is made.

Both a local and a national advisory council provide guidance regarding federal and regional legislation that is relevant to the work, and offer insights at all levels from equipment modifications to interpretations of the political climate in special education.

Currently SAVI has prepared seven of a proposed nine modules, each with four to eight activities. The module titles reflect the content areas covered: *Structures of Life, Scientific Reasoning, Communication, Environments, Mixtures and Solutions, Environmental Energy,* and *Measurement.* The selection of activities within each module represents a range of low or entry level experiences as well as higher level activities. However, all the activities have an identical format.

SAVI EXPECTATIONS

SAVI adheres to the philosophy that students learn best by direct hands-on experiences with materials that demonstrate the learning objectives. Because the population of learners is blind or visually impaired, the use of other senses for making observations and gathering data has been accentuated. And we have found in the process that a multisensory approach to learning is appropriate for all students, handicapped and otherwise.

Perhaps the most noticeable outcome of the use of SAVI activities with visually impaired students has not been the science or related academic strides, but the growth in social areas. SAVI activities become the medium for breaking down social isolation experienced by visually limited students. Sighted peers share in the SAVI experiences, which results in a growth of self confidence and self esteem in the visually impaired student. As such the SAVI project materials can help integrate handicapped children into the mainstream of education.

VISUALLY IMPAIRED

Chisanbop for
Blind Math Students

by Nancy L. Struve, Karen M. Cheney and Charlotte Rudd

Abstract: The severely visually impaired child has difficulty with the study of mathematics for several reasons. One of these is the lack of a tactile equivalent to paper and pencil for carrying out calculations.

At present, the adapted abacus is most widely used for this purpose, but not all children are successful with abacus. Chisanbop, a Korean system of using the fingers for calculating, bears marked similarities to abacus, but avoids most of the difficulties inherent in abacus use.

The potential uses for Chisanbop in the education of the visually impaired are explored.

The study of mathematics presents many difficulties for the severely visually impaired child. Typically he/she lacks many of the experiences upon which mathematical concepts are based. Sometimes the language which is used in mathematics teaching is confusing, especially to the child who must rely on the braille math code in which, for example, the quantity 3/4 does not appear as "three over four" (Nemeth, 1959). However, the lack of a braille equivalent to pencil and paper for carrying out mathematical calculations is perhaps the most severe disadvantage for a blind child studying mathematics. All of the alternatives, which include slate and stylus, cube slates, Taylor Arithmetic Type Slate, braille writer, and Cranmer Abacus, have inherent weaknesses which render them markedly inferior to the simple paper and pencil methods used by sighted children.

Of the means available for carrying out mathematical computations, however, the adapted abacus has become the method of choice for most blind students. The Cranmer Abacus is a variation of the Japanese Soroban, with one bead above the bar and four beads below. With it one can add, subtract, multiply, divide, extract roots, and handle decimals, fractions and trigonometric functions. Because the beads are held in place by pressure applied to them from behind, friction keeps them from sliding out of place when they are being read (Jackson, et al., 1970). Although the abacus is pocket-sized and has the potential for becoming an extremely flexible and efficient calculating instrument, it is not without disadvantages. First, the beads are difficult for some children to manipulate. Those who have small or weak hands, or limited coordination and control of their hands do not do well with abacus.

Second, one becomes an efficient operator only after hours and hours of drill. For a blind child in regular public school, practice is usually limited to times when he/she can receive help from the resource or itinerant teacher for visually handicapped children. Thus, progress may be slow. Also, because neither the classroom

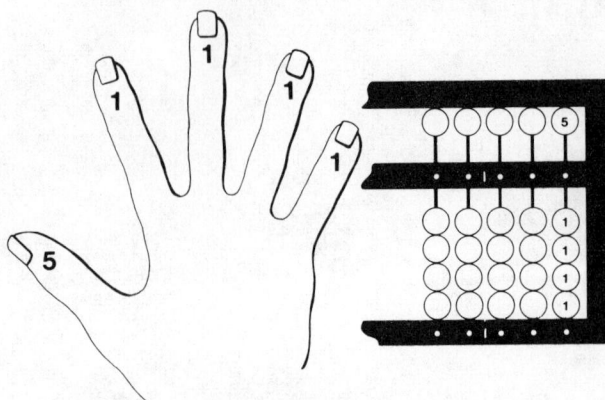

Fig. 1. Mathematical value of each finger of the right hand in Chisanbop, and of each bead in the first column from the right on the abacus.

teacher nor classmates usually have any knowledge of abacus, he/she cannot get help when unable to work a problem, nor much reinforcement when successful.

For mentally handicapped or learning disabled blind children, who require extra time to accomplish a task, these problems are even more acute.

Chisanbop, a Korean system of using the fingers for calculating which has been introduced recently in the United States, may help overcome some of these difficulties, for, although it is not immediately apparent, abacus and Chisanbop are similar in many ways. In fact, it was the Korean mathematician Sung Jin Pai, an authority on the use of abacus, who designed the system now known as Chisanbop for use by his students; and it was the mathematician's son, Hang Young Pai, who became fascinated with the possibility of adapting the system to elementary math instruction, and brought it to the United States in 1976 (Pearson, 1978).

A few examples will illustrate the similarities between Chisanbop and abacus.

The values assigned the fingers of the Right Hand in Chisanbop are the same as those assigned the beads in the extreme right column on the abacus. The total value in both cases is nine (see Figure 1).

The values assigned the fingers of the Left Hand in Chisanbop are the same as those assigned the beads in the second column from the right on the abacus. The total value in both cases is 90 (see Figure 2).

"Exchanging" fingers of the Right Hand for those of the Left Hand in Chisanbop follows the same patterns as those defined by the "secrets" of abacus. For example, adding one to nine requires "the simultaneous Pressing of 10 on the Left Hand and the Clearing of the entire Right Hand" (Lieberthal, 1978). On the abacus the secret "Clear nine, set one left" refers to the same procedure.

Solving the problem 2 + 4 = ? provides another example of these similarities. In Chisanbop (in the Second Stage of Manipulation, where it is no longer necessary to press each finger in sequence), one goes through the following steps: Press Two (Press the first and second fingers of the Right Hand). Next Press Five (Press the fifth finger or thumb). Then Clear One (Clear the second finger of the Right Hand) (Lieberthal, 1978).

On the abacus one sets the two, then uses the secret "Set five, clear one." Whether obtained by fingers or beads, the answer is six.

Although Chisanbop and abacus have many similarities and produce identical results, it appears that Chisanbop would avoid some of the disadvantages which use of the abacus involves for blind students.

First, the finger motions of Chisanbop are much simpler than the manipulations required to set and clear the beads on the Cranmer abacus. Lieberthal (1978) compares the finger motion "Press" with the striking of a piano key. The arms are held parallel to the top of a table with the

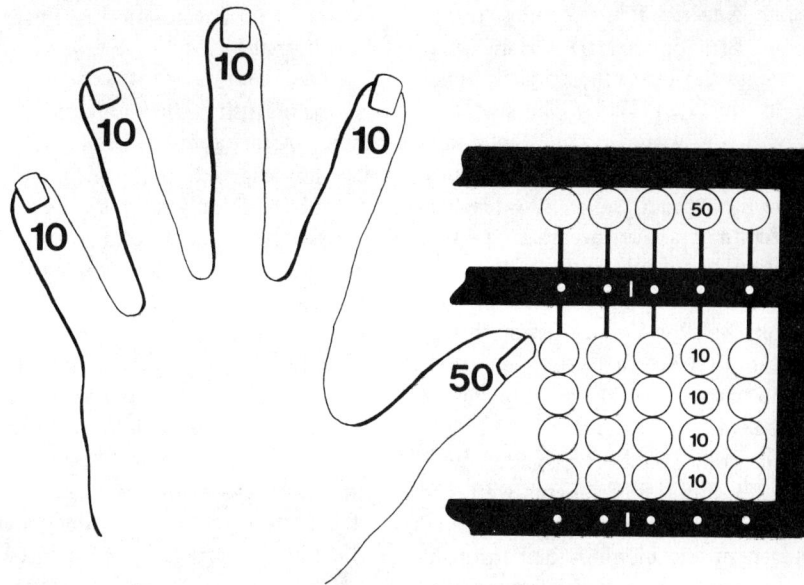

Fig. 2. Mathematical value of each finger on the left hand in Chisanbop, and of each bead in the second column from the right on the abacus.

fingers suspended slightly above it. The fingers drop to contact (or "press") the table top as the quantities they represent are required in computing.

Second, in contrast with any system for calculating which relies on special equipment, the tools of Chisanbop are constantly present. The process of familiarizing the student with a new instrument is eliminated; and, since there is no need to purchase equipment to do so, whole classrooms of children can be introduced to Chisanbop after their teachers have received basic instruction at one of the workshops being taught throughout the country. By the summer of 1978, Pearson (1978) estimated that up to a thousand teachers and supervisors had been involved in such training programs.

Thus, it is reasonable to anticipate that as time goes on, the blind child who uses Chisanbop in a public school classroom will have an increasingly better chance of being surrounded by sighted classmates using the same computational method as he/she is. Even more exciting is the possibility that for the first time in the history of public school education for the blind, this child might have a classroom teacher prepared to include him/her fully in the classroom mathematics program—to instruct him/her in the problem-solving pro-

cess, observe the computations and correct where necessary.

As far as limitations in the use of Chisanbop are concerned, the difficulty of recording answers must be considered. On abacus, of course, once an answer is obtained, it can be left in place as long as necessary and referred to as needed while it is recorded on the braille writer or typewriter. After using Chisanbop to solve a problem the answer must be memorized so that the hands can be used to record it. In solving addition problems which involve more than one column, another difficulty lies in the fact that the fingers of the Left Hand are supposed to remain pressed, holding the number to be carried, while the Right Hand records the sum of the numbers in the right column. The blind child who needs both hands to record answers is at a disadvantage here.

It is possible that educators will find that Chisanbop can be used most effectively with blind children as a computational system in the elementary grades and as a foundation for adapted abacus in junior high and high school. One of the authors (C.R.) introduced Chisanbop to a totally blind, developmentally delayed child in January of her kindergarten year. The child first learned the number names of all her fingers: first, second, third, fourth, and fifth on the Right Hand, and tenth, twentieth, thirtieth, fortieth, and fiftieth on the Left Hand. She was unfamiliar with the word "press." Since this movement is important in obtaining and identifying the correct answer, the teacher had the child practice pressing, as she learned the value of each finger.

Unlike sighted students who can look at their fingers to "read" an answer, blind students cannot verify a tactual sensation visually. So, correct identification of numbers pressed was emphasized.

After the child could identify any number up to 99, addition problems were introduced. At first these involved adding one to each of the numbers one through nine. By the end of the school year, the student was able to add one, two, three, or four to any number if the total did not exceed 10.

This youngster seemed to grasp the basics of Chisanbop with no difficulty. Perhaps because she had never used her fingers for adding before Chisanbop was introduced, there was no confusion with the conventional, western method of "counting on your fingers" in which each finger and thumb equals one. Indeed, Chisanbop seemed to the teacher to be a very "natural" method for this six-year-old blind child to use for calculating.

Another author (K.M.C.) found that Chisanbop has great potential for use with multiply handicapped blind students. A sixteen-year-old cerebral palsied boy was introduced to it three times a week for fifteen-minute sessions, because he was still functioning on a first grade level in arithmetic. The boy was legally blind, but had much useful vision. He was able to do simple one-digit addition and subtraction problems on paper by counting on his fingers and laboriously recording the answer with a black lead pencil.

When the Chisanbop sessions first started, the youth had trouble remembering that his right thumb was worth five units; but after a brief review at the beginning of each session, he had no trouble for the remainder of the session. Counting to ten was accomplished quickly, even after

years of counting on his fingers in the traditional way.

The next step was simple addition problems using the numbers one through nine. After a quick review of counting, the boy did well at this also. He had some trouble mainipulating his fingers correctly, but he always knew what answer his fingers showed. His physical therapist also endorsed this manipulation of his fingers as good exercise.

Since the program was not started until the middle of the school year and the boy was absent because of illness for weeks at a time, the progress with Chisanbop was very slow and review often necessary. However, it did improve the boy's understanding of the addition process as he worked through the actual finger manipulations, and his speed doing addition with Chisanbop was much greater than when he used his fingers in the usual way to do his addition problems. Considering the amount of time available for work with this boy, the progress was considered sufficient to justify continuing and expanding the Chisanbop program the following school year.

In conclusion, although the psychodynamic processes linking hand use and cognition are not fully understood, they are of necessity central to the education of blind children. Considering that Chisanbop was originally designed to be "internalized to the point where no finger movement was needed at all" (Pearson, 1978), it seems to provide not only a practical approach to solving math problems for blind children, but an opportunity for their teachers to learn more about the use of hands as an extension of the mind.

REFERENCES

Davidow, M.E. *The Abacus Made Easy*. Louisville, American Printing House for the Blind, 1977.

Jackson, G., et al. *Developing Mathematical Concepts in Visually Handicapped Pupils in the Secondary School*. Cincinnati, Ohio: Cincinnati Public Schools, 1970.

Lieberthal, E.M. *Home Study Book: Chisanbop, Finger Calculation Method*. Mount Vernon, N.Y.: Chisanbop Enterprises, 1978.

Nemeth, A. Teaching meaningful mathematics to blind and partially sighted children. *New Outlook for the Blind*, 1959, 53, 318-319.

Pearson, C. Do you know how to Chisanbop? *Learning*, Aug./Sept., 1978, 134-138.

ACOUSTICALLY IMPAIRED

Stutterers Challenge
DSM-III Classification

by *Psychiatric News*

THE NATIONAL ASSOCIATION of Councils of Stutterers has appealed to Robert Spitzer, M.D., chair of the APA task force that authored the *Diagnostic and Statistical Manual of Mental Disorders-III (DSM-III)*, to remove the classification of stuttering from the manual because of the stigma associated with psychiatric disorders.

The stutterers' group says that it "is not trying to change *DSM-III*" but is concerned with the Defense Department's using the presence of the stuttering classification in *DSM-III* to support the inclusion of stuttering in the "Psychoses, Psychoneuroses, and Personality Disorders" section of its own classification system, Army Regulation 40-501. Acknowledging the difficulty of knowing where to classify stuttering, National Association Executive Secretary Michael Hartford says, "The National Association has little concern for where DOD hangs stuttering except for the particular discriminations that are attached to psychiatric problems . . .." Hartford, in a letter to Spitzer, said his group would prefer to see stuttering classified under the neurological disorders since the Army has no heading for functional speech disorders.

In a letter from the stutterers' group to the Army surgeon general, its presi-

dent, Kenneth T. Turley, states, "The association feels that stuttering should be classified by the body system that is the origin or root cause of the behavioral deviation. And while it concedes that no researcher has proved any one cause of stuttering conclusively, it submits that far more evidence supports a neurological base for stuttering than supports a psychiatric base for the problem . . .. The great preponderance of evidence suggests that stuttering is, at its root, a neuromuscular problem. Like other neuromuscular problems, it is exacerbated by stress . . .. And it is this apparent link with stress that has led a minority of health workers in psychiatry to posit a psychological base for the problem."

The Army sent the National Association's request for reclassification to its medical consultants, but there was no consensus of opinion supporting a classification change. The National Association also sent Spitzer a letter asking for his comments as something of an "amicus curiae" in the discussion between the Army and the National Association.

Spitzer responded by quoting what is included in *DSM-III* about the category in which stuttering is placed—the class of *Disorders Usually First*

5

Evident in Infancy, Childhood, or Adolescence, under the subclass *Other Disorders with Physical Manifestations.* "The introduction to this section," wrote Spitzer, "makes the following point: 'The inclusion of these categories (*Stuttering, Enuresis, Encopresis, Sleepwalking, and Sleep Terrors*) in a classification of mental disorders is justified partly by tradition in that, formerly, psychological conflict was thought to play a central role in all of these disorders, and it was thought that these conditions were almost always associated with other signs of psychopathology. Recently, however, many have come to question these assumptions, at least with regard to some of these categories. Further, there is evidence that most of the children with these disorders do not have associated mental disorder.' "

Spitzer added, "We would agree with you that the preponderance of evidence suggests that stuttering is at its root 'a neuromuscular problem.' However, tradition dictates, at least for now, that it be classified as a mental disorder. Were we not to classify it in *DSM-III* there would be no place else for it to be classified, since within international classification of diseases it is classified in Section V, the chapter reserved for mental disorders."

ICD-9 does, however, have a section of "Symptoms Involving Head and Neck," which includes such problems as aphasia, dysarthria, and slurred speech, although it specifically excludes stammering and stuttering.

Meanwhile, the National Association of Councils of Stutterers has sent the Army a copy of Spitzer's letter, asking for reconsideration since Spitzer said he basically agreed that the preponderance of evidence suggested a neuromuscular root for stuttering. So far the Army has not responded to the request.

ACOUSTICALLY IMPAIRED

A Task-Response Analysis Approach to Language Assessment

by Billie J. Rinaldi

What do you think when one of your students does not follow verbal directions? Do you attribute this problem to hearing, understanding, or listening? Each interpretation might be a natural response of the teacher who is trying to instruct a group of students or an individual. However, to design an effective instructional program, time must be taken to analyze the interaction that has taken place.

A referral for formal evaluation might be made. Standardized tests may assist in diagnosing the learning problem, however, it is most effective when paired with teacher observation. In fact, teacher observation can detail or pinpoint language problems most efficiently for the purpose of planning appropriate instructional strategies.

Communication is such an integrated and early learned skill that teachers take it for granted. By kindergarten age the child's basic constructs of language have developed. For most children the further development that occurs is a refinement and expansion in the complexity of their communicative skills. However, for children who have not yet reached proficiency in communication, the problem must be addressed in a systematic way. The child who enters school without age level listening and speaking skills needs early and specific help in learning those communicative skills prerequisite to survival in the academic classroom. Communicative skills are the prereadiness skills for academic instruction.

Such students in the regular or special classroom tend to be management problems in terms of behavior and learning. They frustrate the teacher because of the individualization they need; often their diagnosis is misleading. The student may be classified as intellectually limited, learning disabled, and/or emotional disturbed as well as language disabled. It is often difficult to determine where in the language task the child is having his primary problem. It is receiving, comprehending, processing and/or expressing language?

To approach the observation of language, the teacher must understand the basic language system and address the task from a behavioral point of view. This discussion will include recommendations and suggestions for a systematic approach through observation, assessment, and instruction of students exhibiting problems in language-learning. Strategies for collecting and analyzing data as well as suggestions for building language instruction are included.

The Language System —
A Framework for Observation

Teachers usually consider language to include listening, speaking, reading, and writing for instructional purposes. For assessing language-learning competencies a different framework is needed to assist the teacher in the task. To this purpose language-learning is defined as the acquisition of skills and knowledge through auditory/verbal interaction with visual/verbal and visual/motor interaction considered supplementary. The language component of the process of communication is addressed as follows: input stimuli - reception - comprehension - processing - expression. The output or expression provides feedback to the listener as well as to the speaker allowing for communication to proceed. The input stimuli is provided by the teacher and sets the task. The student receives the stimuli. The comprehension step implies understanding of the stimuli and the ability to associate; the processing step implies the ability to remember, to sequence, and to formulate a response; and the expression step is the ability to produce a response.

To assess a student's response it is necessary to analyze the input stimuli or control the input stimuli to record and analyze the student's response easily. In other words the teacher must first set the task or input stimuli carefully, keeping in mind what exactly is being required of the student, and record the student's response as a behavioral ob-

From The Directive Teacher, Vol. 2, No. 3, Winter 1980, published by NCEMMH, The Ohio State University.

5

servation. Once the response is recorded, the teacher can analyze the response utilizing the language interactive model to determine the student's language competency in reception, comprehension, processing or expression. The input as well as the response are determining factors in deciding which language skill is being assessed. This approach might be termed a "task-response analysis" of language.

Task-Response Data — the Observation

Preparation for the observation should include task selection, organization of materials needed for stimuli and for response, and setting up a recording format. The record form should be of the teacher's own design and should enable the teacher to record a description of the task or input to the student, the student's response, teacher comment, and the language skill that was assessed. The record form is an observation log.

Example:

Task	Response	Comment	Language Skill
Follow two step command with motor response	Omitted first step, completed second	Listened closely to whole command	Auditory processing

Task selection should be done carefully and should be based on the student's overall functioning level in the classroom. The purpose is to determine specifically where the student is having difficulty and where the student is successful. Necessarily the tasks should be sequenced carefully starting with receptive skills. Tasks may be added or restructured during the observation at a point of breakdown in response so long as each task-response is recorded. This allows the teacher to pinpoint the student's problem and to seek successful intervention strategies through paired stimuli, simplified stimuli, or alternative response models as a part task-response analysis.

As a general rule the teacher should select auditory stimuli requiring motor or visual-motor response to check the language skills of reception, comprehension, and processing. To check the language skills of processing and expression, auditory and then visual stimuli should be selected and a verbal response required. Another way to describe the task-response sequence would be to do so in more simplified

terms such as "hear-do" for listening; "hear-say" and "see-say" for speaking; "see-say" for reading; and "see-do" and "hear-do" for writing. Adding this type of description to the task-response analysis allows the teacher to relate directly back to the instruction of basic language skills. Listening and reading are primarily receptive language tasks, whereas speaking and writing are primarily expressive language tasks.

Task-Response Analysis

When the observation data has been recorded, the teacher must review the log to determine strengths and weaknesses in the student's ability to do language tasks. A variety of questions should be asked. Which types of responses are learned and which are not yet learned? Was the response directly related to the stimulus? Was the response an associated response rather than direct? Did the response indicate that the student missed or mixed the stimuli? Could the student respond more appropriately when stimuli were simplified, when stimuli were paired, and/or when response modes were paired? Was there a time delay between task stimuli and response? Could the student remember the stimuli, short term and long term? In verbal response did the student appear to have word recall problems, e.g. "I can't remember," or "I know it but I can't say it"? Did the student use self-cuing to assist in the response? Did self-cuing help? The student's help in determining which task were easier or harder is valuable; students can assist in pinpointing their own strengths and weaknesses if they are asked to do so.

Once the teacher has reviewed the observation data, a written summary should be prepared as part of the educational evaluation report. At this point appropriate referrals should be made for testing of hearing and vision, for formal evaluation, or for resource services such as speech/language therapy.

Instructional Suggestions

The teacher who uses a "task-response analysis" approach can move easily into diagnostic or directive teaching as an on-going instructional strategy. Using a well-structured language curriculum that follows a hierarchy of skill development, the teacher can build in

individualization using the task-response models that were found to be most successful in the analysis. Remedial tasks can be selected and sequenced to teach pre-requisite skills. Teacher strategies for style of instructional presentation to a particular student or group of students should be based on the strength of receptive skills of the student(s). The teacher, the speech and language clinician, and the learning disabilities teacher should work closely together sharing observations and successful strategies to assure that the student's needs are met and that learning occurs.

References

Bloom, Lois. *Language development.* Cambridge, Massachusetts: M. I. T. Press, 1970.

Hardy, William G. Childhood aphasia. In Rober West (ed.), *Proceedings of the institute of childhood aphasia.* San Francisco: California Society for Crippled Children and Adults, 1962.

———— .Human communication: Ordered and disordered. *The Volta Review,* 1962, *64,* 354-362.

———— . On language disorders in young children: A reorganization of thinking. *Journal of Speech and Hearing Disorders,* 1965, *30* (1), 354-362.

Kavavagh, J. & I.G. Mattingly, (eds.), *Language by ear and by eye: The relationships between speech and reading.* Cambridge, Massachusetts: M.I.T. Press, 1972.

Miller, Jon F. & David E. Yoder. *An ontogenetic language teaching strategy for retarded children.* Paper presented for National Institute of Childhealth and Human Development Conference, Wisconsin, June 1973.

Newby, Robert. Language and reading: A visual structure. *American Annals of the Deaf,* October 1974.

Petty, Walter T., Petty, Dorothy C. & Becking, Marjorie F.: *Experiences in language: Tools and techniques for language arts methods.* Boston: Allyn and Bacon, 1973.

Waugh, R. P., Relationship between modality preference and performance. *Exceptional Children,* March 1973, *39* (6), 465-469.

ACOUSTICALLY IMPAIRED

The Language Impaired Child in the Preschool: The Role of the Teacher*

by K. Eileen Allen

A major developmental task of young children is to learn the language of their native community. Traditionally, the family has been the basic source of such learning. Patterns are changing, however. Many children under six are dependent upon infant and toddler centers, day care programs, and preschool classrooms for much of their language learning. As a consequence, teachers of young children are playing an increasingly significant role in the language development of the children in their charge.

It can be argued that young children require little or no direct teaching where language development is concerned. Such learning appears to be almost automatic, rooted in earliest infancy (Horowitz, 1978), and progressing in fairly predictable patterns and sequences. Developmentally delayed children may not acquire language so spontaneously. For these children, teachers need to be highly directive in their efforts to move each child toward attainment of individualized language goals. Directive must not be construed

*The work in this paper was supported in part by the Kansas Institute for Early Childhood Education of the Handicapped, supported by a grant from the Bureau for the Education of the Handicapped (USOE 300-77-0308).

to mean sit down, repetitive, "listen to the teacher and repeat after me" type drills. Such activities are often important parts of clinical intervention where improved topography of responses may be the goal. In the preschool the goal is usually broader - children must be taught that language is functional. They must learn, as do normally developing children, that language works - language will help them to get what they want and need from the environment. Thus, the term "directive" should be interpreted as a set of teaching strategies which utilize the total program, *all day long, as a context for helping* to develop language skills in certain specifiable ways in accord with the particular needs of each child. The basic measure of successful intervention should be *how much* the child talks (Allen, 1967; Rieke, Lynch & Soltman, 1977). Such a measure is consonant with several years of research indicating that the more a child talks the better the child talks (Hart & Risley, 1975). To fulfill individualized program goals for language-impaired children within the total program format, teachers must have a thorough understanding of child development and a broad repertoire of early childhood education skills. They must be able to formulate direct and specific intervention procedure for individual children. As an example, teachers must know that re-

ceptive language - the ability to understand what is said - often precedes and frequently exceeds expressive language, just as motor and facial responses such as pointing, tugging, smiling, frowning usually precede and come to accompany vocalizations; and that vocalizations usually give way to step-by-step acquisition of speech sounds and language patterns.

Closely related to understanding developmental sequences is recognition of the interrelatedness of the various developmental areas. Thus, for a low-verbal child who has poor large motor skills and a marked tendency to avoid contact with other children, teachers must shape basic motor and social skills concurrently with their work on language development. Such an approach recognizes that until a child learns to romp and play and join in a variety of peer group activities, that child will not have much to talk about nor many people to talk with.

Skill in observing children within the context of the total environment and recording these observations objectively is another necessary skill. The recording of verbatim language samples is an effective way of determining a child's functional language. When the observations also record what preceded and followed each verbal response, (communicative interactions in terms of an-

5

tecedents and consequences) the value of the observations is greatly enhanced.

"It is in the natural environment that communication needs are identified" (Rieke *et al*, 1977). Repeated direct observations of a child can serve as a basis for assessment; they serve, too, in structuring a program that is orderly and developmentally appropriate. Missing prerequisite skills can be pinpointed and realistic goals, both long and short-term, can be specified. Thus, for a child with only one-word utterances, (sometimes called holophrastic-type speech) the use of complex sentences may or may not be a realistic long-term goal. However, a simple increase in number of one-word productions may be a functional short-term objective with a longer range objective set at the child using two-word or so-called telegraphic utterances.

The foregoing sketch of in-class observations is not to imply that the assessment and diagnostic services of communication specialist can be eliminated - *quite the contrary*. The communication specialist and the classroom teacher need to share information and skills to ensure that the preschool environment supports and extends the expectations for each language-impaired child (Rieke & Thompson, 1978; Hart & Rogers-Warren, 1978). There are occasions when clinical-type interventions have been conducted successfully within the classroom itself (Appleman, Allen & Turner, 1975; Radgowski, Douglas, Allen & Le Blanc, 1978). By and large, however, in regular or mainstreamed preschool settings teachers must rely upon strategies other than one-to-one tutorials; they must provide specific and direct language intervention for particular children. Essentially, teachers do three things to insure effective intervention for language-impaired children:

1. They arrange the environment in ways demonstrated to be conducive to promoting language: a) by providing several interesting learning centers (blocks, housekeeping and dramatic play, creative and manipulative materials); b) by organizing a balance of activities in terms of child-initiated and teacher structured; and c) by presenting materials and activities that children enjoy (Allen, 1977).

2. They manage their own interactions with children so as to maximize effective communication on the part of each language-impaired child, and use every opportunity to teach "on the fly" (White, 1975).

3. They monitor, on a regular basis, the appropriateness of a) environmental arrangements; b) their own behavior; and c) that of the children, in order to validate child progress and thus program effectiveness.

A number of efforts are afoot to analyze these seemingly casual procedures by which children appear to acquire so much of their language learning. Two of the more systematic analyses provide models for exemplary classroom intervention. One is the *incidental teaching model* (Hart & Risley, 1975); the other is called a *communicative interaction model* (Rieke, 1974; Rieke *et al*, 1977).

Incidental Teaching Model

Child-initiation is the essential feature of incidental teaching - it means that the child *wants* something from the teacher: attention, assistance, approval, permission; or items more concrete in the form of materials, food or drink. In other words, the preschool environment provides the teacher with an array of reinforcers (things that the child wants) that can serve to promote better communicative skills on the part of the child. To insure frequent teacher-child contact (thus increasing the number of teaching opportunities), teachers must be available, responsive, and positive. Each initiation by a child is a signal to the teacher for prompting the best possible language that the child can manage at that moment. The child must never be put "on the spot," nor should the child's play or ongoing activity be interrupted unduly. The important dimension in incidental teaching is to keep the contact brief and pleasant so there will be more and more opportunities for the teaching of language. Following is an example of an incidental teaching episode as described by Hart (quoted in Allen, 1980):

A four-year old girl with delayed language stands in front of the teacher with a paint apron in her hand. The teacher says, "What do you need?" (Teacher does *not* anticipate the child's need by putting the apron on the child at the moment.)

If the child does not answer, the teacher tells her and gives her a prompt: "It's an apron. Can you say apron?" If the child says "apron" the teacher ties it while giving descriptive praise, "You said it right. It *is* an apron. I am tying your apron on you." The teacher's last sentence models the next verbal behavior, "Tie my apron" that the teacher will expect once

the child has learned to say apron.

If the child does not say apron, the teacher ties the apron. No further comments are made at this time. The teacher must not coax, nag or pressure the child. If each episode is kept brief and pleasant the child will contact the teacher frequently. Thus, the teacher will have many opportunities for incidental teaching. If the teacher pressures the child such incidental learning opportunities will be lost. Some children may learn to avoid the teacher - they will simply do without; other children may learn inappropriate ways, such as whining and crying to get what they want.

In the foregoing example the teacher's language was adjusted to the level of the child's language. Through repeated episodes of this type, children learn that their language gets them what they want; their language is important. They learn, too, that teachers listen when they speak and want to hear more about topics that are important and of interest to each child.

Communicative Interaction Model

The communicative interaction model (Rieke, Lynch, & Soltman, 1977) stresses the role of the teacher as a facilitator, an adult who listens, helps, models, and reinforces desired responses or approximations to such responses. The teacher-facilitator "makes things happen" by saying or doing those things which evoke communicative responses from the child. The teacher-facilitator also expects the child to initiate and to respond so that dialoguing — exchanges of communicative responses — is established. In other words, this model requires the child and the teacher to initiate and to respond in ways commensurate with the child's level of language development. Thus, the child can be successful both as initiator and as responder. Failure is prevented.

Rieke, Lynch, and Soltman, (1977) suggest that the typical two-unit communication pattern be avoided at all costs. This is the questions and answer routine, with the adult doing most of the questioning. Such interactions, so dominant in teacher-child interactions (Allen, Ruggles & LeBlanc, 1980), rarely prompt the child to continue the interaction; more often they lead to quite the opposite - avoidance of the interrogating adult. The model that should be invoked has a three-unit format where the child initiates either verbally or nonverbally and the teacher responds in a fashion that will evoke still another response from the child. Following are several examples:

Child: points

Teacher: "You want the car? Say 'car'."

Child: nods and makes sound approximating "car"

Child: "Look at my painting."

Teacher: "You used red, blue and ____?"

Child: "and green and yellow and some more red."

Child: "What you doing?"

Teacher: "Watch me and see if you can tell *me* what I am doing."

Child: "play dough - me help?"

In the communicative interaction model the adult is also a frequent initiator. However, the three-unit model is just as important to maintain when the adult is the initiator as it is when the child is the initiator. Thus, when the teacher initiates, the child is expected (and helped) to respond; the teacher then puts the third unit in place by reinforcing the child's response in some fashion—acknowledging, inquiring further, or expanding upon the child's idea. Example of teacher as the initiator follows:

Teacher (to nonverbal child): "Where did you park your trike?"

Child: points to shed.

Teacher: "In the *shed*; you remembered!"

Teacher: "What a pretty new dress!"

Child: "my birthday"

Teacher: "Your birthday dress! What else did you get for your birthday?"

Teacher: "You have a new baby at your house! Is it a boy or a girl?"

Child: "boy"

Teacher: "A new boy baby! What's his name?"

Conclusions

In the foregoing examples, whether child or teacher initiated, the important dimensions are that children are *expected* to communicate, and the teacher helps so that the child is successful and eager to continue his or her efforts. *The facilitative teacher does not let the child fail!* (Rieke, Lynch, & Soltman, 1977).

The two models have a number of characteristics in common. Both view materials, equipment and a rich variety of experiences (in other words, reinforcers that are readily available in most good preschool programs) as a necessary backdrop for an effective intervention program. Both view the teachers as 1) an astute and systematic observer and recorder of child behavior; 2) as a sensitive and willing listener; and 3) as a systematic and discriminative responder who helps each child to "say it better" through differential feedback. Both models stress that teaching episodes be kept relatively brief, always pleasant, and geared to the language level of the individual child. Inherent in both models is the belief that progress for the language-impaired child is not measured by such things as perfect articulation or syntactical elegance; instead the measure is the child's ability to communicate ever more effectively in the natural environment. Finally, both approaches believe that progress measurement involves careful monitoring of environmental arrangements and teacher behaviors to ensure properly implemented plans and producing the intended effects.

Again, verbatim language samples, taken in the naturalistic environment of the preschool, often prove to be the best measure of child progress. Teachers can take many such samples while supervising. It takes only a moment to record on a 3X5 note pad, "Paul approached the easel and said to Michael, 'You my friend; we paint together?'"; yet a great deal of information is inherent in several such brief samples collected periodically on each language-impaired child.

Finally, no intervention program can claim to be effective without ongoing evaluation. Only through such feedback can program alterations be made and teachers' responses and initiations be directed toward specific intervention strategies. When objective records on language-impaired children indicate teachers are talking less and listening more, and children are talking more and talking better, a picture is given of a truly effective classroom intervention program.

References

Allen, K. E. *Mainstreaming in early childhood education.* Albany, New York: Delmar Publishers, 1980.

Allen, K. The least restrictive environment: Implications for early childhood education. *Educational Horizons,* Fall 1977, *56* (1), 34-41.

Allen, K. E. Reinforcement contingencies in preschool education. Symposium paper presented at annual meeting of American Educational Research Association, New York, 1967.

Appleman, K., Allen, K. E., & Turner, K. D. The conditioning of language in a nonverbal child conducted in a special educational classroom. *Journal of Speech and Hearing Disorders.* February 1975, *40* (1), 3-12.

Douglas, P. S., Radgowski, T. A., Allen, K. E., & LeBlanc, J. M. A simple intervention program for the remediation of the misarticulated '1' in a preschool child's speech. *Education and Treatment of Children,* Summer 1978, *1* (4).

Hart, B., & Risley, T. R. Incidental teaching of language in the preschool. *Journal of Applied Behavior Analysis,* 1975, *8,* 411-420.

Hart, B. & Rogers-Warren, A. A milieu approach to teaching language. in Richard L. Schiefelbusch (Ed.) *Language intervention strategies.* Baltimore: University Park Press, 1978, 193-235.

Horowitz, F. D. (Ed.), 1974. Visual attention, auditory stimulation, and language discrimination in young infants. *Monographs of the Society of Research and Child Development. 39* (158).

Quilitch, H. R., & Risely, T. R. The effects of play materials on social play. *Journal of Applied Behavior Analysis,* 1973, *6,* 573-578.

Rieke, J. A. Facilitatiing communicative interaction in the classroom. Paper presented at the Council for Exceptional Children, New York City, April 19, 1974.

Rieke, J. A., Lynch, L. L., & Soltman, S. F. *Teaching strategies for language development.* New York: Grune & Stratton, 1977.

Rieke, J. A., & Thompson, G. The communication specialists: The speech pathologist and audiologist. In K. Eileen Allen, Vanja A. Holm, and Richard L. Schiefelbusch (Eds.) *Early intervention - A team approach.* Baltimore: University Park Press, 1978, 245-267.

White, B. L. *The first three years of life.* Englewood Cliffs, New Jersey: Prentice-Hall, Inc., 1975.

5

ACOUSTICALLY IMPAIRED

Programmed Language Instruction for the Severely Developmentally Retarded

by James W. Tawney

Education for the handicapped, particularly lower functioning students—the moderately and severely retarded, has been shaped by a number of forces in the last 15 or 20 years. These include the use of applied behavior analysis or behavior modification in classroom settings, the development of speech and language training for teacher use in classroom settings, and an emphasis on direct or systematic instruction.

Since 1968, I have been involved with the development of two curricula which reflect and incorporate the attributes of behaviorally based systematic (or direct) instruction procedures. *Systematic Language Instruction* (SLI) (Tawney & Hipsher, 1970) is one of a four part program also known as *Systematic Instruction for Retarded Children*. The *Programmed Environments Curriculum* contains language and concept learning, structured programs in motor, self-help and social skill development. The description here of a structured language program generally cuts across both programs although there are procedural differences which distinguish them.

The underlying philosophy of these programs is that even the most handicapped students can learn when the environment is programmed or structured to facilitate the development of a response repertoire. Language (or communication skill) development is considered to be a high priority for this student population.

The general goal of these programs is to accelerate the development of a language skill repertoire.

The scope of instructional programs across both curricula includes prerequisites to instruction (attending skills), speech sound production for children who are nonvocal or emit only cries, shrieks, or other nonreferential sounds, the development of receptive language skills (motor responses to teachers' requests and objects/events in the environment), expressive language, or vocal production (shaping words, identifying objects and actions). The SLI program also, teaches responding to question forms, verb forms, adjectives, pronouns, plurals, adverbs, multiple commands, and finally a repertoire of simple sentence production skills and reading behaviors (action sentences— say and do—"Alice open a door"). The scope of the *Programmed Environments Curriculum* is shown in Table 1. The child populations for these programs are reflected in the different levels of skills. SLI was developed on a population of young Down's Syndrome children. The *Programmed Environments Curriculum* was validated with approximately 300 children—in 7 locales in Massachusetts, Kentucky, Virginia, and New Mexico—who are

described as severely developmentally retarded.

The theoretical basis underlying the development of both programs is behavioral. Bijou and Baer (1961) extended a behavioral system of psychology to child development. Later, Bijou (1966) extended that analysis to retardation, describing conditions that might retard the development of a repertoire of behaviors. His functional analysis of retarded development has enabled us to focus on behavioral events, to develop strategies to enhance or accelerate the development of a language repertoire.

Readers are referred to *Programmed Environments Curriculum* for detailed lesson plans. A definition of common terms is given below:

1. A *4/5 data* program is one which requires four correct out of five responses to meet criterion to pass to the next more complex step of a program.
2. A *cycle* program can be used to teach many different concepts, or activities, with the same lesson plan.
3. The *skill* statement contains a rationale for teaching each lesson.
4. The term *entry* behaviors is generally synonymous with pre-requisites to instruction—behaviors the child must perform to complete the task.
5. The *objective* follows the Mager (1961) format. These objectives may

From *The Directive Teacher*, Vol. 2, No. 3, Winter 1980, published by NCEMMH, The Ohio State University.

TABLE I

Receptive Skills

1 Responding to Social Interaction	5 Responding to Signal Words
2 Attending to Voice	6 Identifying Objects
3 Following Cued Commands	7 Identifying Body Parts
4 Attending to Own Name	8 Identifying People

Expressive Skills

1 Making Sounds	5 Shaping Words
2 Responding Vocally to Model	6 Naming Actions
3 Indicating Preferences	7 Naming Objects
4 Producing Sounds on Requests	

Cognitive Skills

1 Focusing Attention	10 Putting Objects in Sequence
2 Attending to Objects	11 Lining Up Objects
3 Responding to Teacher Model	13 Sorting
4 Repeating Teacher Model	14 Selecting Equivalent Amounts
5 Finding Hidden Objects	15 Matching Equal Sets
6 Finding Source of Sound	16 Counting Rationally
7 Imitating Actions	17 Selecting a Specified Quantity
8 Matching	
9 Identifying Simple Pictures	

serve, also, as short term objectives in a child's individual education plan.

6. Follow-up activities (generalization) suggest ways to increase the child's repertoire.

Each lesson plan consists of two parts, the Overview, just described, and the Program how to conduct the lesson.

1. The materials are specified, unique to each task.

2. For some programs, there is a chart, e.g., the Common Objects Chart, which suggests which concepts might be taught.

3. The general strategy differs among programs but note that here it specifies how to cue; how to arrange materials, what to say (command), how long to wait for a response (latency) and what to do, contingent upon a child's correct or incorrect response. Here,

(a) If the child responds correctly the natural consequence is handling the object. This may be paired with praise or tangible reinforcers, depending upon the child's preferences.

(b) If the child errs, the correction procedures would include one of these,

(i) Refocus (interrupt the incorrect response and repeat the command).

(ii) Demonstration (interrupt—demonstrate—repeat)

(iii) Guidance (interrupt—repeat command)

4. The other trial section indicates how to proceed from trial to trial.

5. The modification component specifies when the teacher must modify the lesson. In other sections of the curriculum, modification procedures, strategies, and alternatives are listed.

The program shows how the instructional task increases in complexity through four steps in this lesson. Special attention should be focused on the three posttests. When a child has completed this program, he has demonstrated the behavior under four different conditions:

1. in the last step (S/4) with correction and contingent reinforcement.

2. in Posttest 1—S/4 without correction and with noncontingent general reinforcement (you're sitting well, etc.).

3 and 4. in Posttest 2 and 3, where generally the teacher, the environment, objects, or the commands change.

The *Programmed Environments Curriculum* follows a pretest, teach, posttest procedure. The unit of instruction is the learning trial which includes these components.

1. Teacher insures readiness (gets attention).

2. Teacher presents task stimulus events (materials — cues — commands).

3. Child responds (or does not respond and the trial ends after five seconds).

4. Teacher feedback (reinforcement or correction).

5. Teacher records responses.

Four program types yield different data statements. 4/5 programs yield a percent correct response measure; rate data programs show the increase in the rate of responding during a defined and constant instructional session (10 minutes). Skill and behavior chain acquisition programs allow documentation of increases in parts completed in an integrated behavior chain. These enable teachers to be quite specific in describing the outcomes of instruction.

Above, the structure of two language curricula and the scope of behaviors they may teach were described as part of a lesson plan from the *Programmed Environments Curriculum*. I wish to introduce another term. I indicated another level of focus on instruction. I expect to abandon the term curriculum and substitute, in its place, the phrase integrated learning system. Again, I can best explain by example. The *Programmed Environments Curriculum* is an integrated learning system. It contains, in addition to the 79 lesson plans (what to teach), a set of seven instructional modules which describe how to teach the curriculum; and, in addition, modules that review basic concepts of reinforcement and list the strategies for developing one's own lesson plans and incorporating the curriculum into IEPs. On another dimension, the product contains a general assessment strategy (classroom observation form), a Profile (matrix of arrangement of lessons within category by levels of presumed increasing complexity) and data recording systems. These components enable the teacher to use the system for each step in the instructional process, and using existing lesson plans and procedures as a model to develop her own curriculum.

There is yet another dimension to this integrated learning system especially critical to training and evaluation for teachers. The *Programmed Environments Curriculum* was validated through a rigorous process. Trainers who received extensive training at the project site taught local site teachers to content (module) criterion and direct instruction (program administration) criterion. Once met, the teacher's data could then be entered in the computer systems. The materials used to accomplish this training included a video tape and a trainer's manual. These have also been produced commercially so that a school system can set up an integrated training and supervision system

5

for its teachers.

Public education for the severely handicapped is a newly emerging field in special education. The majority of instructional materials for this group are likely to follow a structured model, some more than others. Our language programs have been designed as highly structured systems, which may serve as examples for others to follow. Moving from curriculum to integrated learning systems reflects an intent to integrate, on several dimensions, often disparate or uncoordinated steps in the instructional process for teachers and for children. In conclusion, let me rephrase the goal statements for our products, and for child achievement in general: to structure environments to increase the probability that children will perform at high and relatively error—free rates and to record the effects of intervention to document the extent to which we are successful.

References

Bijou, S.W. A functional analysis of retarded development. In N. Ellis (Ed.), *International review of research in mental retardation* (Vol. 1). New York: Academic Press, 1966.

Bijou, S. W., & Baer, D. M. *Child development I*. Englewood Cliffs, N.J.: Prentice-Hall, 1965.

Tawney, J. W., & Hipsher, L. W. *Systematic language instruction: The Illinois program*. Washington, D.C.: USOE, Bureau of Education for the Handicapped, Grant No. 7-1025, 1970.

Tawney, J. W., Knapp, D. S., O'Reilly, C. D., & Pratt, S. S. *Programmed environments curriculum*. Columbus, Ohio: Charles E. Merrill Publishing Company, 1979.

ACOUSTICALLY IMPAIRED

Stereotype of Deaf Child Said Useless, Inaccurate

by Margaret Markham

Is THE classic portrait of the deaf child as impulsive, hyperactive, rigid, and suspicious valid? Or is it a stereotype that can't stand the glare of scientific scrutiny?

In the view of psychiatrist Stella Chess and psychologist Paulina Fernandez of New York University Medical Center, the time has come to abandon the concept of any specific constellation of behavior symptoms attributable to deafness per se. Such a stance raises major implications for the handling of deaf children both in everyday life and in a clinical setting.

"It is true that many social and academic situations can be stressful for deaf children because of their problems of communication. Such stress may either be resolved constructively or lead to a behavior disorder," the two researchers pointed out in their report to the recent meeting of the American Academy of Child Psychiatry in Atlanta.

"As indicated by our data, deaf children with other handicaps are likely to develop behavior symptoms, often because of the neurological dysfunction associated with mental retardation and chronic brain syndrome. All too often, however, we have seen parents or teachers 'explain' the symptoms as due to the deafness; or in the case of deafness due to congenital rubella, the child is labeled as a 'rubella' case which is presumed to explain his special difficulties."

After a long-term, exhaustive, prospective study of 243 children with congenital rubella, Chess and her co-worker concluded that the traditional concept of a "deafness personality" is unfounded.

Initially, the project examined these youngsters at ages two–five, again at eight–nine, and most recently, a follow-up on 205 of them at the 13–14-year age level. Of this adolescent sample, 34 are without any physical defect, while 89 suffer from deafness alone, and 82 have one or more handicaps in addition to deafness. The study protocol covered each child's behavior in a wide range of everyday functioning. Such data were gathered both by interviews with parents and teachers and by psychologic and psychiatric examinations. The physically and intellectually normal children were used as the control group. Comparisons were made between these youngsters and those with deafness as the sole physical impairment and with each subgroup of those with deafness and other deficits, such as mental re-

5

tardation, blindness, or cerebral palsy.

Over the years, many reports have emphasized that the deaf child has specific deviant personality characteristics, but the results of studies were frequently inconclusive and often suffered from methodological weaknesses. "Deaf populations have also frequently been treated as homogeneous groups, without consideration of the effect of other co-existing handicaps or pathology in some of the subjects," Chess noted. "Other studies have reported contrary data, namely the absence of significant differences between deaf and hearing groups. However, these investigations have been based on small samples whose special features limit the generalizability of the findings."

Refutes Positions

The Chess study clearly refutes both these positions. While the deaf children do not fit into a preconceived personality profile that includes impulsivity, hyperactivity, rigidity, and suspiciousness, neither are they entirely free of adverse symptomatology. Among the deaf without other defects 75 percent were free of any target symptoms. The one symptom significantly higher among the deaf as compared with the normal group was impulsivity. However, the New York researchers emphasized, this was true in only 20 percent of the deaf group. Moreover, a high prevalence of target symptoms was characteristic to a varying extent only among those with other handicaps in addition to deafness. Chess considers these results "especially impressive" in view of the fact that a symptom was tabulated as present even if it was reported via only one of the four sources used for obtaining the pertinent data.

"When we took a closer look at impulsivity, we found some important differences between the type of impulsivity in the deaf only group, compared with that present in the deaf multihandicapped group. In the deaf multihandicapped group, 63 percent of the children who were impulsive turned their aggressiveness against themselves. They hit, pinched, scratched, and bit themselves while

having an explosive episode in which they also were aggressive toward other people. In the group in which deafness was the sole handicap, none of the children engaged in this self-abusive behavior during tantrums," Chess emphasized.

In the course of the longitudinal study, it became clear that nearly 50 percent of the group with deafness as the only deficit had engaged in self-abusive behavior at ages two-five, but within a few years more than half of them had abandoned such practices. By contrast, in those with deafness plus other handicaps, self-abuse remained constant from early childhood through adolescence.

"The continuity of self-abuse over several developmental periods differentiates in a clear-cut manner the qualitative aspects of the impulsivity of the child whose sole handicap is deafness from the deaf child with additional physical and/or intellectual barriers. The gradual diminution of self-aggression over time in the deaf only group has social implications in that it represents communication and relationship with other people and responsiveness to social signals by attainment of self-control," the investigators explained.

"Conversely, in the deaf multihandicapped, we have indication of inadequate social awareness and incapacity for self-control. Thus, the two groups show different levels of interaction with their social environment. This differentiation also has outcome implications. The greater severity both quantitatively and qualitatively of impulsive behaviors of deaf multihandicapped children further reduces their responsiveness to educational measures."

Defensive Behavior

In view of their results, the New York University researchers urge professionals involved in evaluation of a deaf child to be aware of the defensive behavior that the problems of communication may evoke in such a youngster. Once constraints on communication are lifted and possible embarrassment for the child eliminated, protective behavioral devices tend to vanish.

"As with any child with specific needs and difficulties, once the professional gets past the protective responses of the deaf child, he or she will be gratified at the level of positive communication it is possible to establish with such a child. But this will only happen if he is first clear that deafness itself does not create fixed pathological behavioral deviations," Chess reiterated.

5

PART 6

LEARNING/BEHAVIOR HANDICAPS

by Lynne Reynolds, Ph.D.

6

While developmental psychology is important to all teachers, understanding normal child development is especially important to the teacher of those children and youth who have been classified as being behavior disordered and/or emotionally disturbed or as having problems in academic learning. To understand deviant social, emotional and/or learning behavior, it is first necessary to understand that which is accepted as normal and the vast range of behaviors that are considered normal. From this basic understanding, the teacher of children with disturbances in their social/emotional adjustment or in academic learning is then prepared to look at deviant behavioral characteristics, causes, clinical assessment, clinical treatment, and methods of teaching.

Since the topic of concern is students with behavior/learning handicaps, it follows that what is happening in the fields of psychology and psychiatry is relevant. While these fields are still involved in treating patients with deviancies, the trends here are to • identify temperament and look at environmental match to temperament, • identify those who are at risk and perform preventative intervention, milieu therapy and shape family systems, and • identify and treat biochemical disorders that may be the cause of various emotional problems. Extensive work is now being performed with infants and preschoolers that parallels the trends in special education.

The teacher of the behavior disordered/emotionally disturbed is expected to understand and have skill in dealing with a large continuum of students with deviant behaviors—from those who are unable to maintain appropriate behavior in the regular classroom to those children who have been diagnosed as psychotic, schizophrenic and autistic. The teacher of mentally retarded students is expected to understand and have skill in dealing with a wide range of intellectual-academic problems, as well as with problems in social and emotional behavior.

The trend today is to classify students by the behaviors evidenced, via diagnostic tests and behavioral checklists, into categories used in other areas of special education: mild, moderate, severe and profound. This classification system is helpful as the characteristics, treatments and methods of teaching are quite different for those students who are aware of reality and able to communicate, though unable to control their behavior consistently, when compared to those students who are unaware of reality and their surroundings and are unable to communicate. Behavior modification has been, perhaps, the dominant method of teaching these students to control their behavior and to function educationally. However, it must be understood that there will be little carry-over or long term effect if the student does not develop inner controls or does not develop a feeling of self worth. The key is to find that which is reinforcing to each individual, which is not an easy task.

Behavior modification has been largely unsuccessful with those students who are depressed and withdrawn or very bright. The trends today are to combine several approaches—such as the humanistic and behavioral applied with consistency, human warmth and energy on the part of the teacher. Since the majority of these students are not academically motivated, emphasis is being placed upon life skills and vocational preparation, especially at the high school level.

Due to the teacher's observational skills and length of time spent with the student who has behavior problems, he/she is often able to give valuable input to the student's therapist, which allows for adjustment in the therapeutic program. While this is not always the case, the use of an interdisciplinary team approach to educational planning is providing more teacher-therapist contact and an opportunity for the exchange of ideas. The overall goal is for the student to gain control and understanding of his or her own behavior and become a productive and happy member of society.

BEHAVIORALLY DISTURBED

Check of Suicide Potential Urged for Child Patients

by Margaret Markham

THERE IS LITTLE debate today over the merits of the maxim that every child who threatens or attempts suicide requires psychiatric evaluation. But according to Cornell University's Cynthia R. Pfeffer, M.D., the other side of the coin has been neglected. She and colleagues at the Albert Einstein College of Medicine told the American Academy of Child Psychiatry that all children undergoing psychiatric evaluation should be assessed for suicidal potential.

Contrary to earlier reports, their study finds a much higher rate of suicidal potential in youngsters attending an outpatient psychiatric service than generally believed. The Cornell-Einstein team said that 33 percent of the 39 children in their study displayed such a tendency as indicated by their ideas, threats, or actual attempts.

"To date, there have been few systematic studies of suicidal latency-age children evaluated in psychiatric outpatient settings. Previous reports have estimated that between seven and ten percent of latency age children in psychiatric outpatient care were suicidal. Unfortunately, the previous studies had a variety of methodological shortcomings," Pfeffer pointed out.

In the latest study presented at the Atlanta meeting, the 39 children were selected from the waiting list of the Child Psychiatry Outpatient Clinic at the Bronx Municipal Center, which is affiliated with Einstein. These youngsters, aged six to 12, were chosen "randomly" when a child reached the head of the waiting list and if a child psychiatry fellow or child psychology intern was then available to evaluate the patient. All the children in this selected group remained as outpatients for the duration of the project.

A battery of structured suicidal potential scales were administered in addition to the standard clinical evaluation of children in such a service. This special battery of eight aspects of the child's status was designed to provide the following information:

a) Spectrum of Suicidal Behavior Scale—Documented nonsuicidal behavior, suicidal ideation, suicidal threats, mild suicide attempts, and serious suicide attempts.

b) Precipitating Events Scale—Documented environmental and family stresses within six months preceding the evaluation.

c) Affects and Behavior Scale (recent)—Documented feelings and symptomatic behavior during the six months preceding the evaluation.

d) Family Background Scale—

6

Documented history of family stress and psychopathology.

e) Affects and Behavior Scale (past)—Same as scale *c* except it covers time preceding the six-month period before the evaluation.

f) Concept of Death Scale—Documented the child's experiences and preoccupations with death and the child's cognitive concepts of death.

g) Ego Functioning Scale—Documented the child's cognitive abilities, affect regulation, impulse control, reality testing, and object relations.

h) Ego Defense Mechanism Scale—Documented a profile of defenses utilized by each child.

The researchers said that each scale thus contained a number of items which could produce a score for each variable to be analyzed, and comparisons between the suicidal and nonsuicidal children were based on these scores.

"We defined suicidal behavior as thoughts and/or actions which may lead to death or serious injury to the child. The spectrum of suicidal behavior ranged from nonsuicidal behavior to suicidal ideas, threats, and attempts," Pfeffer explained.

In addition to this special test schema, the evaluation of each child also included individual, family, and group diagnostic interviews, psychologic testing (WISC-R, WRAT, Rorschach, TAT, Bender-Gestalt Test, and Human Figure Drawings), as well as a neurological examination.

The Cornell-Einstein investigators found no significant differences between the suicidal and nonsuicidal children with respect to sex, race (ethnicity), or diagnosis. Among the variety of suicidal methods favored by these children, jumping from a height was the one chosen most frequently. This technique was either contemplated or actually occurred in 38 percent of the children in the study.

No differences were noted between the suicidal and nonsuicidal children with respect to specific types of acute environmental stresses they experienced. However, the suicidal children were significantly more chronically depressed and anxious as evidenced by sadness; withdrawal; frequent crying spells; feelings of worthlessness, self-blame, hopelessness; and the wish to die. The suicidal patients had also had significantly greater psychomotor activity during the six months preceding their evaluation. Such hyperactivity may represent a form of masked depression or depressive equivalents. It may also serve as a very early alternative for coping with painful feelings, thus possibly indicating the potential for dangerous acting out is on the rise, Pfeffer noted. The youngsters with suicidal potential also tended to be much more preoccupied with questions of death.

While there was no difference in the degree of psychopathology among the parents of one group as compared with the other, the mothers and fathers of the suicidal children had significantly more suicidal ideation than the parents of the nonsuicidal children, Pfeffer underscored. In comparison to a similar inpatient group, the outpatient population had a higher incidence of neurosis; the inpatients had a higher incidence of multiple deficits in ego functioning and significantly more serious suicidal behavior, including threats and specific attempts.

"The outpatient children seemed to grow up in families chronically affected by family tensions resulting from marital concerns, parental separations, and parental intrapsychic conflicts. Frequently, parents seemed incapable of appropriately responding to their child's developmental needs because of lack of awareness and knowledge of child development and, most significantly, because of serious problems with object relations," Pfeffer commented.

"Many of the parents themselves seemed to have grown up in circumstances that were devoid of appropriate empathy, support, and nurturance. The parents appeared to be very dependent, lacked ability to delay gratification, and were subject to intense mood shifts."

Within such family settings, the children were frequently anxious and maintained symbiotic-like relationships with their parents by identifying with parental affective states. When inconsistencies in parenting were sensed, the children felt hopeless and worthless, and frequently blamed themselves for family problems. Not surprisingly, they were unable to develop trust and considered themselves bad and in need of punishment.

"They often believed that they could solve the problems in the family and depreciated themselves when met with disappointment. Fantasies of escape from such disturbing circumstances were prevalent. Often death was evidenced as a means of eliminating stress and as an attainment of peace and satisfaction," Pfeffer explained. Collaborating with her from Einstein were Hope R. Conte, assistant professor of psychiatry; Robert Plutchik, professor of psychiatry; and Inez Jerrett, research assistant in the same department.

6

BEHAVIORALLY DISTURBED

Haloperidol Use
For Autism Investigated

by *Psychiatric News*

A CONTINUING STUDY on the effects of haloperidol in altering the behavior of autistic children was reported at the meeting of the American Academy of Child Psychiatry in Atlanta. Initial results of a double-blind, placebo-controlled trial in 40 autistic children have been sufficiently promising to encourage further investigation by researchers at the departments of psychiatry and psychology at New York University and Tulane University in New Orleans to broaden the scope of their efforts.

Ira L. Cohen, Ph.D., and associates expanded their protocol to determine if the significant reduction in the severity of the two cardinal symptoms of autism noted on such therapy could be readily confirmed. They had originally observed that stereotypy and withdrawal were favorably affected by such medication in children between 4.5 and seven years of age, but not in those who were younger. At the same time, they had observed that the older group tolerated haloperidol at higher doses than did the younger children.

Because of the innate difficulty of rating such responses objectively and because of the tremendous variability of children, especially such a category of patients, the investigators have modified their approach to psychiatric rating and have resorted to the so-called ABAB design in which each subject serves as his own control. To this end, their present study utilizes objective rating scales and a within-subjects reversal design.

"We developed two objective rating scales designed to record the presence or absence of a given behavior. This is done with a timed instrument that notes the presence or absence of a predefined behavior in 20 successive 30-second time bins," Cohen explained.

The second scale was designed to assess the extent to which a child would respond when asked to react to the rater. For instance, when the children were not attending to the rater, they would be directed to look at him. The rater would then note whether the child simply oriented toward the rater, or made eye contact, or echoed the question, and/or responded in a positive social manner.

Fifteen autistic children were enrolled in this phase of the study, and nine of them completed the course of therapy. Their ages ranged from just over two to seven, and in all instances the diagnosis had been made independently by two research psychiatrists. The dosage of haloperidol was regulated over a range of 0.5 to 4.0 mg during the first week in order to determine the optimal level for each child. The optimal dosage was set as the highest therapeutic dose the child could tolerate without showing side effects, Cohen reported. This dosage was then maintained during the second week of the study.

"The effects of haloperidol on behavior essentially represent a replication of our previous study. The drug significantly reduced the frequency of occurrence of stereotypy, but the effect depended on the baseline level. Haloperidol also facilitated attending to the rater by the child as assessed by the "look at me" scale in those patients who tended not to respond on placebo," Cohen said.

Haloperidol appeared to have no ef-
fect on motor activity levels, affect, speech, or irritability in this autistic population.

"It should be noted that the results of the present pilot study are based on a small sample and a short duration of drug treatment, and clearly require replication," Cohen emphasized.

"We are, at present, examining the effects of haloperidol on the behavior, attention, and learning ability of a new sample of preschool autistic children using both subjective and objective rating scales and automated operant conditioning techniques." This extended study, he added, involves a larger patient sample and treatment lasting for four weeks.

Collaborating in this study were Magda Campbell, Donn Posner; Douglas Triebel; Arthur M. Small, and Lowell T. Anderson.

6

BEHAVIORALLY DISTURBED

Psychiatric Self-Rating Test for Child Developed

by *Psychiatric News*

EVER SINCE Joseph Breuer and Freud soon thereafter, first experienced the exhilaration and enlightenment of sudden glimpses into the tortured inner world of their now classic patient, Anna O., psychiatrists have sought to discover equally effective means for uncovering the inner workings of a child's mind. Their efforts all too often have been crowned with frustration rather than success.

Now a group at the University of Ottawa have devised a do-it-yourself psychiatric scale in which the active participation of the child is a key element. Their efforts, Joseph H. Beitchman, M.D., told the American Academy of Child Psychiatry in Atlanta, have yielded an unexpected dividend. This approach has the "ability to tell us something about the child's inner world. Parent and teacher inventories, by contrast, are based on observational methods, and provide descriptions of the child's behavior. The self-reporting scale does provide a profile that corresponds to one of the three descriptive clinical groups. But more important, however, this instrument will also tell us something of the child's thoughts and feelings, something that is, in the final analysis, the major determinant of the child's emotional health and well-being. . . .

It can help chart aspects of the child's inner world about which little is known."

The new Children's Self-Report Psychiatric Rating Scale has been tested initially in two sample populations. One consisted of 420 normative children, ages seven to 12, drawn from Ottawa schools. The second included 126 youngsters of comparable age who attended the outpatient, inpatient, or day-care facilities at the Royal Ottawa Hospital. Both groups were also matched with respect to geographic and social backgrounds. A pool of items, adapted from various other procedures currently in use, were put into a format that would elicit a "yes" or "no" answer. The wording in the questionnaires was simplified to assure comprehension by even the youngest participants. The roster of 164 items was designed to include several that were factually untrue. The method of administering the tests involved the reading aloud of each question to groups of ten among the normative subjects and individually in the case of those in the clinical sample, Beitchman explained. The tests were finished in little more than half an hour, and each child was able to complete the questionnaire. When a child asked a question about the item under consideration, the youngster was instructed to put down what he thought was true for him.

Discriminant function analysis of the data obtained in this procedure yielded results that the investigators regard as "highly encouraging." Beitchman noted, "The validity of this rating scale has been shown in its ability to discriminate between clinical subgroups and between normals and those that are clinical."

Specifically, he added, "Using this Self-Report Psychiatric Rating Scale, a child can be categorized as normal or abnormal; and if abnormal, the child can then be classified into one of three major clinical subgroups, and the deviant symptom dimensions specified. For instance, a child categorized as neurotic could show deviant scores on the positive peer relations factor, the leadership factor, and the obsessive factor. The ability to specify the deviant dimensions has obvious implications for the focus of treatment efforts. Furthermore, the opportunity to evaluate treatment efforts and observe long-term outcome is facilitated by an approach such as this."

The inadequacies of other approaches now generally in use for the detection and diagnosis of childhood psychopathology are perhaps best reflected in the fact that they have not yielded reliable estimates of the prevalence of childhood disorders, the Canadian psychiatrist pointed out. While the new self-reporting method is still in its infancy, and both repeated testing of the same groups and extension of the procedure to larger groups of normal and abnormal children need to be done to substantiate its usefulness, the Ottawa group believes that such an effort is warranted. With additional refinements in their protocol, they expect to improve further on the reliability of the method and to sharpen diagnostic accuracy.

"The clinical sample, especially for the neurotic and mixed group disorders, was not large enough to rule out chance factors contributing to the excellent success at predicting severity. Nevertheless, the high rate of success at predicting severity warrants an opportunity to replicate our findings," Beitchman stated.

6

BEHAVIORALLY DISTURBED

New Scale Developed To Gauge Autism

by *Psychiatric News*

PROBABLY no other childhood deviant behavior has so baffled clinicians attempting to evaluate young subjects as autism in the preschool years. Equally frustrating have been most attempts to objectively gauge the effect of therapeutic measures in such patients.

While various checklists and psychiatric rating scales have been suggested, some rely on parent reporting, others on observations by school personnel. Many procedures, however, are either not sufficiently sensitive to changes over a brief span of time or, on the other hand, are so sophisticated as to require a high degree of training for their use, according to Theodore Shapiro, M.D., and associates at Cornell University Medical College.

"Our studies of prior scales suggested a need for the development of a scale for rapid and reliable use by clinicians involved in serial assessment of young children in research and other settings," Shapiro declared at the recent meeting of the American Academy of Child Psychiatry in Atlanta.

To bridge this gap the Cornell group has come up with their form of a Behavioral Scale for Deviant Preschoolers (BSDP). They believe it has thus far yielded more meaningful data

than prior scales and with relative ease. They have also found it educationally useful in the training of medical students and psychiatric residents, according to Shapiro, who is professor of psychiatry at Cornell and director of the department of child and adolescent psychiatry at New York Hospital—Payne Whitney Clinic.

"The specificity of this scale for children between the ages of two and six years of age permits the examiner to achieve a reasonably objectified view of varying diagnostic categories and to rate progress in treatment," Shapiro said.

"Why are we offering yet another scale in a climate where there seems to be a proliferation of scales — especially a scale designed to deal with children from two to six where the incidence of deviance is not substantial? Firstly, it seems clear that diagnostic criteria for children in the severely deviant group now called pervasive developmental disorders must be objectified at least to the degree that similar populations are being considered not only for varying therapies but also with respect to their characteristics as development proceeds. Recent restrictions of the syndrome of autism away from other severely deviant young children may require re-evaluation."

To further substantiate his point, Shapiro maintained that any activity referred to as treatment must be monitored by repeated observations on a reliable scale that can indicate either profile and developmental change or severity of modification.

"New suggestive diagnostic groups as well as progress of individual children within groups could accrue from such data. Investigative time is at a premium, and assessments ought to be reliable and also valid in relation to more global clinical judgments — with a third and necessary feature that the effort expended not be so extensive as to make the task an effort disproportionate to the gain."

The scale developed by the Cornell group consists of 29 items covering five sectors that can be scored in five minutes by easily trained observers. A total symptom scale may be achieved to measure severity as well as to yield a profile breakdown of the five sectors. A global assessment rating scale is also provided, which consists of detailed descriptions of mild, moderate, and severe behavior disturbance. These are then scored in six dimensions. No complex key or glossary is required—only simple descriptions of each behavior that permits the examiner to make scaled judgments about the presence or absence of each behavior. The behavior description can, in turn, be broken down into two degrees of severity so that raters can make judgments on a scale of six. This then provides an overall clinician's rating to be compared to the total symptom score as well, in addition to the basic sector analysis of the BSDP.

The scale, designed to be used in brief clinical interviews, in open play sessions, or on brief video taped sessions, has been tested on children in the therapeutic nursery at the Payne Whitney Clinic. They ranged in age from 30 to 66 months; and their conditions were diagnosed as autism, childhood psychosis, mental retardation, primary childhood aphasia, or developmental lag. All had severe problems that prevented their attending regular nursery schools. To check the reliability of the BSDP procedures, the tests were recorded on video tapes, which were later judged by three observers independently. Psychologist Rochelle W. Austrian, as well as psychiatrists Theodore Shapiro, M.D., and Miriam Sherman, M.D., rated each child independently.

The highest overall reliability in the procedures employed was found in the area of relationship of the patient to physical surroundings, and language, the investigators reported. They noted that to their surprise the motor scale achieved the lowest degree of reliability, but they attributed this drawback to the difficulty of assessing mild motor deviance through the medium of video tapes. Specifically, for example, the autistic child has the highest scores in the affective and language deviance levels; and the relationship to social and physical surroundings follows next, with the motor area relatively intact. On the other hand, the retardation syndrome falls below the symptoms profile of the autistic patients with relatively little impairment of affect.

Shapiro emphasized that other professional raters familiar with these particular patients also ranked them independently in terms of degree of disturbance, and their results concurred with the numerical estimates of severity obtained by the BSDP method. The Cornell researchers recommended their 29-item scale because of its specificity, its simple application, and the ease with which agreement can be achieved among observers.

6

MENTALLY RETARDED

Preparing Teachers of the Severely, Profoundly Retarded

by M. Angele Thomas

Current Trends in Preparing Teachers of the Severely and Profoundly Retarded: A Conversation with Susan and William Stainback

The influx of severely and profoundly retarded students into community based public education programs has unquestionably called for a cadre of teachers who possess the knowledge and skills to teach these students. The onus of responsibility for preparing competent personnel rests on colleges and universities. At this critical stage in history, Susan and William Stainback analyze, question, and react to some of the emerging trends and new priorities that are developing and influencing the quality of teacher training program structures.

Susan Stainback is a former teacher in the area of mental retardation and has had numerous other involvements in this field in the form of research, publications, consultancies, and conference presentations. William Stainback has been associate professor of special education at the University of Northern Iowa, Cedar Falls. In other professional capacities, he has served locally and nationally in The Council for Exceptional Children and as a consultant to many school districts throughout the United States. His writing concentrates heavily on teaching methodologies for seriously handicapped children. Both husband and wife are presently on the faculty of Exceptional Student Education, Florida Atlantic University, Boca Raton. One of their responsibilities at Florida Atlantic is the development of a personnel preparation program for prospective and practicing teachers of severely and profoundly handicapped students.

Only a few years ago training teachers of the severely and profoundly retarded was considered a new frontier. Is this area still considered a new frontier and, if not, what strides have been made in teacher preparation programs to get beyond that frontier?

Dr. Susan Stainback: We can now consider the training of teachers to be beyond the frontier stage. Over the past several years considerable awareness, interest, and concern have been generated among educators, medical personnel, parents, and other community members. This awareness and interest have provided the impetus to get a better grasp of what the terrain of this new area is like. All of these factors have helped us to better understand what to do in regard to teacher preparation. Through experience and research (primarily the direct applied type) directions in educating the severely and profoundly handicapped are beginning to emerge. Whereas previously we were grasping in the dark to some degree, and relying heavily on intuition as a guide, we now have a basis in experience and research from which we can infer possible directions to take.

In addition, advances have been made relative to the sheer availability of personnel preparation programs. There is no longer the paucity of training opportunities for potential teachers that existed just a few short years ago. Based on these advances, from our point of view, personnel preparation in the area of teaching the severely and profoundly retarded probably can no longer be considered a new, uncharted frontier. This is not to imply that it is a well developed and advanced field, however. While we can now recognize and better understand the population and areas of concern in personnel preparation to some extent, we are still functioning on a very basic level of knowledge and skill. While the research and experience base provides some direction, it is minimal and we will need to put forth greater effort to enhance progress. In essence, then, while personnel preparation can no longer be considered a new frontier, it nevertheless presents a challenge with room for discovery.

Has there been a substantial increase in the number and types of personnel preparation programs for teachers of severely and profoundly retarded students since the passage of Public Law 94-142?

Dr. William Stainback: Yes, there has been a fairly rapid growth in personnel preparation programs across the nation. They vary in type, level, purpose, and quality depending on the resources and needs of the area in which they are located. Some of the programs result in both a degree and state approval to teach while others provide only state approval to teach. Programs also range in quality and depth, from comprehensive, well developed, integrative sequences to a few isolated courses. It also should be noted that programs have been developed at various levels. Some programs for training paraprofessionals have been developed at the associate of arts degree level. Teacher training programs have been developed at the undergraduate and graduate levels. However, the most common approach is to provide training for teachers of the severely and profoundly handicapped at the graduate level while reserving the undergraduate level more exclusively for learning the basic teaching skills.

In addition, a few doctoral level programs have been developed to train researchers, teacher trainers, school administrators, and consultants. We should add here that while some progress has been made, there remains a real and significant need for well developed and comprehensive preservice and inservice personnel preparation programs.

What is your reaction to this rapid growth in the number of training programs?

Dr. Susan Stainback: The impetus for the rapid growth in training programs was precipitated by a quantitative factor. This quantitative factor constituted an immediate need for trained teachers to provide programming for severely and profoundly retarded children who had not previously been provided educational services. So the educational systems were put into a position of needing a population of teachers for the severely and profoundly retarded who were, for all practical purposes in education, nonexistent prior to this time. As a response to this need various types and levels of training programs were developed. This rapid development of preparation programs has the potential to harbor both advantages and dangers. For example, some advantages might be that with the increased number of programs more teachers can be trained more quickly. Also, more information about the need for and importance of educating the severely and profoundly handicapped can be spread to greater numbers of individuals. This will tend to enhance the potential for services, advocacy, understanding, and cooperation. However, a potential disadvantage may be that if the intensive rigorous training required by a teacher is sacrificed for speed to meet immediate service needs, the damage could be considerable. Once a teacher is fully and permanently certified to teach — even though he or she has not been given the training necessary to provide optimal programming — this teacher, in many cases, has the right and option to remain in the teaching position. The cumulative effect of poor servicing to students could have a serious detrimental effect on the education of severely and profoundly retarded children.

It should be noted that this concern is not to imply that present training programs are not providing quality training. There are some excellent, well planned, sequential training programs. But what Bill and I are trying to say is that we must be consistently cognizant of qualitative factors. Unfortunately, there have been some cases in which short term programs were designed to get enough teachers certified to cover the classes of children without considering the long term effects. While we want services to be provided to all children as quickly as possible, the teachers who are certified to work with severely retarded children should have intensive initial training. They also should be required to engage

6

in continuous and ongoing learning opportunities through inservice training. This is important since the area of educating the severely and profoundly retarded is in its infancy stages and new ideas, research, and information are becoming available every day. Bill and I feel it would be unwise at the present time to allow teachers to be permanently certified to teach severely and profoundly handicapped individuals without the stipulation that they be required to engage in ongoing inservice learning experiences. It would be presumptuous to assume at this initial stage of knowledge regarding the teaching of severely and profoundly retarded children that in their initial training teachers can be provided all they need to know to optimally teach these individuals for the many years ahead. While we are advocating, in answer to your question, that we need to plan carefully, we are not saying that we should stand still and wait until we are sure of all the answers before doing anything. While caution must be exercised, we cannot expect to progress if we do not try to investigate and move ahead in this new area. Lack of positive attempts under the guise of caution can lead to stagnation and the potential annihilation of advancement.

You have repeatedly mentioned the importance of the qualitative factors in personnel preparation for the severely and profoundly handicapped. In an earlier publication on teacher training you outlined several needed components, such as diagnostic evaluation, curriculum, methodology, interdisciplinary teamwork, field experience, and parent involvement. Would you discuss a few other components that have emerged as important factors in influencing the quality of a personnel preparation program for severely and profoundly retarded students?

Dr. Susan Stainback: In our article (Stainback, Stainback, & Maurer, 1976), we focused primarily on some of the training areas that we considered to be important to the prospective teacher in programming for severely and profoundly involved individuals. What we would like to mention here involves important components of a personnel preparation program that have in many cases been overlooked, or at least have not been stressed in some programs. These factors are ones that can greatly influence the quality of personnel preparation, which in turn has a considerable impact on the entire field. These factors are the faculty, the students, community relationships, and university or college interdepartmental relationships. The faculty and

staff in the severe/profound personnel preparation program must include persons who are actively participating in and contributing to the progress and generation of new information in the field. Due to rapid development of this educational area the faculty and staff must spend a considerable amount of time keeping abreast of new information and ideas as well. They also must become actively involved in the progress of the field by engaging in research and direct experiences that will enable them to share new and important information with their students and other professionals. These attributes, in combination with a positive and objective approach toward the education of severely and profoundly retarded children, are required to provide the strong faculty and staff needed to present an appropriate model for both practicing and potential educators. These attributes will also lead to progress and advancement of other fields.

Regarding attributes of students, while all programs encourage bright individuals, students preparing to teach severely and profoundly retarded children require several attitudinal attributes in order to succeed comfortably in such a position. First, the students must recognize that severely and profoundly handicapped children can indeed learn. Second, the student should be reinforced by small as well as large increments of child change. And finally, the student should have the potential to program objectively for these individuals while being positive in his or her teaching approach. In addition, strong interpersonal relationships with peers are extremely helpful in working with other professionals. If a student either does not exhibit these attributes or lacks the potential to develop them, that student's chances of succeeding in and enjoying a position teaching severely and profoundly retarded children are slim.

Another factor that influences the strength of a personnel preparation program in the area of severely and profoundly handicapped involves cooperative relationships with community individuals and agencies that work for severely and profoundly handicapped children. When strong relationships are developed and maintained, both the faculty and the students have the opportunity to directly interact, work, and do research with severely and profoundly handicapped children. Similarly, the faculty and students can gain practical first hand experiences by working with and understanding the considerations of personnel in a variety of disciplines. Without such resources available training programs cannot be expected to prepare teachers who are knowledgeable and proficient in changing children's behavior or in working with professionals beyond the superficial level.

The last component we would like to mention in response to your question is the need for strong interdepartmental relationships throughout colleges and universities. These relationships invariably enhance and strengthen personnel preparation programs. Due to the wide variety and complexity of expertise needed to program optimally for severely and profoundly retarded children in such areas as human growth and development, speech, basic eating skill development, motor training, as well as in basic teaching and monitoring skills, it would be illogical and inefficient to expect any one department to develop the expertise in every area when some may already be available in other departments. For example, the Speech and Hearing Department may have faculty with expertise in basic speech development. Home Economics may have child development experts, and Occupational or Physical Therapy may offer courses in developing eating skills and in using adaptive equipment. While Special Education can provide the educational expertise required and can coordinate the efforts for training, there is generally no need to develop a large number of courses and hire many faculty for this relatively low incidence area. In order to accomplish such an approach to training, a strong, interdisciplinary teamwork approach must be developed and maintained within as well as outside the university.

The answer to this question is not intended to downplay the importance of the content considerations of a personnel preparation program. It is simply intended to recognize that the quality of content and product of the program will be heavily influenced by these other factors.

Would you discuss for us some empirical evidence emerging from research that may influence the content or direction of personnel training?

Dr. William Stainback: Over the past several years a great deal of research has been conducted and the results are very promising. Paul Wehman, for example, at Virginia Commonwealth University, is showing how play and leisure skills can be taught to severely handicapped individuals. Rincover, Lovass, and others have conducted research that is pointing to ways of teaching basic discrimi-

nation to the severely handicapped. Diane Bricker and Doug Guess have conducted research that points to ways of offering functional language to severely retarded students. Wesley Williams, Robert York, and James Tawney have also conducted research related to teaching preacademic and academic skills to some severely retarded individuals. Thomas Bellamy is demonstrating how prevocational and vocational skills can be taught to the severely handicapped. One other researcher that we might mention is Bud Fredericks, at the University of Oregon, who has conducted research to determine competencies needed by teachers of the severely handicapped. All of this, and much more, is giving direction to personnel preparation programs. For instance, in the study conducted by Dr. Fredericks, it was found that one competency among others needed by teachers is the skill to orchestrate the classroom environment in order to maximize the actual instructional time. One of the implications of this particular study is that training institutions are going to have to foster in teachers good organizational skills so that they can get the most instructional time out of the school day. In other words, teachers need to be able to synchronize curricula, management techniques, fun, play, and rest times into a smoothly functioning, efficient schedule. It also should be noted that some excellent ideas and concepts in addition to research have been generated over the past several years.

Lou Brown and his associates at the University of Wisconsin have pointed out the problems involved in always making curricula content decisions strictly based upon theories of human development that track stages of sequences through which all children develop. They also have offered alternative strategies for developing chronologically age appropriate and functionally appropriate curriculum content for severely retarded youngsters, especially the older adolescents. For example, in our "frontier" article we stated that knowing human growth and development principles was a must for teachers but, while that statement still remains true, Brown and his associates have rightly pointed out much more is needed to determine curriculum content. There are factors to consider other than what step a child is on within a human growth and development sequence chart. For example, are the skills we are teaching in our curriculum functional? Can they be used in the natural environment? Are they chronologically age appropriate?

At this point I would like to change the

focus of discussion a bit and ask about the degree of professional agreement in personnel preparation for severely and profoundly retarded students. What controversies have surfaced in this area?

Dr. William Stainback: One of the major controversies in personnel preparation that has recently received much attention involves the level and extensiveness of training required by teachers. On one side of the controversy some individuals advocate minimal training at the two year college level in which potential teachers are trained in basic behavioral management and child development areas. The rationale for minimal teacher training is the attitude that severely and profoundly retarded individuals have limited potential for gain. Thus, educational services for this population should be predominantly different and limited in nature.

The other approach to this controversy is the position that teachers preparing to work with severely and profoundly retarded children should be provided rigorous and extensive training. This approach is based on the premise that all equal rights to the best education possible should be provided to severely and profoundly handicapped students just as they should be provided to every other student, handicapped or not. Susan and I agree with the advocates of extensive training of teachers for severely and profoundly retarded children. Our decision is based on our experience of working with severely and profoundly handicapped students and discovering that they can learn so many things we never thought possible. Some youngsters have learned to ride school buses, shop in stores, read labels on cans, and interact socially with others when we thought it would be impossible for them to do such things. Others have learned to sit up and eat independently when we just knew they could never accomplish such difficult tasks. Others have learned some basic academic skills we thought were beyond their capabilities. With such a variety of possibilities opening up for severely retarded children, it would seem unwise for us not to provide them with the very best teachers.

This posture is not to indicate that we expect all severely retarded individuals to learn all of the things necessary to become doctors or lawyers. However, the maximum potential expected of an individual should not be limited by a preconceived notion. Training or content areas should be based on an individual and specific educational need at a particular point in time. For some

severely and profoundly retarded children, learning how to sit up or to walk, talk, and eat may constitute what they need to learn at a particular point in time, while others may need a higher or lower level of skill development. But simply because some of these skills are generally considered to be more basic does not necessarily justify providing the teacher with less training. Teaching eating skills is a very complex thing. In fact, we have found that teaching eating skills can often require a great deal of expertise. We agree with the position of Sontag, Certo, and Button (1979) which notes that there is a direct positive relationship between the degree of the handicapped condition and the degree of skill and expertise needed by the teacher. In other words, the more severe the disability, the more complex are the competencies required by the teacher.

As a final question, what is the current trend in BEH funding priorities for training teachers of severely and profoundly retarded children?

Dr. Susan Stainback: Personnel preparation in the area of the severely and profoundly handicapped has been a priority with BEH for the past several years. It is our understanding that this area will remain a priority for funding for some time to come. A few of the critical areas of concern in proposal consideration include that the proposed training program have field experiences as an integral part of training, a well trained staff, and an organized, sequential, comprehensive curriculum. Also the trend appears to place funding emphasis on programs designed to train teachers of the severely and profoundly handicapped to work effectively in the public schools setting, which corresponds to the mandate for programming and delivering services to all children in the least restrictive environment. Ongoing inservice training has also received considerable attention in this BEH priority area. In essence, funding trends generally correspond with the concepts set forth in Public Law 94-142 in combination with the findings of recent research described earlier.

References

Sontag, E., Certo, N., & Button, J. On a distinction between the education of the severely and profoundly handicapped and a doctrine of limitations. *Exceptional Children*, 1979, *45*, 604–616.

Stainback, S., Stainback, W., & Maurer, S. Training teachers of the severely and profoundly handicapped: A new frontier. *Exceptional Children*, 1976, *42*, 203–210.

MENTALLY RETARDED

Adaptive Behavior In the Definition Of Mental Retardation

by Thomas J. Huberty, James R. Koller and Terry D. Ten Brink

Abstract: Results of a recent survey of state education agencies indicated that many states emphasize intelligence in the definition and diagnosis of mental retardation and deemphasize or exclude adaptive behavior. The rationale for a renewed emphasis on adaptive behavior and IQ in the identification and education of the mentally retarded is discussed. The establishment of uniform definitions of mental retardation, the inclusion of adaptive behavior and IQ in defining mental retardation, objective and standardized assessment of adaptive behavior, and the establishment of criteria for adaptive behavior, are encouraged for use in the diagnosis, classification, and education of the mentally retarded. Without these emphases, misdiagnosis, inappropriate placement, and improper treatment of the mentally retarded can occur.

■ The methods by which mentally retarded children are placed in special education programs have become a source of controversy in recent years, particularly in light of new legislation such as Public Law 94-142 (the Education for All Handicapped Children Act of 1975) and various court litigations. Referral and placement procedures seem to have improved significantly since the proposal by Binet and Simon that a child's current intellectual functioning should be the sole determinant for his or her special placement (Edwards, 1971).

A child who is identified as mentally retarded is often initially detected by a teacher who notes that the child is not able to progress with the regular class. The teacher is likely to refer the child for psychological and educational assessment, and if the child attains certain scores, he or she may qualify for special education services. Often, if the IQ score falls below a certain point that is consistent with the child's academic performance, he or she may then be eligible for placement in classes for the mentally retarded. As a result, however, the IQ has been emphasized as the primary, if not single, criterion for placing children in special education classes (Baroff, 1974). The ultimate criteria for placement in special classes or institutions are usually determined by state education guidelines and are influential in a school district receiving state funds for special education services.

The procedures for placing children in special classes have become the subject of much controversy in recent years. For example, in the *Larry P.* v. *Riles* court case, the use of the IQ score in determining special class placement was challenged. Although "Larry P." obviously functioned well in his environment, his IQ score would indicate that he should have been placed in a class for the mentally retarded.

6

Mercer (1972) addressed the issue of the psychometric criterion as a determinant of mental retardation, particularly in reference to minority groups. Her position was that there are biases in our present measures of intelligence that favor the Anglo, middle class child. She concluded that

> the primary criterion for mental retardation—the IQ test—is inaccurate and, when it is used on minority groups, unfair. However retardation is measured, minority groups suffer as a result of the Anglo, middle-class content of the tests. . . . While the schools do most of the labeling, they do not agree with other agencies on the proper criteria for mental retardation. (p. 44)

As a result, Mercer contended that many misdiagnoses and placement errors can occur from emphasizing only the IQ score without reference to adaptive behavior.

Adaptive behavior is a concept that has been emphasized in recent years as being essential to the definition of mental retardation. *Adaptive behavior* is defined as the "effectiveness or degree with which the individual meets the standards of personal independence and social responsibilities expected of his age and cultural group" (Grossman, 1973, p. 11). The American Association on Mental Deficiency (AAMD) includes adaptive behavior in the definition of mental retardation: "Mental retardation refers to significantly subaverage intellectual functioning existing concurrently with deficits in adaptive behavior and manifested during the developmental period" (Grossman, 1973, p. 11).

The AAMD definition thus stresses that both IQ and adaptive behavior have equal importance in describing and defining mental retardation. This is a significant and apparently justifiable alteration of the historical unitary emphasis on the IQ score in defining mental retardation. A child who has a low IQ score, but functions well in his or her environment, should not be classified as mentally retarded. A familiar example is the Black ghetto child who may score relatively low on IQ tests in comparison to others of similar age, but has learned to function quite well in daily living. According to the AAMD definition, such a child should not be diagnosed mentally retarded.

Since both IQ and adaptive behavior are important in the definition of mental retardation and education of mentally retarded children, we were interested in determining whether or not there is consistency in state education agencies' definitions of mental retardation. Thus, we attempted to obtain information about various education guidelines in order to analyze current trends and practices. Although it was anticipated that some states would be in the process of revising their guidelines, we were still interested in the consistency and accuracy of these procedures.

METHOD

A letter was sent to all the state departments of education including the District of Columbia specifically requesting material on the definition and classification of all types of exceptionality used in their programs. Of 51 requests, 36 responses were received. A second letter and followup phone calls to the remaining 15 produced 5 additional responses. The data were compiled and the definitions analyzed as to whether they included IQ and/or adaptive behavior, and, if so, what the specific criteria were for each. A review of the literature for related research failed to locate any similar compilation of data, except for one reference dealing with definitions of legal voting privileges of the retarded (Olley & Ramey, 1978).

RESULTS

Of the 41 guidelines, 8 quoted the AAMD definition, while 6 employed slight modifications of it—usually altering only a few words. Twenty-seven states reported their own definitions, none of which were the same. Iowa used the term *mental disability*, but the definition was similar to the others, and included both IQ and adaptive behavior. All states except Alaska included the concept of deficient intellectual ability as a prime characteristic of mental retardation. Alaska defined *mental retardation* as generally deficient functioning with no specific reference to IQ or adaptive behavior.

Fifteen states did not give specific criteria for IQ scores, 13 used standard deviation measures, 12 used an IQ of 80 or less, and one used combinations of both. IQ score ranges varied a great deal from state to state, although several criteria included an IQ of 75 (including an error estimate of 5 points) as the delineating score.

Nine states elaborated on the intelligence concept by proposing that mentally retarded children have a fraction of the intellectual capacity of an average child. A frequent statement was that children with IQ scores of 50 to 75 have one-half to three-fourths the intellectual capacity of an average child. This is a misinterpretation of the IQ score, since the IQ is actually based upon an interval scale of measurement. With an interval scale, there is no

TABLE 1

Summary of States' Guidelines Concerning IQ and Adaptive Behavior in the Mentally Retarded

State	Date of guidelines	Type of definition	Intelligence criteria	Include adaptive behavior in definition	Adaptive behavior criteria indicated	Adaptive behavior measures indicated	Incorrect use of ratio IQ concept
Alabama	1973	Other	30-80-IQ	No	No	No	Yes
Alaska	1975	Other	Not specified	Yes	No	No	No
Arizona	1977	Other	Not specified	No	No	No	No
Arkansas	1977	Other	≤ −2.0 S.D.	Yes	No	Yes	Yes
Colorado	1976	Similar	≤ −1.75 S.D.	Yes	No	No	No
Connecticut	1976	Other	Not specified	No	No	No	No
Delaware	1974	Other	Not specified	No	No	No	No
District of Columbia	Not specified	AAMD & BEH	≤ −2.0 S.D.	Yes	No	No	No
Florida	1976	AAMD	≤ −2.0 S.D.	Yes	Yes	Yes	No
Georgia	1975	Similar	≤ −2.0 S.D.	Yes	No	No	Yes
Hawaii	1966	Other	Not specified	No	No	No	Yes
Idaho	1975	Similar	≤ 75 IQ	Yes	No	No	Yes
Illinois	1976	Other	Not specified	Yes	No	No	No
Indiana	1973	Other	≤ 75 IQ	No	No	No	Yes
Iowa	1974	Other	≤ 1.0 S.D.	Yes	No	No	No
Kansas	1976	Other	Not specified	Yes	No	No	No
Kentucky	1975	Other	Not specified	No	No	No	No
Maine	Draft	Other	Not specified	No	No	No	No
Michigan	1973	Other	Not specified	Yes	No	Yes	No
Missouri	1976	AAMD	≤ −2.0 S.D.	Yes	No	No	Yes
Montana	Not specified	Similar	≤ 75 IQ ≤ −1.6 S.D.	Yes	No	No	No
Nebraska	1975	Other	Not specified	Yes	No	No	No
Nevada	1976	Other	≤ 75 IQ	No	No	No	No
New Hampshire	1976	Other	Not specified	No	No	No	No
New Jersey	1976	Other	≤ −1.5 S.D.	Yes	No	No	No
New York	1975	Other	≤ −1.5 S.D.	No	No	No	No
North Dakota	1976	Other	≤ 75 IQ	No	No	No	No
Ohio	1973	Other	≤ 80 IQ	No	No	No	No
Oklahoma	1976	Other	≤ 75 IQ	No	No	No	No
Oregon	1976	AAMD	≤ −2.0 S.D.	Yes	No	Yes	No
Pennsylvania	1976	Similar	≤ 80 IQ	Yes	No	No	No
Rhode Island	1963	Other	Not specified	Yes	No	No	No
South Carolina	1972	Other	≤ 70 IQ	Yes	No	Yes	Yes
South Dakota	1974	Similar	Not specified	Yes	No	No	No
Tennessee	1976-77	Other	Not specified	Yes	No	No	Yes
Utah	1975	AAMD	≤ 75 IQ	Yes	No	Yes	No
Virginia	1972	Other	≤ −2.0 S.D.	No	No	No	No
Washington	1976	Other	≤ 75 IQ	Yes	Yes	No	No
West Virginia	1974	AAMD	≤ 75 IQ	Yes	No	Yes	No
Wisconsin	Not specified	AAMD	≤ −2.0 S.D.	Yes	No	No	No
Wyoming	1975	AAMD	≤ −2.0 S.D.	Yes	No	No	No

Key to abbreviations:

AAMD = American Association on Mental Deficiency
BEH = Bureau of Education for the Handicapped

Other = definition other than AAMD & BEH
S.D. = standard deviation(s)
Similar = similar to AAMD definition, with only minor variations
≤ = less than or equal to

6

zero point and thus a "zero" IQ does not exist. To say that a child has fractional ability is to assume a ratio scale with an absolute zero point, implying that there are upper and lower measurable limits to intelligence. To our knowledge, no one has yet concluded that either of these phenomena exist.

Of the 27 states who did not use the AAMD definition, 26 made some reference to adaptive behavior or a similar concept. Thus, it would appear that some attention is being given to adaptive behavior. However, many states listed the instruments used to measure IQ, but few indicated those used to assess adaptive behavior. Of the states who did not mention or include adaptive behavior, five referred to it more indirectly as "deficiencies in social adjustment" (a term that was often not defined). We concluded that *social adjustment* refers essentially to adaptive behavior, while assessment of social maladjustment typically is accomplished by such traditional methods as personality testing and observation. No standards or criteria were presented, however, in the data furnished. (See Table 1 for a summary of the data.)

DISCUSSION

The analysis of the data suggests that there are some serious inconsistencies between states in their definitions of mental retardation, and some important omissions concerning the role and assessment of adaptive behavior. It seems possible, under current conditions, for a child to be classified as mentally retarded in one state and not in another, if IQ is used as the primary criterion. Furthermore, even if two children have the same IQ, that is, less than 70, they might not be classified as retarded if their adaptive behavior levels are not the same.

As the situation presently exists, professionals in the education and care of the mentally retarded may unknowingly be contributing to some of the problems that Binet and Simon were trying to correct:

> In the absence of definite guidelines, they [Binet and Simon] indicate that decisions are apt to be haphazard, subjective and uncontrolled. Though some such decisions may turn out to be just and correct, just as often they will be merely capricious. . . . One of the drawbacks recognized by Binet and Simon in this lack of agreement was in comparative statistics from place to place and country to country. If there is such disagreement in medical diagnosis, how may incidence figures for deficiency be compared from country to country? What will be the meaning of school records

where children have widely divergent terminology applied to essentially the same conditions? (Edwards, 1971, p. 22).

It appears that, with the obvious inconsistencies among state guidelines, a problem exists similar to that considered by Binet and Simon. Admittedly, the situation is not as severe as it was when Binet and Simon began their work. The improvement of testing techniques and measurement have facilitated the assessment of exceptional children. Nevertheless, special educators still need to ask similar questions. If, as a result of these diverse criteria, the field cannot agree on the definition of mental retardation, how can it make comparisons, compile incidence figures, and evaluate the effectiveness of educational/remedial programs? More importantly, how can teachers be confident that they are providing the best appropriate education for a child needing special help?

This article has discussed some of the historical developments of IQ testing, the inadequacy of the IQ score alone in diagnosis, the concept of adaptive behavior, and the definition of mental retardation. One may conclude that, although adaptive behavior has been established as a necessary consideration in diagnosing the mentally retarded, it is all too frequently ignored. The reasons why professionals do not systematically consider adaptive behavior remain unexplained.

As the states continue to revise their definitions, the data from this study may eventually be outdated. Nevertheless, they indicate the present state of the issue, and may serve as a barometer for determining whether states actually are becoming more responsible in addressing the IQ/adaptive behavior issue.

CONCLUSIONS

After interpreting the guidelines, the following conclusions may be made: (a) all definitions of mental retardation should be the same from state to state and correspond with that given by the AAMD or some similar standard; (b) these definitions should include both the concepts of adaptive behavior and IQ; (c) adaptive behavior should be objectively determined; (d) adaptive behavior criteria should be established at minimum levels, as is the IQ; and (e) these criteria should be used with IQ in the identification of the mentally retarded.

To include adaptive behavior in state definitions, to measure it, and to implement it in educational planning will be beneficial in helping to better identify mentally retarded students and meet their educational needs and in helping to prevent further misuse of the IQ. Only when consistent, systematic attention is given to intelligence and adaptive behavior will special educators begin to approach an adequate description of and programing for the mentally retarded. The time has come to include adaptive behavior as well as IQ in the definition of mental retardation. This position will not be a panacea to the diagnosis and education of the mentally retarded. It is apparent, however, that a systematic, comprehensive approach to adaptive behavior will help to alleviate some of the problems discussed. Educators should give serious consideration to adaptive behavior for mentally retarded students in the public schools. The concept is already well established, and there are ways of measuring it. Baroff (1974) suggested that sufficient norms exist based upon mental age, chronological age, and degree of retardation. These norms indicate rough behavioral expectations that can be useful in describing the range of adaptive behavior.

Binet's goal of the correct identification of mentally retarded individuals and appropriate educational planning for them is a worthy objective. The state departments of education are in a position to demonstrate this leadership.

REFERENCES

Baroff, G. S. *Mental retardation: Nature, cause, and management.* New York: Wiley & Sons, 1974.

Edwards, A. J. *Individual mental testing: Part I. History and theories.* Scranton PA: International Textbook Co., 1971.

Exhibit A: IQ trial. Plaintiffs take the stand. *APA Monitor,* December 1977, *8*(12), pp. 4-5.

Grossman, H. (Ed.). *Manual on terminology and classification in mental retardation.* (Special Publication No. 2). Washington DC: American Association on Mental Deficiency, 1973.

Mercer, J. I.Q.: The lethal label. *Psychology Today,* September 1972, *6*, pp. 44: 46-47; 95-97.

Olley, J. G., & Ramey, G. Voter participation of retarded citizens in the 1976 presidential election. *Mental Retardation,* 1978, *16*, 255-258.

6

MENTALLY RETARDED

Intellectual and Special Aptitudes of Tenth Grade EMH Students

by Marley W. Watkins

Abstract: Special aptitude scores of a group of 84 tenth-grade Educable Mentally Handicapped (EMH) students were obtained with the Nonreading Aptitude Test Battery (NATB) while intelligence was quantified with the Wechsler Intelligence Scale for Children-Revised (WISC-R). It was hypothesized that aptitudes would emerge from the NATB which would have been overlooked by sole reliance on the WISC-R. Low to moderate correlations between NATB and WISC-R scores prevented immediate extraction of aptitudes independent of intelligence but cross-tabulations of NATB aptitude scores across IQ levels revealed that students often scored at average or above levels on such NATB factors as Form Perception, Clerical Perception, Spatial, and Dexterity. It was concluded that EMH students possess a variety of special aptitudes which could broaden their vocational choice and dissipate the myths surrounding their place in the world of work.

It has long been known that mentally retarded persons could take part in the useful work of society (Cowdry, 1922), and a new appreciation is growing that mentally retarded workers may have a more extensive work potential than was previously thought possible (Blackman & Siperstein, 1968; Gold, 1973). However, efforts to predict this work potential have generally been restricted to standardized intelligence tests that may not adequately measure other specific abilities crucial for vocational prediction for retarded persons (Taylor, 1964). Perhaps because of this oversight, stereotypes of mentally retarded persons persist.

Standardized tests of vocational aptitude have been developed to sample a wide range of abilities and have found wide use with general populations but have been considered to be inappropriate with even the

borderline retarded (Neff, 1966). For example, the General Aptitude Test Battery (GATB) is reported to be the most highly validated multiple aptitude test battery in existence for use in vocational guidance (U.S. Department of Labor, 1970a,b), but is designed for persons with a sixth-grade education and may not appropriately serve people with educational handicaps (Cronbach, 1970). An alternative to the GATB, the Nonreading Aptitude Test Battery (NATB), was developed by the U.S. Department of Labor (1971) to measure essentially the same aptitudes as the GATB but within a disadvantaged population. Although not specifically normed on a mentally retarded sample, the NATB seems to hold promise for use with mentally retarded persons. It has been successfully used to select vocational trainees from an institutionalized men-

TABLE 1

Nine NATB Aptitudes and a Brief Description of Each

Attitude	Description
G—Intelligence	General learning ability
V—Verbal	Ability to understand meaning of words and to use them effectively
N—Numerical	Ability to perform arithmetic operations quickly and accurately
S—Spatial	Ability to think visually of geometric forms and the movement of objects in space
P—Form Perception	Ability to perceive pertinent detail in objects, pictorial, or graphic material
Q—Clerical Perception	Ability to perceive pertinent detail in verbal or tabular material
K—Motor Coordination	Ability to coordinate eyes and hands or fingers to make a movement response accurately and swiftly
F—Finger Dexterity	Ability to manipulate small objects with the fingers, rapidly and accurately
M—Manual Dexterity	Ability to work with the hands in placing and turning motions

tally retarded population (Carbuhn & Wells, 1973) and its application with EMH and borderline intelligence high school students reveals that NATB scores can be viewed more positively than GATB scores and can provide valuable counseling information (Halloran, 1974; Hull & Halloran, 1976).

The present investigation used the NATB with a group of 10th-grade educable mentally handicapped (EMH) students and was designed to display vocational aptitude scores in relation to intelligence test scores. It was hypothesized that aptitudes would emerge from the NATB which would have been overlooked by reliance on intelligence test scores alone, and that these aptitudes could be presented as a method to use in dispelling the myths which equate subaverage general intellectual functioning with inability to perform other than menial work tasks.

Method

Subjects

Subjects were 84 tenth-grade EMH students, identified by state certified school psychologists, receiving special education services in a large urban Southwestern high school district. The students ranged in age from 15 to 18.5 years (Mean = 16.3, SD = .7), were members of several racial/cultural groups (56 Anglo, 18 Mexican-American, and 10 black), and were primarily male (55 male and 29 female). Their Wechsler Intelligence Scale for Children-Revised (WISC-R) Full Scale IQ scores ranged from 44 to 84 (Mean = 66.74, SD = 8.87).

Procedure

Ninety-five 10th-grade EMH students were administered the NATB during the fall semester of the school year as part of a routine vocational assessment program. Of this group, 84 students' psychological records contained complete and current WISC-R scores. The remaining 11 students were assessed with alternate instruments, had WISC-R scores more than two years old, or were missing WISC-R data, and so were eliminated from further consideration in the present investigation. NATB testing was accomplished on the students' home campus by two vocational examiners (1 male and 1 female) with the assistance of the students' counselor and/or teachers so that the examiner-to-student ratio ranged from 1:1 to 1:8. Protocols were hand scored with the appropriate scoring keys and the obtained raw scores converted to aptitude scores following procedures outlined in the NATB manual (U.S. Department of Labor, 1971). These aptitude scores were compared to 10th-grade norms for minimum scores "required to perform satisfactorily the major tasks of the groups of occupations identified with each . . . Occupational Aptitude Pattern" (p. 97). Table 1 lists the nine NATB aptitudes and presents a brief explaination of each.

Results

One initial area of interest was to quantify the relationship between NATB and WISC-R scores. This was accomplished by calculating the Pearson product-moment coefficient of correlation among the WISC-R verbal (VIQ), performance (PIQ), and full scale (FSIQ) scores, and the nine NATB factor scores. For a normal population (i.e., the standardization sample), the WISC-R has a mean of 100 and a standard deviation of 15; the

TABLE 2

Correlations Between WISC-R and NATB Factors

	PIQ	FSIQ	G	V	N	S	P	Q	K	F	M
VIQ	.36	.79	.55	.40	.25	.37	.28	.28	.20*	.33	.19*
PIQ		.85	.45	.16*	.44	.45	.67	.40	.24	.44	.36
FSIQ			.61	.33	.42	.51	.59	.43	.27	.49	.36
G				.62	.64	.73	.40	.31	.07*	.28	.26
V					.40	.08*	.02*	.08*	−.05*	−.10*	−.03*
N						.39	.44	.44	.24	.40	.35
S							.51	.31	.08*	.40	.36
P								.56	.39	.48	.49
Q									.45	.36	.49
K										.37	.29
F											.52

Note: $p < .05$ unless marked by * which indicates ns.

NATB, 100 and 20. The resulting correlation matrix is presented in Table 2. The observed low to moderate correlations indicate that WISC-R scores are related to both verbal and performance NATB factor scores so no clearly defined aptitudes, independent of intelligence, could be extracted from this particular comparison.

To extricate NATB aptitudes from intelligence, students' WISC-R scores were divided into five categories to display the number and pattern of average or above NATB factor scores associated with each FSIQ category. These cross-tabulations reveal that 100% of the students with IQ's between 80 and 84, 77% with IQ's between 70 and 79, 45% with IQ's between 60 and 69, and 18% with IQ's between 50 and 59 obtained a score of 100 or larger on at least one NATB factor. Form Perception, Clerical Perception, Spatial, Manual Dexterity, and Finger Dexterity were the NATB factors on which students most often scored at average levels or above. Student NATB mean factor scores were above mean IQ on the Clerical Perception (92.93), Form Perception (92.68), and Spatial (80.85) factors but were essentially equivalent to mean IQ on the other six factors (58.55 to 63.58). Form Perception and Clerical Perception, in particular, appear to be aptitudes which would have been overlooked had the WISC-R not been supplemented by the NATB.

A final cross-tabulation was undertaken to display the number and variety of Occupational Aptitude Patterns (OAP) associated with each FSIQ category. An OAP is a group of occupations having similar aptitude requirements and was formed by the U.S. Department of Labor on the basis of validity

studies and job analysis extrapolations. Sixty-two OAP's are reported for the GATB and NATB (U.S. Department of Labor, 1970b) and thus students could qualify for a total of 62 separate job families. WISC-R FSIQ scores were again divided into five categories and the number of students within each category who qualified for an OAP was tabulated. These cross-tabulations indicate that 100% of the students with IQ's between 80 and 84, 57% with IQ's between 70 and 79, and 34% with IQ's between 60 and 69 qualified for at least one OAP while only those students with FSIQ's below 60 failed to qualify for at least one family of jobs. Overall, 40% of these students qualified for at least one OAP and aggregately they qualified for 39 of the possible 62 job families.

Discussion

People with low general intelligence may have average or high ability in other aptitudes yet there is still a tendency to rely on intelligence tests and stereotypic notions when considering retarded people for employment. The present investigation revealed a relationship between WISC-R and NATB aptitude scores of low to moderate magnitude for this group of EMH students who often scored at average or above levels on such NATB factors as Form Perception, Clerical Perception, Spatial, and Dexterity. These results are similar to those reported by Murray (1956) where the GATB was used and to those published by Hull and Halloran (1976) where the NATB was used. They also parallel the dichotomy of intellectual abilities versus special abilities formulated by Nunnally (1978). Thus, while performing at subaverage levels in the intellectual class of aptitudes, many students performed at average or better levels in the special class of aptitudes. This special ability was reflected in OAP qualification rates where 40% of the students met cutting-point scores for at least one OAP and where, as a group, they qualified for 39 of the possible 62 OAP's.

Present results suggest that EMH students possess a variety of special aptitudes which are sufficient in many cases to qualify them for several job families if no other factors are considered. It is obvious, however, that a diverse array of factors other than intellectual and special aptitudes may be closely related to prediction of vocational success: social, economic, personality, physical, interest, educational, training, and experience, to name only a few. None of these factors can be arbitrarily omitted when considering vocational prediction but no single factor should be sufficient to cause a priori narrowing of the deliberation process. A more complete consideration of all factors (intellectual, special, and others) will serve to broaden the vocational choice of mentally retarded workers and to dissipate the myths surrounding their place in the world of work.

References

Blackman, L. S., & Siperstein, G. N. Job analysis and the vocational evaluation of the mentally retarded. *Rehabilitation Literature*, 1968, *29*, 103–105.

Carbuhn, W. M., & Wells, I. C. Use of Nonreading Aptitude Tests (NATB) for selecting mental retardates for competitive employment. *Meas-urement and Evaluation in Guidance*, 1973, *5*, 460–466.

Cowdry, C. M. Measures of general intelligence as indices of success in trade learning. *Journal of Applied Psychology*, 1922, *6*, 311–330.

Cronbach, L. J. *Essentials of psychological testing.* New York: Harper & Row, 1970.

Gold, M. Research on the vocational rehabilitation of the retarded: The present, the future. *International Review of Research in Mental Retardation*, 1973, *6*, 97–147.

Halloran, W. D. The validity of the Nonreading Aptitude Test Battery for educable mentally retarded and borderline intelligence students (Doctoral Dissertation, University of Connecticut, 1974). *Dissertation Abstracts International*, 1974, *34*, 2132A–2133A.

Hull, M., & Halloran, W. The validity of the Nonreading Aptitude Test Battery for the mentally handicapped. *Educational and Psychological Measurement*, 1976, *36*, 547–552.

Murray, E. The vocational potential of the retarded. *Vocational Guidance Quarterly*, 1956, *4*, 87–89.

Neff, W. S. Problems of work evaluation. *Personnel and Guidance Journal*, 1966, *44*, 682–688.

Nunnally, J. C. *Psychometric theory.* New York: McGraw-Hill, 1978.

Taylor, J. B. The structure of ability in the lower intellectual range. *American Journal of Mental Deficiency*, 1964, *68*, 766–774.

U.S. Department of Labor. *Manual for the General Aptitude Test Battery. Section III: Development.* Washington, D.C.: U.S. Government Printing Office, 1970 (a)

U.S. Department of Labor. *Manual for the General Aptitude Test Battery. Section II: Norms, occupational aptitude pattern structure.* Washington, D.C.: U.S. Government Printing Office, 1970. (b)

U.S. Department of Labor. *Manual for the Nonreading Aptitude Test Battery. Section I: Administration, scoring, and interpretation.* Washington, D.C.: U.S. Government Printing Office, 1971.

6

MENTALLY RETARDED

Teaching Moderately and Severely Handicapped Adolescents To Shop in Supermarkets Using Pocket Calculators

by Jill Wheeler, Alison Ford, John Nietupski, Ruth Loomis and Lou Brown

Abstract: Seven moderately and severely handicapped adolescents based in a regular middle school were involved in an instructional program designed to teach selected independent supermarket shopping skills. At the end of one year of instruction (June, 1978) three students completed the program. That is, after a parent dictated a 10-item list of groceries, the students could make a grocery list, go to an actual supermarket, purchase the items, and bring them home. Three students required additional instruction and completed the program by December, 1978. The results suggest that moderately and severely handicapped students can and should be exposed to educational curricula and service delivery models that result in the acquisition and performance of age-appropriate functional skills in natural community environments.

Educational programs for moderately and severely handicapped students should arrange for the acquisition and performance of many of the skills necessary to function as independently as possible in a wide variety of current and subsequent natural environments (Brown, Branston, Baumgart, Vincent, Falvey, & Schroeder, 1979; Brown, Nietupski, & Hamre-Nietupski, 1976). One curriculum domain that should be included in educational programs for moderately and severely handicapped students is referred to here as the Community Functioning Domain (Brown, Branston, Hamre-Nietupski, Pumpian, Certo, & Gruenewald, 1978). Recently, instructional programs have been reported in which moderately and severely handicapped students have been taught such community functioning skills as bus riding (Certo, Schwartz, & Brown, 1975), street crossing (Vogelsberg & Rusch, 1979) and telephone use (Nietupski & Williams, 1976). An additional skill area within the Community Functioning Curriculum Domain is supermarket shopping. Supermarket shopping skills have both immediate and long term functional utility in that students presently can use such skills to engage in an important family activity, and that such skills will allow students to function more independently in group homes or other community based domestic environments in the future.

Nonhandicapped adolescents typically develop the skills necessary to shop in supermarkets without specific and direct training provided by educators. Severely handicapped adolescents, however, need to be specifically taught to perform such essential independent living skills. This paper describes an instructional program designed for specific moderately and severely handicapped adolescents and implemented in the Madison Metropolitan School District. More specifically, students were taught the skills necessary to print a shopping list in response to cues provided by one of their parents, locate needed items in a supermarket, determine the cost of the items, determine whether they had enough money to cover total cost using a pocket calculator, and pay for the items at the checkout counter.

The decision to teach the use of pocket calculators was made for at least four major reasons. First, while the students had acquired several rudimentary paper and pencil addition, subtraction, and coin counting skills, the performance of these skills in natural environments required a great deal of time and supervision and thus was functionally inefficient. In addition, the skills in their repertoires were not adequate for shopping independently for grocery items totaling several dollars or more. The use of the pocket calculator is a more efficient computational strategy and allows the use of rudimentary math and money skills in highly functional ways. Second, the use of a pocket calculator in a public facility is associated with little negative social stigmata. In fact nonhandicapped shoppers are often observed totaling the cost of their purchases using such devices. Third, the pocket calculators are relatively inexpensive. Fourth, the calculators are small and convenient to transport and thus can be used in a variety of other shopping and related activities and environments.

This instructional program also included teaching skills necessary to prepare and use a shopping list. The decision to include the preparation and use of a shopping list was made for two major reasons. First, shopping lists are widely used by nonhandicapped persons so negative stigmata are rarely attached to their use. Second, the use of lists allows the purchase of a greater number of actually needed items than would reliance upon memory skills alone. It should be noted that the shopping lists contain preprinted category headings that coincided with the printed aisle headings consistently utilized by a large supermarket chain in the state of Wisconsin; that the students were taught to print the names of selected nontaxable food items on

their shopping lists beneath the printed category aisle headings; that initially the names of the food items to be purchased at the supermarket were dictated by the teacher; and that as the students started to demonstrate criterion performance in instructional environments, their parents were asked to dictate lists of needed food items at home and the students were taught to actually purchase those items.

Method[1]

Students

Seven ambulatory students, six females, were involved in the program. Chronological ages at the initiation of the program ranged from 13-3 to 17-3 ($\bar{X} = 15$-2). Obtained IQ scores ranged from 38 to 53 ($\bar{X} = 45$). Student records contain the following labels: trainable mentally retarded; moderately retarded; severely retarded; severely handicapped. In order to avoid both the outdated term "trainable mentally retarded" and the artificial categorical systems fostered by the use of IQ scores (i.e., moderate, severe, profound) the students are referred to as moderately, and severely handicapped. In accordance with Bellamy, Horner and Inman (1979) the labels moderately and severely handicapped are ascribed to students who require intensive, systematic, and longitudinal instruction even for the acquisition of only rudimentary skills. Since the students in this program rarely perform at acceptable criteria from casual, unplanned, and episodic exposure, the labels moderately and severely handicapped seem appropriate.

All seven were members of a self-contained classroom for moderately and severely handicapped students based in a regular middle school in the Madison Metropolitan School District and had been in public school educational programs for at least five years prior to the initiation of the program. Table 1 contains a summary of the CA, IQ score, and superficial medical information.

Relevant Entry Skill Clusters

The seven students exhibited at least the following skill clusters prior to the initiation

[1] Space limitations do not permit a detailed presentation of the entire instructional program. For more detailed information regarding the skill analyses of each strand, instructional materials, specific teaching procedures, data collection strategies, cumulative student performance, etc., the reader is referred to Wheeler, Ford, Nietupski, and Brown, 1979.

TABLE 1

CA, IQ, and Medical Information Concerning Students Involved in the Program

Student	Sex	CA	IQ Score	Medical Information
S_1	F	13-3	53	No medical diagnosis available
S_2	F	13-3	44	Down's Syndrome
S_3	F	16-9	42	Brain Damaged
S_4	F	13-7	48	Down's Syndrome
S_5	M	17-0	49	Epileptic
S_6	F	17-3	38	Down's Syndrome
S_7	F	15-0	43	Down's Syndrome

of the program:

1. They could locate the matching numeral when the teacher presented a random array of the numerals 0–9, displayed a printed numeral which was identical to one of the numerals in the array, and said, "Touch/where is/show me another number like this."
2. They could verbally label 30 packaged grocery items when presented with each of the items and the verbal cue, "What is this?/Tell me what this is."
3. They could print each letter of the alphabet in either lower case or upper case when the teacher said, "Print/write the alphabet."
4. They could touch the price on packaged food items when asked, "Where is the price?"
5. They could sort money from things that were not money when given money and non-money items.
6. They could demonstrate some understanding of the use of money by responding to the question, "What is money used for?" by indicating that money is used "to buy things," or the equivalent.

The design of the program did not allow the authors to determine whether the skill clusters described above were empirical prerequisites. However, they appeared, at least, to facilitate acquisition of the skills of concern.

Instructional Objectives

The instructional program was divided into the following strands:

Strand Ia: Teaching students to perform selected calculator related subtraction skills.

Strand Ib: Teaching students to perform selected food classification skills.

Strand IIa: Teaching students to utilize selected food classification skills and calculator related subtraction skills to purchase non-taxable food items in a simulated classroom supermarket.

Strand IIb: Teaching students to utilize selected food classification skills and calculator related subtraction skills to purchase non-taxable food items in an actual supermarket.

Strand III: Verifying that students can utilize selected food classification skills and calculator related subtraction skills to purchase nontaxable food items in an actual supermarket when directed to do so by parents.

Concurrent instruction was provided on the skills delineated in Strands Ia and Ib. Once students acquired these skills, concurrent instruction was provided on Strands IIa and IIb. That is, students received instruction in a simulated classroom supermarket (Strand IIa) *while* they received instruction, *not prior to* receiving instruction, in an actual supermarket. Upon completion of Strands IIa and IIb, student performance of the supermarket shopping skills in the presence of parents (Strand III) was verified.

The terminal objectives for each instructional strand are provided below. It should be noted that each strand was further analyzed so that students might acquire the supermarket shopping skills in a sequential fashion.

Terminal Objective for Strand Ia: When students are presented with (a) a whole dollar amount of money from $1 to $10, (b) a pocket calculator, and (c) as many as 10 price marked food items, they will engage in the following sequence of actions across two consecutive measurement probes:

Count the amount of money given;
Activate the calculator;
Enter the amount of money given on their calculator;
Locate the price of each item;
Use the calculator to *consecutively subtract*[2] the price of each item; and
Determine which of the 10 items they have enough money to purchase.

Terminal Objective for Strand Ib: When the teacher dictates the labels of up to 10 nontaxable food items, students will engage in the following sequence of actions within a 45-minute time period across two consecutive measurement probes:

Print the labels of the 10 food items under the appropriate aisle headings printed on their shopping lists;

Verbally label the food items to be purchased;

Locate the appropriate aisle headings in a simulated classroom supermarket; and

Obtain each item on the 10 item list in a sequence in which items from one aisle heading are obtained prior to items from subsequent aisle headings.

Terminal Objective for Strand IIa: When students are presented with (a) a whole dollar amount of money from $1 to $10, (b) a shopping list containing the labels of up to 10 nontaxable food items previously printed by the students, and (c) a pocket calculator, they will engage in the following sequence of actions within a 30-minute time period across two consecutive measurement probes in a simulated classroom supermarket:

Verbally label the food items printed on their shopping lists;

[2] *Consecutive subtraction* refers to a procedure whereby students successively subtract the cost of each food item as those items are obtained. For example, if students are given $2.00 and required to purchase 2 items which cost $.59 and $.75 respectively, they will enter the given amount on their calculators ($2.00), subtract the cost of the first obtained item ($.59), reach a subtotal ($1.41), and upon obtaining the second item, subtract its cost from the subtotal reaching the final subtotal ($.66). Should the subtraction of subsequent items result in a negative number, students were taught to return that item to the shelf and proceed to the checkout counter.

Count the money given and enter the total amount on the calculator;

Obtain a shopping cart;

Maneuver the shopping cart up and then down each aisle of the simulated class-room supermarket utilizing the aisle headings on the right to locate the listed food items and obtain all food items listed under one aisle heading prior to obtaining food items listed under the subsequent aisle headings;

Use calculators to *consecutively subtract* the price of each food item; and

Retain only those food items that they have enough money to purchase.

Upon obtaining the food items for which they have enough money, students will:

Take the shopping cart to the checkout lane;

Remove all items from the shopping cart, and place them on the checkout counter;

Give the money to the cashier;

Receive the change (if any) and place the

change in purses/wallets/pockets; and

Leave the simulated classroom supermarket with the groceries.

Terminal Objective for Strand IIb: When students are presented with (a) whole dollar amount of money from $1 to $10, (b) a shopping list containing the labels of up to 10 nontaxable food items previously printed by the students, and (c) a pocket calculator, they will engage in the sequence of actions described in Strand IIa within 30 minutes, across two consecutive measurement probes in an actual supermarket.

Terminal Objective for Strand III: When a parent (a) presents his/her child with a shopping list, (b) dictates a list of 10 non-taxable food items chosen from the 30 items used in Strands I and II, (c) presents a calculator and a whole dollar amount of money less than $10, which is *less* than the amount of money needed to purchase all the listed food items[3], and (d) provides trans-portation to an actual supermarket, his/her child will independently engage in the sequence of actions delineated in Strand IIa within 30 minutes.

Instructional Materials and Teaching Arrangements

While the program was designed to teach the performance of shopping skills in actual supermarkets, it seemed necessary and appropriate to conduct a majority of the instructional sessions in simulation. The simulated supermarket in the classroom consisted of four aisles of shelves "stocked" with items found in actual supermarkets. Included on the shelves were both actual grocery items and empty containers. Category headings corresponding to the headings in the actual supermarket were constructed of tagboard and suspended from the ceiling above the shelves containing the correspond-ing grocery items. An actual shopping cart, borrowed from the supermarket, was utilized. Students used pocket calculators their parents purchased prior to the initiation of the program. Real money ($1 and $5 bills) was utilized in both the simulated and actual supermarket environments. In Strand Ia instruction took place at tables in the class-

[3] A whole dollar amount of money *less* than that required to purchase all items on a list was provided in an attempt to insure that the calculator was used to determine which items they could actually afford.

6

TABLE 2

Summary of Objectives Realized

| Stu-dents | Strand Ia Calculator Use Phases | | | | | | Strand Ib Food Classi-fication Phases | | Strand IIa Simulated store Phases* | | | | Strand IIb Actual Store, Teacher Dictated Phases* | | | | Strand III Actual Store, Parent Dictated |
	I	II	III	IV	V	VI	I	II	I	II	III	IV	I	II	III	IV	
S_1	X	X	X	X	X	X	X	X	X	X	X	X	X	X	X	X	Criterion reached in December, 1978
S_2	X	X	X	X	X	X	X	X	X	X			X	X			Student was transferred to a high school before criterion was reached.
S_3	X	X	X	X			X	X	X	X	X	X	X	X	X	X	Criterion reached in December, 1978
S_4	X	X	X	X	X	X	X	X	X	X	X	X	X	X	X	X	Criterion reached in June, 1978
S_5	X	X	X	X	X	X	X	X	X	X	X	X	X	X	X	X	Criterion reached in June, 1978
S_6	X	X	X	X	X	X	X	X	X	X	X	X	X	X	X	X	Criterion reached in June, 1978
S_7	X	X	X	X	X	X	X	X	X	X	X	X	X	X	X	X	Criterion reached in December, 1978

* Phases I through IV refer to the number of grocery items students were to purchase (3, 5, 7 and 10, respectively).

room. In Strand Ib and IIa, instruction took place in the simulated classroom supermarket. In Strands IIb and III instruction took place in an actual supermarket.

Instruction and measurement sessions were implemented by the classroom teacher, an instructional aide, university graduate and practicum students, and parents. Several instructors and a variety of verbal language cues were utilized in an attempt to promote criterion performance across persons, places, materials, language cues, etc. (Brown, Branston, Hamre-Nietupski, Pumpian, Certo, & Gruenewald, 1979; Williams, Brown, & Certo, 1975).

Cues and Correction Procedures

The cues and correction procedures used were arranged according to the amount of assistance/intervention required to perform the skills of concern (Falvey, Brown, Lyon, Baumgart, & Schroeder, 1978). Six kinds of cues and correction procedures, arranged from most to the least amount of assistance/intervention, were utilized: primed correction procedures, modeled cues and correction procedures, direct verbal cues and correction procedures, indirect verbal cues and correction procedures, gestural cues and correction procedures, and pictorial cues and correction procedures.

Stimulus fading strategies were utilized until the skills of concern came under the control of a cue or correction procedure that required less assistance/intervention.

Measurement Procedures

Measures of each student's ability to perform the skills delineated in each instructional strand were obtained prior to and during instruction. More specifically, students were pretested on their ability to perform the skills delineated in Strand IIb, the skills necessary to shop in actual supermarkets. Thereafter, a test-teach design was utilized. Students were tested on the terminal objective of each strand and, if necessary, taught to criterion. Measurement probes were administered approximately twice weekly, with criterion performance for each objective established as 100% accuracy across two consecutive probes.

Results and Discussion

Table 2 contains a summary of the instructional objectives reached by each of the seven students. As can be discerned from Table 2, three students (S_4, S_5, and S_6) completed the entire program by June of 1978. That is, three students were taught the food classification and calculator related subtraction necessary to independently purchase as many as 10 nontaxable food items in an actual supermarket when the food items were dictated by parents.

Three students (S_1, S_3 and S_7) completed Strands Ia and Ib, and partially completed Strands IIa and IIb by June of 1978. These three students were taught the skills necessary to independently purchase as many as seven nontaxable food items in an actual supermarket when the names of the items were dictated by their instructors. For these students the program was continued in the fall of 1978. As can be discerned from inspecting Table 2, three (S_1, S_3 and S_7) completed the entire program by December of 1978.

One student (S_2) completed Strands Ia and Ib and made some progress in Strands IIa and IIb by June of 1978. This student was taught the skills necessary to independently purchase as many as five nontaxable food items in an actual supermarket when the names of the items were dictated by an instructor. In the fall of the 1978 S_2 was moved to a high school and her teacher chose not to continue the program.

While the students acquired and performed a number of functional community living skills, there are a number of programmatic limitations that deserve mention. First, the students were taught to locate and purchase only 30 nontaxable food items. These 30 food items were chosen on the basis of inventories of parental buying habits. It was judged that the use of nontaxable food items would minimize the complexity of the supermarket shopping tasks. The list of 30 food items, however, did not contain produce, meat products, or taxable nonfood items (laundry detergent, pet supplies, paper products, soda, etc.) which might be purchased by the members of a "typical household." Obviously, the students should now be taught to purchase both taxable and nontaxable food and nonfood items.[4] Second, students were not taught to prioritize the food items printed on their shopping list. Rather, they were taught to select food items in the order in which they were encountered in the supermarket. Thus,

students might purchase low priority items (e.g., cookies) located in the first aisle and then not have enough money to purchase higher priority items (e.g., bread, milk) located in subsequent aisles. An extension of this program might involve teaching students to prioritize shopping lists and to purchase at least high priority items if enough money to purchase all listed items is not available. Third, students were taught to perform the skills of concern in only *one* actual supermarket. An extension of this program might involve an ecological inventory of other neighborhood supermarkets and instruction in the food classification skills necessary to apply acquired skills in similar but different settings. Fourth, the students exhibited a number of relatively sophisticated entry skill clusters. Additionally, they were taught to label and demonstrate comprehension of over 30 printed words and to print the labels of the food items on their shopping lists. One modification of this program for students who do not exhibit these entry skill clusters and who have limited reading skill repertoires might involve the provision of shopping lists containing printed aisle headings paired with pictures of the corresponding food groups. For example, the printed words "Dry Cereal" might be paired with pictures of several brands and types of dry cereal. A second modification might involve teaching students to circle pictures of dictated food items rather than to print shopping lists.

Finally, the success of this instructional program is interpreted as suggesting that the use of such simple and ordinary adaptive-prosthetic devices as pocket calculators and shopping lists can greatly enhance the potential for independent performance of crucial community functioning skills by adolescent moderately and severely handicapped students with minimally developed math, money, and reading skills. Obviously, care should be taken to avoid the overuse of adaptive/prosthetic devices in that over-reliance might unduly burden students, making their use difficult, inefficient, and possibly embarrassing, and/or promote the unnecessary use of prosthetics in situations where students might be taught to perform the skills of concern without them. On the other hand, the judicious selection of efficient, portable, and nonstigmatizing adaptive/prosthetic devices might provide the initial means by which many moderately and severely handicapped students can be taught to perform a variety of chronological age

[4] Since the completion of this program, a functional procedure for dealing with taxable food items has been developed. The reader interested in such information should contact Jill Wheeler, Madison Metropolitan School District, 545 West Dayton Street, Madison, WI 53703.

6

appropriate functional skills in natural environments.

References

Bellamy, G. T., Horner, R. H. & Inman, D. P. *Vocational habilitation of severely retarded adults.* Baltimore: University Park Press, 1979.

Brown, L., Branston, M. B., Baumgart, D., Vincent, L., Falvey, M., & Schroeder, J. Utilizing the characteristics of a variety of current and subsequent least restrictive environments as factors in the development of curricular content for severely handicapped students. *AAESPH Review,* in press.

Brown, L., Branston, M. B., Hamre-Nietupski, S., Pumpian, I., Certo, N., & Gruenewald, L. A strategy for developing chronological age appropriate and functional curricular content for severely handicapped adolescents and young adults. *Journal of Special Education, 13*(1), 1979, 81–90.

Brown, L., Nietupski, J., & Hamre-Nietupski, S. The criterion of ultimate functioning. In M. A. Thomas (Ed.), *Hey! Don't forget about me.* Reston, Va: Council for Exceptional Children, 1976.

Certo, N., Schwartz, R., & Brown, L. Community transportation: Teaching severely handicapped students to ride a public bus system. In L. Brown, T. Crowner, W. Williams, & R. York (Eds.), *Madison's alternative to zero exclusion: A book of readings* (Vol. V). Madison, Wis.: Madison Public Schools, 1975.

Falvey, M., Brown, L., Lyon, S., Baumgart, D., & Schroeder, J. Curricular strategies for teaching severely handicapped students to acquire and perform chronological age appropriate functional skills in natural environments in response to naturally occurring cues and correction procedures. W. Sailor, B. Wilcox, & L. Brown (Eds.), *Instructional design for the severely handicapped.* Baltimore: Paul H. Brookes, Publishers, in press.

Nietupski, J., & Williams, W. Teaching selected telephone related social skills to severely handicapped students. *Child Study Journal,* 1976. *6*(3), 139–153.

Vogelsberg, R. T., & Rusch, F. R. Training severely handicapped students to cross partially controlled intersections. *AAESPH Reveiw,* 1979, *4,* 264–273.

Wheeler, J., Ford, A., Nietupski, J., & Brown, L. Teaching adolescent moderately/severely handicapped students to use food classification skills and calculator-related subtraction skills to shop in supermarkets. In L. Brown, M. Falvey, D. Baumgart, I. Pumpian, J. Schroeder, & L. Gruenewald (Eds.), *Strategies for teaching chronological age appropriate functional skills to adolescent and young adult severely handicapped students* (Vol. IX, Part 1). Madison, Wis.: Madison Metropolitan School District, 1979.

Williams, W., Brown, L., & Certo, N. Basic components of instructional programs. *Theory Into Practice,* 1975, *14*(2), 123–136.

MENTALLY RETARDED

An Integrative Model For Designing Instructional Programming for Trainable Mentally Retarded Children

by Jimmy D. Lindsey and Frances W. Beck

Special education professionals recognize the need for a valid rationale when designing academic programs for trainable mentally retarded (TMR) children. Burton (1976) stated,

> The early lack of appropriate or well-defined procedures for training was considered to contribute significantly to the limited impact of past efforts in training programs . . . and there has been an emerging and widely acknowledged concern for an instructional system that is based on some sort of educational technology. (p. 139)

According to Mann (1971), research has confirmed the availability of appropriate educational technology through many classical and contemporary learning theories (e.g., Gagné, 1970; Klausmeier, Ghatala, & Frayer, 1974; Thorndike, 1931) and instructional theories (e.g., Bruner, 1966; Glaser, 1962; Skinner, 1968). Examples of teaching technology which can be adopted and applied in the classroom are available (Becker, Engelmann, & Thomas, 1971; Brown, 1973; Williams, Brown & Certo, 1975). In view of the many diverse theories that have been verified by research, it may not be in the best interests of TMR students to adopt one theoretical rationale, especially with respect to concept learning, a task which is very difficult for TMR students.

It is imperative that special educators have a valid rationale for teaching concepts. The adoption and integration of more than one theory might provide a sound theoretical foundation for special education. For example, to create a concept learning foundation we could utilize an instructional and a learning theory in combination. We would select an instructional theory to structure the learning system and to delineate important instructional components, then choose a learning theory to guide the selection of appropriate learning activities and sequence these activities within the instructional system. By adopting and integrating the two theories into an "integrative model," we could "crystallize" the theoretical position of our concept teaching because we logically delineate and sequence our instructional system and learning activities.

Two theories that lend themselves to developing an integrative model are the Instructional Theory by Glaser (1962) and the Concept Learning and Development (CLD) Model by Klausmeier, Ghatala, and Frayer (1974). Glaser's theory is appropriate

6

because it is based on "time-tested" empirical data and it relates psychological theory and research to educational practice. Also, and more importantly for the teacher, the theory prescribes a pragmatic schema that not only structures the learning environment but also structures the development of applied curriculum guides. In contrast, the Klausmeier CLD Model is a relatively new approach to viewing cognition and learning and the procedure teachers should undertake to teach concept formation. The CLD Model's major advantage is that it is hierarchial in nature, i.e., it delineates sequential and higher order levels of cognitive processing. Additionally, the CLD Model provides the special educator with the basis for formulating specific behavioral objectives and designing assessment instruments and procedures.

The integrative model to be presented demonstrates the applicability of integrating two theories for designing concept learning environments. Glaser's theory was selected to structure the instructional environment. His instructional theory identifies three domains— input, instructional system components, and output. The input domain would be the behaviors students bring to the instructional setting. The instructional system domain (a) identifies the teacher's behavioral objective, (b) assesses the student's entering behaviors through pretesting, (c) implements the instructional procedures (IP), and (d) evaluates (through posttesting) students' performance after participating in the instructional procedures. The output domain is student performance as was stated in the behavioral objective.

The CLD Model advanced by Klausmeier et al. directs the selection and sequencing of activities in Glaser's instructional procedures (IP). The CLD Model postulates the use of five domains for concept learning and development: attending to relevant attributes; discrimination of relevant attributes; memory to store relevant attributes; generalization of relevant attributes across changes; and hypothesis testing to identify relevant attributes.

What follows is an example of the application of the integrative model. The specific concept to be taught is the "Stop Sign." A self-contained class with six TMR children, teacher, and teacher aide was the learning environment. Each of the main headings follow Glaser's instructional theory with the CLD Model used to identify and sequence instructional procedures. The instructional procedure (task) is outlined with cogent authoritative sources (theories) cited to document the relationship between the IP selected and the CLD Model.

Input

Subjects were six moderately and severely retarded males in the classroom classified as trainable mentally retarded. An analysis of their cumulative folders revealed the following:

1. Chronological age ranged from 7 years, 5 months to 8 years, 1 month.

2. Mental age ranged from 2 years, 9 months to 4 years, 2 months.

3. Intelligence quotients ranged from 39 to 50 as measured by the WISC-R.

4. Students were sensorially intact, i.e., no motor, visual, or hearing handicaps.

5. Students were capable of communicating needs.

6. Students were ambulatory, i.e., none were dependent upon wheelchairs or dependent upon assistance from peer, teacher, or aide.

7. Students were toilet trained.

System Components

Statement of Behaviorial Objective

Given pictures of a stop sign, a speed limit sign, and a yield sign, each student upon verbal request will identify the stop sign four out of four times within five minutes.

Assessment of Entering Behaviors

Task. The teacher, in a one-to-one relationship with the six students, presented pictures of three signs. She asked each student to point to the "Stop Sign." No student was able to point to the correct sign.

To determine whether or not the students understood the concept "Stop," the teacher asked the students to clap their hands. While the students were clapping, the teacher said, "Stop." All students stopped clapping, which indicated they understood the meaning of the verbal command "Stop."

Theory. Gibson (1969) hypothesized that differentiation of pictured objects is learned as the same distinctive features of real objectives are learned. Therefore, using pictures is a valid procedure for assessment of attainment of the behavior objective.

Instructional Procedures (IP)

Attending Task. The attending tasks

required students to work with a nine-inch plastic stop sign, two pieces of paper, and a red crayon. Students were directed according to the following task requests:

1. Use the stop sign as a templet and trace the outline on both pieces of paper.

2. Color within the outlines (the teacher cuts out the outlines for the students).

3. Go to the front of the room and put one cutout in the red bucket and the other cutout on a nine inch octagonal outline.

4. Go to the front of the room and put the plastic stop sign on an identical plastic stop sign at the front of the room. (No other signs are present, therefore no discrimination occurs at this cognitive level.)

The task ended by playing a game called "Stop." Students marched in place but stopped marching when the teacher held up a stop sign.

Theory. According to Klausmeier et al. (1974), attending to distinctive features must precede all other operations in concept learning. However, retarded children have difficulty with simple concept learning tasks because of their inability to select and attend to relevant stimuli (Luria, 1963). Zeaman and House (1963) have shown, however, that once retarded children attend to the relevant features of a task, they learn at the same rate as normal children. One of the major variables that affect the retardate's attention is the nature of the stimulus (Scott, 1966).

Gibson (1969) postulated that distinctive features selected for students to attend to depend on other objects. The shape and color of stop signs correspond to Gibson's principle of attending and to the concept of relevant stimuli espoused by Zeaman and House (1963). The procedures utilized in the attending task are also supported by Bruner, Oliver, and Greenfield (1966) who found evidence that young children tend to classify on the basis of perceptual attributes, e.g., color, shape, and size.

Discriminating Task. For the discriminating tasks, the students were given a nine-inch plastic stop sign, two pieces of construction paper, and a box of eight colors. Students were given the following directions:

1. Trace the outline of the stop sign on both papers.

2. Color the outline black.

3. Color within the outlines red (the teacher cuts out outlines but in this task the students paste the letters S T O P on the outlines).

4. Go to the front of the room and put one cutout in the correct colored bucket (red, white, or blue).

5. Go to the front of the room and put the nine-inch plastic stop and the other cutout on the correct nine-inch plastic sign. [Stop, speed limit, and yield signs (hexagonal, rectangular, and triangular) are at the front of the room.] This lesson would end with the game described in the attending task.

Theory. Acquiring a concept at the concrete level involves internal representation so that it is recognized as the same object when it is seen and distinguished from similar objects (Klausmeier et al.) Gibson (1969) reported that discrimination between objects is achieved by discovering those features which are present and those features which differ, e.g., color, size, and shape. Additionally, children tend to solve discrimination tasks more readily where both color and form differ than when only one of the dimensions differs (Scott, 1966).

Learning to detect and attend to distinctive features of stimuli is important for the retarded (Zeaman & House, 1963). In the discriminating task presented, students must attend to and discriminate the multiple relevant stimuli, i.e., shape and color. The difficulty that retardates have in discrimination learning is related to limitations in the first tasks of attending.

Memory Task. The tasks to develop memory follow very closely the discrimination tasks. Variation was the multisensory approach designed to accentuate the octagonal shape, the color red, the letters STOP, and the concept "stop" when the sign was presented. Students were given a nine-inch plastic stop sign, two pieces of construction paper, and a box of eight colors. In the memory task students were instructed as follows:

1. Trace the outline of the stop sign on both papers.

2. Color the outlines black.

3. Trace the outlines with your fingers as the teacher said "stop."

4. Color within the outlines red (the teacher cuts out outlines and the students paste the letters S T O P on the outlines).

5. Go to the front of the room and put one cutout in the correct red colored bucket and say, "Red means stop."

6. Go to the front of the room and put the nine-inch plastic sign and the other cutout on the octagonal outline and say, "A stop sign means stop."

These lessons ended with two games. The first game was the same as in the attending and discriminating tasks, but with the variation of students taking turns stopping and marching by holding up the stop sign. The second game involved students walking around the room and stopping in place every time the teacher held up a stop sign.

Theory. The importance of attention and discrimination in establishing memory have been well documented (Zeaman, House, & Orlando, 1958). According to Klausmeier et al., young children rely more heavily than adults on information stored in nonverbal form. Attending and discriminating distinctive features are initial operations in developing a concept. A memory image is the result of these operations, i.e, being able to attend and discriminate.

Children who can spontaneously name the stimuli learn more quickly. Teaching the names of the stimuli to retarded subjects tends to speed their learning, as required in the memory task (Barnett, Ellis, & Pryer, 1960; Cantor & Hottel, 1955). Fernald's (1943) procedure of requiring the child to trace as he repeats the verbal response ensures attention to the relevant and promotes memory of the form dimension.

Generalizing Task. The generalizing tasks began with the teacher taking the students on a field trip. The field trip consisted of stopping the car at stop signs, where safety permitted. The students were required to say, "A stop sign means stop," every time the car stopped at a stop sign. The teacher also parked the car and allowed the students to get out and touch as many stop signs as possible.

When the students returned from the field trip, they constructed a giant STOP sign measuring four feet across. While making the sign, the students listened to taped recordings about Stop signs. Stop sign games were also played around the four foot sign.

Theory. Piaget's (1954) developmental theory asserts that children make auditory and visual pattern associations. Vernon (1970) stated that observations of an object allow for recognitition across projected sizes. Howard and Templeton (1966) and Ghent (1960) found that an individual's ability to recognize an object in different orientations could depend upon the frequency with which an object was seen in various orientations.

Experience with various size signs was necessary for the TMR students to ensure generalizations over size. The generalization tasks provided observations of the stop sign in one of its natural orientations. Perceiving and conceptualizing a stop sign across environmental configurations is also important for generalizing abilities (Williams, Brown,

& Certo, 1975).

Hypothesis Testing Task. The hypothesis testing tasks were one-to-one activities. The teacher utilized 10 signs having various shapes (square, circular, rectangular, triangular, pentagon, etc.) and colors (red, pink, orange, etc.). Students were given the nine-inch plastic sign to facilitate their responding "yes" or "no" to whether or not a sign shown was an actual representation of a stop sign. The task was then repeated, but the second time the students were not given the plastic signs. In addition to the verbalization of "yes" or "no," when the response was no the students were also asked, "Why isn't this a real stop sign?" The different levels of intellectual functioning required the teacher to review the contributing attributes, color (red) and shape (octagonal), with some presentations.

Theory. Klausmeier et al. (1974) accepted and advanced hypothesis testing as a level of cognition necessary for attaining a concept. The concept to be learned was defined by combinations of attributes, and the learner's task was viewed as looking for those attributes which are the basis for correct identification or classification. Shape and color were attributes in this learning situation.

Levine (1966) developed a procedure for directly assessing the nature of the students' hypothesis testing in simple concept identification tasks. He found students used hypothesis testing behavior in conceptual learning. Other researchers have also reported that students' prior experience influences hypothesis testing. The octagonal shape and the color red are salient attributes and the preceding attending, discriminatory, remembering, and generalizing tasks provided valuable prior experiences influencing the students' choices.

Performance Assessment

The teacher assessed (posttested) the students individually. Students were shown three pictures (Stop, Speed Limit, and Yield signs) and were asked to point to the Stop sign. Students were assessed four times. At this point the students should have correctly identified the Stop sign. If a student pointed to the wrong sign, however, that student was reassessed that day. If that student again pointed to an incorrect sign, the student was "recycled" through the IP activities, e.g., attending, discriminating, memory, etc. This "recycling" also dictated that the teacher establish stringent terminal behavior for each IP activity and the CLD cognition domains, as well as utilize additional sensory stimulation (auditory, visual, tactile, and kinesthetic) where possible.

Output is the final domain in Glaser's instructional theory. As would be expected, the teacher is concerned with the behavior acquired in the system, terminal behavior. The validation of that behavior has occurred in the Performance Assessment component. The teacher has used Glaser's instructional system, and terminal behavior as stated in the behavioral objective has been demonstrated. One of the more difficult tasks facing special educators is designing instructional environments to develop TMR children's concept learning. The integrated model presented provides a pedagogical-learning technology that logically structures, sequences, and delineates the instructional environment (Glaser's theory) and the instructional procedures and learning activities (Klausmeier's theory) to promote concept learning. As stated earlier, the literature offers us a number of instructional and learning theories that are applicable for designing instructional programming, as well as helpful reviews and critiques of these theories (e.g., Bigge, 1964; Gage, 1963; Hilgard & Bower, 1966; Snelbecker, 1974). However, as we peruse the literature we must remember that practitioners cannot afford the luxury of relying on one learning theory and that some form of teaching theory should be developed (Snelbecker, 1974). To this end we have also been warned that "theories of teaching need to develop alongside, on a more equal basis with, rather than by inference from, theories of learning" (Gage, 1963, p. 133). The integrative model presented provides a sound theoretical foundation for developing concept learning environments for TMR children because it does not rely on one theory and it attempts to develop a unique pedagogical model based upon sound principles.

References

Barnett, C. D., Ellis, N. R., & Pryer, M. W. Learning in familial and brain-injured defectives. *American Journal of Mental Deficiency*, 1960, *64*, 104–111.

Becker, W. C., Engelmann, S., & Thomas, D. R. *Teaching: A course in applied psychology*. Chicago: Science Research Associates, 1971.

Bigge, M. L. *Learning theories for teachers*. New York: Harper & Row, 1964.

Brown, L. Instructional programs for trainable-level retarded students. In L. Mann & D. Sabatino (Eds.), *The first review of special education* (Vol. 2). Philadelphia: Journal of Special Education Press, 1973.

Bruner, J. S. *Toward a theory of instruction*. Cambridge, Mass: Belknap Press, 1966.

Bruner, J. S., Oliver, R. R., & Greenfield, P. *Studies in cognitive growth*. New York: Wiley, 1966.

Burton, T. A. *The trainable mentally retarded*. Columbus, Ohio: Charles E. Merrill, 1976.

Cantor, G. N., & Hottel, J. V. Discrimination learning in mental defectives as a function of magnitude of food reward and intelligence level. *American Journal of Mental Deficiency*, 1955, *60*, 380–384.

Fernald, G. M. *Remedial techniques in basic school subjects*. New York: McGraw-Hill, 1943.

Gage, N. L. Paradigms for research on teaching. In N. L. Gage (Ed.), *Handbook of research on teaching*. Chicago: Rand McNalley, 1963.

Gagné, R. M. *The conditions of learning* (2nd ed.). New York: Holt, Rinehart, & Winston, 1970.

Ghent, L. Recognition by children of realistic figures presented in various orientations. *Canadian Jounal of Psychology*, 1960, *14*, 249–256.

Gibson, E. J. *Principles of perceptual learning and development*. New York: Appleton-Century-Crofts, 1969.

Glaser, R. Psychology and instructional technology. In R. Glaser (Ed.), *Training research and education*. Pittsburgh: University of Pittsburgh Press, 1962.

Hilgard, E. R., & Bower, H. B. *Theories of learning*. New York: Appleton-Century-Crofts, 1966.

Howard, I. P., & Templeton, W. B. *Human spatial orientation*. New York: Wiley, 1966.

Klausmeier, H. J., Ghatala, E. S., & Frayer, D. A. *Conceptual learning and development: A cognitive view*. New York: Academic Press, 1974.

Levine, M. Hypothesis behavior by humans during discrimination learning. *Journal of Experimental Psychology*, 1966, *71*, 331–338.

Luria, A. R. Psychological studies on mental deficiency in the Soviet Union. In N. R. Ellis (Ed.), *Handbook of mental deficiency*. New York: McGraw-Hill, 1963.

Mann, L. Psychometric phrenology and the new faculty psychology. *Journal of Special Education*, 1971, *5*, 3–14.

Piaget, J. *The construction of reality in the child*. New York: Basic Books, 1954.

Scott, K. G. Engineering attention: Some rules for the classroom. *Education and Training of the Mentally Retarded*, 1966, *1*, 125–129.

Skinner, B. F. *The technology of teaching*. New York: Appleton-Century-Crofts, 1968.

Snelbecker, G. E. *Learning theory, instructional theory, and psychoeducational design*. New York: McGraw-Hill, 1974.

Thorndike, E. L. *Human learning*. New York: Century Company, 1931.

Vernon, M. D. *Perception through experiences*. New York: Barnes & Noble, 1970.

Williams, W., Brown, L., & Certo, N. Basic components of instructional programs. *Theory into Practice*, 1975, *14*, 123–135.

Zeaman, D., & House, B. J. The role of attention in retardate discrimination learning. In N. R. Ellis (Ed.), *Handbook of mental deficiency*. New York: McGraw-Hill, 1963.

Zeaman, D., House, B. J., & Orlando, R. Use of special training conditions in visual discrimination learning with imbeciles. *American Journal of Mental Deficiency*, 1958, *63*, 453–459.

6

MENTALLY RETARDED

A Word List of Essential Career/Vocational Words for Mentally Retarded Students

by Jeffrey Schilit and Mary Lou Caldwell

Abstract: The Delphi Technique was used with 100 professionals involved with or interested in career/vocational education to ascertain the primary 100 words with which mentally retarded students should be conversant prior to their formal entry into the world of work. The first word list distributed contained 300 words. This list was reduced to the third list of 148 words from which was determined the 100 words considered by these professionals to be crucial for the successful transition of mentally retarded children from school to work. The 100 words are presented with implications for both teacher-trainers and teachers of mentally retarded individuals.

According to a recent priority listing by the Department of Health, Education, and Welfare (1976), career education for the handicapped is an area of high interest. Currently, there are several projects operational that concern themselves with the concept of career education. Project PRICE (Programming the Retarded into Career Education) developed appropriate curricular activities and programs to prepare mentally retarded (MR) individuals to enter the world of work and succeed (Brolin, 1976). A second project, funded by BEH to the Teacher Education Division of the Council for Exceptional Children, is Project RETOOL, which has as its purpose the upgrading and updating of the skills, knowledge, and abilities of current university and college special education personnel in two areas: (a) general special education, and (b) career education for the handicapped (Heller, 1977).

Both of these projects deal with and provide services to special education personnel either in public education or in higher education. These projects, however, like many others, are not dealing directly with MR students in relation to the career education concept.

Many studies have been conducted in the area of word association with MR individuals (see Goulet, 1968; Hall, 1971; Kaufman & Prehm, 1966). A search of the literature reveals that little has been done in the area of associations with MR individuals in relation to career education terminology. Goldstein and Mann (1949), Borreca, Burger, Goldstein, and Simches (1953), and Shawn (1962) have separately developed the most comprehensive lists of vocabulary words that have direct implication for career education and MR persons. However, these lists do not differentiate the primary from the secondary or tertiary words that MR individuals must know in order to survive and succeed in a vocational setting. Even the recent publication, *Work Oriented Rehabilitation Dictionary and Synonyms* (1976), does not develop a succinct list of essential terms.

In a study by Gallagher, Baumeister, and Patterson (1968) word association techniques were used to establish norms for institutionalized and noninstitutionalized MR and normal individuals on the Kent-Rosanoff list. The major finding of this study was that the individual's environment and his "educational experience" were the most dramatic influences in relation to the population's word association response to the 100 word list.

One of the major concerns of word association researchers in the field of mental retardation was the feasibility of doing this type of research with institutionalized MR and being able to use the results to develop functional norms. Gerjuoy and Gerjuoy (1965) indicated that word association research was possible with institutionalized MR individuals and that the results of such investigations were capable of norm development. The words used in the Gerjuoy study were the Kent-Rosanoff list which have little or no relevance to career education.

The previous findings indicate the feasibility of word association research involving mentally retarded and normal individuals and the reliability and validity of both the procedures and findings. However, the words used in all of these studies had little or no relevance to career education for educable MR individuals. Similarly, *The Dictionary of Occupational Titles* (1965) and the comprehensive lists by Borreca et al. (1953), Goldstein and Mann (1949), and Shawn (1962) include thousands of words but none of the previously mentioned lists prioritize their words for relevancy, frequency, or commonality. With the current emphasis on career education for the handicapped, similar research is needed in developing a list of words that have direct bearing on career education and vocational training and then replicating the word association studies with various populations using this list.

The intent of this study was to develop a list of 100 essential career/vocational terms needed at graduation by MR students for successful entrance into the world of work.

Method

In order to establish an initial list of words, several sources were searched: Borreca et al. (1953), *The Dictionary of Occupational Titles* (1965) and its Supplements (1965, 1975), Goldstein and Mann (1949), Kent and Rosanoff (1910), Palermo and Jenkins, (1964), Shawn (1962), and *Work Oriented Rehabilita-*

tion Dictionary and Synonyms (1976).

This search yielded over 600 words that had significance in relation to career and vocational employment. In order to reduce the total number of words found during the initial search to a workable number, the American Heritage Word Frequency Book (Carroll, 1971) was used to identify the 300 words to be used in this study. The criterion was a frequency of use greater than 75 times per million.

The Delphi Technique, as described by Pfeiffer (1968), was employed. Therefore, the instrument had to be set up to meet process criteria. The first instrument was developed containing all 300 words in alphabetical order. Parallel to each word were three cells, labelled Essential, Desired, and Reject. The second and third instruments used in this study were set up in the same fashion except for the decreasing number of words per instrument.

One hundred participants were selected from the membership list of the Council for Exceptional Children's Division for Career Development. The authors assumed that individuals belonging to this Division had experience or were interested in the area of career education. Participants were randomly selected from the membership list. The authors paid particular attention to ensure that an equal number of university faculty and public school professionals were included in the population used to develop the word list.

Word lists were sent to the subjects along with preaddressed stamped envelopes. Subjects were instructed via a cover letter to judge each word as Essential, Desired, or Reject. The second and third lists were developed by analyzing the data from the previous list and constructing a word list consisting of few words.

Analysis of the Data

A word was removed from the original list if there was a 20% greater level in the Reject column of that word from the combined totals of the subjects. The levels of response to each word by category was accomplished by use of a frequency distribution by word, by category (Essential, Desired, Reject). This procedure allowed the development of the second word list.

A word was removed from the second list if there was a 50% or greater response of the combined Desired and Reject column for the word. This analysis allowed for the

6

TABLE 1

100 Most Essential Career/Vocational Words

1. rules	26. supervisor	51. entrance	76. withholding
2. boss	27. vacation	52. responsible	77. vote
3. emergency	28. apply	53. hospital	78. break
4. danger	29. fulltime	54. hourly rate	79. cooperation
5. job	30. income	55. schedule	80. dependable
6. social security	31. quit	56. instructions	81. money
7. first-aid	32. check	57. save	82. physical
8. help wanted	33. careful	58. union	83. hazardous
9. safety	34. dangerous	59. credit	84. net income
10. warning	35. employee	60. elevator	85. strike
11. signature	36. layoff	61. punctuality	86. owner
12. time	37. take-home-pay	62. rights	87. repair
13. attendance	38. unemployed	63. hours	88. alarm
14. absent	39. cost	64. payroll	89. gross income
15. telephone	40. deduction	65. attitude	90. manager
16. bill	41. fired	66. reliable	91. reference
17. hired	42. closed	67. work	92. uniform
18. overtime	43. parttime	68. caution	93. hard-hat
19. punch in	44. correct	69. license	94. authority
20. directions	45. foreman	70. poison	95. training
21. paycheck	46. time-and-a-half	71. office	96. holiday
22. wages	47. worker	72. power	97. late
23. appointment	48. buy	73. qualifications	98. personal
24. income tax	49. raise	74. earn	99. tools
25. interview	50. on-the-job	75. transportation	100. area

development of the third list. The results of the third list were used to develop the 100 core words for the career/vocation word list. The top 100 words were determined by using the frequency distribution in the Essential column and ranking the words according to their frequency percentage score in the Essential column.

Results

A total of 100 word lists were sent out with the first mailing to professionals involved with or interested in career education who were selected from the roster of the Division on Career Development of the Council for Exceptional Children. Sixty subjects returned their word lists. Using the 20 percent or greater frequency in the Reject column criteria, 62 words were eliminated from the original list of 300 words.

The second word list comprised of 238 words was sent to the 60 subjects who returned the first mailing. Fifty (83.3%) of the subjects returned the second word list. Using the criteria of eliminating any word that had a 50 percent or greater response of the combined Desired and Reject columns, an additional 90 words were eliminated from the original word list. This left 148 words for use with the third word list.

Of the 50 subjects sent the third word list, 48 (96%) returned their completed form. This allowed for the elimination of the surplus 48 words in order to arrive at the 100 words that are essential in the career/vocational education of MR students. The top 100 words were ascertained by rank ordering the remaining 148 words based on responses to each word using the Essential column. The 100 words deemed most important by professionals in the area of career and vocational education can be seen in Table 1.

As seen in Table 1, the first five words in order of priority are *rules, boss, emergency, danger,* and *job*. The significance of these words lie in the fact that they relate to either authority or safety. In essence, the subjects sampled in the study are indicating that these two areas are of prime importance and special education personnel training MR individuals to enter into the vocational society ought to deal heavily in these related areas. In contrast, the lowest five words (*area, tools, personal, late,* and *holiday*) do not deal with a centralized theme. Instead, they relate to the processes of work. This would imply that the processes involved in the world of work are not as crucial or as important as is the concept of work and the rules, regulations, and authority figures of the industry or company.

Discussion

"There are increasing attempts on the part of public education to serve as effective preparation for, as well as provide transition to, employment for the mentally retarded. This has resulted in the development of cooperative programs between education, vocational rehabilitation and other community agencies" (Cegelka, 1974, p. 101). America is just beginning to see the light about MR employees and is just beginning to allow them full acceptance into the labor market. According to the President's Committee on Mental Retardation (1972), there are job openings for MR individuals and there are a growing number of employers in all vocational areas who are willing to accept MR individuals as employees. However, there are often not enough trained and competent MR workers available to fill the positions. Concomitant to this lack of trained MR employees is the problem of their not being skilled, sophisticated, or proficient in the language of the world of work.

The benefits from this study have direct implications for teacher trainers and teachers of MR students. The impact is greatest for those preparing MR students to enter the working society. These benefits are

1. The collapsing of the thousands of words used in career and vocational education and the world of work to a list of 300 words that have the highest frequency count as indicated by the *American Heritage Word Frequency Book*.
2. The identification from this list of 300 most frequently used words in terms of careers and vocational survival of the top 100 high priority terms MR individuals must understand to "make it" in a vocational world.
3. The hierarchal ordering of the top 100 words from the most to least important.

In conclusion, the results and benefits of this study have applicability to all facets of training and programming MR individuals, from education to work, from training to research, and from new conclusions to new curricular design and implementation.

References

Borreca, F., Burger, R., Goldstein, I., & Simches, R. A functional core vocabulary for slow learners. *American Journal of Mental Deficiency*, 1953, *58*, 273–300.

Brolin, D. *Project PRICE* (Programming the retarded into career education). Columbia, Mo.: University of Missouri, 1976.

Carroll, J. B. *The American heritage word frequency book*. New York: American Heritage Publishing Co., Inc., 1971.

Cegelka, W. J. A review of the development of work-study programs for the mentally retarded. In L. K. Daniels (Ed.), *Vocational rehabilitation of the mentally retarded: A book of readings*. Springfield, Ill.: Charles C Thomas, 1974.

Department of Health, Education, and Welfare. *Application for grants under handicapped personnel preparation program*. Washington, D.C.: Author, 1976.

Department of Labor. *Dictionary of occupational titles*. Washington, D.C.: Author, 1965.

Gallagher, J. W., Baumeister, A. A., & Patterson, G. A. *Word association norms for institutionalized retarded, non-institutionalized retarded and normal children*. University, Ala.: University of Alabama Press, 1968.

Gerjuoy, I. R., & Gerjuoy, H. Preliminary word association norms for institutionalized adolescent retardates. *Psychonomic Science*, 1965, *2*, 91–92.

Goldstein, I., & Mann, H. An occupational vocabulary for retarded adolescents. *American Journal of Mental Deficiency*, 1949, *54*, 38–72.

Goulet, L. R. Verbal learning and memory research with retardates: An attempt to assess developmental trends. In N. Ellis (Ed.), *International review of research in mental retardation* (Vol. 3). New York: Academic Press, 1968.

Hall, J. F. *Verbal learning and retention*. Philadelphia: Lippincott, 1971.

Heller, H. W. *Project RETOOL*. University, Ala.: University of Alabama Press, 1977.

Kaufman, M. E., & Prehm, H. J. A review of research on learning sets and transfer of training in mental defectives. In N. Ellis (Ed.), *International review of research in mental retardation* (Vol. 2). New York: Academic Press, 1966.

Kent, G. H., & Rosanoff, A. J. A study of association in insanity. *American Journal of Insanity*, 1910, *67*, 37–96; 317–390.

Northwest Association of Rehabilitation Industries. *Work-oriented rehabilitation dictionary and synonyms*. Seattle: Author, 1976.

Palermo, D. S., & Jenkins, J. J. *Word association norms: Grade school through college*. Minneapolis: University of Minnesota Press, 1964.

Pfeiffer, J. *New look at education: Systems analysis in our schools and colleges*. New York: Western Publishing Co., 1968.

President's Committee on Mental Retardation. *These, too, must be equal; America's needs in rehabilitation and employment of the mentally retarded*. Washington, D.C.: Author, 1969.

Shawn, B. *Foundations of citizenship, Book II*. Phoenix, N.Y.: Frank E. Richards Publishing Co., 1962.

6

PART 7

GIFTED AND TALENTED

by Edmund Hunt, Ph.D.

An old Chinese curse observes hopefully, "May you live in interesting times'" Gifted education is currently experiencing the mixed blessings of such a period. There are many conflicting trends, both within the specialty and outside it, that are tugging it in several directions simultaneously.

Politically, economically and socially, the citizens of the United States are living in their own trying times, which both support and undermine gifted education. Politically, the U.S. seems to be moving toward the right and the resultant individualism that implies. During such a swing, special education programs come under increased scrutiny. Concurrently, there is less patience with institutional restraints on the ability and creativity of the individual.

Economically, the recession is in full swing. Money for education programs in general does not extend as far as it once did. Gifted programs in particular usually are the first to be deleted when the purse strings tighten. However, many terrific gifted programs are already on-line, fully justifiable and almost self-perpetuating, partially because aware, articulate and dedicated parent groups support them.

Socially, the American people are still not decided on whether or not they want to finance the educational programs that would truly develop the gifted and talented to their potential. At the same time, many Americans are disgusted with mediocrity, incompetence and ineptitude and are willing to extend the effort, time and money to make the nation's educational system the finest in the world.

In addition, there are different objectives, perceptions and perspectives operating at the federal, state and local levels within gifted education. Special education would benefit if all of these goals and objectives were congruent. But since each level serves different constituencies with differing needs, responsibilities and ideas, they coincide only on the larger issues. Such crosscurrents can produce a whirlpool that could undertow a program that does not possess a sturdy framework and a well-planned hull. The program that does not possess a crafty pilot can be smashed on the rocks of the recession. However, it does not require an Odysseus to avoid the two monsters—Charybdis, the maelstrom of elitism, and the many-headed Scylla of triviality.

As presently constructed, many gifted programs are trivial, silly or pointless. They have no direction, let alone philosophy or rationale. In hard times, they will be the first to be devoured because they may fail to accomplish their objective and cannot defend themselves from attack.

The criticism of elitism is more difficult to defend because of the almost traditional allegation in the democratic U.S. that special education for exceptionally intelligent or creative individuals is anti-egalitarian and un (if not anti) American. Apologists for gifted education attempt to answer such an indictment in a variety of ways. Isaac Asimov (*Newsweek,* June 16, 1980) maintains people who cry "elitism" are closet elitists, ashamed of their own education.

7

Possibly those closet elitists' backgrounds do not include much history. Recorded history (5,000 years or so) indicates a penchant for "gifted" education. Priestly tax collectors probably invented writing to keep tabs on who owed how much to whom and when it was past due. The scribes underwent long, arduous training before they ascended to the temple or palace. But their privileged status in society made the education worth the effort.

We know the priests and scribes of Sumeria and Egypt literally felt they were the gods' gifts to mankind. And throughout most of history, specialized professions requiring considerable training and intelligence have garnered some political, religious or economic aristocratic recognition.

With the advent of civilization, education has been the domain of the privileged few. The Spartans tried to isolate and kill the most intelligent and aggressive Helots. The British made reading a capital offense in Ireland. And the post bellum South used literacy laws to prevent Blacks from voting.

Today, the thrust of gifted education is to open specialized, intensive education to every single individual who has the ability, regardless of ethnic, religious, social or political factors. Rather than fostering elitism, gifted education is trying to develop every individual to the limit of his or her potential. How is this elitism?

In the most loudly egalitarian societies such as eastern Europe, there is not a hint of embarassment at discovering the finest talent available and developing it to the nth degree. The snide remark that the U.S. boycotted the Olympics out of fear finds some listeners. East Germany builds special schools for its future scientists and athletes. Russia erects cities for its academics. Our ally, Japan, has a brutally competitive educational system that rewards the gifted hard worker.

While the U.S. does have special schools for gifted children, a number of them are open only to the wealthy and a few scholarship students. An interesting exception is the Governor's School in North Carolina—a good idea whose time has been here for awhile.

Corporately, the gifted and talented are being recognized. McDonald's headquarters features a special room devoted to thinking, for instance. Even straight-arrow IBM has special rules for the beard and sneaker set that does the corporation's creative thinking. These companies recognize that investing in thinkers may not pay off next week. But they're willing to wait.

The scientific community here also is howling for long-range, low-application today, blue-sky research funding. Researchers know there is a need to invest time and money in strange ideas, such as talking to a neighbor without shouting over the fence. In Alexander Graham Bell's day, few people on the street saw much need for a telephone. Today, it's crucial to communication.

So there is a need for educating our gifted and talented to maintain open minds to brainstorming —a period when ideas are generated without criticism. The gifted or talented student is a complex, integral human entity with specific needs and aspirations that can be partially met by a holistic, balanced educational program matched to those individual cognitive, conative and effective requirements.

Educating the Gifted

by Jeanne Paul

The concept of giftedness has sparked great debate among educators for decades. Even the definition of giftedness is an issue of considerable controversy, and the schools vary radically in their response to the special needs of youngsters who are identified as gifted. The question of whether such children can best be educated in isolation from mainstream children, through special projects, or by leaving them to their own devices may never be settled.

Dr. E. Paul Torrance, Alumni Foundation Distinguished Professor at the University of Georgia, is an internationally noted authority on the education of the gifted and the talented. To him, "giftedness" and "creativity" are words that describe many more people than those delineated by I.Q. tests. Dr. Torrance is an outspoken opponent of an approach to education for the gifted that simply increases the volume of regular classroom assignments.

Paul: *What is giftedness?*

Torrance: It is excellent performance in any area of human behavior that is important to society. At least that's my definition of it. It isn't a very widely accepted definition.

Paul: *How does the gifted mind work?*

Torrance: There are many kinds of giftedness, and there are many kinds of gifted minds. The creatively gifted mind functions somewhat differently from the intellectually gifted mind, the artistically gifted, or some other type. One of the things that muddies the waters a great deal is the oversimplified approach taken by most people, who are searching for one kind of giftedness.

Paul: *Are creativity and giftedness synonymous?*

Torrance: No, they are not. There are individuals who are intellectually gifted who are mediocre or below average in creativity.

Paul: *How do you determine giftedness?*

Torrance: A lot of states and local school boards define a gifted child as a child with an I.Q. above 130 or as a child within the upper 2 percent of the local population. Some even define giftedness as an I.Q. above 150 or 160. There has been a trend in recent years toward multiple criteria, but most school systems are still trying to put all gifted children into one package.

Paul: *What are your criteria?*

Torrance: Just yesterday I had people from another state here to consult with me. They are from Tennessee, a state that does define giftedness in terms of I.Q. They had permission from the state department of education to use multiple criteria for the selection of the gifted so that they would be able to include in the gifted population some blacks and other culturally different children who simply don't make it on mainstream intelligence tests. Yet, with other criteria, many of them would be highly gifted. My visitors had worked out a point system, in which they would give so many points for an I.Q. at this level and so many at that level. And they were going to give a creativity test. This was weighted not nearly as heavily as I.Q. Then they were giving a few points for evidence, submitted by teachers or community agencies, of outstanding achievement in some area. So I worked with them as best I could, selecting instruments and helping them make as intelligent a use as possible of the different ways since those were the constraints with which they had to work. But I made it clear to them that in my opinion this was far from an ideal approach.

Paul: *What is your ideal approach?*

Torrance: We would accept as gifted a wide variety of kinds of giftedness. I think probably I might start with the criteria of the U.S. Office of Education's Office of Gifted and Talented. They started with six

7

criteria, but they eliminated one, which I think was a mistake. The academically gifted, of course, is one type. Then there are those with some special academic aptitude, such as a youngster who is extremely gifted in mathematics but may be mediocre, below average, or even poor in language or some other area. You can get precocity in foreign languages, or English, or science, or any other area, as far as I'm concerned. A third is the creative and productive thinker. A fourth category is visual and performing arts. Another is the leadership gifted. Originally, the kinesthetically gifted—the psychomotor gifted—were included, but that was never really understood. Most people felt that this had reference only to gifted athletes and that in the U.S. we already had an adequate program for them.

Paul: *So a gifted person need not be gifted in all of these areas?*

Torrance: No. If a person is gifted in the visual arts, such as painting or sculpture, I say meet that need, give him a chance to achieve excellence in that area, use it to help him achieve in other areas. People are motivated most to do things they do best.

Paul: *We've all heard that Einstein failed math. How could that have happened?*

Torrance: Einstein was always good at math and science. The reason he was asked to leave high school, as I understand it, was that he asked so many questions that the teachers didn't have answers to. This angered them, and they felt that it undermined their position. He sought admission to a university in Switzerland and passed the admissions tests in math and science but failed in other areas, so he had to spend a year preparing these other areas before getting admitted. Now, Werner von Braun did fail math and physics, but he joined the rocket society and found out that he needed mathematics and science. Very soon he had gained so much competence that he was teaching these things to the other members of the rocket society. Prior to that, he hadn't been motivated. He had seen no percentage in it.

Paul: *Are there gifted children in every classroom?*

Torrance: I don't know whether I could be that absolute about it. I think it would be rare that you wouldn't find some in regular classes. If you go into segregated classes where students have been classified as mentally retarded you might not, but even there you very well might. Let me give you an example given to me by a colleague in Japan. In a group of mental defectives in a junior high school, he found a boy who was a genius in physics. So my friend managed to arrange for this boy to be in a regular high school class in physics. Soon he led the class.

When he was given an individual I.Q. test, it was found that he had an above-average I.Q. It wouldn't have put him in a gifted class, although he was gifted in physics; but he wasn't mentally deficient.

Paul: *I imagine a lot of children who have been classified as mentally retarded simply have disabilities.*

Torrance: The mainstreaming of deaf and other children with disabilities is a controversy that has been going on for a long time. A lot of it is determined by the way in which people are asked to manifest their intelligence. In New York, Rawley Silver was working several years ago on art with some deaf children. Most of them were in classes for the mentally retarded. She was trying to get state rehabilitation to provide some of them with art training because she felt they were so extremely gifted that they could earn a living and manifest their abilities through art. The state said this couldn't be done because they were mentally retarded. Dr. Silver was convinced that they were not only gifted in art but in some other ways as well. She had seen their problem-solving behavior in other areas of life and knew that what they were doing couldn't be done by the mentally retarded. So she wrote to ask me if there was any test she could give that would help get these kids out of their classes for the mentally retarded. I suggested that they take a creative thinking test. We scored them, and the whole group she had tested was in the upper 2 percent of the national norm on the figural creativity test. She finally did succeed in getting a few of them out.

Paul: *What about those classified as learning disabled or emotion or behavior disorded?*

Torrance: We gave a verbal test of creativity to children in a local program who are classified in those ways. We found the group as a whole scored significantly higher on the test than the national norm. Over half were in the upper 10 percent.

Paul: Psychology Today *called you the "father of creativity research." What does this mean?*

Torrance: Well, creativity research is the whole matter of trying to understand man's creative function—creative behavior both as creative expressive behavior and as creative thinking ability. It deals with the assessment and development of the conditions that facilitate creative function. I think it's erroneous to call me the father of creativity research. I have probably done more creativity research with children than anyone else, but research is always dependent upon instruments that permit you to study, scientifically and empirically, a kind of behavior. So, the development of my tests did make it possible for a lot of people to do research that otherwise wouldn't be done. The Torrance Test

> We've reached a point in civilization when we need to devote more of the curriculum to helping youngsters enlarge, enrich, and make more accurate their images of the future.

of Creative Thinking is, I guess, one of the reasons people get that impression about me. But creativity research has been going on for a long, long time—even before the turn of the century.

Paul: *Let's talk about the Future Problem-Solving Program you have developed for children from the elementary grades through high school.*

Torrance: I've been ambitious for a long time about getting creative problem solving into the curriculum of the schools. I'm also convinced that gifted children need to learn to work in teams. We've reached a point in civilization when we need to devote more of the curriculum to helping youngsters enlarge, enrich, and make more accurate their images of the future. It's one way that gifted education can stem the label of elitism. Societies throughout history have always had to depend upon the gifted minority for images of the future, and the images they have had of the future have determined whether they survived or not. When images of the future became weak, societies decayed. The images of the future of individual children are also important and determine, to a great extent, what they are motivated to learn and achieve.

The Future Problem-Solving Program is a year-long program in which children get training in the creative problem-solving process. Most of the children across the country who participate have been identified as gifted. First, they get an introduction to futurism, and then they start working with practice problems. They project themselves twenty-five years into the future and are given a problem that might be important then. We give them a lot of information and sources of information, including an annotated bibliography; they're supposed to delve into those before solving the problem. Then they come up with future occupations growing out of the problem. They write scenarios of the future that include some of the solutions they've worked out. Then we ask them, if the world selected those solutions, what changes would there be that would describe that period of time? This year the first practice problem was new modes of transportation of the future. The following month they dealt with space travel, then ocean farming. Now they're working on hypnosis.

Paul: *Are all of the children who are participating across the U.S. dealing with the same "fuzzy" problem, as you call it, at the same time?*

Torrance: Yes, they are. We call it the "fuzzy" problem because we want to give them some information, but we want them to develop the skills of defining the problem. They learn that if they can define a problem then they have it half solved. That is one of the things that differentiates creative problem solving from other types of problem solving.

Paul: *How exactly do they work on problems?*

Torrance: First, they spend some time getting information, in whatever way they can, about the problem.

Paul: *Is this usually limited to reading?*

Torrance: They read, they interview people, they make field visits where it's possible. Some of the kids in Kalamazoo, Michigan, called a leading economist at the University of Chicago to ask him about the balance of trade. Dean Rusk spent half a day in an elementary school here in Athens, Georgia, talking with the children about global interdependence. Then there's a high school student—a real space nut—who was invited by the same local elementary school to teach the kids about space. Incidentally, we were somewhat undecided as to how well the study of ocean farming would work in the Midwest and the Plains states. But the Nebraska people reported that the children were enormously interested and enthusiastic about getting informed about sea fishing.

Then, after they have studied the problem, they work it out in teams of four. They send their solutions to a coordinating agency.

Paul: *Does the process end there?*

Torrance: No, the solutions are evaluated on the basis of a scorecard that we devised, and then feedback is given to the team about their performance.

Paul: *If one group came up with ten ways of solving a problem and another group came up with four ways, could the second group actually score better than the first group?*

Torrance: If they were of a high quality, yes, they could. First, the evaluators look to see if the team has given evidence of understanding the basic problem, then they look at the variety and flexibility of seeking information, then at the quality of problem ideas in relation to their level in school, then finally at the statement of the problem itself—where they boil it all down and state it for creative attack. Then the scorers look at the alternative solutions proposed. Is there fluency in the ideas? Are they flexible in their focus? Did they have ten ideas that were really only one idea? Then they look at the originality of the solution. Did the team completely describe the solution in detail? The top teams are invited to state competitions, and then there are national competitions. This program is one place where they can use absolutely everything they know and everything they are capable of thinking.

Paul: *Do the brightest children always do best in the Future Problem-Solving Program?*

Torrance: Success is more than just having four

> The images of the future of individual children are also important and determine, to a great extent, what they are motivated to learn and achieve.

7

bright kids. Three or four years ago, we had one team in the southern part of Georgia that had been number one in all the practice problems. Then, when they came to the state competition, they fell to seventh place out of ten. So we wondered what had happened. Finally, the kids themselves told me. They said, "In all those practice problems, we had Robert. He would give an idea that we could hitchhike on. But Robert's father got transferred, and he was replaced by the best student in the class. And he didn't have what we needed." Robert had had the spark that the bright, studious, logically oriented thinkers needed to send them in new directions and stimulate their ideas.

Paul: *Do you have any plans for the future of the Future Problem-Solving Program?*

Torrance: It's become almost too big for us to handle right here. We have a chance of finding a permanent home through the University of Nebraska Foundation, if they can get support. Then we hope to get national support.

Paul: *How do you visualize the future of the education of gifted children?*

Torrance: It's difficult to predict because there are so many counterforces that I don't know who's going to win. There are still those who want to limit gifted education to the high I.Q. students. Then there are others who want special categories. Then there are oddballs like me who hold out for an even more complex concept of giftedness. There's also the question of mainstreaming versus segregation of gifted students.

One of the trends we're seeing right now is that more colleges and universities are setting up programs for training teachers who will specialize, although many of the programs are of very poor quality. But I have confidence that eventually the quality will increase and that will increase the quality of education that will result. I think that, in the future, we're going to see more self-directed learning connected with new technologies. Mentorship relationships may also be a wave of the future. Older people, and even the elderly, will go into the schools; or the children will go into mentors' laboratories, or wherever, and work with them.

I think some of the models being developed in gifted education for training both students and teachers will probably be copied by other areas of education. But it will take a lot of imagination, a lot of cooperation, and a lot of work. □

On Educating the Gifted

by Julian C. Stanley

This article explores current thinking on ways to improve the education of intellectually talented youths. The term "intellectually talented" seems, for several reasons, preferable to the more commonly used expression "gifted." In this article, I consider just those specific developed abilities that make some students especially educable within the broad context of schools. The aggregate of several such abilities can provide a measure of general intellectual ability, usually represented by an age-adjusted score called the IQ. In essentially its present form, the concept of general intelligence dates back to Spearman (1904) and Binet (see Binet & Simon, 1905). Perhaps this construct-validated concept is still operationalized best via a child's carefully ascertained standard-score IQ on the Stanford-Binet Intelligence Scale when he or she is about 7 to 12 years of age. If the educator could have but *one* indication of a youth's intellectual ability, this would probably be the best. Later, I shall question the wisdom of relying heavily on a single such score.

To most knowledgeable adults, a "gifted" child is one whose Stanford-Binet-type IQ is "high." Typically, the minimum criterial score is set at 130, 132, 140, or occasionally 150 or even 180 (e.g., see Hollingworth, 1942). It is usually assumed, often tacitly, that all students with a given IQ such as 140 are equally educable in the usual school subjects. For example, when a high-IQ youth performs poorly in a mathematics class set up for intellectually brilliant students, the teacher is likely to conclude that he or she is not adequately motivated and, therefore, not "working up to capacity." Actually, of course, some students reason mathematically far better than do others of exactly the same chronological and mental age. Using only IQ or MA scores to group pupils homogeneously for instruction in mathematics is foredoomed to be inefficient compared with grouping based on more relevant criteria.

This points up the need for frequent use of tests or other assessments of special abilities that, singly or in combination, provide a more valid basis than the IQ for instruction of youths talented in a given school subject. Which measures prove optimum will depend considerably on the type and pace of instruction in the special class. For the 12 fast-paced mathematics classes conducted thus far by the Study of Mathematically Precocious Youth (SMPY) at Johns Hopkins, a high score on a difficult test of mathematical reasoning ability, augmented by a good score on a test of reading comprehension and vocabulary, has been found to be powerful. Many 10- to 12-year-olds who are in this category have been able to get certified via standardized achievement tests for more than 600 hours of precalculus mathematics (Algebra I through analytic geometry) in approximately 40 hours of instruction and testing.

This, then, is my first point about the state of the art concerning education of the gifted: there seems to be too much emphasis on IQ as the primary homogeneous grouping variable for instruction.

Even more troubling to me, however, are the flight from the use of tests for identifying talented youths and the strong prejudices held by many educators

7

and parents against accelerating these youths academically. These are not new concerns, of course. They are featured prominently in Spaulding's (1975) "review of the state of the art on research on the gifted and talented . . . for the period 1969-74" that was done for the American Psychological Foundation. In fact, the prejudices were obvious in 1921 when Terman began his now classic *Genetic Studies of Genius* (see Gowan, 1977; Terman et al., 1925). The perennial arguments against and for standardized tests are not reviewed here, but probably you, too, are concerned lest certain alleged or real misuses should cause them to become unavailable. I realize poignantly, on the basis of my testing experience since 1938, the great value of standardized tests for *finding* talent (Stanley, 1977-78). We appear to be in danger of losing some of that capacity in the name of the current "truth in testing" legislation.

Accelerating the subject matter and/or school grade progress of intellectually talented youths has a long history of successful outcomes. As far as Daurio (1979) could ascertain in his recent, comprehensive review of the acceleration versus enrichment controversy, not a single substantial *study* has found the educational acceleration of intellectually talented youths harmful. Also, Daurio could locate almost no studies of so-called educational enrichment that found it as effective as acceleration. Apparently, successful subject matter enrichment at one level must lead to acceleration later in order to avoid boring the student and causing him or her to lose interest in the subject. This certainly has been SMPY's finding with many hundreds of youths over a 10-year period. (See Fox [in press]; George,

Cohn, & Stanley [1979]; Keating [1976]; Keating & Stanley [1972]; Stanley, Keating, & Fox [1974]; Stanley, George, & Solano [1977, 1978]).

As concluded by Daurio and others contributing to SMPY's most recent book (George, Cohn, & Stanley, 1979), properly conducted acceleration tends to be enriching, and appropriate enrichment is deliberately accelerative. Thus, as the subtitle of the book (Acceleration and Enrichment) indicates, it seems advisable not to contrast acceleration with enrichment as if they were mutually exclusive. Various combinations have produced happy, effective students who completed their baccalaureates 0 to 8 years early.

This leads, naturally, to the concept of a smorgasbord of special educational options that might be sampled freely by intellectually talented youths. Some of these will be primarily enriching, whereas others will be chiefly accelerative. Each intellectually talented youth must have considerable guidance in order to use these options to further his or her own education most effectively.

First, though, the various abilities of the intellectually talented youth must be well known. Some multiability method such as administering the eight Differential Aptitude Tests (DAT) is needed to find those youths who meet a criterion such as scoring in the upper five percent of their age group on the national norms for at least one ability. In a typical school, that will yield far more than five percent of the students tested. The criterial percentage should be set so that false negatives will be minimized. For example, SMPY permits youths of upper-three-percent mathematical aptitude to enter its talent search in

order to make fairly certain of screening in for more difficult testing students who reason better mathematically than do 99 percent of their agemates.

After identifying the high scorers on one or more of the eight tests, it is necessary to administer a much more difficult test of the specific ability or abilities on which the individual excelled. In addition, various self-reports and other information about the student should be secured; these help determine which youths have the ability to forge ahead fast and well in certain subjects or other activities. The titles of the DAT tests suggest ways to relate them to school subjects, but far more research on this is essential: Verbal Reasoning, Numerical Ability, Abstract Reasoning, Mechanical Reasoning, Space Relations, Language Usage, Spelling, and Clerical Speed and Accuracy.

A rather recent development that, as usually applied, seems to me unfortunate is preparation of "teachers of the gifted." Who can be trained to meet all the subject matter needs of youths highly talented in one or more subjects? In mathematics, the situation is especially difficult because most elementary or junior high school teachers simply could not provide or supervise suitable experiences in this subject for highly talented youths.

Instead of teachers of the gifted, it seems to me that coordinators of special experiences for these youths are needed. These coordinators are a special kind of educational guidance counselor seeking resources and flexibility suited individually to each student.

Related to teachers of the gifted is strong emphasis on what I would term "creativity in a vacuum"—that is, creativity essentially divorced from academic subject matter. Such activity, carried along partly by the glamour of the word "creativity," seems to have been derived chiefly from the important work of Guilford (see Michael, 1977) and Torrance (1977). Such approaches often strike me as erring in much the same way that the training of mental "faculties" did many years ago. Even if stable mental factors can be isolated via factor analysis (and Harris & Harris [1971], and Horn & Knapp [1973, 1974] have cast doubt on Guilford's Structure of Intellect model), this does not mean that they can be improved by training, or, even if they can, that this would have beneficial effects for learning school subjects.

Torrance's emphasis on making students "creative" often leads to the teacher's spending considerable time trying to train the presumed trait, creativity. Since two educational activities cannot occupy the same space at the same time, I wonder to what extent the displacement of emphasis on school subjects instruction in favor of such "academically irrelevant enrichment" (Stanley, 1976) (as much creativity training is), has contributed to the present test-score decline. To me it would seem better to handle subject matter, itself, "creatively" rather than to work directly on creativity. Even such activities as "brain-storming" can readily be related to specific subjects. In my opinion, much of the recent emphasis on so-called creativity in our schools is faddish and naive.

It is at the level of differences *within* individuals across abilities that the most glaring problems become apparent. No single school program for "the gifted" can adequately meet these differential needs. For example, if Susan reasons extremely well mathematically and is eager to move ahead faster and better in

mathematics, her most pressing intellectual needs will not be met well by even the best imaginable special course in social studies, French conversation, or even computer science or chess. She needs the appropriate level and pace of *mathematics* now, not as a sit-in-the-corner, independent studier but, preferably, with several other students who are also math-able and eager. Perhaps a mathematics course such as college algebra and trigonometry, taken as a part-time student in college or in high school several years ahead of her grade placement, will be excellent for her. Perhaps, instead, she needs a fast-paced math class on Saturday or Sunday afternoons for herself and students like her.

As noted earlier, since June 1972 SMPY has run a dozen such classes. Their chief purpose was to help well-qualified youths learn mathematics from Algebra I through the first year of college calculus as quickly as possible, depending on their abilities and motivation. While doing this, SMPY developed its "diagnostic testing followed by prescriptive instruction" (DT ♦ PI) method of individualizing the learning of mathematics in a class context (Stanley, 1978). This approach owes much to Glaser's (1977) individually programmed instruction procedures, but little to "[t]he dominant instructional model within special education, Differential Diagnosis - Prescriptive Teaching" (Arter & Jenkins, 1979, p. 517).

In principle, the DT ♦ PI method is simple. We find out what the math-able student does *not* yet know about a school subject such as Algebra I and help him or her learn just that. No time is wasted on repetition of what is already known, as must be done in the usual school class

where there are many pupils who cannot easily grasp the concepts.

A brief description of how SMPY's fast-paced math classes were conducted last summer might help make the DT ♦ PI model clearer. In SMPY's January 1979 search for youths who reason extremely well mathematically, 3,675 boys and girls of upper-three percent math ability, most of them seventh-graders 11 or 12 years old, participated. Nearly 300 of these from a six-state area met the Scholastic Aptitude Test (SAT) score criteria for being invited to be in a fast-paced precalculus class last summer. Of those, 96 accepted the invitation. All but two of these completed the program.

The students came for 5 hours per day, one day per week, for 8 weeks. This was preceded by a day-long standardized testing to help determine initial placement. Thus, about 32 enrolled for Tuesdays, 32 for Wednesdays, and 32 for Thursdays. To work with the 32 on a given day were three instructors and four teaching assistants, all of them graduates of SMPY's earlier math-facilitation efforts. These teachers ranged in age from a 13-year-old Johns Hopkins' junior to 20-year-old David Meyer, who had recently completed his B.A. and M.A. degrees in mathematics at Johns Hopkins after having been elected to membership in Phi Beta Kappa as a junior.[1] All seven were already experienced instructors and/or tutors.

The 10-12 students who on the basis of the pretesting already knew the most mathematics were put into the "top" section, and David and the 13-year-old junior worked with them on an individualized basis. The next most knowledgeable group of 11 or 12 students received their individualized instruction from another instructor and his teaching assistant, both of whom were especially skilled in working at this level. The group with the least background, who did not even know Algebra I very well, had its own specially trained instructor and teaching assistant. (The fourth teaching assistant helped where needed). Some shifting among the groups occurred as students forged ahead at considerably different rates. Each student was encouraged to proceed as far as possible along the route from Algebra I through analytic geometry. Five of the 96 went the whole distance, thereby becoming prepared for calculus by the beginning of the eighth grade. In the approximately 35 hours of working time, the typical participant demonstrated mastery of 2 school years of mathematics beyond where he or she had begun.

Results during the fast-paced summer math program of 1978 had been even better, probably mainly because the selection criteria were higher then: only 62 of the 2,800 upper-three-percent youths had qualified. Thirty-three attended, and 12 of them completed all the precalculus subjects well.

While highly successful, SMPY's various procedures occur only because the age-in-grade, Carnegie-unit lockstep of schools, both public and (especially) private, makes such heroic measures essential. If schools were organized differently, SMPY would not have been necessary—nor, indeed, would the present special provisions for most slow learners. In my opinion, age-grading for instruction in academic school subjects has crept insidiously upon us as we have moved from tutorial instruction and the one-room schoolhouse to the current situation. It needs to be reversed. But, of course, that will not be done

easily or quickly.

My proposal in the area of mathematics is for a longitudinal teaching team that spans kindergarten through the 12th grade in a school system. Working from a mathematics learning center, the various members of this team would be responsible for meeting all the mathematics needs of all the students in the school system. The buck would stop with them. Every student would be helped to meet clearly stated, rather substantial criteria of mathematical competence. A few students would accomplish these early, perhaps by age 8; a few others would have to work hard until age 18 or so in order to attain the minima. Some students would proceed far beyond the minimum essentials; others would stop with them and devote their efforts thereafter to other subject matter.

Much of the instruction might still be in groups, but not age-graded ones. Attaining levels of achievement instead of A, B, C grades would be stressed. All members of the longitudinal mathematics team would have to be highly competent, but some would specialize in helping slow learners and others in helping fast-moving students.

Obviously, this longitudinal-teaching-teams model could be applied to other subject matter areas such as language arts, social studies, science, and foreign languages. There might also be art, music, drama, physical education, and social and emotional development teams. Attention to individualized differences, both within areas and across areas, would be increased vastly.

I should certainly like to see a sizable public school system pioneer this approach for at least 25 years. Because of problems that one can readily anticipate and many that one cannot, almost cer-

tainly this would be extremely difficult. I believe strongly, however, that some such plan is our only hope for the educational future of America's youths. All else will be sorry stop-gaps.

Although increasingly there is much drum beating for the gifted by various associations, including parent groups, a great deal of it seems poorly focused. Avoidance of subject matter by most of them, especially, dooms their efforts to be ineffectual. They place nearly all their gold and energy on the irrelevant-enrichment bandwagon; in my opinion, far too little of it goes into subject matter emphasis and acceleration. This leaves the typical intellectually talented youth unsatisfied because his specific intellectual hungers are not being met. "Let them eat cake" is as poor advice in this matter as it was in the historical context. We should, and certainly can, do far better than that for the intellectually talented. Intervening strongly on their behalf educationally, rather than mainly researching the status quo, is crucial. The National Academy of Education is uniquely able to promote that.

Note

During the 1979-80 school year, Mr. Meyer is studying mathematics and physics at Cambridge University as a Churchill Scholar.

References

Arter, J. A., & Jenkins, J. R. Differential diagnosis—prescriptive teaching: A critical appraisal. *Review of Educational Research*, 1979, 49(4), 517-555.

Binet, A., & Simon, T. Méthodes nouvelles pour le diagnostic du niveau intellectuel des anormaux. *L'année Psychologique*, 1905, 11, 191-244.

Daurio, S. P. Educational enrichment versus acceleration: A review of the literature. In W. C. George, S. J.

Cohn, & J. C. Stanley (Eds.), *Educating the gifted: Acceleration and enrichment*. Baltimore, Md.: The Johns Hopkins University Press, 1979, 13-63.

Fox, L. H. (Ed.). *Women and the mathematical mystique*. Baltimore, Md.: The Johns Hopkins University Press, in press.

George, W. C., Cohn, S. J., & Stanley, J. C. (Eds.). *Educating the gifted: Acceleration and enrichment*. Baltimore, Md.: The Johns Hopkins University Press, 1979.

Glaser, R. *Adaptive education: Individual diversity and learning*. New York: Holt, Rinehart and Winston, 1977.

Gowan, J. C. Background and history of the gifted-child movement. In J. C. Stanley, W. C. George, & C. H. Solano (Eds.), *The gifted and the creative: A fifty-year perspective*. Baltimore, Md.: The Johns Hopkins University Press, 1977, 5-27.

Harris, M. L., & Harris, C. W. A factor analytic interpretation strategy. *Educational and Psychological Measurement*, 1971, *31*(3), 589-606.

Hollingworth, L. S. *Children above 180 IQ, Stanford-Binet: Origin and development*. Yonkers-on-Hudson, N.Y.: World Book, 1942.

Horn, J. L., & Knapp, J. R. On the subjective character of the empirical base of Guilford's structure-of-intellect model. *Psychological Bulletin*, 1973, *80*(1), 33-43.

Horn, J. L. & Knapp, J. R. Thirty wrongs do not make a right: Reply to Guilford. *Psychological Bulletin*, 1974, *81*(8), 502-504.

Keating, D. P. (Ed.). *Intellectual talent: Research and development*. Baltimore, Md.: The Johns Hopkins University Press, 1976.

Keating, D. P., & Stanley, J. C. Extreme measures for the exceptionally gifted in mathematics and science. *Educational Researcher*, 1972, *1*(9), 3-7.

Michael, W. B. Cognitive and affective components of creativity in mathematics and the physical sciences. In J. C. Stanley, W. C. George, & C. H. Solano (Eds.), *The gifted and the creative: A fifty-year perspective*. Baltimore, Md.: The Johns Hopkins University Press, 1977, 141-172.

Spaulding, R. L. *Summary report of recent issues and trends in research on the gifted and talented*. San Jose, Calif.: The author, San Jose State University, no date [1975].

Spearman, C. "General intelligence," objectively determined and measured. *American Journal of Psychology*, 1904, *15*, 206-219.

Stanley, J. C. Identifying and nurturing the intellectually gifted. *Phi Delta Kappan*, 1976, *58*(3), 234-237.

Stanley, J. C. The predictive value of the SAT for brilliant seventh- and eighth-graders. *College Board Review*, 1977-78, Winter (No. 106), 30-37.

Stanley, J. C. SMPY's DT ♦ PI mentor model: Diagnostic testing followed by prescriptive instruction. *ITYB* (Intellectually Talented Youth Bulletin), 1978, *4*(10), 7-8.

Stanley, J. C., George, W. C., & Solano, C. H. (Eds.). *The gifted and the creative: A fifty-year perspective*. Baltimore, Md.: The Johns Hopkins University Press, 1977.

Stanley, J. C., George, W. C., & Solano, C. H. (Eds.). *Educational programs and intellectual prodigies*. Baltimore, Md.: SMPY, Department of Psychology, The Johns Hopkins University, 1978.

Stanley, J. C., Keating, D.P., & Fox, L. H. (Eds.). *Mathematical talent: Discovery, description, and development*. Baltimore, Md.: The Johns Hopkins University Press, 1974.

Terman, L. M., et al. Mental and physical traits of a thousand gifted children. *Genetic studies of genius* (Vol. 1). Stanford, Calif.: Stanford University Press, 1925.

Torrance, E. P. Creatively gifted and disadvantaged gifted students. In J. C. Stanley, W. C. George, & C. H. Solano (Eds.), *The gifted and the creative: A fifty-year perspective*. Baltimore, Md.: The Johns Hopkins University Press, 1977, 173-196.

7

Four Faces of Creativity: The Continuing Plight of The Intellectually Underserved

by Daniel P. Keating

Despite much recent attention to the topic of "gifted" children, the vast majority of highly academically able children and youth are poorly served by the present educational system. Although there are exceptions, a number of which have been documented in this journal and elsewhere, it remains true that these students are not, by and large, receiving the kind of education best suited to their needs.

The Problem

Why is this so? One would think that the cumulative effect of over 50 years of attention, effort, and research devoted to this topic would have been a massive change in the orientation of the educational establishment, and a concomitant change in practice. Although economic considerations have frequently been cited as a major obstacle to the initiation of adequate educational opportunities for this large group of students, the evidence points towards attitudinal factors as the primary source of difficulty.

The most compelling evidence that economics is a secondary rationalization rather than a primary cause is the failure of schools to vigorously pursue cost-free (or nearly so) alternatives for these children, such as acceleration through grade-skipping, subject-matter acceleration, early entrance, advanced placement, and so on. Opposition to these administrative remedies is almost by definition based on opinion and attitudes, because the findings from well-designed research studies are unanimous in their support of the benefits of accelerative alternatives, both academically and socio-emotionally (George, Cohn, &

Stanley, in press; Stanley, Keating, & Fox, 1974; Keating, 1976).

The second kind of evidence that attitudinal factors are the major obstacle to progress is that even modest expenditures for programs for highly able children are implicitly (sometimes, explicitly) among the lowest priorities for school systems. The argument that schools would very much like to do something for this group but just cannot afford it really means that such help has lower priority than all the other things on which schools *do* spend money. A simple listing of all expenditures for most school districts would be quite revealing in terms of what priority, in deed rather than in word, is placed on developing an adequate educational program for the academically able.

Let us for the moment then accept the thesis that the major problem in establishing useful programs for these children is not economic but rather attitudinal. What are the attitudes creating the greatest hindrance, and are they in any way malleable? Others have analyzed this issue previously (e.g., Bereiter, 1976), and a number of societal attitudes have been frequently cited as running counter to the development of effective programs (e.g., anti-intellectualism, egalitarianism, conformity). Rather than reiterate those analyses, I will focus on two areas which are more directly under the control of educators and researchers associated with attempts to improve education for these children. A more critical way of stating the same thing is that these are areas that I believe we have collectively misconstrued and have consequently generated poor or borderline programs as well as unconvincing argu ments to the general public. By clarifying our arguments and assumptions, and by offering solid research evidence when available, we will have a better opportunity of informing public opinion accurately and gathering reasoned support for desired educational alternatives. The two areas I focus on here are creativity and the working conception of academic ability.

Four Faces of Creativity

Historically, the scientific study of creativity in this country is usually dated from Guilford's (1950) presidential address to the American Psychological Association. In that address, he challenged investigators to understand one of the major species characteristics of humankind, creativity. He went on to offer a suggestion that an important unanalyzed component was divergent thinking, the activity of the mind when there is no set solution, and perhaps not even a well-defined problem. This is, of course, contrasted with convergent thinking, or more traditional problem solving. Torrance (1977) and others picked up the gauntlet, and during the 1950's and 1960's an impressive amount of research was generated on creativity and creative thinking, or more specifically on divergent thinking. A number of educational programs were developed and used which had as their goal the fostering of "creative thinking."

In the rush to pursue this area of research, some unreflective inferences were drawn regarding the primacy of the cognitive skill called divergent thinking. It came to be identified as equivalent in all respects to creativity itself. It seems crucial to pause and ask whether or not that is indeed all we mean by creativity, or even all that we include among the cognitive components of creativity. By creativity here I mean socially relevant creativity, in the sense that the individual's creative act is meaningful in the short or long run to society and not only to him/herself. Clearly the acquisition of a complex syntax is astoundingly creative for the toddler, but by this definition it is not creativity because it is derived from rather than contributing toward the society's storehouse of knowledge and experience.

In this light, divergent thinking is seen as but one component, albeit a crucial one, in the creative act. A number of other components are, however, equally crucial. One sensible division of these components follows. Other analyses are of course possible and equally valid, but I propose this one because the educational implications are the most straightforward. The components are listed here in a vaguely temporal sequence, although this is not essential to the argument.

1. Content knowledge. Since this component has served as the "straw man" for arguments that divergent or creative thinking offers a better conception of the creative process, it needs some rehabilitation. Logic of course argues for its necessity to the creative act, and accumulated expe-

rience supports the logical inference. Unless one has a thorough working knowledge of the current status of a discipline or art form, it is virtually impossible to advance beyond the status quo, that is to be creative in the strict sense. The progression in science is often more visible than elsewhere, with innovators "standing on the shoulders" of predecessors. Kuhn (1970) argued convincingly that major paradigm shifts are more meaningful markers in the history of science than the slow accumulation of "ordinary science." But by the same token, it is the accumulation of ordinary science that displays the seams of the existing paradigm and makes shifts necessary and possible. Such trends are often less visible outside the scientific realm, but Shakespeare without Sophocles or O'Neill without Aeschylus is nearly as unthinkable as Einstein without Newton.

These simplified arguments are not meant to downplay significant, unresolved issues in the history of philosophy, science, literature, or art. The point is simply that deep and thorough familiarity with the work of one's predecessors in any field, is, if not an absolute prerequisite, at least a virtually universal concomitant of creative breakthroughs. The denigration of intensive study within any field as rote learning or fact memorization fails to recognize the crucial point that one must master a field before one can surpass it.

This is not meant as a defense of the methods sometimes used in standard curricula to convey content, but rather to emphasize that its importance is equal to divergent thinking. Curricula and teachers are capable of making any content either dull or exciting, and of course we would always prefer the latter. Too often, however, the seeming drudgery of drill, practice, homework, and hard work are seen as inimical to learning and/or creativity, making it less fun, when in fact, the effects of rehearsal are among the few stable findings in all the learning literature.

The Study of Mathematically Precocious Youth (SMPY) project by Stanley and his colleagues (Stanley, Keating, & Fox, 1974; Keating, 1976; Stanley, George, & Solano, 1977, 1978) has focused on the rapid acquisition of content knowledge since its inception. The working premise is that students who are academically able to work at level L + 1 or L + 2 or L + n should not, for the lack of programs or administrative initiative, be left to languish indefinitely at level L. Working rapidly through the content of a specific discipline is seen as helpful rather than harmful to the creative prospects of the learners for several reasons. First, it provides them with this first component at an early enough age to explore beyond it during their intellectual prime (Horn, 1976). Second, the absence of boredom and frustration from years of level L stagnation permits the retention of excitement and initiative. In sum, the focus on the content of a discipline and the acquisition of that content is a priori as much oriented toward creativity as is a program whose focus is

7

on divergent thinking.

2. *Divergent thinking.* As noted above, this area has been more closely identified with creativity than any other. In order to make creative advances, it is, of course, necessary to master the content of a given field, but it is also necessary to avoid being forever bound by the current understanding within the field (Kuhn, 1970). Being flexible and ideationally fluent is an important antidote to excessive reliance on contemporary wisdom, and this was and is the conception underlying much of the research effort in this area.

Critical evaluations of these research efforts have concentrated on two areas, the measurement of creative thinking (especially discriminant and predictive validity) and the effects of intervention programs on creativity. Wallach (1970) thoroughly reviewed the literature to that date, and Torrance's (1977) review contains some crucial follow-up data.[1]

The most significant stumbling block has been the inability to empirically demonstrate variance on creative thinking which at the same time is adequately discriminable from standard intelligence and achievement test variance and predictive of criteria of real-world creativity. Wallach's (1970) conclusion was that creative thinking tests generally intercorrelated no better than their average correlation with standard intelligence tests. The only component of the creative thinking measures reliably discriminable from intelligence test variance was pure ideational fluency, the total number of different ideas an individual could produce in a specified time.

Torrance's (1977) follow-up data tend on the whole to reinforce this inference. Subjects selected as extreme scorers (high and low) on creative thinking tests in high school were asked to report on their creative achievements twelve years later (N=52). Despite the built-in advantage of selecting on the creativity measures, the correlations of these measures with three criteria of post-school creativity are not much higher than standard intelligence on achievement measures ($\bar{r}=.53$ vs $\bar{r}=.44$). If the groups had been selected on the latter measures, the likelihood is that they would have worked as well or better in predicting the real-world creativity criteria used in this study.

What are the educational implications of these research findings? First, most programs which focus on excellent educational achievement in the traditional sense, while maintaining learner interest, would presumably touch upon nearly all the components typically subsumed under the creative thinking label, since the developmental and individual variance in the various measures appear nondiscriminable in terms of both concurrent measurement and long-range predictive validity.

Second, the only discriminable component seems to be ideational fluency, which by itself is of dubious educational value. Interventions aimed toward increasing fluency per se may in fact be somewhat counterproductive if they implicitly or explicitly convey the impression to students that the rapid, unfettered, uncritical production of ideas is as valuable in itself as the acquisition of knowledge or the critical analysis of ideas.

Two criteria regarding "creative thinking" interventions may be inferred from this analysis. The first is that the promotion of ideational fluency in the absence of solid content acquisition is of unknown worth, and *may* be more harmful than helpful. The second is that labeling this activity creativity, thus singling out for special attention what is just one component of creativity, may be inappropriate if it leads students and educators to regard it as more deserving of attention than the other, apparently more mundane components.

Programs which employ the limited notion of creativity and ignore these criteria are likely to be, and often are, ephemeral and diversionary. They may concentrate on the 1% inspiration and ignore the 99% perspiration in creative production. When this occurs, responsible educators begin to look askance at all programs claiming to benefit the gifted or creative student. Programs which propose non-substantive solutions to clearly substantive problems deserve such skepticism.

In sum, the evidence shows that the prominence given to "creative thinking" is undeserved, and that it is properly regarded as only one of several important components in creative activity. Furthermore, programs designed to foster it in isolation are of dubious value, and may well lead to decreasing support for programs for high-ability students within the educational community. They should be undertaken only in conjunction with solid content-oriented programming, and the relative importance of ideational fluency *vis à vis* other components of creativity should be recognized.

3. *Critical analysis.* This, unfortunately, has not been an area often identified with creativity. Indeed, it has frequently been seen as occupying an opposite end of the dimension of intellectual activity in that its major goal is the "cutting-up" of creative productions rather than contributing toward production. Hence its role in creative activity requires clarification.

Let us return briefly to our hypothetical temporal sequence. The individual has acquired sufficient familiarity with a field to be at its frontier. Being ideationally fluent, the individual has generated a large number of possible avenues for solving or conceptualizing a problem in a new way. What next? Certainly, the simultaneous pursuit of all those avenues is almost never possible, and thus there must be some judgments made so that highly promising ideas may be separated from unpromising ones. This is of course the source of creative tension, avoiding on the one hand the useless exertion of intellectual effort on ideas which hold no promise, but on the other hand avoiding the discarding of ideas which may seem preposterous at first blush but in fact hold the seeds of a major advance.

Critical analysis has an undeserved reputation as the tough heel on the fragile throat of creativity. *Good* critical analysis serves exactly the opposite function. To switch metaphors, it selectively removes useless weeds so that the flower of creativity has room and energy to prosper. For some reason we have seemed to assume that this essential tension would occur by concentrating only on fluency and brainstorming, as if solid critical skills would be a natural, unplanned result of the existing educational system. Judging only on the basis of hundreds of undergraduate term papers, I find defense of that assumption difficult in the extreme. Widespread reports of consumers' gullibility in the face of advertising claims and the almost equally frequent belief in parapsychological phenomena in the absence of solid, painstakingly examined evidence are other anecdotal supports for doubting this assumption.

To my knowledge, there have been no extensive, evaluated programs for high-ability children with critical skills as their primary goal. Good models exist, of course, in the form of college-level courses in logic, rhetoric, philosophical analysis, scientific methodology, and so on. In fact, to the extent that such experiences raise students' skeptical awareness, they may have as strong an influence on ideational fluency as do programs intended to foster that directly. If students are well-trained to examine all conveyed knowledge critically, they are more likely to consider a variety of alternatives, even improbable ones. It is instead the student untrained in critical analysis who is more likely to accept on face values claims of wisdom or truth, however unfounded.

Such critical skills may be taught in isolation or incorporated into content-oriented programs. The intellectual challenge of such learning is likely to appeal to high-ability students, and one hopes the establishment and evaluation of such programs will be forthcoming.

4. Communication skills. An idea or artistic conception which exists only in the head of the potential creator, but never escapes, cannot be considered creative in the strict sense. Something must be made, produced, concretized in some fashion before it has a chance to succeed in contributing to the collective human experience. Whatever the creative production, it requires, by our definition, the communication of the idea or concept. Although communication is really the mirror image of critical analysis, that is, being a competent sender as well as a thoughtful receiver, it deserves separate mention on two counts. First, it is the culmination of the creative act. Second, it is an area with important educational implications.

The literature on the development of communication skills is extensive, and there has been considerable attention paid to it in programs for high-ability students. Programs focusing on creative writing are ubiquitous, although less attention has typically been given to expository writing. It is included here primarily to emphasize that the imperative to communicate is one that should be paramount in any successful programs for high-ability students.

Summary. A model for expanding and clarifying the nature of creativity was proposed. It has four components in a vaguely temporal sequence: 1) the individual must have thorough familiarity with the accumulated base of knowledge and experience in whatever field he/she is working; 2) the individual must not be so rigidly tied to that knowledge base that new conceptualizations are blocked, that is, he/she should entertain and generate new ideas easily; 3) the individual must have adequate critical skills to separate promising from unpromising avenues, since not all ideas can be pursued simultaneously; 4) the individual must have adequate communication skills, so there is a production to be evaluated in a social context — that is, outside the individual.

Much of the effort in developing "creativity" has concentrated to date on the second component, even though it is clearly no more important than the others and despite the fact that programs focusing more or less exclusively on that aspect of the creative process are likely to lack substance and definition. When these ephemeral and diversionary programs are seen by the educational community at large as characteristic of efforts on behalf of high-ability students, the predictable effect is declining support for such efforts. The obvious way to counter this unfortunate trend is first to recognize the importance of content learning and critical and communication skills acquisition, and second to design programs for high-ability students which reflect that recognition. In practice, strong programs aimed at any of these three components will probably have greater credibility than "creative thinking" interventions, and may well aid the student more in developing his/her full potential, creative or otherwise.

Connotations of Academic Ability

A common experience of professionals in gifted child education is to be asked, "What IQ is the cut-off for the gifted? What is the difference between bright, very bright, and gifted?" Such questions clearly reflect an unsophisticated understanding of the nature and development of ability (Horn, 1976), but more importantly they reflect the unnecessary and frequently harmful connotative baggage that burdens the term "gifted" and indeed the whole field of gifted-child education.

Either by omission or commission, we have allowed these unnecessary perjorative connotations to continue, and they have led to much of the underlying negative reaction to programs for high-ability students. Here I will highlight four common misconceptions about high academic ability which have special educational implications.

1. Absolute vs. relative definitions. Probably the most common misconception in this regard is the assumption that there exists somewhere a realistic definition of "giftedness" such that some people have it and others do not. Using such an absolute definition, so this logic goes, we should discover how to identify the possessors of this quality of giftedness, and then seek to work with these individuals in the way that best helps them. By this set of assumptions, our task would be much easier if there were perhaps a physical mark of some kind (maybe a "g" in the small of the back?) which would alleviate difficulties of identification.

This is of course facetious, but only partly so. Educationally speaking, the important components of "giftedness" are those defined relative to the school in which the individual student finds him/herself. I have argued elsewhere (Keating, 1979) that much of the confusion in what we are doing in gifted-child education results from a failure to keep rational goals in the forefront. A major goal of gifted-child education should be to provide novel, challenging, and educationally relevant material to all students, regardless of ability, on a reasonably regular basis. For academically bright students, this of course means special programming of one kind or another. The amount and kind of special programming, however, will depend on the kind of education available on a standard basis, that is, without special programming.

The question then ought not to be primarily what the criterion is for some abstract notion of gifted, but rather what is the degree to which a given individual student is intellectually underserved by the standard educational offering. In fact, for educational purposes, it might be more advantageous to define the target of our efforts as the "intellectually underserved" rather than as the "gifted." Consider two students from different schools, both of whom score at about the 90th percentile on tests of mathematical aptitude and achievement. Student *A* goes to a school where the average student scores at about the 85th percentile on these tests; student *B* goes to a school where the average score is about the 30th percentile. *B* will almost certainly be intellectually underserved by the standard in-grade offering in his school, whereas *A* is likely to be getting material at just about the right pace and level of complexity. *B* is intellectually underserved, *A* is not. But by any rational use of terms, they are equally gifted or bright. Educational programming must reflect a recognition of this interaction of learner characteristics and available instruction.

There will always be a sizable number of children, of course, who are intellectually underserved by any standard curriculum. Stanley and his SMPY colleagues have found many such students, and they will nearly always require special programming. But another advantage of the notion of the intellectually underserved is that it tends to define the solution much more straightforwardly, i.e., find the level which serves them adequately. For most academic areas, at least though high school, there exist reliable means of assessing the aptitude and achievement level of the student. Having done so, the solution is simply to arrange in any of a myriad of ways for that student to receive instruction at the next appropriate level. We need not wring our hands and wonder what to do for the gifted (or the intellectually underserved), but rather use the assessment tools and curricula we already have in abundance to eliminate the discrepancy between what they are being taught (level L) and what they are ready to learn (level L + 1, …, L + n).

2. The burden of innate superiority. From the very beginning, the gifted-child education movement has been closely identified in the public eye with notions of genetic superiority, eugenics, an hereditary elite, and so on. In that context, proposals for special efforts on behalf of gifted students is likely to be as popular as welfare subsistence for the Rockefellers, Vanderbilts, and Kennedys. If they already have everything, why strain the public trough to give them even more?

Clearing up all the misunderstandings on this issue is obviously impossible at this point, but several observations are appropriate on the role of gifted-child education in this controversy. The first is that the typical layperson's conception of the nature of genetic transmission of behavioral tendencies is simplistic in the extreme. The reality, of course, is that the models and evidence are quite complex, and on many crucial points there is little consensus among experts (Loehlin, Lindzey, & Spuhler, 1975).

It should be recognized, however, that accounts and explanations of the *origins* of high intellectual or academic ability are for the most part irrelevant to problems of practical planning educationally. Consider the possibilities. If ability were in fact 100% under genetic control, then environmental alterations within the normal range are meaningless anyway. This is the most unlikely possibility, however. Almost certainly, abilities are the result of gene-environment interactions. For educational programming, the relative proportions of each are essentially irrelevant; *whatever* the proportion of environmental influence, it represents the full leverage that educational intervention can have. Our goal should be to design the best possible interventions, since firm knowledge of the behavior genetics involved would not alter the success of those interventions in either direction.

For purposes of public discussion and rational values, it is also crucial to keep firmly in mind the realization that ability or intelligence is but one of a significant number of socially relevant behavioral characteristics. Traits such as energy level (drive), temperament, social competence, and so on are as or more important than mental ability to any definition of success in the society and high ability clearly does not guarantee superior stature on these traits. Notions of "superiority" based on any one human characteristic are extremely foolhardy.

3. Developmental emergence of ability. A corollary of the innate superiority assumption is what we may call the indelibility assumption, which holds that if a child is gifted, it will be clearly evident and expressed as soon as reliable measurement is possible. Working on this assumption, one might reasonably propose the identification of the gifted population at an early age, say first or second grade, which would be followed by special interventions for that identified group through their school career. Those not identified, of course, would be ineligible indefinitely.

No evidence supports such an assumption, and no reasonable theory of human ability, genetic or environmental, requires it. Although the correlation of age 6 or 7 years IQ with age 17 years IQ is approximately + .7 (Bloom, 1964), this does not mean that there can not be individual differences in the developmental emergence of ability. A useful way of viewing this is that less than one-half of the adult-ability variance is accounted for by primary-grade IQ scores. In addition, developmental data strongly suggest that different patterns of ability emergence are present in longitudinal studies (McCall, Applebaum, & Hogarty, 1973).

The educational inference is thus quite clear. The selection of students for special programs should be a recurring activity, *not* a one-shot affair. Multiple entry, exit, and re-entry points should be available, and are far preferable to fixed selection for a several-year (or longer) period.

4. General intelligence vs. specific abilities. Despite a consensus within the psychometric community that "g" does not offer the fullest or most useful account of the development and nature of ability (Horn, 1976), many if not most gifted education programs still employ the IQ or other composite score as the sole or major selection criterion. This is unfortunate, since the educational implications of high IQ are not specific enough to offer much help in practical programming (Keating, 1975). Because of the nature of composite scores, selection on them normally produces a group which is not much less heterogenous in any given subject area than an unselected sample.

The six-fold division of areas (general intelligence, specific academic aptitudes, creativity, social/leadership, artistic, and psychomotor), which has been common in the field for some time, harbors some unfortunate biases which appear to give equal priority to areas which are of demonstrably different importance to the educational facilitation of high-ability children. The vast majority of effort within schools, as measured by time or amount of curriculum or in other ways, is undeniably devoted to academic

learning. Consequently, the most underserved, and hence bored and frustrated students, are those with high intellectual and academic ability. Since academics constitute the part of schooling universally required, our highest priority should be to improve the poor educational options for students underserved in these areas. As argued above, the focus on general intelligence is inadequate to address this problem. Creativity, as defined in most cases, should be a minor priority as a separate topic, but instead should be incorporated into substantive educational programs (see above). Only through a united effort with a focus on students who are especially able in specific academic areas, and who are selected for solid programs on the basis of those abilities, are we likely to have much of an impact on the continuing plight of the intellectually underserved.

Proposals

Based on the above review and analysis, I would argue for the following proposals as the most effective means for working toward the highest priority goals in the area of gifted education.

1. We should disavow clearly non-substantive or diversionary programs which claim to benefit the gifted but actually do not. The temptation is naturally to applaud any efforts on behalf of these students, using as a rationalization to justify poorly conceived programs the belief that any beginning is better than none. I believe instead that they are more often counterproductive, generating skepticism and lack of support among key groups inside and outside the educational community.

2. To distinguish among programs for the gifted, we should welcome, and even insist upon, rigorous evaluations with clearly defined achievement criteria. Solidly conceived and executed programs will show clear positive effects, and on this basis efforts on behalf of the intellectually underserved can continue and expand.

3. We should consider the full range of educational alternatives, whether they are called enrichment or acceleration or something else. Teachers are sometimes urged to find something to do with these students, as long as it does not involve moving ahead in a core area and impinging upon next year's curriculum. Such recommendations are pedagogically unethical. The educational priorities are or ought to be primary; administrative convenience is a priority far down on the list.

4. Whenever possible, we should clarify misconceptions about the nature of ability and abandon unnecessary assumptions. Many issues interesting and important as research topics are irrelevant in terms of educational planning at the present.

5. The educational responsibilities toward the intellectually underserved should be asserted on a firm, rational basis. At a minimum, explanations for assigning a low

7

priority to this problem when that situation exists, should be required from school officials. The arbitrary definition of such programs as luxury items in the school budget rather than necessities should be cogently contested. Advocates will be in a better position to make those arguments if they have theoretically practically defensible alternatives available.

Footnote

1. Research into other aspects of creativity is extensive, including life history motivation, and affective and personality factors. For reasons of space these will not be dealt with here, but obviously they also are important to a full understanding of creativity.

References

Bereiter, C. E. SMPY in social perspective. In D. P. Keating (Ed.), *Intellectual talent: Research and development.* Baltimore: Johns Hopkins University Press, 1976.

Bloom, B. S. *Stability and change in human characteristics.* New York: Wiley, 1964.

George, W. C., Cohn, S. J., & Stanley, J. C. (Eds.). *Acceleration and enrichment: Strategies for educating the gifted.* Baltimore: Johns Hopkins University Press, in press.

Guilford, J. P. Creativity. *American Psychologist,* 1950, 5, 444-454.

Horn, J. L. Human abilities: A review of research and theory in the early 1970's. *Annual Review of Psychology,* 1976, 27, 437-485.

Keating, D. P. Testing those in the top percentiles. *Exceptional Children,* 1975, 41, 435-436.

Keating, D. P. (Ed.). *Intellectual talent: Research and development.* Baltimore: Johns Hopkins University Press, 1976.

Keating, D. P. Secondary-school programs. In A. H. Passow (Ed.), *The gifted and the talented: Their education and development.* 78th Yearbook of the National Society for the Study of Education. Chicago: University of Chicago Press, 1979.

Kuhn, T. S. *The structure of scientific revolutions* (2nd ed.). Chicago: University of Chicago Press, 1970.

Loehlin, J. C., Lindzey, G., & Spuhler, J. *Race differences in intelligence.* San Francisco: Freeman, 1975.

McCall, R. B., Applebaum, M. I., & Hogarty, P. S. Developmental changes in mental performance. *Monographs of the Society for Research in Child Development,* 1973, 38(3), Serial No. 150.

Stanley, J. C., George, W. C., & Solano, C. H. (Eds.). *The gifted and the creative: A fifty-year perspective.* Baltimore: Johns Hopkins University Press, 1977.

Stanley, J. C., George, W. C., & Solano, C. H. (Eds.). *Educational programs and intellectual prodigies.* Baltimore: Study of Mathematically Precocious Youth, 1978.

Stanley, J. C., Keating, D. P., & Fox, L. H. (Eds.). *Mathematical talent: Discovery, description, and development.* Baltimore: Johns Hopkins University Press, 1974.

Torrance, E. P. Creatively gifted and disadvantaged gifted students. In J. C. Stanley, W. C. George, & C. H. Solano (Eds.), *The gifted and the creative: A fifty-year perspective.* Baltimore: Johns Hopkins University Press, 1977.

Wallach, M. A. Creativity. In P. H. Mussen (Ed.), *Carmichael's manual of child psychology* (3rd ed.). New York: Wiley, 1970.

Achievement Test Performance of Intellectually Advanced Preschool Children

by David N. Shorr, Nancy E. Jackson and Halbert B. Robinson

An implicit assumption of the publishers of academic achievement tests seems to be that children below school entrance age have little competence in formal academic skills (e.g., solving arithmetic problems, reading, writing). This is evidenced by the fact that no achievement test has been standardized on such samples despite the documentation of academic skills among preschool age children, particularly in the area of reading (Durkin, 1966; Terman & Oden, 1947). Also, contemporary preschool age children in particular may be expected to have advanced academic skills. Their rate of general intellectual development is superior to that of earlier cohorts (Garfinkel & Thorndike, 1976). The increasing popularity of preschools, their more academic orientation, and the variety of educational programs available for children on television should have contributed to an increase in academic skills among young children.

The present study attempted to assess the feasibility of using an established achievement test, the Peabody Individual Achievement Test (PIAT) (Dunn & Markwardt, 1970), with intellectually precocious preschoolers. The PIAT was selected for a number of reasons, chief among these being its individual administration, its sensitivity to differences among young school age children, and the nonverbal (picture-pointing) response required for the ma-jority of its items. Also, the content validity of the test is sound and its field testing and standardization on school age children (K-12) were comparatively thorough (Proger, 1970).

METHOD

Subjects

The sample consisted of 13 male and 11 female children between 35 and 60 months of age ($M = 48.3$, $SD = 8.0$) at initial PIAT testing. The children were enrolled in a university sponsored preschool for gifted children. They had qualified for the program on the basis of parental reports and their performance on tests of general intelligence, memory, and spatial reasoning.

Procedure

The short form (starred items only) Stanford-Binet Intelligence Scale (Terman & Merrill, 1973) was administered to all children between April 1976 and January 1977. An adjusted MA score was derived from this test. This was that MA score necessary to obtain the same IQ had the Stanford-Binet been administered to the child on the same date as was the PIAT. This adjustment was appropriate in that the interval between intelligence testing and initial achievement testing was not the same for all children.

7

Initial PIAT testing was done between October 1976 and February 1977. In May and June of 1977 the PIAT was successfully readministered to 21 of the 24 children. One child had withdrawn from the program and another refused to leave the classroom for testing. Retesting data for a third child were excluded because the child refused to complete portions of the test. PIAT retesting was done by an examiner who had not tested the children previously and did not have access to records of the children's test scores.

RESULTS AND DISCUSSION

Table 1 lists Kuder-Richardson 20 (KR 20) internal consistency coefficients for four of the PIAT subtests at initial testing. A KR 20 was not computed for the Reading Comprehension subtest items because only eight children were administered this subtest proper.* All KR 20 coefficients approached or exceeded the conventional minimal standard of .90 and are comparable to those reported for first grade children by Lamanna and Ysseldyke (1973). These coefficients suggest an adequate reliability of the PIAT for the sample.

Table 1 also lists the test-retest correlations for the subtests and total PIAT scores. The mean test-retest interval was 6.2 months. These coefficients are consistently higher than those reported for first grade children over a 6 month test-retest interval by Lamanna and Ysseldyke (1973). The coefficients are indicative of good moderate term stability of PIAT scores for the sample.

All mean subtest scores were greater at retesting. The total PIAT raw scores obtained for 20 children at retesting (see note, Table 1) were significantly greater than those at initial testing ($t = 5.55$, $df = 19$, $p < .01$). The mean retest gain was approximately 7 months according to PIAT age equivalency norms (M grade equivalency score 1.1 at initial testing and 1.6 at retesting). The magnitude of this time related increase in PIAT scores is congruent with reasonable expectations for such increases in school age children.

The correlation between total PIAT score at

---

* The administration of the Reading Comprehension subtest proper is dependent on the child obtaining a score of 18 or greater on the Reading Recognition subtest. When the Reading Comprehension subtest items are administered, the child's score for the subtest is the number of correctly answered items *plus* 18. A further peculiarity of this subtest, however, is that *all* children receive a score for it. When the subtest is not administered, the child's score becomes the same as that entered for the Reading Recognition subtest.

TABLE 1

Internal Consistency at Initial Testing and Test-Retest Correlations for PIAT Subtest and Total Scores

PIAT Subtest	KR 20	Test-Retest Correlation
Mathematics	.88	.70
Reading Recognition	.96	.92
Reading Comprehension	—	.81
Spelling	.94	.80
General Information	.90	.82
Total PIAT		.93

Note: All test-retest correlation coefficients are significant at the .01 level and are based on an N of 21 for the Mathematics and Reading Recognition subtests and an N of 20 for the remaining three subtests and Total PIAT. One child was incompletely administered the Reading Comprehension subtest at retesting. Scores for this and the subsequent subtests and Total PIAT were not computed for this child.

initial testing and adjusted Stanford-Binet MA score was .73 ($df = 22$, $p < .01$). The age controlled partial correlation was .53 ($df = 21$, $p < .01$). These correlations at retesting were .63 ($df = 18$, $p < .01$) and .55 ($df = 17$, $p < .01$) respectively. The sample's performances on the intelligence and achievement tests were similar in another respect. The mean Stanford-Binet "test age" (Salvia, Ysseldyke, & Lee, 1975) was 71 months and the mean total PIAT age equivalency score at initial testing was 74 months, both approximately 2 years beyond the children's mean chronological age.

SUMMARY

The performances of the children in the present study suggest that the PIAT is an appropriate instrument for assessing the academic skills of intellectually advanced preschool children. The test demonstrated acceptable levels of internal consistency and stability. Adequate concurrent validity was suggested in its relationship to general intelligence test performances. While the appropriateness of the PIAT for use with less highly selected groups of preschool age children cannot be established without further research, the present findings suggest that such an effort would be worthwhile.

REFERENCES

Dunn, L. M., & Markwardt, F. C. *Peabody Individual Achievement Test: Manual.* Circle Pines MN:

American Guidance Service, 1970.

Durkin, D. *Children who read early.* New York: Columbia Teachers College Press, 1966.

Garfinkel, R., & Thorndike, R. L. Binet item difficulty then and now. *Child Development,* 1976, *47,* 959–965.

Lamanna, J.A., & Ysseldyke, J. E. Reliability of the Peabody Individual Achievement Test with first grade children. *Psychology in the Schools* 1973, *10,* 437–439.

Proger, B. B. Peabody Individual Achievement Test. *The Journal of Special Education,* 1970, *4,* 461–467.

Salvia, J., Ysseldyke, J. E., & Lee, M. 1972 revision of the Stanford-Binet—A farewell to the mental age. *Psychology in the Schools.* 1975, *12,* 421-422.

Terman, L. M., & Merrill, M. A. *Stanford-Binet Intelligence Scale.* Boston: Houghton Mifflin, 1973.

Terman, L. M., & Oden, M. H. *The gifted child grows up.* Stanford CA: Stanford University Press, 1947.

7

Genius Creativity and Eminence

by C. K. Rekdal

ABSTRACT

Large bodies of literature have supported the necessity of gifted programs for either the intellectually superior or the creative-productive thinker, but few have actively sought to establish programs which systematically combine the two. A promising union of these two categories may identify a group previously ignored, but whose characteristics merit closer examination. This paper attempts to establish a theory of eminence based on the notion that the potential genius will very likely be found among this special group. While eminence is viewed as a rare ability which is to some extent predetermined, the capacity of society to significantly influence its fruition is regarded as dependent on its power or skill to increase individual faculty for creative behavior.

Gifted students have been identified according to certain categories of excellence as specified by federal definition. They are: the intellectually superior, the academically able, the creative-productive thinker, the performing artist, those high in leadership ability, and those outstanding in psychomotor skills (Marland, 1972). Gifted programs may provide for one or more of these abilities.

While large bodies of literature have supported the necessity of programs for either the intellectually superior or the creative-productive thinker, few have actively campaigned for programs which systematically combine the two beyond a haphazard or inconsistent method of implementation. A promising union of the intellectually superior and creative thinking categories may in fact identify a group previously ignored, but whose characteristics merit closer examination.

The intent of this paper is to construct a theory of eminence based on the notion that the potential genius will very likely be found among those high in both intelligence (IQ) and creative thinking ability (CQ). The intelligence metric, however, contrary to popular thought, may not be necessarily as important in locating the eminent as creative thinking ability. The degree of intelligence necessary for the actualization of genius, as currently measured, may in fact be acceptably lower than reported. Gifted programs have not adequately addressed this notion in the past.

Creativity and intelligence as they interact with one another are considered a means of increasing the frequency and potential for eminence in our society in the future. If the theory holds true, several very important considerations should be made in re-establishing criteria for gifted programs and prioritizing goals of education in general. Important psychological and curricular ramifications in regards to education should become increasingly apparent within the context of this theory.

DISCUSSION

The intellectually superior are operationally defined as 140 or above on intelligence tests such as the Stanford-Binet and WISC. This is the level Terman suggests as near genius. The creative thinker is operationally defined and identified by scores on creativity measures such as the Alpha Biographical Inventory (ABI) and the Torrance Tests of Divergent Thinking. Both represent two distinctly different kinds of measures used in assessing creative ability. The ABI is based on personality and historical correlates of creativity, while the Torrance Tests are based on productive thinking abilities stressing fluency, flexibility and originality.

Although there are many problems associated with both IQ and CQ tests -- disputes range from charges of bias in regards to factors such as sex, culture and age to heated debate involving the issues of validity and reliability -- the fact remains that some means of identification is necessary, and of those available the current tests in use appear to be our best alternatives of locating students of high intellectual and creative-thinking abilities at the present time. Measures of creativity in particular have been seriously challenged as inadequate in terms of identification, resulting in highly questionable research findings (Rekdal, 1977).

With improved means of locating students high in IQ and CQ a unique group would be formed, one which Torrance (1960) estimates as 30 % of the students who score within the top 20 % on both IQ and CQ. This group could very well account for society's geniuses or eminent: the two in a million who, Guilford (1968) asserts, become truly distinguished in terms of achievement. Evidence is mounting against the notion that high IQ is necessarily imperative in the achievement of eminence. This has lead many, such as Gowan (1971) to suggest that in the future we may wish to move instead to creative ability as the criterion of excellence.

Conceptions of Genius:
There are several prevalent views of genius which the literature

7

evokes. Broadly categorized, they are often explained to this extent:

From the earliest times genius has been regarded as a link with divinity, which, according to Plato and Socrates, calls upon the activities of demons and gods acting through human organisms. Depending on which source, the results may or may not promote a positive influence on one's life.

Genius is frequently viewed by some as a negative quality demonstrated by insanity, degeneracy, imbicility. It is a form of deviation or maladjustment which Moreau (in Hirsh, 1931) describes as a neurosis and often a psychosis. Its inspiration to create is the result of illness and suffering. Often exemplified in the weak, uncoordinated guise of the child prodigy, it is destined for early death or madness.

A diametric view is one in which genius is regarded positively. Usually described as an extreme form of intelligence or ability, qualitatively distinct from the circumscription of normal capacity, it is considered an increase in human potential.

As a natural ability derived through inheritance, genius is considered by others to be a genetically based quality not readily altered by society. According to Ellis (1904) and Galton (1962) it is a condition imposed and explained by heredity.

To others, the emergence of genius in clusters of time and place has established credence to speculations that particular environmental factors are what is required. Genius, according to this viewpoint, is a product of social forces created accidentally or through special circumstance (Hirsh, 1931; Simonton, 1978).

Finally, genius is perceived as conditioned by mutually supporting socio-biological influences. Its actualization is made possible when the cultural milieu facilitates innate characteristics (aptitude, attitude, interest and temperament) held by those who have the potential for eminence. (Cox, 1926; Guilford, 1950; Cropley, 1961; Grubner, Terrell & Wertheimer, 1962; Arieti, 1976)

Criterion for Eminence:
Albert (1975) behaviorally defines a person of genius as one who produces a large body of work significantly influencing many persons for a number of years, chiefly by requiring an alteration of some basic and widely held assumptions. Persons who achieve eminence, he maintains, begin productive careers significantly earlier than the less productive.

Genius, according to Barlow (1952), implies the capacity for extraordinary achievement without the corresponding effort necessary for most persons. It is regarded as the ability to exercise a wider range of faculties than most.

The problem of securing an operational definition has been managed historically through quantitative means dependent on longitudional information. Because genius implies social recognition, a primary criterion of its achievement has utilized measures reflecting fame. Such a standard for genius is not without controversy since cultural values vary and are subject to limitations of time and place. A sample of past studies indicate the nature of the dilemma inherent in research of this kind.

Cattell (1903), in locating 1,000 of history's most eminent persons born after 1450, uses as a means of selection, persons mentioned in at least two of six biographical dictionaries in America, England, France and Germany. Although eminence within the literature is generally considered to be synonymous with genius, Cattell distinguishes between persons of greatness (George Washington), persons of eminence (Napoleon) and persons of genius (Einstein). The distinction drawn between genius and eminence is also made by Galton who hypothesizes that eminence occurs approximately once in a population of 4,000, whereas genius occurs only once in a million.

Weyl (1966) in an attempt to locate the ethnic origins of those of superior talent compiles 1,514 of the most common surnames on Social Security rosters and compares them with their frequency of occurrence on 75 specialized leadership rosters such as Phi Beta Kappa and Who's Who.

Galton (1926) and Ellis (1904) select their eminent using space alloted in the pages of the Dictionary of National Biography. Like others, they make ommisions for entries such as royalty, inherited positions, or those who display little evidence of high intellectual ability.

Goertzels and Goertzels' study (1962) select 400 subjects living in the 20th Century based on the number of biographies of each on the shelves of the Montclair, New Jersey Public Library.

Characteristics of Genius:
Researchers throughout the literature on genius comment on the chief characteristics seemingly necessary for achievement at this level of productivity.

Galton and Freud describe this group as the product of a rare combination of high general ability coupled with an overwhelming energy which is continuous over most of a lifetime. Eminence among researchers, according to Cattell and Drevdahl (1955) is correlated not only to high general intelligence, but to personality dimensions reflected in factors such as ego-strength, stability, dominance, adventurousness, emotional sensitivity, self sufficiency and radicalism. Albert (1975) lists the following qualities as necessary for eminence: perceptiveness, persistence, endurance, productivity and influence. Preconditions of the capacity for what he calls genius level work are high general ability and prolonged personal motivation. Roe (1951), in studies of eminent biologists, uncovers personality patterns of persistence and intensity of devotion to work -- traits which do not differ from non-scientists or between fields of study. Hudson (1966) identifies motivation as an important characteristic.

7

Cox (1926) perceives the essential attributes of genius as self-confidence and unusual persistence. She declares that a high intelligence when combined with a high degree of persistence is more necessary in the achievement of eminence than the highest degree of intelligence coupled with a lack of motivation or persistence. Barron (1969), MacKinnon (1962) and Bloom (1964) also support the notion of differential factors beyond IQ as necessary to success once a particular intelligence level is achieved.

The personality correlates between and among these studies provide a means of hypothesizing a personality of genius based on traits such as persistence and productivity. How these characteristics interact with intelligence can best be understood through a closer examination.

The Factor of IQ:
Since the inception of the IQ test, genius has most often been equated with high IQ. To be sure, estimates of the IQs of geniuses have been made, but for the most part these have been primarily speculations not supported by empirical evidence. A review of the literature reveals that high IQ as a characteristic of genius is not always the case, and that other factors enter into its fruition. Guilford (1962) states that genius is not a function of difference in intelligence. Above an IQ of 120, he contends, other variables become increasingly important.

Research on the ability of IQ tests to tap intelligence correlates, according to Dissinger (1975) is not as extensive as one is lead to believe. The typical IQ test, states Guilford (1950), measures no more than half a dozen of the intellectual factors, which to a large extent have been considered largely the ability to master subjects such as reading and arithmetic.

Nonetheless, there is overwhelming dependence on it largely for reasons of convenience. While the notion of IQ as the criterion for achievement has been debated for years, the fact that intelligence is highly related to convergent achievement, and closely associated with grades, aptitude tests and classroom success, has been documented well enough. But it seems equally clear that classroom achievement is not related to achievement in general.

IQ and Achievement:
In a study of over seven thousand college freshmen, Holland and Richards (1965) conclude that academic and nonacademic accomplishment are relatively independent dimensions of talent. Confirmation of this is produced in a later study (Holland & Richards, 1966) of over eighteen thousand college applicants. Although Biard and Richards (1968) allege that both academic and nonacademic accomplishments can be predicted to a useful degree, the correlations between the two according to Richards, Holland and Lutz (1966) are negligible.

This charge is supported by Jennings and Nathan (1977) who conclude that the ability of measures such as the Scholastic Aptitude

Test (SAT) to predict accomplishments beyond the classroom is extremely poor. College grades, according to Elton and Shevel (1969) are equally unreliable in indicating any relationship to measures of adult accomplishment in real life. Taylor (1958), investigating grades as a means of locating research scientists, arrives at a similar conclusion and suggests that grade point averages be given no weight at all in their selection. IQ scores, which Jencks (1972) equates with measures of aptitude and achievement, only identify those who will perform well in the clasroom, and are not, according to Sharp (1972), related to attainment beyond grades. Guilford (1950) relates that graduates from the same institutions with high scholastic records and strong recommendations differ widely in the output of new ideas.

Schools of higher learning, charge Baird and Richards (1968) should be concerned with finding students who accomplish outstanding things outside the classroom and in later life, not only those who can achieve satisfactory grades in school. The inability of conventional IQ tests, says Hudson (1966), to predict who will do outstanding work in science or any other field is unquestioned. Terman's 1,500 subjects, according to Goertzels, et al (1962), selected at IQ 140 and above, although successful, have only enhanced rather than advanced the status quo.

The use of grades, achievement and IQ scores in the selection of college students center on only one dimension of talent to the neglect of others. Holland and Kent (1960) warn that concentration of funds based on a restricted type of giftedness reflected in grades and test scores could have effects which are not in the best interest of the total society. Feibleman (1960) charges that it is this oversight which explains why much of the knowledge transmitted by universities is not necessarily produced in them. America, he says, has its geniuses, but an astonishing number come from other places than its universities.

The magnification of mass testing, emphasis on grades, achievement and aptitude scores, says Pang (1968), eliminates many potentially creative persons. Achievement, prescribed by college standards, does not automatically determine the eminent scientists, engineers, businessmen, artists or writers. The number of distinguished persons with undistinguished or difficult school careers is lengthy and includes Copernicas, Einstein, Pasteur, Hobbes, Darwin, Freud, John Locke, Auguste Comte, Frank Lloyd Wright, Isaac Newton, to name a few. Mediocre performance, examination failures and expulsion problems plagued these individuals. Edison was asked to leave schools after the first grade; his teacher thought he was "dull". Einstein complained that he could not think well until a year after completing his university examinations.

The consensus of opinion expressed here indicates that IQ as currently defined and measured reflects an ability to think and absorb information, but beyond the confines of the classroom it does not, by itself, advance the cause of achievement. What then does

7

contribute significantly to future performance in adult life? What factors of human potential have not been evaluated by IQ tests and therefore remain either ignored, overlooked or unmeasured? Has intelligence as historically perceived presented a myopic vision of human ability?

Guilford (1967) contends that there are alternative views regarding intelligence, one being that there are two kinds: ability and creativity, which he asserts, is far more fundamental. Others have preferred to address creativity and intelligence as two fairly discrete elements of human capacity, acknowledging only that intelligence, while necessary, does not insure the presence of creativity (Rossiman & Horn, 1972; Schubert, 1973).

The Factor of CQ:

Creativity is not the same wherever you find it (Guilford, 1968), nor is it a normally distributed trait among the general populace (Rosner & Abt, 1974) or the gifted (Gowan & Torrance, 1967). Creativity occurs at all ages, in all fields of human endeavor, in all cultures (Reitman, 1972). The idea that all people are to some degree potentially creative is shared by many investigators (Bruch & Torrance, 1972). However, the difference in kind is in terms of frequency, level, time (Reitman, 1972) and degree (Taylor, 1964). Arieti (1976) points out that ordinary creativity is attainable for many while great creativity is present only in a few which he terms, genius.

To Gruber, Terrell and Wertheimer (1962), the heredity-environmental issue - whether a creative person is born or bred - is not nearly so clear cut as to Cropley (1967) who asserts that heredity imposes the upper limit in terms of creative ability, while environment regulates the extent to which that potential is realized. Arieti (1976) argues that the ability to synthesize cultural elements occurs in a very small percentage of the population. In order to nurture creative talent, a proper social climate or environment is necessary.

To attempt to address the critical question of identifying the creative person, it may be necessary to rid ourselves of the misleading views centering around it. We continue to refer to creativity as though it were a singular process, neglecting the reality that it is in fact a complex set of cognitive, motivational and emotional processes. A review of the literature on creativity reveals the complex nature of the creative act.

Jackson and Messnick (1962) view creativity in five perspectives: (1) cognitive style of the creator, (2) personal qualities of the creator, (3) properties of the product, (4) standards for judging, and (5) aesthetic responses drawn. They suggest four behaviors by which creative responses may be judged: (1) unusualness, (2) appropriateness, (3) transformation in the sense of the new form overcoming the constraints of reality, and (4) condensation, or the degree to which the product manifests a unified and coherent relationships between the simple and complex.

Gowan (1971) defines creativity in terms of five distinct views represented by several personalities: (1) the cognitive/rational/semantic/problem - solving view of the Buffalo School, Guilford's Structure of the Intellect, and others, (2) the personality and environmental view of Taylor, (3) the mental health/self-concept/self-actualization view of Maslow and Rogers, (4) the Freudian/Neo-Freudian/psychoanalytic/oedipal pleasure and preconscious view, and (5) the psychedelic/existential/nonrational view of Huxley, Barron, Koestler and Krippner in which drugs, hypnosis meditation, exercise and mysticism play a large part.

Taylor (1958) believes creativity exists at five different levels -- expressive, productive, inventive, innovative and emergent -- suggesting a hierarchical ordering of ability. Chambers (1968) views creativity in three dimensions: (1) level, which he regards as either low or high, (2) field, which he describes as the medium in which the creative process occurs, and (3) type, which is defined as theoretical, developmental or scholarly. Theoretical creativity deals with the production of new ideas while developmental creativity occurs as a result of recombinations of pre-existing knowledge or theories, the origins of the creative process having been pre-established. Scholarly creativity is concerned with both the generation and development of new ideas.

Lescher (1973) sees creativity as having in the past been an examination of four major approaches: (1) product, (2) process, (3) person, (4) place/environment.

By far the most generally agreed upon definition -- the one which the majority of the literature invokes in discussing creativity -- is that which involves divergent thinking and the production of unique and useful products (Taylor and Getzels, 1975).

In an attempt to identify the creative individual, a great many tests have been developed (Davis, 1975). They can be classified into two general categories: divergent thinking tests and biographical or personality inventories. Recent investigation denotes a shift in emphasis from divergent production to bio-inventories as a means of locating the creative-productive thinker. These inventories are based on differential factors reflected in personality and motivational characteristics gleaned from studies of creative persons.

Confirmation that traits of personality determine the appearance of creative products is still under intense research. Several observations, however, have been made during the course of investigation. Personality characteristics tend to be associated with a medium or field of expression rather than the level of expression. Massialas and Zein (1967) state that although certain traits have been identified as creative descriptors, there is a great difficulty in evaluating between the highly creative and the less creative person. That there are field or medium differences is also noted. Kagan (1967) reports that both the competent and the incompetent poet resemble one another more in terms of personality than the com-

7

petent and incompetent creative scientist.

Nonetheless, creativity research has uncovered considerable information on the differences between creative and less creative individuals. While the less creative individual tends to be good natured, conventional, moralistic, rigid, authoritarian (Zahn, 1966), the highly creative, according to Galton (1962) display energy, health, steadiness of purpose, independence of views, enthusiasm, rapid, fluent, firm mental associations, vivid imagination.

Roe (1951), in her studies of eminent scientists finds two particularly strong traits among them: self sufficiency and independence.

Barron (1969), in analyzing the personal characteristics of architects, scientists, writers and mathematicians, determines that they have a preference for complexity, are independent in judgment, have complex personalities, are self assertive, dominant and impulsive. Gold (1965) classifies creatives as having a positive self-image, drive or involvement, openness to experience, high aesthetic sensitivity, intuitive perception, a capacity to entertain many ideas simultaneously and independence of judgement.

Taylor (1964) declares that there is a widespread belief by practically everyone that motivation is a strong component of creativity. Motivational factors are drive, dedication to work, resourcefulness, desire for discovery and desire to bring order from disorder. Other factors, he asserts, are intellectual and personality factors. Personality traits are independence, self-sufficiency, tolerance for ambiguity, professional self-confidence and femininity of interests.

Particular personality and motivational characteristics continue to reappear in study after study associated wtih creative ability. Upon close examination they either strongly resemble or are identical to those qualities identified as necessary for the achievement of eminence. How are these factors of creativity related to intelligence?

IQ and CQ:
The past three decades of research in creativity measurement has attempted with limited success to demonstrate a substantial independence of creativity from IQ (Wallach in Rosner & Abt, 1974). Evidence as to degree of IQ supports the notion of an average IQ as more highly correlated with creative ability. Hollingworth (1942) comments that this phenomenon is more likely due to the numbers represented by the average range of IQ than to IQ itself -- that is, since there are greater numbers of persons with an average IQ, the chances of locating more people in this range who are creative is greater. In working with subjects of IQs at 180 and above she was puzzled that only one-third displayed any remarkable creative ability.

Torrance (Gowan & Torrance, 1971) asserts that many creative children do not have IQs as high as 130. Intelligence tests, he claims, miss 70 % of those who score in the top 20 % in creative thinking tests. This fact, he says, is constant in hundreds of studies. MacKinnon (1962) in his studies of creative persons, states that only a minimum level of intelligence is necessary. This level varies from field to field and in some cases may be surprisingly low. Getzels and Jackson (1962) report that only a certain amount of intelligence is required for creativity and that the factors are not synonymous. Highly intelligent creative individuals, they find, are more the exception than the rule. At higher levels of IQ, the relationship between IQ and creativity is extremely unreliable. Above a certain point, a high IQ is reportedly of little advantage.

MacKinnon (1962) alleges that highly original/productive subjects do not differ from one another in terms of intellectual abilities, but in personality characteristics. Barron (1969) concludes that stylistic and motivational variables are more important in determining creative productivity than intelligence, beyond an IQ of 120. This IQ threshold is supported by Ogletree (1967) who reports that beyond a certain level, the more intelligent individual is not necessarily the more creative. Guilford (1968) cites 120 as the point below which creativity and intelligence are highly correlated. Above this, he says, there is very little correlation. There are many cases of low divergent production among those of high IQ, he claims. This group he refers to as the creative underachiever.

Johnson and Fogel (1974) in studies of creative aptitude among highly intelligent subjects (the top 2 % on standard IQ test norms) also report infrequent manifestations of high creative aptitude among those tested. Wallach and Kogan (1965) conclude that there is little doubt that within the upper ranges of IQ the relationship between creativity and IQ is minimal. Scores of nearly all of MacKinnon's eminent men and women are above 120, but among them the relationship between IQ and creativity is almost nonexistent. A mature scientist with an adult IQ of 130, he says, would be as likely a candidate for a Nobel Prize as one with an IQ of 180. Most of Terman's subjects, selected on the basis of IQ made their way effectively through life, but very few, says Gold (1965), distinguished themselves creatively. The relationship of creativity to IQ is, according to Getzels and Jackson (1962), close to zero with groups of superior IQ.

There is no support for creative ability being related to those of low IQ (MacKinnon, 1962). Of the two IQ groups discussed, superior and above average, it is obvious that creative acts are more often associated with the latter. Those of high IQ represent the upper 2 % of the population, a distinct and select gifted group. Of these individuals, less than half are expected to be likewise invested with creative ability. How creativity will serve to differentiate among high IQ group members is, at this point, based more on conjecture than empircal evidence. However, evidence that creativity does enhance intellectual achievement exists.

In an achievement study by Getzels and Jackson (1962) equally superior scholastic performance between two groups of high IQ as measured by standardized achievement tests were obtained despite a difference of 23 points in IQ. The difference in IQ, they contend is balanced by high creative ability. There appears, according to the authors, to be a positive relationship between performance on tests of creativity and scholastic achievement. Their work is substantiated by Torrance, who, they report, in a similar experiment between groups with a sizeable difference in IQ, replicated their study. The interpretation of these results lead to these assumptions: (1) that creativity enhances achievement, and (2) that overachievement is a consequence. However, one of the issues they raise is the need to re-examine the concept of overachievement. The IQ metric, they assert, simply does not sample all cognitive functions. Therefore, they charge, achievement beyond certain levels of IQ is a functional problem of the test itself and the concept of overachievement is simply not valid.

Creativity and Eminence:

According to Albert (1975) and Arieti (1976), genius is defined as exceptionally creative behavior -- the highest degree of creativity. The outstanding genius, says Guilford (1962), simply stands out because he is at the top of the creativity continuum. Several researchers have drawn similar conclusions conceptualizing their views with various educational learning models. These models have all had one common element among them: the uppermost level of achievement has been associated with creative ability.

Hughes and Miller (1963) in outlining the importance of creativity to higher level thinking skills place creativity at the top of their taxonomical model, "The Hierarchical Schema of Mental Processes".

Arlin (1975) hypothesizes the existence of a fifth Piagetian stage beyond the formal operational level. Identified as the problem-solving stage, she states that it is characterized by that of creative thinking. Only a very small percentage of persons will ever enter this hypothesized fifth stage since, she says, only half of the adult population ever attains Piaget's fourth level of formal operational thinking.

Smith (1971), using achievement tests based on Bloom's Taxonomy of Educational Objectives, identifies lower levels of the taxonomy as convergent achievement levels, and upper levels as divergent achievement levels. Intelligence, he reports, is the major variable related to convergent achievement. Creativity along with ingelligence is the necessary prerequisite for divergent achievement.

SUMMARY

The existing research indicates a concensus on the following points: (1) the capacity for achievement of eminence is based on the prerequisites of an above average intelligence, (2) creativity, while not tied necessarily to high IQ, but more often is associated with above average intelligence, is an important factor in the function of higher level cognitive abilities and achievement, (3) the use of the IQ metric and other measures highly correlated with it in educational decision making is seriously challenged by current research which indicates the effects may in fact inhibit the development of eminence, reducing the potential for genius to emerge, (4) certain personality and motivational characteristics not measured by IQ tests, but highly correlated with creativity, appear as important if not more important in the achievement of eminence, and (5) the importance of creative functions in defining genius is, according to many, attributed to the creative act, the uppermost level of achievement by which society measures it eminent.

CONCLUSION

Current information regarding studies of genius, achievement, creativity and its relationship to intelligence supports a theory of eminence which suggests that the potential genius will most likely be found among those high in two particular areas of ability -- creative thinking and intelligence. The degree of intelligence necessary for eminence may be dependent on field of endeavor, but it is estimated to be above average, and in some rare instances extremely high. While the necessity of superior intelligence has historically been equated with eminence, empirical evidence has not supported this assumption. According to recent research, beyond certain limited ranges, intelligence by itself does not insure achievement. While it is reasonable to expect to find some correlation between intellectual quantity and capacity, intellectual functions extend much further than the boundaries of the traditional IQ metric. Intelligence as it is now conceived is a pale reflection of what the real world demands as a prerequisite for success. What we have managed to measure so far is only paper and pencil success, and in a very limited environment at best. Other factors, more closely associated with creative ability, insure the advance of potential beyond the confines of schools to achievement in real life. Research provides evidence that creativity, as a complex of personality, motivational and intellectual factors beyond the bounds of currently prescribed intelligence measures, is a necessary condition for the achievement of eminence.

There are several implications which this theory holds for gifted programs as they are now conceived. First, if the metric for success is not accounted for by intelligence alone, then its role in student selection must be altered. The majority of gifted programs presently serving academically able students use intelligence and achievement scores (both highly correlated psychometric measures) as major program entry criteria, and in some cases they are the only means of selection. If creativity enhances or supports intellectual ability as it is assumed by this theory, then the use of some criteria to establish creative capacity should be included in student selection. Gifted programs at present do not generally incorporate creativity measures as part of the selection process. They are more often used as pre and post tests, measuring creative gains after certain kinds of instruction have occurred.

Second, a large group of individuals with high IQ provides a pool of promising talent which in the past has not been adequately tapped. These individuals have often been referred to as creative underachievers. Speculations as to their potential for achieving eminence is predicated on the assumption that by increasing creative

7

behavior this capacity is positively affected. What role education should play in this effort is an important consideration. Certainly it must be more willing than it has in the past to address basic issues and needs. The field must undertake more than it has by way of clearly defined terms and providing a more comprehensive delineated theoretical framework if creativity in education is ever to extricate itself from the intimations of frill and marginal necessity to a more substantive perception of its function relative to productive thought, problem solving and achievement in the real world.

Third, the need to develop more valid and reliable means of measuring creative potential becomes more apparent within the context of this theory. The task is more challenging still at the early childhood and elementary age level, since there is little available at present in the area of creativity measurements.

Fourth, programs for academically and intellectually gifted students tend to be oriented to left hemispheric function of the brain. Creative thinking is hypothesized to be a primary function of the right hemisphere. An estimated 50 % of an individual's capacity to achieve is lost through either disuse or misuse of the total spectrum of potential available. To what extent gifted programs, and schools in general, alter their approaches to learning in order to utilize the resource of the intellectually creative student has yet to be accomplished. The influence of stimulus and task on information processing as it relates to cerebral dominance is significant to the functional aspects of program planning. Curricular considerations in regards to supporting both areas of the brain's functions are not only of importance to gifted, but provide important implications for all student learning in our educational institutions.

The literature on gifted programs consistently point to the reasons for supporting special programs for the gifted as having a basis in future societal contributions, or as a nurturing force in support of the growth of real talents. It is the aim of this paper to point out that the eminent persons in our culture have contributed most generously to their society in the past, and with support, and aid, will no doubt continue to do so in the future. What programs for gifted must seek in coming years are means of locating those capable of achieving eminence. The literature reviewed here has hopefully given some direction toward that search. The notion that a means of uncovering the nature and development of eminence with a prospect of increasing its fruition in the future is an exciting one, worthy of pursuit.

BIBLIOGRAPHY

Albert, R. S. Toward a behavioral definition of genius. *American psychologist,* 1975, *30,* 140-151.

Arlin, P.K. Cognitive development in adulthood: a fifth stage? *Developmental psychology,* 1975, *11,* 602-606.

Arieti, S. *Creativity the magic synthesis.* New York: Basic Books, 1976.

Baird, L.L., Richards, J.K., Effects of selecting college students by various kinds of achievement. *American college testing program research report,* 1968, *23,* 1-30.

Barlow, F. *Mental prodigies.* New York: Philosophical Library, 1952.

Barron, F. *Creative person and creative process.* New York: Holt, Rhinehart,

Winston, 1969.

Bloom, B. *Stability and change in human characteristics,* New York: Wiley, 1964.

Bruch, Torrance, J.P. Reaching the creatively gifted. *National elementary principal,* 1972, *51,* 69-75.

Cattell, J. Mck. A statistical study of eminent men. *Popular science monthly,* 1903, *5,* 359-377.

Cattell, R. B., Drevdahl, J. E. A comparison of the personality profile of eminent researchers with that of eminent teachers and administrators and of the general population. *British journal of psychology,* 1955, *46,* 248-261.

Chambers, J.A. Beginning a multidimensional theory of creativity. *Psychological reports,* 1969, *25,* 779-799.

Covington, M.V. Promoting creative thinking in the classroom. *Journal of experimental education,* 1968, *37,* 22-30.

Cox, C. M. *Genetic studies of genius Vol. II.* Stanford: University Press, 1926.

Cropley, A. J. *Creativity.* New York: Humanities Press, 1967.

Davis, G.A. In frumious pursuit of the creative person. *Journal of creative behavior,* 1975, *9,* 75-87.

Dissinger, A. *Studies in the psychological foundations of exceptionality.* Monterey, Cal.: Brooks/Cole, 1975.

Ellis, H. *A study of british genius.* London: Hurst, 1904.

Elton, C.F., Shevel, L.R. Who is talented? An analysis of achievement. *American college testing program research report,* 1969, *31,* 1-30.

Feibleman, J.K. Genius vs. the American University. *Journal of higher education,* 1960, *31,* 139-142.

Galton, F. *Hereditary genius.* New York: Meridian Books, 1962.

Getzels & Jackson *Creativity and intelligence.* New York: Wiley, 1962.

Goertzel, V., Goertzel, M.G. *Cradles of eminence.* Boston: Little, Brown, 1962.

Gold, M.J. *Education of the intellectually gifted.* Columbus, Ohio: Charles Merrill, 1965.

Gowan, J.C. The relationship between creativity and giftedness. GIFTED CHILD QUARTERLY, 1971, *15,* 239-43.

Gowan, J.C. Torrance, E.P. *Educating the ablest.* Itaska, Illinois: Peacock Pub., 1971.

Grubner, H.E., Terrell, G., Wertheimer, M. *Contemporary approaches to creative thinking.* New York: Prentice Hall, 1962.

Guilford, J.P. Creativity. *American psychologist,* 1950, *5,* 444-454.

Guilford, J.P. Creativity and our future. In Rubin, R.J. *Creativity its application to the classroom.* Ventura County: Office of the superintendent of schools, 1962.

Guilford, J.P. *The nature of human intelligence.* New York: McGraw-Hill, 1967.

Guilford, J.P. *Intelligence, creativity and their educational implications.* San Diego: Knapp, 1968.

Hirsh, N.D.M. *Genius and creative intelligence.* Cambridge, Mass.: Sci-Art Publishers, 1931.

Holland, J.L., Kent. Concentration of scholarship funds and its implications for education. *College and university,* 1960, 35, 471-483.

Holland, J.L., Richards, J.M. Academic and nonacademic accomplishment: correlated or uncorrelated? *American college testing program research report,* 1965, *2,* 1-23.

Holland, J.L., Richards, J.M. Academic and nonacademic accomplishments in a representative sample taken from a population of 612,000. *American college testing program research report,* 1966, *12,* 11-17.

Hollingworth, L. *Children above 180 IQ.* New York: World Book, 1942.

Hudson, L. *Contrary imaginations.* New York: Schocken Books, 1966.

Hughes, M., Miller, G. *Frontiers of thinking.* Salt Lake City, Utah: University of Utah, 1963.

Jackson & Messnick. The person, the product and the response: conceptual problems in the assessment of creativity. *Journal of personality and social psychology,* 1965, *33,* 309-329.

Jencks, C. *Inequality a reassessment of the effect of family and schooling in America.* New York: Harper & Row, 1972.

Jennings & Nathan. Startling disturbing research on school program effectiveness. *Phi delta kappan,* 1977, Mar., 568-572.

Johnson & Fogel. Creative aptitudes in a high intelligence population. *Journal of general psychology,* 1974, *91,* 93-104.

Kagan, J. *Creativity and learning.* Boston: Houghton Mifflin, 1967.

Lescher, R. *Assessment of creativity.* Trenton, N.J.: New Jersey Dept. of Education. 1973.

MacKinnon, D.W. Nature and nurture of creative talent. *American psychologist,* 1962, *17,* 484.

Marland, S.P. *Education of the gifted and talented.* Report to the Congress of the U.S. by U.S. commissioner of education. Wash., D.C.: U.S. Government Printing Office, 1972.

7

Massialas, B.G., Zevin, J. *Creative encounters in the classroom.* New York: John Wiley, 1967.

Ogletree, E. IQ as index of creativity. *Times London educational supplement.* June 2, 1967, 2715, 1858.

Pang, M. Undistinguished school experiences of distinguished persons. *Adolescence*, 1968, 319-326.

Parnes, S.J., Harding, J.F. *A source book for creative thinking.* New York: Charles Scribner, 1962.

Reitman, S. The reconstruction of Harold Rugg. *Educational theory*, 1972, *22*, 47-57.

Rekdal, C.K. In search of the wild duck personality inventories as tests of creative potential and their use as measurements in programs for the gifted. GIFTED CHILD QUARTERLY, 1977, *XXI*, 501-516.

Renzulli, J.S.   Callahan, C.M. Developing creativity training activities. GIFTED CHILD QUARTERLY, 1975, *19*, 38-45.

Richards, J.M., Holland, J.L., Lutz, S.W. Prediction of student accomplishment in college. *American college testing program research report*, 1966, *13*, 1-29.

Roe, A. A psychological study of eminent physical scientists. *Genetic psychology monographs*, 1951, *43*, 121-239.

Rosner & Abt. *Essays in creativity.* Croton-on-Hudson, New York: North Riverside Press, 1974.

Rossiman & Horn. Cognitive motivational and temperamental indicants of creativity and intelligence. *Journal of educational measurement*, 1972, *9*, 265-286.

Schubert. Intelligence as necessary but not sufficient for creativity. *Journal of genetic psychology*, 1973, *122*, 45-47.

Sharp, E. *The IQ cult.* New York: Coward, McCann & Geoghegan, 1972.

Simonton, D.K. The eminent genius in history: the critical role of creative development. GIFTED CHILD QUARTERLY, 1978, *XXII*, 187-195.

Smith, L. IQ, creativity and achievement: interaction and threshold. *Multivariate behavioral research*, 1971, *6*, 51-62.

Taylor, C.W. *Second university of Utah research conference on the identification of creative scientific talent.* Salt Lake City, Utah; University of Utah Press, 1958.

Taylor, C.W. *Creativity: progress and potential.* New York: McGraw-Hill, 1964.

Taylor & Getzels *Perspectives in creativity.* Chicago: Aldine Press, 1975.

Torrance, E. P. *Talent and education.* Minnesota: University of Minnesota Press, 1960.

Torrance, E. P. Can we teach children to think creatively? *Journal of creative behavior*, 1972, *6*, 114-133.

Treffinger, D. J., Speedie, S. M., Brunner, W. D. Improving childrens' creative problem solving ability: the Purdue Creativity Project. *Journal of creative behavior*, 1974, 8,

Wallach, M.A., Kogan, N. *Modes of thinking in young children.* New York: Holt, Rinehart & Winston, 1965.

Weyl, N. *The creative elite in America.* Wash., D.C.: Public Affairs Press, 1966.

Zahn, J. C. *Creativity research and its implication for adult education.* Center for study of liberal education for adults,, Boston, U., 1966.

The Pied Piper's Magic Endures

by Bryna Paston

In a suburban Philadelphia school 20 sixth graders are savoring the afterglow of a hit. The run is over, the reviews are raves, and now they're remembering more than the moments onstage—a whole year of learning, planning, improvising, and rehearsing.

"I'd have to be honest and say I was nervous about the whole thing," admits Matt. The 20 youngsters are sitting in a circle. "But I've discovered that we're all kids."

"I found out it was okay if I made mistakes," says Bobby. "At first I worried a lot about that. Especially the teasing I might get."

"Here," says Carol, "almost no one teases us."

"Some kids in the school still tease us, though," Bobby reminds her. "Oh, sometimes they call us slow, sometimes even weird."

Peggy speaks up, "Some kids don't associate with us because they say we're eggheads."

"It helped to have Obie in the play," says Steve. (Obie, a main character in *The Pied Piper,* is crippled.)

"Because Obie was different from the other children in the town," says Lisa, "they teased him. He was lonely. He wanted to be able to run and dance. But more than anything, Obie wanted to be accepted by the other children."

"Obie," says Ted, "is a lot like us." The 20 sixth graders divide equally between learning disabled and gifted students. Bobby, Carol, and Steve spend part of the time in a regular classroom at Round Meadow Elementary School in Pennsylvania's Upper Moreland School District and, depending on each one's needs, are also receiving special education. Matt, Peggy, and Lisa are in the school's gifted program. Last year, they and the rest of the 20 sixth graders produced a two-act play, *The Pied Piper.* How they grew to feel comfortable and candid with one another is a story in itself.

The whole idea began as two separate thoughts in one teacher's mind. For two years, Michael Rothstein had watched the learning disabled students in the Round Meadow school cafeteria sitting off to themselves at a corner table. Being in regular classrooms did not seem to change the youngsters' social isolation.

Rothstein was also thinking about how to challenge his class of gifted children with whom he'd been working for three years. Although Rothstein and the youngsters had done many creative projects together, he worried that if they were to become leaders, they should be getting to know other youngsters better than they had. He also worried that they considered themselves to

From *American Education,* October 1979, published by the U.S. Department of Health, Education and Welfare.

be too perfect.

Why not, thought Rothstein, challenge his gifted students by having them work with learning disabled students and, at the same time, help bring the learning disabled out of their social isolation? Rothstein recalled how his gifted group had taken to *The Wiz* (based on *The Wizard of Oz)* during a field trip to Philadelphia last term, particularly the feat of reshaping a classic.

Using theatrical experiences as a teaching tool is a natural technique for Rothstein, who has done this throughout his 17 years as classroom teacher and crisis counselor.

But Rothstein wanted to avoid the easy cliché of gifted kids tutoring the learning disabled. Rothstein suspected that each group had help for the other. "My gifted youngsters, if anything, were overconfident. They needed to discover that handicapped youngsters have leadership qualities, too. On the other hand, LD youngsters fear criticism and shun leadership roles."

As a child, Rothstein had his share of adjustment to school and he got some help from teachers along the way. Back in Trenton, New Jersey, in the 1940s, his fifth grade teacher Lois Tobish was a stern schoolmarm with rigid standards. "But her kids," says Rothstein, "knew she cared. Even the ones from poor homes. She'd come in with dresses that she told us she'd bought for her niece. Mumbling something about the dresses not fitting her niece, she'd give them to different girls in the class. Years later, I realized she didn't have a niece.

"I used to beg my father for a crewcut so Miss Tobish couldn't grab my hair. You know, she was the only teacher who ever whacked me with a ruler, but she was also the only one who ever hugged. me."

He also remembers his eighth grade history teacher Bill Carnigan. Hating school, Rothstein often played truant, taking out a boat on the Delaware River —as he says, "to read stories I liked, not school stuff. But," says Rothstein, "Carnigan had a way of filling his classes with juicy tidbits about the doings of kings and queens, much like a soapie that is continued tomorrow. It got so I had to keep coming back to find out what happened.

"Anyway, I owed him 15 written as-signments and I wasn't doing anything about them. Some kids stole my private notebooks of poems and stories and showed them to Carnigan. He told me to write a book report on my own work and that would count for all 15 assignments. It was an offer I couldn't refuse.

"He made me see myself as a writer and as someone who is competent. It made quite a difference to me. I started coming regularly to school and doing well in classes. Four kids from that history class became teachers because of Bill Carnigan." One of the youngsters, of course, was Rothstein.

For Rothstein, now fortyish and settled in at Round Meadow, ideas like mixing gifted and LD students come naturally. The real challenge is to do them. Rothstein sought out Beverly Sigafoos, special education teacher for the school district, then teaching a class of learning disabled sixth graders at Round Meadow. She warmed to the idea, volunteering her help. One firm rule they agreed upon: *no script.* A learning disabled youngster generally has trouble with reading, and a script would be too threatening. "We hatched a way around that by having one of us write down the dialog as the youngsters improvised. When they forgot a line, we fed it to them. We also used a tape recorder and videotape. Being able to see and hear their performances caught the youngsters' fancy so that mistakes became less important."

Once the principal approved the project, Rothstein approached his gifted students. "They reacted enthusiastically," he remembers, "particularly with *The Wiz* fresh in their minds."

He went down to Sigafoos's class and explained the play and what they would be doing—improvising a script based on a legend, and then acting out and producing the show. "We talked," says Rothstein, "about the characters." He found the youngsters less than lukewarm to the idea. "I couldn't seem to bring them out, get them to talk beyond the usual polite yes or no," says Rothstein, who usually has a knack for putting youngsters at ease. "I didn't know enough then to realize they were full of fears, self-doubts about performing and goofing up lines and risking ridicule from the gifted students, whom they didn't know."

It wasn't easy to get Sigafoos's students to attend the first joint meeting. "We practically had to push them there," says Rothstein. To break the ice, he asked each student to make name tags that gave more than just the name. "I suggested they give a hint about themselves, tell something on the tag that they might want people to know," ex-plains Rothstein. "Well, they tried, but most didn't get beyond their names."

What surprised Rothstein more than anything was the reserve of his own gifted students. He had been counting on them to open up Sigafoos's youngsters. But no. They hung back awkwardly and volunteered nothing. The two groups sat on opposite sides of the room and stared uncomfortably. "Instead of a group, we had Beverly's group and mine. And somehow we had thought that the two groups would hit it off instantly."

Not one to be discouraged, Rothstein held a second meeting. He subdivided the youngsters into random groups of three or four, mixing gifted with learning disabled. "For the moment we forgot about the play and turned to improvisation," he says. "I asked each subgroup to 'be' a piece of equipment—in 60 seconds or less. Bobby, one of the learning disabled students, caught the idea immediately and inspired his group to become a pinball machine. The skit drew warm applause from the group. It was a breakthrough. A learning disabled student had picked up the ball as group leader."

It was time to turn to the play. "I eased them into it, talking about how a play is built around a problem and then the search for a solution," explains Rothstein. "We did some research on the Pied Piper legend. The students discovered that a town called Hamelin really does exist in West Germany, and the legend is believed to have grown out of an actual incident sometime in the 13th century. They also found that poets and storytellers sometimes draw upon a classic like the Pied Piper—as did Goethe, Robert Browning, and the brothers Grimm.

"We pieced out the basic legend. A magician, the Pied Piper, appears one day in the town of Hamelin, and for a fee, agrees to rid the town of rats. He keeps his promise by playing a flute and luring the rats into the Weser River. When the town reneges on its promise to pay him, he also charms away the children."

With the storyline clearly in mind, Rothstein turned to casting. Each weekly session of several hours was built around one main character, particularly mannerisms, feelings, and phrasing. Everyone who wanted to try out for the character would then take a turn auditioning. "We started with Obie's mother," recalls Rothstein, "how hard her life had been and how she was strong because of this. The youngsters admired her.

"To ease the way, Beverly and I got up in the middle of the circle and did some impromptu dialog. Then various youngsters auditioned as the mother. We never hurried anyone. If someone was partway through and wanted to start over, we let them. In fact, we hadn't even set dates for the performances. We wanted them to take their time."

Neither Rothstein nor Sigafoos did the casting. Instead, the group voted. To spread the lead roles around, Rothstein double-cast. One youngster might be the Pied Piper one evening and a town resident the next. With six performances, each cast would appear three times in a role. Without anyone intending it, the leads were split between gifted and LD students.

Julie, a learning disabled student with dyslexia, expressed a wish to try out for the mother's part. But she would not ask to audition. "I knew she wanted the part," says Rothstein, "but she was terrified of getting up to audition. She didn't really trust the group. Finally one youngster said to Julie, 'I was so sure when I got up there that nothing would come out. But it did. You'll see. Go on and try. If you're stuck, we'll help you. We'll give you the words.'

"Julie got up," Rothstein continues. "Taking a breadbasket for a prop, she approached the youngster playing Obie as he sat alone on the stage. She knelt down and said, 'Didn't I hear children here?' He nodded. Putting her arm around Obie, Julie whispered, 'Were they teasing you?' "

Rothstein looked over and saw that

Ted, a youngster who is seldom still, was glued to his chair and listening intently. "Nobody made a sound," he recalls. "Julie got the part. I must add, however, that she didn't learn her songs. I decided to let the situation go. But during one rehearsal, she got up there, opened her mouth to sing, and nothing came out. She was embarrassed into going home that evening and learning all three songs for the next rehearsal."

With Rothstein's encouragement, the youngsters made some changes in their version of the Pied Piper legend. They had one of the town children who had been teasing Obie in the first scene show sympathy for the boy. Further, they decided to bestow upon the Piper human emotions, particularly anger at the mayor's refusal to pay as promised. The group saw the piper in more human than mythical terms.

As a gesture to women's equality, it was decided to create the character of Katrina, a vegetable vender who leads the women into pressuring the mayor and his two aldermen to act on the rat problem. Later, when the mayor has messed things up by refusing to pay the piper, Katrina is compassionate, telling the mayor he has done some good things too. Government, the youngsters concluded, means working things out. They felt the mayor was the wiser for his mistakes.

Throughout the rehearsals, if anyone was having trouble with a part, the group would return to games or exercises. "We'd just stop," says Rothstein. "Maybe we'd do trust activities. I might ask, Whom do you trust in the group enough to fall backward against? or Who are the characters in the play who really trust each other? Who are the ones who don't?"

After a nervous couple of months, friendships began to form. Julie and one of the gifted students, for instance, became pals. Rothstein's gifted students took to going down to the LD classroom to try out the air hockey game. "I could really feel they were accepting one another," says Rothstein, "when that single table of learning disabled students in the school cafeteria became two tables pushed together so cast members could work on the play while they ate lunch."

The only formality connected with the play was a run-of-the-play contract specifying that each performer and crew member be on time, give and take positive criticism, and respect others' opinions. The idea of spelling out their responsibilities appealed to the youngsters. On the day the contracts were signed, Rothstein recalls, each youngster brought along a trusted friend to witness the agreements and also sign the paper. The youngsters even suggested that Rothstein and Sigafoos draw up contracts, which both did.

As the play progressed, so did the youngsters. There was Ted who has a non-retentive memory. With the others learning lines quickly, those on stage with Ted had to listen to every word he said because it always came out differently. All the same, he was never at a loss for words and his fellow performers learned to accommodate themselves to his non-retentive memory.

Ted also had trouble remembering the words to his songs. A parent watching one rehearsal suggested writing the lyrics on a menu that Ted held in one scene. Once Ted had the words on the menu, he never needed to look at them. Just knowing the words were there was enough.

There was an unplanned addition to the crew. "We had a fifth grader — neither gifted nor learning disabled — who came to every rehearsal," says Rothstein. "He desperately wanted to be in the play, to be involved." Rothstein invited him to work with the group. "I put him in charge of the lights and he was terrific," says Rothstein. "The group voted him an associate member for the rest of the year."

Parents had a way of coming for a session and staying, getting involved. A mother volunteered to play the piano. A former professional dancer, a friend of Rothstein's who has her own dance group, donated her time. She did all the choreography. Many others gave hours of their time to sew costumes and help build sets.

When the final evening performance played to a capacity crowd of 350 last June, the parents, teachers, and community loved it. The question Rothstein heard the most that evening was, Which are the LD children and which are the gifted? □

Identifying and Programming For Highly Gifted Underachievers In the Elementary School

by Joanne Whitmore

It is easy for anyone – parents, teachers, neighbors, or community workers – to recognize as gifted the young child who fits the descriptive mold of the Terman well-rounded high achiever. Such a child gains our attention by his/her provocative and persistent questions, bright-eyed enthusiasm for discovering new ideas, cleverness and wit, a surprisingly advanced and appropriately used vocabulary, a remarkable memory for facts and events, and a wealth of information which humbles even the most learned adult. This child is readily identified as gifted because his/her self-confidence, created by a history of success and approval, encourages him/her to be continually self-expressive, to tackle any task, and to participate actively in social and academic endeavors within and outside the classroom.

It seems equally easy for many adults *not* to recognize signs of giftedness in the highly gifted young child who is not achieving in school. In contrast to the high achiever, this child has been conditioned by a sense of failure or rejection to withdraw from difficult tasks, to withhold self-expression, and to find some relief in nonacademic activities such as daydreaming, socializing, or disrupting. The gifted underachiever is most often recognized for his "problem behavior". Teachers and parents usually become concerned about the child's withdrawal, signs of emotional disturbance, or aggressive disruptive behavior within the classroom and/or at home.

For at least fifty years, professional educators have commented occasionally on the fact that some gifted children fail to achieve in school. Today, however, one can see little evidence that school systems are seriously attempting to identify gifted underachievers in the early grades and to systematically provide special educational opportunities for those children. Most identification is occurring through parent or teacher requests for placement of the child in a special education class, usually a class for the educationally handicapped, emotionally disturbed, or behaviorally disordered. Sometimes they are referred for special placement because of obvious learning disabilities or physical handicaps. Therefore, at present only the most severely disturbed gifted underachievers are receiving special educational programming.

The purpose of this paper is to focus our attention on the need for early identification and special educational opportunities for those youngsters who

From *Gate: Gifted and Talented Education*, Vol. 1, 1979, Journal of the World Council for Gifted and Talented Children, published by courtesy of the Bulgarian Government's Committee for Culture.

7

are highly gifted and nonachieving. The results of a program designed to meet the needs of highly gifted underachievers is expected to provide strong evidence that early identification and special programming should be a priority in our schools.

Indeed, the identification of potential gifted leaders for the future – particularly in the fields of science, government, and economics – must become an intentional worldwide priority. All people of the world are dependent upon the development of leaders who can bring the highest mental powers to bear upon the problems facing humankind today. We desperately need brilliant thinkers whose creative, constructive problem-solving can help us resolve the perplexing problems of overpopulation, world hunger, diminishing natural resources, recurring wars, crime, corruption, and mental illness. The gifted children of today are the hope for a better tomorrow. Therefore, if some of our most brilliant minds are being crippled and hidden beneath masks of failure, emotional instability, and "problem behavior" people around the world cannot afford to allow this waste to continue. Not only is the problem of early identification and intervention critical to the development of future leadership for the world, but it is also important for preventing those brilliant minds from turning against society and using their wits to mitigate against the effectiveness of social institutions and the maintenance of democratic social order. The frustration and rejection experienced by many highly gifted youngsters has the potential of producing emotionally disturbed adults who, in hostility, become powerfully destructive forces in society.

The program for highly gifted underachievers, upon which this paper is based, was first implemented in 1968 and continues today in Cupertino Union Elementary District, Cupertino, California. During the early 1960's, the Cupertino system developed an outstanding program for gifted children which was called The Extended Learning Program. By 1965 early identification of the gifted had become a major goal and screening tests were administered in the kindergarten and primary grades. In the course of extensive testing, psychologists and teachers increasingly became aware of youngsters with an exceptionally high potential for learning who were not achieving satisfactorily in kindergarten or grades one and two and had not been recognized as mentally gifted. At the time, in order for the child to be placed in an Extended Learning Program class, it was necessary for the teacher to recommend placement with assurance that it would be an optimal environment for the child's development – i.e., that the child would be a successful achiever in the class. Teachers were reluctant to recommend placement in the gifted program for youngsters not excelling in classroom learning activities. They were even more reluctant when the child manifested patterns of emotional disturbance, social immaturity, and inability to function effectively in a group or to follow directions. Consequently many underachievers had been required to repeat one of the early grades and/or to work in the low-ability group of heterogenous classes.

To reverse this pattern of early failure, a special program was designed for highly gifted youngsters. In 1968 the Board of Education accepted the proposed program, and a class for highly gifted underachievers was established.

To identify children for participation in the special class for underachieving gifted (UAG), the teacher-counselors, classroom teachers, and school psychologists were asked to identify youngsters in the primary grades who evidenced many of the following characteristics:

1. An IQ score of over 140 on Stanford-Binet or WISC.

2. A level of achievement one year or more below grade level in one or more of the basic skills, particularly reading and language arts.

3. "Problem behavior" preventing a recommendation of placement in the Extended Learning Program (classes for the gifted).

4. Superiority in comprehension and retention of concepts, though he/she may accomplish no work in applying or reinforcing concept (e.g., math); learns very quickly and easily *when interested.*

5. Vitality of imagination when stimulated; is creative, inventive in

thought, and divergent in thinking. This characteristic is often first observed in the arts and sciences.

6. An exceptionally large repertoire of "facts" – knowledge independently acquired, usually through experience outside of school.

7. Superior oral expression – uses appropriately an advanced vocabulary and concepts.

8. Acute sensitivity and perceptiveness about self, others, and life – at a level not expected for his/her age.

9. Persistent dissatisfaction with work accomplished (even in art!) and tends to be severely self-critical; is a discontented perfectionist.

10. A wide range of interests outside of school; often has profound interest in a single area – is an "expert" on some subject of special interest, most frequently in the sciences.

11. Initiative in pursuing self-selected projects for fun at home or school.

12. A low self-concept; does not seem happy with self, others, or school.

The characteristics of underachieving gifted children were described to groups of principals, psychologists, teacher-counselors and teachers in the Extended Learning Program during regularly scheduled meetings for the dissemination of information and in-service activities. The referral form which was distributed subsequently simply identified the problem and the purpose of the special class:

> Many students who are identified for the Extended Learning Program on individual IQ tests have a significant discrepancy between potential and achievement. They are not able to perform at grade level, much less being able to handle advanced or enriched curriculum. Special classes for underachieving gifted students with an IQ score of 140 or higher in grades two through five are available. The classes emphasize helping these bright students to bring up their performance levels to the point which might be expected from able students.
>
> The purposes of these classes will include motivation to learn, development of research skills, strengthening of weak skills and deficient areas, and improvement of self-concepts. The classes will be very flexibly planned and will be continually modified to better meet the needs of the pupils. A maximum amount of freedom to choose and pupil involvement in planning will be provided and all activity will be oriented toward developing self-respect, self-confidence, self-control, self-direction, and self-evaluation for the individual. Success experiences, fun in learning, and thus enthusiasm for exploring fields of knowledge will be the focus.
>
> Please list below the names of students in your school whom you would recommend for screening for this special program for next year, indicating the present grade and weak areas of performance.

The key persons involved in the referral process were the teacher-counselors who, as resource teachers, assisted classroom teachers by working with children having special educational needs. These resource teachers helped classroom teachers evaluate whether or not individuals should be considered for placement in the UAG program. Together they completed a confidential referral sheet which reported basic information about the child and school performance. The form included identification of the current placement, parents, test scores, and summary reports of the child's social adjustment, emotional growth, academic needs and strengths, and other pertinent information for evaluation in the referral process.

After referrals were obtained, the teacher(s) of the special UAG class(es) and the Coordinator of the Extended Learning Program, rank-ordered them according to their professional judgment regarding the child's degree of need for special class placement. Students were not eliminated from consideration if the IQ score obtained was not quite 140 if the examining psychologist reported that the child's performance was judged to be minimal and there were significant indications of greater potential than was demonstrated.

The next stage of screening involved a multidisciplinary team conference for each child ranked in the top twenty. Conferences were held at each child's

7

school, involving the parents, classroom teachers, the special education resource teacher, and occasionally the school psychologist and principal. If all members of the conference agreed that placement in the special class would seem appropriate for the child, the teacher of the special class involved the student in considering that option. After observing the child in the present classroom, the UAG teacher interviewed the child and invited him/her to join the class. The child made the final decision, none refusing the opportunity for help. After the first year of the program, the child usually visited the class in session prior to placement in the class. When the decision was made to place the child in the UAG class, parent commitment was obtained for regular participation in monthly parents' meetings, monthly parent-teacher-child conferences, and in seeking the services of other community agencies as appropriate.

SPECIFIC CHARACTERISTICS OF THE CHILDREN

All of the children referred for the special class were identified as highly gifted and functioning as nonachievers (i.e., were completing no work and failing to pass minimal requirements in a primary grade). All of the children potentially could have been labelled according to one or more of the following special education classifications: learning disabled, behaviorally handicapped, health impaired, or even mentally retarded! Most of the youngsters could be classified accurately by popular definitions of learning disabled and/or behaviorally disordered.

Learning disabled: A disorder in one or more of the basic psychological processes involved in understanding or in using language, spoken or written; imperfect ability to listen, think, speak, read, write, spell, perceptual handicaps, brain injury, minimal brain disfunction, dyslexia, and developmental aphasia. The result is a severe discrepancy between achievement and intellectual ability in one or more of several areas — at or below 50% of the child's expected achievement level.

Behavior disordered: The child's behavior deviates from age-appropriate behavior in a pattern which significantly interferes with the child's own growth and development and/or the lives of others. The child exhibits emotional disturbance and social maladjustment which can be best defined by the effect of the child's behavior on himself and others.

The behavior patterns of the students could be generalized as either aggressive or withdrawn. Actual potential for social and academic leadership usually was masked by defense mechanisms to protect low self-concepts. Behavior profiles of the two contrasting responses to stress created by the extreme gap between aptitude and performance level are as follows:

Aggressive, Hostile Response

- refusal to comply with rules, requests
- instead of working, moves about, disrupting others and teachers
- vies for attention in a wide variety of ways
- rejects assignments as "silly, – I know it!" or "I don't want to..."
- exploits any freedom, lacks self-direction and self-control
- alienates peers by constant aggression and derogatory attitude toward them; excessive fighting and quarreling

Withdrawal Response

- no significant communication with peers or teacher
- daydreams, wanders, doodles... lives in a fantasy world
- cannot work in groups – always withdraws alone somehow
- will attempt nothing in work or class activities

– will not even defend self

The following comments were extracted from the referral forms and cumulative records of students referred for placement in the UAG class:

"... has no close friends... easily distracted-daydreams... poor work habits, rarely finishes work... no power of concentration... discipline problem, wanders around the room... vivid fantasy world, walls us all out... appears retarded with glassy eyes and slowness... explosive, irritable, dominating... extremely shy, a complete loner... a rebellious individual... hyperactive since birth... socially rejected."

Most referrals were received because crises had occurred when the child would not or could not adapt to the social environment of school. One could summarize the process by which identification occurred as external and internal pressures increasing to the point of explosion or implosion of the child's mental health. One significant fact which contributed to the success of the program was the intense dissatisfaction the children were feeling with the way in which their personal needs were being fulfilled. In other words, they were intensely unhappy with their sense of social alienation, academic failure, and patterns of aggression or withdrawal in the classroom and often at home. Therefore, they were highly motivated to change, and parent commitment to lend appropriate support facilitated the entire process of rehabilitation.

The characteristics most frequently associated with the children identified as highly gifted underachievers, ages 5 to 9, are listed below. It is important to note that 90% of the referrals in this project were males. The asterisked characteristics were found in more than 80% of the subjects studied. All of the characteristics listed occurred with unusual frequency in this group of children.

* IQ of 140+ on the Binet
* school work had been rather consistently incomplete
* vast gap between qualitative level of oral and written work
* test phobia, poor results on group-administered tests, lack of academic initiative (as defined by school), a rigidity of interests
* profound interest in a single area in which he/she is "expert"
* school phobia – or at least disinterested in school
* very low self-esteem, unhealthy self-concept producing: difficulty coping emotionally, lack of self-confidence, inferiority feelings, sincere belief that no one likes him/her (projection of self hatred), distractibility – inability to focus, to concentrate efforts constructively; lack of selective perception of stimuli, general hyperactivity, hypertensive behavior
* a very autonomous spirit, quite focussed in self and resistant to influence
* general immaturity in all areas – physical, social, emotional
very often young (Fall babies)
chronic inattentiveness – "just cannot listen and absorb"
* inability to function constructively in a group of any size
* psychomotor inefficiency, most often a visual perception handicap
* wide interest range
* tendency to consistently set goals and standards too high; e. g., unrealistic standards of complexity or realism in art
* no apparent satisfaction from *repeated* demonstration of acquired skill – e.g., math facts, cursive writing frequently *not* motivated by the usual teacher devices – e.g., teacher enthusiasm, group interests, an environment set up by the teacher to engender interest, teacher praise or points awarded
* tendency to attribute success and failure to external control
malingering, hypochondria, frequent illness

In light of the characteristics of the easily recognized gifted child cited at the beginning of this paper, it is important to note that highly gifted underachievers were most readily identified in classrooms where there was sufficient flexibility to allow self-expression, exploration of ideas, and sharing of information between children. In highly rigid or traditional classrooms, identification was more difficult and usually occurred in response to a "crisis" situation with the child. It is important to become aware of potential

7

obstacles to the identification of these youngsters as highly gifted. The following list summarizes the most frequent causes of failure to identify early the characteristic of giftedness:

1. *Test scores* are very low on group-administered tests of achievement or aptitude.

2. *"Inability to read"* or reading unsatisfactorily at grade level."

3. Low self-esteem and subsequent anxieties may prevent oral or written participation in class which would reveal advanced thought processes (withdrawn child). Or, the child may be so engrossed in perpetual ego-defensive behavior that he/she does not respond to stimuli for learning activities or demonstrate mental skills in response (aggressive child). Often the child's advanced mental skills are illuminated only in a one-to-one teacher-pupil communication.

4. The assumption that gifted children are easily interested in academic tasks and are naturally motivated to achieve in school – NOT PERCEIVED AS "LAZY," "INDIFFERENT," "UNINTERESTED," OR "UNCOOPERATIVE."

5. Teacher's attitudes toward the nonconformist who "can't even follow directions" and may challenge her with defiance.

6. Teacher's emotional response to a child whose behavior does not indicate effort and positive attitudes but, rather, prevailing negativism and resistance.

7. Teacher's lack of knowledge about a child: especially the medical and family history.

In comparing information about individual children, several characteristics related to the home were suggested as possible accompaniments to the pattern of underachievement. Parents frequently reported anxiety over the child's behavior and indicated that the parental concern had produced considerable conflict and tension in the home. Parents also tended to note excessive conflict or noticeable lack of interaction between the child and siblings. Parents often described the child "as very different from birth," unusually sensitive, desiring much attention, and resistant to "coercion." Parents, describing their observations of the child in the early infant and toddler years, reported an independent learning style rooted in self-gratification and indicating considerable difficulty in assimilating multiple stimuli. This observation suggested inadequate selectivity and over-stimulation as a characteristic of gifted underachievers. This trait may be most closely linked to those possessing some minimal cerebral dysfunction which may interfere with the processing of stimulus input. Numerous parents described their child as "an autonomous spirit" from birth who was not motivated for long by the usual external rewards and often "difficult to penetrate" in communication. It should be noted that all children came from white middle-class homes with no other consistent characteristics evident. There was diversity in family size, composition, parent vocations and level of education.

CAUSES OF THE UNDERACHIEVEMENT OF HIGHLY GIFTED YOUNG CHILDREN

There are two primary causal forces in the underachievement of highly gifted children: (1) personality and physical characteristics including specific learning disabilities; (2) environmental conditions of the classroom. Each of the characteristics of personality which may contribute to adjustment problems in school can be positive strengths in gifted youngsters. For the highly gifted underachiever, the interaction between these traits and the classroom environment they experienced produced severe problems of emotional and social adjustment. Those traits and their concomitant difficulties are summarized below:

1. *Acute supersensitivity, perceptiveness* – produces psychological tension, contributes to hyperactivity and distractibility; creates emotional strain from supersensitivity to interpersonal relationships.

2. *Perfectionism* – can create feelings of inadequacy and can foster unrealistic self-expectations which result in "perceived failures". Perfectionism also makes the child vulnerable to sensing the high expectations of adults for his/her behavior. Intense frustration and self-rejection result when the child perceives a huge gap between his/her goals or expectations and the actual level of performance.

3. *Independence of thinking* – may cause the child to behave in a manner interpreted as "rebellious" or "disruptive"; the response to his independent thinking may foster feelings of resentment toward the structure of the classroom, feelings of alienation, and unhappiness at school. His divergent responses may not be appreciated and, in fact, may evoke punitive responses from teachers or peers.

4. *Initiative* – causes the child to want to have a choice, to resist limitations and unnecessary structure, and to seek opportunities to be self-directive.

5. *Drives toward self-expression, self-fulfillment, and productivity* – can contribute to behavior perceived as stubbornness or uncooperative perseverance as the child is reluctant to cease one task to begin another, or insists upon expressing ideas at inappropriate times. The child frequently perceives social criticism, resentment, or the irritation of others, both adults and peers, when he behaves in response to these drives. The high level of creativity present in most can frustrate the child in a classroom where convergence and conformity are valued and the creative impulse must be strictly controlled.

6. *Skill in problem solving* – may result in the child moving ahead of the class, dominating discussions or activities, or being bored with shallow curriculum.

7. *Learning style* – the specific learning style of the highly gifted child, which responds most to analytical thinking and creative exploration, may cause the student to be unresponsive to any traditional teaching methods and curricula (e.g., pages of math drill, syllabication, reading in groups, waiting your turn, and moving at a slow pace). Teachers sometimes conclude the child is unmotivated and *"lazy"*.

In addition to the personality traits described above, specific physical sources of underachievement may exist. Frequently youngsters in the special class exhibited general immaturity – physical and/or socio-emotional. Specific psychomotor handicaps were common, the most common being in the visual motor skills necessary for writing with ease and the visual-perceptual skills essential to the task of reading. Some youngsters were diagnosed as having minimal cerebral dysfunction or neurological impairment which often was specifically undefined or vaguely diagnosed. These youngsters exhibited great difficulty in gross motor activity as well as in writing or artwork. Most common was the label of "hyperactive." About eight of the children had been placed on medication to control hyperactivity. For several the drug treatment was used for less than two years. Others continued to puberty. High activity levels remained a characteristic of most of these youngsters throughout childhood.

In spite of specific disabilities or handicaps, there was no evidence that problems needed to result in such severe disturbance and underachievement apart from the external pressure created by inappropriate classroom environments, unrewarding curriculum, and teacher insensitivity to the child's specific problem and emotional needs. Children in the experimental class were able in time to specify elements of their previous classroom environments which had contributed significantly to the development of their "problem behavior" at school. Those classroom conditions can be summarazed as follows:

1. *A perceived lack of genuine respect for each individual* – the underachieving child was sensitive to the treatment of others but also perceived himself as the recipient of communicated resentment or hostility from both teacher and peers.

2. *A competitive social climate* – a competitive hierarchy fostered tensions and hostilities which resulted in the alienation of nonconformists or those

7

who were "different".

3. *Inflexibility and rigidity* – of expectations for student performance, curriculum choices sequence of learning experiences (e.g., Chapter 1,2,3, must be completed in sequence), time (e.g., deadlines, sequence of work periods), and lack of time and attention to individual interests.

4. *Stress on external evaluation* – children were aware they had to meet absolute standards set by the teacher and/or district in order to be a "success".

5. *The "failure syndrome" and criticism predominated* – children perceived that respect and rewards were granted only to those who were achieving and striving to conform. The worth of the individual seemed based on the judgment of others through grades, test scores, etc. More attention was given to errors and shortcomings than to progress. The teacher's communication was primarily composed of "you don'ts" and success seemed to be a matter-of-fact expectation of the teachers.

6. *Adult/teacher control* – children perceived the teacher as having a monopoly on all decision-making and as being a source of mandates, orders, and directions which were not to be challenged.

7. *An unrewarding curriculum* – the learning experiences were governed by regulations in the state and district, and little attention was given to the interests and abilities of students. Typically, the curriculum was not individualized and there was little group interaction or discussion.

In summary, it appeared that the stereotypic traditional classroom, focussed on textbook learning and student conformity to expectations, aggravated or created intense emotional problems for highly gifted children who also were highly creative and had developed patterns of poor performance on academic tasks in school. The most critical disturbance had occurred when teachers had been insensitive to the child's inability to perform requested tasks in a manner to meet expectations. An example is the common expectation of first grade teachers for six year olds to be able to write letters neatly between the lines. Where physical immaturity or visual-motor impairment prevented success in writing, extreme frustration resulted for the student. Likewise, for the highly gifted child unable to learn to read with any degree of success, there was a definite tendency toward self-hatred in reaction to the repeated failure. Highly creative individuals with no learning handicap sometimes failed out of emotional rebellion against a perceived press for conformity and devaluation of divergence and imagination. Characteristics of these classrooms gave support and direction to the structuring of the special class which will now be described.

DESCRIPTION OF THE SPECIAL CLASS
FOR UNDERACHIEVING GIFTED CHILDREN

Before constituting the special class of highly gifted underachievers, an attempt was made to meet the needs of such youngsters within the regular Extended Learning class for the gifted. In spite of an individualized approach and flexible planning, this was found to be a very difficult situation in which to achieve success with underachievers because of the invidious comparisons made between youngsters. The underachiever tended to feel hostility toward self when unable to write proficiently like his classmates, to produce outstanding art work, or to read fluently difficult books as did many of his classmates. As a result of this experience, the following rationale for grouping underachieving gifted youngsters together temporarily in a special class was suggested:

1. Underachievers had reacted with a self-degrading response to the superior performance of others in regular classes for the gifted; there was also the negative effect of natural competition between youngsters in a gifted class.

2. Each underachiever would be able to respect the special talents and abilities of others in the special class while also recognizing their "academic failures," personal struggles, and handicaps.

3. Intellectual stimulation through idea play, creative problem solving,

and discussions would be very rewarding for underachievers.

4. Underachievers need genuine success by their standards of giftedness; it would be easier to structure experiences of genuine success in a classroom of highly gifted youngsters than in a class of low-functioning children or high-achieving gifted.

5. These children are uniquely capable of ministering effectively to each other; grouping them together accelerates the socialization process and emotional adjustment.

Further justification for a special class comes through the distinctions made between a class for underachieving gifted and educationally handicapped (or LD and BD children). In the UAG class, a rational approach existed from the beginning, with the children being able to identify and resolve problems through consistent support and guidance from the teacher. Curriculum units, such as study of the human body and psychology of behavior, helped them to understand their difficulty when trying to achieve in school. In most special education classes, the day is shortened and there is increased structure and direction. These children had rebelled against structure that seemed excessive and oppressive and were hungry for freedom and the right to pursue their own interests in a self-directed manner. Consequently, the length of the day was extended an hour to include a workshop period after school. This was their favorite aspect of the program and was most beneficial in facilitating social development as well as pursuit of academic types of projects. Furthermore, the class was identified as part of the Extended Learning Program for gifted and, therefore, avoided some of the negative effects of labelling that these children would perceive if placed in a class for educationally handicapped.

The class was structured with two primary goals in mind: (1) the rehabilitation of poor self-concepts; (2) the remediation of specific learning problems and development of achievement motivation in school. The class was structured from a humanistic philosophy and a psychological theory that the development of healthy self-concepts is the most basic educational need which, to a great extent, has to precede the pursuit and attainment of specific learning goals. Six specific purposes or objectives for the class reflect both the philosophy and methodology:

1. To modify the responses and change basic behavior patterns of individuals so that:

(a) he/she can adjust to the demands of a class situation without feeling that his/her individuality is unappreciated, rejected, or to be suppressed;

(b) response patterns to social and academic pressures can be modified in a constructive direction to improve social relationships and learning behavior;

(c) self-directive behavior is developed in a group context.

2. To promote the emotional adjustment of individuals – i.e., to improve self-concepts and raise self-esteem so that positive attitudes develop toward learning, people, and school, in addition to self.

3. To foster social adjustment – to help the child develop the ability to sit in a group, to contribute to a group effort, to become involved and work with others, to listen and to respond appropriately in social settings.

4. To develop more realistic perceptions of self and life.

5. To prevent continuation of the self-fulfilling prophecy: to reverse the self-destructive patterns perpetuating failure and rejection.

6. To reduce the academic lag so that the child can return to an appropriate classroom and achieve at a level commensurate with his/her ability.

The objectives are listed in order of emphasis in the beginning stages of the program although all objectives were continually in the mind of the teacher.

The teacher's approach to the experimental class could be described as child-centered with an eclectic methodology attempting to create a classroom environment of acceptance, success, and fun. The basic belief was that through successful experiences, socially and academically, the child would develop a more healthy self-concept which would release him/her to develop

7

a natural love of lifelong learning, a zest for the adventures of life, and an energized drive toward self-actualization of potential. The teacher focussed her efforts on developing a sense of community within which there was genuine rejoicing over individual differences.

Five "keys" to self-esteem and academic growth were foremost in the mind of the teacher while establishing the classroom environment and planning for learning activities. Those keys are:

1. To foster the communication of genuine respect between individuals.

2. To focus first on the child as a person; to treat the student as an active participant and problem solver.

3. To design individualized learning experiences which will foster self-management.

4. To decrease and eliminate external and internal pressures having detrimental effects on the child.

5. To provide success experiences – academically, socially, personally.

In designing the program with those keys in mind, six primary tasks for the teacher emerged:

1. To eliminate all need for defenses against failure, criticism, and rejection.

2. To evaluate all curriculum for each individual child, involving him in the selection and evaluation.

3. To identify with the child realistic goals and small steps to be taken in order to reach each goal.

4. To devise ways to develop social skills and to foster leadership potential.

5. To seek alternatives for activities, how to work (e.g., individually? in teams? in pairs?), and when to work (i.e., a flexible schedule).

6. To motivate achievement through curriculum and instruction involving their individual and collective interests, making meaning and usefulness evident to them.

The author is currently writing a book to describe in considerable detail the characteristics of the children and the content of the program. In this paper, only a very sketchy description can be provided. The basic methodology of the course can be outlined in terms of major objectives.

Objective: To increase self-esteem, to change a negative self-concept.

Communicated respect, experienced success, shared and independent decision-making, and self-evaluation are primary methods for increasing self-esteem in children. Genuine respect for the child is conveyed by the teacher as she listens, evidences interest and a desire to help, honestly trusts the child, and shares personal feelings with the child. Much respect is communicated as the teacher allows the student to make decisions relative to curriculum options and alternative methods of learning. Utilizing self-correcting work and student charts of personal progress and involving students in goal-setting, selection of materials and methods, and self-evaluation are methods which communicate trust and respect to the child. Prescriptive teaching and the use of programmed materials are helpful in guaranteeing success but discovery of learning through problem solving is even more motivating and self-enhancing.

Objective: To increase socialization and social adjustment

Group sharing through class meetings involving open discussions of problems helps youngsters discover that others have the same feelings as they do and heightens social sensitivity and awareness. Role playing and sociodrama also help children to develop empathy. After-school workshops allow students to pursue their own interests in an informal social atmosphere which encourages learning to work in pairs and teams requiring cooperative effort. Social studies and science projects involving group planning and evaluation also contribute to the development of social skills.

Objective: To change the behavioral response to curriculum and academic work from negative avoidance to positive attack

In the early months of the student program, behavior modification was used to eliminate undesirable behaviors and to increase the frequency of appropriate behavior. In addition, attitudes toward work were significantly modified by allowing students increasing responsibility for selecting the content of their work, for setting goals, and evaluating their own efforts. The involvement of the child's interest in planned activities and the development of a rational understanding of the gap between the child's thinking and performance levels also contributed significantly to changing behavior during work periods.

Objective: To develop self-discipline and improve work habits

All instruction in the basic skills was accomplished through an individualized format and afternoon activities in the arts and sciences involving various forms of group work. In both types of activities, extensive involvement in planning and evaluation motivated students to develop a high level of self-discipline. They internalized responsibility for the outcomes of their behavior during work periods and began to take pride in their accomplishments. In addition, teaching methods of reducing muscle tension or appropriately ventilating frustration or anger, helped them to improve work habits and concentration. Children had freedom to move, leave the classroom, work anywhere they desired with the ultimate evaluation of the appropriateness of the decisions always returning to the child in a conference with the teacher. The youngsters developed a remarkable level of self-management as a group and individually.

Objective: To reduce the academic lag

It is easy to see how interrelated the first four objectives are. As those are attained, rapid academic progress can be expected. With increased emotional stability and reduced conflict, the highly gifted child becomes more able to direct his mental abilities and emotional energies toward the pursuit of academic learning. Some specific techniques of prescriptive teaching and remediation facilitated academic progress. An effort was made always to pair strengths with weaknesses or pleasurable activities with less rewarding tasks. In that manner, specific learning activities were designed where the student could remedy weaknesses through a pleasurable medium or in some way that was gratifying. The utilization of a wide variety of methods and content was necessary in order to capitalize upon and stimulate interest which would motivate academic learning. To say the methodology was eclectic is perhaps an understatement. Frequent trips to the Instructional Materials Center were essential to rummage through new and old, discarded curricula in order to find possible materials which would heighten motivation and accomplish specific learning objectives. Numerous packaged programs were very effective – e.g., Sullivan Reading Program (for junior high remedial readers), MacMillan Reading Spectrum, SRA Think Lab, etc.

RESULTS OF THE PROGRAM

Twenty-nine students participated in the experimental class during the first two years (1968-70): six for both years, thirteen for only one year, and ten for the second year plus one or more additional years in the intermediate level UAG class. Scores on standardized achievement tests and measures of self-concept and locus of control, plus anecdotal records of the teacher regarding behavioral changes, comprised the data for evaluation of the results.

It is significant that this study began as an educational intervention rather than a research project. The consequence is that data analysis is limited by the usual problems of missing data, pre-intervention scores only on comparable rather than identical measures (i.e., achievement test scores,) and the variability among subjects on such variables as length of time enrolled in the special class, age and baseline data collected prior to entry into the UAG program. The most appropriate and accurate use of the collected data is for the purpose of evaluating the growth of individuals in a clinical model or case study approach to program evaluation. Group statistics obscure the meaningful changes which occurred in individuals. For example, self-concept scores tended to be extremely high; or low, producing a group mean approximating the norm.

7

The initial data collected on student behavior, self-concept, and perceived locus of control were used to set educational goals and plans for individuals. Later data obtained were a basis for evaluating the effects of individualized programs. Pauline S. Sears, Stanford University professor, assisted as an external evaluator with the collection of information about self-perceptions and with behavioral observations. She observed students in the class one half day per week for the first year. Her observational reports and the classroom teacher's anecdotal records provided the basis for evaluating pupil behavior.

For some youngsters, behavioral changes occurred rather suddenly in the new climate of the classroom, but for most it was a very gradual and painful process of growth. In the end, however, changes were dramatic for each student. By the end of the second year, and usually by the end of the first, students had established new behavior patterns which reflected significant social and emotional growth and revealed leadership potential in many. All students responded to "failure" more constructively, participated enthusiastically in school activities, gave more realistic self-evaluations and goal setting, were able to make decisions and be highly self-directive, and evidenced significantly improved peer, sibling, and parent relationships.

Responses on the Sears Self-Concept Inventory (1966) at the beginning of the experimental program indicated self-concepts were often unrealistic (i.e., defensively high with highest scores on all items) or very negative, especially regarding school subjects and social relationships. After participation in this program, students reported more differentiated and realistic self-concepts which corresponded more accurately with the child's strengths and weaknesses as revealed in observed academic performance and social behavior (e.g., low in social relations and high in work habits). Group mean scores were comparable in the spring to the mean responses reported by Sears. The value of the results, however, was in the analysis of the changes in self-reported perceptions of individual students.

In addition to the self-concept inventory, the students were asked to respond to the Intellectual Achievement Responsibility (IAR) Questionnaire constructed by Crandall, et. al. (1946). Responses on the initial administration revealed several critical patterns associated with poor attitudes toward self and school. Withdrawn students tended to have developed beliefs that a) success and failure experiences in school were externally controlled, or b) responsibility was primarily internal, especially for failure experiences with success being seen as more "luck" or external "charity." Aggressive UAG students reflected ego defensive, "I'm okay!" behavior through reporting that a) failure is more a consequence of external factors and success is internally controlled, or b) success and failure experiences are internally determined and external factors have little influence. After participation in the UAG program, students reported desirable shifts in perceptions which indicated more typical pupil perceptions and more accurate perceptions of reality, i.e., causes of failure and success experiences in school. Table 1 shows the first year shifts in group means toward the Crandall norms. At the end of the second year, most students scored higher on internal control and lower on

Table 1

Responses to the Intellectual Achievement Responsibility questionnaire. UAG students, first year in program

	Internal responsibility				External responsibility	
	Success		Failure		Success + failure	
	Fall	Spring	Fall	Spring	Fall	Spring
X males	11.31	12.23	9.15	9.92	13.23	11.85
X females	10.33	11.50	8.33	10.33	15.16	12.17
X total	11.00	12.00	8.89	10.05	13.84	11.95
norm, males	12		11		11	
norm, females	13		10		11	

No 19, 13 males and 6 females

external control than the norms Crandall reported for the measure.

At the end of the first year of the class, scores on standardized achievement tests showed highly significant gains. Twelve out of eighteen students scored a gain of 1.5 to 3.0 years on reading tests and the same number were above grade in math. All students scored at or above grade level in language skills and only three remained below grade level on tests in math or reading.

At the end of the second year, the average reading gain for class participants was 2.9 or 3 school years. Of 14 third graders, the average reading score was fifth grade level, and eight out of the fourteen scored above 5.5 (fifth grade, fifth month). Only two students scored below grade level in reading and were not accelerating in all basic subjects.

In 1972 a follow-up study was conducted to begin to assess the long-term effects of the program. None of the students remained in a class for underachieving gifted. The "graduates" of the program were compared to a group of students who qualified for placement in the program but were not selected to participate. The two groups were compared on measures of classroom behavior, self-perception, attitudes toward school, and academic achievement. Parents and teachers rated the behavior of the students (*Behavior Rating Form*) and scores were obtained for all subjects on measures of self-concept (*Sears Self-Concept Inventory*) and attitude toward school (*Thinking About My School* questionnaire). In addition to providing standardized achievement test scores, teachers were asked to rate the academic performance of the students in comparison with their peers. The results of data analysis indicated that the students who participated in the program for underachievers were significantly different on all measures from similar students not in the program. Teacher reports indicated that changes which occurred in behavior and attitude while the child was in the UAG class remained stable over time. The UAG graduates had classroom behavior that was more positive and constructive, higher self-esteem, more positive attitudes toward school, and more self-directed work habits than comparable students who were not participants in the program.

The students in this study are now approaching graduation from high school. Continued contact has indicated that many of them have been highly successful and have emerged as influential social leaders as well as competent scholars. Many are planning toward careers in government, science, and law. It is obvious that these young people, once failing in school, may make very significant contributions to our society. A few, about three, of the students were unable to sufficiently overcome their handicaps so that they could fully develop their potential for academic achievement. In each case, the student had a health impairment or severe learning disability. A longitudinal study of the educational experiences and accomplishments of the students in the first UAG class continues. It is hoped that more controlled research evaluating this type of program will be conducted in the future.

DISCUSSION OF THE RESULTS OF THIS EXPERIMENT

The individual achievement gains at the end of one or two years of participation in the UAG class appeared inextricably linked to the development of anxiety produced by a desire to protect self from social or academic failures. New self-concepts and loss of anxiety resulted in freedom to respond with reasonable confidence in testing situations and to strive to achieve according to personal and institutional standards on daily work as well as on tests. Essentially, the children became free to enjoy learning, which is their innate desire.

The changes in behavior and attitudes are sustained best when successful transition has been made to regular classrooms. This is accomplished by careful placement of the students into classroom situations which will: (1) accept and encourage individuality; (2) result in more success than failure; (3) include healthy social relationships; (4) provide individualized instruction to allow continued efforts to remedy weaknesses. Most important, probably, is the selection of a teacher who delights in individual differences, divergence,

7

creativity, and nonconformity.

The findings have specific implications for regular classrooms. The first question raised pertains to the tendency of teachers to apply pressure to obtain student effort and achievement. Previous research studies have established the fact that pressure is more detrimental than facilitative for all kinds of individuals, including "high achievers," when it exceeds a tolerable level. Perhaps these youngsters have less tolerance for pressure but, in any event, it was obvious that the application of pressure was the most destructive technique that could be used.

In the experimental class, the subjects or tasks which created feelings of failure and anxiety were removed for as long as six months until a healthy self-concept and sufficient background of success experiences would allow the child to risk failure again. Although this strategy heightened teacher anxiety regarding ultimate student achievement, it proved successful. Particularly important was the strategy with pleasurable, fun experiences. The implication seems clear that teachers must cease to use the approach that more intense work and pressure in the area of weakness will remedy the problem. In many cases, a period of relief and waiting for conditions to develop which would allow success is a more desirable and effective strategy.

Another direct implication for classroom teachers is the importance of individualization of instruction. When designing programs in the basic skills for individuals, one must allow opportunity for frequent conferences with students. In these conferences information about tests results, and any other information relevant to the prescription of instructional needs, should be shared with the student and together the teacher and child, set goals and select the method by which those goals may be reached. Having available a variety of alternative curricula to accomplish goals in the basic skills is important, and allowing the student to self-pace and self-evaluate his progress in the curriculum is essential. Even in group efforts there should be opportunity for individuals to pursue learning in their own style and according to their particular interests and abilities. Individualization in the truest sense means designing learning experiences optimally valuable to the individual in his present state of ability. The individualization of instruction provides privacy for "failure experiences" and reduces invidious comparisons which tend to arouse anxiety and negative aspects of competition.

A major outcome of the experimental program was the evidence that socialization and the development of social skills is a powerful influence upon classroom behavior. The many hours spent early in the year on class meetings each day paid off in the cohesive sense of community that was developed and the spirit of acceptance and valuing of individual differences which resulted. Through healthy social relationships much healing occured as students made social contracts with each other to help individuals reach their goals for behavior change or accomplishment. Certainly a sense of being worthy is rooted in perceiving acceptance and caring in others around us. A teacher's time spent in designing experiences to enhance the socialization process and development of social skills can reap many rewards and payoffs in the academic area, as well as in social and emotional growth.

The results of the program gave further support to the known importance of success and praise as being more prevalent than criticism and failure in the classroom. It also substantiated the value of students developing skills for self-direction and self-discipline, and, the possibility of those skills being developed in bright children who are considered quite emotionally disturbed or behaviorally disordered. Exceptional potential for self-direction, self-discipline and leadership was evidenced in the classroom for underachieving gifted children.

In summary, the results of the program for underachieving gifted children tend to substantiate our belief in the importance of educating the whole child and preparing children for lifelong learning – nurturing the curiosity present when children ask questions, developing interests children possess, helping children build a repertoire of tools by which they can find answers to the questions they will raise throughout their lives. A repertoire of factual knowledge is not valuable in and of itself; knowledge must be useful and lay a foundation for further learning. With that philosophical approach, a curriculum that appears meaningful and relevant to children results. Teaching the whole child also requires providing social experiences which begin to equip these youths to become the leaders of tomorrow's world. Therefore, the results of this program suggest that humanizing and personalizing the educational activities in classrooms, establishing social and emotional development as a priority in teaching, increasing flexibility and individualizing for learning styles for different needs seem mandatory for the effective education of children – especially the mentally gifted.

In conclusion, I would urge all of us to relate the findings of this study to the current national movement in America called "Back to the Basics." Many parents as well as teachers are sensing that highly structured classrooms devoted almost solely to traditional instruction in basic skills will eliminate the problems which have been cited recently of graduting high school students lacking sufficient reading, writing and mathematical skills. The assumption seems to be that giving children more of the same instruction, increasing the pressure on the child to master the learning, and demanding more of children even at an early age will bring the desired result. I challenge all of us to consider the effects of such pressure on highly gifted children who became underachievers. It seems evident that more may be gained by creating classrooms in which efforts to motivate learning that is rewarding and enjoyable may obtain the results desired far more effectively than the "Back to Basics" approach. Mental health should be a top priority in our classrooms and the building of positive self-concepts in a humanistic environment seems essential to release youngsters for learning. Furthermore, pressing children to master skills for which they are physically or psychologically incapable at that point in time will only increase the damage and difficulty in learning. Accuracy in diagnosing educational needs and in prescribing appropriate learning experiences is critically needed. If that is attained, inappropriate expectations will be reduced and the probability of success and achievement increased for students.

To summarize the conclusions of this project, the following program elements are listed which reversed the trend and made underachievers successful learners in school:

1. Releasing the potential power within a group of individuals with similar needs to aid each individual in –

(a) raising his/her self-esteem, self-respect, and confidence in his/her ability and work through recognizing and valuing strengths;

(b) developing more realistic self-expectations through knowing others and his/her own potential and present capacity for achievement;

(c) experiencing true belonging in the peer group and school community;

(d) learning to relate effectively socially – in interpersonal relationships with peers and adults;

(e) developing skills for self-governance – self-direction, discipline, evaluation and skills in all types of problem solving, decision-making, and choosing in relation to values.

2. Guaranteeing that children experience success more often than failure in academic tasks through prescriptive teaching.

3. Teaching children techniques for self-treatment – setting reasonable goals, selecting means and materials, evaluating, employing methods of self-modification and self-control.

4. Correcting the learning deficiency – making up for lost time once the psychological obstacles to learning in that area are removed.

5. Developing an exciting curriculum relevant to their interests, meaningful, rewarding and appropriate to their learning styles.

A 1972 report on the gifted and talented distributed by the U.S. Office of Education stated:

"Research on large-scale studies has concluded that gifted and talented children are disadvantaged and handicapped in the usual school situation. It has been observed, in fact, that when mental age and

7

chronological age are compared, the gifted are the most retarded group in the schools. The boredom that results from discrepancies between the child's knowledge and the school's offerings leads to underachievement and behavior disorders affecting self and others. Early identification would enable schools to prevent rather than to attempt later on to cure underachievement. Further, there is evidence that efforts later on are wasted, as underachievement patterns are so strongly set by then."

Underachieving gifted children who may not be as critically impaired as the youngsters in this study should also be considered. Although there undoubtedly are many thousands of brilliant young children who are being turned off toward school and are developing patterns of aggression or withdrawal which result in underachievement, there probably are many thousands more who adapt to the school situation so that their giftedness is hidden under average performance and conforming behavior. All wasted human potential should be of critical concern to us in the world of 1977. We cannot afford not to cultivate all potential leadership which may contribute to the betterment of humankind.

REFERENCES

Crandall, V.C., Katkovsky, W., Crandall, V.J. Children's belief in their own control of reinforcement in intellectual academic achievement situations. *Child Development.* 1965,36, 91-109.

Fine, B. *Underachievers: How They Can be/ Helped.* New York: Dutton, 1967.

Gallagher, J. J. *Teaching the Gifted Child.* Boston: Allyn and Bacon, 1975.

Kornrich, M. (Ed.) *Underachievement.* Springfield, Illinois: Thomas, 1965.

Newland, T.E.~ *The Gifted in Socioeducational Perspective.* Englewood Cliffs, New Jersey: Prentice-Hall, 1976.

Sears, P.S. Memorandum with respect to the use of the Sears Self-Concept Inventory Stanford, California: Stanford Center for Research and Development in Teaching, R&D Memorandum No. 125, August 1974.

Whitmore, J. R. Thinking about my school (TAMS): The development of an inventory to measure pupil perception of the elementary school environment. Stanford University Center for Research and Development in Teaching, R & D Memorandum No. 125, August 1974.

Zilli, M. G. Reasons why the gifted adolescent underachieves and some of the implications of guidance and counseling to this problem. *Gifted Child Quarterly.* 1971, *15* (4), 279-292.

Giftedness and Creativity In Young Children: An Annotated Bibliography

by Nancy L. Quisenberry and John Casey

GIFTEDNESS AND CREATIVITY IN YOUNG CHILDREN:
AN ANNOTATED BIBLIOGRAPHY

This annotated bibliography pulls together articles which report research on giftedness and creativity in the early years. Research on these topics with young children, ages three to eight, appears to be sparse. These annotations provide the reader with a range of findings on these topics.

Abravanel,Eugene Intersensory integration of spatial position during spatial position during early childhood. *Perceptual and Motor Skills,* 1968, 26, 251-256.
Studying perceptions of spatial position, 96 subjects ranging in age from 3-6 were used. Subjects aged 3-4 showed little accuracy in sameness-difference judgments, whereas, significant increases in accuracy were found by ages 5 and 6.

Biller, Henry B. Singer, David L. and Fullerton, Mary Ellen. "Sex' Role Development and Creative Potential in Kindergarten-Age Boys." *Developmental Psychology* 1. 291-296. 1969.
Creativity was unrelated to IQ across ten different measures of creativity. Creativity was not significantly associated with sex-role orientalism or preference; but boys with mixed sex-role patterns demonstrated higher creativity than those with a consistent pattern.

Cathcart, W. George. "The Relationship Between Primary Student's Rationalization of Conservation and Their Mathematical Achievement. 'Child Development,* September 1971, *42,* 755-C5.
Primary aged children who use several rationalizations; instead of one for conservation tasks based on Piagets task have higher mathematical achievement.

Davis, F. B., Lesser, G. S., French, E. G., and others, Identification and Classroom Behavior of Gifted Elementary School Children. THE GIFTED STUDENT, U.S. Department of HEW Monograph, 2, 1970, 19-32.
Intellectual abilities can be accurately measured in children as young as four and five in at least five areas.

Dreyer, Albert S. and Wells, Mary Beth. "Parental Values, Parental Control, and Creativity in Young Children." *Journal of Marriage and the Family 28.* 83-88. February, 1966.
Parents of high creative children had less domestic value consensus and more role tension than the parents of low creative children.

Dudek, S.Z., and others. "Relationship of Piaget Measures to Standard Intelligence and Motor Scales. *Perceptual and Motor Skills* 28. 351-362, 1969. Piaget's Tests of Thinking as a measure of children's ability were slightly higher than the WISC at the kindergarten level.

7

Ellison, Odia. Identifying racial minority second grade gifted students. (Doctoral Dissertation, United States International University. 1972), *Dissertation Abstracts International*, 1972, *32*, 3783A-3784A.

Working with Negroes, Mexican-American, and white children, a battery of individual and group tests were administered. Grade point averages and teacher ratings were also used. Findings: rating scales and grade point averages identified the same percentage of gifted candidates in each ethnic group; there were significant mean differences between the white group and the minority groups on the standardized tests; the pupil rating scale and the grade point averages had the highest number of significant interest correlation coefficients.

Franklin, Margery B. *A Study of Non-Verbal Representation in Middle-Class and Lower-Class Preschool Children.* Research Division, Bank Street College of Education, New York.

Using a group of preschool children from middle and lower class backgrounds, they were tested on two tasks: (1) picture-object matching, and (2) spatial arrangement. The middle class children tended to make more correct choices than the lower-class children and received higher total scores than the lower-class group.

Gollin, Eugene S. Developmental studies of visual recognition of incomplete objects. *Perceptual and Motor Skills*, 1960, *11*, 289-298.

In an experimental study using subjects ranging in age from preschool-kindergarten, the task investigated was visual recognition of incomplete objects. The following conclusions were drawn: (1) amount of completeness required for recognition was greatest for the youngest subjects, (2) training decreased the amount of completeness required for recognition, (3) greater developmental differences were found when subjects were trained with the complete object pictures.

Gollin, Eugene S. Factors affecting conditional discrimination in children. *Journal of Comparative and Physiological Psychology*, 1965, *60*, 422-427.

The investigators worked with a group of middle class preschool children on a conditional discrimination (CD) task, which included a training and a testing phase. It was found that success in training did not assure success in the CD phase of the task for the youngest children.

Harris, Joan, Quisenberry, Nancy L. and Litherland, Ralph. "Identification of Leadership Abilities of First Grade Subjects Using the Primary Leadership Identification Instrument (PLII)," Mimeograph Copy, Southern Illinois University-Carbondale, 1974.

Leadership abilities can be identified in first grade children. Few children demonstrate leadership abilities in all areas.

Lichtenwalner, Joanne S. and Maxwell, J. W. "The Relationship of Birth Order and Socioeconomic Status to the Creativity of Preschool Children." *Child Development* 40. 1241-1247, 1969.

Middle socioeconomic Anglo young children had a mean inability score higher than lower socioeconomic children on Starkweather Originality Test. Oldest and only children made higher mean scores than later born preschool children.

Machen, Orellle H. A validity and reliability test (SIT) with an atypical population--gifted children (Doctoral dissertation, The Catholic University of America, 1972). *Dissertation Abstracts*, 1973, *33*, 329A.

This study investigated the reliability of the SIT and its concurrent validity with the WISC, using gifted children. The results indicated that the SIT is a reliable and valid instrument for use by school personnel in the identification of gifted children.

Martinson, R. A. & Seagoe, M.V. *The Ability of Young Children.* Council for Exceptional Children Research Monograph, 1967, ED 019770, 72 pp.

A significant relationship was found between high IQ and high quality of creativity.

Pohl, Rudolph Gustave. Teacher nomination of intellectually gifted children in the primary grades. (Doctoral dissertation, University of Illinois, 1970). *Dissertation Abstracts*, 1970, *31*, 2337A.

Working with teachers in self-contained classrooms and team-teaching situations, a comparison study was conducted to see how closely teacher nomination of gifted children would correlate with those designated as gifted by an individual intelligence test. The investigator found a low correlation.

Terman, L.M. *Genetic Studies of Genius.* Stanford University Press, 1959, 5 pp.

Terman's studies of children with unusually high IQ have provided much of the basic information about the characteristics, backgrounds, and development of the gifted.

Torrance, E. Paul "Current Research on the Nature of Creativity Talent." *Journal of Counseling Psychology* 6:309.16, Winter, 1959

Growth did occur in five year olds with whom a Creative-Aesthetic Approach to School Readiness was used during the kindergarten year.

Torrance, E.P. Explorations in creative thinking in the early years: VI Highly intelligence and highly creative children in a laboratory school. University of

Minnesota Bureau of Educational Research, 1959, 14 pp.

Children rated as both highly creative and of high IQ are generally leaders in al! areas.

Torrance, E. P. Educational achievements of the highly intellectual and highly creative; Eight partial replications of the Getzels-Jackson Study. Research Memorandum, University of Minnesota Bureau of Educational Research, 1960, 8 pp.

Torrance, provides data on clues to determine when the Getzels-Jackson results are likely to hold.

Torrance E. Paul and Phlips, Victor K. A three-year study of continuity of creative growth under a cognitive structure approach to educational stimulation, research, and development center in educational stimulation, University of Georgia, September, 1969, 9 pp. typed.

Ward, William C. Creativity and Environmental Cues in Nursery School Children. Developmental Psychology, 1969. 1. 543-547.

Children identified as "high creative" scan their environment for task-relevant information "Low creative" showed no environmental effect.

7

PART 8

THE PROFESSIONALS

by Glen Thompson, Ph.D.

Over the years, special education has developed as a profession. The movement is most clearly evidenced in the quality, depth and breadth of presentations at state and national Council for Exceptional Children conventions. Then there are the effectiveness and efficiency of special education's professional activities as they relate to the identification, diagnosis and education of exceptional children, as well as the quality and quantity of professional articles published.

Teaching is an art. The art is based on scientific data and textured by a humanistic regard for children and human kind in general. So teaching should never be rigid or ritualistic. A particular technique must never be employed merely because "that's the way I was taught to do it." Or because some famous educator "felt that was the way it should be done."

What teachers must do is always bring to education the best of current knowledge and practice. But they must always recognize that tomorrow can bring change and improvement. Institutions of higher learning must instill this attitude in their teacher candidates. And teachers, once they commence educating, must keep abreast of developments in the profession.

Traditionally, education was one profession that was not problem oriented. Lawyers handle legal problems; doctors, medical problems; and dentists, dental problems. Educators, in contrast, frequently wanted to deal with children who had no educational problems.

In fact, special education may owe much of its early growth to the fact that special ed removed problems from regular classrooms and segregated them in isolated areas. Some early special educators saw their primary task as keeping their charges happy rather than educating them. This philosophy may explain why efficacy studies showed retarded children learned at least as much in regular classrooms as they did in special rooms.

Today, the complexion of education is finally changing. Teachers are being trained to be problem oriented, and educational problems are no longer referred out of regular classrooms, unless the teacher can demonstrate that such a transfer would be educationally beneficial to the student.

When the "least restrictive alternative" is considered for any given student, it must always relate to the competency of the educators most directly involved. Is the regular teacher trained to be able to deal effectively with special children? Does the special education teacher have helping skills that allow him or her to serve as a professional support for the regular teacher?

The answers to these questions determine the least restrictive alternative for the special child. Mainstreaming is least restrictive only if the mainstreaming teacher is prepared to accept special students, with available support help. So, components of teacher preparation programs that address these issues are critically important, as are in-service programs.

The special educator's role requires working with regular teachers in preparing teaching pro-

8

grams for mainstreamed students in a cooperative, consulting and demonstrative manner. Teacher certification should consider these skills or competencies and devise a system for insuring that teachers receiving certificates possess them.

As new areas of specialization emerge, new problems surface. How should teachers of autistic children be prepared, for example? Or teachers of severely mentally retarded children? Or pre-school children with handicaps? One method would employ surveying the most advanced programs available and employing the results as a basis for developing a model. Another way might use specialists as consultants, perhaps in tandem with survey results, to design model programs. In either case, the preparation programs should relate directly to those competencies deemed important for teachers of such children.

Preservice Changes In Teacher Education Relative to Mainstreaming

by Julius B. Roberson

In our increasingly complex society, schools of education are being called upon to assume unparalleled obligations. Multicultural education, environmental education, nutrition, communications, health education, career education, and economic education are among the priority areas being promoted by various interest groups to be dealt with in teacher preparation programs. One of the major responsibilities being assumed by college preservice teacher preparation programs results from recent federal (and state) legislation for the handicapped.

Federal legislation can be traced to P.L. 89-10 (Elementary and Secondary Education Act of 1965) and subsequent amendments, the most significant of which were P.L. 93-380 (Education Amendments of 1974) and, in 1975, P.L. 94-142, the Education for All Handicapped Children Act. States have adopted (or are in the process of adopting) legislation and state requirements to be compatible with the federal legislation. Teacher preparation programs of colleges and universities, like the public schools of our nation, are directly affected by federal legislation and state mandates relative to the education of the handicapped. The required implementation of P.L. 94-142 in the public schools necessitates that the preparation of preservice teachers change also. Hermanowicz (1978) has cited P.L. 94-142 as one of the major developments that will quickly affect teacher education, stating, "Provisions of the Act will alter much of the conventional practice found in schooling, teacher education, in-service education, and the preparation of teacher educators" (p. 13).

Unlike the public school sector, there has been little concerted nationwide or statewide effort to bring about changes in higher education curricula and faculty to satisfy the law. Grosenick and Reynolds (1978) have indicated that two basic problems faced by institutions are how to find the most effective way to bring about a change of attitude among educators toward the handicapped child per se and how to prepare the faculties for the reconceptualization of the teacher-training curricula (p.3). In addition, Grosenick and Reynolds have said:

> Changing human behavior can be a long, laborious process. Changing societal institutions often appears an impossibility. Yet, education today finds itself in an era mandating significant change, particularly as it relates to the education of handicapped children.
>
> Colleges, schools, divisions, and departments of education in institutions of higher education must examine their training of educational personnel in light of the realities of "mainstreaming" handicapped students. (p.7)

The earlier record for institutions of higher learning providing faculty development for instructional change and improvement has not been particularly impressive. Miller and Wilson

8

(1960) concluded that there was a dearth of well-articulated, comprehensively designed programs for faculty development. During the 1970s, interest in faculty development has increased, but not to the point where there is universal practice of planning faculty development programs. Centra (1978) reported that about 60% of the accredited, degree-granting colleges in the U.S. have some sort of program or set of staff development activities for its faculty. Institutions which have programs found that faculty participation was the highest for the good teachers who want to get better. The least actively involved were those faculty who really need to improve (Centra, 1978).

A review of the literature indicated little evidence as to how public laws, especially P.L. 94-142, have affected staff development and curricula development in institutions of higher education. The purposes of this study were (a) to determine the degree to which colleges and universities in the southeastern region of the U.S. are modifying their preservice curricula to satisfy federal and state laws in the preparation of regular teachers to address the needs of "mainstreamed" handicapped children; (b) to determine the degree to which opportunities are being provided to better prepare the non-special education higher education faculty members in special education methodology. By examining the results of this study, we may determine the level of difficulty NCATE-approved teacher education programs in the SACS region are experiencing in bringing about changes in curriculum and faculty to satisfy the federal and state legislation.

METHOD

A survey instrument was developed to help investigate the difficulty which the National Council for Accreditation of Teacher Education-approved teacher education programs in the Southern Association of Colleges and Schools are experiencing in regard to curriculum changes and faculty development in order to comply with federal and state legislation. The instrument was developed in the summer of 1978. It was mailed out in September, with return requested by December 1.

Sample

The sample for this survey consisted of 128 institutions listed by the National Council for Accreditation of Teacher Education (NCATE, 1978) in the region of the Southern Association of Colleges and Schools (SACS, 1976). Of the 128 institutions surveyed, 64 (or 50%) useable questionnaires were received. Ten percent of the survey instruments were contaminated (failure to include all data asked for) and eliminated from the study.

RESULTS AND DISCUSSION

Curricula (Program) Changes

Results from the study indicate that 31% of public institutions have implemented a plan for faculty development, as compared to 9% of the private institutions. Of the larger institutions (over 10,000 enrollment), 33% had implemented their plan, as compared to 19% of the smaller institutions (under 10,000 enrollment). Of those institutions located where states have certification regulations for preparing regular teachers to teach handicapped children, 30% have implemented their plan, as compared to 12% where these regulations are not in effect. Of the 64 institutions of higher education used in the study, 24% indicated they had fully implemented curriculum changes necessary to prepare preservice teachers in regular preparation programs to teach handicapped children in the mainstream.

How Special Education Topics are to be Presented

For those institutions who have or plan to implement curricula changes, 43% indicated they would present the special education topics through a required course, 46% through modules in a required course(s), and only 11% through an elective course. Results from the study indicate that courses within the curriculum would be the major method of presenting information regarding the public laws.

In-service Plans for Nonspecial Education Faculty

Further analysis indicated that 32% of the total group reported they have no in-service plans to better prepare their nonspecial education faculty in the area of special education. This number indicates a substantial time lag for a significant number of institutions in preparing their nonspecial education faculty to meet the federal mandate of P.L. 94-142.

Of the public institutions, 76% have completed or are planning a faculty in-service program, as compared to 58% of the private institutions. This finding suggests that the public sector of education is meeting and dealing with the Public Law more expeditiously than are the private sectors of higher education. For the larger institutions, 81% indicated they have completed and/or are planning such a program, as com-

TABLE 1
*Status reports of preservice teacher preparation programs for
nonspecial educators and the education of the handicapped*

	Curricula (Program) Changes					Method of Presentation			
	No Plan	Plan Being Developed	Complete Plan	Partially Implemented Plan	Fully Implemented Plan	Through Required Course	Through Modules In Required Course(s)	Through Elective Course	N
Public inst.	2%	26%	11%	29%	31%	41%	46%	12%	44
Private inst.	24%	26%	16%	26%	9%	48%	40%	12%	20
Under 10,000 enrollment	12%	25%	19%	24%	19%	45%	42%	13%	44
Over 10,000 enrollment	.02%	27%	.01%	36%	33%	37%	52%	10%	20
State cert. reqs.—yes	8%	21%	14%	27%	30%	45%	44%	11%	44
State cert. reqs.—no	12%	36%	11%	29%	12%	36%	50%	14%	20
Summary	9%	26%	13%	28%	24%	43%	46%	11%	64

TABLE 2

	Institutional Plans for In-Service for Nonspecial Education Faculty			Method of Presentation			
	In-Service			In-Service			
	No In-Service Plan at this Time	Plan Being Developed	Complete In-Service Plan	Individual Faculty	Seminars or Workshops on Campus	Credit Courses	Other
Public inst.	24%	54%	22%	21%	68%	8%	2%
Private inst.	42%	53%	5%	41%	52%	2%	4%
Under 10,000 enrollment	39%	46%	15%	32%	60%	.05%	.03%
Over 10,000 enrollment	15%	57%	24%	20%	64%	.09%	.06%
State cert. reqs.—yes	30%	53%	17%	26%	63%	6%	5%
State cert. reqs.—no	35%	42%	23%	32%	60%	7%	1%
Summary	32%	49%	19%	29%	65%	6%	Less than 1%

pared to 61% of the smaller institutions. Results from the survey indicate that the larger universities are planning to use in-service training or workshops as the major method of staff development. However, the smaller, private institutions are leaving the staff development to the responsibility of individual faculty members. Of the institutions located in states with the previously mentioned certification requirements, 70% have or will have a program of in-service for their nonspecial education faculty with no reference to a schedule for completion. This is compared to 67% of the states where no such state regulations are currently in effect. Of the total group, 68% are now completing or have completed their in-service plans for their non-special education faculty.

How In-service Will Be (or Is Being) Accomplished

For those institutions who have a plan or a completed program for faculty in-service, 65% indicated they will hold inservice seminars on their campuses and 29% will allow this professional development to be undertaken by the individual faculty. For the various categories of institutions in the study, over 50% indicated the

8

in-service would be accomplished in the same manner. Less than 10% of the total group have indicated the use of credit courses for this purpose.

SUMMARY

The larger public institutions appear to be progressing more rapidly towards the two-fold task of making curriculum changes and faculty development in the area of special education. The smaller, private institutions appear to be having more difficulty in modifying their curricula and bringing about faculty development. Institutions indicated three options in presenting handicapped topics to preservice teachers: through a single, required course, through modules in several courses, and through an elective course. The institutions that have modified (or will modify) their curricula are about evenly divided between the first and second options, both requiring their students to enroll in either a single course or incorporating selected elements of handicapping topics into a series of courses. Institutions within states that now have state certification requirements for addressing handicapped topics are moving more rapidly towards incorporating mainstreaming into their preservice curricula.

About one-third of the institutions have no in-service plan for their faculty. For those institutions that have plans, about two-thirds will hold faculty workshops or seminars on their campus. The results would indicate that the professional organizations, the state and federal levels of special education services, should perhaps develop a network whereby the large public institutions can provide collaborative assistance to the small private institutions in developing individual plans to meet the federal mandates. For professional faculty growth to occur, there must be significant involvement on the part of the affected faculty (in both planning and implementation), a commitment on the part of the total faculty (especially those in positions of leadership), and the financial capability to secure resources and expertise not available on their respective campuses. Without more significant progress, the regular classroom teacher will continue to enter the teaching profession ill-prepared to deal with the "mainstreamed" child. Without planned in-service for higher education faculty, the capability to prepare these preservice teachers will not be fully realized.

REFERENCES

Centra, J.A. Faculty development in higher education. *Journal of Higher Education* 1978, *80* (1).

Grosenick, J.K. & Reynolds, M.C. (Eds.). *Teacher education: Renegotiating roles for mainstreaming.* Minneapolis: National Support Systems Project, University of Minnesota and The Council for Exceptional Children, 1978.

Hermanowicz, H.J. Teacher education: A retrospective look at the future. *Journal of Teacher Education,* 1978, *29*(4).

Miller, W.S., & Wilson, K.W. *Faculty development procedures in small colleges.* Atlanta: Southern Regional Board, 1960.

National Council for Accreditation of Teacher Education. *24th Annual List 1977-78,* Washington, D.C., 1978.

Southern Association of Colleges and Schools. *Procedures of the 80th Annual Meeting,* Atlanta: March, 1976.

Preparing Teachers of The Severely Handicapped: Responsibilities and Competencies of the Teacher Trainer

by John Umbreit, George Karlan, Robert York and Norris G. Haring

The preparation of teachers of the severely handicapped is a fairly recent endeavor in the field of special education. Only a decade ago, few people believed that severely handicapped people could benefit from educational services. The idea of training professionals to serve this population in public school settings was seldom considered. The changes since then which have affected education for the severely handicapped can be traced to several events, including significant litigation (*Pennsylvania Association for Retarded Children v. Commonwealth of Pennsylvania*, 1971; *Mills v. Board of Education of the District of Columbia*, 1972) and legislation (P.L. 93-380; P.L. 94-142), the formation of a professional organization (The Association for the Severely Handicapped[1]), recognition and acceptance of concepts such as normalization and desegregation (Wolfensberger, Nirje, Olshansky, Perske, & Roos, 1972), and developments in applied behavior analysis (cf. Mercer & Snell, 1977; Snell, 1978).

Despite dramatic changes and the rapid development of the field, a number of problems remain. One of the major problems is that severely handicapped people gained the legal right to an appropriate education before a suffi-cient number of well-trained teachers could be provided (McDowell & Sontag, 1977). Although substantial progress has recently been made, we must be careful to view teacher preparation critically, rather than lauditorily, or continued progress will be less likely to occur.

Previous analyses of teacher preparation (cf. Burke & Cohen, 1977) have focused on identifying the skills a teacher should possess by the time preservice training is completed. There has been an almost *a priori* assumption that the battle has been won once a set of posttraining behaviors has been identified. Our intent is to analyze the teacher education process by focusing on an often-ignored critical element—the teacher trainer.[2] What are the responsibilities of those who train teachers of the severely handicapped? What kinds of competencies do they need to fulfill their responsibilities and to

1. Formerly the American Association for the Education of the Severely/Profoundly Handicapped

2. When we use the term "teacher trainer," we are referring to university faculty who prepare professional educational personnel. Because our intent is to focus on the teacher trainer, rather than to define the term *severely handicapped,* we refer the interested reader to Baker (1979) for a recent review and critical analysis of the definition of the latter.

8

From *Teacher Education and Special Education*, Vol. 3, No. 2, Spring 1980. Copyright 1980, Special Press. Reprinted with permission.

achieve their goals? We will consider the teacher trainer's role in regard to five important issues—competency-based training, field-based training, in-service training, the desirable qualifications of the teacher trainer, and conflicts between the different roles a trainer must fulfill. If our paper generates thoughtful consideration and discussion, even controversial discussion, of these issues, then our goal will have been achieved; and our field and the population we serve should be the ultimate benefactors.

COMPETENCY-BASED TRAINING

Special educators are now required to demonstrate higher levels of competence than the field has ever seen before (Haring, 1978). Although a variety of approaches to teacher training may be found in the literature (cf. Dunn, 1973), the competency-based approach is becoming more common in special education, particularly among those who train teachers of the severely handicapped (Bricker, 1979; Horner, 1977; Wilcox, 1977). The trend is not surprising if we consider that few teacher trainers in our area would question the appropriateness of applying a behavioral approach to teaching the severely handicapped (Burke & Cohen, 1977) and to the process of preparing teachers to serve the population (Bijou & Wilcox-Cole, 1975). In fact, employing a competency-based approach to teacher preparation may well be the logical result of adopting a behavioral approach to the education of students with severe handicaps.

Brown and York (1974) have defined "teaching" as the process of creating or arranging an environment in ways that produce specified changes in a student's behavior. If you accept this view of teaching, as we do, then the ultimate goal of a competency-based approach to preparing teachers of the severely handicapped must be to have student teachers acquire the competence to produce observable, desired changes in the behavior of the students they will teach. If a prospective teacher acquires competencies which do not relate either directly or indirectly to changing his or her students' behavior in specified ways, then those "competencies" are of little no value to the student or teacher or to the severely handicapped student.

The process of training teachers of the severely handicapped can be viewed as involving three major levels of training. The first level is the level of *skill development;* the second is the opportunity to *practice* target skills until an individual reaches an acceptable level of proficiency; and the third provides the opportunity and training to *apply* and *adapt* skills and knowledge in the actual education setting. Naturally, the measure of competency through these advancing levels will need to be applied somewhat differently in each case.

Starting at the first level, with the building of targeted teacher skills, many skills that teachers must acquire involve the ability to make very quick and accurate responses, and to respond to the severely handicapped child during an emergency (e.g., recognizing seizures and taking appropriate action, dealing with choking, intervening when a child with a sharp object advances on another child, identifying and counting behaviors targeted to be measured, charting, analyzing charts and making instructional decisions, lifting children, and carrying children). All of these behaviors are part of the daily teaching routine.

The next level of training requires the individual to apply and practice these skills in the classroom. Prospective teachers must achieve a reasonable level of generalization and integrate skills into a fluent sequence. Teacher trainers not only must set specific criterion levels for the trainee, but must also assess and reassess the trainee to insure that these well-coordinated teaching procedures are maintained over time.

The third and highest level of training requires adaptive teaching behaviors. This training involves an opportunity for the individual to develop the skills needed to adapt to a wide variety of instructional settings, including the classroom, the community, and the home. Each can and should be an instructional setting but each requires flexibility and adaptability.

Clearly, teacher trainers need to devote considerable attention to the process by which prospective teachers acquire specific skills or competencies, apply and integrate these skills, and learn to make necessary adaptations. As Meyen (1975) stated, we must be careful to prevent situations in which we "find the 24-hour retarded child being taught by teachers who run out of skills after an hour and a half" (p.144). In response to this concern, two major approaches to preparing teachers of the severely handicapped have emerged. These approaches involve either identifying a large number of *specific competencies*, or identifying certain *general strategies* for changing behavior. Both approaches, which are described below, are intended to enable teachers to produce verifiable changes in the behavior of their students.

Approaches to Competency-Based Training

The approach of identifying large numbers of specific competencies is probably best exemplified by Horner's (1977) description of the training program which operates at the University of Kansas. The program is based largely on a set of 322 informational competencies and 128 performance competencies (Horner, Holvoet, & Rinne, 1976) which were compiled "through an analysis of the literature, expert opinion, direct observation of teacher behavior, and lists prepared by teachers in the field and students in the program" (Horner, 1977, pp. 431-432). *Informational competencies* specify the information a teacher must acquire in order to achieve a performance competency. *Performance competencies,* which specifiy the behavior to be demonstrated by a student teacher, presumably enable one to effectively change the behavior of severely handicapped students. These competencies are included within 25 modules which comprise the teacher-training program. Haring (1978) suggests that the vast number of competencies identified by Horner et al. (1976) can be subsumed within nine general areas:

1. Techniques for managing severe behavior problems;
2. Procedures for developing teacher-made instructional materials;
3. Engineering physical properties of a classroom;
4. Basic principles of the acquisition of operant behavior;
5. Basic principles and techniques of measurement;
6. Basic principles of imitation training, generalization, discrimination, and maintenance;
7. Basic principles of task analysis;
8. Development and implementation of instructional programs; and
9. Procedures used to develop curriculum sequences. (Haring, 1978, p. 412)

One should note Horner's admission that the list of competencies he and his colleagues developed "probably has omitted many required competencies and may include many that are not required" (1977, p. 431). Nevertheless, their efforts represent a major approach to preparing teachers of the severely handicapped.

A different method, which involves identifying general strategies for changing behavior, is probably best exemplified in the model which was described by Bricker (1976), and later extended by Iacino and Bricker (1978). Their system, which was developed and implemented at the University of Miami, tried to avoid the situation in which trainees must acquire "1008 essential competencies" (Bricker, 1979, p. 5).

Rather, they suggest that the process of teacher preparation should focus on developing global areas of expertise such as content knowledge, instructional strategies, synthesis and evaluation.

Content knowledge refers to developing in the student teacher certain conceptual skills, such as knowledge of behavioral technology, awareness of developmental processes, and familiarity with the broad content of curricular domains. *Instructional strategies* involve training teachers to serve as "instructors" for at least three distinctly different targets—severely handicapped students in the classroom, parents of these students, and preservice or inservice trainees seeking practical experience with severely handicapped students in a classroom. Skills at *synthesis* involve training teachers to draw information and materials from a variety of relevant disciplines and professionals, and to integrate these resources into a comprehensive intervention program. *Evaluation skills* involve training teachers to assess a student's current level of functioning, to determine appropriate training targets, to set priorities, and to monitor the overall effectiveness of an intervention program.

Underlying Iacino and Bricker's approach is their belief that prospective teachers of the severely handicapped should be trained to employ general strategies which transcend any particular student or problem, but which can be applied to the needs and problems of any particular student. They call a teacher with these global competencies a "generative teacher."

The primary difference between the Horner (1977) and Iacino and Bricker (1978) approaches to competency-based training stems from a difference in their points of view about how competencies should be delineated. For Horner and his colleagues, competencies are precise statements that describe the expected behavior of a trainee. They have identified a large number (450) of these competency statements and apply them as objectives to be met by trainees in the same way that teachers would apply behavioral objectives in their classes. On the other hand, Iacino and Bricker prefer to delineate only four global competencies (i.e., content knowledge, instructional strategies, synthesis, and evaluation) and the general areas (e.g., behavioral technology, developmental process, etc.) that comprise each of the competencies.

The advantage of using Horner's approach lies in the opportunity to precisely define and measure a trainee's performance in relation to each informational and performance competency. Iacino and Bricker's approach does not allow for this same degree of precision. For exam-

8

ple, how do you reliably define and measure the degree to which a trainee "draws information and materials from a variety of relevant disciplines and professionals"? However, the Iacino and Bricker approach allows for a good deal more flexibility in training than does Horner's approach. Furthermore, their system of training would seem to be much more easily managed than Horner's, and possibly equally as effective.

Quality and Relevance

Regardless of which approach is adopted, those who train teachers of the severely handicapped must strive to make the content and sequence of their training programs relevant and functional. To do so, teacher trainers will need to keep up-to-date on the latest techniques and information from the literature, to continually review and revise the content and sequence of the courses they offer, to carefully select students who will enter a training program, and to continually monitor student progress.

As we stated earlier, preparing teachers to serve severely handicapped sudents is a recent development. However, within the past few years, we have witnessed a dramatic increase in the amount of available, pertinent literature. At least a dozen major books have been published. In addition, a professional journal (the *Journal of the Association for the Severely Handicapped*[3]), which publishes research and other material specifically for educators of the severely handicapped, has now completed its fourth volume of quarterly issues. When one considers that other journals and books may include some coverage of topics which relate to severely handicapped persons, and that much of the most current information must be found in reports of special project and personnel preparation grants, it becomes obvious that "keeping up-to-date" is no easy task. Nevertheless, teacher trainers must surmount this obstacle if their training programs are to be current and functional. To do less is to shirk a basic responsibility in training teachers.

The need to review and revise the content and sequence of courses also relates to the recent explosion in available literature. Courses which contain out-dated, irrelevant, or erroneous information serve only to weaken the quality and skills of personnel who will teach the severely handicapped. The demands and difficulties which teachers must face every day when dealing with this most difficult and heterogenous population mandate that teacher training be the best that can be provided. As Sontag, Burke, and York (1973) state:

There is a direct relationship between the level of a student's disability and the competencies

of the teacher, i.e., the more pronounced the level of disability, the more specific and precise are the competencies required of the teacher. (p.23)

Without repeated review and revision of course content, teacher trainers will not be providing the quality of preparation that prospective teachers and severely handicapped students deserve

Similarly, teacher trainers must recruit and accept only the most highly qualified and capable students into their training programs (Sontag, Smith, & Sailor, 1977). Teacher training must be rigorous and demanding if severely handicapped students are to be well served (Sontag, Certo, & Button, 1979; Stainback, Stainback, & Maurer, 1976). Only the most qualified and capable students will be able to survive a quality training program and to provide quality educational services to the severely handicapped.

Finally, if teacher trainers do not continually monitor the progress made by students in their programs, "rigorous and demanding" training will be rendered a farce. Without careful evaluation, efforts to train teachers would become a "hit-and-miss" affair. No one could conclude that the training given to prospective teachers in any way helped prepare them to teach the severely handicapped. The accountability now required of special education teachers should apply also to those who prepare professional personnel. Careful monitoring of student progress is a necessary element in establishing the accountability which is critically needed in teacher-training programs.

Competency Validation

Despite a number of impressive efforts to establish competency-based teacher preparation programs (for a review and evaluation of several programs, see Burke & Cohen, 1977), certain problems remain. Probably the most far-reaching problem is the general lack of empirical validation for any of the competencies identified for teachers of the severely handicapped (Bricker, 1979). Certainly, training programs will not be truly competency-based until we, as teacher trainers, can verify that acquiring certain competencies does produce reliable, observable changes in the behavior of severely handicapped students. Only through carefully conducted research will we obtain the kinds of information and documentation that are critically needed.

Fortunately, initial attempts to document the

3. Formerly the *AAESPH Review*.

validity of certain teacher competencies have begun. For example, a recent study by Fredericks, Anderson, and Baldwin (1979) examined 86 variables which measure teacher behavior and its relationship to desired changes in the behavior of severely handicapped students. These investigators found that only two of the variables (amount of instruction time and percentage of curriculum materials task analyzed) accounted for nearly 80% of the variance. One should not conclude that these are the only competencies, nor even the most important competencies, which teachers of the severely handicapped need to acquire; the results are suggestive, not conclusive. However, this study is an example of the kind of research which is needed before training programs can become truly competency-based. Teacher trainers have the responsibility to be informed about this kind of research, to incorporate research findings into their training programs, and even to advocate and possibly participate in the conduct of the research. Only this way will competency-based education for teachers of the severely handicapped rise above the level of opinion-based education (Shores, Cegelka, & Nelson, 1973).

FIELD-BASED TRAINING

Prospective teachers cannot develop useful skills unless they have opportunities during training for extensive direct, daily contact with severely handicapped students (Burke & Cohen, 1977; Horner, 1977; Iacino & Bricker, 1978). At present, the only viable method for affording this opportunity is through a series of carefully supervised practica with a variety of severely handicapped individuals (Brown & York, 1974; Meyen, 1975; Sailor & Haring, 1977; Sontag, Certo, & Button, 1979; Sontag, Smith, & Sailor; Wilcox, 1977). Furthermore, practica conducted solely within university laboratory schools are helpful, but not sufficient, to adequately prepare teachers to teach severely handicapped students in public school settings. Therefore, during training, experience with severely handicapped students should move away from the university campus and into the community. Field-based training is a necessary component of teacher preparation.

No professional has the range and depth of skills necessary to single-handedly develop and implement a comprehensive intervention program for severely handicapped students (Iacino & Bricker, 1978). Therefore, it seems appropriate to consider the need for multiple inputs from a variety of resources (Bricker, 1976). Wilcox (1977) has suggested that we need to align ourselves with people from other areas of education and from other professional fields. In particular, teacher trainers must form alliances with professionals in other disciplines who have skills or information relevant to the severely handicapped.

Similarly, if severely handicapped students are to benefit from educational services, the professional educators who work directly with them must become familiar with the roles, responsibilities, and abilities of a variety of professionals, including physical and occupational therapists, speech and language pathologists, pediatricians, school nurses, building principals, school psychologists, counselors, regular classroom teachers, and parents (Haring, 1978). Teacher trainers need to give prospective teachers the skills necessary for working in public school settings with professionals from other disciplines. We believe that student teachers will not acquire these kinds of skills unless they have the opportunity to participate in training which is field-based. However, as Wilcox (1977) pointed out, field-based training is destined to fail unless we break down traditional barriers between the university and community.

Use of Community Resources

One approach to breaking down these barriers requires that professionals from the local community be made an integral part of the teacher-training process. To do this, teacher trainers must be skilled at identifying and managing available community resources. For example, physical and occupational therapists who work in public schools which serve the severely handicapped may be asked to give invited lectures in university courses, as well as to provide demonstrations and supervision at the practicum site. Similarly, if a medical school is not available in the immediate area, school physicians or nurses could provide information regarding the use of medications to control seizures, typical and atypical physiological development, or general programming considerations for students affected by progressive or terminal diseases.

Current teachers of the severely handicapped, as well as social service personnel, should also be made an integral part of training. For example, teachers could give lectures on methods of adapting to the social organization of a school, in addition to providing information on specific curriculum domains or demonstrating methods for reducing the amount of time required for accurate and effective data recording. These activities, of course, go beyond the

8

usual requirements involved in the daily supervision of student teachers in the classroom. Social service personnel could provide information, as well as some supervision, so that student teachers will be better able to understand and more fully use community resources related to providing direct educational services to severely handicapped students. If field-based training is to succeed at all, teacher trainers must develop the ability to identify, organize, and orchestrate the use of available community resources as they relate to the operation of a comprehensive training program.

Practicum Site Selection

Despite the viability of the approach just described, certain cautions and problems should be noted. A primary concern is that field-based training sites must be selected very carefully. Here we are really talking about the need to select practicum sites that will provide the opportunity for the trainee to observe and model after a comprehensive educational management-team—a team which includes a special educator, a developmental therapist, a communication disorders specialist, etc., who work together in a single setting arranging instructional contingencies and procedures. In addition, the trainee should have experience in working with the family service worker and the nurse. Although these two individuals often do not function as essential team members, they are crucial to the comprehensive educational team management of the severely handicapped student.

Bricker (1976) has suggested that the most effective training is likely to occur in settings which have the following components: (a) an ongoing intervention program in which students can participate in practica on a full-time basis; (b) representatives from a number of relevant disciplines who have demonstrated an interest in severely handicapped students; and (c) faculty and/or trainers who are enthusiastic about operating within an applied setting. "The key to successful training is the content of the instruction offered during the practicum placement" (Bricker, 1976, p. 91). Unfortunately, as Wilcox (1977) pointed out, public school programs have few teachers who teach severely handicapped students and who are able to serve as appropriate models for student teachers. As one method for solving this problem, teacher trainers could encourage local schools to hire competent graduates of the teacher-training program. These people, in turn, could assume some responsibility for supervising future student teachers.

Feedback to Trainees

Another concern in field-based training is the need for student teachers to receive adequate feedback regarding their interactions with severely handicapped students (Meyen, 1975). In response to this need, Horner (1975) developed a series of "Teacher Proficiency Checklists" which can be used to observe a student teacher's skills as they develop during baseline, acquisition, and maintenance. The Checklists focus on a number of teacher behaviors, such as appropriately presenting discriminative stimuli, appropriately presenting or withholding reinforcers, and managing innappropriate behaviors. According to Horner (1979), experience with the Checklists has shown that their primary value lies in providing feedback to student teachers immediately after an observation session.

Another system which can be used to provide feedback to trainees is the Comprehensive Analysis of Special Education (CASE). Volumes 3 and 4 of CASE (Tawney, Blum, & Donaldson, 1979a, 1979b), were designed as training and observation systems to be used, respectively, with preservice and in-service trainees. CASE includes a series of instruments which are used to directly observe a student teacher's performance in regard to (a) assessment, (b) individualized education programs, (c) facilitating skill acquisition, (d) reducing inappropriate behaviors, and (e) arranging the learning environment. The initial field test data on the CASE instruments suggest that they may provide a useful system for providing feedback to both preservice and in-service trainees in field-based settings.

A Model for Field-Based Training

A final concern involves the systems or models used to facilitate field-based training. Meyen (1975) has suggested that we may need to adopt a completely different system of training teachers for the severely handicapped than has been used in training teachers for other areas of special education. As he stated, "Our tradition of how we involve teachers in training is working against us" (p. 143). One model that seems particularly well-suited to field-based training was actually presented more than a decade ago by Tharp and Wetzel (1969). Writing about methods for establishing behavior modification programs in the natural environment, these authors suggested the use of a "triadic" model which involves a consultant, a mediator, and a client. The *consultant* is a person who has needed information. A *mediator* is a person who has some control of the reinforcers for a client. Finally, the *client* is the person whose behavior will be

changed in some way. The triadic model requires that the consultant focus attention on
his or her target—the mediator. Similarly, the
mediator's attention should focus on his or her
target—the client.

Applied to field-based training, the model
would operate in the following way. The consultant would be the teacher trainer, the person
who has the information which is needed. The
mediator would be the practicum-site supervis-
or, the person who, through observation and
evaluation, controls at least some of the reinforcers for the student teacher. In practice, the
mediator could be any appropriate professional, most likely *from the community*, who is
assigned the responsibility for direct supervision. In turn, the client would be the student
teacher, the person whose behavior is to be
changed. As indicated earlier, the teacher trainer's primary goal would be to provide the information and other assistance needed by his/her
target—the practicum-site supervisor. Similarly, the practicum-site supervisor's primary goal
would be to provide the direction and feedback
needed by the student teacher.

Use of the triadic model for field-based training would enable available resources to be used
effectively and efficiently. Teacher trainers
could use their time and talents to focus on providing direction and assistance to the practicum-site supervisor, who is, after all, the person
with the most direct contact and influence on a
student teacher functioning in a field-based setting. Similarly, given adequate support from the
teacher trainer, practicum-site supervisors
should be better able to provide the kinds of attention, direction, and feedback which are so
critically needed by a teacher in training. In addition, practicum-site supervisors, through frequent contact with the teacher trainer, are likely
to become aware of information, additional curricula, and refinements in teaching techniques
which can be applied to their daily work in the
classroom. Astute teacher trainers not only will
accept, but will welcome and actively seek opportunities to provide this kind of assistance to
teachers and other professionals in the field.

Another advantage of using the triadic model
for field-based training is that professionals
from the community, by serving as mediators,
would become an integral element of the
teacher-training process. Professionals from
the community would be brought into a direct
line of training designed to prepare competent
teachers to serve severely handicapped students. In this way, the traditional barriers which
have separated the university and the community might be effectively surmounted, to the
benefit of all involved.

In-service Training

To most professionals involved in the education
of students with severe handicaps, the need for
continuing in-service training seems obvious.
Many professionals have been required to
assume roles in which they must provide direct
services to the severely handicapped, even
though they have not had extensive training or
experience in this area. Others have received
training, but that training has only highlighted
their need for additional skills.

The need for continuing and in-service training is currently acknowledged, and receiving a
great deal of attention. However, it is important
to realize that this concern is not temporary; it
will not be resolved by a few years of attention
and effort. If our field is to remain strong and
dynamic, those interested in educating severely
handicapped students will need to update their
skills periodically through additional training.

Placing programs of continuing and in-service education in this light should help remove
the negative connotations frequently associated with post-employment training programs. The purpose of this training is *not*, as
many assume, to correct the deficits of incompetent professionals in the field. Rather, the purpose of continuing in-service education is to re-
fresh and reinforce existing competencies, and
to provide information and training on new techniques and innovations.

The challenge to universities and colleges to
assist in providing the necessary training is
enormous (Martin, 1977; Saettler, 1976). Universities and colleges must be willing to move off
their campuses and into the public schools to
deliver training. This training must be practical,
current, and yet retain the rigor associated with
"on campus" instruction.

Characteristics of In-service Training
Continuing and in-service education differs in
several important ways from the typical preservice training model found at most colleges and
universities. Several of these differences are
discussed below.

Personnel. The personnel to receive training
are more experienced and typically demand a
more relevant training program than do preservice students. The nature of their job is clear to
them, and they want specific information or
skills to assist them in completing that job.

Time. The time available for training is different than that available to the preservice student. Hour-long classes which meet many times
a month are usually impossible for working professionals. However, time spent actually per-

forming their job represents training time unavailable to even the richest practicum-based preservice program.

Need. Although preservice programs can generally describe the past training received by their students and predict future training needs, continuing and in-service education programs have less knowledge about their students' past training. Thus, students' needs must be assessed, and some individualization in training must be provided.

Location. For preservice students who live on or near campus, the college or university represents a practical location for attending classes, buying books, and meeting with instructors. For continuing and in-service students, the more practical location is often their place of employment. This location is often near the trainees' homes and convenient for training just before or after work.

Effectiveness. Continuing and in-service education is provided to individuals currently serving pupils with severe and multiple handicaps. This situation represents an almost unmatched opportunity to test the effectiveness of training. Services provided to pupils should change as a result of training, and these changes should lead to changes in pupil behavior. Measuring these two factors—changes in services and in pupil behavior—provides the basis for evaluating the effectiveness of in-service training.

Models of In-service Training

To account for these characteristics of continuing and in-service education, several models of in-service training have been developed. Although none of the models provides a complete solution to the problems and demands teacher trainers encounter in in-service training, each model has been successful in satisfying at least some of the needs.

Consultative Triad. The "consultative triadic" model of training (Reynolds & Birch, 1977; Tharp & Wetzel, 1969) was discussed earlier in regard to field-based training. Because quality in-service training is likely to be field-based, the model can be used for in-service training as well. The primary difference between this model's application in in-service versus preservice training is that the target is a teacher who is already employed by a school and who works daily with severely handicapped students. Another difference is that the ultimate measure of

the effectiveness of training can be obtained by monitoring the progress made by the severely handicapped students in the teacher's (i.e., the target's) own classroom.

Active Response In-service Training Model—University of Virginia. This model uses the triadic model discussed above and has been successfully applied to the in-service training of teachers of the severely handicapped (Snell, Thompson, & Taylor, 1979). Training focuses upon both consultant and teacher-identified problems and is applied directly to the individual trainee's classroom. The active response in-service training model consists of six steps:

1. Problem identification and assessment of needs;
2. Assessment of targeted students' skills;
3. Joint planning of an intervention program;
4. Consultant demonstration of classroom procedures;
5. Teacher imitation of the procedures, with feedback provided by the consultant; and
6. Monitoring the effect of the intervention program over time.

In-service M.Ed. Program—University of Vermont. This model provides training on a regional basis throughout the State of Vermont. Competency-based training is organized around traditional university courses that are delivered at regional sites. Practicum experiences are provided by using the trainee's own classroom. Trainees may enroll in courses for audit, continuing education credits, or for an M.Ed. program in the area of educating the severely and multiply handicapped. Summer school training, complete with practicum experiences, is made available to all trainees in the program (Christie, Williams, Edelman, Hill, Fox, Fox, Sousie, & York, 1977).

Content of In-service Training

The content of each training program should be determined by the needs of the trainees. However, certain topics appear repeatedly in nearly every needs assessment. The following is a list of repeatedly requested topics:

1. Assessment of pupils;
2. Selection of curricular materials;
3. Materials and equipment;
4. Evaluation of pupil progress;
5. Use of classroom aides;
6. Interdisciplinary expertise;
7. Classroom organization;
8. Maximizing instructional time;
9. Maintenance and generalization of skills;
10. Physical care and management of stu-

dents;

11. Behavior problems;
12. Restrictiveness of environments; and
13. Interactions between handicapped and nonhandicapped students.

The list of topics for in-service training often seems endless, as do the problems of providing such training. However, by beginning the process of providing in-service training, local educational agencies and institutions of higher education can form a partnership which will yield positive, productive, and even exciting results. The reciprocal knowledge flow and practical experience which result from such a partnership will strengthen both training and service programs.

Teacher trainers should be urged to attack the problem of credit loads and the threat of dusting off old service delivery skills and begin providing vital, field-based continuing and in-service education. Once in this position, opportunities for research and training will more than justify the effort required in delivering quality in-service training (Marotz & Nelson, 1978).

QUALIFICATIONS OF THE TEACHER TRAINER

Three questions must be answered in order to determine the qualifications the trainer of teachers of the severely handicapped must possess in order to perform his or her job. (a) What skills are necessary to carry out the function of teacher trainer? (b) What are the roles and responsibilities of the teacher trainer in relation to the training settings and agencies involved in the process? (c) What is the appropriate background for the teacher trainer, either to serve as a teacher trainer or to enter a teacher-trainer preparation program? In many ways these questions, especially the first two, have already been discussed in this article, particularly those portions concerning the competency-based and the field-based approaches to teacher training.

What Skills Are Needed?

The job of teaching the severely handicapped requires a large and diverse repertoire of competencies (Burke & Cohen, 1977; Horner, 1977; Sontag, Certo, & Button, 1979; Stainback, Stainback, & Maurer, 1976; Wilcox, 1977). Using Burke and Cohen (1977) as an example, the teacher trainer must have expertise in at least 17 areas and 20 subgroups of information and performance competence. However, the teacher trainer also generally serves as a supervisor of teacher trainees at the field site, whether at the pre- or in-service level. Walker (1978) has discussed the importance of field-based supervision, the functions and roles of the practicum supervisor, and most importantly, the woeful fact that supervision is often the least systematic portion of the teacher-training program. Walker's basic point is that the teacher trainer must be prepared to apply the same process of assessment, individualized planning, instruction, evaluation, feedback, collection, and recording of progress, etc., that is used with handicapped students, *but* must apply the process to mature, independent, verbal, reasoning, adults.

What Are the Roles and Responsibilities?

The discussion so far reflects the minimum process of preparing a teacher of the severely handicapped. The **context** of teacher training must also be considered. To comprehend more fully the qualifications the teacher trainer needs, we must reflect upon the constraints and demands of the training setting that confront the teacher trainer. The field base upon which most successful, quality teacher-training programs rest presents demands upon the teacher trainer for service to the local and state community in areas of case consultation, evaluation, program development, recruitment, etc. However, if one were to apply a "criterion of ultimate functioning" (Brown, Nietupski, & Hamre-Nietupski, 1976) to the teacher-trainer role, it probably would need to involve the university and its "academic reality." The university demands that the teacher trainer participate in the great triad of academic endeavor—Teaching, Research, and Service. In this section, these demands will be considered only with respect to the qualifications of the teacher trainer; the potential for conflict inherent in these demands will be discussed later.

The teacher trainer will be an administrator who will be called upon to recruit, to give academic or career-choice advice, to respond to the requirements of granting undergraduate and/or graduate degrees, to respond to the requirements of certification of educational personnel, and to interact with Colleges of Education, Schools of Graduate Studies, other governing bodies within the university, and the various sections of state educational agencies which are concerned with teacher preparation.

Recent debate makes it clear that, despite disagreement on style, research on the education of and the learning processes demonstrated by severely handicapped students continues to be an important need in this field (Burton & Hirshoren, 1979; Sontag, Certo, & Button,

8

1979). This fact probably provides slightly less motivation for the academic professional involved in teacher training than does the simple fact that the demand for research and scholarly writing is an academic reality. This reality is especially important for those engaged in the preparation of new teacher trainers, because the ability of new trainers to continue in the field depends upon their continuation as members of the academic community. To be explicit, teacher trainers must eventually receive tenure if they are to become "respected and experienced" trainers of teachers, and research and writing are an integral part of the attainment of tenure.

Another factor which contributes to the need to include research and evaluation among the qualifications of the teacher trainer is the need for the field to validate our past assumptions. As mentioned earlier, only a very small body of work (e.g., Fredericks, Anderson, & Baldwin, 1979) addresses itself to the empirical identification and validation of skills and competencies needed to educate the severely handicapped. It seems reasonable to assume that the long-term success of our efforts at teacher training and at educating the severely handicapped will depend upon our continued rigorous and systematic examination of our assumptions and processes.

Finally, although the necessity for skills in the area of service to the severely handicapped, to the local community, to the state, and to the university has already been established, an additional area of service in which the teacher trainer will undoubtedly be called upon to perform needs to be discussed. It is a service that holds great value to the teacher-training program itself—the successful gathering of financial support for the teacher-training effort. As Meyen (1975) indicated, "it is unlikely that many universities will be able to independently underwrite the costs of quality training programs to prepare personnel for the severely handicapped" (p.138). By 1976, 13 Special Projects related to personnel training were already receiving financial assistance from the Bureau for Education of the Handicapped (Burke & Cohen, 1977). Teacher trainers must, therefore, be prepared to secure additional local, state, or federal funds to help underwrite the costs of training.

If we assume that all of the qualifications discussed thus far are important to the teacher trainer, what then is their impact upon programs designed to prepare teacher trainers? The primary impact is to affirm that the principles of instructional accountability and minimization of instructional interference apply to the preparation of teacher trainers as well as they do to the preparation of teachers of the severely handicapped and to the education of severely handicapped students. Programs need to arrange for potential teacher trainers to gain field-based experience in *all* phases of the job. It is not enough for the potential teacher trainer to spend the greatest, if not the entire, part of his or her time supervising teacher trainees and perhaps teaching an occasional course. The best strategy may be to adopt a "junior colleague" model, in which the potential teacher trainer (i.e., the potential academic professional) is actively brought into the entire process of teacher training and is not protected from what might seem to be the "tiresome" and "mundane" aspects of the job.

The opportunities for the potential teacher trainer to perform the job, and the opportunities for those responsible for preparing the teacher trainer to observe, assess, individually plan for, instruct, and provide feedback to the future trainer, should be arranged systematically. The process of preparing the teacher trainer/academic professional could begin to move toward a competency-based approach that provides maximum individualization and flexibility in recognizing the competence of the person entering the process. The very factors that may best serve as background qualifications may also introduce to the process persons who are most likely to have very diverse areas of competence. These same people are also least likely to be willing, because of professional standing or economic considerations, to submit to the traditional program of preparation that (a) emphasizes minimum, but lengthy, time periods, (b) has requirements seemingly rooted in nothing but tradition, or (c) fails to recognize incoming competence, relying instead upon the notion that the particular program is the only path toward the development of the necessary skills. Given the size and complexity of the task of educating the severely handicapped and of preparing personnel to serve them, the field can ill afford to discourage such needed individuals from participating in teacher-trainer preparation programs.

What Is the Most Appropriate Background?

Because the preparation of teachers of the severely handicapped is a relatively new endeavor in the field of special education, the preparation of teacher trainers is also in its early stages. Thus it is possible that the demand for teacher trainers cannot be met through the usual inter-program hiring practices. Perhaps also selecting teacher trainers only from the field of special education is not appropriate. Meyen (1975) noted that in "the typical special education faculty. . .most faculty members are totally inexperienced in dealing with the behavioral characteristics of the severely and profoundly handicapped" (p. 138).

Although this situation certainly has improved since 1975, the areas of competence required of teachers of the severely handicapped clearly involve more than mere academic or simple self-help concerns (Burke & Cohen, 1977; Wilcox, 1977). Because teachers must also be competent in physical handling and prosthesis, auxiliary communication techniques, life-skill training, parent training, vocational preparation, community survival, and more, faculty for teacher-training programs should be recruited from areas other than special education. Persons from related fields such as physical therapy, occupational therapy, social work, rehabilitation, and vocational education should be given serious consideration in the process of assembling personnel to staff teacher preparation programs.

In time, teachers being trained to take their place in the classroom with the severely handicapped will certainly become prime candidates for advanced training to become teacher trainers. However, two factors weigh heavily against considering classroom teaching to be the most appropriate background. First, recent events, up to and beyond the passage of P.L. 94-142, and including such cases as *PARC v. Pennsylvania*, must be taken as an indication that traditional programs for the severely handicapped did not measure up to the demands of the job. If they had, the call for change is likely to have been less dramatic. Therefore, depending upon the experiences of those who have served in these "classrooms" does not seem logical, particularly because classrooms did not even exist in many cases. As with any generality, there are no absolutes. Although we can look to those who were doing exceptional work under difficult situations, we can by no means depend upon former teachers as the primary source for teacher trainers.

Secondly, because competency-based and field-based preparation for teachers of the severely handicapped are also recent developments, there has not been sufficient time for evolution—the developmental process by which teachers are trained, enter the teaching field, return for advanced training after a period of time in the field, and finally take their place as teacher trainers.This process has not yet occurred, although notable exceptions (e.g., the University of Wisconsin–Madison) can be found. Nevertheless, until this process of evolution becomes a more general phenomenon, determining the most appropriate background for a teacher trainer will continue to be a matter of matching the needs of a training program with the competencies of people whose backgrounds are in diverse areas relating to educating the severely handicapped.

CONFLICT IN ROLE AND PROCESS

Many of the problems facing the teacher trainer result from the conflicting demands of the university and the demands of the job of training teachers. These conflicts are not without resolution, but they are often exacerbated by the need to secure funding to support the efforts of the program. Competency-based and field-based teacher training is expensive in terms of faculty time for training and supervision. When this is combined with the time that trainers devote to more direct services to handicapped individuals or to programs serving them, available time for research and scholarly pursuit may diminish, or even disappear completely. In addition, the field's need for inservice training and the development of appropriate materials and efforts to fund these endeavors often further reduce available time. Where, then, can the teacher trainer find the time to devote to the development of research? The answer involves taking a different perspective when examining those activities already being undertaken.

The process of teacher training itself is a rich area for undertaking research and evaluation efforts. Because preparing personnel to teach the severely handicapped is a new undertaking, expectations have been created among educators and the public concerning our abilities to educate (i.e., to change the behavior of) severely handicapped students. Therefore, we need to test our assumptions, question our methodology, and critically examine our curricula while the progress of the field is in its early stages.

We always need to know why something is operating properly so that we can be sure to maintain the factors responsible for success. For example, if we can discover which components of the teaching strategy are most responsible for performance change by severely handicapped students (such as the number of behaviors which have been task analyzed by the teacher or the amount of direct instructional time achieved in the classroom [Fredericks, Anderson, & Baldwin, 1979]), then we can also determine the most efficient ways to help teachers develop these skills. As Nelson (1978) has suggested, the traditional model by which the university shares its knowledge—the lecture or seminar—may be the most **inappropriate** model to be presenting to the trainee. Very different models and priorities for handling in-service and preservice training will need to be developed (Callander, 1978; Intrilligator & Saettler, 1978; Mercer, Forgnone, & Beattie, 1978). The resolution to the problem of how research can be undertaken by the trainer of teachers of the severely handicapped is to suggest that the process of teacher preparation itself should become a focus of serious empirical study.

In the area of materials development, we need to empirically validate materials as they become available. Given the diversity of problems exhibited by the students enrolled in any particular program, the generality of most materials or curricula will need to be rigorously tested. Rather than using large *N* validation studies, most validation efforts probably will result in valuable information on modifications and adaptations if they relate to small clusters of students (possibly as few as three or four) within the educational program. However, several different clusters may exist in any one program. Therefore, efforts could focus on establishing the demonstration components of programs whose goal is to examine and modify, rather than create anew. Such efforts will provide settings in which the teacher trainer can train, provide service to the community, and respond to the demand to produce imposed by academic reality.

Another area which can create the potential for conflict for the teacher trainer is in the scope of the job itself. As we have discussed already the teacher trainer must have a wide base of knowledge and performance skills in order to effectively change the behavior of prospective teachers. It seems unreasonable to presume that any person can singlehandedly assume the job of training teachers of the severely handicapped for any one Department of Special Education. Meyen (1975) has warned that "the role of the faculty in special education is changing....We are being reminded that we are employed by universities for particular roles and not to create roles for ourselves....Unilateral effort is not being reinforced to the degree that departmental unity is " (p. 138). As a general working strategy, we believe that programs which prepare teachers of the severely handicapped should not be "one-person shows." With the roles and responsibilities that teacher trainers must undertake in order to train teachers and to prosper in the academic community, the staffing of teacher preparation programs should be a process that selects individuals whose strengths blend into a whole. One-

person training programs probably would lead to a new burn-out phenomenon—teacher trainer burn-out.

The final conflict facing those who train teachers and those who prepare teacher trainers is a logistic one. Several writers have warned of the dangers of overproducing teachers of the severely handicapped (Meyen, 1975; Wilcox, 1977); by extension, there is also a danger of overproducing teacher trainers. The combined needs of preparing personnel for a low-incidence group within the general population, and the great need to produce high quality rather than high quantities of personnel suggest that we must emphasize quality rather than quantity in producing teacher trainers. The inherent danger for teacher-training programs that are also responsible for doctoral training is that the demand for personnel generated by field-based training may be met by a tactic of overrecruiting doctoral candidates whose entire responsibility will be to supervise the teacher trainees. As a result, personnel will be prepared only for teacher training and not for other roles which might be required at the doctoral level in state-level educational agencies, in the administration of public or private programs for the severely handicapped, in research and development centers, in vocationally-oriented programs, etc. The preparation of doctoral-level personnel to work with the severely handicapped should provide for a variety of experiences that will address ultimate functions other than only that of teacher trainer.

PROBLEMS AND FUTURE DIRECTIONS

As we stated at the outset of this paper, substantial progress has been made in our ability to prepare competent teachers of the severely handicapped. Furthermore, this progress has been made largely in just the past few years, a relatively short period of time. However, the progress which has been made should not overshadow our need to resolve a number of problems which are critical to the teacher-training process. Perhaps the most important concern is our need to not only identify but *empirically* validate the competencies needed by a teacher of the severely handicapped. Thus far, teacher trainers in our field have engaged in a primarily developmental process, i.e., a process of identifying the competencies which we *believe* are needed by teachers. The process of developing effective teacher-training programs requires not only this stage of development, but also the stages of evaluation, revision, and refinement. At present, we are entering a stage of evaluation which calls for the empirical validation of the competencies we have identified.

Another major concern involves the need for data-based research, particularly as it relates to the development and implementation of field-based programs. The models for field-based training which we suggested and described in this paper are still largely untested. Although we have some initial data which suggest their effectiveness, these data represent only a beginning. Additional research is needed, and teacher trainers are the most likely source of leadership in the effort to establish and validate various field-based training models.

A final concern involves the standards which should be used to certify teachers of the severely handicapped. Those who advocate a competency-based approach to training are likely to advocate that certain competencies should be used as the criteria for certification. The problem, of course, appears in determining which competencies should be required. This problem is complicated further by a lack of empirical validation for the competencies which have been identified. However, as we stated earlier, a "competency" should directly or indirectly enable teachers to produce observable, desired changes in the behavior of their students. Therefore, we believe that the *ultimate* criterion for teacher certification should be the trainee's demonstrated ability to produce desired changes in the behavior of severely handicapped students. However, the problems we have already identified dictate that we must view this criterion for teacher certification as a goal to be worked toward in the next several years. Furthermore, any satisfactory achievement of this goal will occur only through cooperation between universities and state departments of education.

One effort to resolve some of these problems is being made by the Southeastern Regional Coalition (SERC), an innovative approach to personnel preparation funded by the Bureau of Education for the Handicapped. SERC is a cooperative effort at teacher training being made by seven universities—the Universities of Alabama, Kentucky, North Carolina, and Virginia, and Peabody College of Vanderbilt University, Georgia State University, and Virginia Commonwealth University. The objectives of SERC are to develop (*a*) guidelines on how programs may cooperate in teacher certification, (*b*) a common method of evaluating trainees, (*c*) a system of regional cooperation for preservice and in-service training, and (*d*) guidelines for collaboration in research on teacher training.

The SERC cooperative training program involves several unique features. First, master's and doctoral-level students at one university have the opportunity to receive training at another cooperating university. These exchanges of students are carefully designed so that the resources for training at each of the cooperative universities can be more fully used both by the teacher trainers and by the trainees. Another feature of SERC includes the system of cooperation in collecting data on performance by students in the exchange programs. A third feature of SERC includes the opportunity for students to participate in intensive two-day workshops on specific topics which are selected based on needs assessment. SERC is an innovative, cooperative approach to preparing teachers of the severely handicapped. Through this cooperative effort we may begin to identify the solutions to a number of the problems in teacher training which were mentioned earlier.

A FINAL COMMENT

Our intent has been to take a critical look at the role of the teacher trainer in preparing educational personnel who can reliably and efficiently change the behavior of severely handicapped students. Teacher trainers have certain responsibilities to their field, and need certain competencies if they are to function effectively. We have outlined some of these responsibilities and competencies in regard to five issues—competency-based, field-based, and in-service training, desirable qualifications, and conflicts in roles. We offer our views in the hope that they will stimulate additional consideration and discussion.

In a field such as ours which is young, emerging, and expanding rapidly, a proliferation of instant experts and instant programs is likely (Wilcox, 1977). We believe that the only way to combat this problem, and to foster the growth and development of our field, is to take an occasional critical look at our efforts, and to suggest some standards to be upheld. Otherwise, we run the grave risk of failing to fulfill our responsibilities to the teachers we train and, ultimately, to the severely handicapped individuals they will serve.

REFERENCES

Baker, D.B. Severely handicapped: Toward an inclusive definition. *AAESPH Review*, 1979, 4(1), 52-65.

Bijou, S.W., & Wilcox-Cole, B. The feasibility of providing effective educational programs for the severely and profoundly retarded. In *Educating the 24-hour retarded child*. Arlington, Tex.: The National Association for Retarded Citizens, 1975.

8

Bricker, D. Educational synthesizer. In M.A. Thomas (Ed.), *Hey, don't forget about me! Education's investment in the severely, profoundly, and multiply handicapped.* Reston, Va.: The Council for Exceptional Children, 1976.

Bricker, D. *Educating the severely handicapped: Philosophical and implementation dilemmas.* Paper presented at the conference of the Teacher Education Division, Council for Exceptional Children, San Antonio, Texas, January, 1979. Reprinted in *Teacher Education and Special Education*, 1979, (3), 59-68.

Brown, L., Nietupski, J., & Hamre-Nietupski, S. Criterion of ultimate functioning. In M.A. Thomas (Ed.), *Hey, don't forget about me! Education's investment in the severely, profoundly, and multiply handicapped.* Reston, Va.: The Council for Exceptional Children, 1976.

Brown, L., & York, R. Developing programs for severely handicapped students: Teacher training and classroom instruction. *Focus on Exceptional Children*, 1974, 6, 1-11.

Burke, P., & Cohen, M. The quest for competence in serving the severely/profoundly handicapped: A critical analysis of personnel preparation programs. In E. Sontag, J. Smith, & N. Certo (Eds.), *Educational programming for the severely and profoundly handicapped.* Reston, Va.: The Division on Mental Retardation, The Council for Exceptional Children, 1977.

Burton, T.A. & Hirshoren, A. The education of severely and profoundly retarded children: Are we sacrificing the child to the concept? *Exceptional Children*, 1979, 45(8), 598-602.

Callander, B.D. An in-service model for implementation in an institutional setting. *Teacher Education and Special Education*, 1978, 2, 24-29.

Christie, L.S., Williams, W., Edelman, S., Hill, M.G., Fox, T.J., Fox, W.L., Sousie, S.P., & York, R. *A master's level training program to prepare teachers serving learners in need of intensive special education.* Burlington: Center for Developmental Disabilities, University of Vermont, 1977.

Dunn, L. (Ed.). *Exceptional children in the schools: Special education in transition (2nd ed.).* New York: Holt, Rinehart, & Winston, 1973.

Fredericks, H.D.B., Anderson, R., & Baldwin, V. Identifying competency indicators of teachers of the severely handicapped. *AAESPH Review*, 1979, 4(1), 81-95.

Haring, N.G. Conclusion: Classroom two. In N.G. Haring (Ed.), *Behavior of Exceptional Children* (2nd ed.). Columbus, Ohio: Charles E. Merrill, 1978.

Horner, R.D. *Teacher Proficiency Checklist.* Lawrence: Department of Special Education, University of Kansas, 1975.

Horner, R.D. A competency-based approach to preparing teachers of the severely and profoundly handicapped: Perspective II. In E. Sontag, J. Smith, & N. Certo (Eds.), *Educational programming for the severely and profoundly handicapped.* Reston, Va.: The Division on Mental Retardation, The Council for Exceptional Children, 977.

Horner, R.D. Personal communication, April, 1979.

Horner, R.D., Holvoet, J., & Rinne, T. *Competency specifications for teachers of the severely and profoundly handicapped.* Lawrence: Department of Special Education, University of Kansas, 1976.

Iacino, R., & Bricker, D. The generative teacher: A model for preparing personnel to work with the severely/profoundly handicapped. In N.G. Haring & D. Bricker (Eds.), *Teaching the severely handicapped* (Vol. 3). Seattle: AAESPH, 1978.

Intrilligator, B., & Saettler, H. In-service training: A federal perspective. *Teacher Education and Special Education*, 1978, 2, 56-60.

Marotz, B.A., & Nelson, C.M. Field-based in-service special education teacher training. *Teacher Education and Special Education*, 1978, 1(2), 1-4.

Martin, E.W. Foreward. In J. Smith (Ed.), *Personnel/preparation and Public Law 94-142: The map, the mission, and the mandate.* Washington, D.C.: Division of Personnel Preparation, Bureau of Education for the Handicapped, Second Annual Regional Conference, 1977.

McDowell, F.E., & Sontag, E. The severely and profoundly handicapped as catalysts for change. In E. Sontag, J. Smith, & N. Certo (Eds.), *Educational programming for the severely and profoundly handicapped.* Reston, Va.: The Division on Mental Retardation, The Council for Exceptional Children, 1977.

Mercer, C.D., Forgnone, C., & Beattie, J. In-service and the large university: Perspective, issues and recommendations. *Teacher Education and Special Education*, 1978, 2, 30-34.

Mercer, C., & Snell, M. *Learning theory research in mental retardation.* Columbus, Ohio: Charles E. Merrill, 1977.

Meyen, E.L. Preparing educational personnel for the severely and profoundly mentally retarded. In *Educating the 24-hour retarded child.* Arlington, Tex.: National Association for Retarded Citizens, 1975.

Mills vs. Board of Education of the District of Columbia, 348 F. Supp. 866 (D.D.C., 1972).

Nelson, C.M. Field-based special education teacher training and the university: Mismatched or match made in heaven? In *Field-based teacher training: Applications in special education.* Minneapolis: Department of Psychoeducational Studies, University of Minnesota, 1978.

Pennsylvania Association for Retarded Chilren vs. Commonwealth of Pennsylvania, 334 F. Supp. 1257 (1971).

Public Law 93-380, *Education Amendments of 1974,* August 21, 1974.

Public Law 94-142, *Education for All Handicapped Children Act,* November 29, 1975.

Reynolds, M.C., & Birch, J.W. *Teaching exceptional children in all America's schools: A first course for teachers and principals.* Reston, Va.: The Council for Exceptional Children, 1977.

Saettler, H. Current priorities in personnel preparation. *Exceptional Children*, 1976, 43(3), 147-148.

Sailor, W., & Haring, N.G. Some current directions in education of the severely/multiply handicapped. *AAESPH Review*, 1977, 2(2), 67-87.

Shores, R.E., Cegelka, P.T., & Nelson, C.M. Competency-based special education teacher training. *Exceptional Children*, 1973, *40*, 192-197.

Snell, M. (Ed.). *Systematic instruction of the moderately and severely handicapped.* Columbus, Ohio: Charles E. Merrill, 1978.

Snell, M.E., Thompson, M.S., & Taylor, K.G. Providing inservice to educators of the severely handicapped: The active response inservice training model. *Education and Training of the Mentally Retarded*, 1979, *14*(1), 25-33.

Sontag, E., Burke, P., & York, R. Considerations for serving the severely handicapped in the public schools. *Education and Training of the Mentally Retarded*, 1973, *8*(2), 20-26.

Sontag, E., Certo, N., & Button, J.E. On a distinction between the education of the severely and profoundly handicapped and a doctrine of limitations. *Exceptional Children*, 1979, *45*(8), 604-616.

Sontag, E., Smith, J., & Sailor, W. The severely and profoundly handicapped: Who are they? Where are we? *Journal of Special Education*, 1977, *11*(1), 5-11.

Stainback, S., Stainback, W., & Maurer, S. Training teachers for the severely and profoundly handicapped: A new frontier. *Exceptional Children*, 1976, *42*(4), 203-212.

Tawney, J.W., Blum, K.M., & Donaldson, R.M. *Comprehensive analysis of special education: Volume 3—Pre-service version.* Lexington: University of Kentucky, 1979. (a)

Tawney, J.W., Blum, K.M., & Donaldson, R.M. *Comprehensive analysis of special education: Volume 4—In-service version.* Lexington: University of Kentucky, 1979. (b)

Tharp, R.G., & Wetzel, R.J. *Behavior modification in the natural environment.* New York: Academic Press, 1969.

Walker, J.A. The practicum supervisor inches toward competence. *Teacher Education and Special Education*, 1978, *1*, 14-27.

Wilcox, B. A competency-based approach to preparing teachers of the severely and profoundly handicapped: Perspective I. In E. Sontag, J. Smith, & N. Certo (Eds.), *Educational programming for the severely and profoundly handicapped.* Reston, Va.: The Division on Mental Retardation, The Council for Exceptional Children, 1977.

Wolfensberger, W., Nirje, B., Olshansky, D., Perske, R., & Roos, P. *The Principle of normalization in human services.* Toronto: National Institute on Mental Retardation, 1972.

Wilcox, B. A competency-based approach to preparing teachers of the severely and profoundly handicapped: Perspective I. In E. Sontag, J. Smith, & N. Certo (Eds.), *Educational programming for the severely and profoundly handicapped.* Reston, Va.: The Division on Mental Retardation, The Council for Exceptional Children, 1977.

8

Moving the University To the Student: A Model for Special Education Training

by Sidney R. Miller, Robert L. Stoneburner and Ted L. Miller

The passage of Public Law 94-142 initially prompted the focus of teacher preparation in special education to move toward providing in-service training for personnel already working with handicapped students. Today, professional school personnel who are receiving in-service training include special education teachers, regular classroom teachers, and ancillary professionals (Harvey, 1976; Seattler, 1976). This new focus is prompted by at least two factors: (1) the need to keep all teachers abreast of new strategies and materials to meet the educational needs of the handicapped; and (2) upgrading the training of teachers and the treatment that educationally handicapped students receive (Burke, 1976; Wiederholt, Hammill, & Brown, 1978).

Since the early 1970s, the validity of categorical definitions and the training of teachers to these conceptual frameworks have been challenged (Forness, 1974; Mann, Goodman, & Wiederholt, 1978; Reger, 1972; Wiederholt, 1974). As a result, the United States Office of Education (USOE) and the Bureau of Education for the Handicapped (BEH) recently have supported the training of personnel who can identify and service generic needs rather than a single educational disability (Seattler, 1976). The BEH indicated in its 1979 guidelines for personnel preparation that it was placing an emphasis on generic training, holding that the mandates of 94-142 encourage the mainstreaming of educationally handicapped students. As a result, many teachers, even the more recently trained, now will be required to serve students for whom their training was incomplete. To meet this need, primary teacher training institutions, universities and colleges, are being called upon to develop procedures for providing in-service education for the teacher who has been working with handicapped children in either a resource/self-contained special education environment or in a regular classroom. For some teachers, in-service education could be directed toward obtaining a master's degree, while for others it could consist of a limited sequence of courses that result in the development of identified competencies. In both cases, the instruction from the university should feature direct classroom observation and teaching (Strauch & Affleck, 1976).

An approach to training

Since institutions of higher education began eliminating on-campus laboratory schools because of their high costs, the frequency of simultaneous presentations between theory taught in courses and actual application of the information has been lowered. In addition, the effectiveness of in-service training has been limited since it primarily involved course work with minimal concurrent

Semester	Course sequence			Practicum activities/ emphases
Fifth Semester			1. Educational Research 2. Electives	Design and carry through research project
Fourth Semester		1. Methods and Materials 2. Advanced Reading		Management of behavior and evaluation of student projects
Third Semester	1. Diagnosis 2. Methods and Materials			Programming and instruction for children, personal program evaluation
Second Semester	1. Characteristics 2. Methods of Behavior Analysis			Analysis of skills and tasks of children
First Semester	1. Foundation of Exceptional Children 2. Characteristics			Identification of learning problems in the classroom

Figure 1. Course sequence and practicum activity within the five-semester program

field experience. In order to correct this situation, Northern Illinois University's Department of Special Education has developed and tested off-campus, in-service delivery systems through four different mechanisms: (1) one- and two-day institutes; (2) individual courses; (3) off-campus master's degree programs with the practicum occurring at the conclusion of the course work; and (4) off-campus master's degree programs with a concurrent practicum. Of these alternatives, the off-campus master's degree in conjunction with the concurrent practicum has received the strongest internal and external support from both higher education and public school personnel.

To assure that the educational objectives of both the university and the local educational agencies are considered in establishing the master's degree program's operational goals and objectives, concurrent practicum programs are established through local school districts and special education cooperatives. In addition to determining local needs, the off-campus, in-service model maintains as general performance criteria that each of the participatory teachers:

1. Are required to work directly with educationally handicapped pupils while simultaneously taking courses;

2. Must develop and demonstrate a set of diagnostic skills that enable them to employ both formal and informal procedures to identify learning handicaps;

3. Are required to develop and demonstrate a range of instructional methods

that can be used and adapted to meet the needs of individual handicapped students;

4. Must develop and demonstrate a range of behavior management skills that can be used in conjunction with the instructional phase of the teaching process;

5. Must develop programming skills that integrate the methodological and behavioral management findings into a comprehensive educational plan;

6. Are required to develop methods and procedures to monitor each public school student's progress and continually evaluate the program's effectiveness for meeting individual needs; and

7. Must develop research skills that will enable them to measure and determine the efficiency of their personal programmatic efforts (self-evaluation).

All course work is offered in the geographic region of the school district or special education cooperative. The courses—including the practicum—are offered during five semesters. During the experience, the participants are required to take seven credit hours per semester in the sequence outlined in the program specifications (see Figure 1). Those few persons unable to take the courses in the required sequence are not allowed to remain in the off-campus program.

Admission and completion criteria

Admission to the off-campus program has the same requisites as admission to the on-

8

campus program. The same minimum grade-point average and Graduate Record Examination Scores, and the same number of letters of recommendation, are required for admission. Satisfactory performance in the prescribed sequence of courses and a research paper are required for completion. In general, in-service teachers must demonstrate the same level of competence as on-campus students.

Practicum experience

One of the strongest features of the off-campus master's degree program is the continuous mix of theory and application achieved through practice. The practicum offered each semester is concurrent with course instruction and requires the participants to implement a facet of the course work. The specially designated practicum coordinator of the specified site, along with other university instructors and the public school personnel, determine the content of the practicum and the performance criteria required of each of the enrolled teachers. The individual is visited at least three times by the university coordinator and the public school supervisor. The visitations are designed to fulfill several purposes:

1. To assist the teachers in implementing particular aspects of their course work in their classrooms;

2. To evaluate the teachers' performance in implementing the task in order that final objective grading can be established;

3. To determine the efficacy of the practicum requirements so that course content and the realities of the practicum can be better integrated; and

4. To keep the university personnel abreast of the needs and expectations in the public school setting.

The inclusion of public school supervisors in determining practicum requirements has promoted an ongoing dialogue between public school personnel and university faculty. Through this dialogue, a more complete view of the practicum has been achieved and modifications have been brought about to better align the legitimate concerns of all parties.

Results and conclusions

The field based program is in the initial phases of implementation, and no empirical results have yet been generated. However, some preliminary anecdotal data and observations have been collected by public school and university personnel. The participating teachers have reported that the field based off-campus programs have:

1. Enabled them to offer a more comprehensive program that meets the schools' and the teachers' specific operational and theoretical needs;

2. Made it possible to identify regular classroom teachers who can effectively service handicapped children from either a resource or self-contained classroom environment;

3. Allowed the school to hire apprentice teachers and, through observation and training, determine whether they meet the district's short- and long-term needs; and

4. Enabled the district to maintain a close liaison with the university, thus facilitating a continual exchange of information and data.

University personnel reports suggest that the programs have:

1. Enabled the university to structure the course sequence and thus the flow of the training program and content;

2. Promoted knowledge of student's previous courses, thus enabling university personnel to offer information without spending excessive time reviewing information to determine the proper instructional level;

3. Enabled the university to predetermine and thus plan for the courses and students that will be serviced over a two-year period; and

4. Allowed the university to maintain open communication with the public schools.

Summary

Other institutions may consider establishing similar models of in-service training so that the in-service education intent of Public Law 94-142 can be achieved. Because good professional preparation best occurs when there is a well-established, closely monitored procedure for training, previous models of one- and two-day institutes and weekend workshops, in most cases, have failed to meet the needs of the schools and teachers. The in-service program described above overcomes that problem since it contains a well-structured set of theoretical and practical activities within which university personnel follow the teacher into the classroom to determine the efficacy of the theory and the appropriateness of the application. Preliminary acceptance has been noted, and it is believed that other training institutions may find the approach beneficial.

REFERENCES

Burke, P. J. Personnel preparation: Historical perspective. *Exceptional Children*, 1976, *43*, 144-146.

Forness, S. R. Implications of recent trends in educational labeling. *Journal of Learning Disabilities*, 1974, *7*, 445-449.

Harvey, J. Future trends in personnel preparation. *Exceptional Children*, 1976, *43*, 148-150.

Mann, L., Goodman, L., & Wiederholt, J. *Teaching the learning disabled adolescent*. Boston: Houghton-Mifflin, 1978.

Reger, R. Resource rooms: Change agents or guardians of the status quo? *Journal of Special Education*, 1972, *6*, 355-359.

Seattler, H. Current priorities in personnel preparation. *Exceptional Children*, 1976, *43*, 147-148.

Strauch, J. D., & Affleck, G. G. Competencies for cooperating teachers in special education. *Exceptional Children*, 1976, *42*, 403-405.

Wiederholt, J. L. Historical perspectives on the education of the learning disabled. In L. Mann and D. Sabatino (Eds.), *The second review of special education*. Philadelphia: JSE Press, 1974.

Wiederholt, J. L., Hammill, D. D., & Brown, V. *The resource teacher: A guide to effective practices*. Boston: Allyn and Bacon, 1978.

8

A National Survey of Preservice Programs on Law and the Handicapped

by Michael E. Gallery and John McLaughlin

INTRODUCTION

Today's educators are faced with a multitude of challenges precipitated by recent litigation and federal legislation concerning the education of the handicapped. This legal activity has culminated in the enactment of P.L. 94-142, the Education for All Handicapped Children Act. The Act mandates that schools provide a *free* and *appropriate* education to *all* children. Priority must be given to those heretofore excluded from the educational community (Abeson & Weintraub, 1977).

The degree to which educators will successfully comply with this and other Acts is largely dependent upon their understanding of their present legal responsibilities. To that end, the Bureau of Education for the Handicapped, as well as state departments of education across the country, has been sponsoring in-service training for educators on laws related to the handicapped as well as on ways in which schools can best comply with these laws (Harvey, 1977).

While this in-service activity has been highly visible, preservice training with regard to legal issues has been, by virtue of its nature, less apparent. Thus, we were interested in determining the degree to which colleges of education are preparing their trainees to meet the legal responsibilities with which they will be presented upon entering the field.

METHODOLOGY

Sample

The target population for this study consisted of colleges of education throughout the United States. The accessible population was comprised of colleges of education which are members of the American Association of Colleges for Teacher Education. Membership of the association includes American colleges of education, both privately and publicly supported. A stratified random sample of 170 schools was selected from the accessible population; school size was used as a classification variable.

Instrumentation

A mail survey questionnaire was developed to generate responses from deans of the selected colleges. A panel reviewed the instrument to ensure that the items addressed the survey objectives. Deans of the colleges of education were asked to either complete the instrument themselves or to submit it to someone within the college who could supply the requested information. A total of 140 schools (82% of the sample) returned completed instruments.

RESULTS

The results of the survey are summarized in Table 1. Absolute frequencies and percentages

From *Teacher Education and Special Education*, Vol. 3, No. 2, Spring 1980. Copyright 1980, Special Press. Reprinted with permission.

(in parentheses) are presented for responses to each item in the survey. The percentage figures are based upon the total responding to each item rather than the grand total. The results of the survey, as they pertain to the original research questions, appear below.

What Percentage of Respondents Disseminate Information on Laws Related to the Handicapped?

A total of 77% of those responding to question 1 indicated that they disseminate information. Those answering in the negative most frequently cited lack of staff (62%) and lack of funding (50%) as their reasons.

What Percentage of the Respondents Have Future Plans to Offer Coursework in Law and the Handicapped?

Of those responding, 64% indicated plans to offer courses sometime in the future. Furthermore, 10% of this group was composed of schools not presently disseminating any information on law.

On What Laws and Through What Media Do Schools Disseminate Information?

Not surprisingly, more schools disseminate information on P.L. 94-142 than any other law listed, as evidenced by the 11 schools (8%) indicating they did not disseminate information relative to their respective state laws and regulations.

While coursework appears to be the most common method of presenting information on laws related to the handicapped, use of the library and lectures seemed to be popular alternatives and/or supplements.

What Percentage of the Schools Offer Classes in Laws related to the Handicapped?

A total of 76 schools (54%) offer courses in law related to the handicapped. However, only 33 schools (24% of the total sample) indicated that those courses are required. Of those requiring classes, 61% require them for graduates and 55% for undergraduates, an indication that colleges offering these courses view the acquisition of this knowledge as essential at all levels of instruction.

Five schools reported that they plan to discontinue courses presently being offered. Two of these five cited lack of funding as a major reason for that action.

What Percentage of Respondents Perceive a Need for Training Faculty

Members to Teach Classes in Law related to the Handicapped?

Seventy-nine schools (62%) perceived a need for training faculty members. Among those schools not presently offering courses in law, 67% indicated that there was a need for training faculty members to teach those classes.

There was no significant relationship between whether schools were presently disseminating information on law and whether they perceived a need for training faculty in this area ($\chi^2 = 1.77$, $p > .05$). However, the schools' plans to offer coursework in the future were significantly related to their perception of the need to train faculty ($\chi^2 = 12.25$; $p < .01$); 73% of those planning to offer courses in the future acknowledged the need for staff training, while 62% of those not planning future courses did *not* perceive such a need.

Is There a Significant Relationship Between School Size and Whether Schools Disseminate Information?

A point-biserial correlation coefficient was computed to determine the relationship between school size and the dissemination of information on the law and the handicapped. The resulting coefficient of .14 was not significant ($t = 1.59$; $p > .05$), which indicates there is no significant relationship between the variables investigated.

Is There a Significant Relationship Between School Size and Whether Schools Perceive a Need for Faculty Training in Laws Related to the Handicapped?

A point-biserial correlation coefficient was also computed to determine the relationship between school size and the perception of a need to train faculty. The resulting coefficient of .13 was not significant ($t = 1.41$; $p > .05$), indicating that there was no significant relationship between the variables studied.

DISCUSSION AND CONCLUSIONS

Colleges of education are a major vehicle for information dissemination to persons preparing for and working in the educational community. The purpose of the investigation was to determine the extent to which these institutions of higher education have established methods through which information is provided to their trainees concerning law as it relates to the education of handicapped children.

The survey results suggest that the majority of colleges of education do disseminate infor-

8

Table 1

Table 1

College Survey Questionnaire Results

1. Does your school disseminate information on law related to the handicapped?

yes 106 (77)   no 32 (23)

A. If no, reason(s): *

(50) 16 Lack of funds   (13) 4 Lack of interest

(66) 21 Lack of staff   (22) 7 Other (Please specify)

* Multiple responses were possible.

B. Do you plan to offer course work in this area in the future?

yes 79 (64)   no 45 (36)

2. Please indicate how information on each of the following topics is disseminated by placing a check mark (✓) in the appropriate column(s). If information on a particular item is not disseminated check the column marked "None".

		Course-work	Seminar	Library	Lectures	Work-shops	None
a.	Elementary and Secondary Act of 1965 (PL 89-10)	74 (53)	16(11)	34(24)	29(21)	18(13)	22(16)
b.	Rehabilitation Act of 1973 (PL 93-112)	70 (50)	18(13)	33(24)	33(24)	23(16.5)	22(16)
c.	Education of the Gifted and Talented (PL 93-380) Title III	66 (47)	19(14)	31(22)	30(21)	24(17)	25(18)
d.	Title II, Rights of the Developmentally Disabled (PL 94-103)	63 (45)	16(11)	30(21)	26(19)	17(12)	31(22)
e.	Education of All Handicapped Children Act (PL 94-142)	97 (69)	39(28)	45(32)	58(41)	55(39)	11(8)
f.	Educational Amendment of 1974 (PL 93-380)	48 (34)	17(12)	21(15)	29(21)	13(9)	18(13)

Multiple responses to this item were appropriate.

3. If your schools offer courses in law related to the handicapped:

A. Are these courses required?

yes 33 (48)   no 36 (52)

for graduates?   yes 20 (61)   no 8 (39)

for undergraduates? yes 18 (55)   no 13 (45)

B. Do you plan on continuing these courses?

yes 56 (81)   no 5 (7)   no response 8 (12)

If no, reason(s):

(40) 2 Lack of funding   (0) 0 Lack of students

(0) 0 Lack of interest   (0) 0 Lack of personnel

Other (Please specify) (0) 0

4. Do you perceive a need for training faculty members to teach classes in law related to the handicapped?

yes 79 (62)   no 48 (38)

mation on law and the handicapped. Not surprisingly, information on P.L. 94-142 is the main focal point of the information. Coursework is the most prevalent vehicle for training, followed by lectures and workshops.

When respondents were asked to suggest reasons for not offering experiences in law and the handicapped, the majority responded that lack of staff and funds are primary reasons. Given the trainees' presumed critical need for legal information, a reordering of administrative priorities to obtain the necessary staff and funds is perhaps needed.

The finding that many of the respondents

perceive a need for faculty trained in law and the handicapped seems interesting. Although many colleges may have staff, funds, and facilities, they may not be offering the information because of a lack of trained staff. A "Catch 22" situation may exist. That is, there is a discrepancy between the perceived need to train students in litigation and legislation concerning the handicapped and the ability to deliver this service. Thus, we may need to establish or identify component resources where faculty may receive the appropriate training to fulfill this need.

The data revealed that less than half of the institutions offering coursework in legal issues required those courses for their trainees. If knowledge of legal issues is a necessary professional competency, then it seems imperative that those courses be required. This should hold true not only for trainees in education (both special and regular), but also for related fields as well (i.e., speech pathology, physical and occupational therapy, social work, and school psychology). Further, the issue of "quality" needs to be addressed. Not only is it important that personnel know the law, but it is critical that they be able to *implement* the law as well (e.g., write appropriate IEPs). Thus, it must be insured that both knowledge and skill objectives be addressed.

Finally, the data indicate that there is no significant relationship between school size and the degree to which experiences in law and the handicapped are provided. Further, size of college is not significantly associated with the school's perceived need for the training of staff in the area of law and the handicapped. However, there is a significant relationship between the schools' intent to offer coursework in law and the handicapped and their perception of a need for trained faculty. Thus, those who see the endeavor as important seem to be recognizing future program needs.

In review of the data dervied from the investigation, we can make the following recommendations:

1. Although colleges of education are providing experiences which produce information on law and the handicapped, more emphasis should be placed on this topic. This emphasis on legal issues should also be reflected in training of ancillary personnel.
2. In order to increase the probability that offerings will be made, opportunities for faculty enrichment in the area need to be established. Federal agencies should identify and encourage resources to provide such enrichment opportunities.
3. The agencies primarily responsible for providing support monies for colleges of education must establish incentives for those institutions to organize experiences in the area of law and the handicapped.
4. Colleges of education should initiate or continue evaluation activities to assess the degree to which they are adequately preparing staff to successfully meet legal responsibilities.

REFERENCES

Abeson, A., & Weintraub, F. Understanding the individualized education program. In S. Torres (Ed.), *A primer on individualized educational programs for handicapped children.* Reston, Va.: The Foundation for Exceptional Children, 1977.

Harvey, J. Regional collaboration. In J. Smith (Ed.), *The map, the mission, and the mandate: Second annual regional conferences.* Washington, D.C.: Division of Personnel Preparation, Bureau of Education for the Handicapped, 1977.

8

Measures of Regular Classroom Teachers' Attitudes Toward Handicapped Children

by Thomas M. Stephens and Benjamin L. Braun

Regular classroom teachers of children in kindergarten through grade eight were asked to respond to a questionnaire concerning their willingness to accept educable mentally handicapped, physically handicapped, and emotionally handicapped students into their classrooms.

A questionnaire was developed as a means of obtaining information concerning the teachers' training, their prior experiences with exceptional children, and their attitudes toward such children. Ten school districts were randomly selected from the 20 districts in the Southwest Cook County (Illinois) Cooperative for Special Education. An explanatory cover letter was attached to the questionnaire which was then distributed to all (1,034) teachers (kindergarten through eighth grade) in the 10 selected school districts.

RESULTS

Of the sample population 83.66% returned the questionnaires. However, not every teacher responded to all 20 items.

Primary and middle grade teachers were more willing to integrate handicapped students than were teachers of grades 7 and 8 ($p < .01$). Of the 795 teachers responding to this question, 481 (61%) indicated a willingness to integrate the handicapped and 314 (39%) said they would not be willing to do so.

A multiple correlation coefficient of .44, accounting for 19% of the variance, was obtained between the weighted sum of three teacher variables and their willingness to accept handicapped students. As indicated in Table 1, in descending order of their contribution to the multiple correlation, these variables were: teachers' confidence in their ability to teach exceptional children; a belief that exceptional children are capable of becoming useful members of society; and teachers' beliefs that public schools should educate exceptional children.

The relationship between each variable and willingness to integrate the handicapped was examined further by means of chi square tests for independent and contingency coefficients. In addition to confirming the significance of the three most effective predictors in the multiple regression analysis, the chi square analyses identified present grade level of teaching assignment and number of special education courses taken as variables related to willingness to integrate.

Those teachers who had taken courses in special education were more willing to accept handicapped students into their classes ($p < .01$) than were those who had not taken such courses. Those confident of their abilities to teach exceptional children were more willing to integrate them than were teachers who were

TABLE 1

Chi Square Analysis of Association Between Teachers' Willingness to Include Handicapped Children in Regular Classrooms and Selected Teacher Variables

Item	Variables	Chi square	Degrees of freedom
1	Sex	.65	2
2	Age	6.30	2
3	Marital status	1.78	2
4	Parental status	1.39	6
5	Size of municipality of residence	1.50	2
6	Number of years since earning bachelor's degree	11.43	4
7	Bachelor's degree major	7.89	3
8	Credit hours beyond bachelor's degree	11.73	4
9	Number of courses in special education	52.82*	3
10	Years of elementary teaching experience	10.08	4
11	Years of Southwest Cook County teaching experience	5.09	4
12	Present grade level teaching assignment	12.23*	2
13	Exceptional child(ren) in family	1.58	1
14	Exceptional child(ren) in neighborhood	2.35	1
15	Confidence in ability to teach exceptional children	33.20*	1
16	Teaching experience in a school containing special education classes	5.77	1
17	Recommend a child for special education placement	4.33	1
18	Belief that public schools should educate exceptional children	57.13*	1

* significant beyond $p < .01$

not confident.

Teachers who believed that handicapped children can become useful members of society were more willing to integrate them than were teachers who did not share this belief ($p < .01$).

Those who believed that public schools should educate exceptional children were more willing to integrate them than were teachers who did not endorse this position ($p < .01$).

DISCUSSION

While identifying the relative contributions of the three most effective predictors, the moderate multiple correlations indicate that the domain of teacher variables related to willingness to integrate the handicapped includes factors beyond those considered in this study. Since these three predictors—confidence in teaching exceptional children; a belief that handicapped children can become useful members of society; and a contention that public schools should educate the handicapped— represent only 19% of the variance; 81% is unaccounted for in this study.

Regular classroom teachers' willingness to integrate handicapped children into their classrooms increased as the number of special education courses increased.

Confidence in their abilities to teach exceptional children was also significantly related to their willingness to integrate such children into their classrooms. Future studies could fruitfully consider teachers' self confidence as an essential factor for accepting students who are handicapped.

Primary and middle grade teachers' willingness to more readily accept children with handicapping conditions into their classes as compared to teachers of grades 7 and 8 could imply that as subject matter becomes more important, teachers become less accepting of individual differences.

It appears that sex, age, marital status, size of municipality of residence, number of years since earning bachelor's degree, years of teaching experience, having exceptional children in the family or neighborhood, teaching experience in a school in which there were special education classrooms, and experience in recommending students for special education evaluations were not significantly related to classroom teachers' attitudes toward integrating handicapped children into regular classrooms.

8

Issues in the Professional Preparation of Secondary School Special Educators

by Sidney R. Miller, David A. Sabatino and Roger P. Larsen

Abstract: The purpose of this study was to contrast university views with those of practitioners in defining professional preparation program efforts for secondary special educators. The impetus for the study was the paucity of secondary special education preparation programs (distinct from elementary, with clearly identifiable course patterns) in university catalog copy in the six states that comprise the US Department of Health, Education, and Welfare's Region Five.

Discrepancies were noted between administrators in local education agencies and those in universities on three issues: (a) the preparation of secondary special educators in language remediation, (b) the restructuring of the standard K-12 teaching certificate into a K-6 and 7-12 licensure, and (c) the identification of teaching competencies necessary to the successful implementation of mainstreaming.

■ Perhaps the most populous category of underserved—frequently unserved—handicapped youth in response to Public Law 94-142 (the Education for All Handicapped Children Act) are the mildly handicapped adolescents found in today's secondary schools. Proportionally, only one-fifth of secondary students receive the required special education services, while elementary school aged handicapped pupils receive almost four-fifths of the required special education services (Metz, 1973). Malouf and Halpern (1976) have advanced a strong argument that few high school aged handicapped students are served by special education programs because they are encouraged to drop out or are excluded from general school activities.

There is evidence to indicate that many secondary youth who have records of nonattendance are properly considered handicapped. For example, Burke and Simons (1965) reported that 76% of nonattenders were reading below grade level, 73% had been retained in school 2 or more years, and only 59% had normal IQ's (90-110 range). The majority of those who did function in the normal IQ range experienced failure in at least one academic subject area and over two-thirds failed at least one grade.

The US Office of Education conservatively estimates that 1.8% of the population in the secondary schools, or approximately 314,000 youths, are learning disabled. Estimates of behavioral disorders range from approximately 1% to 10% (Clarizio & McCoy, 1976) to 0.5% to 15% reported in a national survey by Schultz, Hirshoren, Manton, and Henderson (1971). The incidence of mildly mentally retarded high school students is conservatively estimated at 0.75%. However, since most states accept an IQ score of at least the upper 70's for special education placement or services, the prevalence of mildly retarded youth may well exceed 10%.

Despite the need, special education programs exist for only 85% of the mentally retarded, 54.8% of the learning disabled, and 44.1% of the behaviorally disordered youth in the United States. The following discussion will explore the relation of this phenomenon to the paucity of personnel who have been professionally trained to provide educational services to mildly handicapped adolescents.

PROBLEM

A recent survey of professionals working with secondary handicapped youth suggests that the majority of teaching activities directed to adolescent handicapped pupils should be spent on skills for coping with daily living, occupational preparation, and psychosocial problems. However, in actual practice many secondary educators have long emphasized the remediation of basic reading, mathematics, and social skills, with little emphasis on career education (Miller, 1975). The continuation of elementary educational practices in secondary schools is in part due to the fact that many professionals working in secondary special education were trained in instructional and behavioral management college courses directed toward the elementary level.

Special education has not yet developed a strong, on-going secondary programmatic effort, and it rarely encourages regular (basic) and vocational educators to initiate program development for handicapped adolescents. The special education literature is filled with the term *child*, while references are rarely made to the term *youth* and then only in the last few years.

Historically, special education teachers have not been professionally prepared to develop or implement secondary level programs that address the issue of employment. Thus, the absence of appropriate secondary special education services has encouraged the use of traditional approaches to solving student problems such as expulsion from school as a "treatment" procedure. If the data being reported are accurate, there is little evidence to support the continuation of current secondary treatment procedures, since only 21% of handicapped adolescent students leave high school each year with employable skills (Martin, 1972); 2.5 million handicapped youth will leave school over the next 4 years (Barone, 1976); and 59% will be unprepared for community living and the world of work and will seek solutions for unemployment in welfare, out-patient assistance in clinics, and other public aid programs. The students falling between those qualified for work and those totally unquali-

fied often occupy positions requiring minimal skills and providing a bare modicum of reimbursement.

The availability of specific secondary special education teacher preparation programs at colleges and universities in the United States does little to offset this bleak picture. Miller (1975) reported that in a survey of 243 state colleges and universities only 5 listed either a specific secondary special education preparation program, a single career education course, or a secondary special education course entry in their catalogs. This supports Clark and Olverson's (1973) contention that training and certification in special education are failing to represent current influences in the field and are artifacts of an earlier time.

PURPOSE OF THE STUDY

The literature reviewed supported the supposition that universities and practitioners are not in agreement on the critical aspects of teacher preparation (Brolin, 1973; Clark & Olverson, 1973; Miller, 1975). The available literature does not indicate the degree of agreement among these two groups on teacher preparation or secondary program development issues.

The purposes of this study was, therefore, to assess the degree of agreement and disagreement between college/university and local education agency (LEA) administrators of special education on selected professional preparation and secondary special program development issues. A questionnaire was designed to measure the respondents' thinking on these issues.

PROCEDURE

The study was restricted to the six states that comprise the US Office of Education's Region Five. The reason for selecting Region Five was that the American Association of Colleges of Teacher Education reported (Reynolds, 1978) that more than 50% of the nation's teachers are prepared in these six states. The names of state recognized local directors of special education were obtained by contacting each of six state directors of special education and obtaining directories. The *Education Directory: Colleges and Universities* (Podolsky & Smith, 1977) was consulted to identify colleges of education housing special education departments or programs with special education teacher education components. Once the two lists were compiled, cover letters and the questionnaire were mailed to the 308 local directors of special education who administer state recognized special education programs in cooperatives, regional offices, intermediate districts, or large city schools in Illinois, Indiana, Michigan, Minnesota, Ohio, and Wisconsin. The questionnaire was also mailed to the 46 college/university departments of special education in those same states listing special education courses or programs.

The questionnaire was developed to measure 10 selected areas of focus. Five areas were viewed through the dimension of professional preparation and the questionnaire items were phrased in teacher competency language. The other five items were programmatic counterparts of the first five, but were phrased in program delivery language. The first eight questions required a forced choice, yes/no response. Questions 9 and 10 required the respondent to estimate the percentage of time mildly handicapped adolescents could be successfully mainstreamed and should receive special education consultive assistance. The questionnaires, which were sent to the university/college departments and local education agency special education administrators, contained the same items developed in parallel form to address that particular group of respondents. The essential research questions underlying this work assumed that:

1. University and local education agency administrators of special education do not agree ($p < .01$) on the basic competencies needed to teach mildly handicapped students in secondary special education programs.

2. University and local education agency administrators of special education do not agree ($p < .01$) on the principal teaching tasks required of secondary special educators.

RESULTS

The mailing resulted in a 79% questionnaire return from local directors (243 responses) and an 85% response from colleges and universities (39 responses). Table 1 provides the frequency, percent of agreement and disagreement, and level of statistical significance for each item between the two groups of respondents using a chi-square analysis.

The 10 items from the questionnaire are shown in the extreme left-hand column of Table 1. The first five questions measured preferences of the two groups (college and university educators versus special education directors) with respect to desirable competen-

cies in the preparation programs for secondary special education teachers. Statistically significant differences were found between the two groups on the necessity of language remediation ($p < .05$) and differentiation of the K-12 certificate into a K-6 and 7-12 licensure. The data indicated that local special education directors supported language remediated competency while university educators did not. With respect to licensure, local directors preferred that state certificates for secondary and elementary special educators include a distinct K-6 and 7-12 split. University personnel preferred to remain with a K-12 licensure. The two groups did not disagree significantly with respect to teacher competencies in behavior management, remedial reading, and career education.

The second section of the questionnaire dealt with delivery of services in terms of actual programs and yielded significant ($p < .01$) differences for four of the five items. Both groups were in agreement as to whether or not secondary special education programs should require remedial reading.

An interesting reversal of beliefs took place on an item that addressed collapsing special education categories into a high incidence handicapping cluster by grouping mental retardation, behavior disorders, and learning disabilities. The university personnel supported the high incidence concept, the practitioners did not. Conversely, the local directors supported career education as a mainstay principle in secondary special education. The universities did not see career education as a programmatic mainstay in secondary programs.

A dichotomy in the respondents' position was found over the "success of mainstreaming" item on the questionnaire. There were 38% of the local directors and 47% of the university departmental representatives who did not view mainstreaming as a successful practice at the secondary level. Of the local directors, 26% believed that 50% to 74% of the secondary students can be successfully mainstreamed, while 41% of the university representatives believed that 1% to 25% of the mildly handicapped students can be successfully mainstreamed.

There was a significant disagreement between groups on the percentage of time secondary special educators should work as consultants. University personnel generally felt that secondary special educators should not work as consultants, although 26.5% felt that up to 25% of professional time could be spent consulting. Local special education directors

TABLE 1

Agreement on Selected Professional Preparation and Program Delivery Issues Between Universities and Local Special Education Directors

| | | Professional Preparation for Secondary Special Educators | | | | | |
| | | Yes | | No | | Statistics | |
Question	Statement	Colleges and Universities	Special Education Directors	Colleges and Universities	Special Education Directors	Chi Square[1]	Significant
1.	The primary student management competencies needed by secondary special educators are in behavior management.	54.1% 21	48.4% 118	45.9% 18	51.3% 125	0.376	N.S.
2.	The primary instructional competencies needed by secondary special educators are in remedial reading.	48.6% 19	37.6% 91	51.4% 20	62.4% 152	1.79	N.S.
3.	The primary information processing competencies needed by secondary special educators are in language remediation and development.	45.9% 18	63.4% 154	54.1% 21	36.1% 89	4.18	.05
4.	The primary program delivery competencies needed by secondary special educators are in career education.	51.4% 20	55.7% 135	48.6% 19	44.3% 108	.248	N.S.
5.	The state certification for teachers should differentiate the K-12 certificate into a K-6 and 7-12 licensure.	18.9% 7	48.1% 117	81.1% 32	51.9% 126	12.44	.001

		Program Delivery of Secondary Special Educators					
1.	Generally, secondary special education programs should require remedial reading to be taught.	54.3% 21	54.5% 132	45.7% 18	45.5% 111	.003	N.S.
2.	Generally, secondary special education programs may serve high incidence handicapped (educably retarded, behavior disordered, and learning disordered) students in the same program.	83.3% 32	34.6% 84	16.7% 7	65.4% 59	31.92	.001
3.	Generally, special education programs should employ vocational or career education specialists to implement a career education component (minimizing the career education role of the special educator).	37.0% 13	63.2% 154	63.0% 26	36.8% 89	7.51	.005

continued on next page

8

TABLE 1 (Continued)

Program Delivery of Secondary Special Educators

Ques- tion	Statement	0%	1-25%	26-49%	50-74%	75-99%	100%	Statistics Chi square	Significant
					Special Education Directors[1]				
4.	Percentage of mildly handicapped adolescent youth that could be successfully mainstreamed in secondary special education programs?	38.2 93	8.8 21	14.7 36	26.5 64	11.8 29		40.83	.001
				Colleges and Universities					
		46.9 18	40.6 16	6.3 2	6.3 2				
					Special Education Directors[2]				
5.	Percentage of professional time per week secondary special educators should work as consultants with regular or vocational educators?	35.1 85	10.3 25	10.3 25	21.6 53	21.6 53		136.99	.001
				Colleges and Universities					
		67.6 27	26.5 11				2.9 1		

[1] degrees of freedom= 4
[2] degrees of freedom= 5

were much more divided in their opinions, as the data in Table 1 indicate. In short, universities and practitioners were not in agreement in their thinking on preparing secondary educators to work in support of mainstreaming through consultation models, or on the success of mainstreaming activities in secondary schools.

DISCUSSION

The social organizational pressures in any society tend to influence the responses to issues for a particular period of time. Special education's very being, its growth, and the current mandates by the courts and the Congress suggest that human rights issues include handicapped children. However, the word *children* in the Public Law 94-142 legislation may tend to exclude youth to age 21 until 1980.

The problem is compounded by regular and vocational educators who are aware that there is little help available at this time and as a result remain subject matter oriented. University special educators have also contributed to the dilemma by not developing training programs to prepare personnel to work specifically with handicapped adolescents and by maintaining K-12 course and program preparation patterns, as opposed to age sensitive programs.

The result is that the focus in most special education teacher preparation programs is on elementary remediation, rather than on high school age youth, who are more difficult to program for both in behavioral areas and in curriculum content.

Universities and local special education directors do agree that career education, reading remediation, and behavioral management are primary competencies. Universities do not agree that competencies as reflected in age sensitive certification patterns should be established or that language remediation is an important preparation competency.

Universities tend to feel that categorization of the handicapped is a poor practice. They could easily accept cross categorical high incidence programing including the mildly mentally retarded, behaviorally disordered, and learning disabled. The local special education directors had difficulty with the high incidence concept programmatically. It is certainly true that when characteristics, diagnostics, and instructional management courses are collapsed across categories and are not taught to any specific age group, the cost of university special education instruction is mitigated. Equally influential from a university cost standpoint is the fact that most states require a practicum or student teaching in the area of certification. If specific area certificates for age sensitive levels are to be issued, practicum sites must be sought. Such sites are not easy to find in the secondary schools. Then too, additional practica mean additional university supervisory resources, sometimes a difficult element to obtain in an era of retrenchment in higher education.

The last two issues, which delve into the success of mainstreaming at the secondary level for mildly handicapped students and the consultation time needed from special educators, generated diverse intergroup and intragroup responses. It appears that both university and local program directors have mixed positions about mainstreaming. The analysis of the obtained data indicates that local administrators view secondary special education consultation as a highly specific role requiring university preparation which at present is not commonly available. Therefore, the cost of developing resource rooms and consultation models at the secondary school level falls to the local district.

It appears from the extent of agreement between university and local administrators of special education on what constitutes both program and preparation competencies that cooperative model program efforts could be initiated. It also appears that communication among departments of communication disorders, remedial reading, vocational education, trade and industry, counseling, and other areas is needed if secondary programs are to offer the required competencies agreed upon by the two groups of respondents. The professional preparation of secondary special educators may need more drastic reorganization as well as more diverse types of competency requirements than is currently the case, at least as reflected in university catalogs. This is especially true given the current elementary age orientation and K-12 licensure in most states.

In conclusion, it appears that Public Law 94-142 may serve as an impact measure primarily at the elementary school level unless specifically prepared special educators are available to implement appropriate secondary programs for mildly handicapped adolescents. The onus is therefore on universities to initate new programs capable of providing an age sensitive structure, and it is the responsibility of the public schools to develop sufficient resource training programs that will provide cooperative student teaching placements.

REFERENCES

Barone, S. Career education and the handicapped. In R. D. Bhaerman (Ed.), *Career education and basic academic achievement: A descriptive analysis of the research.* Washington DC: US Office of Education, May 1976.

Brolin, D. Career education needs of secondary educable students. *Exceptional Children*, 1973, *39*, 619-624.

Burke, N. S., & Simons, A. F. Factors which precipitate dropouts and delinquency. *Federal Probation*, 1965, *29*, 28-32.

Clarizio, H. F., & McCoy, G. F. *Behavior disorders in children* (2nd ed.). New York: Crowell, 1976.

Clark, G. M., & Olverson, B. S. Education of secondary personnel: Aspiration and preliminary data. *Exceptional Children*, 1973, *39*, 541-546.

Malouf, D., & Halpern, A. A review of secondary level special education. *Thresholds*, 1976, *2*, 6-7.

Martin, E. W. Individualism and behaviorism as a future trend in educating handicapped children. *Exceptional Children*, 1972, *38*, 517-527.

Metz, A. S. *Number of pupils with handicaps in local public schools* (Bureau of Education for the Handicapped, Report No. DHEW-OE-73-11107), Washington DC: US Government Printing Office, 1973.

Miller, S. R. Secondary programming. In D. A. Sabatino (Ed.), *Learning disabilities handbook: A technical guide to program development.* DeKalb IL: Northern Illinois University Press, 1975.

Podolsky, A., & Smith, C. R. *Education directory: Colleges and universities.* Washington DC: US Government Printing Office, 1977.

Reynolds, M. C. Basic issues in restructuring teacher education. *Journal of Teacher Education*, 1978, *29*, 25-33.

Schultz, E. W. Hirshoren, A., Manton, A. B., & Henderson, R. A. Special education for the emotionally disturbed. *Exceptional Children*, 1971, *38*, 313-318.

8

The Implementation of Statewide Early Education Plans: A Two-year Report

by Julie Anne Carter, Charlene Imhoff, Ronald LaCoste, Brian McNulty and Pamela Peterson

The Bureau of Education for the Handicapped initiated the State Implementation Grant (SIG) program in 1976–77 with the funding of 13 states. Twenty states were funded in 1977–78 and 23 states were funded for 1978–79. The intent of the grants is to assist states in the implementation of Early Childhood State Plans and to develop a statewide network of services for young handicapped children. This report summarizes the observations of five State Implementation Grant directors for the first two years of program operations.

Rationale

There are few traditions or precedents regarding public education for children below kindergarten age. In addition, there are attitude barriers which have been created by those who are uncomfortable with the idea of young children being involved in public education. Our society is oriented toward providing public school programs for children aged 6 through 18; consequently, there is an uneven commitment to early education programming at the state and local level. SIG directors are beginning to confront these barriers by providing information and public awareness as to the benefits of early intervention and by serving as advocates for young children with special needs.

Local Education Agencies need support from the state level before they can implement early childhood programs. Coordination of resources, standards, and program models must be created at the state level in order to build program consistency and accessibility throughout the state. Again, the Implementation Grant provides asistance in the form of organized state support for early childhood/special education and in the coordination of existing resources as well as the development of novel solutions to emerging issues.

Another problem is posed by the scarcity of reliable instruments, procedures, and criteria for identifying young children in need of services. Implementation Grant activities which include data collection, monitoring, evaluation, and development of technical assistance networks will result in improved identification capabilities.

Professionals generally agree that even minimal intervention during the crucial early years of development yields greater returns than later intervention. The cost efficiency of the early intervention greatly outweighs the burden of providing funds for special education services later in life. Thus, lack of funds should not be a barrier to program development.

Existing programs for young handicapped children have been implemented primarily

From *Education and Training of the Mentally Retarded*, Vol. 14, No. 12, February 1980. Copyright 1980, The Division of Mental Retardation, The Council for Exceptional Children. Reprinted with permission.

by staff who are not specifically trained in early childhood/special education. State Implementation Grants are providing inservice training programs in an effort to retrain current personnel to be proficient in the necessary skills. Many teachers lack knowledge of child development in the early years and this information must be provided through inservice training.

Finally, State Implementation Grants are providing the impetus to develop guidelines and standards for early childhood/special education programs. New standards are necessary because of the unique characteristics of very young handicapped or at-risk children.

Commonalities

Although different states have focused attention on different areas of emphasis, a review of the data clearly identifies major areas in which all State Implementation Grants have been involved. These areas include system development, needs assessment, planning, program management, coordination of resources, personnel training, parent involvement, and technical assistance. The fact that a number of common factors exist in the various SIG grants demonstrates the similarity of needs which occur nationwide in this new educational program area.

System Development

A review of existing grants show that there is a central focus throughout all the grants. This focus is system development. Regardless of the priorities established by each grant, the common overall goal is to develop and establish a system whereby all early childhood programs within a state, whether public or private, can be blended into a comprehensive system of service for young handicapped children.

The development of this system is tied to an existing delivery system which includes the Department of Education, Division of Special Education, and other state human service agencies. It is imperative for the Implementation Grants to coordinate with all the human service agencies, (e.g., Head Start, Welfare) because the educational system serves only children who are in need of special educational services. These other agencies, in conjunction with educational services, provide the necessary continuum of program alternatives. Coordinating with these

other delivery systems provides the opportunity for facilitation and advocacy for all early childhood programs within their states as they assist in policy and procedural development, program development, and personnel training. Additionally, the Implementation Grants serve as advocates for the expansion of services to greater numbers of children at increasingly younger ages.

Within the development of a system of early childhood services, it is necessary and advantageous to develop a close relationship with the Handicapped Children's Early Educational Program (HCEEP) Model Demonstration and Outreach projects in each state. These projects provide a key component within the comprehensive system of services to young handicapped children. Through this cooperative effort, the State Implementation Grants support the dissemination and replication efforts of the Model Demonstration and Outreach projects within their own states. State Implementation Grants are catalysts for the increased replication of model programs; model programs, in turn, enrich each state's system of service for young handicapped children.

Needs Assessment

All Implementation Grants are involved actively in needs assessments. A majority of the grants have assessed the states' needs in the following areas: program inventories, interagency coordination, and training (inservice and preservice). Other topics of needs assessments include parent training, fiscal needs, local education agency early childhood planning, private day care service, administrative needs, population census, curriculum, legislation, and policy. One state's entire Implementation Grant revolves around the assessment of local school districts' early childhood needs and the subsequent provision of technical assistance to meet these identified needs.

Planning

Planning is an essential component of State Implementation Grants for two reasons: (a) goals and objectives written in the grant must be implemented through specific procedures, which are developed through planning, and (b) ongoing planning is necessary as a result of the domino phenomenon. That is, while one objective is being pursued, other related areas surface, and these must be addressed as well. For example, if one sets

8

forth to develop programs, one quickly realizes the need to develop program standards, a certification pattern, university training programs, and other areas of support. Currently, one state's planning effort will result in the development of a tracking system to aid its legislatively-supported child identification efforts and a data system containing a profile of services for which each child is eligible.

Program Management

Program management involves policy and procedures development as well as fiscal management. Nearly all Implementation Grants are working actively on interagency agreements and new legislation. A majority of grants are in the process of developing regulations, guidelines, and certification in the area of early childhood/special education. Several states have already adopted certification patterns through the efforts of their Implementation Grant staff. Nearly all are involved in fiscal management of various resources and are cognizant of the need to use the most restricted dollar first.

Additionally, several State Implementation Grants are involved in program monitoring and evaluation to determine both compliance with regulations and quality of programs. One Implementation Grant developed a comprehensive model for monitoring early childhood programs that the Division of Special Education adopted for use in monitoring all local Education Agency programs in the state.

Coordination of Resources

Another endeavor engaged in by all State Implementation Grants is that of interagency coordination. States have learned that an interagency agreement must be realistic and workable. The development of these agreements necessitates a lengthy process of communication among the involved parties. Both programmatic and fiscal resources must be considered and coordinated. Some states have approached this planning effort from the state level, others have begun at the local level, and still others have tried a combination state/local approach. Implementation Grant directors are also represented on advisory boards of other related agencies and in early childhood consortia.

Personnel Training

Personnel training is one of the most im-

portant functions performed by State Implementation Grants. Every Implementation Grant is involved heavily in conducting in-service training workshops, which may take the form of a half-day presentation, a six-week summer program, or anything in between. Trainees include school administrators, education program personnel, community agency personnel, parents, university faculty, and legislators.

Parent Involvement

State Implementation Grants are committed to the belief that parents are primary teachers of their children. Because of this commitment, parent involvement is a key component of each grant. Many activities focus on parents, and the scope of emphasis is broad. Some states have used parents as presenters at conferences, describing to professionals both their feelings about having a young handicapped child and the necessary ingredients in an effective parent involvement program. Other Implementation Grants are working to organize parent support groups and respite care services. Many states are training parents in methods which will enhance the liaison between home and school. Parents are frequently involved in interagency planning efforts as valuable contributors from the consumer perspective.

One exciting example of service to parents is found in a state whose Implementation Grant has organized a state-wide toy lending library. The toys have been carefully selected for educational value and are categorized by developmental level. They are distributed through public libraries and are targeted toward young children with handicaps. A card which accompanies each toy describes suggested activities and solicits parents' comments regarding additional uses for the item.

Technical Assistance

The final component which is common to all State Implementation Grants is the provision of technical assistance. For a few grants, technical assistance is the primary activity, while for others it is at least one significant part of the total work scope. The following types of technical assistance are being provided by a majority of Implementation Grants: interagency coordination, program development (screening, assessment, program planning), inservice training, parent training, and the development of program standards.

Technical assistance is provided primarily in a responsive manner, that is, following a needs assessment or a specific request for assistance.

Fiscal and Program Coordination

Many states do not mandate programs for handicapped children below the age of five. The approach to early childhood planning and program development in these states differs considerably from the methods used in states with mandatory legislation below five years of age. One state with permissive legislation is using its Implementation Grant to assess local district needs in planning and preparing for early childhood education. That state believes it will have a firm foundation in place when its mandatory age limit is lowered.

The states' priorities for service needs are increasingly met and coordinated through the direction and support provided by the Implementation Grants. Regardless of the priorities established by the states, there is a real need for the State Implementation Grants to provide the management function necessary to allow for the most effective use of all early childhood dollars and programs. This system development process, through the operation of an Implementation Grant, provides the states with the opportunity to cooperate with all service providers to design and deliver quality services for young handicapped children and their families.

The catalytic activities of State Implementation Grants are responsible for the first large-scale surge of interest and program development in early childhood/special education in many states. By operating from the State Education Agency, Implementation Grants are in the unique position of being able to coordinate existing resources in a systematic manner. The grants provide a network for linking model demonstration programs and outreach projects with Local Education Agency and community-based services for young handicapped children and their families. Their impact is strongly felt in each state which operates a State Implementation Grant; for without them, early childhood/special education service delivery systems are destined to remain fragmented at best.

State Implementation Grants and Preschool Incentive Grants: Some Distinctions and an Illustration

Perhaps because of the relative newness of special education and related services to handicapped children under the age of 6 or because of the recent availability of these two funding sources, there currently exists some confusion as to the distinction between State Implementation Grants and Preschool Incentive Grants. An attempt will be made here to clarify the major distinctions.

First, State Implementation Grants are competitive grants with eligibility limited to State Education Agencies. Funding is authorized from the Handicapped Children's Early Education Program (HCEEP), a program which primarily provides discretionary grants for the purpose of developing exemplary programs in the area of early childhood education for the handicapped. Preschool Incentive Grants, on the other hand, supplement General Aid to States under Part B of P.L. 94-142. General Aid, based on a formula grant applied to the information provided in the State Plan, is made available to states to assist in ensuring a free and appropriate public education to all handicapped children. The Preschool Incentive Grant is based on attachments to the State Plan and differs from General Aid by existing specifically to provide special education and related services to 3-, 4-, or 5-year-old handicapped children.

8

Direct Observation Approach to Measuring Classroom Behavior

by Stanley L. Deno

Virtually every teacher has at least one student who might variously be described as "a behavior problem," "inattentive," "hyperactive," "acting out," or "disruptive." The problems of managing social behavior in the classroom are so pervasive, in fact, that lack of discipline has been identified by the American public as the major problem facing the schools in 8 of the last 9 years (Gallup, 1978). Disorderly classroom behavior is so common that it has become normal for a child to be identified at least once as a behavior problem during the elementary school years (Rubin & Balow, 1978).

At the same time the courts have acted clearly to establish the basic rights of students under the US Constitution. Lawmakers have made it clear to educators that despite the ease with which they might identify children as socially deviant, they must not selectively segregate a child without ensuring that the child's rights to due process of law have been met (*Mills* v. *Board of Education*, 1972). Further, if the school's recommendation is to make substantive revisions in the child's environment, not only must those revisions include due process protections, but their effects must also be carefully monitored. As a result of the countervailing pressures both to respond effectively to classroom disorder and yet to protect the student's rights, principals, teachers, special educators, and school psychologists are becom-

ing sensitive to the need for objectively documenting the basis for interventions.

One approach to documentation has been to use behavior checklists or rating scales completed by the classroom teacher or someone who has observed the student in question. When such instruments are used, however, the probability of bias is significant (Foster, Ysseldyke, & Reese, 1975; Ysseldyke & Foster, 1978). A preferable alternative seems to be the use of direct observation and recording of behavior, which is less susceptible to biasing (Madle, Neisworth, & Kurtz, 1978) and, consequently, better meets the requirement that behavioral difference be documented objectively.

Since 1972 staff at the University of Minnesota have been involved in training special education resource teachers to become intervention managers. In this role the teachers have learned to assess differences in classroom behavior using a direct observation system developed in connection with a special project funded by the Bureau of Education for the Handicapped.

The observation system is based on the assumption that any label applied to a child identifying him or her as a conduct problem implies that the child's behavior differs significantly from that of the peer group. Proceeding from that assumption, the observation system has been used to objectively determine the

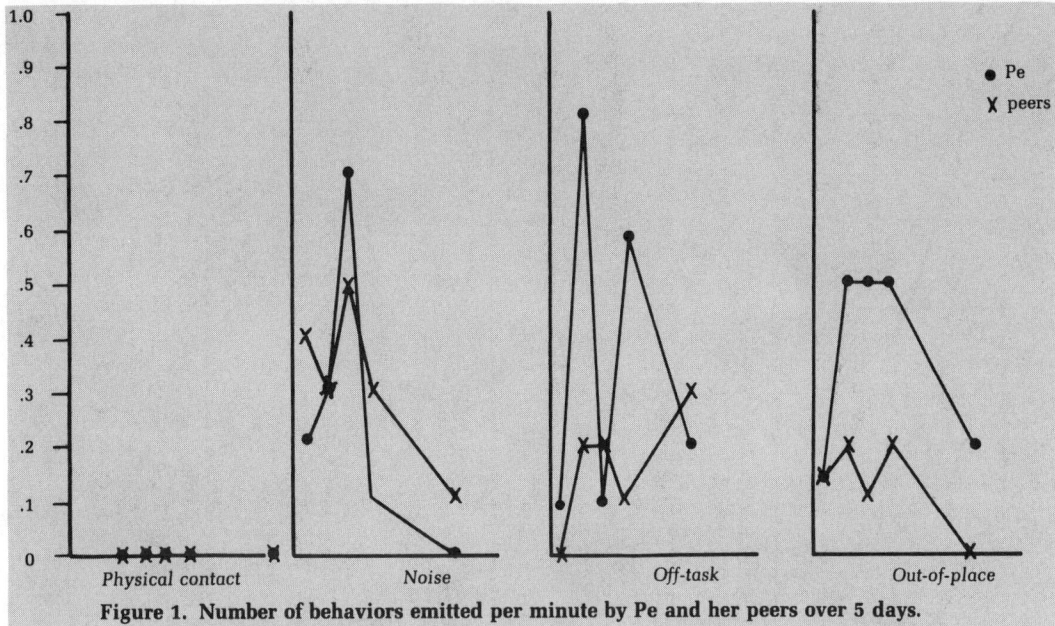

Figure 1. Number of behaviors emitted per minute by Pe and her peers over 5 days.

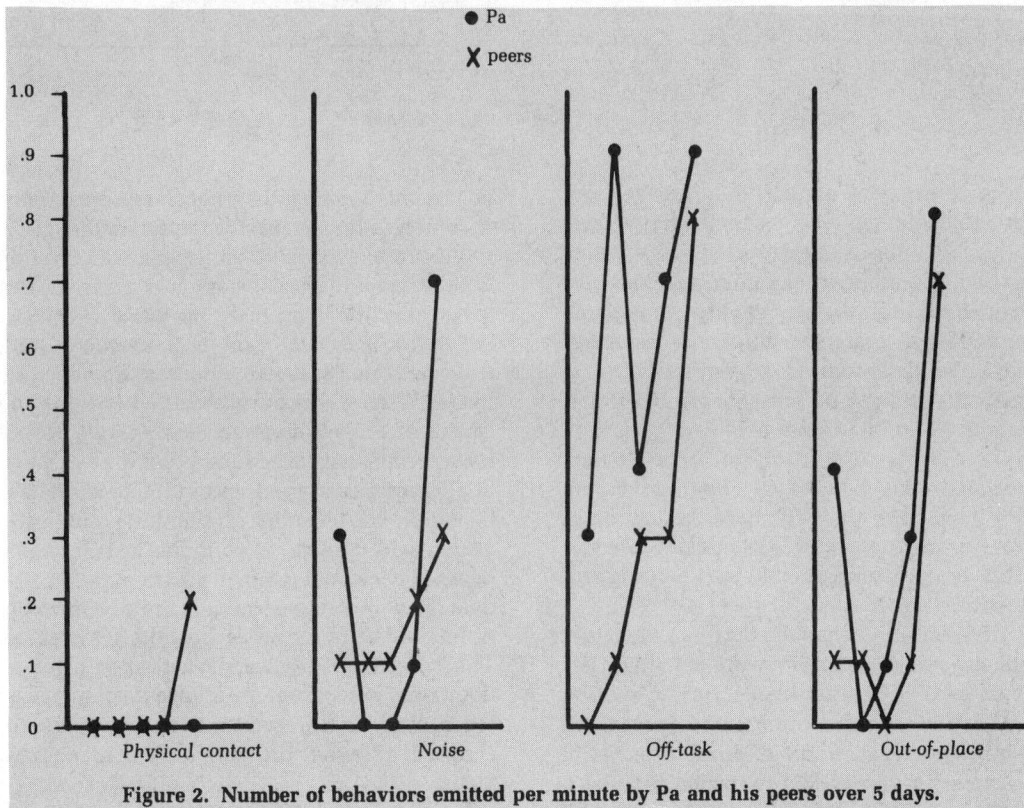

Figure 2. Number of behaviors emitted per minute by Pa and his peers over 5 days.

existence, and the extent, of that implied behavioral difference.

THE OBSERVATION SYSTEM

The recording procedures are briefly described here to provide a general understanding of the observation system. The system involves rec-

ording the frequency of four key target behaviors (noise, out-of-place, physical contact/destruction, and off-task) emitted by the referred student and by a normative peer sample. Peer sampling is a procedure developed by Cobb and Ray (1970), subsequently modified by Patterson, Cobb, and Ray (1972), and recently used by Walker and Hops (1976). The advantage of peer sampling is that data on the fre-

8

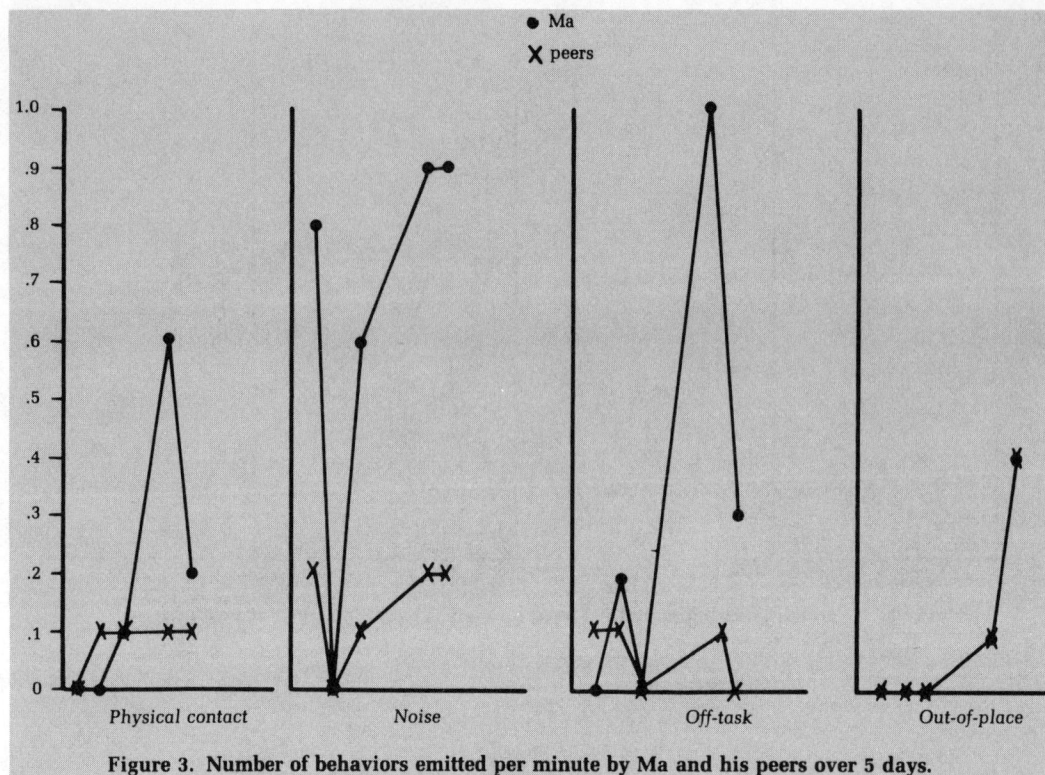

Figure 3. Number of behaviors emitted per minute by Ma and his peers over 5 days.

quency of behavior emitted by a referred student can be considered on both relative and absolute grounds. A student's behavior, which may seem excessive if considered alone, may in fact be quite consistent when considered relative to peer behavior within the context of a particular classroom. This point is illustrated graphically in the data presented in Figures 1, 2, and 3. These data were obtained by observing three different students in three elementary classrooms who were identified as socially deviant by their teachers. Inspection of the graphs reveals the differences between students, between classrooms, and within students from day to day.

A difference in behaviors between the target child and the peer sample was obtained on the category called "out-of-place" for Pa and Pe, but not for Ma, while a difference was obtained in "off-task" for Pa and Ma, but not for Pe. In the "noise" category, Ma exceeded his peers, Pa did not differ, and Pe was actually less noisy than her peers. Although none of the three target students differed in median frequency of occurrence for the category "physical contact," a difference is obtained for Ma if the mean rather than the median is used to summarize the data. Further inspection of the graphs reveals that the differences obtained for "physical contact/destruction" between target students and peers was smaller than the differ-

ences obtained among the classrooms. Such variation in the levels of behavior among classrooms underscores the importance of sampling both target and peer behavior.

An additional point to be made regarding the individual data bears on the value of multiple behavior samples when assessments are made. Were we to have observed Ma only on Day 2 of the observation sessions we would have erroneously concluded that if he differed at all from his peers it was in terms of off-task behavior. His behavior on the three other categories was either equal to or less than his peers. That conclusion is contradicted in the data from multiple samples. Similar contradictions may be found in each of the other cases. The conclusion is clear: When attempting to document behavioral difference through classroom observations, multiple observations are essential to avoid drawing erroneous conclusions.

A CAVEAT

The data obtained through using the discrepancy observation system described here can be summarized and presented in a variety of ways. How the data are summarized is, of course, less important than how they are interpreted. Great care must be taken to use the data fairly for all persons involved. That means that once differences in behavior are empirically established, the importance of that difference in each individual case must be addressed by all parties (i.e., students, parents, teachers, etc.) who have a vested interest in that difference. To paraphrase Mager and Pipe (1970) on this point, "If a discrepancy can be ignored it should be." A person who is doing something different from the peer group is not ipso facto behaving wrongly. The value of a discrepancy cannot be established by determining either its existence or its magnitude.

REFERENCES

Cobb, J. A., & Ray, R. S. *Manual for coding discrete behaviors in the school setting.* Unpublished manuscript, Social Learning Project, Oregon Research Institute, Eugene, Oregon: March, 1970.

Foster, G. G., Ysseldyke, J. E., & Reese, J. H. "I wouldn't have seen it if I hadn't believed it." *Exceptional Children,* 1975, *42,* 469-473.

Gallup, G. H. The 10th annual Gallup poll of the public's attitudes towards the public schools. *Kappan,* 1978, *60,* 33-45.

Madle, R. R., Neisworth, J. T., & Kurtz, P. D. Biasing of hyperkinetic behavior ratings by diagnostic reports: Effects of observer training and assessment method. *Journal of Learning Disabilities,* in press.

Mager, R. F., & Pipe, P. *Analyzing performance problems or 'You really oughta wanna'.* Belmont CA: Lear Siegler, Fearon Publishers, 1970.

Mills v. Board of Education of the District of Columbia, 348 F. Supp. 866 (D. D. C., 1972).

Patterson, G. R., Cobb, J. A., & Ray, R. S. Direct intervention in the classroom: A set of procedures for the aggressive child. In F. W. Clark, D. R. Evans, & L. A. Hamerlynck (Eds.), *Implementing behavioral programs for schools and clinics.* Proceedings of the Third Banff International Conference on Behavior Modification. Champaign IL: Research Press Co., 1972.

Rubin, R., & Balow, B. Prevalence of teacher identified behavior problems: A longitudinal study. *Exceptional Children,* 1978, *45,* 102-111.

Walker, H., & Hops, H. Use of normative peer data as a standard for evaluating classroom treatment effects. *Journal of Applied Behavior Analysis,* 1976, *9,* 159-168.

Ysseldyke, J. E., & Foster, G. G. Bias in teacher's observations of emotionally disturbed and learning disabled children. *Exceptional Children,* 1978, *44,* 613-615.

8

Certification Requirements Of General Educators Concerning Exceptional Pupils

by James E. Smith, Jr., and W. Jean Schindler

As the trend toward mainstreaming exceptional pupils grows (Chaffin, 1974) and as the mandate of Public Law 94-142 (the Education for all Handicapped Children Act) for an appropriate education in the least restrictive environment (Ballard & Zettel, 1977) becomes more of a reality, professional educators need to consider carefully the degree to which teachers are prepared for these developments. This investigation sought to ascertain what requirements each state imposed on general education teachers in training so that they would be able to work with and effectively teach exceptional children and youth.

PROCEDURE

Questionnaires were sent to the superintendents or commissioners of education in the 50 states and the District of Columbia asking whether or not preservice general educators in those states had to meet any requirements in their coursework relative to the characteristics and needs of exceptional learners. All states responded to the questionnaire in writing or by telephone.

RESULTS

The responses to the questionnaire can be summarized as follows: (a) 25 states and the District had no such certification requirement, nor were these states contemplating such a requirement; (b) 11 states were either considering such a requirement or anticipated instituting such a requirement in the near future; and (c) 15 states required all preservice educators to be exposed to the characteristics and needs of exceptional children and youth. Of the states that did require coursework concerning the exceptional learner for preservice general educators, only Oklahoma required more than one course. The course required by states with the certification requirement was usually entitled "Education of Exceptional Children" or "Psychology of Exceptional Children." Several states did not require that specific coursework be taken, but these states did require that certain competencies relating to exceptionality be fulfilled in state approved teacher training programs (see Table 1).

An additional question asked during the survey was: "How would teachers who are already in the field be affected by such a requirement?" Two principal responses emerged regarding this question: (a) the requirement did not have any effect on persons presently certified to teach, or (b) teachers presently teaching would gain the same competencies through inservice training. However, detailed analysis of questionnaire responses failed to show a clear or consistent pattern for delivering this inservice training.

TABLE 1
Disposition of Exceptionality Coursework Requirements for Certification

State	No require-ment	State require-ment	State require-ment in ap-proved pro-grams	Requirement by year indi-cated	Requirement contemplated	Requirement pending in state legisla-ture
Alabama	X					
Alaska	X					
Arizona		X				
Arkansas	X					
California				1979		
Colorado		X				
Connecticut	X					
Delaware	X					
District of Columbia	X					
Florida	X					
Georgia		X				
Hawaii			X			
Idaho	X					
Illinois	X					
Indiana	X					
Iowa	X					
Kansas					X	
Kentucky		X				
Louisiana			X			
Maine				1981		
Maryland	X					
Massachusetts					X	
Michigan	X					
Minnesota			X			
Mississippi				1980		
Missouri		X				
Montana					X	
Nebraska			X			
Nevada						X
New Hampshire	X					
New Jersey	X					
New Mexico	X					
New York	X					
North Carolina		X				
North Dakota	X					
Ohio				1980		
Oklahoma		X				
Oregon	X					
Pennsylvania			X			
Rhode Island	X					
South Carolina	X					
South Dakota	X					
Tennessee				1980		
Texas		X				
Utah	X					
Vermont	X					
Virginia		X				
Washington	X					
West Virginia		X				
Wisconsin					X	
Wyoming				1979		

8

DISCUSSION

The results of this study clearly indicate that a very large number of general education teachers will be unprepared to work with exceptional children and youth if the present situation continues. In order to eliminate this problem (at least at the undergraduate level), it is recommended that all states begin to require teachers in training to take a minimum of two 3 hour courses dealing with exceptional learners. These two courses should expose the prospective teacher to (a) characteristics of exceptional learners, that is, how these learners are similar to and how they are different from the typical student; and (b) methods for effectively teaching exceptional pupils. The same procedure should be followed with teachers who are already in the field. These teachers should be required by the state and the local school system to become knowledgeable about the characteristics of and methods for working with exceptional pupils. In this case, the local school system can either contract with the state to provide the inservice training, work with nearby colleges and universities, or provide the services directly by using personnel from the local system.

It would appear that for the states that have a certification requirement concerning the exceptional learner for general educators, one would expect to find less money being spent on inservice training in this area; a more consistent mode of training being employed to expose teachers to the exceptional learner; and less frequent due process hearings being convened because of miscommunications between teachers, parents, and students regarding the appropriateness of educational placement and instruction.

While a number of states have shown a purposeful movement toward requiring that all teachers be exposed to the special needs learner, this exposure is at a minimal level. Therefore, a goal for all professional educators should be to acquire an in-depth knowledge of the special needs learner.

REFERENCES

Ballard, J., & Zettel, J. Public Law 94-142 and Section 504: What they say about rights and protections. *Exceptional Children*, 1977, 44, 177-184.

Chaffin, J. P. Will the real mainstreaming program please stand up: (Or . . . Should Dunn have done it?)? *Focus on Exceptional Children*, 1974, 6(5), 1-18.

Training and Certification Of Administrators In Special Education

by Stephen W. Stile and Timothy J. Pettibone

Abstract: A national survey of state certification offices was conducted to determine requirements for administrator certification in special education. In addition, the status of special education training programs was assessed. A 100% return was achieved. Over half of the states offer separate special education administrator certification and over half have at least one training program available. Some inconsistencies of the data are apparent, indicating possible transition or communication problems.

■ In recent years, the tasks and social systems of educational administrators involved with programs for exceptional learners have been subjected to many forces for change. As seen by Burrelo and Sage (1979) these forces include

such externally based sources as the general social climate, actions of the courts, and legislation at both the state and federal levels. In addition, forces internal to the education establishment, generating from professional doubts, questions, and innovative ideas, suggest new policies, new models, and new approaches to serving new populations .... The pervasiveness and potency of these forces seem to leave little chance for anything but accelerating change. (p. 57)

It is axiomatic, therefore, that a need exists for reorientation in educational administration programs. Clearly, if all exceptional children are to be served well in our regular and special classrooms, in addition to teachers such personnel as principals, supervisors, and superintendents must receive specialized training (Behrens & Grosenick, 1978). Such training would include learning what the recent research data indicate regarding effective instructional programs for exceptional children, as well as keeping data based records, planning programs, interpreting mandates, assisting in program redesign, assessing training needs and using evaluation data for program revision (Gearheart, 1977; Nevin, 1979).

The purpose of this study was to determine the current status of training/certification of educational administrators in the field of special education throughout the United States.

PROCEDURES

Hirshoren and Umansky (1977) conducted a parallel survey regarding certification requirements for teachers of preschool handicapped children. Through their courtesy, a list of offices of certification in the 50 states and the District of Columbia was obtained. A questionnaire was mailed to these offices together with a letter of explanation. After 6 weeks, a followup letter and second questionnaire were mailed to the 8 nonrespondents. Three states failed to respond to the followup materials and

8

TABLE 1

Current (1979) Coursework, Authorization, Certification, and Training Program Requirements for Special Education Administration in the United States

State	Coursework required for general administration certificate	Separate special education administrative credential	Existing training program	General certificate includes special education authorization
Alabama	Yes	Yes	Yes	No
Alaska	No	Yes	No	No
Arizona	No	Other	No	Yes
Arkansas	No	Yes	Yes	No
California	Yes	No	Yes	Yes
Colorado	Yes	Yes	Yes	No
Connecticut	No	No	No	No
Delaware	No	Yes	No	Yes
Florida	No	No	No	Yes
Georgia	Yes	Yes	Yes	No
Hawaii	No	No	No	Yes
Idaho	No	Yes	Yes	No
Illinois	No	Yes	Yes	No
Indiana	No	Yes	Yes	No
Iowa	No response	Yes	Yes	No
Kansas	No	Yes	Yes	No
Kentucky	Yes	Yes	Yes	No
Louisiana	No	Yes	Yes	No
Maine	Other	Yes	No	No
Maryland	No	Yes	No	No
Massachusetts	No	Yes	Yes	No
Michigan	No	Yes	Yes	No
Minnesota	No	Yes	Yes	No
Mississippi	No	No	No	No
Missouri	Yes	No	No	Other
Montana	No	No	Yes	No
Nebraska	No	Yes	Yes	Yes
Nevada	Yes	No	No	Yes
New Hampshire	No	No	No	Yes
New Jersey	No	No	No	Yes
New Mexico	No	No	No	Yes
New York	No	No	No	Yes
North Carolina	No	No	No	Yes
North Dakota	No	Yes	No	No
Ohio	No	No	Yes	Yes
Oklahoma	Yes	No	No	Yes
Oregon	No	No	Yes	Yes
Pennsylvania	No	Yes	Yes	Yes
Rhode Island	Yes	Yes	No	No
South Carolina	No	No	Yes	No
South Dakota	No	Yes	Yes	No
Tennessee	Yes	No	Yes	No
Texas	Yes	No	No	No response
Utah	No	No	No	Yes
Vermont	No	Yes	Under development	No
Virginia	Yes	Yes	Yes	Yes
Washington	No	No	No	No
West Virginia	No	No	No	Yes
Wisconsin	No	Yes	Yes	No
Wyoming	No	No	No	Yes
Washington DC	No	No	Yes	No

were contacted by telephone. Ultimately, the desired information was obtained from all 50 states and the District of Columbia.

The questionnaire consisted of four items printed on a self addressed, stamped postcard enclosed with the explanatory letter. These items were:

1. Is special education coursework required for the general administration credential?
2. Is a separate special education administration credential issued in your state?
3. Does a formal special education administration training program exist in at least one of your state's institutions of higher education?
4. Does the general administration credential include authorization in special education?

These questions required a simple *yes-no* response. However, room was left for further explanation if the respondent so desired (unfortunately, few comments were received). Several states supplied the authors with materials such as standards for special education administrative certification or endorsement.

FINDINGS

Results of the survey are shown in Table 1. Of the 51 respondents, 26 (51%) offer separate certification as a special education administrator while 20 (39%) include special education authorization as part of the general adminstrator's certificate. Of the states offering separate certification, four (8%) include authorization in the general certificate as well. Only 12 (24%) states require special education coursework for general administration certification. Special education administrator training programs exist in 26 (51%) of the states, but seven (14%) of these states have no separate special education administrator credential. Six (12%) of the states offering separate special education administrative certification have no training programs. Only one (2%) state not currently having a training program claimed to have one under development.

DISCUSSION

Twenty-six states offer a separate credential in special education administration. Only seven states offer neither a separate certificate nor an endorsement of the general administrator's certificate. Clearly, special education administration is currently recognized in one form or another. The form taken probably reflects philosophical differences among the states. It seems that separate certification indicates a posture of specialization while endorsement indicates a more generalist position.

Of the 12 states requiring education coursework for the general administrative credential, six do not offer a special education endorsement of the certificate and five of these require a separate certificate for special education. Some of these findings seem inconsistent. Obviously, some states are in a transition stage, but it does appear that state certification requirements and availability of training programs do not match in several states. It may be that this discrepancy reflects a lag in institutional response to changing requirements. Another possible reason for the discrepancy may be, as Hirshoren and Umansky (1977) concluded in their preschool study, that there is a lack of communication between state education agencies and institutions of higher education.

It seems appropriate that all educational administrators become "special" administrators through training in special education competencies. In our view, however, separate administrative certification in special education is *not* desirable. If, as Corrigan (1978) has pointed out, the special education/regular education dualism that exists in the public schools, is to be eliminated, it must be eliminated in the colleges of education. Admittedly, this goal may not be reached for some time and, realistically, separate certification may need to be pursued as an interim measure. The survey results indicate that such an interim period is well underway.

REFERENCES

Behrens, T., & Grosenick, J. K. Deans' grants projects: Supporting innovations in teacher-education programs. In J. K. Grosenick & M. C. Reynolds (Eds.), *Teacher education: Renegotiating roles for mainstreaming.* Reston VA: The Council for Exceptional Children, 1978.

Burrelo, L. C., & Sage, D. D. *Leadership and change in special education.* Englewood Cliffs NJ: Prentice-Hall, Inc., 1979.

Corrigan, D. C. Political and moral contexts that produced P.L. 94-142. *Journal of Teacher Education,* 1978, *29*(6), 10–14.

Gearheart, B. R. *Organization and administration of educational programs for exceptional children* (2nd ed.). Springfield IL: Charles C Thomas, 1977.

Hirshoren, A., & Umansky, W. Certification of teachers of preschool handicapped children. *Exceptional Children,* 1977, 44, 191–193.

Nevin, A. Special education administration competencies required of the general education administrator. *Exceptional Children,* 1979, 45, 363–365.

8

Index

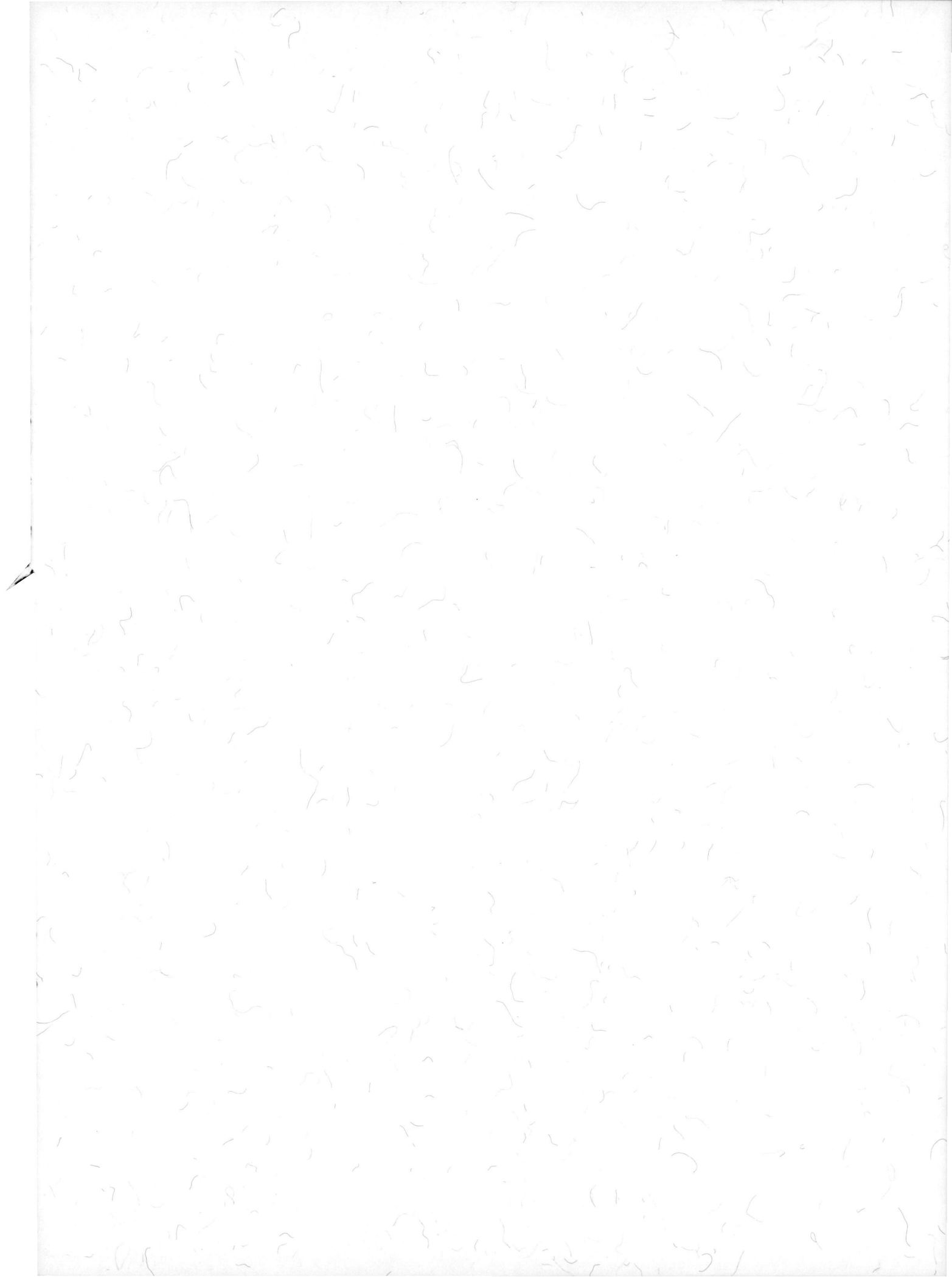